Building the American Republic

VOLUME 1

Building the American Republic

A NARRATIVE HISTORY TO 1877

Harry L. Watson

The University of Chicago Press CHICAGO AND LONDON

This is volume 1 of a two-volume narrative history of America by Harry L. Watson and Jane Dailey. Volume 1 is written by Watson; volume 2 is written by Dailey. To read digital editions of both volumes and more, please visit buildingtheamericanrepublic.org.

The University of Chicago Press, Chicago 60637
The University of Chicago Press, Ltd., London
© 2018 by Harry L. Watson
For more information, contact the University of Chicago Press, 1427 East 60th Street, Chicago, IL 60637.
Published 2018
Printed in the United States of America

27 26 25 24 23 22 21 20 19 18   1 2 3 4 5

ISBN-13: 978-0-226-30048-1 (cloth)
ISBN-13: 978-0-226-30051-1 (paper)
ISBN-13: 978-0-226-30065-8 (e-book)
DOI: 10.7208/chicago/9780226300658.001.0001

Library of Congress Cataloging-in-Publication Data
Names: Watson, Harry L. | Dailey, Jane Elizabeth, 1963–
Title: Building the American republic.
Description: Chicago ; London : The University of Chicago Press, 2018. | Includes bibliographical references and index.
Identifiers: LCCN 2017026856 | ISBN 9780226300481 (vol. 1 ; cloth : alk. paper) | ISBN 9780226300511 (vol. 1 ; pbk. : alk. paper) | ISBN 9780226300658 (vol. 1 ; e-book) | ISBN 9780226300795 (vol. 2 ; cloth : alk. paper) | ISBN 9780226300825 (vol. 2 ; pbk. : alk. paper) | ISBN 9780226300962 (vol. 2 ; e-book)
Subjects: LCSH: United States—History.
Classification: LCC E178.B955 2018 | DDC 973—dc23
LC record available at https://lccn.loc.gov/2017026856

Contents

5 · The Era of Independence, 1756–1783   147

6 · A Federal Republic, 1783–1789 195

7 · Federalists and Republicans, 1789–1815 231

9 · Northern Culture and Reform, 1815–1860 311

14 · "A New Birth of Freedom," 1861–1865 493

Preface

When Benjamin Franklin left the Constitutional Convention in Philadelphia in July 1787, a bystander reportedly asked him what sort of government the delegates had created. "A republic," he replied, "if you can keep it."

Keeping a republic is no easy task. The most important requirement is the active involvement of an informed people committed to honesty, civility, and selflessness—what the Founders called "republican virtue." Anchored by its Constitution, the American republic has endured for more than 220 years, longer than any other republic in modern history.

But the road has not been smooth. The American nation came apart in a violent civil war only 73 years after ratification of the Constitution. When it was reborn five years later, both the republic and its Constitution were transformed. Since then, the nation has had its ups and downs, depending largely on the capacity of the American people to tame, as Franklin put it, "their prejudices, their passions, their errors of opinion, their local interests, and their selfish views."

Our goal in writing *Building the American Republic* has been to craft a clear, engaging, readable, and thoughtful narrative history of the United States. In a world of increasing complexity and danger, America's civic tradition, both past and present, is a vital public asset and a continuing source of national renewal. Those who want to build a better America, however they define it, must understand the nation's history, its place in the world, the growth of its institutions, and their own role in preserving and reinvigorating the Republic.

Harry L. Watson
Jane Dailey

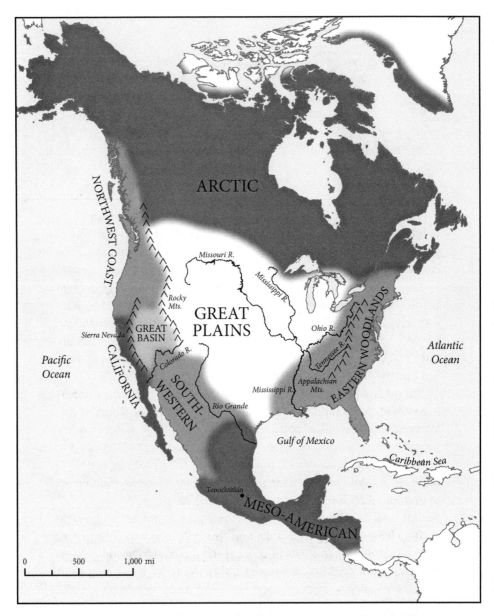

MAP 1. North America and its major cultural groups, ca. 1500. Map by Gabriel Moss.

CHAPTER 1

First Americans, to 1550

The island's name was Guanahaní. It shimmered in the sunlight of a calm, fragrant sea, and the sailors gazed on its palms and beaches with unspeakable relief. Their commander undoubtedly shared his men's excitement, but he controlled himself in a dry notation to his diary. "This island is quite big and very flat," the admiral reported. "[It has] many green trees and much water and a very large lake in the middle and without any mountains." Allowing his feelings to escape momentarily, he added, "And all of it so green that it is a pleasure to look at it."

Nor was Guanahaní empty. "These people are very gentle," the admiral marveled. "All of them go around as naked as their mothers bore them. . . . They are very well formed, with handsome bodies and good faces. . . . And they are of the color of the [Canary Islanders], neither black nor white." Certain that he had reached the outer shores of India, the explorer called the people "Indians" and their home the "Indies." His blunder still persists.

It is no wonder that Christopher Columbus rejoiced to see green branches and gentle people on October 12, 1492. Columbus and his crew had been sailing for 33 days, westward from the Canary Islands off the west coast of Africa. They traveled in three small ships, the *Niña*, the *Pinta*, and the *Santa Maria*, and they were searching on behalf of the king and queen of Spain for a western passage to the fabled ports of China. No one had ever done such a thing, and they did not yet know that they had failed at their task, while succeeding at something they had never dreamed of.

The villagers who met the sailors were members of the Taíno, or Arawak, people, who uneasily shared the islands and coastlines of the Caribbean Sea with neighbors they called the Caribs. Their home lay at the eastern edge of an island cluster later called the Bahamas. We cannot know how they felt when the white sails of the little Spanish fleet loomed out of the sea that fateful morning, nor what they thought of the bearded strangers who cumbered themselves with hard and heavy clothing, and busied themselves with puzzling ceremonies involving banners, crosses, and incomprehensible speeches. The Taínos were certainly curious, however, and gathered around the landing party to receive gifts of red caps and glass beads, and to examine the Spaniards' sharp swords. In return, the Taínos swam out to the boats with parrots and skeins of cotton thread, and then with food and water.

Neither the Taínos nor their visitors could know it, but their exchange of gifts that morning launched the beginning of a long interaction between the peoples of Europe and the Western Hemisphere. Interaction would have profound effects on both sides. The Europeans gained new lands, new knowledge, new foods, and wealth almost without measure. Tragically, the exchange brought pestilence, enslavement, and destruction to the Taínos, but Native Americans managed to survive through a tenacious process of resistance and adaptation. Interaction was unequal, but it also produced a multitude of new societies and cultures, among them the United States of America. For the Taínos as well as the Spanish, therefore, the encounter on that fateful October morning was the beginning of a very new world.

Land, Climate, and First Peoples

The Taínos of Guanahaní were among the thousands of tribes and nations who inhabited the continents of North and South America at the time of Columbus's voyages. The Native Americans were people of enormous diversity and vitality, whose ways of living ranged from migratory hunting and gathering to the complex empires of Mexico and Peru. Each people had its own story to explain its origins, but modern anthropologists have concluded that most of their ancestors crossed a land bridge that connected Siberia and Alaska between 11,000 and 15,000 years ago.

FROM THE LAND BRIDGE TO AGRICULTURE

The earliest Americans traveled widely, eventually spreading across North and South America as they hunted huge mammals that are now mostly extinct: elephant species called mammoths and mastodons, wooly rhinoceroses, giant bison, horses, camels, and musk oxen.

When these animals died out, they turned to other foods, according to their local environments.

Coastal people gathered fish and shellfish. Great Plains hunters stalked a smaller species of bison (often called buffalo), and eastern forest dwellers sought white-tailed deer and smaller game. Women everywhere gathered edible plants and prepared them for meals with special grinding stones. As people adjusted to specific local environments, they traveled less and lost contact with other bands. Individual groups developed their own cultural styles, each with its own variety of stone tools. Linguistic and religious patterns undoubtedly diverged as well, as local populations assumed their own unique identities.

One of the most important adaptations occurred when women searching for a regular supply of seeds began to cultivate productive plants. The earliest Indian farmers grew a wide variety of seed-bearing plants, but those of central Mexico triumphed by breeding maize, or "Indian corn," from native grasses about 3,000 years before the Common Era (BCE). Mexican Indians also learned to grow beans, squash, and other crops—an important improvement since the combination of corn and beans is much more nutritious than either food alone. Knowledge of corn spread slowly north from Mexico, finally reaching the east coast of North America around the year 200 of the Common Era (CE).

Agriculture brought major changes wherever it spread, and often replaced the older cultures based on hunting and gathering. Farmers had to remain in one place, at least while the crop was growing. Village life became possible, and social structure grew more complex. Artisans began making and firing clay pots to store the harvest. Baskets, strings, nets, and woven textiles made many things easier, from storing food to catching fish to keeping warm. Hunters exchanged their spears for more effective bows and arrows. More elaborate rituals appeared as planting peoples made corn the center of their religious life and made the endless cycles of sun, rain, and harvest the focus of their spiritual lives. In Mexico, farming led to village life by about 2500 BCE and supported a major increase in population.

The new tools did not spread everywhere, but Native American cultures became increasingly diverse. California Indians did not adopt agriculture, for example, but gathered bountiful harvests of wild acorns. In the Pacific Northwest, salmon and other fish were so plentiful that the Haida, Tlingit, and Kwakiutl tribes built elaborate and complex cultures based on the sea. The buffalo herds supported hunting cultures on the Great Plains. After the coming of the Spanish, tribes like the Comanche, Lakota (Sioux), Cheyenne, Arapaho, and Kiowa acquired European horses to pursue their prey and their enemies, laying the basis for powerful images of American Indians as mustang-riding warriors who lived in teepees made of buffalo skins.

Living very differently from the Plains Indians, four native North American cultures joined the Taínos in bearing the first brunt of the European encounter. All four depended on farming more than hunting, and all lived in permanent settlements that ranged in size from simple villages to impressive cities. The Pueblo villagers of the area that became the southwestern United States met the Spanish explorer Coronado as he wandered north seeking the mythical Seven Cities of Gold. In the future southeastern states, the mound-building Mississippian people resisted the march of Hernando de Soto, another probing Spaniard. The Woodland peoples of eastern North America received the first English explorers, from Virginians to New Englanders. And south of the future United States, the empires of Central America astonished the Spanish with their wealth and sophistication, and sharpened the invaders' appetites for gold.

PUEBLOAN VILLAGERS, THE FIRST TOWNSPEOPLE

The introduction of agriculture brought permanent villages, with pottery making and extensive systems of irrigation, to the area that would become the southwestern United States. The earliest American townspeople lived in circular pit houses roofed against the elements, but by 700 CE they were building large, multiroom apartment houses out of stone and mud (adobe) brick. The Spaniards would later call these communities pueblos, or villages, and these Puebloan Indians built the largest residential buildings in North America until the construction of modern apartment houses in nineteenth-century cities.

The ancestral Puebloan people built some of their earliest and most elaborate structures in Chaco Canyon, New Mexico, between 900 and 1150 CE. Chaco was a large and well-planned urban community, containing 13 pueblos and numerous small settlement sites, with space for 5,000–10,000 inhabitants. Linked by a network of well-made roads, the people of Chaco drew food from 70 surrounding communities. Farther north, another major Puebloan culture developed around Mesa Verde, in what is now southwestern Colorado. The Mesa Verdeans, perhaps numbering 30,000 people, built elaborate structures under cliffs and rock overhangs and also lived in scattered villages and outposts surrounding the larger settlements.

By 1300 CE, both the Chaco and Mesa Verde communities lay deserted amid evidence of warfare and brutal conflict, but refugees seem to have built new pueblos to the south and west. The Hopi and Zuñi tribes of Arizona and the modern Pueblo people of northern New Mexico are their descendants. One of their settlements, Acoma Pueblo in New Mexico, dates to 1250 CE and is the oldest continuously occupied town in the modern continental United States.

MISSISSIPPIAN CHIEFDOMS

Long before European contact, some North American Indians lived in socially and politically complex societies known as chiefdoms, with hereditary leaders who dominated wide geographical areas. The Mississippian people, as archaeologists call them, built large towns with central plazas and tall, flat-topped earthen pyramids, especially on the rich floodplains adjoining the Mississippi and other midwestern and southern rivers. Now known as Cahokia, their grandest center lay at the forks of the Mississippi and Missouri Rivers. At its height between 1050 and 1200 CE, Cahokia held 10,000–20,000 people in its six square miles, making it the largest town in the future United States before eighteenth-century Philadelphia. Its largest pyramid was 100 feet tall and covered 16 acres, and over 100 other mounds stood nearby. Other large Mississippian complexes appear at Moundville, Alabama; Etowah, Georgia; and Spiro, Oklahoma.

Mississippian mounds contain elaborate burials of high-status individuals, often accompanied by finely carved jewelry, figurines, masks, and other ritual objects made of shell, ceramics, stone, and copper. Long-distance trading networks gathered these raw materials from hundreds of miles away and distributed the finished goods to equally distant sites. With many similar motifs, these artifacts suggest that Mississippians used their trading ties to spread a common set of spiritual beliefs, which archeologists call the Southeastern Ceremonial Cult. With more ritual significance than practical utility, the cult's ceremonial objects were often buried with their owners for use in the next world rather than hoarded and passed through generations as a form of wealth.

Mound construction clearly required a complex social and political order in which a few powerful rulers deployed skilled construction experts and commanded labor and tribute from thousands of distant commoners. The Spanish conqueror, or conquistador, Hernando de Soto encountered many such chiefdoms in his march across the

American southeast between 1539 and 1541. Survivors from his expedition described large towns of thatched houses, surrounded by strong palisades and watchtowers. Borne on a cloth-covered litter, the queen of a major town called Cofitachique showed de Soto her storehouses filled with carved weapons, food, and thousands of freshwater pearls. Almost two centuries later, French colonists in Louisiana described the last surviving Mississippian culture among the Natchez Indians. Their society was divided by hereditary castes, led by a chieftain called the "Great Sun," and included a well-defined nobility, a middling group called "Honored People," and a lower caste called "Stinkards." As in Mexico and Central America, the Natchez pyramids were sometimes the scene of human sacrifice.

Wars and ecological pressures began to undermine the largest Mississippian chiefdoms before de Soto's arrival, and epidemics apparently depleted most of the others by the time English colonizers arrived in the seventeenth century. The survivors lived in smaller alliances or even single towns without large mounds or powerful chiefs, but governed themselves by consensus. They also coalesced in larger confederacies when necessary; Europeans would know them as Creeks or Choctaws.

WOODLAND PEOPLES OF THE EAST

On the Atlantic coast, Eastern Woodland Indians lived by a combination of hunting, fishing, and farming, and dominated the area when the Mississippians declined. Woodland women had developed agriculture independently, by cultivating squash, sunflowers, and other seed-bearing plants as early as 1500 BCE. They adopted corn around 900 CE and added beans and tobacco.

Woodland Indians practiced a slash-and-burn agricultural technique, in which men killed trees by cutting the bark around their trunks and then burned them to clear a field. Women then used stone-bladed hoes and digging sticks to till fertilizing ashes into the soil and to plant a mixed crop of corn and beans in scattered mounds. When the field's fertility declined, the villagers would abandon it and clear another, returning to the original plot when a long fallow period had restored its fertility. Anthropologists have found that slash-and-burn agriculture is very efficient, generating more food calories for a given expenditure of energy than more modern techniques, but it obviously requires ample territory to succeed in the long run.

Woodland Indians lived in semipermanent villages for the growing season. They made houses from bent saplings covered with bark, mats, or hides, and sometimes surrounded their villages with log palisades. During the fall and winter, men frequently left their villages for extended hunting trips. Spring could bring another migration to distant beds of shellfish or to the nearest fishing ground. Coastal peoples developed complex systems of netting, spearing, and trapping fish later copied by Europeans. With appropriate variations according to climate and other conditions, this way of life prevailed extensively up and down the Atlantic coast, from Florida to Maine.

Woodland villages ranged in size from 50 inhabitants to as many as several hundred. Adjacent villages usually spoke the same language, and several large families of languages prevailed across most of eastern North America: Algonquin on the Atlantic coast and around the Great Lakes, Iroquoian in the Hudson River Valley and parts of the south, Muskogean in the southeast. Europeans usually referred to the speakers of a common language as members of a "nation" or "tribe," but the Indians themselves did not feel the same degree of political unity that the Europeans expected of them. Village chiefs normally ruled by custom and consent, and individual clans and families were responsible for avenging any injuries they received. Related tribes might come together in confederacies, like the League of the Iroquois, or Haudenosaunee, in western New York or the Powhatan Confederacy of Chesapeake Bay, but these loose-knit federations needed charismatic leadership and continual diplomacy to hold them together. Each tribe claimed its own territory for hunting and tillage, and specific plots belonged to different families or clans, but tribes owned their lands in common and individuals did not buy or sell land privately. Like the Mississippians and most other Native Americans, Woodland peoples traded raw materials and finished goods, including strings or belts of shell beads called *wampum*, over wide areas, and cherished fine objects for their *manitou*, or spiritual power. These exchanges were not barren commercial transactions but forms of reciprocal gift giving that bound the givers into valued social relationships ranging from loyalty between leaders and their supporters to alliances between towns.

Woodland men were responsible for hunting and war, while women took charge of farming and childcare. Most Woodland Indians practiced matrilineal kinship, which meant that children belonged to the families and clans of their mothers. In contrast to the women of sixteenth- and seventeenth-century European societies, Indian women took an active role in political decision making and often made critical decisions regarding war or peace as well as the fate of military captives.

Woodland tribes fought frequent wars against one another, but usually not to expand their territories. Instead, warriors gained personal honor by demonstrating bravery and avenging old injuries. They might adopt their captives to replace lost relatives, or torture them to death to satisfy the bereaved. Native warfare changed dramatically after the Europeans arrived, as some Woodland tribes fought for favorable positions in the fur trade or sold their prisoners to the colonists as slaves.

THE EMPIRES OF CENTRAL AND SOUTH AMERICA

The most spectacular civilizations in precolonial North America emerged in Mexico and Central America, also called Mesoamerica. When the Spanish arrived in the sixteenth century, many Mesoamericans lived in cities that dwarfed the capitals of Europe, with stone palaces and pyramids that provoked the newcomers' envy and amazement. Mayas and Aztecs made gold and jeweled objects of exquisite beauty, cloaked their leaders in shimmering feathered robes and luxurious textiles, and recorded their deeds in brilliantly colored books. It was an impressive record of power and material achievement, but the Spanish destroyed most of it in their zeal to stamp out the Indians' religion and amass their treasure. What we now know about these civilizations comes from reports by the conquerors and a few survivors, from archeology, and from the painstaking decoding of surviving inscriptions.

Mesoamericans began living in cities as early as 1200 BCE, but the cultures who met the Spanish had appeared more recently. In Yucatán and adjoining areas of Central America, the Mayan people built numerous city-states between 300 and 900 CE, with a total population of some five million. Each city featured one or more stone temples and a hereditary nobility supported by tribute from peasants. The Mayan city-states made frequent wars on their neighbors to obtain more tribute and to capture victims for sacrifice atop their dizzying pyramids. They also devised the only written language in the Americas before European contact and used a precise calendar to record key dates from the reigns of their kings. Unlike the ancient Romans, Mayan mathematicians used a zero in their calculations and accurately measured the movement of heavenly bodies. Though remnants of elite Mayan culture persisted until the era of the Spanish conquest, the Mayas abandoned most of their cities for unknown reasons by about 950 CE.

The Aztecs (or Mexica) were the most powerful people the Spanish conquerors met in the sixteenth century. About 1325 CE, ancestors of the Aztecs migrated to the central valley of Mexico and founded the city of Tenochtitlán on an island in a lake there. By 1434, Tenochtitlán had become the dominant power in a coalition of three city-states that eventually collected tribute from 10 million subjects who lived across 125,000 square miles. The city of Tenochtitlán held 200,000 people, more than any city in Spain and five times the population of sixteenth-century London. Its largest pyramid was 200 feet high and crowned by temples to the gods of rain and war. Highly skilled artisans created a wide array of luxury goods and ordinary consumer items that wealthy merchants traded all over Mesoamerica, and a powerful army made almost perpetual war on surrounding peoples. Successful warfare provided the Aztecs with an endless stream of sacrificial victims, whose blood, they believed, was essential nourishment for the sun god. Endless raiding made many enemies, however, and the Aztecs' victims would later become indispensable Spanish allies in the conquest of 1521.

Farther to the south, in the Andean region of South America, large chiefdoms and city-states had emerged even earlier than in Mexico, and a succession of powerful empires had ruled for many centuries. The Andean Indians cultivated maize and potatoes, domesticated herds of llamas and related animals, wove complex wool and cotton fabrics, and became expert artisans in gold, silver, copper, and bronze. Early in the fifteenth century, the Incas created a powerful chiefdom in southern Peru, with its capital city at Cuzco. A century later, their empire extended more than 2,500 miles along the crest of the Andes Mountains, from northern Ecuador to central Chile, and contained 6-12 million people. A sophisticated bureaucracy and almost 19,000 miles of stone highways held the empire together. Like their Aztec contemporaries, however, the Incas did not remain in power for long. A war between rival claimants to the throne divided and weakened their government just as the Spanish approached in 1525, with fateful consequences for their empire.

The Expanding Nations of Europe

As the Incas and Aztecs rose and flourished, forces were stirring across the Atlantic that would utterly transform the society of the Americas.

Fifteenth-century Europe slowly emerged from poverty and isolation to launch a wave of expansion into Africa, Asia, and finally America. Europe's invasion of the Western Hemisphere would devastate Native American cultures and create a set of colonial societies ruled and largely populated by newcomers from across the ocean. Thousands of the immigrants were Europeans, but thousands more were African slaves. Interacting together, Indians, Europeans, and Africans created new American societies that borrowed heavily from their old customs but sharply differed from what had come before.

POPULATION GROWTH AND PROSPERITY

The first Europeans to reach America were almost certainly Scandinavian Vikings from medieval Iceland and Greenland. According to Viking epic poetry, Leif Erikson sailed west from Greenland about the year 990 CE and established a small settlement in a distant land he called Vinland. His relatives sustained the outpost for about two decades. Archeologists in the 1960s confirmed this story by recovering Viking artifacts from a small excavation at L'Anse aux Meadows on the northeastern coast of Canada. The Vikings' toehold remained unknown to the rest of Europe and had no major impact on the Native Americans.

The contact between Europe and America that would transform both continents grew out of deep social and economic changes. Earlier, a social and economic system known as feudalism had dominated most of medieval Europe. In feudal society, a king parceled out lands to his leading noblemen, or vassals, and they subdivided it among vassals of their own in a descending series of ranks that followed the allotment of land. At the bottom, impoverished serfs or peasants lacked freedom of movement, toiled by compulsion, and split their crops and their labor with their lords. In theory, every vassal owed loyalty, obedience, and service to his lord and protection to his own dependents in a long chain of mutual obligations. In practice, leading noblemen maintained private armies of vassals and waged nearly endless warfare with other nobles or even the king. By comparison to later periods, towns were small, trade was limited, and economic change came very slowly.

In the mid-fourteenth century, Europe suffered a devastating epidemic of bubonic plague, or the Black Death, which killed as many as one-third to one-half of its people, and contributed to the breakup of feudal society. Noblemen's armies were decimated, allowing fifteenth-century kings to assert their own authority and restrain the private wars that had devastated the medieval countryside. Surviving peasants escaped serfdom and gained land through a combination of rental and individual or common ownership. Artisans turned out plentiful goods like woolen cloth and metalwork in growing numbers of market towns, selling to merchants who shipped crops and handicrafts to distant consumers by pack trains and sailing vessels. Responding to prosperity, Europe's population rebounded between 1400 and 1500. Most of its inhabitants still struggled against poverty, famine, and early death, but greater stability and prosperity encouraged the daring to look for further improvements.

Europe's expanding economy fed a parallel cultural change, a rebirth of art and learning following the end of feudalism that historians call the Renaissance. Newly rich rulers, merchants, and churchmen celebrated their ascent with displays of beautiful and costly goods that ranged from silks and spices to stunning works of painting, sculpture, and architecture. Their patronage encouraged a dramatic outpouring of artistic achievement that started in Italian city-states like Florence and Venice but spread across the Alps into northern courts and cities. Successful princes supported intellectuals who could recover the lost learning of the ancient Greeks and Romans, often by studying with Arab or Turkish scholars and copying manuscripts from their libraries. Broader knowledge led scholars from the study of theology to the nature and needs of humanity, a movement historians have called humanism. More practical experts struggled to learn the secrets of mathematics, navigation, metallurgy, and cannon making. Perhaps their most significant innovations were movable type and the printing press, which made books cheaper and spread the new learning widely. Europe's new hunger for luxurious goods, new information, and, above all, the money to buy these things would soon power its seemingly insatiable drive for overseas expansion.

RELIGIOUS RIVALRY AND TRADE

Christianity was the professed religion of almost all Europeans of the fifteenth century, and most in western Europe were Roman Catholics who acknowledged the spiritual leadership and worldly power of the pope in Rome. The Catholic Church owned extensive lands throughout the continent and collected substantial taxes from the population. An elaborate hierarchy of bishops, archbishops, and cardinals governed the church, while thousands of men and women devoted their lives to its service as priests, monks, and nuns. Princes might struggle with the papacy's worldly power, and moralists might condemn its corruption, but the truth of the Gospels and the spiritual authority of the church were deeply venerated, even where magic and the remnants of pre-Christian religions continued to coexist with orthodoxy in popular culture.

On its southern and eastern borders, Christendom faced Islam, its powerful rival for spiritual and material supremacy. Expanding from the Arabian Peninsula in the eighth and ninth centuries CE, Muslims had conquered all the lands from Mesopotamia to North Africa. Known as Moors, Muslim Arabs from North Africa then crossed the Mediterranean and captured the Iberian Peninsula, now the location of Spain and Portugal. Embracing and protecting the secular scholarship of the ancient world, Islamic civilization far outshone Europe in wealth, technology, science, mathematics, and commerce with India and East Asia. Crucial navigational instruments like the magnetic compass, for example, and the astrolabe (used for measuring latitude) probably reached medieval Europe from the Muslim world.

Arab advances had frightened Christians as early as the eleventh century, when Pope Urban II first called for a massive campaign, or crusade, to free the holy places of Jerusalem from Muslim "infidels." The crusaders founded a temporary Christian kingdom in Palestine, and there the roughhewn knights of medieval Europe first met the luxuries of the distant Orient. Silk for the warrior's body, perfume for his nostrils, spices for his meat, and sugar for his sweet tooth were all part of the successful crusader's experience, and he brought home an enduring taste for such finery. Even when Muslims retook the Kingdom of Jerusalem, a hunger for the exports of Asia still persisted among the European upper classes.

Happy to oblige, Muslim merchants disregarded religious rivalries to trade extensively with Venice, Genoa, Pisa, and other city-states of northern Italy. The most popular commodities were silk from China and pepper, cloves, cinnamon, ginger, and nutmeg from the coasts of India and the islands of what is now Indonesia. Aromatic spices were immensely prized in Europe, where salted and tasteless meat and fish were staples of even the most opulent tables. Passing through the hands of countless middlemen as they passed from Sumatra to India to Arabia to Syria and finally to Italy, these lightweight and compact cargoes were the most profitable commodities of international trade. Merchants were as eager to join this commerce as monarchs were to tax it, and the spice trade became one of the most important aspects of the fifteenth-century economy. At the same time, the need for something to offer in exchange for spices gave European traders a special incentive to find new sources of gold and silver to spend in eastern markets.

PORTUGAL'S FIRST STEPS

Hunger for Asian riches and rivalry with Islam drove the first expansion of Europe across the oceans. One motive fed on the other, since campaigns for the Christian faith would require funds, while displacing Muslim states and merchants might be the fastest way to get rich. These dual motives kindled expansionist dreams in the poor and tiny kingdom of Portugal, which bordered the Atlantic Ocean, along the western edge of Spain. Once Portugal succeeded in its drive for wealth and Christian victories, international rivalry tempted the other Atlantic powers to imitate it.

Medieval Christian kings had fought a long and bitter *reconquista* to retake the Iberian Peninsula from its Muslim rulers. Their struggle was almost complete in the fifteenth century, with only a single Moorish enclave, the kingdom of Granada, still remaining in southern Spain. Determined to continue the war against Islam, Portugal seized the city of Ceuta in northern Morocco in 1415 and followed this with a series of penetrating voyages along the west coast of Africa.

A younger brother of the king of Portugal, known in English as Prince Henry the Navigator, became the principal sponsor of Portuguese voyages to Africa. After distinguishing himself for valor at the capture of Ceuta, Henry became intrigued with Africa, especially in the possibility of harassing the Muslims from its western side. He considered forging an anti-Muslim alliance with Prester John, the mythical king of a Christian realm beyond the Sahara. More practically, Henry wanted to follow the African coastline southward to find the source of the gold Arab camel caravans had long carried north across the desert.

Though he did not set sail personally, Henry used his considerable wealth to send a series of small fleets down the west coast of Africa. His mariners faced considerable difficulties, because prevailing winds in the eastern Atlantic made it easy to sail away from Portugal but very hard to get back. Henry's role in solving such nautical problems by founding a special school of ship design, mapmaking, and navigation has been exaggerated. Instead, the Portuguese relied on a series of

small practical refinements of existing knowledge, especially in adapting a traditional vessel, the caravel, to the demands of Atlantic sailing.
Using these means, Henry's men successfully located and colonized
the uninhabited island clusters of the Madeiras and the Azores. By
1434, they had returned safely from farther south than traditional Arab
and Christian authorities ever thought possible. A decade later, the
voyagers finally passed the southern border of the Sahara and located
traders who would barter with them for gold. More ominously for the
future, they also returned with cargoes of human slaves.

The World of West Africa

To the south of the Sahara, Africa contained a wide range of climates
and natural environments. The desert gave way to a band of semiarid
grasslands near the mouth of the Senegal River, at about the 15th parallel. Tropical forests began farther to the south, where the African coast
turns eastward. The 2,600-mile Niger River bends across the entire
region, beginning in the highlands of modern Guinea, then flowing
northeastward toward the heart of the Sahara before turning south-
eastward and entering the Atlantic Ocean through a fan-shaped delta
in modern Nigeria. The Senegal and Gambia Rivers arise nearby but
flow roughly westward to the sea, creating three major water highways
that tie interior districts to each other and to the coast.

West Africa contained a diverse assembly of peoples, cultures, languages, and religions with their own long and complex histories. Kinship knit together most of its societies, and some sustained no governments larger their own villages, but large and prosperous empires also
flourished in the area, complete with complex economies, populous
cities, powerful armies, and well-developed bureaucracies. Elaborate
trade routes crossed the Sahara, tying southern parts of the continent
with the Arab north. Islam spread southward along these connections,
but traditional African religions were also widespread. Indigenous
African languages remained unwritten, but especially under Islam,
religious and political elites used written Arabic much as contemporary Europeans used Latin as their international scholarly language.

THE PEOPLE OF WEST AFRICA

Most West African cultures shared features that underlay their diversity. Cattle herders dominated the northern grasslands, while the for-

est people practiced agriculture. The farmers tilled their fields with hoes instead of plows, since draft animals were likely to die from diseases carried by the tsetse fly. Residents of both regions were very familiar with metalworking and used iron tools. In some areas such as the kingdom of Benin in modern Nigeria, artists created magnificent portraits and bas-relief sculptures in iron and bronze.

Extensive trading networks had shaped the creation of African states. Treacherous winds and currents hampered the development of ocean navigation, so commerce traveled inland toward overland routes that began along the Niger and stretched across the Sahara. Whoever controlled the upper Niger and the nearby headwaters of the Senegal and Gambia Rivers could dominate the region, so from as early as the ninth to the seventeenth centuries CE ambitious rulers made this area the seat of three extensive empires: Ghana, Songhai, and Mali. Their princes embraced Islam and made lavish pilgrimages to Mecca, and also fostered a famous center of trade and Muslim learning in the ancient trading city of Timbuktu. Farther south and west, smaller kingdoms lined the coasts of the Atlantic and the Gulf of Guinea, some the size of England or France and others no larger than city-states. Farther south, in West Central Africa, the coastal kingdoms of Loango and Kongo dominated a cluster of smaller states around the mouth of the Zaire (Congo) River from modern Gabon to Angola.

The gold sought by the Portuguese came from inland deposits in the forested coastal region that runs roughly parallel to the equator between modern Sierra Leone and the Bight of Benin. Local rulers sent it north to trading centers such as Timbuktu where they exchanged it for salt with Arab and Berber merchants, whose camels then carried it to Mediterranean ports. Coined by Continental monarchs, West African gold supplied the currency for Europe's growing trade and inspired Prince Henry to find its source.

SUGAR AND SLAVES

Europeans first came to Africa for gold, but they kept coming back for slaves. The colonization of America gave rise to an international traffic in human beings that saw the capture, deportation, and exploitation of millions of African people. The cost in human suffering was immense, and the impact on the history of Africa and the Americas was equally profound.

Slavery had been the fundamental economic institution of the ancient world, but it had given way to serfdom in northern Europe without disappearing from the Mediterranean basin. Unlike American slavery, however, ancient and medieval slavery had no connection with modern concepts of race. Greek and Roman slaves had been military captives of every color. Medieval Europeans had hesitated to enslave their fellow Christians, but Muslims and other non-Christians were fair game. In the tenth century, German emperor Otto the Great sold his pagan Slavic captives into slavery, giving us the word "slave." Arab Muslims also seized white Slavic people from the Black Sea region to sell throughout the Mediterranean basin.

The revival of human slavery, and the exclusive targeting of Africans as its victims, grew out of the culture of sugarcane, a plant that Crusaders had learned about from the Arabs. The tantalizing crystals of the sugarcane plant produced a far sweeter taste sensation than honey, the strongest sweetener known to medieval Europeans, and sugar had joined the other spices as an expensive and exotic item of eastern trade. Crusaders grew sugar on the islands of the eastern Mediterranean, and knowledge of the crop spread westward in the Middle Ages, gradually coming to the western Mediterranean and the southern tip of the Iberian Peninsula. Fifteenth-century Spaniards found that sugar grew well on the Canary Islands off the coast of Morocco. The same was true on the islands the Portuguese found and claimed on their way to West Africa, beginning with the Madeiras, the Azores, and the Cape Verdes, and later São Tomé, Fernando Po, and Príncipé farther south.

Sugar was not easy to make. Cane required enormous amounts of very hard labor to grow and especially to harvest, when workers had to cut and process the crop very quickly, using expensive machinery to grind the stalks and boil the juice. Free workers often refused this drudgery, so many sugar growers used forced labor. The need for costly equipment and a bound workforce kept small farmers out of the sugar business, moreover, and encouraged the rise of plantations, or large estates that often used unfree workers to concentrate on a single commercial crop. Mediterranean sugar planters used slaves. Off the coasts of West Africa, the Spanish and Portuguese did likewise.

THE EARLY SLAVE TRADE

While many of the slaves who toiled in Mediterranean cane fields were white, some also came from West Africa. Like many ancient and medieval societies, the African kingdoms commonly enslaved their military captives. It did not occur to the enslavers that they were victimizing their "own people," just because both parties were black, any more than Russians or Italians used skin color as an excuse to refrain from enslaving alien whites. African captives could become laborers or domestic servants. They might be adopted by their masters' families, and their children might go free, but some were sold to the caravans heading north. Those who somehow survived the march across the desert were important articles of trade in the markets of North Africa. Purchased there by Europeans, African slaves became commonplace in fifteenth-century Italy, Spain, and Portugal, usually as domestic servants. When the Turks took Constantinople in 1453, the trade in Black Sea slaves declined, with the fateful result that western slavery became closely associated with Africans alone.

The mariners of Prince Henry the Navigator readily joined the slave trade when they rounded the capes of West Africa, initially seizing their own captives and later purchasing them from local kings. European involvement increased dramatically when the Portuguese began to grow sugarcane on their offshore African islands and purchased their workforce from local traders. Sugar was so profitable that planters could pay top prices for slaves and make exorbitant profits for chieftains whose only expense was the cost of capturing and transporting the victims. Some rulers declined the bargain, so European slavers avoided their domains. Others found the opportunity irresistible, but strictly controlled the trade by limiting sales to enemy captives, collecting stiff taxes from European captains, insisting on high-quality textiles, alcohol, and guns in exchange, and imposing their own conditions on prospective buyers. West African warfare inevitably escalated as rival rulers raided each other's villages to supply more captives to the traders on the coast.

The slave trade flourished as sugar culture spread, and soon it outpaced the export of gold from West Africa. As early as 1482, the Portuguese built a massive fort at Elmina ("the mine") in modern Ghana, complemented by a massive sugar colony on the offshore island of São Tomé. Elmina's first purpose was protecting the gold trade, but its dungeons soon became holding pens for slaves as well. Other forts and markets soon sprouted along the West African coast, and Europeans began calling its different stretches by their major exports: the Grain Coast, the Ivory Coast, the Gold Coast, the Slave Coast.

Once established on São Tomé and other islands, the Spanish and Portuguese might have expanded their sugar plantations eastward to the African mainland, but its powerful rulers strictly confined them to coastal trading posts. Plantations in the Americas were an obvious alternative. When Spain and Portugal established their American colonies in the sixteenth century, the transplantation of slavery and the sugar plantation became an easy, almost automatic extension of their activities on the eastern side of the Atlantic. In America, European colonizers readily imposed terms of forced labor on captives, convicts, and paupers from their own societies, but reserved lifetime slavery for Africans and some Indians. Their African victims were enslaved already and apparently seemed so alien that harsh treatment came easily. Masters also found that Africans were somewhat resistant to Eurasian diseases like smallpox, and also to malaria and the other tropical fevers that proved so fatal to Europeans. Every colonizing nation in the Western Hemisphere would eventually follow the Spanish and Portuguese example, and African slavery became a deeply entrenched institution of colonial America. In the sixteenth, seventeenth, and eighteenth centuries, enslaved Africans were by far the largest group of people who crossed the Atlantic to America, possibly numbering as many as 10 million people over four centuries.

Europe Comes to America

Portugal was not alone in seeking new wealth from overseas. Searching for an alternate route to the Indies, the king and queen of Spain financed the voyages that led Columbus to America, where the Spanish built an empire that soon eclipsed the achievements of its Portuguese rival. Spain's successes brought more imitators, as England, France, the Netherlands, and other rivals scrambled to match its conquests.

Like Columbus himself, Spain's American empire mixed high adventure and breathtaking ambitions with cruelty and exploitation. The invaders overwhelmed most of the Indian societies they confronted, from the Taínos of the Caribbean to the civilizations of Mexico and Peru. Obsessed with finding gold and silver, the Spanish forced the Indians to mine these metals wherever they could. If local Indians died out, and especially where plantations seemed more profitable than mines, slaves from Africa took their places. The Spanish investigated North America but mostly abandoned it when their search for precious metals yielded nothing. These lands remained available to Spain's competitors.

THE VOYAGES OF COLUMBUS

The Portuguese did not halt their voyages when Prince Henry died in 1460. In 1488, a captain named Bartolomeu Dias finally reached the southernmost tip of Africa, which he called the Cape of Good Hope, and safely returned to Portugal. Nine years later, in 1497, Vasco da Gama led a fleet around this cape and did reach India, finally returning home with a fabulously profitable cargo of pepper. Others quickly followed, and soon the tiny kingdom of Portugal had established a line of forts and trading posts around the west and east coasts of Africa, to India, to the Spice Islands, and on to China and Japan. It was a stunning imperial achievement, and wealth from the royal monopoly on the spice trade made the kings of Portugal the envy of all their neighbors.

Portugal's success invited competition, but opportunities for direct trade with the East remained limited. The Italians controlled direct contact with the Middle East, and Portugal would not tolerate rivals in Africa, so challengers needed to find an alternative. Since the time of the Greeks, all educated Europeans had known that the earth was round, and that it was theoretically possible to make direct contact with Asia by sailing west across the Atlantic Ocean. Most experts believed, however, that the size of the earth made such a voyage impractical and that any sailor who foolishly attempted to cover the immense distance between Europe and China would surely perish in the attempt.

Christopher Columbus was an Italian sailor who disagreed. The son of a weaver and wool merchant of Genoa, Columbus had become an experienced mariner in the Mediterranean and the Atlantic, ranging as far south as Elmina on the Gold Coast and north to England and possibly Iceland. He was fascinated by sailors' tales of land in the western Atlantic, and convinced that Japan lay no more than 2,400 nautical miles west of Spain's colony in the Canary Islands. In fact, Japan is 10,600 nautical miles from the Canaries, so the experts were much closer to the truth than Columbus. The determined sailor could not be dissuaded, however, and he begged a number of European monarchs for ships and men to test his theories.

Rejected by Portugal, Columbus approached King Ferdinand and Queen Isabella of Spain. Isabella was an especially pious Catholic who was determined to increase the power and extent of the church, and in 1492 Spanish armies had just conquered Granada, the last Muslim foothold in Spain. In the same year, she and Ferdinand demanded the conversion or expulsion of all Jews from their dominions, and later extended the order to Muslims. When Columbus came to them with a plan to enrich the monarchy and spread Christianity by a westward voyage to China, the sovereigns were reluctant at first, but Isabella became more and more interested. In 1492, she granted Columbus three ships and permission to sail west in search of unknown islands or continents, naming him "Admiral of the Ocean Sea" and governor and viceroy of any lands he might claim for Castile. Not expecting him to claim China itself, she also gave him a letter of introduction to its emperor. In return, Isabella asked for 90 percent of the voyage's profits.

Admiral Columbus set out in two caravels, the *Niña* and the *Pinta*, and a larger flagship, the *Santa Maria*. His little fleet stopped for fresh food and water in the Canary Islands, and then caught the trade winds for a relatively quick and uneventful 33-day voyage across the Atlantic. Toward the end of the journey, the sailors began to grumble, not because they were afraid of falling off the edge of the earth, but because they did not know how they would ever get home in the teeth of such a steady eastern breeze. To cheer them on, Columbus pointed to the driftwood and shorebirds around them and predicted that land could not be far distant. Guanahaní came into sight soon afterward, and Columbus quickly claimed the island for the crown of Castile. Ignoring its Taíno name, he rechristened it San Salvador, or "Holy Savior," in honor of Jesus Christ.

Almost immediately, Columbus and his men began to mingle arrogance and violence with piety and garbled good intentions in a pattern that scarred European relations with Native Americans for centuries. The Taínos puzzled the voyagers, for they bore no resemblance to travelers' descriptions of the Chinese, but Columbus thought they could make good Christians and perhaps good slaves as well. He was even more interested in the Taínos' golden ornaments and longed to find their source. He needed interpreters, moreover, so he did not hesitate to kidnap six islanders to teach them Spanish. On his next voyage, Columbus sought to cover his expenses by seizing Indians for sale in Seville.

The admiral completed his first voyage with a series of exploratory cruises that took him to Cuba, Hispaniola (now divided between Haiti and the Dominican Republic), and to numerous other islets in the eastern Caribbean. Everywhere he looked for signs of India, China, or Japan, or at least for some valuable commodity to make his voyage worthwhile. Asia proved maddeningly elusive, but gold turned up on Hispaniola, and Columbus began to realize that colonizing these islands might yield just as much wealth as direct trade with China. Leaving a contingent of men behind him, he turned back to Spain and arrived in the spring of 1493 after a long and very difficult passage.

Ferdinand and Isabella were so pleased by Columbus's voyage that they sent him back with 17 ships and 1,200 men, clearly intending to add his "discoveries" to their realm. Arriving at Hispaniola, the admiral discovered that the Taínos had killed the men he left behind and destroyed their fort, acts which he punished by attacking and enslaving the supposed perpetrators. He followed his second voyage with two more, eventually sailed as far as the coasts of Central and South America, and founded Spain's Caribbean empire. Until his death, the admiral remained convinced that he had found a water route to the Orient. A clumsy administrator, he quarreled with his subordinates and brooded on the religious implications of his travels, hoping to find the original Garden of Eden and to finance the recapture of Jerusalem. On one occasion, when Columbus interfered too much in the work of other officials, he had to be arrested and returned to Spain in chains and disgrace. Though he managed to regain the confidence of the king and queen, Columbus proved to be a courageous but eccentric and intransigent visionary rather than a level-headed colonial governor. Consumed with boundless ambition, passionate curiosity, and a thirst for personal advancement, he was also capable of heedless brutality to the people he encountered. The conquerors who followed him — English, French, Spanish, and Portuguese — would all share many of the same characteristics.

Spanish authorities attempted to displace Columbus himself, but they clearly saw the value of his discoveries and quickly took possession of the largest Caribbean islands. Technically, the conquistadors were not supposed to enslave the Indians they controlled, but they did confine them to private estates called *encomiendas* and forced them to work as a form of tribute. Priests and friars arrived to convert the natives, and those who resisted faced terrible tortures. When tales of cruelty reached the queen, Isabella ordered that her newest subjects must not be mistreated, but her directives proved impossible to enforce. As the Caribbean Indians succumbed to mistreatment and alien diseases, the Spanish replaced them with Africans.

SPAIN'S RIVALS AND IMITATORS

The news of Columbus's voyages touched off a burst of European exploration. The volume of international commerce had grown all over Europe, feeding the appetites of monarchs for more trade, more profits, more islands, and more gold. Columbus had proved there were riches in the west; if he had failed to find China, the next voyager might succeed. Suddenly, almost every kingdom on Europe's Atlantic coast showed interest in exploration.

English, French, and Basque mariners had been catching codfish in the northwest Atlantic for several decades before Columbus's voyages. They may even have made a landfall in Newfoundland as early as 1480, but if so, they did not share their secret with the world. In 1497, the English king supported a voyage to the same region by the Italian Giovanni Caboti, known to the English as John Cabot, once more looking for a passage to Asia. When Caboti returned empty-handed, the English went back to fishing and made no further efforts in America for almost a century.

The Portuguese were still deeply interested in the African route to India, though da Gama would not return with his cargo of pepper until 1499. When Columbus proclaimed that he had found a western route to the Indies, the Portuguese hastened to protect their own outposts from Spanish incursions. With papal approval, the two kingdoms negotiated the Treaty of Tordesillas in 1494, agreeing that all new lands more than 1,100 miles west of the Canary Islands would belong to Spain, while lands to the east would go to Portugal. Unknown to the negotiators, their line crossed eastern Brazil, so Portugal gained its own American colony when a storm-tossed vessel reached its shores. Soon afterward, a Florentine geographer named Amérigo Vespucci visited the area, and later declared in print that the lands that Columbus had called the Indies were actually a continent previously unknown to Europe. Mapmaker Martin Waldseemüller promptly suggested that the continent bear Amérigo's name and "America" it has been ever since.

Geographers did not begin to realize just how big this continent really was, however, until Ferdinand Magellan led a Spanish fleet around the tip of South America in 1519. Magellan himself died in the Philippine Islands, but survivors of his expedition brought home a single ship around the coast of Africa, becoming the first men to circumnavigate the globe. The length of their trip across the Pacific proved that older ideas about the size of the earth had been fairly accurate, and that Asia was indeed much farther from Europe than Columbus had ever imagined.

In 1524, shortly after the return of Magellan's last ship, Giovanni da Verrazzano, an Italian sailing for France, became the first European to explore the coast of North America, tracing the shoreline from North Carolina to Cape Cod, fruitlessly searching for a northwest passage that would break through the continent to the ocean beyond. In 1534 and 1535, another French explorer, Jacques Cartier, continued the search in Canadian waters and spent a winter at the head of navigation on the St. Lawrence River, but to no avail. Slowly, Atlantic captains absorbed the reality that an immense tract of territory barred their way to Asia, but that the riches of this new world might actually surpass those of the old.

THE CONQUEST OF MEXICO AND PERU

As the Spanish established themselves in the Caribbean, they expanded their American empire with astonishing rapidity. After securing the main islands, they sent exploring parties to the surrounding mainland, perhaps as far as Chesapeake Bay, often in search of Indian slaves. Juan Ponce de Léon visited the mainland north of Cuba in 1513, naming it La Florida on account of its flowers. In the same year, Vasco Núñez de Balboa crossed the Isthmus of Panama and became the first European to view the Pacific Ocean.

The most momentous probe took Hernán Cortés to the coast of Mexico in 1519. Resentful local Indians complained to him of the oppressive empire of the Aztecs, or Mexicas, and Cortés marched inland to find it. Accompanied by 1500 Spanish men-at-arms, prancing horses, snarling war dogs, a handful of cannon, and an army of several thousand allies from the Tlaxcalan Indians, Cortés entered the city of Tenochtitlán as a guest, but quickly subdued its ruler, the emperor Montezuma II, and attempted to use him as a Spanish puppet. After several months of uneasy standoff, angry Aztecs attacked the Spanish and murdered Montezuma as a traitor. Fighting his way out of Tenochtitlán in a desperate midnight battle, Cortés regrouped with his Indian allies and besieged, captured, and destroyed the city in 1521. The remainder of the Aztec Empire fell quickly thereafter.

The spectacular conquest of Mexico stemmed partly from Spanish advantages in armor, firearms, and horses, partly from Cortés's own brilliance as a leader, partly from the assistance of Indian allies, and partly from an epidemic of smallpox that decimated Aztecs and Tlaxcalans alike. The victorious conquistadors placed themselves atop the Aztecs' existing system of tribute and forced labor and made themselves the rulers of an Indian empire. They called it the Viceroyalty of New Spain, and they built its capital, Mexico City, on the ruins of Tenochtitlán.

Eleven years later, in 1532, a similar conquest by Francisco Pizarro gave the Spanish control of the South American realm of the Inca. The Aztecs and Incas had possessed great quantities of gold and silver, and the Spanish promptly melted all the sacred and precious objects they could find. By the 1540s, they had finally located the rich deposits they had longed for, and put the Indians to work in the silver mines of Zacatecas and Potosí. During the second half of the sixteenth century, an immense American treasure flowed steadily into the coffers of Spain, and its sovereigns used its buying power to make Spain the mightiest kingdom in Europe.

SPAIN IN NORTH AMERICA

Discoveries of gold and silver did not halt the Spanish search for wealth. Intoxicated by the vision of personal enrichment and the glory of expanding the power of their king and church, conquistadors probed every accessible corner of the Americas in hopes of replicating the deeds of Cortés and Pizarro. Most of their North American efforts proved unsuccessful. In 1527, Pánfilo de Narváez attempted the conquest of Florida with 600 men, but most of them died in shipwrecks and Indian attacks. Only four survivors, who included the officer Álvar Núñez Cabeza de Vaca and an African slave named Estaban, stumbled back to Mexico in 1536, after years of wandering and Indian captivity. They bore fantastic tales of the Seven Cities of Cíbola, made entirely of gold and located somewhere to the north. In 1540, guided by Estaban, Francisco Vásquez de Coronado pursued the rumor with an expedition to the southwestern region of the future United States. Instead of golden cities, Coronado found the Zuñi pueblos.

Coronado easily captured these villages and his men raped and pillaged their inhabitants, but they could not find any gold. Refusing to give up, Coronado kept searching. On a side trip, one of his lieutenants gazed into the vast depths of the Grand Canyon. Coronado himself reached Kansas and witnessed the Great Plains, the buffalo herds, and the teepee-dwelling Indians who hunted them, but finally returned to Mexico empty-handed. It would be more than half a century before Juan de Oñate successfully followed up Coronado's expedition by founding New Mexico in 1598, in the northern valley of the Rio Grande, but his settlement remained small and isolated, focused on farming and converting the Pueblo Indians, not gold mining.

Most Spanish expeditions to southeastern North America were even less rewarding. After surveying the shores of modern Florida, Georgia, and South Carolina in 1525, Lucas Vásquez de Allyón established a small settlement on what became the Carolina coast, but died with most of his companions a year later. In 1539, Hernando de Soto led over 600 men into Florida, determined to find the rumored riches of the Indian city of Cofitachique. When Cofitachique disappointed him, de Soto kept marching from one Mississippian chiefdom to the next, fighting several pitched battles and kidnapping Indians at the slightest provocation, but never finding the gold he longed for. Death overtook him on the banks of the Mississippi River, and his survivors committed his body to its waters before retreating hastily to the Caribbean.

In succeeding decades, other Spaniards made intermittent efforts to occupy the southern Atlantic coast. In 1565, Pedro Menéndez de Avilés wiped out a French settlement on the northern coast of modern Florida and replaced it with a post he called San Agostín. Known in English as St. Augustine, this settlement has become the oldest continuously occupied European town in what is now the United States. In 1566, Juan Pardo reached farther with a fort at Santa Elena, on what is now Parris Island, South Carolina, followed by six inland garrisons along a route to the Appalachian Mountains. Indians burned these forts and killed their residents two years later. In 1570, a party of Spanish Jesuits established a mission to the Indians at Ajacán by Chesapeake Bay, and sent "Don Luis," a local Indian youth, to Spain for education. On his return, "Don Luis" turned on his patrons and helped his people kill them. Santa Elena did not survive past 1587.

Over the course of the sixteenth century, the Spanish gradually realized that their greatest interests in America lay to the south. The mines of Peru and Mexico were phenomenally successful, and a combination of Indian labor and African slavery supported a growing colonial economy elsewhere in their dominions. Though the Indian population declined drastically, it did not disappear. Spanish men made marriages and informal unions with Indian women, giving rise to a large mixed, or *mestizo*, population, particularly in Mexico. The wealth of New Spain gave the colonial authorities every incentive to maintain tight control, so colonial Latin America developed without the tradition of local self-government that would prevail in North America.

Spain made only limited efforts to carry its colonial system north of Mexico. Until the founding of California in 1769, only New Mexico, St. Augustine, and even smaller stations in Arizona and Texas remained as small but enduring beachheads of Hispanic culture in North America. Spain took over New Orleans and nearby districts from France in the eighteenth century, and claimed the entire Mississippi basin, but French influence still dominated the region's European culture. In the following century, the conquest and colonization of this portion of the Americas would mostly fall to kingdoms in northern Europe: the Dutch, the French, and especially the English.

After Columbus

Human affairs changed dramatically after Christopher Columbus came ashore on Guanahaní. People had long interacted across cultural and geographical distances, but the pace and intensity of worldwide interactions radically increased in the aftermath of the Columbian encounter. And despite the first peaceful exchanges between Columbus and the Indians, the encounter soon became a conquest, as the Native Americans proved vulnerable to foreign weapons and diseases, and the Europeans pressed their advantages. The most obvious result was the eventual colonization of the Western Hemisphere and the creation of new nations in North and South America. In addition, the transfer of plants and animals across the Atlantic in both directions changed economies, environments, and daily life in both hemispheres. Eventually, Europeans and their descendants would extend their power across the globe, directly colonizing Africa and much of Asia, while dominating most of the rest of the world. Less tangibly, the encounter brought cultural changes to every society it touched, from the Aztecs to the Guineans to the Chinese.

As they contemplated their conquests and struggled with their numerous failures, moreover, Europeans struggled to understand what they had started. Was America a place of moral and physical peril, or a providential opportunity to create a new and better world? How should the colonizers carry out that task? A struggle to answer these questions would preoccupy the colonizers and the colonized for centuries to come.

MODES OF CONQUEST

Native Americans had developed the bow and arrow, pottery making, weaving, agriculture, metalworking, irrigation, and vast construction projects. They domesticated a wide variety of plants that human beings use heavily today, including maize, potatoes, beans, tomatoes, peanuts, squash, gourds, cassava, chocolate, and—less happily—tobacco. From elaborate empires to small villages, the Indians displayed a sensitive and intelligent adaptation to their various surroundings and sustained complex and populous cultures. Demographers now estimate that at least 10 million and perhaps as many as 18 million people lived north of the Rio Grande in 1492, while the more urban civilizations to the southward may have supported as many as 25 million people in central Mexico alone.

Paradoxically, the Aztec and Inca Empires proved more vulnerable to foreign conquest than the smaller, decentralized tribes of North America. The Spanish could take over Mexico and Peru by destroying the Indian leadership and placing themselves at the top of an existing imperial structure. In North America, Europeans confronted a large number of distinct Indian societies, each composed of mobile and semiautonomous villages that could only be taken individually. Their skilled warriors could attack without warning at any time and then slip away to fight again later. European military commanders consistently reported that Indian archers could fire deadly arrows faster and more accurately than the clumsy matchlock guns of the explorers. Cortés could thus conquer and keep the Aztec Empire relatively quickly, but Juan Pardo could not preserve his forts in the Carolina backcountry. The arrival of Europeans did not mean instant defeat, therefore, but the beginning of a long continental struggle. North American Indians would hold their own for centuries by adopting European military methods such as guns and horses, and by pitting one imperial power against another.

Native Americans suffered a massive loss of life from their encounters with Europeans, though exact numbers and proportions are very hard to determine. Twentieth-century estimates of North America's Indian population ranged from 1 million to 18 million, with suggestions that their numbers fell by as much as 90 percent by the mid-seventeenth century. More recent estimates of peak Indian population fall between two and seven million. Thereafter, scholars now stress, mortality was serious, but varied by time, place, and circumstances.

Epidemic diseases certainly played an enormous role in decimating

Native Americans. Europeans and Africans lived in very close quarters, with poor sanitation, and often side by side with domestic animals. Germs spread quickly in these environments, often from livestock to people, so epidemics of smallpox, bubonic plague, cholera, and other deadly maladies repeatedly appeared and took millions of lives. Native Americans also suffered from diseases, but they had no prior exposure to the germs brought by the newcomers. Smallpox was certainly a serious killer. It appeared on Hispaniola in 1518 and quickly swept through the Caribbean, possibly killing a majority of the native Carib and Taíno people in a decade or two. The epidemic reached Mexico within a year and devastated the Aztecs, including the heir to the throne and his most talented generals, while leaving the Spanish invaders relatively unscathed. The Incas suffered a similar fate, and the same smallpox epidemic may have spread as far as California before subsiding. By 1548, a veteran Spanish colonist estimated that the population of Hispaniola had fallen from as many as 300,000 Indians to no more than 500.

Disease was not the only cause, however, for wars between Europeans and Native Americans also took countless lives. Anxious for labor and profits, colonists subjected survivors to cruelty, malnutrition, and overwork, leading to even more casualties. As late as 1715, a flourishing Indian slave trade spread deadly violence through southeast North America. Disease and exploitation could work together, moreover, since people weakened by hunger and overwork were more likely to get sick and die. It is quite possible that trade, slaving, and warfare conducted or inspired by English settlers spread far more germs among Indians than the marches of Spanish conquistadors. Over time, moreover, some Indian groups would begin to grow again, and keep a large presence in eastern North America well into the nineteenth century.

Experts dispute whether the transfer of diseases worked in reverse, bringing new ailments from America to Europe. Syphilis may have crossed the Atlantic with the crews of Columbus, for its first European outbreak coincided with their return in 1494. Contemporary physicians thought it came from America, and there is archaeological evidence that the disease had long existed among the Indians. The infection quickly spread along routes of commerce and warfare, and like smallpox among the Indians, it brought agony and relatively rapid death to previously unexposed populations.

For centuries after the arrival of Columbus, epidemic diseases repeatedly swept through Indian communities, often far in advance of the Europeans themselves. Smallpox was the worst killer, but waves of measles, influenza, typhus, cholera, scarlet fever, diphtheria, and even bubonic plague were almost as bad. The epidemics played a crucial role in sweeping native peoples from the colonists' path and breaking the morale of the survivors. In the southeastern United States, most of the chiefdoms visited by de Soto had vanished by the time Europeans revisited his line of march, while the Pilgrims discovered that a deadly plague had almost wiped out the Indians of coastal Massachusetts shortly before their arrival in 1620. "They not being able to bury one another," reported William Bradford, governor of the Plymouth colony, "their skulls and bones were found in many places lying still above the ground where their houses and dwellings had been, a very sad spectacle to behold."

The statistics of Native American population and depopulation have very important implications. North America was not an empty continent in 1492, waiting to be filled by European colonizers. Instead, its population density probably exceeded the definition of "frontier" later adopted by the US Census Bureau. The drama of the earliest "frontier," therefore, was not acted out between civilized Europeans and an empty wilderness, but in a vibrant zone of interaction between diverse cultures. Without knowing the true cause of infection, moreover, less vulnerable Europeans readily attributed the Indians' decline to divine providence, and Native Americans at times feared that their own gods had deserted them.

THE COLUMBIAN EXCHANGE

Deadly germs were not the only organisms to follow Columbus across the Atlantic, for a "Columbian exchange" of living things brought many varieties of plants and animals from each hemisphere to the farmers and consumers of the other. As food for people and animals alike, maize began spreading across southern Europe in the sixteenth century and soon reached Africa before expanding worldwide. Domesticated by Andean Indians, white potatoes fed millions of Europeans from Ireland to Russia by the eighteenth century and kept expanding thereafter. Sweet potatoes from South America spread almost as widely. The manioc root (also called cassava or tapioca) migrated from South America to the fields of Africa, India, and Indonesia, as farmers carefully copied the technique for removing its deadly poison first developed by Amazonian Indians. The world's cooks embraced American varieties of beans and also took up peanuts, squash, pumpkins, and tomatoes, together with delicacies like pineapple and chocolate. Native Americans also gave the world tobacco and the most widely cultivated variety of cotton.

In the opposite direction, the Western Hemisphere imported major species of domestic animals from the east. Native Americans kept dogs, llamas, turkeys, and guinea pigs, but Europeans added cows, horses, pigs, and sheep. The availability of horses especially transformed the lives of buffalo hunters on the North American Great Plains and strengthened many tribes militarily. Rats were far less welcome immigrants.

Colonists also brought their favorite plants to America, especially wheat and sugarcane, and both became very profitable staples. They also planted European fruits and vegetables in their American gardens. Bananas spread from Asia to Africa and followed the slave trade to the Caribbean. Rice took a similar path from Africa to South Carolina and Georgia, and southeastern Indians learned to plant peach orchards. Inedible plants crossed the Atlantic as well, from grasses and ornamental flowers to dandelions. The vast transfer of organisms from each hemisphere greatly increased the world's production of food, providing essential nutrition as human population doubled between 1650 and 1800, and radically altering ecosystems throughout the planet.

UNDERSTANDING AMERICA

The encounter with America presented learned Europeans with a series of profound intellectual challenges. The scholars of medieval Europe had little direct contact with the outside world, but they knew about Africans and Asians and argued theology with Muslims and Jews, so these different societies puzzled them far less than reports of an entirely "new world." They wondered why America was completely unmentioned in the Bible, the foundation of all human knowledge. Why had God allowed almost 1,500 years to pass before permitting its inhabitants to hear the Christian gospel? Observers of the natural world likewise wondered at the enormous diversity of American plants and animals, and the differences between the species of each hemisphere. They noticed that the commonest animals of Europe—from chickens to war-horses—were completely unknown in America, but America contained an astonishing variety of species that seemed completely new. Had all these creatures wandered from the landing place of Noah's ark to different continents without leaving any traces along the way?

The biological questions would puzzle Europeans for centuries, until Charles Darwin proposed his answers. More urgent questions concerned the American Indians. Theologians seriously debated whether Indians were truly human beings with souls who could convert to Christianity, or animals or devils in human form. If they were indeed human, should they be forced to accept Christianity, as Ferdinand and Isabella had demanded of the Jews and Muslims of Spain? Were compulsory labor and the seizure of Indian lands necessary for spreading the Christian faith? The conquistadors themselves spent little time on such issues. They were already accustomed to combating and enslaving non-Christian peoples, and they did not question their rights to American land and gold. Some of the Catholic clergy who came with them were more sensitive, however, and pushed for answers to difficult questions.

As early as 1511, the Dominican monk Fray Antonio de Montesinos had outraged the rulers of Hispaniola by denouncing their treatment of the Indians. "Are these not men?" he demanded. "Have they not rational souls? Must you not love them as you love yourselves?" Pope Paul III agreed, and declared in 1537 that "the Indians are truly men and that they are not only capable of understanding the Catholic Faith but, according to our information, they desire exceedingly to receive it." But what if the Indians rejected Christianity? Fray Bartolomé de Las Casas, who grew up on Hispaniola and became the bishop of Chiapas, Mexico, denounced the use of violence and the *encomienda* system to force the conversion of Indians. In his voluminous writings, Las Casas protested Spanish cruelty to Native Americans so powerfully that King Charles I (also known as Emperor Charles V of the Holy Roman Empire) convened a special council in 1550 to thrash out the lawfulness of compulsory labor and conversion. Held in the Spanish city of Valladolid, this extraordinary debate over Indian policy pitted Las Casas against another monk, Fray Juan Ginés de Sepúlveda, but ended inclusively. As a practical matter, the Spanish government halted the worst abuses of the *encomienda* system but still required labor tribute from conquered Indians. When Spanish demands for labor exceeded the local supply, they substituted African slaves for Indian workers, a policy Las Casas first supported but later opposed. Since the Spanish had long bought and sold Africans at home, their enslavement in America apparently touched fewer consciences.

Las Casas was not alone in defending the humanity of Native Americans. Some Renaissance thinkers praised the Indians as innocent "noble savages" whose natural virtues mocked the vices of civilized Christians, though exaggerated accounts of Indian innocence were as unrealistic as contrasting reports of Indian savagery. In a famous book of essays published in 1580, Frenchman Michel de Montaigne described Brazilian Indians who lived in a land of plenty, shared all their possessions in common, and spent their days hunting and dancing. Europeans called these Indians barbarous, he observed, but only because their customs were unfamiliar. Montaigne admitted that visitors called the Brazilians cannibals, but he mocked the moral pretensions of Europe by dryly observing that eating prisoners was kinder than torturing them, as Europeans did in their wars of religion. "We may then call these people barbarous, in respect to the rules of reason," he concluded, "but not in respect to ourselves, who in all sorts of barbarity exceed them."

Few Europeans were willing to go so far as Montaigne in comparing themselves to alleged cannibals, but America still challenged their sense of superiority and forced them to reckon with a vaster range of human possibilities than they had ever known before. If America was inferior to Europe, then the empire builders felt obliged to uplift it, perhaps by civilizing and Christianizing the Indians. If the Indians were somehow superior to their conquerors, then Europeans might justify their conquest by the creation of new societies that corrected the deficiencies of Europe and America. The Spanish responded to the moral challenge of America with fervent efforts to convert the Indians, but they were not the only colonizers to feel a moral imperative. English religious reformers revealed similar emotions when they chose a symbol for their colony on Massachusetts Bay: the image of a half-naked Indian calling, "Come over and help us." The utopian pressure represented by that symbol would continue its potent influence on the nation that the English colonists created.

*

The Native Americans were complex and diverse peoples whose histories were 15,000 years old in 1492. Their lifestyles ranged from simple hunting and gathering to large urban civilizations, and they had developed a wide variety of cultural practices, from archery to agriculture to building stone pyramids. Most North American social structures were less complex than those of Mexico and Peru, but from the

Pueblos to the Mississippians, many of its people created impressive urban settlements and intricate social hierarchies.

The European explorers who first encountered these Indians came from other complex cultures that suddenly expanded in the fifteenth century. Driven by a craving for Asian luxuries, a lust for gold, an immense curiosity, a yearning to save souls, and a fierce competition with each other and their Muslim rivals, European Christians began the voyages to West Africa that eventually led them to America. Soon after their arrival, Europeans combined slavery with plantation agriculture in a system that would profoundly shape the history of America, Europe, and Africa.

The invasion of Indian societies, the enslavement of Africans, and the founding of colonial empires was not a one-sided process of subjugation. The experience brought Europeans, Indians, and Africans close together for the first time and launched a course of interaction and exchange that would create new societies with fundamental contributions from all three. It was a highly unequal development in which Europeans benefited from stronger governments and economic systems, as well as superior weapons, and resistance to deadly epidemics. But Native Americans exerted their own pressures on Europeans and did not leave the colonists unmoved or unscathed. When Columbus died in 1506, the physical and cultural demands of empire building had just begun.

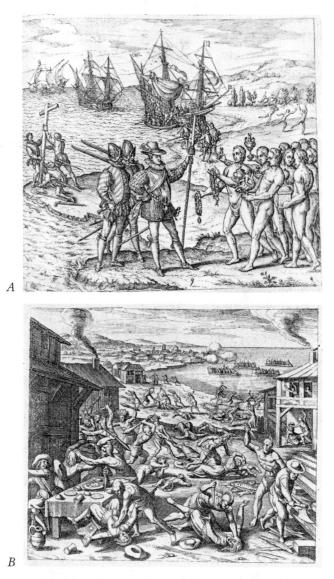

A

B

FIGURE 1. Colonizing Europeans depicted Native Americans in widely diverging
ways to reflect both their fantasies and their fears. *A*, Theodor de Bry, *Columbus, as
he first arrives in India, is received by the inhabitants and honored with the bestowing of
many gifts*, 1594. Engraving. Theodor de Bry's America, Special Collections, University of Houston Libraries, accessed November 11, 2016, http://digital.lib.uh.edu/col
lection/p15195coll39/item/84. *B*, Matthaus Merian, after a work by Theodor de Bry,
The Massacre of the Jamestown Settlers, 1634. Engraving. John D. Rockefeller Jr. Library, Colonial Williamsburg Foundation, accession no. 1986-15, image no. C86-461.

CHAPTER 2

The First English Colonies, 1584–1676

The captured Englishman stared death in the face. Guards pinned his head on two large stones as mighty executioners raised their clubs, awaiting the king's signal to dash his brains out. After a life of escapades that stretched from England to Turkey to Russia, was this bold adventurer really about to die at the far end of the earth, at the hands of half-naked strangers? No, not yet. The king's favorite daughter suddenly rushed forward and cradled the captive's head in her arms. John Smith was spared.

Pocahontas's rescue of Captain John Smith is one of the most melodramatic stories in American memory, the subject of endless retellings in print and on-screen. As Smith recalled some 20 years later, the incident took place in December 1607, eight months after a tiny contingent of Englishmen reached the shores of Chesapeake Bay in a country they called Virginia. Assuming leadership of a weak and bitterly divided band of colonists, Smith had gone to the local Indians for desperately needed food. Instead of trading, however, the Indians seized Smith and took him to their leader Powhatan, whom the English called an emperor. Smith certainly thought Powhatan had decided to put him to death when Pocahontas intervened and allowed him to obtain the food he had come for.

But what had really happened? Pocahontas was no more than 13 years old at the time, and probably less. Had she fallen in love with this bearded stranger, as mythmakers have imagined? Did Providence move Powhatan to compassion, as Smith later concluded? Both explanations are unlikely. Instead, the resourceful chief probably arranged the outcome in advance.

Ever since their arrival, the feeble band of Englishmen had troubled Powhatan's people with endless demands for food that were especially hard to satisfy because recent crops had withered in a massive drought. But the English had also brought valuable objects for trade—iron tools to fight Powhatan's enemies and exotic materials like cloth and bells to impress them. Powhatan had decided that the English could stay, but they must learn his rules and join the government he had worked for decades to create.

Smith's mock execution was probably an initiation ceremony that brought him to the brink of death and allowed him to be reborn symbolically as a dependent who owed the chief his life. Following his supposed rescue, Powhatan adopted Smith as his son, gave him an Indian name, and proclaimed him a *werowance*, or local chief. Henceforth, Powhatan would expect Smith to govern the English as a subordinate tribe, free to manage their internal affairs but subject to his ultimate authority.

Ten months later, it was Powhatan's turn to be initiated. Captain Christopher Newport arrived from England with badly needed supplies, and imposed the emperor's policy in reverse by proclaiming Powhatan a subordinate chief under the authority of King James I of England. Newport carried a copper crown to symbolize the new relationship, but the proud chief refused to cooperate. Finally the exasperated Newport pushed down on Powhatan's shoulders and forced him to stoop low enough to get the circlet on his head. In a more familiar ceremony, the two leaders exchanged gifts. Among other items, Powhatan received a scarlet cloak and gave Newport his beaded deerskin mantle in return. Today the mantle rests in an English museum, a pointed reminder of the mutual incomprehension between Englishmen and Indians.

Neither John Smith nor Powhatan understood or accepted their initiations. Certainly neither one had knowingly agreed to subject himself to the other. Each ceremony was an effort to manage radically different people by assigning them familiar roles. No matter how clumsy, the rituals also embodied hopes for peaceful—though unequal—cooperation between Indians and Englishmen. These hopes were sadly doomed to fail, not only from misunderstanding but also because the two sides' purposes were fundamentally at odds. Some months after his coronation ceremony, Powhatan put his finger on the problem when he told Smith that "many do informe me, your coming is not for trade, but to invade my people and possesse my Country." Despite the niceties of initiation ceremonies, the prediction proved true, not only in Virginia but also farther north, in a region that John Smith had named New England.

The English would extend a chain of colonies up and down the Atlantic seaboard by the end of the seventeenth century, with even more valuable sugar colonies sprinkled among the Caribbean islands. On the mainland, the Chesapeake colonies of Virginia and Maryland came first and flourished from the cultivation of tobacco. These colonies depended on plantation agriculture and forced labor, first with English laborers and later with African slaves. New England sheltered religious dissidents called Puritans, who established an economy based on family farms, small villages, and active commerce. The Puritans hoped to create an ideal Christian community and left an enduring mark on secular and religious culture in the United States. Both sets of colonies reflected important aspects of English society, and both fought bitterly with Indian neighbors like Powhatan, but the contrasts between them became at least as important as the similarities.

England and the Atlantic

The movements that brought John Smith and Powhatan together were part of a vortex of changes in the seventeenth century that transformed people all around the basin of the Atlantic Ocean. Whatever their hemisphere, almost all ancient and medieval people had seen the Atlantic as an impassable barrier, far too dangerous to cross. The sixteenth-century explorers had shown instead that the Atlantic could be a bridge or even a highway. Joined by a sprinkling of other Europeans, the Spanish and Portuguese had crossed this bridge to contact other Atlantic peoples and, often, to sweep them into colonial empires. As the sixteenth century became the seventeenth, several nations of northern Europe, notably England, France, and the Netherlands, challenged Spain and Portugal by using the ocean to greatly expand their contacts with Africa and America. The inhabitants of Africa and America responded in a variety of ways—sometimes by seeking to repel the newcomers and sometimes by enlisting them in their own alliances, but often by agreeing to trade with them, swapping exotic products that the Europeans craved for goods the Europeans could provide. The result was a crisscross of relationships around a new Atlantic world that brought together diverse people who were previously unknown to one another. These relationships brought a dramatic increase of commerce and interaction, as well as a heightened scramble for empire.

Commerce and new empires did not expand in a vacuum, for religious changes had also swept through sixteenth-century Europe. Beginning in the early sixteenth century, the Protestant Reformation split Christians into warring camps that pitted Protestant England against Catholic Spain, and various Protestants against each other. Together, these quarrels interacted with economic and political rivalries to affect the drive for colonization, and especially influenced the English settlements that rose in eastern North America and later became the United States. The forces that brought John Smith and Powhatan to their twin initiations were thus much larger than either could fully comprehend.

A NEW ATLANTIC WORLD

For most of the sixteenth century, the Spanish and Portuguese kept the business of Atlantic trade and empire for themselves. Even before Columbus, the Spanish learned the colonial enterprise by conquering the Canary Islands off the African coast, enslaving most of the natives, and forcing them to make sugar. After the voyages of Columbus, they repeated the pattern on the major Caribbean islands, but then concentrated on the mainland when the mines of Mexico and Peru proved even more profitable than plantations. As provided in the Treaty of Tordesillas, the Portuguese built a different kind of empire by continuing to send voyages southward along the African coast. After Vasco da Gama rounded the Cape of Good Hope in 1497, other Portuguese commanders pressed onward to the Southeast Asian islands where the spices originated, and built strings of forts and trading posts behind them that reached as far as Africa, India, Southeast Asia, and China and Japan. By sailing south and east they finally found the water route to Asia that Columbus had sought by sailing west.

Portugal also took advantage of its treaty rights to develop a colony in Brazil, first as a source of material for making dye and later for sugar plantations. Like the Spanish in the Caribbean, they began with Indian labor before turning to African slaves. To find them, the Portuguese converted their Gold Coast fort of Elmina to slave trading, expanded their contacts with the West Central African kingdom of the Kongo, and laid the groundwork for a colony farther south, in Angola. Portugal dominated the first century of the Atlantic slave trade, sending as many as 650,000 Africans to America before 1640.

The kingdoms of northwestern Europe watched with growing concern as the Spanish and Portuguese empires grew, especially as Spain used American silver to wage war and exert influence throughout Europe. Their concern only deepened after 1580, when Spain briefly took over Portugal, uniting both world empires under a single sovereign. As the Iberian kingdoms grew stronger, their rivals hungered to break their imperial monopolies. These new participants dramatically increased the pace and complexity of the seventeenth-century Atlantic world. They generally began with their own trading companies and voyages, went on to raid Spanish commerce, and finally sought colonies of their own.

A few examples can illustrate the intensity and complexity of what happened. In 1580, Francis Drake became the first English mariner to sail around the world, and he gave captured Spanish treasure to Queen Elizabeth that exceeded the value of her total annual income. Seeking a base to replicate this feat, England tried to colonize Virginia between 1584 and 1587, but did not begin to succeed until the founding of Jamestown in 1607. France put its first permanent settlement on the St. Lawrence River in 1600, while the Netherlands chartered the Dutch East India Company in 1602 to capture the spice trade from Portugal. A year after Jamestown, Samuel de Champlain pushed higher up the St. Lawrence to found Quebec City, future anchor of the fur-trading empire of New France. A year after that, Henry Hudson, an English captain serving the Dutch, stumbled on the river that still bears his name while searching vainly for the Northwest Passage. Calling the surrounding territory New Netherland, the Dutch launched their own fur-trading empire with a post at Albany in 1617. Still searching for the Northwest Passage, this time for England, Henry Hudson sailed into Hudson's Bay in 1610, staking England's claim for its own share of the fur trade. Native American hunters supplied the French, Dutch, and English with the pelts they purchased, and Native Americans replaced their stone technology with the metal tools they took in exchange. Colonization became so popular that even the distant Swedes and Danes got involved by founding New Sweden on the Delaware River south of New Netherland, a Danish sugar colony on St. Thomas in the modern Virgin Islands, and slave-trading companies in both nations.

Soon after the founding of Albany, moreover, English religious dissidents (whom later Americans called the Pilgrims) left their Dutch refuge to start a very different colony in New England, not far from New Netherland. As they did so, the Netherlands gave a monopoly on its African and American trade to a new venture, the Dutch West India Company. In 1628, the company scored its greatest coup by capturing the entire Spanish treasure fleet. Besides running New Netherland, moreover, the company quickly moved on Portuguese Brazil and managed to hold it for three decades. By 1640, it was exporting sugar technology to Barbados, a Caribbean island claimed by the English in 1627. Led by Barbados, England's Caribbean sugar islands were the world's largest sources of sugar by 1700 and the biggest destination for the African slave trade. The islands could not supply themselves with food or fuel, however, but nourished another commercial empire by importing those items from English North America, on ships sailing from New England. The colonies that became the United States grew directly from this dizzying network of Atlantic relationships.

REFORMATION AND EMPIRE

Economic rivalries fed Atlantic expansion, but religious rivalries were also crucial to the motives of kings and settlers alike. Many Europeans had worried that the Roman Catholic Church had become worldly and corrupt, and they joined a sweeping movement to reform and purify it that became known as the Protestant Reformation. In 1517, two years before Cortés invaded Mexico, German monk Martin Luther publicly denounced church abuses and the theological reasoning used to defend them. In place of outward practices like church rites, the veneration of saints, or the bestowal of spiritual promises in exchange for gifts of money, which all reinforced the institutional power of the church and could become moneymaking schemes, Luther insisted that the Bible was the only source of Christian truth and that salvation came only from sincere personal faith. These ideas put private conscience and personal interpretations of scripture ahead of church traditions and authority. Luther's followers also replaced the Latin Mass with services and Bible readings in the worshippers' own languages and allowed their clergy to marry. To loyal Catholics, these changes spelled moral chaos and heresy, or gross violation of religious truth, but Luther's followers found them liberating and consoling, and called themselves Protestants to emphasize their protest against Catholicism.

The Swiss theologian John Calvin took Luther's ideas several steps further. With fierce and unbending logic, Calvin concluded that an all-powerful and all-knowing God must have planned, or "predestined," the salvation or damnation of every human being in advance, even before the creation of the world. Calvin also taught the "innate depravity," or fundamental wickedness, of all humanity, stemming from the disobedience of Adam and Eve. Everyone deserved eternal damnation in this view, but God showed mercy to his chosen few and no one could influence His decision. Paradoxically, perhaps, belief in predestination did not discourage Calvinists from seeking salvation. Instead, they lashed their consciences over every hint of sin or worldly frivolity and fervently prayed for God's guidance. Spiritual improvement might be a comforting sign that God had chosen them for salvation. Rejecting every church practice they could not find in the Bible, Calvinists called for simple worship services centered on Bible reading, preaching, and prayer, and some abandoned all forms of church government beyond the individual congregation. Calvin's demanding faith took deep root in English America, where a search for different versions of religious and moral perfection would be a recurrent cultural theme from the seventeenth century to the twenty-first.

Protestantism spread widely in northern Europe, where resentment of Rome ran deep, but long campaigns against Jews and Muslims left Spain staunchly Catholic. England's King Henry VIII resisted the Reformation at first, but when his Spanish wife did not bear a son, Henry alienated Spain by asking the pope to annul their marriage. When the pope refused, Henry rejected Rome's authority and obtained his divorce from a cooperative archbishop of Canterbury. Henry wanted no radical changes in doctrine or theology, but Protestant ideas spread quickly after his death. Divorce, however, did not bring the healthy son the king had wanted. Henry VIII famously married six wives, but his only son did not survive him long.

Political and religious instability roiled England until Henry's daughter Queen Elizabeth I began a long reign that lasted from 1558 to 1603. With the monarch as its earthly head, the Church of England (or Anglican Church) adopted a conservative form of Protestantism while retaining Catholic rituals, vestments, and holy days, as well as governance by bishops and archbishops serving under the monarch.

Queen Elizabeth won deep love and extravagant praise from her subjects as she guided them successfully through political and military perils. When she came to power, England was a tiny realm on the fringes of Europe, with no more than 3.5 million people—perhaps no more than one-fifth as many subjects as the Aztec emperor Montezuma. Under her leadership, England grew dramatically in economic and military power, and its population rose, reaching 5 million by 1680. Spain had used its American wealth to finance wars against Protestantism, but the English fought back with a deep conviction that the Almighty favored their nation, their church, and their queen. "God is

English," proclaimed one Elizabethan preacher, and few in his audience seemed shocked by the assertion.

Like other English monarchs, Elizabeth shared power with Parliament, a legislature that included the House of Lords for nobles and bishops and the House of Commons for members chosen by townsmen and rural landowners. The English Parliament gained strength in the sixteenth and seventeenth centuries, and new laws and new taxes could not be imposed without its consent. Elizabeth dealt tactfully with the lawmakers, but the next two kings, James I and his son Charles I, were less accommodating. In the 1640s, parliamentary forces overthrew Charles I and put him to death. Establishing the principles of representative government and parliamentary supremacy coincided with the founding of England's overseas empire, with central importance for American history.

THE PRICE REVOLUTION AND ITS CONSEQUENCES

Atlantic empires changed the European economy in ways that made colonization seem more important and more affordable to its rivals. Spain spent its American silver on manufactured goods from other countries, including English woolens. The influx of silver caused inflation, and English consumer prices rose more than fivefold in the sixteenth century. A similar pattern prevailed in most of Europe, leading to what historians have called the price revolution. Wool producers and other exporters benefited from rising prices, but wages usually failed to keep pace with inflation, so laborers and artisans suffered accordingly.

Inflation hit rural areas the hardest. Noblemen and a group of wealthy commoners known as the gentry owned most of England's farmland and rented it to peasant cultivators under long leases and fixed rents. Their real incomes shrank as prices climbed, so innovative gentry tried to repair their fortunes with alternatives to traditional agriculture. The most popular measure was to enter the booming wool market by evicting tenants, consolidating their tiny plots, and enclosing these larger tracts with fences or hedges to make sheep pastures.

Victims of enclosure could toil as day laborers, work in the woolen industry, or turn to beggary and crime. Contemporaries may have exaggerated, but earnest observers worried that enclosure brought private benefits and social catastrophe. "The people ... doe swarme in the land, as yong bees in a hive in June," warned one. "The mightier like strong old bees thrust the weaker, as younger, out of their hives: Lords of Manors convert towneships, in which were a hundred or two hundred [church] communicants, to a shepheard and his dog."

While wandering laborers and improving landlords transformed the countryside, merchants and manufacturers grew rich from trading cloth and other finished goods and looked for new ventures to reinvest their profits. The price revolution thus elevated a group of men with money to spend on colonies, and uprooted others who lacked prospects at home, who were used to moving around already, and who might be willing to try their luck in America.

Religious and political rivalry inspired some Englishmen to break Spain's monopoly of empire, and new wealth gave them means to do so. If American treasure financed war against Protestants, they reasoned, the Almighty would surely bless a counterattack. In 1562, a Plymouth mariner named John Hawkins seized a cargo of African slaves and sold them in the Spanish Caribbean in defiance of Spain's monopoly. In 1573, Hawkins's associate Francis Drake captured an enormous shipment of Peruvian gold as it crossed the Isthmus of Panama. A later raid made him the first Englishman to sail around the world, as he robbed Spanish fleets in the Pacific and kept heading west. Spain denounced Hawkins and Drake as pirates, but Elizabeth knighted them both and the nation acclaimed them as heroes.

The exploits of Hawkins and Drake fired the imagination of English writers and scholars who began to ask why England should not colonize America directly. Richard Hakluyt, an English clergyman and diplomat, collected stories of past English voyages and arguments for western settlement. Somewhere in America, he reasoned, there had to be a northwest passage leading safely to the Orient; the Spanish could not have found all the gold and silver in America, and there must be plenty left over for the English; American naval bases would enable English ships to attack the annual Spanish treasure fleets as they followed the Gulf Stream north and east across the Atlantic; and finally, he predicted, the Indians would remember Spanish cruelties, join the kindly English to oppose them, and embrace Christianity in the bargain.

The Enterprise of Virginia

Wishful thinking inspired all these arguments, but they were persuasive enough to carry English colonists to Virginia. Poor planning and unrealistic expectations undermined their efforts, and England's first attempted settlement on Roanoke Island in modern North Carolina vanished entirely. The Jamestown colony on Chesapeake Bay nearly failed too, as its colonists lived like soldiers, neglected agriculture, antagonized the Indians, and focused on a fruitless search for gold. Virginia would not flourish until its settlers abandoned their initial goals and established private farms, added women and families, and began to feed Europe's new appetite for smoking tobacco.

ROANOKE AND JAMESTOWN

Hakluyt caught the attention of Walter Raleigh, a renowned soldier and favorite courtier of Queen Elizabeth. In 1584, the queen gave Raleigh permission to search for new lands and claim them for England. Later that year, his first exploring party reached Roanoke Island and reported that the natives were friendly and harmless, and the soil and climate were delightful. Collecting his own knighthood, Raleigh named the area Virginia in honor of his unmarried "Virgin Queen."

The next year, Raleigh's second expedition tried to found a permanent base. Commander Ralph Lane's men mapped the area and located Chesapeake Bay to the north while artist John White made sensitive sketches of the native inhabitants. Despite these advances, Lane antagonized the Indians with endless demands for food and by murdering their chief at a supposed peace conference. When Sir Francis Drake visited the colony in the early summer of 1586, the besieged survivors accepted his offer to bring them home, and the colony ended in failure.

Undaunted, Raleigh sent John White back to Virginia in 1587 with a shipload of men, women, and children. They first intended to settle on Chesapeake Bay, but later decided to reoccupy Lane's old fort on Roanoke. Soon after their arrival, White's daughter, Elizabeth Dare, gave birth to a girl, Virginia Dare, the first English child born in America. Without much pause, Governor White then returned to England for more supplies, but while he was there, King Philip II of Spain dispatched an enormous fleet, or armada, to invade England, dethrone Elizabeth, and reclaim her realm for Catholicism. Drake and Hawkins led in England's defeat of the Spanish Armada in 1588, but the emergency delayed White's return for two more years. When he finally arrived, his colonists had vanished, and the fate of the "Lost Colony" remains a mystery to this day.

After the fiasco at Roanoke, Raleigh lost favor at court and abandoned his efforts to settle Virginia. Queen Elizabeth died in 1603 and her cousin James Stuart, who ruled Scotland as King James VI, succeeded her as King James I of England. Within a year, James had made peace with Spain, and a group of London investors had decided to try again in Virginia, hoping to find profits there without challenging Spain. In 1606, they organized the Virginia Company, a joint-stock company which sold shares to investors who expected to split its profits through dividends, much like a modern corporation. On an early April morning of 1607, their three tiny ships entered Chesapeake Bay.

The expedition consisted of 104 men and boys, most of whom were gentlemen who expected to share in the honor, glory, and wealth of the new colony, but not in its manual labor. Others were personal servants, and some were technical experts who could identify the gold and jewels that everyone expected to find. Only a handful had more practical skills and none was a farmer or gardener.

When the leaders opened their locked chest of instructions, they were chagrinned to find that their seven-member governing council included Captain John Smith, a cocksure young adventurer of humble birth who lacked due respect for his superiors. Submitting to Smith's elevation as best they could, the council elected Edward Maria Wingfield as governor and considered where to settle.

They found that Chesapeake Bay penetrated a heavily forested plain that sluggish streams and estuaries had cut into alternating bands of land and water. They called the largest of these the James River after their king and followed it upstream for 60 miles. One enthusiastic colonist later reported that the banks were sprinkled with "faire meddowes and goodly tall Trees, with such Fresh-Waters . . . as I was almost ravished at the first sight thereof." Finally finding an easily defensible promontory with a safe, deepwater anchorage on May 13, 1607, the exhausted men disembarked, named the place Jamestown, and set about making a fort.

SURVIVING IN POWHATAN'S VIRGINIA

The newcomers had unwittingly entered the territory of a confederacy of some 30 small Indian tribes from the Algonquian language group who shared the name or title of their supreme chief, or "emperor," Powhatan. Partly by inheritance and partly by force, the aging Powhatan had brought them together while still a young man and installed subsidiary chiefs, or *werowances* (mostly male but some female), to guide each tribe and village within the group. Like the related tribes who had sparred with the Roanoke colonists, the Powhatans grew corn, beans, and squash, lived in bark-covered houses, and hunted game and seafood with stone-tipped arrows.

The Powhatans already knew about Europeans, for explorers' vessels had occasionally entered the Chesapeake for several decades. The emperor's kinsman and ultimate successor Opechancanough may have been "Don Luis," the youth whom Spanish missionaries had sent to Spain in 1570, but who returned and helped kill them in 1571. Powhatan may also have met survivors from the Roanoke expedition, for he later reported that white people had once lived near the mouth of Chesapeake Bay but died in an intertribal war. He knew the bearded, pale-skinned newcomers could be dangerous, but he also knew they brought valuable trade goods. After several initial skirmishes, the English and the Powhatans settled into a wary truce, occasionally punctuated by murders and violence on either side. Each group wisely distrusted the other but resolved to make use of their antagonists. As Powhatan himself later explained to John Smith, "[I]t is better to eate good meate, lie well, and sleep quietly with my women & children, laugh and be merrie with you, have copper, hatchets, or what I want, being your friend: then bee forced to flie from al[l], to lie cold in the woods, feed upon acorns, roots, and such trash, and so be hunted by you, that I can neither rest, eat nor sleepe."

Not surprisingly, the English first needed the Indians more than the reverse. They did not bring enough food and the river's feeble currents did not flush away their wastes. The leaders quarreled endlessly and the gentlemen would not work. As servants of the Virginia Company, the colonists expected their employer to feed them. Failing that, they might live off the local population like soldiers in enemy territory, but severe drought had left the Powhatans with little to spare. Hungry and wracked by intestinal diseases, only 38 of the original 104 Englishmen were still alive at the end of January 1608.

These were the circumstances when John Smith went looking for food and fell captive to Powhatan. He may never have grasped the meaning of his "rescue" by Pocahontas, but Smith certainly realized that English lives depended on those they called "Salvages." Combining threats with barter, he obtained enough corn from the Powhatans to keep his company alive. As other leaders died or departed, Smith took command and minimized casualties with his famous rule that "he that shall not worke, shall not eate." Smith's blunt speech and stringent methods never endeared him to others, however, and a serious injury forced him back to England in 1609. John Smith never returned to Virginia, though he later explored the northern coasts of America, named them New England, and continued to promote American colonization.

Smith's departure was followed by the "starving times." Over the winter of 1609–1610, Jamestown's population plunged from five hundred to sixty, as Powhatan refused assistance and the frantic colonists ate dogs, rats, roots, and (in at least one grisly case) even one another in a desperate struggle to stay alive. When a new governor landed in May of 1610, he decided the situation was hopeless and ordered everyone into his boats for a return to England. Just as they were passing the mouth of the James, however, the starving colonists met three supply ships laden with provisions, and returned to Jamestown for another effort.

Virginia barely flickered back to life. The countryside seemed devoid of profitable exports, and supplies from home were never reliable. Arriving in 1611, Deputy Governor Sir Thomas Dale attempted to whip the demoralized colonists into shape with a severe legal code, the "Lawes Divine, Morall and Martiall," that imposed the death penalty for crimes ranging from disobedience and desertion to sex offenses and robbing gardens. As in John Smith's day, everyone was required to work and the colonists attempted to grow their own food, but they did not stop raiding the Indians. The result was a bitter war of attrition with the Powhatans that did not abate until 1613, when the settlers captured Pocahontas and held her hostage. Colonist John Rolfe sealed this peace by marrying Pocahontas in 1614. He took his bride and their infant son to England two years later, where she impressed the court with her noble bearing, her command of English, and her conversion to Christianity. Sadly, Pocahontas did not return to Virginia, but sickened and died before the couple's planned return.

TOBACCO

Pocahontas's death did not interrupt John Rolfe's experiments with a new crop that eventually secured Virginia's future. Native Americans grew several varieties of the tobacco plant and used it widely in their ceremonies. Spaniards had taken up smoking in the Caribbean and Sir Walter Raleigh made it popular in Elizabeth's court. The habit caught on quickly among the rich and fashionable, and soon there was a thriving market in Europe for the golden brown leaf. Virginia's native tobacco was harsh to English throats, but Rolfe discovered that the milder Caribbean variety grew well at Jamestown, and he sold a large shipment in 1617 for the tidy sum of three shillings per pound. His fellow colonists scrambled to do likewise and planted tobacco every-where they could, including the streets of Jamestown. Tobacco be-came so important that Virginians soon used it for money.

Potential farmland was plentiful in Virginia but labor was not, and tobacco required enormous amounts of painstaking, backbreaking work. Fields were cleared by axe and fire and prepared for planting by the hoe. Seeds were nurtured in specially prepared beds until the delicate seedlings could be transplanted to a larger field. Workers hoed endlessly to control the weeds and nipped small shoots and flowers to force the growth of larger leaves. At harvest, whole plants were care-fully cut and hung in large, open-air drying sheds until the leaves could be stripped and packed into barrels. All these tasks were done by hand, but with enough effort, even an inexperienced worker could raise be-tween 500 and 1,000 pounds of tobacco per season, and enough corn to eat the following year. At prevailing prices in the 1610s and early 1620s, one worker's crop could be worth as much as £100 in London, more money than most English laborers would see in a lifetime. Any-one who commanded the labor of many workers could gain a hand-some fortune in a few short years.

PLANTATIONS AND BOND SERVANTS

Rolfe's success sparked a clamor for tobacco workers, and the Virginia Company was happy to help. In 1619, a Dutch vessel arrived in James-town and exchanged a cargo of "twenty negars" for food, but we do not know if these first African Americans were held as slaves. More commonly, London officials scoured the docks and poorhouses for un-employed men and women cast adrift by the changing English econ-omy, and offered them passage to Virginia in exchange for a term of service that ranged between four and seven years. They sealed these agreements with documents called indentures, much like apprentice-ship contracts, so the laborers were called indentured servants.

Most indentured servants were single men in their teens or early twenties, but some were women and some were much younger. Not all came voluntarily—some did not understand what they were signing and others were simply kidnapped. Once in the Chesapeake, however, their labor was the personal property of whoever owned their indentures, and they were sold to new masters from the decks of their ships. Until they had served out their terms, servants received no pay and minimal subsistence. They could be sold over and over, bequeathed in a will, or even lost in a card game. Runaways had to repay their masters with at least twice as much time as the length of their absences. Pregnancy cost a female servant two more years of bondage, and her child suffered servitude in turn until the age of 24 — 30 if the father was one of Virginia's slowly growing number of Africans. Whipping was the punishment for disobedience or for running away, and little but the promise of eventual freedom, with the chance to grow tobacco on their own, distinguished their lives from those of slaves.

The Virginia Company encouraged the tobacco boom by allowing settlers to create their own private farms. The company released its veteran employees and gave them each 100 acres of land. Anyone who paid to import a newcomer (either himself, a family member, or a servant) would receive a headright of 50 acres. Well-connected settlers could receive even larger grants, or purchase land for low prices and an annual fee, or quitrent. Responding eagerly, English settlers pressed up and down the James River and throughout the Chesapeake basin to find the best land. Much to the dismay of London authorities, they refused to live in compact towns or villages but scattered widely along the shore of the James and nearby creeks and rivers, with each planter shipping his tobacco to London from his own waterside dock. For centuries into the future, Virginia and the other southern colonies preferred scattered farms over towns and cities.

Tobacco farmers (early Virginians called them all planters, whatever the size of their farms) who gained enough land and servants could become very wealthy. Many hoped to make enough in a few years to return to England, purchase an estate, and escape Virginia's misery forever. This get-rich-quick objective encouraged masters to extract as much labor from their servants as they could, in the shortest possible time and at the lowest possible cost. The most nimble or unscrupulous succeeded in amassing large landholdings and numerous servants, laying the groundwork for a dominant class of wealthy plantation owners. Conditions on their estates were often brutal and life expectancies were very short. One young servant, Richard Frethorne, undoubtedly spoke for many in 1622 when he implored his parents to redeem him. "Wee must work hard both earlie, and late for a messe of water gruel and a mouthful of bread, and beife," he wrote them. "If you love me or respect me, as your Child release me from this bondage, and save my life." Frethorne's pleas were ineffective, and he died within a year like so many others. One careful investigator of 1623 discovered that the Virginia Company had brought 3,570 settlers to its colony between 1619 and 1622, joining 700 who were living there already, but no more than 1,240 were left alive at the end of that three-year period.

Important political changes coincided with the rise of tobacco culture. A new governor, Sir George Yeardley, arrived in 1619. He abandoned the "Lawes Divine, Morall and Martiall" and instead summoned a General Assembly, composed of his appointed Council and a House of Burgesses elected by the colonists, to make laws. In time, the Governor's Council would function as an upper house of the colonial legislature while the House of Burgesses claimed the rights and roles of a colonial House of Commons. No one foresaw this in 1619, as America's first representative assembly seemed to view itself as something like an English town council. The members took their duties very seriously, however, and spent several days in Jamestown's church adopting a code of laws and regulations that settled matters from the prices of commodities to the penalties for swearing.

Stabilizing the Chesapeake

Tobacco production finally created the basis for stability and prosperity in Virginia, especially after the English government took over government from the Virginia Company. Crushing Indian resistance, the colonists re-created as much of English life as possible, including familiar forms of government, an established Anglican Church, and the presence of women and children. Unlike England, however, prosperity rested on the labor of bound workers and the creation of a plantation economy. Virginia was successful enough to inspire imitation in the nearby new colony of Maryland, but it also fostered severe social tensions that brought rebellion and a colonial civil war.

INDIAN WARS AND ROYAL GOVERNMENT

Powhatan died in 1617, just as the tobacco boom was taking off, and any traces of a mutually beneficial Indian-English relationship in Virginia died with him. As the English took more and more land for tobacco planting, his successor Opechancanough plainly saw the balance of power tipping inexorably against his people and decided to strike while he could. On the morning of March 22, 1622, his men attacked without warning and slew 347 colonists in a matter of hours. The "massacre," as white Virginians called it, wiped out one-third of the English population, but it was not enough to kill the colony. Virginians struck back ruthlessly, vowing to root the Powhatans "out from being longer a people uppon the face of the Earth." Powhatan casualties soon exceeded English losses many times over, and sporadic warfare continued until 1632, leaving the tribe barely independent on a fragment of its former territory.

The Powhatans struck once more in 1644, but they were far too weak for victory. Virginians captured and murdered the elderly Opechancanough, while the remnants of the once-powerful confederacy became tributary nations who lived peacefully inside the colony's boundaries in exchange for annual payments and submission to English authority. Tributary Indians traded furs and skins for the English products they now relied on and helped the colonists fight other tribes. The prominent colonists who dominated the fur trade appreciated their presence, but ordinary whites frequently distrusted them and coveted their meager reservations.

Virginia was beginning to succeed, but not the Virginia Company. It never turned a profit and the death rate stayed high, even though individuals prospered on their private plantations. Disgruntled directors complained to King James and appalled His Majesty with their tales of Indian attacks, wholesale death, and general incompetence. In 1623, English courts revoked the charter of the Virginia Company, shortly before the death of King James. Two years later, his son, King Charles I, proclaimed Virginia a royal colony.

Royal government did not change Virginia much in the short term. The king appointed a governor and a council, and the governor became Virginia's chief link to England's monarchy. Grudgingly (for King Charles had no love of elected assemblies) the Crown continued to allow the freeholders, or landowners, of Virginia to select members of the House of Burgesses to represent them. Together, the Governor's Council and the House of Burgesses formed a bicameral, or two-chambered, assembly for the passage of colonial laws. The governor and the Crown could both veto their bills. The result was not democracy, for the majority of Virginia's residents were tenants, bound servants, or other dependents of established planters. Over time, however, Virginia's House of Burgesses would become the institutional basis for an increasingly self-governing colony.

The Assembly divided Virginia into counties and created an English system of local government. In each county, the governor installed a number of substantial planters as justices of the peace, with authority to settle minor local controversies without formality. Sitting together, the justices composed the county court, and met each month to try civil and criminal cases, issue licenses, regulate roads and taverns, supervise the collection of taxes, and generally transact the routine public business of the county. Like their English counterparts, the county justices were never elected, served virtually for life, and, in practice, used the power of recommendation to fill the vacancies in their own ranks. Able justices gained their peers' respect and won election to the House of Burgesses, and the county courts became key institutions for cementing the power of Virginia's planter gentry.

Planters also ruled the colony's Anglican Church. England's national religion had always been legally established in Virginia, but few spared time for religion in the early years of the tobacco boom. As society gradually stabilized, the Assembly created an Anglican parish in each county and ordered a vestry, or committee of prominent laymen who were often justices of the peace, to impose taxes to support a church and a minister and provide local charity. Vestries did not always comply, but churches and Anglican clergy spread gradually over prosperous parishes. Inhabitants were required to attend church, and courts and vestries made conscientious efforts to punish immoral behavior. Like the county courts and the House of Burgesses, the Anglican Church became an important bulwark of the established order and Virginia's dominant social class.

ECONOMIC AND SOCIAL STABILITY

The growth of stable institutions owed much to the passing of the tobacco boom. Tobacco prices fell as production rose, until almost everyone could afford the comfort of a pipe. Falling prices made overnight riches impossible, but the planter with plenty of hands could still become wealthy by remaining in the Chesapeake. More permanent settlers gradually built a society where a small and wealthy upper class controlled vast lands and tilled them with unfree workers whom they bought and sold at will. The majority of residents were small or middling planters who tilled their own fields with the help of their families. The outlines of a plantation society had emerged long before African slaves replaced white Englishmen in the tobacco fields.

Lower profits made it harder to replace dying workers, so even the cruelest masters provided better food and living conditions by the 1640s. With better treatment, more servants survived to seek farms of their own, so settlement spread ever farther along the rivers and creeks of Virginia's tidewater. As they moved inland, more Virginians escaped deadly marshes and bad water, and their lives grew even longer.

Stability also brought more women to the colony. Only a handful of the first settlers had been female, most of them wives of senior commanders. Beginning in 1619, the Virginia Company sent over several boatloads of young single women, rightly expecting they would easily find husbands to pay for their passage. These women suffered from the same poor conditions and high death rates as male newcomers, but their numbers continued to grow. Female servants worked indoors more often than in the fields, but their hard work in the preparation and preservation of food and clothing was indispensable to the colony's success. Female servants faced the threat of sexual abuse, but the unbalanced sex ratio gave poor women in Virginia much more freedom in the choice of marriage partners than they had in England. A high death rate created many widows, and fortunate women could radically raise their standing by marrying a succession of wealthy men and combining their estates. By English law, however, a husband had full control of his wife's property, so men could also improve their fortunes by marriage to wealthy widows.

As white Virginians began to marry, the sounds of their children's games and voices mingled with the din of axes and the calls of working adults. The death rate remained higher in Virginia than in England for most of the seventeenth century, so many of these children died young. Most of the survivors lost one or both parents before reaching adulthood, but the presence of a rising generation was an unmistakable sign of Virginia's growing success. Slowly and unconsciously, Virginians of the 1640s had transformed their settlement from an outpost into a home.

MARYLAND JOINS VIRGINIA

Imitation was another telling sign of success. In 1632, King Charles set off a separate colony on the northern shores of the Potomac River and Chesapeake Bay and called it Maryland in honor of his wife. He granted it to George Calvert, Lord Baltimore, a trusted councilor and tireless colonial promoter who had been active in the Virginia Company and in plans for a colony in Newfoundland. Maryland was a proprietary colony whose owner held full rights to govern as he saw fit, so long as his laws did not conflict with England's. George Calvert died before the grant was complete, but his son Cecilius Calvert became the next Lord Baltimore and first Lord Proprietor of Maryland, developing his colony on familiar lines.

Maryland's economy, like Virginia's, depended on tobacco. Those who brought in new settlers got headrights of land and could purchase more, but owed an annual quitrent in return. Most of the early workers were indentured servants, joined by a sprinkling of slaves. The proprietor appointed the governor, but an elected assembly made the province's laws and county courts administered local government. As in Virginia, a small group of wealthy landowning planters dominated society and government.

Religion formed the greatest difference between Maryland and Virginia. The Calverts were Roman Catholics when most English Protestants still regarded so-called papists as potential enemies of the state and supported strict laws that discriminated harshly against them. The Calverts were mainly interested in Maryland for economic reasons, but they also wanted a haven for their fellow Catholics. England would not have allowed an exclusively Catholic settlement, but Cecilius Calvert protected his coreligionists by refusing to establish an official church and allowing all professing Christians complete freedom to worship as they chose.

The Maryland Assembly ratified the policy of toleration with its Act Concerning Religion in 1649, the first law guaranteeing religious freedom for competing denominations of English Christians. As expected, most Marylanders were nominal Anglicans, but their church remained weak without public funds or official support. Radical Protestants found safe havens in Maryland when they faced persecution in Virginia. The Catholic population remained small but enjoyed a disproportionate share of wealth and political influence. At the end of the seventeenth century, religious and political tensions led Maryland Protestants to defy the Calverts and revoke religious liberty, but until then, the colony demonstrated the feasibility of toleration to the rest of the English world.

BACON'S REBELLION

A violent uprising in 1676 marked the end of Virginia's founding era. By the early 1670s, a ring of counties pressed out from the shores of the

Chesapeake to the fall line, a band of rapids that blocked river passage from the coastal plain or tidewater to the piedmont uplands. Beyond the fall line, the powerful Susquehannocks dominated diverse Indian peoples who surrounded white settlements from a distance, jockeying with colonists and each other for access to trade and safeguards for their independence. Within the white settlements, wealthy planters held most of the best land but depended heavily on the labor of large numbers of discontented servants. Governor William Berkeley and his closest friends enriched themselves with the Indian trade and used their offices for private gain. Ordinary planters complained bitterly of official corruption and the high taxes that top officials did not have to pay, and declining tobacco prices often blighted their dreams of security. Freed servants pressed westward beyond them and collided with the first tier of Indian inhabitants. Often landless, freed servants could be just as discontented as bound ones. Senior officials worried that they were "pressed at our backs with the Indians [and] in our bowells with our servants," and could not tell which group would be more dangerous.

The tension snapped in 1675, when a dispute between whites and Doeg Indians took the lives of some innocent Susquehannocks and ignited a war between their tribe and the Virginians, who promptly split into factions. Hoping to contain the conflict and return to profitable trading, Governor Berkeley would only attack Susquehannocks and asked the Assembly for an expensive line of defensive forts. This decision disgusted backcountry farmers who did not trade with Indians but feared them all. They preferred a full-scale war against all Indians that would pay for itself through the sale of captives. When the governor refused again, an obscure young gentleman named Nathaniel Bacon stepped forward as popular champion.

Bacon had just arrived in Virginia as a high-born but restless young man of 27 and readily agreed to lead a force of angry settlers against all Indians, concentrating on the peaceful tributary tribes and avoiding the more dangerous Susquehannocks. Aroused by Bacon's defiance, a new Assembly passed reforms to empower ordinary settlers and clean up official corruption. When Governor Berkeley resisted, the insurgents burned Jamestown and looted the plantations of his wealthiest supporters. Violence suddenly collapsed in October 1676, when Bacon took sick and the rebellion died with him, but his followers had already defeated most Virginia tribes, allies and enemies alike. Defeat removed restrictions on the Indian slave trade, and warring southern tribes sold the English as many as 30,000–50,000 captives in the next generation. Berkeley retaliated by hanging 23 rebels and annulling their reforms, but the Crown decided he had acted too harshly. When a royal commission arrived to soothe the shattered colony, Berkeley lost his job, returned to England, and died soon afterward.

Bacon's Rebellion uncovered deep rifts in Virginia's social fabric. White farmers were clearly enraged by their subordinate position in Virginia society. They might seek vengeance by attacking people they saw as radically different, especially those of another color, but they could also turn against their social superiors. In the future, great planters who longed for social stability would treat the complaints of small farmers with greater sensitivity. Planters would also benefit when racial hostility between poor whites and black slaves obscured class differences among whites, and when enslaved plantation workers could not become free and rebel. In the generation after 1676, Indian slaves were not enough, so Virginia's great planters gradually replaced their indentured servants with African victims of a growing Atlantic slave trade. The imperial government also resolved to keep Virginia and its other colonies under tighter central control.

Puritan America

The English settlers of Virginia had reacted to the economic and social disruption of their homeland by looking to America for economic opportunity. Facing similar pressures, other English people saw a moral and spiritual crisis that they hoped to reverse by creating a more perfect church and commonwealth in America. Contemporaries called these men and women Puritans, because they wished to purify the English church and nation of deep-seated corruption that they blamed on persisting remnants of Roman Catholicism. Beginning on the margins of the Church of England, Puritans would lead the settlement of the New England colonies and briefly take control of the English government. Their ideals and values would leave a lasting mark on the culture and politics of the United States.

THE PURITAN FAITH

Puritanism was not a clear-cut sect or denomination, but a broad religious movement among English men and women who worried that the Church of England had not done enough to rid the nation of sin or itself of Catholic errors. Under Queen Elizabeth, the Anglican Church had embraced a moderately Calvinist theology, conducted its services in English, and allowed its clergy to marry, but it retained Rome's hierarchy of bishops and archbishops to supervise parish priests or ministers, and church courts to regulate public morals and religious teaching. Ministers wore Catholic-style vestments during services and read from an officially adopted Book of Common Prayer. Strict laws defined all English Christians as members of the Church of England, required them to attend its services, and demanded their acceptance of its doctrines and structure.

Like their fellow English subjects, Puritans took enormous pride in England's leadership of the Reformation. As in the days of the Old Testament, they concluded, God had made a covenant, or contract, with the English and made them his new chosen people, offering them special protection in exchange for their special devotion. This national covenant was a blessing and a burden, for God had held the Hebrews to higher standards than other nations. Surely He would treat the English likewise, but Puritans fretted that England had repaid God's blessings with indifference. They saw shortcomings everywhere: neglect of public worship, sports and games on Sunday, immoral or indifferent clergy, commercial greed, and government corruption. Above all, Puritans complained that the Church of England included everyone in the realm, saints and sinners alike, when a true church should be more selective. With such abounding wickedness, who could escape God's wrath?

Puritan standards for individuals were as strict as their demands for their country. Devoted followers of John Calvin, they denied that anyone became a true Christian by birth or upbringing. Instead, genuine "saints" gained their faith through a lengthy process they called "conversion." Usually beginning in young adulthood, anxious sinners worried that damnation was almost certain. After a long period of agonized study and prayer, however, the "elect" would slowly gain a hope, and then a more confident "assurance," that God had decided to save them after all. In the joyous aftermath, devout converts still worried about overconfidence, and tested their own perceptions by constantly grilling their consciences and struggling to live righteous lives. Like other Calvinists, good Puritans were never certain of salvation—that knowledge belonged only to God—but they fervently hoped that moral progress might be a sign that God had chosen them indeed. By contrast, the Church of England taught that salvation was a lifelong process, not a distinct moment of radical change, and forgave the shortcomings of its members and clergy far more readily than its Puritan critics.

Puritans were keenly aware of England's social and economic ills, and blamed them on sins like greed and pride. No one expressed their concerns more vividly than John Winthrop, a Puritan gentleman and rural landowner. "The land growes weary of her inhabitants," he reflected in 1629, "so that man, which is the most precious of all creatures, is here more vile and base than the earth they tread upon." A stern but loving man, Winthrop immediately worried over the moral consequences of overpopulation. "Children, neighbors and friends," he mourned, "especially of the poore, are counted the greatest burdens which if things were right, would be the highest earthly blessings." Like other Puritans, Winthrop worried about rampant selfishness and dishonesty. As he put it, "All arts and trades are carried on in that deceitful manner and unrighteous course as it is almost impossible for a good upright man to maintain his charge and live comfortably in any of them."

Puritanism grew slowly in the reign of Elizabeth and continued to spread in the early seventeenth century. Reformers did not come from any single class, but they were most numerous in the middling ranks of society. Their movement was especially popular where people were abandoning the traditional economy to take up trading and manufacturing. Ironically, Puritans condemned greed and selfishness but they also praised frugality, self-control, and personal responsibility—useful virtues for worldly success. The sober-minded Puritan who rejected self-indulgence in favor of hard and steady work was more likely to prosper than his easygoing neighbors, so the Puritan faith found an undeniable affinity with the emerging capitalist economy.

The leaders of the English church and government agreed that men and women should have good morals, but viewed their Puritan critics as potential subversives. English leaders believed that God had appointed them to protect righteous government and true religion with a firm hierarchy in church and state, beginning with the king himself and proceeding downward through archbishops and bishops, nobles and magistrates, parish priests, and ordinary parishioners. Puritans threatened this order by disputing Anglican doctrines, rejecting church hierarchy, and demanding a "converted" clergy. Fundamentally, English rulers opposed the Puritans for questioning God's approval of the king, his ministers, and his church.

Puritans were also unpopular among ordinary Englishmen who resented their campaign against minor faults and harmless amusements or hated their eternal soul-searching and fault-finding. Despite official suspicion and popular disapproval, however, most Puritans continued to worship in Anglican churches and refused to break openly with the authorities. Hoping to reform the church and state from within, they tried to stay out of trouble and prayed for the day when their chance would come.

PLYMOUTH'S PILGRIMS

A small number of the most zealous Puritans gave up on the Church of England. Insisting that the Anglican establishment was too corrupt to be a true church at all, Separatists wanted to withdraw from it altogether to form their own tiny congregations of fellow believers. Unlike most others, these Puritans faced serious persecution for their open rejection of the king's religion.

One special group of Separatists launched the first Puritan settlement in New England. Suffering from fines and imprisonment in 1608, a congregation from the village of Scrooby in Nottinghamshire first sought refuge in Calvinist Holland. After years of discouragements there, and worried that their children would grow up Dutch, the people who came to be known as Pilgrims decided to settle in Virginia. Obtaining financial backing and permission from the Virginia Company, their first contingent of 102 passengers set sail for America from the port town of Plymouth in 1620, tightly packed in a tiny ship called the *Mayflower*. Thirty-seven had been members of the Dutch congregation, joined by 22 of their servants and family members. The others were "strangers" who sailed for a variety of motives, including the hope for economic gain, but church members and their values dominated the expedition. Outside of New England, few English settlements would share their religious motives for migration.

The Pilgrims were officially bound for the mouth of the Hudson River, then within the boundaries claimed by Virginia. Blown off course, the *Mayflower* actually landed on Cape Cod in mid-November, and its crew refused to go farther. A few passengers muttered that their settlement was illegal and its rules nonbinding outside of Virginia, so leaders persuaded the other men to sign an agreement later known as the Mayflower Compact, which tied them together as a "civil body politic" and bound them to rules of their own making. They then chose William Bradford as governor and a group of "assistants" to legislate with him, and went ashore to build the community they would call Plymouth, after their port of departure.

The Mayflower Compact did not renounce the English Crown, but king and Parliament had no formal role in the government it created. Practically speaking then, Plymouth was America's first republic, or government that the citizens elected without a functioning monarch or nobility. English authorities would eventually reclaim their authority, but the other early colonies in New England followed Plymouth's example and made self-government a founding principle.

As at Jamestown, conditions were grim during Plymouth's first winter, and almost half the colonists died. Also as in Jamestown, there were Native Americans in the area with prior European contacts. Like "Don Luis" in the Chesapeake, a Patuxet Indian named Squanto had been to England, but returned to find his tribe dead or scattered from an epidemic. Squanto mediated between the Pilgrims and the nearby Wampanoags, interpreting for both sides and teaching the English to plant corn. Massasoit, the Wampanoag *sachem*, or chief, followed the same logic as Powhatan and thought the English could help him deal with rival tribes, and concluded a treaty of friendship. Though the Pilgrims shared the suspicion that most early modern Englishmen felt for those they termed "savages," they refrained from wanton attacks and escaped Virginia's early trauma of Indian warfare.

The Plymouth colony grew slowly through further immigration and gradually gained the power to feed itself. After their first harvest in 1621, the Pilgrims invited Massasoit and his warriors to a five-day feast that later Americans remembered as the first Thanksgiving. They later won a firmer legal foundation when English authorities gave them retroactive permission to settle and govern themselves.

Settled by married couples and their children, Plymouth enjoyed an equal sex ratio and a full range of ages from the outset. Families received land grants and established farms to raise foodstuffs, not tobacco. They bought supplies from England with exports of fish and furs. Until the 1675–1676 Indian war known as King Philip's War, the Plymouth colony quietly grew and prospered in the southeast corner of modern Massachusetts. In 1691, a new royal charter merged the Plymouth colony with Massachusetts, its larger and more turbulent neighbor.

MASSACHUSETTS'S GREAT MIGRATION

King Charles I succeeded his father James I in 1625. Charles was more hostile to Puritanism than James, and even showed signs of nostalgia for Catholicism. William Laud, his archbishop of Canterbury, severely persecuted Puritans to "harry them out of the land." Charles also envied European kings who ruled as absolute monarchs, and tried to rule without consulting Parliament. His religious policies offended Puritans, and his political ambitions outraged the country gentlemen who dominated the House of Commons, many of whom were also Puritans. Rising tensions split the kingdom, with royalists and Anglicans increasingly on one side and parliamentary supporters and Puritans on the other.

As conflict escalated in the late 1620s, John Winthrop and some other leading Puritans considered seeking refuge in America. Safe in the wilderness, they could devise more godly political and religious institutions and bring them back to England when the time was ripe. They would not establish freedom of religion, however. Like their Anglican and Catholic opponents, Puritans were sure that their own religion was the only truth, and that God required them to establish truth and punish falsehood. What they called their "godly commonwealth," or community founded on the common good, would establish their understanding of the true faith in true churches, and nothing else.

To implement these plans, a few Puritan gentlemen took over an existing trading company, renamed it the Governor and Company of the Massachusetts Bay in New England, and won permission to found a settlement. In a daring legal maneuver, the directors then transformed their private company into a civil government located in America. As in Plymouth, the freemen, or free adult males of Massachusetts, chose a council of assistants and made John Winthrop their governor. They soon added that voters must be church members and created a legislature, or General Court, composed of town representatives. Governor Winthrop would serve 13 one-year terms between 1629 and his death in 1649.

In June 1630, Winthrop and the first group of 400 settlers arrived at Massachusetts Bay in the *Arbella* and three other ships. Six hundred others soon followed them. Over the ensuing decade, about 10,000 settlers, most of them English Puritan couples with their children, would come to Massachusetts in an unprecedented mass movement that historians later called the Great Migration.

"God's Commonwealth"

The newcomers built their first towns around the mouth of the Charles River, where it emptied into Massachusetts Bay. John Winthrop's own group founded Boston on a peninsula jutting into the harbor from the river's south shore. More supplies and colonists arrived in February 1631, but 200 still died the first winter, and more than 80 returned to England. Despite this perilous beginning, migrants kept coming. With intense idealism, they tried to create a reformed version of their homeland that conformed as much as possible to their understanding of God's will.

A COVENANTED PEOPLE

The governing principles of Puritan commonwealths differed profoundly from those of the US Constitution, but still left a deep imprint on American culture. John Winthrop spelled them out in a famous sermon he delivered to passengers on the *Arbella*. Unlike Thomas Jefferson's Declaration of Independence over a century later, Winthrop's "A Modell of Christian Charity" began by firmly rejecting any notion of human equality. "God Almightie in his most holy and wise providence hath soe disposed of the Condicion of mankinde," Winthrop explained, "as in all times some must be rich, some poore, some highe and eminent in power and dignitie[,] others meane and in subjeccion." But Winthrop immediately linked inequality to the ideals of justice and mercy. Hierarchy existed to enforce God's will on earth, he reminded his audience, so "no man is made more honorable than another or more wealthy etc., out of any particular and singular respect to himself, but for the glory of his Creator and the common good of . . . man." Bound by the spirit of Christian love, he explained, no man's personal interests should overrule the needs of others, so social rank must support the greater goals of God's service and the common good.

Winthrop thought cooperation was more important in Massachusetts than other places because more was at stake. Proclaiming a national covenant like ancient Israel's, he declared that New England's sacred mission gave it a unique role in history and a special relationship with God. "Wee shall be as a Citty upon a Hill," he admonished. "The eyes of all people are upon us." This did not mean that Massachusetts was already a perfect society, but only that it ought to be. Like a biblical prophet, Winthrop warned his people to put religious obligations ahead of worldly interests, or "the Lord will surely breake out in wrathe against us[,] be revenged of such a perjured people[,] and make us know the price of the breache of such a Covenant . . . till wee be consumed out of the good land whether wee are going." Similar warnings about the special nature of America's covenant with the

Almighty would echo from future generations of religious and secular reformers, endlessly warning backsliders to reclaim the founders' high standards to avoid a terrible fate.

TOWN, CHURCH, AND COLONY

Reflecting their commitment to church and community, the settlers of Plymouth and Massachusetts Bay did not scatter themselves like Chesapeake planters but lived in close-knit "towns" that were not truly urban places, but farming villages that strictly controlled their own local affairs. To create a town, a group of men, mostly heads of families, sought a land grant from the colony and spelled out their guiding principles in a written covenant modeled on the larger covenant they felt they had with God. In a typical example of 1636, the founders of Dedham, Massachusetts, committed themselves to "that most perfect rule, the foundation whereof is everlasting love," and warned away those who could not comply: "We shall by all means labor to keep off from us all such as are contrary minded, and receive only such unto us as may be probably with one heart with us." The founding ideals of these little communities thus linked the duty of mutual support to powerful pressures for conformity.

Town leaders gave each man a plot of land that reflected his family's size and social rank. Some towns distributed strips of land in large fields that the residents tilled together; others gave a separate farm to every household. All retained some common land to share later, and for grazing and timber in the meantime. Reflecting their commitment to mutuality, the adult men of a town continued to make major decisions in a general town meeting, but they often elected a committee of selectmen to handle routine public business.

After some hesitation, Massachusetts Puritans decided to "gather," or assemble, their churches according to their understanding of scripture. In each town, the most pious elders met for lengthy prayer and mutual interrogation until a small number recognized one another as properly converted "visible saints" with the right and duty to form a church. These men signed another covenant that spelled out their religious principles and invited some worthy man to become their minister. Over time, they would extend the privilege of church membership to other men and women who convinced them of their own conversions, but members who broke moral or religious laws could expect to be disciplined or expelled. Whether members or not, all the townspeople were required to attend weekly worship and pay taxes for the minister's salary.

Unlike the Church of England, New England church government was called congregational because each congregation ruled itself and chose its own minister, without control by an outside hierarchy. There was no denominational structure at first, but ministers maintained unity with regular meetings for prayer and consultation. The churches had no formal place in government, but only church members could vote, religious and secular leaders often overlapped, and magistrates punished anyone who strayed from Puritan doctrines. Careful not to press defiance too far, the churches of Massachusetts claimed formal communion with the Church of England while rejecting most of its practices.

Puritan churches required a learned clergy who could properly expound their intricate doctrines. As early as 1636, a pious benefactor named John Harvard left money for the training of godly ministers, and Harvard College in nearby Cambridge was named in his honor. The colonial government also required each town to maintain a common school where children could learn to read the Bible. Even in Massachusetts's earliest decades, Harvard graduates and other well-educated New Englanders began writing and publishing a large body of erudite sermons, tracts, theological treatises, poems, and chronicles, creating a rich intellectual life in the community and laying the basis for an American literary tradition.

The Massachusetts economy rested on farming families who tilled their own land, perhaps with a servant or two. Wives and husbands had equally important responsibilities, with women in charge of cooking, cleaning, gardening, poultry, and the preservation of food, as well as the routines of childcare. Children learned their grown-up roles by helping and copying their parents, a practical education that was just as important as schoolwork. Unwitting agents of the Columbian exchange, husbands planted English crops like wheat, rye, oats, and peas, as well as Indian corn and pumpkins, and carefully tended horses, cows, and pigs. Hay was an important summer crop that carried livestock through bitter New England winters.

Families who arrived first sold some of their harvests to the immigrants who arrived every season, and bought from them items like iron, lead, cloth, and salt. This trade carried the Bay Colony through its own "starving times" relatively quickly, and made it self-sustaining by the mid-1630s. After 1640, however, a looming political crisis in England cut the flow of migrants, forcing New Englanders to shift from supplying newcomers to exporting fish, lumber, and furs instead. In an early sign of business talent, the prudent merchants of Boston, Salem, and other port towns also turned to shipping and shipbuilding as their colony began to flourish.

Massachusetts Bay grew much faster than Virginia in its early decades. Most of the first Virginians were single men, but the Great Migration brought repeated shiploads of married couples with their children. Those who survived the first few brutal winters enjoyed long lives in a healthy climate. In the carefully studied town of Andover, Massachusetts, for example, most of the founders lived into their seventies while raising an average of 7.2 children to adulthood. Even when substantial immigration declined after 1640, the excess of births over deaths pushed the population of Massachusetts as high as 20,000 by 1660 and almost three times that by the end of the seventeenth century.

A growing population spread more towns across eastern Massachusetts. In 1635, a group inspired by the Reverend Thomas Hooker traveled much farther west and founded the town of Hartford in the Connecticut River Valley. Their community became the nucleus of Connecticut, which established its own General Court and frame of government by 1639. Connecticut later absorbed the separate Puritan colony of New Haven. New Hampshire took shape to the north of the Merrimack River, but Massachusetts kept Maine until well into the nineteenth century. These spin-off colonies mostly grew harmoniously with Massachusetts Bay and collectively embraced its sense of mission and Puritan orthodoxy. The founding of the tiny enclave of Rhode Island, however, was not nearly so tranquil.

THE CHALLENGE OF DISSENT

One of the most noted early migrants to Massachusetts was the eloquent and learned young minister Roger Williams. A charming man whom everyone loved, Williams was also a doctrinal purist who could never keep tactful silence when he spotted a sin. Arriving in 1631, he began to preach in the town of Salem and immediately questioned the moral and legal basis for the entire colony. First he claimed that King Charles never owned Massachusetts so he had no right to grant lands there; the colony should invite the king to repent of his sin and correct it. Williams next declared that government had no right to regulate religion, so his Salem congregation should hold aloof from other churches that condoned this error.

Williams's sermons frightened and outraged Governor Winthrop and the Massachusetts leadership. They had no intention of lecturing the king or tolerating heresy. More fundamentally, they feared that Williams demanded an impossible degree of perfection in merely human affairs, rejecting all compromises and undermining the flexibility their godly experiment required. When Williams would neither change his mind nor quit inciting disputes, they reluctantly ordered him to leave Massachusetts. In January 1636, Roger Williams and a small band of followers departed to found the dissenting colony of Rhode Island.

A second controversy erupted the following year. Arriving with her husband in 1634, Mrs. Anne Hutchinson began to hold religious discussions in her Boston home, and suggested to her followers that most of the colony's leaders were hypocrites who went through the motions of good behavior without a genuine conversion. Hutchinson strongly hinted that God identified the imposters to her personally and freed her from the need to obey them—a heresy known as antinomianism.

Once again, an upstart was urging ordinary Puritans to spurn their leaders as damnable sinners. Anne Hutchinson was not only a woman who did not know her place, Puritan leaders feared, but like Roger Williams, her divisive teachings could stir up factions and tear the fragile colony apart. When the General Court summoned Hutchinson to account for herself, she skillfully parried their questions for two days, until she slipped and claimed to hear God "by the voice of his own spirit to my soul." This was flagrant antinomianism. Unwilling to allow anyone's inner voices to overturn authority, the court quickly ordered Hutchinson and a few of her followers to join Roger Williams in Rhode Island. Of her two favorite ministers, John Cotton escaped punishment, but John Wheelwright departed to become a founder of New Hampshire. Mrs. Hutchinson could not settle down, however. After four years, she and her family left Rhode Island for the neighboring colony of New Netherland, where Indians killed her in 1643. The patriarchs of Massachusetts Bay took grim satisfaction from her fate. "The Lord heard our groans to heaven," wrote one, "and freed us from our great and sore affliction."

Rhode Island adopted town government, congregational churches, and many other institutions from the other Puritan colonies, but like Maryland, it granted liberty of conscience, or freedom from religious

dictation, to all its residents. With Roger Williams as one of its leading citizens, Rhode Island became a beacon of religious tolerance, and
irritated its neighbors by sheltering Baptists, Quakers, Jews, and other
dissidents from Puritan orthodoxy.

War and Transition

As in the Chesapeake, the 1670s seemed to bring New England's founding era to a close. Half a century after the Pilgrims established Plymouth, Puritan towns spread westward from Cape Cod to the Connecticut River Valley, and dotted the shores of Long Island Sound. Steady
growth brought the problems of success, including warfare with Indians, whom the colonists defeated with bloody determination. Events
in England forced conscientious New Englanders to rethink their mission, as English Puritans dealt with King Charles and fought a civil
war without their help. As New England's first generation gave way to
the second, many ministers worried that rising prosperity and changing priorities were sapping religious devotion. In 1676, a renewal of
Indian warfare demonstrated that New England could survive these
challenges and keep expanding, redefining its sense of purpose without surrendering it.

THE ENGLISH CIVIL WAR

Back in England, political and religious tensions had continued to
mount while the Puritan colonies were growing. In a bid for absolute power, Charles I had tried to ignore Parliament, until the need
for money finally forced him to relent in 1640. The king resisted when
Parliament tried to limit his power, and in 1642, the English Civil War
broke out between supporters of the king and the Anglican Church
on one side and Parliament and the Puritans on the other. Parliament's army triumphed under Puritan general Oliver Cromwell and
beheaded King Charles in 1649. Cromwell tried to rule England as a
Puritan commonwealth without king or Parliament, but the experiment foundered when he died in 1658. The former king's son had been
waiting in France for just such a moment, and in 1660 he returned to
England as King Charles II. The Restoration, as it was called, reestab-
lished the monarchy, the Parliament, and the Anglican Church, and
England turned firmly away from its Puritan revolution. Like the Puritan "republics" of New England, however, the commonwealth experi-

ment in kingless government held enormous importance for the future American republic and fed many of the ideas that later supported its revolution.

Virginia remained quietly loyal to the Stuart dynasty in the Civil War and Interregnum, as the period between kings was called, but New England's position was more difficult. Its founders had planned to rescue England when its crisis inevitably arrived, but events moved too quickly in the end and English Puritans made their own decisions without consulting Massachusetts. American Puritans felt suddenly irrelevant and intensely disappointed, especially when the Restoration ended their hopes for a Puritan England. If God had further work for his chosen people, they must find it in America.

Governor John Winthrop died in 1649, the same year as Charles I. While he was governor, the people of Massachusetts had gradually given more attention to their own problems than to those of England. They did not abandon the ideals of a covenanted people, but focused more on preserving their own colony than reforming all Christendom. In the future, the Puritans' most serious challenges would come from the conflicts they found between their twin objectives of holiness and prosperity in America.

THE SECOND GENERATION

As New England continued to grow, Puritans increasingly wrestled with a painful contradiction. They worked hard and practiced self-denial to glorify God and avoid temptation, but these frugal habits could bring material success and even more temptation. The contradiction was less severe in rural communities where families struggled to feed and clothe themselves, and could not aspire to much more than supplying the next generation with enough land and household goods to start farms of their own. Family arguments were the biggest source of rural social tension, as long-lived parents tried to keep their lands and their children's labor for as long as possible and young people longed to marry and start their own households.

Most farm families supplied as many of their own needs as possible, but they also traded a bit in market towns, which allowed ports like Boston to swell with Atlantic commerce. New England merchants sent furs, fish, lumber, and foodstuffs all over the Atlantic basin in locally made vessels manned by local mariners. They returned with overseas cargo that ranged from sugar and tobacco to the finest silks and wines. As ports and merchants prospered, pious Puritans worried that the quest for profits and the lure of luxuries could undermine religious zeal.

The most visible sign of spiritual malaise was the failure of the founders' children to join their parents' churches. Young people prayed sincerely for spiritual rebirth, but fewer of them experienced the transforming sensation that was still the test of true conversion. Most of them had been baptized as children because their parents had been church members, but could the children of these pious but officially unconverted Puritans be baptized as well? After long debate, the majority of ministers finally consented, and devised the so-called Halfway Covenant to cope with the new reality. After 1662, the child of a baptized but unconverted person could be baptized in turn, but could not be admitted to full communion until he or she reported a personal conversion experience.

Arguments about the Halfway Covenant seemed to betray disunity and declining faith. Near the end of his life, Governor William Bradford mourned in his chronicle of the Plymouth colony that the founding spirit of mutual love and cooperation seemed to be lost: "I have been happy, in my first times, to see, and with much comfort to enjoy, the blessed fruits of this sweet communion, but it is now a part of my misery in old age, to find and feel the decay and want thereof (in a great measure) and with grief and sorrow of heart to lament and bewail the same." In eloquent sermons known as jeremiads, after the Old Testament prophet Jeremiah, vigilant ministers warned their flocks against declension, or a decline in religious standards. Over and over, they denounced the moral decay that seemed to follow success, and predicted that God's wrath would destroy an errant people unless they repented and returned to primitive purity. "We have in great part, forgotten our Errand in this Wilderness," thundered Increase Mather, president of Harvard. "Although the Lord hath been calling upon us, not only by the voice of His servants, but by awful judgments, that we should return unto Him who hath been smiting us, yet men will not return every one from his evil way." Dozens of less-famous contemporaries added their condemnations to Mather's.

The jeremiads could not bring everyone to repentance or distract many merchants from their business. Even in worldly Boston, however, life in 1660 or 1670 was still simple and straitlaced by the standards of a century later. But the fact that the sermons were preached, published as pamphlets, and purchased in large numbers reveals that the old perfectionist temper was not entirely dead. It had only changed its form, and would keep doing so as the burdens of the covenant continued to weigh uneasily on the spiritual heirs of John Winthrop.

INDIAN WARFARE

Like the Spanish, the French, and the Virginians, the Puritans had partly justified their migration to America by promises to convert the Indians to Christianity. Also like the Virginians (but not the Spanish or French), they did relatively little to practice this intention, and like most Englishmen of their day, distrusted the Indians as savage worshipers of Satan. Soon after his arrival, Governor John Winthrop rejoiced that the Indians "are all neere dead of the small Poxe, so as the Lord hathe cleared our title to what we possess." The Reverend John Eliot worked hard to convert Indians in Massachusetts, and brought about 1,100 "praying Indians" to specifically designated towns by the mid-1670s, but most Puritans assumed that Indians should disappear like the Old Testament nations displaced from Canaan by the children of Israel.

As in Virginia, however, the Indians did not decline nearly as fast as New England expanded, and the result was bloody warfare. In the Pequot War of 1637, Connecticut struck when Indians raided its frontier town of Wethersfield. Militiamen surrounded the Pequots' main town when most of its warriors were away, set it on fire, and shot the old men, women, and children as they fled. Between 300 and 700 Pequots died in an hour. Over the following months, Massachusetts, Plymouth, and Connecticut militias captured most of the stragglers and sold those they spared into Caribbean slavery. The war did not end until settlers had destroyed most of the Pequot nation, but the victors assured themselves that "we had sufficient light from the Word of God for our proceedings."

Metacom's War was an even deadlier conflict that ravaged New England in 1675 and 1676, almost simultaneously with Bacon's Rebellion in Virginia. Both upheavals exposed deep rifts in the white community and aroused fears of a general uprising of Indians up and down the Atlantic seaboard. Whites were finally victorious in both, but the violence shook both colonies deeply and marked the end of their founding eras.

By 1675, whites and Indians lived side by side throughout much of southern New England. Metacom, whom the English called King

Philip, had replaced his father Massasoit as *sachem* of the Wampanoags, and lived on the eastern side of Narragansett Bay near the border between Plymouth and Rhode Island. His traditional enemies, the Narragansetts, held the opposite shore. There were also Nipmuck towns between Boston and the Connecticut River Valley, and the Abenakis held most of inland Maine. As New England grew, whites eyed Indian land with increasing jealousy, and rival colonies competed to acquire it. Indians' resentment also grew as the English demanded more land, livestock raided their fields and clam beds, and colonial governments treated them as subjects instead of independent neighbors.

Relations between the Wampanoags and Plymouth grew especially tense by the early 1670s. Plymouth protested loudly when Metacom sold land to the despised colony of Rhode Island, but Metacom countered that Plymouth was stealing tribal land for its own settlements. Deeply suspicious, colonial leaders listened carefully when a Christian Indian accused Metacom of plotting war, and believed his reports when the informer was found dead, seemingly murdered. Preparing for the worst, Wampanoags readied themselves for combat and struck the border town of Swansea when Plymouth executed the alleged killers. Massachusetts came to Plymouth's aid, and counterattacks soon spiraled into general war, as rival tribes and colonies put aside their differences and united against each other. Powerful bands of English and Indians burned one another's towns throughout New England and drove their inhabitants into fortified garrisons. In one of these raids, a party of Narragansetts kidnapped Mary Rowlandson, a minister's wife from Lancaster, Massachusetts, who lived to publish *The Sovereignty and Goodness of God*, a model for innumerable other tales of frontier capture and rescue and one of the earliest books written by an American woman.

Like the rebellious followers of Nathaniel Bacon, New Englanders responded to Indian trouble with indiscriminate violence against all the Indians in reach, even the "praying Indians" converted by John Eliot. As these measures succeeded in the winter and spring of 1676, Metacom sought the help of Mohawks from the Iroquois Confederacy, but they sided with his enemies instead. When Metacom retreated to the Wampanoag homeland on Narragansett Bay, a combined force of Indians and Plymouth militia captured and killed him, selling most of his people into slavery.

The English lost at least 600 lives, 8,000 cattle, and 1,200 houses in Metacom's War, proportionately the bloodiest in American history. Its expenses ran to £150,000. The Indians lost about 3,000 men, women, and children, their political independence, and most of their land. In the war's aftermath, ministers hurled more jeremiads at their congregations, certain that God had sent calamity to punish a sinful people. Returning to the theme of declension, royal official Edward Randolph reported that the clergy pointed specifically to the declining church attendance, toleration of the persecuted sect known as Quakers, young people who dishonored their parents, men who grew long hair or wore wigs, and women who adopted "strange fashions in their apparel." As Puritan zeal continued to wane, it would be harder and harder to combat the enduring appeal of "strange fashions," despite the ministers' best efforts.

Isolated bands of Indians hung on in southern New England, and their descendants still live there, but the colonists subjected them to English control. The victorious colonies absorbed most Indian lands within their own boundaries, but they failed to wrest territory from their neighbors, except for Massachusetts, which soon swallowed Plymouth. Metacom's War weakened colonies and tribes so badly that neighboring New York (the former New Netherland, which England acquired in 1667) and the Iroquois Confederacy soon replaced them as the dominant military powers in the northeast, the guarantors of its peace, and the lords of its fur trade.

*

Bacon's Rebellion and Metacom's War exposed deep rifts in the colonies they touched. Virginia's poor attacked the rich, and New England colonies turned on each other in a scramble for Indian land. Presented with unmistakable signs of crisis, English authorities began to wonder if the colonies were misgoverned. Certainly New England's semi-independent "republics" could not continue to imitate Cromwell's commonwealth. At the very least, they reasoned, royal governors like Virginia's should rein them in and perhaps impose even stricter controls. The coming years would see other important plans for subjecting all American colonies to tighter English control, and the loss of Massachusetts's own treasured independence.

Despite these setbacks, neither Bacon nor Metacom could permanently damage their targets. By the final quarter of the seventeenth century, Virginia, Plymouth, and Massachusetts Bay had burst their original boundaries to spawn Maryland, Connecticut, New Hampshire, and Rhode Island. Despite early hopes for coexistence, planters and Puritans had both proved willing to strike their Indian rivals with all the violence deemed necessary. Each region had deep roots in its parent culture, but each had developed its own way of life based on varying local conditions and the portions of English culture they imported. Heartened by the examples of Virginia and Massachusetts, other colonizers would continue to imitate them, soon creating a string of English outposts from chilly Newfoundland to the sunny Caribbean.

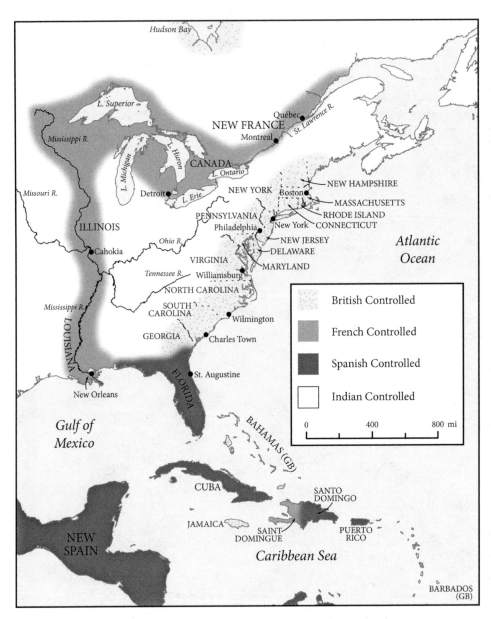

MAP 2. By the early eighteenth century, British, French, and Spanish colonies occupied eastern North America, but Native Americans controlled the continent's interior and most of its land and resources. Map by Gabriel Moss.

CHAPTER 3

The Emerging Empire, 1676–1756

New York militia major Jacob Leisler gave his dying speech on a rainy May morning in 1691. With his son-in-law Jacob Milborne beside him, Leisler tried to explain their recent conduct in "great & weighty matters of State affairs." Though penitent, Leisler still insisted "before god & the world that what I have done was for king William & Queen Mary, for the defence of the protestant religion & the Good of the country." Moments later, the hangman tied his blindfolds, and the bodies of Leisler and Milborne swung lifeless from the gallows of Manhattan. Their severed heads would soon bear public witness to rebellion's awful price.

England had taken the Dutch colony of New Netherland in 1664 and a treaty of 1667 had formalized its new status. King Charles II had given the province to his brother James, the Duke of York, who renamed it New York and installed an autocratic government before taking the throne himself in 1685. At the time of Leisler's Rebellion, a genuine crisis had gripped the colony and its neighbors, for England had toppled King James II in an upheaval known as the Glorious Revolution. The overthrow of New York's official proprietor upset public authority and led to panic over imagined Catholic conspiracies and Indian attack. Ostensibly acting for the new sovereigns, King William and Queen Mary, and traditional English liberties, Leisler and his followers seized local power and held it for nearly two years. When royal authorities finally arrived to reestablish a lawful government, however, Leisler fired on their troops, so newly appointed governor Henry Sloughter resolved to make him an example.

Under other circumstances, the governor might have shown mercy. Colonial upheavals did not always end with bloody reprisals. Leisler had acted in a real emergency, he was basically loyal, and he finally disarmed voluntarily. He and his followers also believed they had defended popular rights against arbitrary power, a belief that English events had seemed to confirm. But the new government was not secure and war had broken out with France. New York was a valuable port, vulnerable to attack by land and sea, and rife with ethnic and religious dissension. Above all, while Leisler had many supporters, he had also made many enemies who now had the governor's ear. Sloughter would take no chances so early in his term, so Leisler's disobedience cost him his life. In short, Leisler and his followers thought the principles of the Glorious Revolution should allow them local autonomy, especially in an emergency, but English authorities insisted on more-central control of their growing empire.

Though founded as New Netherland, New York was otherwise emblematic of the seventeenth-century English empire. It was one of several proprietorships established by the Stuart Restoration, and filled a vital gap between the Chesapeake and New England. In an empire based increasingly on commerce, the Hudson River Valley provided bountiful food exports and a vital highway for the fur trade, but its diverse people were prone to quarreling. James II hated representative assemblies in both his kingdom and his colony, so he would not allow New York to elect a legislature like Virginia's or Massachusetts's, but his appointees had proved inept in the recent emergency and opened the way for Jacob Leisler's coup. In the aftermath of the Glorious Revolution, a more successful imperial system would require enough central authority to maintain stability and protect the interests of empire, balanced by enough flexibility and popular consent to resolve disputes and maintain public support. It was a formula that eighteenth-century colonists and officials worked hard to establish, so incidents like Leisler's execution would no longer be necessary.

Like New York, most of the colonies that became the United States slowly took shape and found stability between the Restoration and the early eighteenth century. Several experienced disruptions, but most escaped political violence. Competition between rival empires spurred the colonies' development, and imperial officials struggled constantly to control trade, but had to balance central control and commercial interests against popular expectations. Though repression ended Leisler's Rebellion, representative assemblies in England's other colonies gained central roles in imperial governance, bolstered by the results of the Glorious Revolution. The new empire would depend on the right combination of imperial requirements, colonial aspirations, and the realities of the American continent.

Rivals for America

American colonial development always took place within the framework of Atlantic imperial competition. Eighteenth-century Spain claimed an immense empire stretching from California and Florida to the southern tip of South America. Its mines still yielded vast quantities of silver, but Spain's economic and military might began to ebb in the early seventeenth century, allowing England, France, and Holland to advance by exchanging America's products for Europe's. With the right balance of trade, commercial countries could divert gold and silver from Spain's treasury to their own. As hopes faded for the discovery of more mineral treasure in America, European statesmen became more and more excited by the possibilities of empires built on Atlantic trade.

SPAIN AND NEW SPAIN

Spain claimed most of North and South America, though much of its territory was still in Native American hands. It divided this empire in quarters, each headed by a viceroy who represented the Spanish Crown and directed the governors of individual provinces. With its capital at Mexico City, the former Tenochtitlán, the viceroyalty of New Spain included all Spanish territory north of Panama. A large bureaucracy administered the affairs of its church and state, and the only elected bodies were local town councils, or *cabildos*.

Spain's American wealth was the envy of Europe, but precious metals actually weakened its economy. The Crown claimed one-fifth of all the silver from the colonies and designed its trade policies to protect this revenue from smugglers, pirates, and foreign enemies. Most of the remaining silver went to the nobility and some of it went to the church. Like the Crown, these recipients were anxious to protect their incomes and avoid risks, and they shunned direct involvement in business as socially degrading. Silver therefore crossed the Atlantic in closely guarded annual convoys and entered Spain through a single port (Seville first, Cadiz later), where a small guild of merchants held a trading monopoly. These policies did not stop smuggling, but they limited the growth of more innovative urban rivals.

Once in Spain, silver paid for expensive armies and navies, the lifestyles of nobles and churchmen, and imported manufactures that undermined Spain's own industries. Though Spain forbade direct foreign exports to its colonies, merchants evaded the barrier by bringing foreign goods to Spain before reshipping them to America. Foreigners also supplied most of the capital for this trade, leaving Spain and its empire economically dependent on other countries. Contemporaries remarked that "the cloth trade is England's Indies," because exchanging textiles for Spanish silver was an ideal path to riches.

The economies of the Spanish colonies centered on mining or supplying the mines with necessities like food, livestock, and leather. If they did not own mines themselves, leading colonists raised these products, as well as sugar and tobacco, on large landed estates called *haciendas*. Some of their workers were African slaves, especially in the sugar districts, but most were Indians laboring under the *encomienda*, or tribute, system or struggling to repay debts that kept them in a state of semibondage called peonage. As in Spain itself, the focus on mines and haciendas discouraged economic diversity and self-sustaining development, and led to a society dominated by a small wealthy elite atop a mass of impoverished laborers. Hostage to the silver trade, the economy of Latin America depended on Spain just as Spain itself depended on Europe.

Latin American society developed patterns of racial and ethnic diversity that sharply contrasted with those in the English colonies. Relatively few Spaniards came to America and many were single men who hoped to return to Spain. These men often had children with Indian or African women, creating a racially mixed population of *mestizos* (with white and Indian parents), *mulattos* (with white and African parents), and all combinations of their descendants. Free, mixed-race people took jobs that might otherwise have gone to poor or middling whites, and they became intermediaries between the white elite and the mass of slaves and Indians. Latin America became a society where light skin was a key to social rank, but with many gradations of color, power, and status between very dark and very light. In the English colonies, by contrast, wealthy whites extended a certain kind of equality to poor and middling whites while treating free people of color almost as badly as enslaved Africans.

New Spain guarded its northern boundaries with a series of frontier outposts, beginning with San Agostino (St. Augustine) in 1565 and followed by New Mexico in 1598, nine years before the English came to Jamestown. Spanish settlements reached Texas in 1691, and finally California in 1769. The Spanish did not find gold or silver in these places, but used them to convert Indians while warding off enemies and preserving their claims against England, France, and (on the

Pacific coast) Russia. When private settlers ventured to these distant outposts, their principal economic activity was cattle ranching and the export of hides and tallow.

Missionary efforts were central to all these border settlements. Members of the religious orders, especially Franciscans, accompanied conquistadors wherever they went, and the government funded their efforts to bring Christianity and Hispanic culture to the Indians. The colonizers typically established themselves near an Indian community and offered it protection in exchange for work and Christian baptism. Participation was supposed to be voluntary, but the Spanish presence might provoke attacks from other Indians, disease was an ever-present menace, and Spanish animals could overrun fields and other food sources. Nearby Indians might thus have little choice but to enter the mission community. Once there, they were not allowed to leave or continue their traditional religions, but forced to practice Christianity and work under conditions of near slavery. Mistreatment and disease soon took their toll, and the population of border areas dropped as grimly as elsewhere.

The most successful rebellion against the mission system erupted among the Pueblo Indians of New Mexico. Scattered in separate adobe villages along the Rio Grande Valley, the Pueblos had accepted the Spanish without much resistance between 1598 and 1680, while their numbers dropped from 60,000 to 17,000. A chain of events then drove them to fury, beginning with a prolonged drought that devastated crops and drew raids from neighboring Navahos and Apaches. Pueblos revived their traditional religion when Spanish soldiers and the Spanish God seemed equally powerless against these dangers. Determined to keep their converts, the Franciscans cracked down on "witchcraft" by whipping and hanging the offenders.

One of these, a young man named Popé, struck back by organizing a rebellion in the summer of 1680, soon after Bacon's Rebellion and Metacom's War in the far-distant English colonies. Using series of knotted cords to count off the days, his recruits struck almost simultaneously in mid-August and quickly killed nearly 400 Spanish settlers and missionaries, while besieging most of the rest in the governor's palace at Santa Fe. One band of survivors immediately retreated to the village of El Paso, then located on the south bank of the Rio Grande. Once the Santa Fe garrison surrendered, Indians allowed its members to join them. The victorious Pueblos destroyed all the signs of Spanish culture they could find, from churches and crosses to livestock and fruit trees, and the Spanish did not attempt to return until 1692, after Popé's death. A smaller revolt followed in 1697, until the warring parties struck a compromise in which the Pueblos tolerated the Spanish presence and ultimate authority in return for greater independence and religious toleration. The Spanish and Pueblos could then unite against their common enemies, the Navajos and Apaches.

THE DUTCH AND NEW NETHERLAND

The Netherlands was England's closest economic competitor in the seventeenth century. The low-lying Dutch provinces on the North Sea had fallen to the Spanish Crown by conquest and marriage, but they outraged its Catholic monarchy by embracing Calvinism in the Reformation. Spanish efforts to crush Dutch Protestantism touched off a prolonged struggle for independence that made the disparate provinces a true nation. Fighting broke out in 1568 and continued sporadically for another 80 years, but the United Provinces of the Netherlands enjoyed de facto independence after 1585, with a republican government that practiced religious toleration. This generous policy not only made the United Provinces a refuge for dissident European Protestants, but it also brought the energy and talents of Sephardic Jews persecuted by Spain and Portugal.

Seafaring skills, a shortage of land, and a weak nobility gave the Dutch a long trading tradition that encouraged economic independence and innovation. Expanding capitalism thus blended with religious and patriotic motives to inspire Dutch attacks on Spanish and Portuguese commerce, particularly after 1580, when the Dutch independence struggle overlapped with the union of the two Iberian kingdoms. Founded in 1602, the Dutch East India Company captured Portuguese trading posts in Africa, India, Ceylon, and Java, gained exclusive trading privileges in Japan, and established the colony that became South Africa. Founded in 1621, the Dutch West India Company seized Elmina on the Gold Coast, Caribbean islands and Surinam on the northern coast of South America, and coastal Brazil, where it briefly took over the sugar industry.

The Dutch West India Company also founded New Netherland, North America's first major mid-Atlantic colony, by settling 30 families there in 1624. Like the founders of New France, the company mostly sought furs, so it first ignored the excellent harbor at the mouth of the Hudson River in favor of Fort Orange, an upstream trading post at the present site of Albany. Two years later, a second group purchased Manhattan Island from the local Indians and established New Amsterdam as the capital of New Netherland. The price was 60 florins' worth of trade goods, not the 24 dollars of legend, but the exact sum is virtually impossible to translate into a modern currency. As often happened, the Manhattan Indians probably thought they were renting the island, not selling it. To stabilize the fur trade, Dutch officials and the Five Nations of the Iroquois formed an alliance that promised mutual friendship and cooperation and recognized Iroquois dominance of the neighboring tribes.

As European population grew, newcomers began building farms along the Hudson to Fort Orange, and beyond there to the Mohawk River outpost of Schenectady. To encourage more immigration without resorting to indentured servants or deported paupers and criminals as the English did, the Dutch made some very large Hudson Valley land grants that gave the owners certain rights of government and the title of patroon if they brought in 50 tenant families. Patroons could operate courts and collect rents and their own taxes, but their tenants escaped colonial taxes for 10 years. The largest of these, the manor, or patroonship, of Rensselaerwyck went to Kiliaen van Rensselaer in 1630, and contained approximately one million acres on both banks of the upper Hudson. In addition to collecting rents and administering justice, the patroons could require tenant labor on their roads and fences, appoint clergymen, and collect taxes to pay them. They did not always exercise these privileges, and many of the largest landholdings broke up after sale or inheritance in the eighteenth century. Other manorial families, including the van Rensselaers, established themselves as enduring rural aristocrats in the Hudson Valley. They attracted tenants by offering low rents on long leases, with the right to sell the improvements to their farms if and when they chose to move. The English continued patroonships and even created new ones when they took over New Netherland, and Rensselaerwyck survived until the early nineteenth century.

The population of New Netherland was never wholly Dutch. The first 30 families were French speakers from what is now Belgium. New Englanders built Puritan townships on eastern Long Island. French Protestants, called Huguenots, fled persecution at home to found New Rochelle, and German refugees came from the Rhine Valley for similar reasons. New Netherland absorbed New Sweden in 1655, and Sephardic Jews arrived from Brazil when Portugal recaptured that colony and ended its religious freedom. The Dutch brought African slaves to their colony, and the Iroquois Indians traded there regularly. Manhattan residents spoke 18 different languages in the seventeenth century, more than any other town in North or South America. The Dutch Reformed Church was New Netherland's legally established faith, but persecution was bad for business and other sects enjoyed de facto toleration.

Commercial competition sparked three Anglo-Dutch wars in the seventeenth century, and New Netherland became a pawn in these conflicts. Coveting the fur trade, England seized New Netherland in 1664, lost it to the Dutch again in 1673, and finally regained it after the Third Anglo-Dutch War of 1674. Renaming its prize New York, England cemented its control of the entire Atlantic coastline from Maine to South Carolina.

NEW FRANCE AND THE "MIDDLE GROUND"

France became England's most enduring rival for control of North America. The kingdom had suffered serious internal conflict during the Reformation, but the Huguenots did not prevail and Catholic France replaced Spain as the strongest and wealthiest realm in seventeenth-century Europe. In the era when Parliament won supremacy in England, French kings and their able ministers concentrated power in royal hands and used their authority to bring stability and prosperity. Like Spain, France became an absolute monarchy, where the king ruled by decree and individual subjects depended on traditions and intermediaries rather than legal safeguards to shield them from the central state. French glory reached its zenith under King Louis XIV, known as the Sun King for the splendor of his reign and his court at Versailles. Louis XIV fought a series of costly wars to assert his kingdom's power and expand its boundaries to the Rhine, challenging most of the surrounding states, including England, for political and military supremacy.

French expansion reached America when sixteenth-century voyages by Giovanni da Verrazzano and Jacques Cartier established France's claims to the St. Lawrence River Valley. French fishermen had long taken codfish from the rich waters of the Grand Banks, just off the coasts of modern Newfoundland, dried their catches on neighboring islands, and traded for furs with nearby Indians. Building on this traffic, an expedition in 1600 established France's first permanent North

American settlement at the village of Tadoussac at the mouth of the St. Lawrence River. Farther upriver, Samuel de Champlain founded the city of Quebec in 1608. The colony of New France took shape along the St. Lawrence between the Atlantic and the Great Lakes, as French fur traders paddled their canoes ever higher up the waterways in search of skins. Jesuit priests frequently accompanied them, earnestly seeking to convert the Indians, and sometimes burning at the stake when their audiences proved unreceptive.

Hearing of the Mississippi River from Indians living near the Great Lakes, Father Jacques Marquette and fur trader Louis Jolliet followed their portage across modern Wisconsin in 1673 and descended the Mississippi to the mouth of the Arkansas River before returning to New France. Robert de La Salle followed in 1682, traveling the length of the Mississippi to the Gulf of Mexico, claiming the lands it drained for France, and naming them Louisiana for its king. La Salle later hoped to found a settlement by ascending the river from its mouth, but in 1687, he died at the hands of his own colonists when he could not find the elusive channel. A permanent French presence on the Gulf began in 1699, followed by the city of New Orleans in 1718. Moving upstream, French colonists slowly built a chain of riverbank trading posts that tied Louisiana to New France. To counter the partnership of the Dutch and the Iroquois, and later the English, the Indians of the *pays d'en haut*, or "upper country," of the St. Lawrence Valley allied with New France to protect their trade and to settle disputes. French, English, and Indian land claims would overlap in the triangle formed by the Ohio River, the Mississippi, and the Great Lakes, and spark bloody struggles for control of the Ohio country.

The fur trade became very important for all its participants. French individuals and trading companies gained commercial profits. The government of New France collected revenue from the sale of trading licenses. More important, the government and the Indians used their trade agreements to stabilize the *pays d'en haut*, reduce the chance of war, and protect each other from their Dutch, English, and Iroquois rivals. Like most native peoples, the Hurons and Algonquian-language speakers of the upper country traded with the French and other Europeans according to their own needs and their older traditions of intertribal trade. They might exchange furs for copper kettles, for example, but cut up the new vessels to make weapons or ornaments instead of cooking food. Rejecting the Europeans' acquisitive or utilitarian attitude to wealth or material possessions, they tapped the *manitou* of foreign products for spiritual power and social prestige as well as practical uses. They also expected generous presents from traders and officials to signify their friendship, whether they had furs to exchange or not. Throughout colonial North America, clashing understandings of trade inevitably led to numerous disputes between Indians and whites.

Settlement patterns created marked differences between the French and English mainland colonies. French officials welcomed immigration, but Canada's stern climate hindered agriculture, and French people seemed reluctant to abandon their homeland. Those who did come built homes and farms along the St. Lawrence River, but many trappers and traders married Indian women and did little to transplant French society into America. By contrast, the English mainland colonies had large and growing populations that outnumbered French Canada by twenty to one in the 1750s. England's expanding colonies always thirsted for more Indian lands, but the French claimed vast territories without fully occupying them.

The upper country has been called the Middle Ground because it bridged the worlds of Indians and Europeans and sheltered a diverse population who needed each other and mingled, intermarried, and did business there on terms of relative equality. The Middle Ground also linked New France to Louisiana, with its Mississippi outposts stretching as far north as modern Illinois. Recognizing the benefits of the Middle Ground, the French supported it with gifts, alliances, and mediation among its diverse inhabitants. Though the French and Indians shared control of this intermediate zone, Indians ruled the territories farther west. There, enduring Indian power safeguarded the fur trade, protected tribal autonomy, and held off land-hungry Anglo-Americas behind an arc of territory stretching from the Gulf of St. Lawrence to the Great Lakes and south to the Gulf of Mexico. Eighteenth-century war and diplomacy would severely test the security of this prized region, until the final expulsion of France from North America on the eve of the American Revolution.

CARIBBEAN SUGAR COLONIES

England, France, Spain, and Holland also competed in the development of West Indian sugar islands that purchased food and timber from the mainland colonies and introduced them to African slavery. Sugar became less important to Spain when silver proved more profitable, but production surged in Portuguese Brazil. The Dutch learned sugaring skills when they occupied Brazil from 1630 to 1654, brought cane cultivation to their own Caribbean colonies, and passed it to nearby English islands.

England's first sugar colonies appeared in the Lesser Antilles, a long chain of islands between Hispaniola and South America that Spain had bypassed on its way to the mainland. England occupied St. Kitts in 1624, soon followed by Barbados (1627), Nevis (1628), Montserrat (1632), and Antigua (1632). Only 166 square miles, Barbados stood out because of its fertility and its closer location to England and Africa. Much as in Virginia, early settlers cleared small farms with help from indentured servants who received some tools, supplies, and land (until it ran out) after five years of service. Also as in Virginia, masters inflicted beatings and other harsh punishments to make their servants work, and bought and sold them freely. The first planters tilled crops of tropical cotton and tobacco, but adopted sugar when Virginia's leaf became more popular.

The need for expensive machinery for grinding cane excluded small planters from the Barbados sugar boom, sending some to other islands and some to the mainland. Wealthier planters bought them out to create large estates of 150–200 acres, engrossed the best land, and established themselves as a small ruling class, even wealthier than Virginia's. Also like Virginia, Barbados and the other islands adopted elected assemblies to represent the interests of their largest planters. Both Virginia and the Caribbean sugar colonies thus found economic success by growing one crop with unfree labor on large plantations. The greatest thing they both still required was a dependable source of labor when indentured servants proved insufficient. Barbados and the other sugar islands adopted slavery about the same time they discovered sugar. Virginia followed the same path, but took a little longer.

By the end of the seventeenth century, a couple of hundred sugar barons owned most of Barbados, each operating one or more plantations of about 200 acres and about the same number of African slaves. The very richest spent their lives and profits in England, and left the management of their estates (and the risk of tropical diseases) to a handful of salaried white employees. Blacks outnumbered whites by as many as ten to one, since European inhabitants were mostly limited to a handful of managers, overseers, artisans, and shopkeepers.

Displaced from Barbados, white ex-servants and small farmers carried the sugar system up and down the Antilles chain. Cane spread to Jamaica after 1655, when Admiral Sir William Penn (father of Pennsylvania's founder) plucked it from Spain. Jamaica eventually surpassed Barbados as the wealthiest English colony. France likewise brought sugar from the small twin islands of Guadeloupe and Martinique to its much larger colony of Saint Domingue (later known as Haiti) on the western end of Hispaniola. Throughout most of the West Indies, a captive African population replaced the native Caribs and Arawaks, and toiled under the whips of European masters and overseers to produce the bewitchingly sweet crystals craved by ever-larger numbers of international consumers.

Like tobacco, the price of sugar fell as production increased. The new sweetener crossed class lines, from flavoring the confections fancied by the wealthy to flavoring more affordable treats like coffee, tea, and chocolate, and providing cheap rum and molasses for the poor. Sugar profits became a treasured source of European prosperity, and the sugar islands far outranked the colonies of mainland North America in the wealth they generated for their respective empires.

Restoration Colonies

When King Charles II gained the English throne in 1660, he owed heavy debts of gratitude to the courtiers and power brokers who had restored him. His chosen rewards were lavish American land grants. Like the Calvert family's venture in Maryland, the king's gifts were proprietary colonies, which belonged to their developers. Proprietors normally received English title to all the land in their colonies and also governing rights, so long as they did not contradict the laws of England or the ultimate sovereignty of the king. After some fumbling with other forms of government, most proprietors ruled their provinces much like the Crown. They granted headrights to settlers and sold much larger tracts of land to developers and speculators, subject to an annual quitrent. Like the king, they normally appointed a governor and an advisory council and allowed the settlers to choose a representative assembly. Most granted religious toleration. The proprietors hoped to profit from their territories by attracting as many settlers as possible, stimulating a prosperous local economy, and collecting plentiful quitrents as immigrants streamed in. Most of the proprietary colonies made good homes for their free settlers, but their proprietors rarely earned as much as they had hoped.

THE TWO CAROLINAS

King Charles I had named Carolina after himself ("Carolus" is Latin for "Charles") when he named Maryland in honor of his wife. In 1663, his son Charles II granted this vast expanse between Virginia and Spanish Florida to eight Lords Proprietors, a mixed group who included some high-ranking Stuart loyalists, some key parliamentary supporters who assisted the Restoration by adroitly switching sides, and some lesser gentry with valuable experience in America. Receiving their charter in 1663, the proprietors employed the philosopher John Locke to draw up a plan of government called the Fundamental Constitutions of Carolina. Locke proposed a feudalistic system with titled nobility ruling a population of serfs, slaves, and smaller landholders. His plans were largely unworkable because free people would not submit to feudal discipline when America offered so many alternatives. Never fully implemented and later discarded, Locke's plans illustrated how the most elaborate plans for settlement could collapse in the face of American reality.

The Carolina proprietors paid little attention to the small band of fugitive Virginians who had already slipped into the far northern corner of their new province. They pinned their hopes instead on a more southern settlement they called Charles Town (later simplified to Charleston), originally located a few miles inland and then moved to a peninsula where the Ashley and Cooper Rivers meet the sea. From its origins in 1670, Charles Town maintained close ties with Barbados and welcomed Barbadian immigrants who were seeking new homes as sugar reshaped life in their parent colony. The more prosperous West Indians brought slaves with them as a matter of course and quickly started trading with their earlier island home. The Barbadians had stripped away their forests for cane fields, leaving little wood behind to fire the sugar boilers or make casks for the finished product, and little space to grow food and livestock. Early Carolinians could easily supply these deficiencies and prospered by sending cattle, hogs, corn, and timber to the Caribbean islands.

This pattern began to change when planters learned how to grow rice in the fertile wetlands of the colony's low country, or coastal region, drawing on the knowledge of slaves who grew it in Africa. Carolinians were harvesting substantial rice crops by 1690, and the fluffy grain became their economic mainstay in the eighteenth century. "The only commodity of Consequence produced in South Carolina is rice," one observer reported in 1761, "and they reckon it as much their staple Commodity as Sugar is to Barbados and Jamaica, or Tobacco to Virginia and Maryland." The main exception to this rule was indigo, a blue vegetable dye from India that Eliza Lucas Pinckney, daughter of the governor of Antigua, a British sugar colony, introduced in the 1740s.

Worked by large forces of slaves, plantations became so widespread and prosperous in coastal South Carolina that the colony contained a black majority by 1708.

The northern part of Carolina developed very differently. Early North Carolinians carved out small farms along the northern shores of Albemarle Sound, not far from the original site of Sir Walter Raleigh's settlement on Roanoke Island. Shallow rivers and a hazardous coastline barred them from easy access to Atlantic commerce and limited the growth of a Chesapeake-style tobacco economy. From the outset, the proprietors seemed to recognize that distance and circumstances required a separate local government for the northern settlement, though formal separation of North and South Carolina did not occur until 1712.

Unruly and independent-minded, the North Carolinians smuggled a little tobacco into Virginia by land and to northern ports through their own shallow inlets, and did not hesitate to rough up any governor or imperial official who tried to interfere. The colony remained poor and underpopulated well into the eighteenth century. In addition to foodstuffs for the West Indies, North Carolina's most valuable commodities were lumber and naval stores, or tar, pitch, and turpentine, which were extracted from the sap of pine trees and used to waterproof wooden ships.

NEW NETHERLAND BECOMES NEW YORK

Soon after England's capture of New Netherland in 1664, King Charles II included the former Dutch colony in a huge proprietary grant to his brother, James Stuart, the Duke of York and the future King James II. Renamed New York, James's province originally embraced the entire Atlantic seaboard between the Delaware and Connecticut Rivers, and territories west and north of New England. James regranted much of this territory to others and did not insist on a Connecticut River boundary, but kept the Hudson Valley for himself.

New York already had as many as 10,000 people scattered among four major regions, so James did not need to recruit new settlers. Tobacco planters spilled over from Maryland and clustered along the southern banks of the Delaware River. Albany thrived on the Indian fur trade, though farms were developing nearby. Connecticut farmers raised grain and livestock on eastern Long Island, where they also prepared whale oil, while Hudson Valley farms grew wheat to export as flour. New York City was the commercial center for all four regions, with a population of some 1,500 residents. The majority were Dutch, but the government stoked ethnic tensions by seeming to favor English newcomers. In rural areas, James continued the Dutch practice of issuing large manorial grants to be tilled by tenants, which made landlord-tenant conflicts a recurrent feature of eighteenth- and nineteenth-century politics.

Dispensing with an elected legislature, James appointed a colonial governor who chose a council to advise him and sit as a court. The governor made laws and set taxes by decree, and enforced the laws that redirected the colony's trade from Amsterdam to London. The first proprietary governor boasted that "our newe Lawes are not contrived soe Democratically as the rest," yet the English settlers in particular rarely stopped agitating for an assembly with the power to control taxation.

PENNSYLVANIA, NEW JERSEY, AND DELAWARE

The last mainland settlements of the Restoration era were also carved from the lands of the Duke of York. Together with New York itself, the proprietorships of New Jersey, Pennsylvania, and Delaware became known as the middle colonies. They were too far north for plantation crops and lacked the exclusively Puritan mission of New England, but the middle colonies contained excellent harbors and river systems that supported two major commercial centers, Philadelphia and New York. Towns encouraged trade and economic development, while the countryside attracted settlers from a wide variety of ethnic and religious backgrounds. Diversity often bred distrust of rival communities and interests, and public life in the middle colonies often featured factional quarrels and political contentiousness. As colonists learned to negotiate their differences, however, diversity could also encourage respect for personal liberty, individual exertion, tolerance of differences, and a drive for personal advancement, characteristics that became boasted aspects of American culture in later centuries.

When he received New Netherland, the duke split off the land between the Hudson and the Delaware Rivers as a proprietary grant to two friends, Lord John Berkeley and Sir George Carteret. They named their province New Jersey after Carteret's birthplace and divided it between them. Carteret took the northeastern half, or East Jersey, and attracted many settlers from Long Island and Puritan New England. Berkeley sold his half, or West Jersey, to a group of investors seeking refuge for the Quakers, or Religious Society of Friends. Repeated sales of the proprietorships brought political uncertainty and bitter disputes over land titles, which prompted the Crown to reunite New Jersey and govern it as a royal colony after 1702.

Quakers, formally known as the Religious Society of Friends, had emerged from the welter of dissenters that blossomed in the era of England's Civil War and Interregnum, and attracted followers who rejected the Puritans' efforts to establish religion by worldly power. They avoided Calvinist-style arguments about the nature of salvation and abandoned external rituals like sacraments, formal preaching, and structured prayers, in favor of quiet meditation to find guidance from the divine spark, or "inner light," that Quakers saw in every human being. Renouncing violence and the trappings of worldly status, Friends enraged English officials by refusing to bear arms, to take oaths, and to bow, curtsey, or doff their hats to social superiors, and by using the familiar pronouns "thee" and "thou" for everyone, regardless of rank. To the committed Puritans who still reigned in Massachusetts, Quakerism recalled the chaotic heresies of Anne Hutchinson and the Antinomians, who had also disrupted public order by claiming to hear God's voice directly.

Unlike most of the splinter sects of the Commonwealth period, the Quakers did not disappear in the Restoration, but continued to win converts and experience persecution. English officials jailed as many as 15,000 Quakers, and their missionaries faced whippings, exile, and even the death penalty in Massachusetts. Most Friends were men and women from modest backgrounds, but some were prominent merchants, intellectuals, and members of the gentry, including one popular and persuasive young gentleman named William Penn.

Penn's father had commanded the fleet that captured Jamaica for Oliver Cromwell's Commonwealth, but he befriended the Stuarts when Cromwell died, loaned money to Charles II, and remained influential in his court. The younger Penn held on to his father's wealth and access to power even after he joined the despised Quaker movement, and he helped the Friends who sought a religious haven in West Jersey. Disillusioned by their disputes over politics and ownership, Penn decided to seek his own colony in the promising territory lying west of the Delaware River.

Though William Penn had been jailed four times for his Quaker faith, he maintained an unlikely friendship with the Duke of York. After breaking with the Church of England, the two shared a common interest in religious freedom, though James had taken the more inflammatory step of embracing Catholicism. King Charles sympathized with James's religious leanings, so the royal brothers were receptive when Penn asked to found a new colony based on freedom of conscience for all. In the spring of 1681, the king awarded Penn a proprietary charter for Pennsylvania, or "Penn's Woods," a huge tract of land lying west of the Delaware River between New York and Maryland, and explained to suspicious Anglicans that the grant would simply repay his large debt to the Penn estate.

Penn saw his grant as a blessed opportunity, not only to shelter persecuted Quakers and demonstrate the benefits of religious freedom, but to establish the ideal Christian society. "I eyed the Lord in the obtaining of it," he explained, and "desire that I may not be unworthy of his love, but do that which may answer his kind providence and serve his truth and people." Like the Puritans before him, Penn wanted Pennsylvania to be "an example . . . set up to the nations," and earnestly prayed that "there may be room there . . . for such a godly experiment." At the same time, he expected his province to turn a profit, explaining that "I desire to extend religious freedom, yet I want some recompense for my trouble."

To raise capital for an initial settlement, Penn sold large land grants to wealthy Friends and devised the first of several "Frames of Government" to protect landowners while extending liberty of conscience to all settlers. His plans won enthusiastic support from English and Continental Friends, and 23 ships brought supplies and 2,000 passengers to Pennsylvania in 1681. Penn himself and 2,000 more settlers arrived the following year. Taking the post of governor, Penn led his colonists in forging friendly relations with the Lenni Lenape, or Delaware Indians, establishing a record of honesty and fairness that remained firm until after his death. Penn went back to England after a two-year stay in Pennsylvania, and only spent another two years there in 1699–1701, but his influence on the colony and its capital of Philadelphia remained strong.

The bulk of early settlers in Pennsylvania were English, Irish, and Welsh Quakers. Many were attracted by the commercial possibilities of Philadelphia, but some of the early merchants were closely connected to Penn and shared his confidence, while others felt more isolated from the center of power. Other differences arose from the fact that Quaker settlers dominated the three counties around Philadelphia, while inhabitants of the three Lower Counties near the mouth of the Delaware were very similar to their neighbors in nearby Maryland and tended to favor the claims of its proprietor, Lord Baltimore. These differences bred an early pattern of political dissension, with proprietary and anti-proprietary parties taking shape among the Quakers, and the Lower Counties agitating for their own particular interests. Fervent opposition prevented Penn from collecting most quitrents, while the Lower Counties gained their own legislative assembly and eventually became the separate colony of Delaware.

Step by step, Penn retreated in the face of demands for more powerful and more representative legislative institutions, though the constant clamor for new laws and more legal protections distressed him. "For the love of God, me, and the poor country," he wailed at one point, "be not so *governmentish*, so noisy and open in your dissatisfactions!" The fractious colonists of Pennsylvania were reluctant to obey, however, and continued a lively sparring contest with Penn and his successors for the remainder of the colony's existence.

CHARITY AND GEORGIA

Georgia, the southernmost colony to join the American Revolution, did not take shape until the 1730s, long after the establishment of the other twelve. Led by James Oglethorpe, a group of English humanitarians known as the Trustees of Georgia obtained a charter in 1732 to found a refuge for debtors, petty criminals, and other poor persons, as well as persecuted foreign Protestants, on lands to the south of the Savannah River that were included in the original grant to Carolina. Calling the settlement Georgia in honor of King George II, they gave free transportation, supplies, and land to hard-pressed artisans, laborers, and their families, but rejected actual debtors and convicts. The trustees banned slavery to preserve Georgia as a society of small farmers supporting themselves by their own labor, but the settlers themselves were unhappy with this policy, and cast envious eyes on the prosperity of South Carolina's nearby rice plantations. After years of complaints and economic stagnation, the trustees abandoned their utopian plans, lifted the ban on slaves, and surrendered the colony to royal government in 1752. For most of the eighteenth century, colonial Georgia remained a fringe settlement along the Savannah River, smaller and weaker and exposed to attack from Spaniards and Indians, but otherwise very similar to the neighboring colony of South Carolina.

The Operations of Empire

The growth and social development of the English colonies in the late seventeenth and early eighteenth centuries took place within a larger framework of Atlantic commerce and empire. By the middle of the 1680s, all the colonies (except Georgia) that later formed the core of the United States had taken shape on the Atlantic seaboard. Other colonies flanked them, including Spanish Florida, the sugar islands, and the fur-trading empire of New France. Political and economic structures varied widely, but kings, ministers, and lawmakers governed all these empires to enrich their own countries through trade.

MERCANTILISM AND TRADE

Following the thought of Adam Smith, a Scottish author whose pathbreaking book, *The Wealth of Nations*, appeared in 1776, modern economists usually argue that profits and growth are greatest when businesses are free to buy and sell as they choose. During Smith's lifetime, however, most imperial administrators believed no such thing. For them, colonial trade was much too precious to be left to chance or the unreliable choices of individuals, so the colonizing countries all enacted strict rules to govern what their colonists could sell to whom, and from whom they could buy.

Imperial regulation took shape within a body of intellectual assumptions that later analysts called mercantilism, because it favored the merchants who conducted imperial trade. Every leading nation of Europe tried to sell more to its neighbors than it purchased, hoping that the difference between the value of its exports and imports would remain in the kingdom as specie, or gold and silver coin. By definition, not every country could succeed in creating a favorable balance of trade, for no country could acquire a surplus unless one or more of its partners ran a deficit. Mercantilists thus saw trade as a zero-sum game in which one country's gains always spelled losses for another. Nevertheless, monarchs hoped to use trade to accumulate a hoard of cash that they could tap to maintain their armies, their courts, and their kingdoms' larger interests. As part of this strategy, each empire sought to prevent the escape of specie to its neighbors by using its colonies to supply commodities and purchase finished goods. English mercantilists also tried to encourage overseas commerce by granting certain corporations monopoly privileges in certain areas of business, like the East India Company in South Asia, Hudson's Bay Company in northern Canada, or the Royal African Company in the slave trade.

The broad outlines of English mercantile policy appeared in a series of basic laws called the Navigation Acts, successively adopted by Parliament between 1650 and 1698. Pinpointing their imperial purposes, one observer called the Navigation Acts "a true way to enlarge dominions throughout the world, the most easy for conquests, and the least costly for appropriating the property of others." The acts were complicated and often amended, but their basic intent was to create a closed trading universe among the colonies and the mother country. A set of enumerated goods that included sugar, tobacco, indigo, and other valuable commodities could only be shipped in English or colonial vessels, manned by English or colonial crews, and sent to English or colonial ports. Once in England, these goods could be unloaded, taxed, and then reloaded and sold to another country, but colonists could not sell enumerated goods directly to foreign buyers, nor could they purchase goods abroad without paying English taxes. American products such as flour and fish, which England could supply for itself, could be sold anywhere, usually in the West Indies. The duties imposed by the Navigation Acts were quite valuable to the Crown, and produced as much as £140,000 per year as early as 1670.

England enforced the Navigation Acts by a combination of prohibitions and taxes designed to make certain forms of commerce too expensive to pursue. Regulatory taxes were supposedly collected in the colonies, but unlike more lucrative levies, they normally yielded little or no revenue, either because they made a given trade too costly or channeled it to smugglers who paid no taxes at all. Special vice-admiralty courts, which did not use juries, tried all violations of the Navigation Acts, so colonial lawbreakers could not count on sympathetic neighbors to protect them from convictions.

Slavery was an important aspect of imperial trade that tied all the colonies together, regardless of its local importance. Slavery was essential to the cultivation of the empire's most valuable commodities, including sugar, tobacco, rice, and indigo, and made the West Indies, the Chesapeake colonies, and South Carolina into full-fledged slave societies very early. Caribbean colonies were especially valuable. As early as 1700, for example, Barbados, Jamaica, and the Leeward Islands were annually producing about £768,600 in sugar, rum, and molasses, while the Chesapeake's annual exports only equaled £218,300. By the time of the American Revolution, the annual value of British West Indian sugar products had risen to some £3.9 million. Sugar, molasses, and rum were so valuable that the sugar colonies produced virtually nothing else, and imported all their other necessities from England or the mainland. The slave economies of the Caribbean thus supported the economies of the other colonies, providing crucial markets for such products as foodstuffs, livestock, and wood for fuel, building, and sugar barrels. In the late colonial years, for example, New England sold well over half its total exports in the West Indies and the proportion for the middle colonies was almost as high.

The Navigation Acts were particularly important to colonists who participated directly in international trade, especially the merchants who bought and sold the colonies' principal products, and the planters and farmers who supplied them. These men held the highest and wealthiest ranks in colonial society, dominated the assemblies, and paid close attention to the twists and turns of English politics. The fall of a minister, the rise of a privileged new interest group, the hint of a tightened or loosened approach to commercial regulation, all received anxious and intense attention in the taverns and coffeehouses where men of business gathered to discuss the news. During the 1680s, these were the men who paid closest attention to the English political crisis that led to the overthrow of King James II. Unexpectedly, the crisis also affected the views of many other Americans on the proper relationship between liberty, property, religion, kingship, and representative government.

JAMES II AND THE GLORIOUS REVOLUTION

King Charles II had no legitimate children, so when he died in 1685, his brother James became the new king. Repeating the mistakes that dethroned his father, James also ignored the Parliament and seemed to prefer ruling England as an absolute monarch. He and his ministers also worried about the colonies' tendencies to go their own way, especially Massachusetts, which governed itself under the charter of the old Massachusetts Bay Company.

As early as 1676, the Crown had sent its trusted emissary Edward Randolph to investigate the Massachusetts government in the aftermath of Metacom's War. Randolph was astonished to discover that officials in Boston, the largest port in North America, were completely ignoring the Navigation Acts on the grounds that their colony's charter exempted it from acts of Parliament. Randolph struggled to correct that situation, but met only limited success and bitterly complained that Boston's defiance cost the kingdom more than £100,000 annually. Randolph's protests finally led English courts to revoke the charter of Massachusetts in 1684, but King Charles had not decided on a new government before his death the next year. The new king and his ministers sought an administration for Massachusetts and all the colonies that would protect English revenues, enforce the mercantilist system, and firmly bind them to imperial rule.

James also distrusted New England on religious grounds. All the Stuart kings had resented what they viewed as the disorderly and anti-monarchical tendencies of radical Protestantism, but only James II repudiated the Reformation and tried to restore the Catholic Church. As we have seen, this step gave him an interest in religious toleration and strengthened his friendship with William Penn. James also married an Italian Catholic princess who gave birth to a healthy son in 1688 and was promptly baptized in his parents' faith. Under James II, England seemed poised for a return to Catholicism.

Most Protestant Englishmen were deeply prejudiced against "popery," which they associated with treason and tyranny, and supported discriminatory laws against Catholics as potential public enemies. James tried to help the Catholic minority by promoting toleration, but he did so by defying anti-Catholic laws and asserting his right to ignore the will of Parliament. These claims frightened English and American Protestants who remembered the struggle against the absolutist ambitions of Charles I. They worried especially in New England, where Puritan leading ministers and magistrates still believed that Puritan uniformity was essential to public order and the preservation of New England's sacred covenant with the Lord.

James's religious and constitutional views reinforced each other and inspired an attack on New England's independence. In 1686, he revoked the charters of Connecticut and Rhode Island, and lumped them together with Massachusetts, Plymouth, and New Hampshire in a new entity called the Dominion of New England. Citing the need for stricter enforcement of the Navigation Acts, he appointed as governor-general Sir Edmund Andros to rule the new government without an elected assembly, and added New York and New Jersey two years later. While eliminating self-government, the new administration ended legal privileges for Puritanism and even seized Boston's South Church for Anglican services. Going further, James hinted that he would like to subject all the other colonies to a similar consolidated arrangement, which resembled a Spanish viceroyalty more than a traditional English colony.

Unfortunately for him, James's religious and political views were as unpopular in England as they were America. Political leaders divided into rival camps: those who opposed his policies were called Whigs and his supporters were called Tories. Profoundly fearful of Catholicism and absolutism, a handful of prominent Whigs reached out to James's Protestant daughter Mary, wife of the leading Dutch nobleman, Prince William of Orange. At their invitation, William crossed the English Channel with an army in 1688, and James fled to France. Early the following year, Parliament proclaimed William and Mary the joint sovereigns of England and Scotland, with executive power held by William. War broke out between France and England, as James got help from King Louis XIV in an unsuccessful effort to reclaim his crown.

To prevent future monarchs from repeating James's offenses, Parliament required William and Mary to accept a statute called the English Bill of Rights. Still a pillar of the British constitution, this far-reaching law defined James's flight as an abdication of the throne, required all future kings to be Protestant, and praised King William as "the glorious instrument of delivering this kingdom from popery and arbitrary power." It further declared that the monarch could never set aside a law, raise taxes or maintain a peacetime army without Parliament's consent, or detain any subject contrary to established law. It guaranteed free and frequent elections to Parliament and protected freedom of speech in Parliament. It barred cruel and unusual punishment and excessive bail, while protecting free deliberations by juries and the right of Protestants to bear arms. Many of its provisions were later included in the Bill of Rights of the United States Constitution.

The Bill of Rights established the supremacy of Parliament in English law. While the absolute monarchs of the Continent continued to claim that Almighty God had placed them on their thrones with the "divine right" to rule with no restraint but God's own laws, the future kings of England were constrained by the will of their subjects. This did not mean that seventeenth- or eighteenth-century England had become a democracy. The subjects' "consent" was conveyed by Parliament, and Parliament obeyed the titled nobility, the rural gentry, urban businessmen, and the great merchants and bankers who dominated the city of London, not the ordinary population of the realm. Even so, Englishmen became so pleased with the events of 1688–1689 that they called James's overthrow their Glorious Revolution, and they began to make the liberty of the English government their proudest national boast.

In the aftermath of the revolution, John Locke, the philosopher who had earlier composed the authoritarian Fundamental Constitutions of Carolina, found it safe to publish his *Two Treatises of Government*, attacking the divine right of kings. Locke argued that men (not women) had created governments to protect their natural rights, especially to their lives and personal liberty, and their property or the fruits of their labor. A just government was thus founded on a voluntary agreement, or social contract, between the people and their rulers in which the people surrendered some of their natural liberty to their rulers in exchange for protecting the rest. When rulers violated men's rights, as James II had done, they broke the compact, and the people had a right to replace them. The spirit of the *Two Treatises* differed sharply from the feudalistic measures of the Fundamental Constitutions and gave strong philosophical support to the Glorious Revolution. Locke's new thinking had a profound impact on subsequent British and American ideas about the nature and value of public and private liberty.

THE GLORIOUS REVOLUTION IN AMERICA

The Glorious Revolution had immediate repercussions in America. James's efforts to cancel colonial charters, abolish assemblies, and replace elected officials with appointees had been very unpopular. When rumors arrived that the king had been overthrown and war had broken out with France, colonists celebrated the end of a hated reign and struck out against imagined Catholic conspiracies to restore it. In Massachusetts, a popular uprising toppled the Dominion of New England and jailed Governor-General Sir Edmund Andros and most of his top lieutenants. As we saw earlier, a militia led by Major Jacob Leisler overthrew the Dominion in New York, while Connecticut, Rhode Island, and Plymouth quietly resumed their former governments. Protestants seized power in Maryland, convinced that their Catholic proprietor would inevitably side with James and the French.

When the dust settled, colonists discovered that King William disapproved of these disruptions and did not believe that a change of kings gave them new powers or permitted disobedience of established authority. Imperial officials continued to believe that the purpose of the empire was to benefit England through trade, and enforcing the rules of a trading empire could require a firm hand and a strong measure of central control. If colonial governments needed adjustments, the king and his ministers would attend to those themselves. If their governments needed adjustment to comply with the revolution, they would deal with that too. William accordingly released the former officials whom rebellious colonists had sent home for trial and slowly considered his next steps. Eventually he decided to give up the Dominion of New England and allowed Connecticut and Rhode Island to resume their previous governments. He joined Plymouth to Massachusetts under a new royal charter that balanced an elected assembly with an appointed governor and gave all Protestants legal equality. In Maryland, William confirmed the overthrow of the Catholic proprietorship and installed a royal government, though the Calverts regained their property when they joined the Church of England in 1715.

The Glorious Revolution left its deepest mark in America on New York. In the spring of 1689, local administration had collapsed along with the Dominion of New England. Panicked rumors swirled that French Catholics would revenge the overthrow of King James by sending Indians to attack the Hudson Valley, scalping and pillaging everywhere. A committee of safety formed in New York City and handed power to militia commander Jacob Leisler, who repeatedly invoked the language of popular rights and Protestant radicalism to justify his authority. But Leisler was a clumsy politician who manipulated elections, jailed all who crossed him, and saw papists everywhere. Fears of French and Indian attack came true with a serious raid on Schenectady, but Leisler could not respond effectively and became increasingly unpopular.

Jacob Leisler finally overstepped in 1691 when he refused to surrender Manhattan's fort to the duly appointed new governor. After his execution, New York became a royal colony with an elected assembly like the others, but Leisler's bitter legacy remained. His rebellion had revealed serious class and ethnic rivalries, with poorer Dutch residents tending to support him against wealthier English settlers. In addition to these ongoing tensions, Leisler had treated his opponents so harshly and his own punishment was so severe that the surviving leaders of each side fiercely hated each other, leaving New York divided between Leislerians and Anti-Leislerians for a generation to come.

Old-line Massachusetts Puritans mourned their lost charter and lost independence, but most colonies welcomed the Glorious Revolution. Most whites were devoted English subjects who held the same religious and political values as their kinfolk back home. The events of 1688–1689 seemed to confirm that English government rested on popular consent, that representative bodies must approve all taxes, and that popular liberty required strict legal protection and a balance between the power of the king (known as the royal prerogative) and the power of legislative assemblies. Colonial Englishmen assumed that these guarantees applied to them as much as to Englishmen at home.

English leaders drew a different lesson from the revolution. They concluded that Parliament alone was supreme within the empire, not representative institutions in general. The colonies still existed to serve the mother country, so they could not be entirely equal to it. In practice, this meant that if the combined will of the king and Parliament clashed with the views of colonial assemblies, the assemblies would have to give way. The conflict between these two points of view would later have a crucial significance that few people noticed in the jubilant aftermath of the Glorious Revolution.

The Empire and the British Constitution

As the revolution's turmoil gradually subsided, colonial governments settled into stable routines. One major theme in the prevailing pattern was the importance of international rivalries, particularly the rivalry between England, France, and their Native American allies for control of North America. Another was the continued relevance of events and developments in Britain.

FIGHTING THE FRENCH AND INDIANS

Britain and France clashed frequently in the eighteenth century and all their wars involved America. Indians played an active role, carefully choosing and changing sides and recruiting Europeans to their own quarrels, just as Europeans sought Indian allies for theirs. American-based combat could take the form of colonial assaults on strongholds of the enemy, or it could erupt from skirmishes in Indian country between the English colonies and New France. All contestants between the Ohio River and the Great Lakes tried to play their multiple adversaries against each other, striving to protect their independence and the terms of trade. Parallel contests emerged in the similar space where the claims of Spanish Florida, French Louisiana, and English Georgia overlapped in the homelands of the Choctaw, Chickasaw, and Creek Indians.

For all sides, the most immediate stakes of colonial war were control of the interior fur trade, though the balance of power in Europe also worried diplomats. From the colonial perspective, all the major military conflicts from 1689 to 1763 were really French and Indian wars, though only the last one, known in Europe as the Seven Years' War (1756–1763), was remembered by that name in America. Instead, Americans called the others by the name of the reigning monarch, while the English named them after relevant events in Europe: King William's War (War of the League of Augsburg, 1689–1697), Queen Anne's War (War of Spanish Succession, 1702–1713), and King George's War (War of Austrian Succession, 1740–1748).

Other wars pitted groups of tribes against white Americans and their Indian allies, without the involvement of European powers. Resenting white incursions on their lands, for example, Tuscarora Indians descended on North Carolina settlements in 1711 and killed hundreds of whites. Unable to defend itself, North Carolina sought aid from South Carolina, which sent a party of Yamasee Indians under white command. They crushed the Tuscaroras by 1713 and repaid themselves by selling hundreds of captives into slavery. Most surviving Tuscaroras then joined their kinfolk in New York to become the sixth nation of the Iroquois Confederacy. Only two years later, the Yamasees and their allies among the Catawbas, Creeks, and neighboring tribes launched their own war against South Carolina and killed approximately 7 percent of its white population. The colony survived by recruiting Cherokees to counterattack and kill or enslave most of the Yamasees.

The outcomes of the Tuscarora and Yamasee Wars were conspicuous examples of the widespread enslavement of Native Americans by colonial whites. Columbus himself had originated the practice, but King Ferdinand and Queen Isabella had banned it in favor of forcing Indian labor through the *encomienda* system. New Englanders had enslaved captives in their wars with the Pequots, Wampanoags, and other tribes. Carolinians were especially active slavers, and sold as many as 30,000–50,000 Indians between 1670 and 1715. To reduce the chance of uprisings, most went to the West Indies instead of local plantations. Across the Southeast, slave raids by whites and by other Indians wiped out numerous small tribes such as the Westos of South Carolina, as well as most of the native inhabitants of lowland Georgia and Florida and the coastal tribes of Louisiana, and even struck large groups such as the Creeks, Choctaws, and Chickasaws. Native combatants did not believe they were fighting "their own people" in these conflicts because they did not embrace a common identity. As always, tribes

fought one another for revenge, but also to gain resources like hunting grounds or favorable trading positions. As their numbers declined,
tribes could try to rebound by consolidating with others or adopting
captives, but they could also sell their prisoners to the whites.

Each of these conflicts brought terror and destruction to colonial
frontiers and their Indian neighbors. In Queen Anne's War, for example, a party of French, Mohawks, and other Indians attacked the
town of Deerfield, Massachusetts, killed over 40 inhabitants, and captured 112 for ransom. Other campaigns saw large colonial mobiliza-
tions to attack the enemy's military strongholds. Creeks and Carolinians besieged St. Augustine in 1704, and a New England expedition in
King George's War took the massive French fortress of Louisburg on
Cape Breton Island in northeast Canada. War also changed or strengthened imperial claims. In Queen Anne's War, for example, Britain took
Canada's Nova Scotia, Newfoundland, and Hudson Bay, while France
strengthened its hold on the Mississippi Valley.

THE EIGHTEENTH-CENTURY
BRITISH CONSTITUTION

In 1707, Parliament passed the Act of Union to merge the previously
separate countries of England and Scotland into the new kingdom of
Great Britain. The change gave Scots access to American markets, and
Scottish merchants came to have an increasingly important role in the
eighteenth-century tobacco trade. Americans also attended closely to
the succession of British monarchs. Worried that the Catholic Stuarts,
supported by plotters called Jacobites, might once more try to seize the
throne and undo the Glorious Revolution, Parliament passed the Act
of Settlement in 1701 to reemphasize that no Catholic could occupy
the throne. When Queen Anne (Mary's sister, who succeeded the joint
monarchs) died childless in 1714, the new king was accordingly her
Protestant cousin George I, from the German principality of Hanover.
Taken all together, these laws and actions became major features of
the eighteenth-century British constitution, which was never written
down in a single place or adopted in a formal deliberative process, but
won deep popular loyalty as the freest government in the world.

Britain's constitution was based on a theory of mixed, or balanced,
government. Political thinkers assumed that there were three fundamental divisions in society: the king, the nobility, and the common
people. Each of these segments underpinned one of the three classic
forms of government: monarchy, or government by one; aristocracy,

or government by a few; and democracy, or government by many. By themselves, theorists agreed that each of these systems was vulnerable to a corresponding abuse—tyranny, oligarchy, or anarchy—that could overturn liberty and order.

Eighteenth-century Englishmen believed that the rest of Europe and Asia already suffered from varying degrees of tyranny, but their own mixed constitution protected liberty by combining the best parts of monarchy, aristocracy, and democracy. Each segment of society supposedly controlled a different branch of the British government: the Crown, the House of Lords, and the House of Commons. Each of these institutions provided government with a different benefit: firmness and single-mindedness from the Crown, stability and wisdom from the Lords, and love of liberty from the Commons. New laws required the consent of all three branches, so the liberties promised by the Glorious Revolution to Englishmen of every rank were considered safe. Boasting of their freedom from arbitrary power, Englishmen and Americans embraced the new philosophical theories of John Locke, and proudly claimed that any future would-be tyrant would suffer the fate of James II.

The British government operated very differently in practice. The German-born King George I could not speak English, so Sir Robert Walpole, First Lord of the Treasury and the king's principal minister, led the government without much royal interference. The appearance of parliamentary supremacy remained, but Walpole managed to control opinion in the House of Commons by distributing government jobs and patronage to its members and their relatives and other dependents. Though Crown and Parliament jointly ruled the country, Walpole prevented serious conflict between them while dominating both between 1721 and 1742.

Though the House of Commons spoke for the people of the realm, moreover, it did not represent them directly. Property requirements limited voting rights, most members came from medieval towns, or boroughs, with widely varying populations, and some large cities sent no representatives at all. Rotten boroughs had lost so much population that the remaining voters could be bribed or intimidated. Some ancient boroughs had entirely disappeared, leaving pocket boroughs owned by a single person, who chose the representative himself. Members of the House of Commons did not have to live in the districts that sent them, and most members were landed gentlemen whose social and economic interests overlapped with the hereditary members of the House of Lords. Others represented financial interests in the city of London, but Walpole made sure these interests did not clash, so no fundamental power struggles disrupted the harmony of British government.

Aggressively promoting Britain's commerce, Walpole laid the basis for a future acceleration of economic development that came to be called the Industrial Revolution. Founded in 1694, the powerful Bank of England already existed to facilitate government borrowing, but with firm support from financiers, Walpole strengthened it and made reliable payments on the sizable national debt. The mercantilist empire approached its heyday, harvesting profits from a worldwide network of colonies and business partners that stretched from Hudson's Bay to the Caribbean, and from African trading posts to the subcontinent of India. Walpole also created a large navy to protect British shipping and a professional standing army to deploy at will on land. The British people paid heavy taxes for these costly measures, but the government could always borrow more money in times of war or other emergency because Walpole had made government bonds a supremely secure investment.

In accordance with the Glorious Revolution, the British government continued to respect the personal liberty of individual subjects more fully than any other monarchy in Europe, but the majority of Britons had no vote in elections and no significant voice in the government. Hungry laborers could riot from time to time, but the government did not depend on their approval. Subsequent kings and ministers followed Walpole's example, so British society and government became far more stable in the eighteenth century than it was in the seventeenth. Politically active Englishmen liked to believe that the balance of king, Lords, and Commons created this stability, but it actually resulted from a fundamental consensus among the governing classes and the undisputed control of Parliament by the Crown and its ministers.

THE OPPOSITION TRADITION

Not all Englishmen were satisfied with Walpole's version of balanced government. A small group of disenchanted radicals hated the manipulation of elections, the high taxes, and the corrupt distribution of jobs and favors that the government routinely used to control the House of Commons. Deeply distrustful of human nature, they were certain that strong ministers would always use their powers for personal gain instead of the public welfare. Abuses would breed more abuses, taxes would skyrocket, elections would become meaningless, and a standing army would crush dissent. Freedom's only hope, they argued, was a truly balanced government overseen by a virtuous and hypervigilant populace. Without immediate and radical reforms, corruption would overwhelm the kingdom and liberty would perish.

Foremost among these self-styled Real Whigs were John Trenchard and Thomas Gordon, authors of a series of essays signed "Cato," which first appeared in newspapers between 1720 and 1723 and were followed by at least six bound editions before 1755. Also calling themselves the Country Party (in opposition to Walpole's Court Party), Trenchard and Gordon and a vocal band of imitators sang the praises of British liberty, calling it "the divine source of all human happiness," but endlessly warned that it hung by a thread. "Liberty chastises and shortens Power," they cautioned, "therefore Power would extinguish Liberty; and consequently Liberty has always exceeding cause to be jealous, and always upon her Defence." To safeguard liberty, Trenchard and Gordon stressed the importance of public virtue, or the willingness to sacrifice personal interests for the good of all. In their minds, self-indulgent citizens would readily surrender their liberties in exchange for immoral personal benefits ranging from frivolity and vice to corruption and government favoritism. Without strict public virtue, they pleaded, liberty would be lost.

Generally satisfied with their government, most influential Englishmen dismissed such alarms, but many Americans read them eagerly. Wide distribution of property, relatively simple lifestyles, and feisty colonial assemblies made free Americans especially proud of their liberty and virtue, while the arbitrary power and seductive allure of royal government might threaten them both. Far from the seats of real power, even the most powerful Americans easily believed in conspiracies against them. Their newspapers reprinted selections from *Cato's Letters* endlessly and bound copies appeared in over one-third of American private libraries. Politically active colonists repeatedly invoked Cato's ideas to justify resistance to imperial policies. For most of the eighteenth century, they did not go on to reject royal power altogether, but when relations with Britain turned sour, they would blend English radical suspicions with the revolutionary ideas of John Locke to interpret the crisis and prescribe a remedy.

The radical, or Real Whig, tradition appealed to colonists who could read, vote, and freely participate in public affairs, but it was not the only cultural framework available for resisting established authority. Below the ranks of land-owning white men were thousands of artisans, wage earners, tenants, sailors, and laborers who claimed the rights of freeborn Englishmen even though they might not vote or read political theories. They usually deferred, or submitted, to upper-class rule, but in return, they expected the authorities to treat them fairly and preserve a moral economy, or decent conditions for the poor. When the elite failed in these duties, as in times of famine or oppressive taxation, for example, poor people in England, America, and continental Europe often formed crowds or mobs to protest and correct their grievances. These crowds could include women, free blacks, and young people as well as adult white men. Up to a point, the authorities often tolerated such outbursts and acted on their complaints, believing that stable government required a minimum level of popular support. In this irregular fashion, even the poorest free subjects thus claimed the right to influence public affairs. In times of political crisis, these crowd actions could bring elite and popular protesters together.

BALANCED GOVERNMENT IN THE COLONIES

With all their suspicions of centralized power, colonial Americans still shared British enthusiasm for parliamentary supremacy, the Protestant succession, the House of Hanover, and the freedom and stability they seemed to produce. The widespread enslavement of Africans radically contradicted their boasts of British liberty, but few whites seemed troubled. Their own colonial governments shared many features of Britain's constitution that they were quick to magnify. The royal or proprietary governors were obviously the local representatives of the king, and the governors' councils, appointed from the very wealthiest and most distinguished colonial families, resembled the House of Lords. The elected assemblies were apparently analogous to the House of Commons, and colonials made much of their power to initiate legislation, to control their own membership, to approve all public taxes, and to control all public expenditures.

The king's ministers and governors scoffed at these claims. So far as they were concerned, the colonial assemblies were inferior local bodies more like boards of village aldermen than the august House of Commons. Without the will or resources to create a large imperial bureaucracy like Spain's, it was more convenient to leave the colonials in charge of their own local affairs, but that was not at all the same as conceding that the assemblies had equal powers with Parliament itself. In 1760, Governor Arthur Dobbs of North Carolina reported with mixed anger and incredulity that "the Assembly think themselves entitled to all the Priviledges of a British House of Commons and therefore ought not submit to His majesty's honorable Privy Council further than the Commons do in England, or to submit to his Majesty's instructions to His Governor and Council here." Despairing of proper government under such conditions, Dobbs demanded more power to "oppose and suppress a republican spirit of Independency rising in this colony." Like other governors, he was largely disappointed, for most British ministers had more important things to worry about.

London expected governors to control their assemblies. In Britain itself, the Hanoverian kings abandoned their personal control of legislation, including the power to veto acts of Parliament, and relied on their ministers to cajole or manipulate the lawmakers to obtain the results they wanted. The case was far different in the colonies, where governors used the veto with great frequency, and the Crown often disallowed, or vetoed, laws that the governor had approved. Colonial governors could also call and dismiss assemblies without restraint, demand new elections or forbid them as they wished, and exercise far more powers over courts than the Crown claimed in Britain.

Royal governors provoked endless controversy when they tried to flex these executive muscles. About a fifth of them were born in America, but most were career bureaucrats or the needy relatives of some powerful person in Britain. They were usually honest and conscientious, but frequently knew little or nothing about America. They typically arrived at their posts with a sheaf of official instructions about what they were supposed to accomplish and how they were to go about it, but eventually clashed with their assemblies and found that their supposedly extensive powers were difficult to exercise. Unlike the ministers back home, governors lacked authority to entice assemblymen with offers of jobs and patronage. Unpopular governors could also face dismissal, as resentful colonial leaders pulled every string they could find to undermine their standing with the home government. It was therefore very difficult for the typical governor to gain an assembly's compliance without granting equal or greater concessions in return.

Unlike Britain, moreover, colonial society was often bitterly divided. Backcountry representatives frequently wanted more protection against Indians and coastal towns wanted to avoid the expense of war. Ambitious speculators wanted handsome land grants and their rivals wanted to stop them. Religious dissenters quarreled with the established church. A faction from one section of a colony struggled with enemies from another over place and preferment, and so on.

Also in contrast to Britain, many of the malcontents could vote,

for land was so cheap that many colonists could meet the property requirements for the suffrage. Historians estimate that as many as one-
half to three-quarters of free white men in America could cast a ballot,
while the corresponding number in Britain was no more than one-
third. Enfranchised Americans also had closer ties to their elected representatives than most Britons had, for their assembly districts were
more equally apportioned and assemblymen were more likely to live
among their constituents. While the eighteenth-century British Parliament was a model of stability and decorum, quarrels with governors
and among internal factions bitterly split its colonial counterparts.

Most of the time, governors and assemblies reached the agreements
they needed. Many assemblies controlled the governor's salary and
refused to pay it without his cooperation. Others could make generous land grants to governors who pleased them. The endless cycle of
colonial wars forced governors to go repeatedly to assemblies with
requests for men and money, and assemblies demanded recognition
of their powers before granting the supplies. Successful governors
learned to play one faction of the assembly against another or grant
the majority's demands in exchange for cooperation. "A governor is
no sooner appointed than the first question is, Into whose hands shall
I throw myself?" wrote one experienced veteran in 1752. "The answer
is ready, Into whose but such as can best manage the Assembly. Hence
prime ministers and courtiers are established, and, of course, anti-
courtiers."

In the course of these disputes, the gentlemen who dominated the
assemblies grew accustomed to thinking of themselves as the real
rulers of their own colonies, despite the grumbles of their governors.
They consistently thought of themselves as loyal and dutiful subjects
of the British Crown and contented members of the larger empire, but
regarded local control of colonial society as their fundamental right.
This assumption would eventually drive them away from the king and
toward an American republic.

*

British North America changed a great deal between the twin crises
of Metacom's War and Bacon's Rebellion in the late seventeenth century and the eve of the Seven Years' War in 1756. Colonies that had not
even existed in 1676 had grown and flourished. Extravagant blueprints
for imaginary utopias had given way to more practical arrangements

worked out by endless negotiation. Most important from a political standpoint, colonists and administrators had absorbed many lessons from England's Glorious Revolution and attempted to apply them to colonial conditions. The results were a ragged and uneven approximation of Britain's balanced government that combined popular liberties with centralized powers for protecting trade, but leading colonists took pride in this achievement. Though they frequently quarreled with specific imperial demands, they cherished their membership in the British Empire.

The triumph of William and Mary seemed to settle the most pressing issues of colonial governance and identity. Eighteenth-century Americans shifted their attention to economic concerns, and varied local resources brought diverse ways of life to different regions. The population of the thirteen mainland colonies would grow dramatically by immigration and natural increase until it almost reached two million whites and blacks. Distinct societies emerged in the South, the middle colonies, and New England, yet the colonies shared common features that resembled and contrasted with conditions in Britain. A provincial elite appeared everywhere, with free subordinates enjoying a simple but substantial prosperity below them. Proud of their achievements, few if any colonists guessed that their loyalty to the British Empire would be strained past the breaking point by events in the third quarter of the eighteenth century.

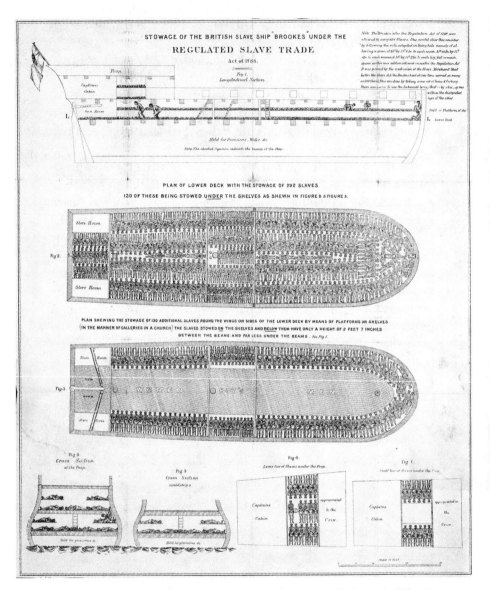

FIGURE 2. The eighteenth-century British slave ship *Brookes*, "tight-packed" for the Middle Passage. Miscellaneous Items in High Demand, Rare Book and Special Collections Division, Library of Congress, LC-USZ62-44000.

CHAPTER 4

Colonial Society and Culture, 1676–1756

In 1798, an elderly African told a listener in Connecticut how he came to America. About the year 1735, Broteer Furro had been a six-year-old boy who later remembered his father as "Prince of the tribe of Dukandarra," somewhere in the interior of West Africa. The Dukandarra had paid invaders to escape attack, but the raiders struck anyway. Broteer watched helplessly from a thicket of reeds as his father fought bravely but alone until he was finally overpowered. Dragging the boy from his hiding place, the attackers beat him, bound him with the women and other children, and tortured his father to death.

Marched overland for months by his African captors and finally delivered to the waiting slave ships, Broteer and his family were among 12 million victims of the African slave trade. Like the Dukandarra, whole nations disappeared in a dragnet for human lives that continued from the mid-fifteenth century to the late nineteenth. Most of those who survived the notorious Middle Passage across the Atlantic Ocean came to the Caribbean or Latin America, but as many as half a million reached British North America, mostly before 1770.

Broteer was among them. A ship's officer bought him as a personal servant and gave him the new name Venture, because his purchase was a private investment. That act may have saved the boy from confinement in the filth and stench that others endured belowdecks, where smallpox killed 60 out of 260 captives on the transatlantic voyage. Eventually it brought him to his master's home in Rhode Island instead of the others' destination, the cane fields of Barbados.

As a man, Venture became famous for his size, strength, and diligence. He used these gifts to "hire his time" — that is, to pay his owners for the privilege of working independently — and to save enough from his remaining wages to buy freedom for himself, his wife Marget, and their three children. Taking the surname of his last master, Venture Smith toiled for years as a farmhand and a woodcutter and later as a shipowner and farmer. Often cheated by customers who scorned to pay a black man, Venture Smith still secured three houses and 100 acres of good farmland in Haddam Neck, Connecticut, before his death in 1805. His memoirs circulated widely for the rest of the nineteenth century.

The remarkable life of Venture Smith was part of the extraordinary growth of the eighteenth-century British colonies. Like many of the new Americans who arrived between 1700 and 1770, Smith came as a slave. Unlike the vast majority of his peers, however, he won his freedom and used it to approximate the success that free Europeans sought when they crossed the ocean voluntarily. Capping his father's achievements with patriotic service, Smith's son Solomon even fought for his country's liberty in the War for Independence. The experience of Venture Smith thus combined slavery and freedom, starkly contrasting aspects of America's colonial history.

The America of Venture Smith had rapidly changed since the Glorious Revolution of 1688–1689. Its population grew dramatically, both from the large families of existing settlers and from free and unfree newcomers. Immigrants brought more social and cultural diversity to the colonies, and distinct regional economies and cultures took shape along the Atlantic seaboard. The Chesapeake and Carolina colonists created tobacco and rice plantations whose slaves produced most of the colonies' exports. The middle colonies of New York, New Jersey, Pennsylvania, and Delaware welcomed thousands of Europeans to growing towns and cities or to their own small farms. New England also fostered productive farms and active commerce, giving Venture Smith his business opportunities, but growth and prosperity strained its Puritan heritage.

The eighteenth-century colonies faced an array of social and cultural challenges. Colonial assemblies governed slaves with labor codes that had no European precedents. Prosperity brought increased opportunities for some, but also sustained a clear social hierarchy. A growing population depended very directly on the presence of women and families, and inspired corresponding laws, ideas, and customs that did derive from English precedents. Eager to share in a broader intellectual community, leading colonists absorbed new ideas about the role of reason and science in human life and embraced the opportunity to join a transatlantic movement called the Enlightenment. Americans also launched a revival of Protestant Christianity that blended vitality and stability amid unsettling change.

A Changing Population

Britain's American colonies expanded dramatically in the three-quarters of a century before the American Revolution, growing from a quarter million inhabitants in 1700 to about 2.5 million in 1775. Much of this growth came from natural increase, as families were large and settlers lived longer, but over half a million people were newcomers. Almost half were captive Africans like Venture Smith, but slightly more came from Europe, especially Britain, Ireland, and Germany. The fate of African exiles would be far different from that of the Europeans, but their contributions to the colonies' society and economy were equally unmistakable. The new Americans added striking diversity to the colonial population and ensured that the future nation would not become a replica of England but a distinctive society of its own.

IMMIGRANTS FROM EUROPE

New migrants dramatically changed the ethnic composition of the colonial population. Most of the seventeenth-century settlers had been English, but a careful recent estimate suggests that England provided less than 8 percent of the migrants between 1700 and 1775, while 14 percent came from Germany, 18 percent from Ireland, 6 percent from Scotland, 5 percent from Wales, and the rest from Africa. About 40 percent of the roughly 300,000 European immigrants were bound servants of some kind, including some 50,000 British convicts.

The largest group of migrants from continental Europe came from Germany, especially from the Palatinate, a mostly Protestant region along the Rhine River whose nobles were pressing for higher rents and feudal dues. When Britain welcomed foreign Protestants to its mainland colonies, as many as 84,000 Palatines and other Germans accepted the invitation. As the first cohort established themselves, they urged their friends and relatives to follow, creating a pattern of chain migration that brought repeated waves of settlers from the same districts. To reach America, Palatines sailed down the Rhine River to Rotterdam and booked passage for Philadelphia, the largest colonial port. If their funds ran low, passengers borrowed from the ship's captain, hoping to find a friend or relative to redeem them in Pennsylvania. If unsuccessful, these redemptioners repaid their debts with stints of indentured servitude.

Many of the new arrivals became urban artisans, common laborers, or domestic servants, but more purchased land from private speculators or Pennsylvania's proprietor and began their own farms. They usually settled near kinfolk, creating German-speaking ethnic enclaves across the countryside. Preserving a non-English culture provoked resentments that would frequently recur in the American immigrant experience. "Why should the Palatine Boors [i.e., peasants] be suffered to swarm into our settlements," grumbled Benjamin Franklin, "and by herding together establish their languages and manners to the exclusion of ours?" Such sentiments encouraged the growth of ethnic blocs in Pennsylvania politics, another recurrent pattern. Corrupting *Deutsch* (the German word for "German"), Anglo-Americans called the Palatines "Dutch," and their descendants are still known as the "Pennsylvania Dutch."

An estimated 66,000 Protestant settlers from northern Ireland joined the Germans in Pennsylvania and the other mainland colonies. Their journey to America had begun in the early seventeenth century when King James I had seized the lands of Irish Catholic rebels, especially in the northern province of Ulster, and awarded them to followers who promised to settle them with Protestant tenants. Thousands of Scottish Presbyterians soon crossed over to Ireland, rented small plots in Ulster, and battled the dispossessed Catholics for control of the territory. England had sponsored these immigrants but discriminated against Presbyterians as well as Catholics, taxing all inhabitants to support the Anglican Church, reserving lands, offices, and even university enrollments for Anglicans, and even denying the validity of Presbyterian weddings. Ulster Protestants endured these burdens and initially prospered by raising flax and making linen. When landlords raised rents and the linen business faltered, first after 1720 and again after 1750, thousands left Ulster for Pennsylvania, where they came to be known as the Scots-Irish on account of their dual heritage.

Europeans came more slowly to other colonial empires. In 1660, the 58,000 inhabitants of British North America far outnumbered the 6,000 residents of New France, for example. Both New France and Louisiana claimed the vast river drainages, with small numbers of French downstream and Indians controlling the interior. French authorities ruthlessly suppressed and exploited the "little nations" who preceded them on the Gulf coast of Louisiana but upstream on the Mississippi and the St. Lawrence, both colonial governments respected Indian sovereignty and depended on Indian allies to maintain their supposed authority. The settlers of New France rented small farms from noble landowners and raised grains and livestock in the short growing season. Louisiana faced additional challenges from heat, floods, hurricanes, and tropical diseases. Over 5,000 whites and 6,000 slaves came to the colony before 1730, but a combined attack by slaves and Natchez Indians killed 10 percent of the population in 1729. As in the Carolinas, the French settlers could not defeat these enemies alone, but used lavish presents to get help from the Choctaws. Their combined forces then killed or enslaved most of the Natchez, scattering the survivors to other southeastern tribes. In the aftermath, no more than 2,000 whites and 4,000 Africans remained in Louisiana, growing indigo and tobacco that sold poorly. Unlike the French sugar islands, both New France and Louisiana languished and their revenues never matched expenses.

In addition to the uncounted Indians who remained independent, the population of New Spain grew vigorously in the eighteenth century, from 1.5 million in 1650 to nearly 5 million in 1790—roughly a million more than the infant United States in the same year. Most of this growth came from Indian and *mestizo* families who survived the earlier epidemics. In Florida, however, the non-Indian Spanish presence dwindled to small garrisons at St. Augustine and Pensacola, and its other borderland settlements were not much larger.

THE EXPANSION OF SLAVERY

Africans came to Virginia as early as 1619, but white servants outnumbered them before 1700. According to current estimates, about 12 million Africans boarded the slave ships in Africa but only 10 million reached the Americas alive, about half of them in the eighteenth century. In all, about half a million came to British North America and the United States, three-fifths of them before 1775.

Much about Virginia's first Africans remains uncertain. Most apparently came from the Caribbean and not directly from Africa. They knew something about European culture and often bore Portuguese and Spanish names like Antonio or Driggus (from Rodriguez), so they may have been baptized Catholics. Some remained slaves for life, but others gained their freedom quickly and may have been released like other servants. Court records show that early slaves and free blacks lived about like other servants—drinking, gambling, thieving, having sex, and running away with their English fellows as if there were few differences between them. Free Africans had fewer rights than the English, but they could still hold property, marry black or white spouses, go to court, testify against whites, and enjoy freedom in ways that later black generations could only dream about.

Conditions worsened after 1660, as planters sought new sources of labor. Indentured servants were increasing in price and decreasing in number, as poor British workers found better opportunities at home. A limited number of Indian slaves were available, but they still suffered badly from diseases and they might help their tribesmen during attacks. Soon after Bacon's Rebellion, however, the Royal African Company started shipping as many as 5,000 captives a year to the West Indies and the Chesapeake, at prices American planters could afford. Virginia's plantation owners soon began shifting from servants to slaves. Small planters in Virginia and Maryland still grew tobacco with their own hands and purchased indentured servants when they could, but by 1700, most tobacco workers were probably black.

Slavery also flourished on the rice plantations of South Carolina. Rice became a valuable export to the Caribbean and southern Europe, but it required frequent flooding, and constant heavy labor was necessary to build and maintain dikes and sluices and to tend the crop in mud and stagnant water. White South Carolinians bought so many slaves for this work that their colony contained a black majority by 1708, and its centers of rice cultivation contained as many as ten Africans for every white.

Slavery scarcely existed in England, so colonial assemblies established it with new laws that defined slaves as personal, or chattel, property, and stripped them of rights that belonged to the poorest Englishman. In Virginia, the first clear distinction between slaves and free servants came in a statute of 1661. "That in case any English servant shall run away in company with any negroes who are incapable of making satisfaction by the addition of time," the House of Burgesses declared, "*Bee it enacted* that the English so running away . . . shall serve for the time of the said negroes absence." The assembly presumed, in other words, that Africans' terms could not be extended since they already served for life. A year later, the House of Burgesses reversed English custom and decreed that children would inherit the status of their mothers, not their fathers, so enslaved mothers' children were enslaved as well. Masters could thus increase their slaveholdings by impregnating female slaves. In 1669, the assembly acknowledged that slavery rested on violence, and protected masters by ruling that any slave's death "from the extremity of . . . correction" must be deemed an accident, for murder required an intent to kill and no one would destroy his property on purpose. The need for repression was so great, in other words, that masters got permission to whip their slaves without limit, even to death.

The greatest number of slaves came from West Central Africa, where the states of Gabon, Congo, and Angola are today, followed by those from the Bight of Biafra, just to the south of the Niger River, and the Bight of Benin to its west. As with Venture Smith, Africans seized most of the victims and sold them to whites along the coast, allowing kingdoms like Ashanti, Dahomey, and Benin to rise and flourish on profits from the trade. One king received £250,000 in 1750, five times the income of the richest English nobleman. The leading European traders came from Britain, Portugal, and France, and usually supplied their own nations' colonies. Captives who survived a kidnapping raid and the brutal march to the African coast were chained and packed together "spoonways" in the holds of slave ships with as little as five feet between floors. The ships carried between 250 and 600 people, who suffered in unbearable filth and stench during a the Middle Passage, which could last for two or three months, before reaching a colonial port such as Charles Town or Savannah.

NATIVE AMERICANS AND COLONIAL EXPANSION

By 1700, coastal tribes like the Powhatans and the Wampanoags had nearly vanished, and survivors had submitted to English authority. Living as inconspicuously as possible, they quietly farmed in unwanted places like swamps and sandy wastes, sometimes selling pottery, baskets, or game, and occasionally working for pay. Farther inland, some of the larger Indian societies began to recover their numbers in the eighteenth century, partly by absorbing survivors from smaller groups. In the Southeast, tribes such as the Creeks, Cherokees, Choctaws, and Chickasaws occupied wide territories beyond the limits of white occupation and held the balance of power among the British, French, and Spanish empires. In a counterpart to the French Canadian fur trade, they conducted a lively trade in deerskins with South Carolina merchants, selling as many as 53,000 hides a year for weapons, cloth, and alcohol.

The Iroquois Confederacy of New York was an especially powerful network with a crucial role in diplomacy and the fur trade. Brought together by Chief Hiawatha in the late fifteenth century, the Five Nations included the Mohawk, Oneida, Onondaga, Cayuga, and Seneca tribes, and occupied the strategic corridor in western New York that connected the Hudson River to Lake Erie and the Ohio Valley. After defeat in North Carolina, the related Tuscarora tribe migrated north to become the sixth member of the confederacy in 1722. Controlling the fur trade of the eastern Great Lakes, the Iroquois expanded by collecting captives and tribute from weaker tribes to their south and west.

Iroquois dealings with Britain and France illustrate the methods of Indian diplomacy. When the English acquired New York, the Five Nations maintained their independence, but as they had with the Dutch, they joined the newcomers in an alliance called the Covenant Chain. Over time, various treaties formalized this relationship between Britain and the Iroquois, and recognized the confederacy as the dominant power in western New York and the Great Lakes basin. The allies of the Covenant Chain thus squared off against New France and its own Indian allies in the upper country, often using diplomacy instead of war to assert themselves. When France used gifts and trade to counteract Iroquois power over weaker tribes, for example, the Six Nations made friendly overtures to Britain, France, and their respective Indian allies, neutralized potential opposition, and then overpowered the Shawnees, Delawares, and other tribes of the Ohio Valley. Iroquois agents, or half kings, remained with subordinate tribes to oversee trade and external relations.

Avoiding dependence on either empire, the Iroquois offered benefits to both Britain and France by allowing the British to trade in the Ohio country and the French to travel through it to Louisiana. When colonial wars broke out, the Iroquois tried to stay neutral, but when that failed, they gave nominal support to Britain while quietly encouraging France. At the height of its power in 1744, the confederacy granted land (which it did not really control) to Virginia in exchange for access to the Cherokees and Catawbas, hoping to reduce them to vassalage as well. Unfortunately for the Six Nations, Virginia took far more land than the confederacy intended to give, and used its advantage to open the upper Ohio Valley to its land speculators. Until then, the Iroquois continued to dominate the territory bounded by the Hudson and Ohio Rivers and the Great Lakes, while Britain and France each courted their favor.

Elsewhere on the continent, Creeks, Cherokees, Choctaws, and the Indians of New France used similar tactics to safeguard their independence by pitting one European power against another. In the words of one New York negotiator, "To preserve the balance between us and the French is the great ruling principle of the modern Indian politics." Though the large native states of Mesoamerica and the Andes had quickly lost independence to the sixteenth-century Spanish, North American Indians used a combination of war and diplomacy to control as much as three-quarters of their continent through the 1780s.

The South as a Slave Society

Historians of slavery make a distinction between slave societies, where slavery dominates the economy and other institutions, and societies with slaves, where slavery is just one of several kinds of labor. In this sense, both South Carolina and the Chesapeake colonies became slave societies by about 1700. Coastal areas of North Carolina and Georgia soon followed, but their upland regions were societies with slaves for much longer. Northern colonies were also societies with slaves, though blacks were 12 percent of New York's population in 1770, 7 percent of New Jersey's, and 6 percent of Rhode Island's.

LIFE IN BONDAGE

There was a very important difference between slavery in North America and slavery in the colonies farther south. In the sugar islands, most slaves were men who died young, and continuous imports were available to replace them. In most parts of the eighteenth-century mainland, however, enslaved women were more numerous, so the slave population began to grow by natural increase, or an excess of births over deaths. In one 50-year period, for example, 150,000 Africans came to Barbados but its slave population only rose by 28,000. At about the same time, Virginia imported 100,000 Africans but its slave force rose from 10,000 to 100,000.

These differences arose from cold calculations. Wealthy sugar planters could afford to pay high prices for enslaved men, overwork them, and replace the dead or disabled with fresh purchases, knowing that a mostly male workforce would yield higher profits than one composed of men and women who would need years of milder and costlier treatment to reproduce themselves. Tobacco plantations were less lucrative, so mainland masters had to buy at least one woman for every two men, pay to protect their lives and health, support child-rearing, and add new workers from the ranks of their children. Planters also realized that men with wives and children would be less troublesome than bachelors. One spoke realistically in 1769:

> I Shd. Be obliged . . . to render the Negroes I now have happy and contented, wch I know they cannot be without having each a Wife. This will greatly tend to keep them at home and to make them Regular and tho the Women will not work all together so well as ye Men, Yet Amends will be sufficiently made in a very few years by the Great Encrease of Children.

Slave owners were not always farsighted, and shocked travelers reported that slaves often lacked adequate food, clothing, and shelter. Poorer masters were less generous than affluent ones, and did not own enough slaves for them all to find spouses nearby. The law did not recognize slave marriages, moreover, so enslaved families had no protection from sale or sexual abuse. But as more and more masters learned the value of a growing workforce, they provided more basic material necessities.

Modest improvements never eased the fundamental brutality of bondage, and slaves resisted their condition whenever possible. Shipboard rebellions happened often enough to keep captains and crews on their guard at all times, and some captives committed suicide rather than submit. Slaves made persistent efforts to escape the plantations. Known as maroons, some found refuge in remote swamps or other hidden places, where they re-created African-style communities and conducted occasional raids on white settlements. These communities were especially significant in colonies with accessible hideouts and large numbers of Africans, such as Jamaica and Brazil, but they also took shape in the Carolina swamplands. When escape seemed impossible, day-to-day resistance could take the form of feigning sick, breaking tools, or working poorly.

In America, well-armed whites usually outnumbered the slaves, so overt rebellions were unlikely to succeed. When Spanish authorities in St. Augustine offered freedom to runaway slaves from the English colonies, however, some 20 Angolans on South Carolina's Stono River somehow heard the news and launched a strike for freedom in 1739. Killing about 20 whites who stood in their way, the original band recruited between 60 and 100 others to make a break for Florida, before being crushed by a massive white counterattack. Louisiana's Natchez Revolt took 200 whites lives in 1729, and the colony stagnated when the danger persisted.

Even while they resisted, African Americans slowly forged their own culture, using their own versions of English with African words and grammatical features. At first, whites made few efforts to convert them to Christianity, but Africans used charms and magic to influence natural forces and made no sharp distinctions between the sacred and the secular. Like their African forebears, African Americans included highly rhythmic music in the tasks of everyday life and kept a place for African instruments like the banjo and the drum. Throughout the Americas, slaves punctuated their worship and their work rhythms with the call-and-response pattern of West African singing in which a leader offers a phrase or a sentiment to a group and the group replies by reinforcing or amplifying the leader's theme. Cultural roots in Africa would sustain and anchor the African American community throughout the brutal centuries ahead.

MASTERS IN A SLAVE SOCIETY

For whites, the spread of slavery reinforced a social structure that already existed by the time of Bacon's Rebellion and reflected patterns on the sugar islands. In the Chesapeake and the Carolinas, a small group of wealthy planter gentry owned most slaves and the best land. Middling farmers bought slaves when they could. A much larger group of common whites, many of them poor ex-servants, struggled to find their own farms, often in hillier or less fertile districts far from the coast.

The great planters dominated society wherever slavery flourished. In Virginia, for example, Robert "King" Carter used marriage, inheritance, and political appointments to get his start in tobacco planting, land speculation, and the slave trade, and he died owning 300,000 acres, over 1,000 slaves, and £10,000 in cash. His sons Landon Carter and Robert Carter III were almost equally wealthy and prominent. Patriarchs of the "first families of Virginia," including the Randolphs, Beverleys, and Lees, ruled their county courts and vestries, filled the House of Burgesses and Governor's Council, and supplied generations of leaders to Virginia and the United States.

Elite families often intermarried to build up fortunes and networks of powerful kin. Virginia law followed primogeniture and awarded a father's land to his oldest son unless a will directed otherwise. Owners could also entail their lands to prevent heirs from selling or subdividing them. Sometimes educating their sons in England, planters used impressive houses, the finest furnishings, elaborate entertainments, and polished manners to display their wealth and claim superior status. Like many successful elites, the Virginia gentry often had roughhewn origins and could make room for some talented newcomers, so lesser planters hoped for the educational opportunities or the advantageous match that might place one of their own children in the ranks of their colony's upper crust.

Farther to the south, in the rice and indigo country of South Carolina and Georgia, leading families like the Rutledges, Middletons, and Pinckneys surpassed even the Virginians in their wealth and flourishes. To avoid the danger of malaria on their swampy plantations, the low-country rice planters built townhouses in nearby Charles Town, where they enjoyed races, balls, and matchmaking in a fashionable social season. Unable to equal this display of elegance, aspiring Georgians strove to imitate it in their own capital of Savannah, and the even less prosperous North Carolinians tried their best in coastal villages like Wilmington and New Bern.

Colonel William Byrd II of Virginia vividly illustrates the achievements, frustrations, and vices of the planter aristocracy. After a polished education in England, Byrd entered the House of Burgesses at the age of 22. Rebuffed when he courted an English heiress, he married the daughter of a planter and imperial official who promised the couple £1,000, and later inherited his father's hundreds of slaves and thousands of acres. Byrd adorned his plantation with Westover, an elegant brick mansion whose symmetrical lines and balanced proportions perfectly embodied the aesthetic ideals of his era. Though hugely rich and successful, Byrd chafed at his colonial status and longed to enter the English aristocracy or to win appointment as governor of Virginia. He never achieved either goal.

William Byrd is best known today for his detailed and perceptive diary. It reveals a man of great learning and sharp wit who excused his nonchalant brutality with superficial piety. Remembering a visit to Williamsburg in October 1709, he noted, "I sent for the wench to clean my room and when she came I kissed her and felt her, for which God forgive me." Another entry complained of a slave's cooking. "Moll had not boiled the bacon half enough," Byrd noted casually, "for which I gave her some stripes under which she beshit herself. . . . I said my prayers and [retired with] good health, good thoughts, and good humor, thank God Almighty." With no restraints on their authority, other slaveholders could be equally callous.

Public institutions in the southern colonies bolstered the actual and symbolic power of men like William Byrd. Planters dominated Virginia's county courts and constructed substantial brick courthouses that resembled their own impressive mansions. They raised an even more splendid edifice for the House of Burgesses and the rest of colonial government, and in 1693 founded the College of William and Mary to train their sons. In South Carolina, westerners had to transact legal business in Charles Town, for its assembly refused to create local governments that might empower nonslaveholders.

Anglicanism was the established religion of the southern colonies, but the Church of England remained weak. In the most affluent parishes, vestries levied taxes to construct substantial churches and fill their pulpits with ministers who blessed the planters' power. Less developed neighborhoods often sheltered religious dissenters or resented a costly establishment, so they neglected church construction and hired poorly qualified clergy or none at all. Unlike the French and Spanish, moreover, the English made few efforts to convert slaves or Indians to Christianity. Anglican weaknesses left the southern colonies open for future generations of evangelists.

Despite the fundamental inequality of white society, its tensions slowly abated as race replaced class as the strongest measure of social distance. Seeking allies against a possible slave revolt, planters reached out to poorer whites. As the Indian population declined, ex-servants gained land more easily and thus the right to vote in provincial elections. Candidates learned to treat their poorer neighbors with greater respect and the simple possession of white skin became a valuable new privilege.

The wealthiest whites did not always welcome this development, but they submitted to it. "I am sensible of many bad consequences of multiplying these Ethiopians amongst us," wrote William Byrd in 1736. "They blow up the pride, and ruin the Industry of our White People, who seeing a Rank of poor Creatures below them, detest work for fear it should make them look like Slaves." Colonel Byrd could commit these words to paper in a letter to an English friend, but he would probably hesitate to utter them at a militia muster or a market day where common white men might overhear. Paradoxically perhaps, the growth of liberty and equality for white men depended in part on the spread of black slavery.

THE BACKCOUNTRY SOUTH

Plantations were scarce in the southern backcountry because high transportation costs absorbed agricultural profits. Most slaveholders owned no more than 5 or 10 workers and lived in sturdy homes of clapboards or squared logs, dressed themselves and their families in rough work clothes, and usually worked in fields beside their slaves. Known as yeomen, after the class of small, land-owning cultivators of rural England, the majority owned no slaves but purchased 100 or 200 acres from the Crown or the Carolina proprietors and cleared out small farms with the labor of neighbors and family. Poorer folk, who rented their land or squatted without permission on clearings in the wilderness, lived in an even simpler style.

Backcountry settlement lagged until the middle of the eighteenth century, when a second generation of Germans and Scots-Irish began to overflow from Pennsylvania. Clearing the Great Wagon Road from Lancaster, Pennsylvania, south into the Shenandoah Valley of Virginia, and across the Carolinas as far as Augusta, Georgia, these migrants became yeoman farmers and the first white inhabitants of the inland South. Far from established authorities, their communities sometimes suffered from corrupt local officials or from crime and social disorder that troubled orderly inhabitants like George Washington, who called the Shenandoah settlers "a parcel of Barbarian's and an uncooth set of People."

The labor of men and women was equally valuable in yeoman households. Men and boys performed heavy field work while women and girls devoted themselves to the preparation and preservation of food, the culture of poultry and vegetables, the production of textiles and clothing, and, of course, the care of many infant children. Westerners traded whatever they could at coastal or fall line settlements for items like iron, salt, and gunpowder that could not be made in their communities, but they had fewer commercial dealings than coastal residents.

Life in the Middle Colonies

Mostly founded after New England and Virginia, the middle colonies of New York, New Jersey, Pennsylvania, and Delaware mushroomed in the eighteenth century, growing from about 50,000 people in 1700 to more than half a million seven decades later. The Penn family's willingness to sell fertile land at low prices made Pennsylvania and Delaware

VENERATE THE PLOUGH

FIGURE 3. The eighteenth century brought growth and prosperity to Britain's mainland colonies, and praise for yeoman farmers as ideal free citizens. Miscellaneous Items in High Demand, Prints and Photographs Division, Library of Congress, LC-DIG-ds-04633.

especially attractive, and their tolerant religious policies made them hospitable to foreign dissenters. New York's policy of renting land within large privileged manors made it less desirable. The middle colonies supported large numbers of modestly prosperous yeoman farms that raised a wide variety of crops for sale and family consumption. Slavery was present, but it coexisted with family labor, hired workers, and indentured servitude. Commerce encouraged the growth of towns, while social, economic, and ethnic diversity marked the entire region and laid the basis for a lively and contentious public life.

FARMS AND RURAL LIFE

Rural dwellers of the middle colonies developed customs and land-use patterns that characterized much of the American frontier in the eighteenth and nineteenth centuries. As many as half the inhabitants were tenants or laborers at any one time, but land was affordable and most white men could reasonably aspire to owning their own farms eventually. Families dispersed their farms across the landscape and did not build large plantations or cluster in villages like some New Englanders. Their farms were about 50–300 acres in size, but few households could till that much at one time.

Much like their kinfolk in the southern backcountry, yeoman families often lived in log cabins that they copied from the early settlers of New Sweden, and raised corn, pigs, and a few cattle. Stout split-rail fences enclosed the fields while the animals fed themselves by roaming the woods until a fall roundup, followed by fattening and slaughter. This system allowed families with little or no land to raise numerous livestock, but prevented them from renewing their fields with the animals' manure. European observers criticized this wasteful practice but farmers persisted, for as Thomas Jefferson said, "We can buy an acre of new land cheaper than we can manure an old one." They also squandered timber by girdling trees to clear land, cutting the bark around their trunks and later burning them. Plowing was impossible until the stumps rotted, so families used hoes to plant corn in hills, or small mounds, instead of rows.

Households concentrated on their own welfare and valued self-reliance, but no family could perform all its tasks alone. Neighbors remained very important for activities like barn raisings, quilting bees, and cornhuskings. Local communities tended to be informal clusters of similar folk rather than government entities like New England towns. To make cooperation easier, relatives and people from the same ethnic groups tended to stick together, seeking out neighbors who knew their language and customs and shared their views about schools and churches. Some rural counties in the middle colonies were virtually all German or all Scots-Irish, while others resembled checkerboards of different religious and ethnic communities.

Families could get by on corn, pork, and garden vegetables, with some wool and flax for simple clothing, but they also needed a cash crop to pay taxes, buy or rent land, and purchase things they could not make themselves, like shoes, tools, iron, and salt, or modest luxuries like sugar and tea. When the fields were ready and the farmer could afford a plow and a team of horses or oxen, he usually supplemented his corn with wheat, the favorite commercial crop of the middle colonies. Wheat suited the local soil and climate, it needed little labor between sowing and harvest, and it did well on farms of any size, so farmers could raise it without slaves or servants. Ground by water-powered grist mills, wheat flour commanded a ready market in southern Europe and in the West Indies, and also provisioned the numerous ships that stopped at Philadelphia. Unwilling to stake all their hopes on one crop, however, farmers also sold corn, livestock, and flaxseed, while farm women sent large quantities of butter and cheese to market.

Unlike large plantation owners, small farmers in the middle colonies and elsewhere had to be cautious about raising crops for sale. If William Byrd faced crop failure or low tobacco prices, he could sell some spare acres or even some slaves to buy food for the rest without damaging his entire plantation. If the same thing happened on a 100-acre farm, the family might go hungry or lose their land and the independence that came with it. Especially where poor transportation or uncertain market conditions made commercial agriculture unreliable, farmers were careful to raise the family's food supply first, selling the surplus only when subsistence needs were satisfied. Unlike tobacco, wheat was an ideal cash crop in this respect, for families could eat it if a short harvest left no surplus.

Judging from their choices of crops and their marketing decisions, mid-Atlantic yeoman families worked hard to attain simple comforts and to leave something for their children, but they avoided commercial gambles that might imperil their competency, or modest financial independence. Economic historians have called this practice safety-first farming. Family farmers sold market crops within safe limits, but they also protected themselves by careful self-sufficiency in food and other basic necessities. They were also reluctant to undertake difficult improvements of doubtful immediate usefulness, like soil conservation. This pattern of semisubsistence farming and extensive land use would be commonplace in the future of rural America, much to the dismay of later commercial boosters and agricultural reformers. The middle colonies prospered under this system, however, and became famous as a fertile region where humble immigrants could flourish by hard work and steady habits. Pennsylvanians liked to call their colony "the best poor man's country."

TOWNS AND CITIES

Rural prosperity encouraged the growth of towns and cities in the middle colonies, for the export of commercial crops required merchant shippers and port facilities, and farmers wanted artisans to make their houses, furniture, shoes, tools, and finer clothing. With 24,000 inhabitants by 1760, Philadelphia was the largest city in the colonies and one of the largest in the empire—about the size of Dublin, Edinburgh, or Bristol—while New York and Boston ranked second and third. A network of smaller towns also dotted the landscape, offering local farmers a place to sell their crops, shoe their horses, order clothes, buy a drink, cast a ballot, or tend to legal business. The top ranks of urban society included the leading merchants and shipowners who controlled the import and export trade, together with the lawyers and imperial officials who made their residences in colonial capitals. Families like the Livingstons and DeLanceys of New York City composed an urban gentry who often competed in factional disputes to control colonial politics and enjoyed an opulent lifestyle in elegant urban townhouses. Their counterparts in Philadelphia were a Quaker elite who lived more simply but exercised a similar power in provincial affairs.

Beneath these wealthy families, a solid stratum of smaller businessmen and successful artisans composed the middle ranks of urban society. Many of these had been among the thousands of skilled redemptioners and indentured servants who entered the middle colonies during the eighteenth century to work in the region's towns and cities. Gaining their freedom, these men and women found that hard work and frugality could bring modest prosperity and respectability. Colonial towns also housed a population of poor and disabled inhabitants who needed public charity, as well as a sometimes-unruly group of laborers, apprentices, sailors, and slaves. Colonial towns were diverse and robust places that offered challenges and opportunity to a variety of inhabitants.

The Philadelphia printer and politician Benjamin Franklin was the preeminent representative of urban life and ambition in the middle colonies. Born in Boston in 1706, Franklin was a talented printer's apprentice when he escaped from his overbearing master (who was also his older brother) to seek his fortune in Philadelphia. Working for wages at first, Franklin later used his own press to publish the *Pennsylvania Gazette*, one of the colony's first newspapers, and his famous pamphlet series, *Poor Richard's Almanack*.

The almanac was an annual calendar of planting directions and astrological data, but Franklin spiced it up with pungent sayings and proverbs that reflected the ambitions and mobility of the surrounding society. "Waste not, want not," Poor Richard reminded his readers, and "God helps those who help themselves," while "A Ploughman on his Legs is higher than a Gentleman on his Knees." Poor Richard's advice to work hard, live frugally, and stay out of debt resonated powerfully with the common sense of farmers and artisans anxious to earn their own competence, even when the lure of imported luxuries outweighed this good advice from time to time. Reflecting the wisdom of semisubsistence farmers who expected to raise their own food but also hoped to sell something in the marketplace, Poor Richard advised readers to "plough deep while Sluggards sleep, and you shall have Corn to sell and to keep." Franklin's own life seemed to be an apt illustration of the benefits of his suggestions, for his successful printing business enabled him to retire at the age of 42, and devote the rest of his long life to science, philanthropy, and public service. Most artisans and apprentices in colonial Philadelphia could only dream of such success, but Franklin's words and example both reflected and encouraged the aspirations of their society.

SLAVES AND FREE BLACKS
IN THE NORTHERN COLONIES

Without plantations, the middle colonies had a limited but still significant demand for slave labor. The Dutch brought slaves to New Netherland and so did the English, initially from the West Indies and later from Africa. The black population of New York's southern counties exceeded 16 percent as late as 1750, and proportions were similar in northern New Jersey. Benjamin Franklin owned as many as five slaves in his early career, and printed advertisements for slave sales and runaways in the *Pennsylvania Gazette*, though he turned against slavery near the end of his life.

Throughout the countryside, most slaves worked by ones and twos for the region's more prosperous farmers, but a few masters held 20 slaves or more. Wealthy urban families used slaves as status symbols, dressing them in velvet coats and powdered wigs to work as domestic servants, while other slaves toiled in the streets as artisans, teamsters, and laborers. One New Jersey iron mine employed over 200 bondsmen.

Northern slaves shared the grievances of their southern counterparts, and northern whites were as likely as white southerners to crush their protests violently. In 1712, two dozen New York City slaves tried to launch a general insurrection by setting a building on fire and then killing 9 whites and wounding 6 others as they rushed to fight the blaze. Whites retaliated by burning 20 convicted rebels at the stake and beating another to death. A generation later, the city panicked again when a series of mysterious fires broke out in the spring and summer of 1741. When a handful of black and white suspects were arrested, an accused white servant launched a spree of executions by describing a widespread conspiracy by slaves and poor whites to burn the city, kill or rape its white inhabitants, and create their own government. Before the summer was over, almost half the city's adult male slaves had been jailed and at least 26 blacks and 4 whites had been hanged or burned. Many of the condemned were surely innocent, but plans for a real insurrection may indeed have inspired the alleged New York Slave Conspiracy of 1741.

Changes in New England

The descendants of Puritans continued to populate eighteenth-century New England. Their farms and towns flourished like those of the middle colonies, but their unique religious heritage made little room for immigrants. By the early eighteenth-century, however, the intensity of early New England had begun to fade. The rising generation honored their faith and the notion of covenant, but hard work and diligence had brought material rewards and accompanying temptations. A bloody purge of accused witches in Salem, Massachusetts, was the most conspicuous symptom of the social strain.

THE TENSIONS OF TRADE AND RELIGION

As in the middle colonies and the South, the population of New England grew sharply in the eighteenth century, rising from about 90,000 in 1700 to almost 600,000 by 1770. Rising generations spilled out from the oldest settled regions, pressing north and west into Maine (still part of Massachusetts), New Hampshire, and the interiors of Massachusetts and Connecticut. Slavery was more limited than in the middle colonies, though Rhode Island merchants and shipowners became leaders in the slave trade and brought home Africans like Venture Smith to work in their fields and households.

New England's economy grew to match its swelling numbers. Its thin, rocky soil favored pasturage over wheat fields, so New Englanders raised livestock and caught codfish instead. Like flour, pickled beef and salted fish would sell in most markets around the Atlantic basin, and New England merchants were particularly active in provisioning the sugar islands. These activities stimulated shipbuilding and commerce, not only in Boston but also in Newport, Salem, and a string of smaller ports. Like the middle colonies, New England continued to develop an urban network, a population of free skilled workers, and a concentration of cash in the hands of merchant families who would finance later developments. Venture Smith likewise found opportunity in this economy to buy his freedom and then secure his livelihood.

The key difference between eighteenth-century New England and the middle colonies lay in the continued importance of religious distinctiveness. Nobody used the word "Puritan" much in the eighteenth century—New Englanders spoke about "orthodoxy" or the "Standing Order" before settling on "Congregational" as the customary label for their region's established churches. Uniformity had eroded since the seventeenth century, for the Crown had finally forced the dissenting colonies to stop persecuting Anglicans, Quakers, and other non-Puritans. Orthodox leaders still believed in their godly covenant, however, and supported their churches with public taxes.

Tensions between religion and material prosperity had long troubled New Englanders and they intensified in the eighteenth century. Preachers demanded that all good Christians work hard in their callings, for honest work was a blessed spiritual discipline. Like living a moral life, worldly success could be a sign (though never a cause) of God's blessing, so ministers expected the saints to prosper. But what if the desire for worldly success overwhelmed the spiritual fervor that should inspire it? "The *Cursed Hunger of Riches*," the Reverend Cotton Mather warned, "will make man *break through* all the Laws of God." Unfortunately, neither Mather nor his colleagues could be sure where godly diligence left off and the sins of greed and pride took over. He could only remind them that "when Wealth is more unto us, than the Creator of all our Wealth; Here, is Criminal Covetousness."

Cotton Mather's own career illustrates the transitional character of New England religion in the early eighteenth century. Born in Boston in 1663, he came from a distinguished line of Puritan ministers. His grandfathers had been towering spiritual patriarchs in early Massachusetts Bay, and his father, Increase Mather, had been minister of Boston's Second Church, president of Harvard College, and Massachusetts's colonial agent. A brilliant youth, Cotton Mather entered

Harvard at the age of 12, already determined to follow his forebears in the ministry, and was ordained in his father's church in 1685. Mather devoted his life to sustaining the Calvinist tradition, but rival denominations and religious indifference kept advancing, along with doctrinal quarrels among the faithful themselves. Groomed to succeed his father as president of Harvard, Mather never won the post, partly because his theology had become so old-fashioned.

Even so, Mather embraced new ideas in other fields. He supported nondenominational benevolent societies to relieve social problems that an earlier generation might have left to God's care. He was likewise an intense and highly accomplished scholar who published more than 400 books, pamphlets, and sermons, and whose thinking reflected an earnest desire to combine conservative theology with a respect for science and the direct observation of nature. Defying public opinion, Mather strenuously defended the dangerous and newfangled idea of inoculation against smallpox. Though he feared witches sincerely and supported the Salem witchcraft trials (see below), Mather's scientific writings won him election to the Royal Society, England's prestigious scientific association. (Benjamin Franklin and William Byrd II also belonged.) Like his father and grandfathers, Cotton Mather longed for weighty political as well as religious influence on the larger society around him, but he never reached their eminence of unchallenged authority. By the time of his death in 1728, the Puritan legacy had loosened its grip on New England, but remained a powerful influence on its broader culture.

WITCHCRAFT IN SALEM

Certainly the most dramatic and tragic illustration of New England's tendency to see change as the work of the devil burst out in a fearful campaign against witches in Salem Village, now Danvers, Massachusetts. The trouble began in 1691, when several neighborhood girls fell to mumbling in strange fits and trances. Pressed by adults around them, the "afflicted girls" began to accuse older, unmarried, or unpopular women of sending invisible spirits to torment them. Arrests and trials only seemed to make the problem worse, and over the course of 1692, almost 200 people in eastern Massachusetts were accused of consorting with the devil. During the same period, 14 women and 5 men were hanged for the crime of witchcraft and another man died under torture.

Like most of their contemporaries, Salem Villagers did not doubt that Satan could grant terrible powers to those who served him. They saw women as especially susceptible to his allure, just as Eve had been vulnerable in the Garden of Eden, and they particularly suspected widows and spinsters. Many believed that Satan worked harder to bewitch New England, for the Puritans had captured his former domain for God's commonwealth. New Englanders tried far more accused witches than other colonial Americans, but only Salem saw mass executions.

Massachusetts faced unusual pressures in 1692. The Glorious Revolution had just stripped the colony of its independence and cherished charter. Many doubted the legitimacy of Sir William Phips, King William's appointed governor. England and France were still fighting King William's War, and France's Indian allies were attacking New England's northern frontiers. Frightened villagers could thus see the devil's handiwork all around them.

Still more subtle factors may have played their part. Salem Village was an agricultural hamlet that lacked the prosperity of nearby Salem Town. Most of the accused witches were somehow connected—often in inferior or dependent roles—to families who shared in Salem Town's wealth and far-flung connections. Town and village factions had recently quarreled about their minister—whose daughter and niece were the first to be afflicted. Did accusers unconsciously blame Salem's mysterious success on black magic? Did they try to strike back by attacking their rivals' wives and servants? We cannot be sure at this distance, but it is tempting to think so.

Certainly no one in 1692 dared to say that the charges were inherently absurd. Increase Mather, Cotton Mather, and other eminent ministers cautioned against the misuse of evidence but warned authorities to take the charges seriously. As investigations continued, most of the accused sought safety by naming alleged accomplices who ranked higher and higher up the social scale. Governor Phips finally called a halt when someone accused his wife. He suspended the trials and executions and freed the remaining prisoners. Belief in witchcraft did not vanish overnight, but most of the colony's leaders soon realized they had made a terrible mistake. Future concern about the tension between Christian devotion and worldly success in New England would not take the form of a witch-hunt but may have encouraged a major religious revival in the 1740s.

Social and Cultural Trends

As the eighteenth-century colonies grew and diversified, social and cultural developments influenced popular ideas, customs, and beliefs, and often crossed regional lines to build up a widely shared culture. Ideas about families and gender, race, and the social order were especially important to this process. At the same time, Americans shared in the cultural and intellectual life of the Atlantic basin. Wealthy and well-educated colonists embraced the ideas of the European Enlightenment, which honored science and reason and stressed the perfectibility of human nature. Others concluded that eighteenth-century society had lost its religious bearings and called for repentance and personal transformation. A revival movement known as the Great Awakening swept the colonies, splitting old denominations, revitalizing personal piety, and encouraging ordinary Christians to decide religious questions themselves. The Enlightenment and the Awakening would both have important roles in the future of American culture.

FREE WOMEN AND FAMILIES

Immigration was one major source of colonial growth; families were the other. The first settlers of New England and the middle colonies came in family groups that included men, women, and children. Women were scarce in the early Chesapeake, but sex ratios were nearly even by 1700, and both African Americans and whites began growing by natural increase.

The family or household was the fundamental unit of free society in the colonies. Almost every free person married, and lived with their parents before then. Most economic activity took place on family farms or in workshops within the owner's home. A "family" in these circumstances usually consisted of a married couple, their unmarried children, and their servants, apprentices, and slaves. While he lived, the father had legal authority over his dependents. He owned the family's labor, earnings, and property, and minor children could not "rob" him by moving away without permission. The father represented the family in all its relations with outsiders, and authorities could hold him responsible for his household's behavior. Fathers even carried out government functions, as some were paid through taxes to care for orphans or needy adults, for example.

English law subordinated women to men, especially inside the family, and conventional wisdom taught that women were the weaker sex both intellectually and morally. Women could not vote, hold office, sit on juries, or serve in the militia. The moment she married, even a technically free woman became a *feme covert* ("covered" or "hidden woman") whose husband absorbed her civil existence. She could be tried and punished for a crime, but she could no longer control property, transact business, make a contract, write a will, obtain credit, or make any legally valid decision for herself. Courts almost always defended a husband's authority, even in cases of gross mistreatment or desertion, and it was nearly impossible for a wife to take control of her earnings or her children from an abusive or absent husband. A widow could use one-third of her husband's land until she died or remarried. It then reverted to his heirs (usually his sons), so she could not sell it or bequeath it as she chose. Divorce usually required a special act of the assembly when it was possible at all, and the husband normally received custody of his children. Though harsh laws and customs governed the lives of free women, enslaved women lived far more harshly, with no recognition of their marriages or other legal protections.

A free widow or adult single woman had the legal status of a *feme sole*, which allowed her to acquire property and do business as if she were male. In extraordinary cases of desertion or abuse, assemblies might grant *feme sole* status to a wife, with the right to hold property and run her own household but not remarry. Prenuptial agreements could safeguard the property rights of heiresses, but these were rare.

Free colonial couples could not easily marry without the resources to form their own households. Except among the poor, groom's families were expected to provide land for a farm while the bride's father gave cash or equipment. It took fathers time to accumulate these goods, so in the mid-eighteenth century, the average age at first marriage was about 26 or 27 for men and 22 for women. Poorer couples had less reason to wait and married somewhat earlier.

Once married, a woman's duty was to bear as many children as possible. Her first child usually followed the wedding within a year and more followed at intervals of two or three years until her death or menopause. In New England, where information is most reliable, most wives bore about seven or eight children and reared about five or six to adulthood, if they escaped the serious danger of death in childbirth. Colonial children were an economic asset, performing small tasks as early as six or seven and working seriously from the time they were young teenagers until their own marriages. Large families, longer lifespans, and continued immigration caused the American population to double almost every 25 years.

A woman's labor was as important as her ability to bear children. Like slaves and servants, poor free women performed hard field labor like hoeing and reaping. Even when mothers were spared from the field, caring for numerous children could be endless and exhausting work. Most housewives were also responsible for cleaning, spinning, and making and mending clothes, as well as cooking and preserving food by drying, pickling, and fermenting. Farm women also cared for milk cows, poultry, and kitchen gardens, and turned milk into cheese and butter. Wealthy families had slaves or servants for household labor and childcare but wives had to supervise their work.

The sale of eggs, butter, cheese, and soap could become a serious business for farm women who lived near urban markets. The wives of urban tradesmen or shopkeepers often helped with their husbands' affairs, but while their husbands lived, law and custom usually kept them from going into business themselves. Widows might continue their husbands' businesses, however, from a simple grocery to a more elaborate inn or workshop. Women could also keep small schools or use their sewing skills to make clothing or hats, but economic opportunities were still scarce outside of marriage. Those who never married faced dependent lives in the homes of relatives, and widows without means or prosperous relatives faced serious danger of poverty.

Colonial children practiced the roles of adulthood by observing their parents and imitating them in small tasks, and their jobs became more demanding as they grew older. Some parents bound out their offspring as servants or apprentices by age 12 or younger, so they could learn their roles from less indulgent adults. Education for the poorest stopped there, but most learned simple literacy from their parents or from a teacher hired by neighboring families. Further schooling was deemed unnecessary for girls. Affluent or ambitious families might send their sons to more advanced academies, and a few of these attended one of the dozen or so colleges that appeared before 1775.

The lives of eighteenth-century children may have changed more than those of their mothers. In the seventeenth century, strict Calvinists taught that even infants were inherently sinful, so the parents' job was to break a child's will and teach him or her obedience to human and divine authority. By contrast, the English philosopher John Locke, whose *Two Treatises of Government* had defended the Glorious Revolution, also published *An Essay Concerning Human Understanding* and

Thoughts on Education in the 1690s, arguing that the human mind began as a "blank slate" that could be trained to good or evil. He encouraged parents to be loving and patient with their children, to avoid physical punishment, and to teach them by good example. Over the course of the eighteenth century, wealthy and well-educated parents grew increasingly receptive to such advice and seemed to soften their strictness with more indulgence and open affection. Love for the unique personality of each child likewise spread among the gentry and gradually seeped downward. The respect for individual rights that later became so important in American public life may have had psychological roots in the changing eighteenth-century family.

DEFINING RACE

Early modern Englishmen had gloried in their own nation and often looked down on everyone else, so their views of the Indians, the Irish, the French, and the Spanish were uniformly negative. These low opinions did not depend on concepts of race, because they rarely distinguished between inherent inferiority (which could not change) and cultural inferiority (which might). When comparing themselves to Indians, for example, seventeenth-century settlers usually spoke of "Christians" and "savages" instead of colors like "white" and "red." All the same, the English could treat the Indians as especially different, inferior, and naturally deserving of violence, as when a roving party of Virginians reportedly amused themselves by "shoteinge owtt [the] Braynes" of Indian children. In other words, early English settlers did not clearly *think* in racial terms, and claimed to believe that Indians could improve themselves by adopting English customs, but they could *feel* and *act* in ways that later generations would recognize as racist. Over the course of the seventeenth century, these feelings and actions intensified, until we can speak of whites' "racial" hostility to Indians, even without well-developed theories of race.

African slavery encouraged the growth of ideas about race. English prejudice against Africans was especially strong, for black was the traditional color of the devil and a powerful synonym for "sinful," "wicked," and "base." Perhaps as a result, early English voyagers did not hesitate to buy, sell, or steal Africans though enslaving Europeans never seems to have occurred to them. From the beginning, they also subjected African women to field labor more readily than whites. People in West Africa wore considerably less clothing than the

Elizabethans, moreover, so startled explorers were quick to imagine that tropical sexuality was as heated as the climate. Viewing sex as a dark and bestial passion, they spread absurd stories of sex between apes and African women, and easily assumed that all Africans were somehow like animals. As early as the sixteenth century, European explorers began creating mental links among Africans, blackness, sexuality, and subhuman creatures that would have long and lethal consequences for African Americans. These early prejudices did not lead directly to slavery but helped convince the English that Africans were especially suited for it.

If early prejudice helped justify enslavement, enslavement also deepened prejudice. The purchase of a human cargo, confinement belowdecks, brutal living conditions, and violent punishments were all part of enslavement. Such cruelties came easier when the perpetrators believed that their victims were innately inferior. John Woolman, an early Quaker critic of slavery and the slave trade, understood the process very well. "Placing on men the ignominious title slave," he reflected, "dressing them in uncomely garments, keeping them to servile labor, in which they are often dirty, tends gradually to fix a notion in the mind, that they are a sort of people below us in nature."

Not all early colonists shared these convictions, for black and white servants mingled freely and sometimes intimately, and cooperated to resist their bondage. As decades passed, authorities fought these alliances and reinforced slavery by imposing legal inferiority on Africans, specifically because of their color. The new statutes defined blackness as a form of gross pollution, especially in connection with sex and mixed-race children. In 1664, for example, Maryland authorities denounced "freeborne English women [who] forgettful of their free Condicion and to the disgrace of our Nation doe intermarry with Negro Slaves." The Virginia assembly imposed its own ban on interracial marriage in 1691, condemning the "abominable mixture and spurious issue" that resulted. The laws also imposed a heavier penalty on free people who aided runaway slaves than on those who aided fugitive white servants, and devised increasingly bloody punishments for Africans who defied white authority.

Legal discrimination reinforced prejudice and supported the belief that Africans were inherently inferior. Theorists would eventually spin this idea into elaborate concepts of race that ranked all human beings in color-based categories, with whites at the top, Africans at the bottom, and Indians somewhere between them. Long before then, however, powerful whites courted their poorer white neighbors with color-based privileges that offered a kind of equality across class lines. In other words, concepts of deep-seated racial identity and inferiority did not arise inevitably from physical differences among Indians, Africans, and Europeans. While prior prejudice played its role, whites began constructing race and racism from the practices of enslavement and conquest.

RANK AND THE SOCIAL ORDER

Seventeenth-century England was a steeply ranked society that extended from the king and a handful of titled aristocrats at the top, down through a larger class of gentry and urban merchants, and on through a mass of yeomen, shopkeepers, artisans, laborers, servants, and beggars. Status corresponded to wealth, power, education, personal refinement, and family connections, and no one expected America to be different. The leaders of Jamestown resisted Captain John Smith as a social climber, and Governor John Winthrop carefully reminded the passengers on the *Arbella* that "some must be . . . highe and eminent in power and dignitie[,] others meane and in subjeccion." The original settlers of the English colonies saw rank as a crucial part of social order.

Despite these expectations, wilderness tended to undermine the hierarchy that crossed the Atlantic. In the rough-and-tumble world of the early Chesapeake, men with strength and cunning might capture more land and labor than those with finer pedigrees, while Bacon's followers looted the plantations of those who claimed unwarranted superiority. Without the violence of class rebellion, the unsettled economy of New England could also humble the distinguished and elevate the obscure. Puritan leaders tried to preserve traditional appearances with laws preventing upstarts from sporting lace and gold braid, but they could not freeze the economic order.

As conditions stabilized in the eighteenth century, the American economy grew more rapidly than its population. While living standards improved for almost everyone, prosperity supported a firmer social and economic hierarchy. In the Chesapeake and South Carolina, successful planter families passed land, slaves, and status to their rising generations. Outside the South, the wealthiest men were merchants and shippers in Philadelphia, New York, Boston, and smaller ports. Whether they were landed magnates like William Byrd II, self-made businessmen like Benjamin Franklin, or respected ministers like Cotton Mather, established leaders were known as the "better sort of people" and enjoyed wealth, political power, and public recognition. Their families enjoyed deference, or voluntary respect and submission, from the lesser folk around them, and deference usually enabled social leaders to monopolize both elected and appointed public offices. Colonists reserved the words "lady" and "gentleman" for adults of the better sort, and only community leaders and their wives could claim the titles of "Mister" and "Mistress."

Most Americans seem to have accepted social inequality as a fact of life. Conventional opinion took it for granted that some people should dominate the rest, so long as they respected the rights of those below them. To receive political power, a gentleman should have the respect and confidence of his community. He should also be affluent, well-educated, supportive of established religion, and distinguished for good taste in art, literature, conversation, and dress. As stable elites emerged in most colonies, the movement of English society across the Atlantic seemed more complete

At the opposite end of the social scale, some Americans suffered long-term poverty. Slaves were the poorest of all, for they did not even own themselves. Cities contained a permanently impoverished class of sailors, laborers, disabled people, and propertyless widows and their families. Rural districts also supported destitute inhabitants or forced penniless wanderers to move on. Even landowners could feel the pinch of inequality, especially in the older towns of New England, where fathers continued to divide their lands equally among their sons and average landholdings shrank from 150 acres in the seventeenth century to as few as 40 in the later eighteenth. Within the colonies as a whole, economic historians estimate that the richest tenth of free Americans owned half their society's wealth while the poorest tenth owned .02 percent. If slaves are included among the propertyless, America's poorer half owned only 3 percent of its wealth. Even so, the poorest Americans ate better and lived longer than their European counterparts, and escaped the disastrous famines that still brought dire suffering and starvation to many in the countries they left behind.

Between the rich and the poor, land-owning yeoman farmers enjoyed higher incomes as they sold a growing surplus to local and Atlantic traders. American leaders had also spread political rights to lure more immigrants, giving average white men far more influence over their governments than elsewhere in the Western world. Foreign observers frequently commented that American society had fewer peaks and valleys than Europe's. "The leveling principle here operates strongly and takes the lead," remarked a typical Boston visitor in 1764. "Every body has property and every body knows it." Though "every body" in America did *not* own property, better and wider opportunities for owning land and making a living clearly joined political protections and religious toleration to inspire the surge in colonial immigration.

Economic growth allowed most free Americans to buy more goods. Especially after 1740, English workshops turned out greater and greater quantities of consumer products that ranged from ordinary cloth and tableware to more elaborate clocks, books, textiles, china, glass, silver, and other luxuries. In the consumer revolution, Americans snapped up these goods as eagerly as the English did, and drove up the value of British imports by 360 percent between 1740 and 1770. Up and down the social scale, Americans enjoyed the opportunity to make their lives more comfortable and more stylish, and to show off their refinement through elaborate social rituals like the proper way of serving tea. "There are zealous efforts in every single Person to imitate the person next above him, and in every Town to equal [the] next [highest] in Wealth, Popularity, and Politeness," one writer protested in the *Connecticut Courant* of 1765. "Thus by a [spread] of the most ridiculous Mimickry, the Fashions of London are communicated to the poorest, meanest town in Connecticut." Moralists protested the love of luxury, but ordinary free Americans joined the gentry in using consumer imports to brighten their lives and display their achievements.

REASON AND THE ENLIGHTENMENT

As colonial society grew more elaborate, a transatlantic movement later called the Enlightenment reached growing numbers of educated Americans. Its ideas had begun to stir as early as 1637, when French philosopher René Descartes made his famous declaration, "I think, therefore I am," and shifted the source of moral and intellectual authority from God and tradition to the rational human mind. Fifty years later, English scientist Sir Isaac Newton offered a practical demonstration of reason's power in his *Principia Mathematica*, showing how natural laws, expressed in a few simple formulas, could explain the behavior of all moving objects, from a falling apple to revolving planets. The political and educational ideas of Englishman John Locke extended rationalist principles to human life, and promoted the perfectibility of human nature, the importance of individual rights and judgment, and the rights of subjects to overthrow oppressive rulers. By the middle of the eighteenth century, French scholars Denis Diderot and Jean le Rond d'Alembert felt ready to catalogue all human knowledge in their comprehensive, 30-volume *Encyclopédie*. The French philosopher Voltaire applied his witty, biting satire to all forms of traditional authority, especially the Catholic Church. From Scotland, pioneer economist Adam Smith attacked mercantilism, the basis of Britain's imperial trade policy. Enlightenment ideas spread when the violence and brutality of religious wars discredited the churches' dogmatism and made theological controversies seem increasingly irrelevant to philosophers and their followers.

In all the leading cities of Europe and America, these educated people gathered in coffeehouses, debating societies, and salons to discuss ideas in a new public sphere, uncontrolled by church or royal authority. Some dared to hope that earthly suffering was not inevitable and that reason and education could improve the human condition. Despising superstition and raw emotion, Enlightenment thinkers made the word "enthusiasm" one of the most negative terms in their vocabulary. Admiring the harmony that early scientists found in nature, they favored balance, calm, order, and uniformity in art and literature. They encouraged the direct observation of the natural world and cheered Benjamin Franklin's famous experiments with electricity. Political thinkers celebrated the balance of the British constitution and insisted that colonial government replicate its virtues. The Enlightenment was an inspiration to optimistic reformers on both sides of the Atlantic, but its emphasis on science and reason necessarily limited its appeal to the educated few.

Some followers of the Enlightenment became deists. Using Newton's findings to compare the universe to a clock, they saw God as the clockmaker who created the world, gave it natural laws, and allowed it to run freely. Deists believed that human reason could discover the laws of nature and morality without religious guidance, and often condemned "priestcraft" as superstitious and fanatical. Without endorsing any sect, they favored toleration for all since persecution could never change anyone's mind. Even some ministers approached deism, particularly in the more prestigious and well-established churches, and tried to explain Christianity by rational proof instead of spiritual conviction or biblical authority. Deism became the favorite philosophical stance of the Enlightenment's most eminent representatives, from the distinguished philosophers of France to Benjamin Franklin, Thomas Jefferson, and other leaders of the American Revolution.

THE GREAT AWAKENING

While the "better sort" flirted with deism, rekindled faith warmed more ordinary Americans. Beginning in the 1730s and continuing through the 1760s, a wave of renewed religious intensity swept through the Protestant Atlantic world. Renewed spiritual fervor and personal conviction gripped the German churches in a movement known as Pietism. The brothers John and Charles Wesley led a Methodist movement to revive personal piety in the Church of England that later became a separate denomination. Americans experienced a wave of religious revivals known as the Great Awakening. Leaders in all these movements visited and corresponded with one another frequently and supported similar goals.

Colonial prosperity had allowed American churches to grow and spread in the eighteenth-century. New towns in northern and western New England included new Congregational churches. German migration brought Lutheran, German Reformed, and Pietist churches to the middle colonies, and the Scots-Irish took Presbyterianism wherever they went. Plantation exports paid for a wave of new Anglican parishes in southern colonies from Maryland to South Carolina. Growth brought diversity; a 1771 image of New York City depicts 18 houses of worship, including a prominent Anglican church, a Jewish synagogue, and an Anabaptist meetinghouse, for its 25,000 inhabitants. Despite the influence of deism, eighteenth-century Americans had clearly not abandoned religion.

A handful of especially zealous ministers still feared that religious devotion had slackened. A generation after the Halfway Covenant, many young New Englanders still lacked life-changing conversions and could not assume full membership in their churches. Despite their best efforts, moreover, established denominations could not keep up with population growth. Many backcountry districts lacked worship facilities, and eastern clergy worried that their inhabitants lived in lawlessness and sin.

From his pulpit in Northampton, Massachusetts, the Reverend Jonathan Edwards began to strike back in the 1730s. A brilliant philosopher and theologian who shared the Enlightenment's respect for human reason, Edwards was also a practical preacher who worried about the coldness of his flock. Fearing that logic could never warm them, he used terror instead. "The God that holds you over the pit of hell, much as one holds a spider or some loathsome insect over the fire, abhors you, and is dreadfully provoked," he reminded the unconverted sinner. "His wrath towards you burns like fire; he looks upon you as worthy of nothing else but to be cast into the fire." Edwards spoke calmly and without gestures, but the solemnity of his bearing only magnified the horror of his words. In the tradition of Puritan jeremiads, his sermons launched an emotional revival in the 1730s that brought tears, shrieks, and fainting spells to his anguished and penitent listeners. Conversions increased dramatically, and word of Edwards's extraordinary preaching spread widely.

Other preachers followed quickly. Also in the 1730s, William Tennent Sr. and his sons, William Jr., Charles, John, and Gilbert, set a blaze among Scots-Irish Presbyterians in the middle colonies. Samuel Davies did the same in Virginia. The most renowned preacher of the Great Awakening was the Reverend George Whitefield, an Anglican missionary with Methodist leanings who repeatedly toured the colonies between 1739 and his death, preaching to immense crowds outdoors. Convinced that mere logic could never crack a hardened heart, Whitefield and the other revivalists appealed to emotions over abstract reason. During Whitefield's visit to Philadelphia, Benjamin Franklin remembered that "it was wonderful to see the Change soon made in the Manners of our inhabitants; From being thoughtless or indifferent about Religion, it seem'd as if all the World were growing Religious; so that one could not walk thro' the Town in an Evening without Hearing Psalms sung in different Families of every Street."

Inspired by Edwards, Whitefield, and the Tennents, dozens of lesser preachers fanned across the colonies. Known as itinerants, the revivalists constantly traveled from one community to another and often accused more settled ministers of neglecting the genuine gospel to drone lifeless dogma in empty meetinghouses. They preached in fields or packed houses, everywhere declaring that stale, superficial worship meant nothing, that the people were drenched in sin, that they must repent and seek forgiveness, and that joyous salvation awaited those who sincerely did so. Like the Puritans, they stressed the importance of personal conversion, a theological stance that is often called evangelical. Without explicitly renouncing predestination, the itinerants undermined it by hinting that everyone who truly sought

God would find Him. Timing of the Awakening varied from place to place, peaking in the 1740s in New England, and continuing into the 1750s in the South and elsewhere. Almost everywhere they traveled, the itinerants won hundreds, even thousands, of weeping, joyful converts who flocked to join old churches or form new ones.

Evangelicals insisted on strict standards of personal conduct that drew sharp lines between their followers and "the world." When mainstream clergy rejected their methods, the evangelicals broke away and split Protestants between New Light supporters and Old Light opponents of revivalism. In New England, the two factions quarreled bitterly over public funds to support their churches. Throughout the colonies, evangelicalism invigorated Baptists, Presbyterians, and, later, Methodists, while Anglicans, Quakers, and Old Light Congregationalists languished. The denominations linked to New Light evangelism would eventually become the leading Protestant churches of the United States.

By opening salvation to everyone, the Great Awakening democratized religion and especially appealed to Americans who did not share the prosperity around them. Denouncing drunkenness, gambling, dancing, card playing, theatergoing, and sexual misconduct, evangelicals won few converts in the upper classes but offered a sober, serious life to humble folk who wearied of disorderly social change. Women and young people converted more readily than older men, the "middling" and "lower" sorts were more receptive than the wealthy, and the first large wave of African Americans entered the Christian churches. Everywhere, revivalists exalted humble converts beyond their rank in worldly society. As Baptist preacher Isaac Backus put it, "The common people now claim as good a right to judge and act in matters of religion as civil rulers or the learned clergy."

Superficially, the Enlightenment and the Great Awakening seemed to have little in common. Intellectuals mocked what they called the "enthusiasm" of self-taught preachers whose pulpit thunder exceeded their formal learning, just as the roughhewn itinerants knew little of Isaac Newton. Fundamentally, however, both movements stressed the importance of direct personal experience as a measure of the truth. For the Enlightenment scientist or statesman, observable facts could overrule tradition. New Lights encouraged believers to reject all religious authorities except the Bible, to think for themselves religiously, and to value a personal sensation of salvation over the bookish debates of the Old Lights. Together, the Enlightenment and the Great Awakening challenged Americans to test received tradition by the light of personal experience, and authorized them to build their lives and institutions according to their own understandings of the truth.

The personal test of truth led easily to religious clashes, especially when New Lights cited their own insights to attack Old Light religious authorities, and both sides battled over limited public funds. Influenced by deistic distaste for sectarian disputes, pragmatic politicians would eventually decide that the best solution was to disestablish the churches and cut off public funding in the name of religious freedom. They would also use Enlightenment reasoning to advance "self-evident truths" about government. In the second half of the eighteenth century, the Enlightenment and the Awakening both had profound effects on American views of public liberty.

*

Developments in the eighteenth century had brought a new population to the English colonies and accelerated the evolution of distinctive regional societies. The expansion of slavery marked the southern colonies as slave societies, while New England and the middle colonies combined commercial and subsistence farming with the growth of towns and handicrafts. Despite these unique regional features, however, growth and stability brought the colonies closer to prevailing patterns of English society and culture, and opened them to such transatlantic movements as the consumer revolution, the Enlightenment, and the Great Awakening. Prosperity and cultural diversity also fostered differences of opinion and public debates, especially in towns and cities where taverns, docks, and squares formed a public sphere between the chambers of government and the privacy of home. As the colonists passed the half-century mark, few had any idea that their increasing similarity to the mother country might also lead to increasing imperial tension.

CHAPTER 5

The Era of Independence, 1756–1783

On the afternoon of May 30, 1765, Virginia's House of Burgesses had nearly finished its spring session, and most of its members had gone home, but one important issue still remained. Virginians had recently learned that the British Parliament had adopted a stamp tax for the American colonies. The law would require an expensive stamp for almost every kind of official paperwork, from a bill of sale to a court decision to a marriage license. Newspapers, college diplomas, and playing cards would carry costly stamps as well. The proceeds would pay for an army of 10,000 men — supposedly to guard the frontier, but perhaps for suppressing political dissent.

Virginians disliked all taxes, but they truly hated the Stamp Act because it came from Parliament, not their own assembly. It thus sought to tax Virginians without the consent of their representatives and, in their view, violated the British constitution. The House of Burgesses had protested when the Stamp Act was only a rumor, but Parliament paid no attention. Now would the assembly truckle to Parliament's authority?

House leaders thought quiet objections would be most effective, but one freshman member felt otherwise. Patrick Henry was a 29-year-old attorney from the rural piedmont who had just won a popular and successful court case against British efforts to control the salaries of Anglican clergy. Rewarded with his first assembly seat, Henry became a firebrand for American rights, most remembered for his later slogan "Give me liberty, or give me death!"

Henry introduced five resolutions of protest. The first four declared that the colonists had kept their English rights when they came to Virginia, that royal charters had confirmed these rights, that Englishmen could not be taxed without their consent, and that neither could Vir-

FIGURE 4. The Boston Massacre and other clashes between Americans and British authorities intensified the dispute over colonial autonomy. Cartoon Prints, American, Prints and Photographs Division, Library of Congress, LC-DIG-ppmsca-01657.

ginians. Later rescinded by the House of Burgesses, a more radical fifth resolution warned that colonial taxation by Parliament could "destroy British as well as American Freedom."

Everyone later agreed that Henry made a fiery speech, but accounts differed over what he said. In 1810, patriotic biographer William Wirt gave stirring details. "Caesar had his Brutus," he had Henry say, "Charles the first, his Cromwell — and George the third —" and then the Speaker of the House of Burgesses interrupted. "'Treason!' cried the speaker — 'treason, treason,' echoed from every part of the house." Would the rash young lawyer physically threaten his august sovereign? No. In Wirt's account, Henry recovered brilliantly. "And George the third . . . ," he concluded, "*may profit by their example. If this* be treason, make the most of it.'"

Wirt's version has thrilled patriots since he wrote it, but other evidence gives different details. In a diary that surfaced later, a visitor who heard the speech reported that Henry backed down when listeners cried "treason." "If he had affronted the speaker or the house, he was ready to ask pardon," he explained, and pledged to support the king "at the Expence of the last Drop of his blood." Unlike Wirt, the only recorded eyewitness mixed Henry's defiance with apologies.

These dueling stories illustrate the challenge of conflicting historical evidence, but they also reflect the hesitation and ambivalence that Patrick Henry and other Americans felt as they challenged the empire of Great Britain. Most white Americans were of British descent, they drew their political principles from English history, and they reverenced the king as protector of his people and their liberties. The Stamp Act was imposed by Parliament, not King George, but Henry denounced the king and linked his name to history's most famous king-killers because history taught Virginians that kings always threatened liberty more than legislatures. Even so, cutting their ties to Britain would not be easy.

Patrick Henry retreated a bit, but his resolutions made a greater impact than he anticipated. Garbled newspaper reports made his resolutions seem more radical than they were, and other assemblies then hastened to match or exceed Virginia's stance. Taking their cue from legislators, violent mobs continued the fight and made the Stamp Act unenforceable throughout the colonies.

The American War for Independence began as a quarrel over taxes that was launched in colonial assemblies by men like Patrick Henry, carried to the streets by violent mobs, and finally decided in battle. The dispute began when officials decided that the empire needed central direction and Americans should pay more of its expenses. Carried to extremes, the new policy could take control of the colonies from men like Patrick Henry and give it to London officials. The House of Burgesses was thus defending its own interests when protesting the Stamp Act, but torrents of rhetoric like Henry's suggest that its constitutional objections to "taxation without representation" were not feigned or consciously hypocritical. Like Patrick Henry, moreover, the other burgesses struggled to balance their constitutional principles and their loyalty to Britain.

The men who made the speeches did not win independence by themselves. They needed volunteers and willing sacrifice. For popular support, they touched the convictions of middling and poorer Americans, and linked legal theories to practical realities. To defend their own privileges, they empowered ordinary freemen and launched a movement that continued long after fighting had stopped. Their principles eventually spread to Americans they had not meant to reach, beginning with common white men and stretching to African Americans and women. In the process, a war for independence became truly revolutionary.

Imperial War and Its Consequences

Henry's resolutions marked a looming crisis in the long relationship between Britain and its colonies that followed yet another war between Britain and France. British victory in a worldwide struggle called the Seven Years' War (1756–1763), known in the colonies as the French and Indian War, had expelled France from the North American mainland, giving Canada and Florida to Britain and Louisiana to Spain. The war had nearly bankrupted the British treasury, however, and further expenses lay ahead. Efforts to cover these costs sparked a bitter and escalating controversy.

THE SEVEN YEARS' WAR

Unlike most of the eighteenth-century conflicts between Britain and France, the Seven Years' War began in America and then spread to Europe, Asia, and Africa as the two empires struggled for global supremacy. The immediate issue was the Ohio River Valley, a rich source of furs that the British wanted for future expansion and the French wanted in order to stop them. Indians wanted to keep it from both empires because they lived there. Other issues concerned the balance of power in Europe and commercial dominance worldwide. Britain and France had long clashed over these issues, most recently in King George's War (known in Europe as the War of Austrian Succession, 1740–1748) but had not settled the fundamental questions. Following King George's War, Britain and France began preparing for the next conflict by adding more Indian alliances, new forts, and additional trading posts in the Ohio country. Hoping to settle the area, the Crown granted 200,000 acres in 1749 to the Ohio Company, a group of Virginia land speculators. They had seven years to build a fort and establish 100 families at the Forks of the Ohio, where the Monongahela and Allegheny Rivers join to form the Ohio River at the modern site of Pittsburgh, Pennsylvania. Exploration and construction began, but progress was slow and France continued to move southward. Fearing that France could lure away their dependent tribes, the Iroquois drew closer to Britain and Virginia to preserve their dominance in the Ohio country.

In 1754, imperial officials, Iroquois representatives, and delegates from all the colonies north of Virginia met in Albany, New York, to foster cooperation in case of war with France. There Benjamin Franklin, a delegate from Pennsylvania, proposed the Albany Plan of Union, which would place the British mainland colonies under a single government to manage Indian affairs, including war, trade, and land purchases, to make land grants beyond the existing colonies, to organize and govern new settlements, to raise and equip armed forces, and to finance them with quitrents and import duties. Each colony would keep its own laws and identity and govern itself internally. This blend of local and central authority foreshadowed the structure of the future United States government, but colonial and imperial authorities rejected Franklin's plan as too ambitious.

A Mohawk chief named Hendrick had warned the Albany Congress that the French and their Indian allies were already preparing for another war by building a string of forts to connect Lake Ontario with the Forks. "Look at the French," he mocked. "They are men; they are fortifying every where; but we are ashamed to say it; you are like women, bare and open, without any fortifications." Recognizing the threat, London officials ordered Virginia to warn them off and protect the interests of the Ohio Company. The task fell to a small expedition commanded by a promising young major named George Washington,

21-year-old half-brother of Ohio Company shareholders Lawrence and Augustine Washington.

Washington had been born into the lesser Virginia gentry in 1732. His father died while he was still a child, depriving young George of the English education received by his older half-brothers. The ambitious youth studied hard to master the science of land surveying instead and grew accustomed to the rough work of measuring large tracts in the backcountry wilderness. Six feet three inches in height, with an athletic build and strength to match, young Washington wanted to excel in public leadership more than planting or surveying, and he pulled hard on his family's connections to win the governor's permission to confront the intruders.

Unsurprisingly, the French refused to blink, and sent Washington back to Williamsburg while they occupied the Forks and began constructing Fort Duquesne to guard the spot. The following spring, Washington returned with Tanaghrisson, the local Iroquois half king, and a larger force of whites and Iroquois, defeating a small French party near the Forks. The sequel might have been a truce, but Tanaghrisson wanted no stalemate that could leave the French in his domain. Probably hoping to provoke a conflict that the French would lose, he stepped forward when the skirmish ended and whispered to the fallen French commander, "You are not dead yet, my father." Then he suddenly tomahawked the stricken officer and defiantly wiped his hands in his victim's brains before scalping him. His tribesmen then fell on the other French prisoners, as Virginians tried to save as many as possible. The Virginians fell back to a small stockade named Fort Necessity but could not hold it against a French and Indian counterattack. Once again, the French sent Washington home with another refusal to move.

If the half king wanted a full-scale war, his tactic worked. Loss of the Forks prompted British authorities to order a major assault on New France while France launched a recruiting drive for Indian allies that would bring in thousands of fighters from the Ohio Valley and as far away as Georgia and modern Iowa. In 1755, London sent General Edward Braddock to the Chesapeake with 2,000 Irish regulars and orders to capture Fort Duquesne. Massachusetts forces headed west to capture another French fort on the Niagara River while New Yorkers marched on Lake Champlain. These offensives all failed disastrously. Accompanied by Washington and his Virginia militia, Braddock blundered into a French and Indian ambush as they approached the Forks.

Braddock died along with half his men, but Washington won credit for bravery in the battle and the subsequent retreat, and gained command of Virginia's battered army. Hearing of Braddock's defeat, the Massachusetts expedition abandoned its attack on Niagara, and the New Yorkers were repulsed from Lake Champlain. Fort Oswego, Britain's outpost on Lake Ontario, fell the following year. France drew heavily on its Indian allies in these victories, but the Iroquois—whose half king had touched off the explosion—gave no active aid to Britain until later in the war.

Britain suffered another painful loss in the summer of 1757, when a mixed force of French and Huron Indians advanced on Fort William Henry, located on Lake George in northern New York. Vastly outnumbered, the British surrendered after a brief siege and accepted French terms that allowed them to withdraw unharmed after laying down their arms. This time it was France's Indian allies who refused to accept the limitations of European warfare. Deprived of the captives and plunder they expected, Indians swept into the nearly empty fort and killed its wounded occupants before turning on the retreating British for booty, prisoners, and more scalps. Exaggerated accounts of the Fort William Henry massacre soon inflamed the British and American side and fed the Americans' fear of Indians for decades to come.

Defeats in America did not stop the British, and fighting spread worldwide. In Europe, France's allies Austria and Russia attacked Britain's partner Prussia in order to reclaim the province of Silesia. French and British trading companies fought each other in India, using local allies and their own troops, while the British navy seized French sugar colonies and African slaving posts. In America, Braddock's defeat emboldened the Shawnees, Delawares, and other western Indians to defy their Iroquois overlords, attack white settlements from Maine to Virginia, and push the frontier back as many as 50 miles eastward in some places.

Though Britain had stumbled at first, the tide of battle slowly turned as William Pitt, a new British minister, borrowed massive sums to assemble major forces and pay the colonies' military expenses. Forts Duquesne and Niagara surrendered, along with the French post on Lake Champlain, which the victors renamed Fort Ticonderoga. Louisburg, the French fortress that commanded the mouth of the St. Lawrence, fell in 1758. A year later, General James Wolfe ascended that river to besiege Quebec. Leading a small force up a steep opening in the cliffs below the city's defenses, the attackers won a short battle at the top in which Wolfe and his French antagonist, the marquis de Montcalm, both died. Montreal fell to Britain the following year, and France's Indian allies dispersed as British naval victories cut the flow of supplies they relied on. In the end, even a Spanish alliance could not stave off French defeat. In the 1763 Peace of Paris, Britain acquired the entire colony of New France and the half of Louisiana that lay east of the Mississippi, while Spain took the western half of Louisiana and passed its own colony of Florida to Great Britain. British allies likewise triumphed in Europe while the British East India Company laid the basis for another future empire by besting French forces in India and acquiring extensive territories of its own. The loss of New France and Louisiana entirely expelled the French from the mainland of North America.

The Seven Years' War had profound consequences for the colonies and the entire Atlantic world. Its costs prompted Britain to tax its colonies, starting a train of events that led to the American Revolution. France lost most of its American empire and incurred massive debts that contributed to its own revolution and the overthrow of its monarchy. And the French Revolution led to a successful slave revolt in the Caribbean colony of Haiti, with massive challenges to slavery throughout the Americas. Despite these momentous changes, the imperial rivalry between Britain and France would continue for decades in wars spawned by the American and French Revolutions.

PONTIAC RISES

A European treaty did not end all the fighting. Combat in America had subsided when Montreal fell, but France's former Indian allies wanted Britain to assume the roles of ally, judge, and benefactor long played by French officials. Using gifts, trade, and diplomacy to reestablish the Middle Ground conflicted with traditional British policies, however, and Lord Jeffery Amherst, commander in chief of Britain's American forces, spurned the Indians' demands as expensive and presumptuous. Instead, he banned the sale of alcohol to Indians and strictly limited their purchases of gunpowder and ammunition, a step that brought famine and severely restricted the deerskin trade. Native Americans responded to this distress with a pan-Indian military and spiritual movement to defend their independence and restore an earlier culture. Similar efforts would also appear in the wake of the American Revolution and the War of 1812. The first began in 1761, when a Delaware prophet named Neolin preached that the Master of Life was punishing Indians for abandoning their traditions. Neolin told his hearers to regain the Master's favor by renouncing white culture, including liquor, guns, and textiles, and returning to traditional clothing and weaponry. The message spread from tribe to tribe in the upper country, the Ohio country, the Illinois country, and even farther, convincing converts that the tribes should unite to expel the British from the Mississippi Valley.

In the spring of 1763, a war chief named Pontiac took the first step by organizing a siege of Fort Detroit by Potawatomis, Hurons, and his own Ottawa tribe. As word spread over the summer, other bands joined in attacking British bases throughout the western territory, from Illinois to the Forks of the Ohio, and captured all but Niagara, Detroit, and Fort Pitt. Amherst was so angered by the wave of assaults that he authorized the distribution of smallpox-infected blankets to one party of besiegers, though the epidemic was already rampant and his proposed experiment in germ warfare may have made little difference. In the east, frontier residents of Paxton, or Paxtang, Pennsylvania, feared attack so much that enraged mobs murdered 20 helpless Indian noncombatants in 1763 before marching on Philadelphia to demand the deaths of 140 more. Patient diplomacy finally deflected the Paxton Boys, but anti-Indian passions ran dangerously high.

Pontiac eventually lifted the siege of Detroit, but other forts kept falling over 1764. Amherst tried to crush the uprising with massive military force, but he failed and was recalled. His successor, Sir Thomas Gage, was no more successful. Fighting gradually subsided into a stalemate. Pontiac himself was only one of the campaign's many leaders, but in a series of 1765 peace conferences, he persuaded most of his allies to accept a return to the prewar status quo. In other words, without expelling the British or surrendering their own lands, the tribes would resume trading and allow the British to reoccupy their forts. The last Indian combatants abandoned the fight that year by crossing the Mississippi into Spanish Louisiana. The British returned to their older policies of gifts and trade and reluctantly accepted the role of paternal leadership and mediation once exercised by the French. War had claimed 2,000 colonial lives and untold numbers of Indians.

A STANDING ARMY AND REVENUE REFORM

Britain and its colonies celebrated the outcome of the Seven Years' War but struggled with its consequences. Wartime expenses had doubled the British national debt, to just under £130,000,000, and interest payments required half the government's annual revenue. Canada, Florida, and the Ohio Valley would all be valuable in the long run, but Pontiac's War helped convince the government that the new territories needed guarding by an army of 10,000 men costing £400,000 per year—as much to guard the Indians from the colonists as vice versa.

Officials also decided to reorganize imperial government. The Treaty of Paris left Britain with an American empire of 26 colonies, including the 13 that later joined the American Revolution, a clutch of sugar islands led by Barbados and Jamaica, East and West Florida, and 5 in what is now Canada: Newfoundland, Nova Scotia, Prince Edward Island, Rupert's Land around Hudson Bay, and Quebec. Most of the North American colonies had elected assemblies that vigorously defended their autonomy. Governors had complained for years that the colonies were too independent and uncooperative, but centralization raised thorny constitutional issues. Most colonies had been founded by royal authority and "belonged" to Britain through their allegiance to the Crown. The Glorious Revolution had subordinated the king to Parliament, however, and Parliament's authority in the empire was unclear. It regulated the colonies' trade with the Navigation Acts, but could it govern their internal affairs? Could it tax them? Britain's authority supposedly flowed through royal governors, but their instructions had no legal force until assemblies enacted them. In practice, the colonies were governed by their own elites instead of king or Parliament, an arrangement that parliamentary leader Edmund Burke later called "salutary neglect."

George III was the young and inexperienced king who oversaw the process of reform. Earnest but dull, George inherited his grandfather's throne in 1760, at age 22. He wanted to be a good king but distrusted politicians and longed to exercise real power. Over the next decade, chief ministers came and went as George struggled to find one he liked, and colonial government suffered from political gyrations that usually had little or nothing to do with events in America. When peace arrived in 1763, George Grenville was Chancellor of the Exchequer and First Lord of the Treasury, and he developed what historians have called a new imperial policy to raise money and control the colonies.

The first step was a proclamation forbidding settlement beyond the crest of the Appalachian Mountains, intended to reduce the chance of costly Indian wars. The new army of 10,000 troops would enforce the Proclamation Line of 1763 from their frontier forts, and the Quartering Act of 1765 required assemblies to shoulder part of the cost. Passed to satisfy London merchants who hated payment in inflated bills, the Currency Act of 1764 made these costs harder to pay by forbidding the use of colonial paper money. All these measures curbed colonial freedom of action and reminded sensitive Americans of power-hungry schemes condemned by the Real Whig, or Country Party, tradition.

Grenville first looked for revenue in the lucrative trade between New England and the Caribbean. New Englanders made large quantities of rum from West Indian molasses, but to keep them from trading with the French, the Molasses Act of 1733 had imposed a tax of sixpence a gallon on molasses imported from outside the empire. When British islands could not supply all the syrup the distillers wanted, they still bought from the French and bribed the ill-paid customs inspectors to look the other way. Even without this abuse, however, the Molasses Act could never have raised much money. The duty made foreign molasses too expensive to use, so strict enforcement would have ended both importation and revenue. As a result, Americans did not think of the Molasses Act as a real tax, but only a trade regulation.

Grenville decided to change that policy. He reformed the customs agency to make it more honest and efficient, and he set the Royal Navy to chasing smugglers. More important, the Sugar Act of 1764 reduced the duty on foreign molasses to an affordable threepence a gallon and tightened collection procedures. Violators still faced vice-admiralty courts, without juries, and could lose their ships and cargoes if convicted. Royal governors, customs inspectors, and naval captains would divide the proceeds, creating handsome incentives for rigorous enforcement. Colonial merchants soon complained that corrupt officials used minor technical violations as pretexts to confiscate their property. Grenville ignored their objections, however, and the Sugar Act began to raise a modest annual revenue of £20,000.

Imperial Crisis

Grenville's new imperial policy proved extraordinarily unpopular in the colonies. Americans claimed they did not object to paying their fair share of imperial expenses, but the Currency Act would make it very difficult to find the cash to pay them. More fundamentally, the new measures reduced the colonies' long-established powers of self-government. The elites who dominated the colonial assemblies naturally resented this loss of authority, but even ordinary subjects began to protest what many came to believe were "unconstitutional" threats to American liberty.

RESISTING THE STAMP ACT

Colonists objected to the Sugar Act, but they were outraged when Grenville announced plans for a colonial stamp tax modeled after a similar levy in Britain. The law required stamped paper for publications and a wide range of legal and commercial transactions. Like the taxes on molasses, moreover, the stamps would have to be purchased with pounds sterling, or official British currency, just when the Currency Act had stretched the demand for scarce coinage even tighter. After spending a year to collect more information, Parliament passed the Stamp Act on March 22, 1765, and set November 1 as the date it would take effect.

A storm of protest followed Patrick Henry's outburst in the House of Burgesses. Every assembly on the mainland and several in the West Indies denounced the Stamp Act for taxing them without their consent, and public anger exploded from port towns to isolated villages. In a typical response, the inhabitants of Leicester, Massachusetts, blasted the new law as "contrary to the Rights of Mankind & Subversive of ye English Constitution," with "a Direct Tendency, to bring us into a State of abject Slavery & Vassalage." Complaints commonly stressed that the old Molasses Act was a trade regulation in the form of a tax, but taxation for actual revenue was "taxation without representation." If the king needed money, he should ask each assembly for an appropriation, just as he asked Parliament. If colonists submitted to the moderate but unconstitutional costs of the Stamp Act, worse impositions would inevitably follow, for illicit power would never restrain itself voluntarily. Before long, the colonists would lose their liberty along with their property, as Country Party writers had predicted.

As protests mounted, Massachusetts called for a meeting of all the colonies to present a united front, so in October 1765, the Stamp Act Congress convened in New York with delegates from nine colonies. It issued the firm but calmly worded Declaration of Rights and Grievances, which promised loyalty to the king and "due subordination" to

Parliament, but insisted that taxation without consent broke fundamental English rights. Less abstractly, the congress also claimed that Americans did not have enough hard currency to pay for the stamps and that commercial restrictions like the Sugar Act would impair their purchases of British manufactures.

The Sugar Act and the Stamp Act touched off a prolonged constitutional debate about colonial rights, mostly conducted through dueling pamphlets and newspaper essays that continued until independence. In this debate, the Crown's writers usually declared that Parliament was the supreme authority in Britain, so British colonies must obey it. Colonial authors denied the claims of Parliament and called for a return to the "salutary neglect" they had enjoyed before 1763. Treasury spokesman Thomas Whately argued, for example, that Americans did not need to elect a member of Parliament to be represented there, because the elected members "virtually" represented the whole realm and not just the voters who sent them. Maryland lawyer Daniel Dulaney struck back, acknowledging that some British towns sent no one to the House of Commons but shared interests with those that did. Since British taxes would fall on everyone there, a member of Parliament might represent voters and nonvoters alike. But who in Britain was affected by a tax in America? Which British borough shared the conditions and circumstances of colonists across the ocean? While "virtual representation" might work in Britain, Dulaney declared, the idea was preposterous for America.

Ministry spokesmen eventually abandoned the argument over representation and declared that every government must contain a sovereign, or ultimate, undivided authority. In Britain, the sovereign power was "the King in Parliament," or the combined will of king, Lords, and Commons. For the empire to have any meaning, sovereign power could not be split between Parliament and the colonies, so Americans must obey Parliament whether they were represented there or not. This position put the colonies in a state of permanent inferiority to Britain itself, a situation they finally rejected.

Unconcerned with theory, the ministry continued its plans to implement the Stamp Act, and colonists responded with direct action. Pressured by public anger, most merchants in New York, Boston, Philadelphia, and smaller ports signed nonimportation agreements pledging not to buy any British goods until the Stamp Act was repealed. Publicists followed with calls to replace British goods with homespun cloth and other colonial products. Semisecret bands called the Sons of Liberty led popular protests in every port. Mostly composed of artisans and shopkeepers of a distinctly lower social class than the merchants and lawyers who wrote the pamphlets and dominated the assemblies, the Sons of Liberty drew on longstanding English traditions of mob protest to completely block the operation of the Stamp Act.

A REVOLUTION FROM BELOW?

Events in Boston set the example for events that followed. Bostonians were well prepared for crowd actions, for lower-class leaders had long organized raucous popular parades to celebrate Pope's Day, the anniversary of a foiled plot to impose Catholicism and "Stuart tyranny." Going further, angry mobs had mobilized in 1747 to protect sailors from impressment, or forced service in the British navy. Over a decade later, when the end of the Seven Years' War left Boston impoverished, a political war broke out pitting Lieutenant Governor Thomas Hutchinson (a wealthy merchant who later became chief justice of Massachusetts) and his privileged friends and family against a popular movement that called itself the Caucus. The two factions battled for years, first over Hutchinson's effort to abolish the Boston town meeting, and then over customs enforcement. Both factions were thus well primed to react to the inflammatory Stamp Act.

Hutchinson had privately lobbied against the law, but still wrangled the profitable office of stamp distributor for his brother-in-law Andrew Oliver. On August 14, 1765, a hanged effigy of Oliver appeared prominently in Boston, and Governor Francis Bernard could not find anyone brave enough to take it down. Ebenezer MacIntosh, a shoemaker and chief organizer of Pope's Day, gathered his followers to denounce the governor, destroy the suspected new stamp office, burn the effigy with its wreckage, and break the windows of Oliver's house. Believing that Hutchinson favored the Stamp Act, MacIntosh led another mob two weeks later in attacking and demolishing his elegant townhouse. Soon afterward, Andrew Oliver stood at the foot of Boston's Liberty Tree to publicly resign the office of stamp distributor.

There was no inherent reason why leading colonists' fight for "liberty," or freedom from British taxation, should also have led to a fight for "equality," or a broader distribution of power within America. In other words, the merchants, lawyers, and gentry who were most affected by the Stamp Act might have opposed it without losing their power over lower-ranking colonists. Nevertheless, protesting gentlemen recruited artisans and laborers by invoking their equal rights to the liberties of freeborn Englishmen. Men like MacIntosh and his followers responded to their appeals, even though the Stamp Act—mostly a tax on legal and commercial documents—was unlikely to weigh on them heavily. Artisans did know that nonimportation would benefit them by cutting off foreign trade and increasing demand for their own products. Just as important, perhaps, they also knew that Thomas Hutchinson and his friends were wealthy, powerful, arrogant, and longstanding enemies of the "mob." Attacking Hutchinson would not only defend their liberty from arbitrary taxation, but it could also bring them more equality, or greater political power in Massachusetts. The entry of men like MacIntosh was therefore a step toward what historians now describe as a "revolution from below" that developed alongside the gentry's "revolution from above," sometimes cooperatively and sometimes in conflict. As political clashes mounted, demands for liberty and equality for those "below" would only grow stronger. In the short run, most (but not all) the participants in this popular revolution were white men of modest means. Over time, their participation set a precedent that other Americans used and still use for broader claims to liberty and equality.

Riots like those in Boston broke out against stamp distributors in Newport, Rhode Island, and New York. Sons of Liberty confronted stamp distributors from New Hampshire to Georgia and forced them to resign. By the time the stamped paper arrived in most ports, there was no one on hand with the authority to receive it, and crowds compelled local officials to resume port business without using it. Mob violence had nullified the law.

Protests did not stop with the future United States. Except for Quebec, all the colonies had significant English populations who boasted of liberty and balanced government, though slaves far outnumbered whites in the Caribbean. Just as in Boston, Newport, and New York, mobs on Nevis and St. Kitts destroyed supplies of stamped paper and forced the stamp distributors to resign. Jamaica's stamp distributor complained of "repeated Threats of Violence, Torrents of Personal abuse and many other very disagreeable Circumstances," and was finally burned in effigy. According to their governor, West Floridians viewed the stamps as "badges of slavery." On the whole, however, the Canadian and Caribbean colonies kept their protests moderate. Britain maintained a strong military presence in both regions, guarding against foreign attack and the very real possibility of Caribbean slave

revolts, but the troops could also silence protesters. West Indies merchants and planters depended on the Navigation Acts for protected
markets in Britain, and while they grumbled at parliamentary interference, they would not endanger their privileged position. Most Nova
Scotians had come from New England, but they depended heavily
on military spending, and the Crown controlled their government
tightly, while French-speaking Quebec lacked British political traditions of self-government. The thirteen mainland colonies from New
Hampshire to Georgia thus remained the centers of protest against the
Stamp Act and subsequent taxes by Parliament, as well as the independence movement that followed.

Back in London, merchants complained that colonial boycotts hurt
their business, and their voices carried more weight than those of the
colonists. Parliament gave in and repealed the Stamp Act in March
1766, but it also passed a Declaratory Act asserting that it had "full
power and authority . . . to bind the colonies and people of *America*
. . . in all cases whatsoever." Ignoring this pronouncement, Americans
greeted repeal with toasts, bonfires, and jubilant celebrations. They
did not ask if Parliament had truly renounced its intention of taxing
them, or if British and American understandings of public liberties
were the same. Time proved that they were not.

POLITICAL THEORY

What can explain the extraordinary upheaval against the Stamp Act?
The tax would cost money, of course, and the combined effects of the
Currency Act and a postwar economic downturn would magnify its
burden, but Americans knew that some taxation was inevitable. Back
in Britain, the common people quietly submitted to a much heavier
tax burden than Americans. Why then should normally law-abiding
subjects resort to violence against this modest and arguably necessary
measure?

As revealed in the language of protest, Americans had absorbed a
set of political ideas that made the possibility of parliamentary taxation
seem not just costly but intolerably dangerous. Some of these ideas
came from the Puritan notion of covenant, which taught that government was a sacred responsibility and that God would punish those
who tolerated its abuses. Enlightenment philosopher John Locke had
likewise argued that human government rested on a social contract
between the people and their rulers. If rulers broke that contract as

James II had done, men could and should resist them. By attempting to take Americans' property without their consent, Parliament appeared to have broken this fundamental bargain.

Americans also remembered the early eighteenth-century English radicals who had called themselves the Real Whigs, or the Country Party. These writers had denounced their own government as massively corrupt, a mockery of rule by consent, and bent on despotism. Almost everywhere they looked, Country Party writers saw secret plots to "enslave" the British people by taking control of their opinions, persons, and property. Following their example, colonial writers like Rhode Island's Stephen Hopkins linked "slavery" to taxation without consent. "Those who are governed at the will of another, or of others, and whose property may be taken from them by taxes, or otherwise, without their own consent, and against their will," he explained, "are in the miserable condition of slaves." The Whig political tradition was so important to protesting Americans that they began to call themselves "Whigs," while condemning supporters of the king and Parliament as "Tories."

The fear of enslavement did not seem far-fetched to many Americans, perhaps because real slavery already surrounded them. "Preferring death to slavery," North Carolina's Sons of Liberty succinctly explained, "we will . . . unite . . . in preventing entirely the operation of the Stamp Act." The Boston town meeting was more elaborate but just as certain. "If Taxes are laid upon us in any shape without ever having a Legal Representation where they are laid," it demanded, "are we not reduced from the Character of Free Subjects to the miserable state of Tributary Slaves?"

Country Party writers stressed the importance of what they called public virtue, which included ordinary morality but also a willingness to sacrifice personal pleasures for the common good. They loudly warned that ambitious tyrants would undermine both. "They will promote luxury, idleness, and expence, and a general depravation of manners," Cato had predicted. "From immorality and excesses [the people] will fall into necessity; and from thence into a servile dependence upon power." A certain measure of economic and social equality was also necessary to protect virtue and liberty, Cato insisted, because "where there is inequality of estates there must be inequality of power," and excessively powerful men would surely take liberty from others to satisfy their own corrupt desires.

Cato's admirers thus tied liberty and equality to a secular version of Puritanism. Boston activist Samuel Adams braided Country Party rhetoric with revival sermons and jeremiads to prophesy that parliamentary taxation would corrupt Massachusetts with "standing armies and ships of war; episcopates [i.e., Anglican bishops] and their numerous ecclesiastical retinue; pensioners, placemen and other jobbers, for an abandoned and shameless ministry; hirelings, pimps, parasites, panders, prostitutes, and whores." In the wake of Boston's anti-impressment riots, his popular newspaper had foreshadowed later disputes by tying political and social or economic grievances together. "All men are by nature on a level," it declared, "born with an equal share of freedom, and endowed with capacities equally alike." His cousin John Adams explained more simply that "liberty can no more exist without virtue and independence, than the body can live and move without a soul."

American realities lent credence to radical Whig predictions. Without intending despotism, the Crown did expect royal governors to strengthen their powers and control unruly assemblies, so colonial politics did resemble the endless struggle between rulers and subjects that Cato had predicted. As America's economy and society grew beyond frontier simplicity, the consumer revolution introduced previously unknown luxuries, distance widened between rich and poor, and overcrowding and land scarcity threatened to bring English-style poverty to America. Pamphleteers warned that the real purpose of parliamentary taxation was to hasten this process, strip American freeholders of their little farms and reduce them all to tenancy and want. "If the breath of a British house of commons can . . . [take] away all our money," a Boston meeting reasoned, "our lands will go next or be subject to rack rents from haughty and relentless landlords who will ride at ease, while we are trodden in the dirt." Prosperity led colonists to import more British products, moreover, and then to fret that luxury might corrupt them. While Englishmen lived with much heavier taxes, even the most moderate and level-headed Americans saw parliamentary taxes as leading to despotism.

The Contagion of Liberty

Wealthy and well-educated Americans had better opportunities to study political theory than artisans, farmers, and laborers. Stamp Act protesters had reached beyond the elite, however, to rally the "lower" and the "middling" sorts against the threat to liberty. As they did, what some writers called the "contagion of liberty" spread through the American social order, arousing rich and poor, town and country, and members of excluded groups such as women and African Americans. Beginning as a defense of privileges for the "better sort," the campaign for colonial rights slowly broadened under new rounds of parliamentary taxes, and led to demands for greater equality inside American society.

PROTESTING THE TOWNSHEND DUTIES

Charles Townshend became the king's chief minister in 1767. Like George Grenville, Townshend believed that the colonies must submit to Parliament and pay their share of imperial expenses. To replace the Stamp Act, he asked Parliament for import duties on certain products that the colonists regularly bought from abroad: lead, paper, glass, painter's colors, and tea. He hoped Americans would accept these duties because they were external taxes (like the Molasses Act and Sugar Act) on overseas commerce, rather than internal taxes (like the Stamp Act) on transactions inside the colonies.

Philadelphia lawyer John Dickinson attacked this distinction in his persuasive pamphlet *Letters from a Pennsylvania Farmer.* The Townshend Duties were just as bad as the Stamp Act, he argued, because they still raised revenue without popular consent. Collections would pay the salaries of governors and other royal officials, moreover, stripping assemblies of the power to coerce officials by refusing to pay them. Instead of backing down, the ministry raised more fears by moving frontier troops to the seaports, supposedly to cut costs, while Parliament strengthened the notorious vice-admiralty courts and created a centralized customs office for America.

Radical minds saw threats to liberty in all these measures, but it was not until February 1768 that the Massachusetts assembly adopted a circular letter to other colonies calling for peaceful measures of resistance. Lord Hillsborough, the newly appointed secretary of state for the colonies, unwisely demanded that Massachusetts rescind this circular and forbade the other legislatures to accept it, which only strengthened their determination to discuss whatever they wished. Governors then dissolved the defiant assemblies, fulfilling radical warnings that corrupt rulers would abolish free government to silence dissent.

Attempted intimidation brought a new round of nonimportation agreements against the Townshend Duties. The Sons of Liberty resumed attacks on defiant merchants, and soldiers could not stop them without provoking further violence. The boycotts brought hard times to the Boston docks, where sailors and laborers competed with off-duty soldiers for scarce employment. Clashes mounted in streets and taverns until March 5, 1770, when sailors, laborers, and apprentices began pelting a small group of soldiers with snowballs, rocks, and catcalls. Pressed too far, the redcoats fired back and killed five rioters, including a free black sailor named Crispus Attucks.

Publicists dubbed this incident the Boston Massacre and illustrated it with gory lithographs depicting the wanton slaughter of aggrieved and harmless civilians. The truth was more complicated, but when soldiers fired on an unarmed mob, ordinary colonists concluded that the orators and pamphleteers were right: British forces threatened liberty. Farmers, artisans, laborers, and even dockside toughs fought back with more demonstrations, hangings in effigy, and rounds of angry speeches fortified with strong drink and stronger language. With tacit approval from colonial leaders, property was damaged and people got hurt. As violence escalated, angry crowds connected the gentry's protests with their own grievances and applied the lessons of liberty to their own lives.

These developments were still invisible in London, where the government had changed hands again. Lord Frederick North, the new chief minister, supported Britain's right to tax the colonies, but he would not fight for the unpopular policies of his predecessor. He responded to the boycotts by asking Parliament to repeal all the Townshend Duties but one, keeping the tax on tea for the sake of principle.

RURAL PROTESTS

Social and economic tension did not stop at coastal ports in the 1760s. When military spending slackened at the end of the Seven Years' War, credit shrank and crop prices fell in a sharp economic contraction, punishing farmers just as tighter enforcement of the Navigation Acts barred their crops from foreign markets. New York's manorial landlords tried to boost their incomes with higher rents and shorter leases, but their tenants fought back with rent strikes and riots. Dispossessed local Indians also came forward and convinced many tenants that the patroons had never purchased their lands, so they had no right to collect rents from their vast manors. In 1765, officials evicted and jailed Philipse Manor tenants when they refused give up their long leases for shorter agreements that could lead to higher rents, but hundreds of angry farmers marched on New York City to free them. "Mobs had overcome Kings before," their leader warned, "and why should they not overcome now?" In this environment, unrest spread quickly to rural districts, and white farmers followed townspeople in protesting with the language of liberty.

Economic problems were especially acute in Virginia, where yeomen and planters had spent freely on expensive imports when tobacco sold well but could not pay their debts when its price fell. Many Virginians blamed themselves and lashed their consciences for overspending, but could not give up the purchases that proclaimed their status. "From immorality and excesses we fall into necessity," wailed a writer in the *Virginia Gazette*, echoing Cato, "and this leads us to a servile dependence on power, and fits us to the chains prepared for us." Others blamed the imperial system itself and decided that conditions would improve if the Navigation Acts allowed them to produce their own manufactures, avoid British middlemen, and trade directly with foreign buyers. "*Britain* from her exclusive trade to these colonies, and from the manner in which she tied up our manufacturing hands," despaired prominent planter Richard Henry Lee, "involved the people here in very heavy debt, which agriculture, without arts, and a trade so confined, will probably never pay."

The Currency Act only made repayment harder. When Virginia sought to loosen credit with a government-owned loan office, and tried to control costs and limit tobacco production by halting slave imports, Britain said no. Nor could Virginians escape their problems on new lands beyond the mountains, for the Proclamation Line of 1763 had reserved this territory for the Indians. Tempers mounted as Virginians realized that liberty had practical as well as theoretical value.

Farther south, rural tension pitted the Carolina backcountry against low-country elites. The great planters who dominated South Carolina's assembly were very suspicious of upland pioneers. Not trusting these poor, unruly strangers with the power to elect assemblymen, the planter gentry refused to give them courts, county governments, or other institutions of law and order. Horse thieves and cattle rustlers roamed above the fall line until vigilantes called Regulators began dishing out rough justice after 1765. Violence did not diminish until 1769, when the legislature finally established courts for the area.

In North Carolina, a different group of Regulators protested corruption in their local governments. Their assembly had been all too ready to establish local courts, stocking them with venal officials who lined their pockets by collecting local taxes with oppressive severity and embezzling the proceeds. "The sons of Liberty withstood the Lords in Parliament in behalf of true Liberty," the Regulators complained in 1766, so "let not Officers under them carry on unjust Oppression in our own Province." When petitions failed and violent mobs disrupted western courts, Governor William Tryon mobilized 1,200 eastern militiamen in 1771 and marched west to crush the disorder. After a two-hour battle at Great Alamance Creek, he scattered 2,000 insurgents and hanged 7 others. Ironically, most of North Carolina's leading revolutionaries were eastern leaders who fought with Tryon in this conflict, but the clash taught frontier yeoman to distrust both coastal slaveholders and British officials.

Whether in New York, Virginia, or the Carolinas, it is difficult to draw direct lines between rural protests of the 1760s and 1770s and the opposing sides of the American Revolution. Sometimes dissenters sided with the drive for independence, sometimes they were neutral, and sometimes they concluded that the Whig gentry were more dangerous than the Crown. It is clear, however, that rural America was subject to increasing social and political tensions in the late colonial era and that frontier farmers were learning to apply the rhetoric of liberty for themselves.

DAUGHTERS OF LIBERTY

Calls for liberty also touched American women, for assumptions about proper sex roles deeply colored ideas about public life. Like most rights, liberty belonged to men, not women. Condemning the effects of the consumer revolution on liberty, virtue, and masculinity, John Adams praised "manly" resistance to tyranny but denounced dependence on British goods as "vicious, luxurious, and effeminate."

Conflict with the "mother country" still had deep implications for American women. Their shopping habits determined the effectiveness of the nonimportation agreements. They spun and wove American cloth when men renounced British imports. Newspapers, essayists, and ministers urged the "Daughters of Liberty" to practice their public virtue by rejecting British frippery and making essentials at home. In an incident known as the Edenton Tea Party, North Carolina ladies committed themselves to nonimportation, while their counterparts elsewhere took their spinning wheels out of storage to make homespun in public displays of patriotism. Milcah Martha Moore of Philadelphia used rhyme to protest the Townshend Duties, explicitly contrasting the patriotism of women, who lacked public rights, to the venality of men, who might succumb to pro-British temptations:

> If the Sons (so degenerate) the Blessing despise,
> Let the Daughters of Liberty, nobly arise,
> And tho' we've no voice, but a negative here
> The use of the Taxables, let us forbear.

Sentiments like these did not lead immediately to legal changes in the position of American women, but they fed the idea that women could and must be public spirited in their own ways. In the generation after independence, American women would continue to build on these ideas to fashion a concept of female citizenship and public service that extended from the home to the larger community.

THE RHETORIC AND REALITY OF SLAVERY

When whites complained of British "slavery," African Americans demanded freedom as well. In 1765, Henry Laurens of South Carolina watched approvingly as Stamp Act protesters chanted, "*Liberty Liberty and stamp'd paper.*" Three months later, he and other white townsmen shuddered and put the whole province on alert when slaves followed suit and shouted "Liberty" in the streets of Charles Town. Some white Americans were painfully aware of the contradictions between their words and their behavior. A Boston firebrand declared in 1774 that "the colonists are by the law of nature free born, as indeed all men are, white or black." Even Virginia aristocrat Arthur Lee agreed. "Freedom is unquestionably the birthright of all mankind," he wrote to the *Virginia Gazette* in 1767, "of Africans as well as Europeans."

Freedom-loving slaveholders drew bitter charges of hypocrisy. "Why is it that we hear the loudest *yelps* for liberty from the drivers of negroes?" mocked English literary lion Samuel Johnson, and black and white Americans raised the same question. "Blush ye pretended votaries for freedom! ye trifling patriots!" cried John Allen, a Baptist minister from Massachusetts. "[You] are making a mockery of your profession by trampling on the sacred natural rights and privileges of Africans." African-born poet Phillis Wheatley of Massachusetts insisted, "In every human Breast, God has implanted a Principle, which we call love of Freedom." Writing to Native American minister Samson Occom in 1774, she acidly remarked, "How well the cry for Liberty, and the reverse Disposition for the exercise of oppressive Power over others agree . . . does not require the Penetration of a Philosopher to determine."

Spurred at first by religious faith and Enlightenment principles, vocal opposition to slavery as an institution had slowly emerged in eighteenth-century America and Europe. Puritan judge Samuel Sewall had denounced slavery in an early pamphlet of 1700. French Enlightenment philosopher Baron Charles-Louis de Montesquieu called slavery contrary to natural law in *The Spirit of the Laws* (1748), and Adam Smith of the Scottish Enlightenment called it backward in his *Theory of Moral Sentiments* (1759). Eccentric Quaker Benjamin Lay scolded Pennsylvania Friends for the sin of slaveholding in the 1740s. Fellow Quakers John Woolman and Anthony Benezet took up the cause in the following decade, leading the Society of Friends to ban slaveholding by its members in 1774. Without freeing his own five slaves, Benjamin Franklin endorsed their views and joined Benezet's Society for the Relief of Free Negroes Unlawfully Held in Bondage, America's first abolition society, and eventually served as its president. In London, a small group of Quaker and Anglican reformers created the Society for Effecting the Abolition of the Slave Trade in 1787, and France's first abolition society, the Société des Amis des Noirs, appeared the following year.

Enslaved Africans in Massachusetts sought their own freedom in a rash of successful lawsuits dating from the 1770s. In 1773, Boston slaves filed the first known petition for complete abolition. They described themselves as "discreet, sober, honest, and industrious," as well as "virtuous and religious," but owing to their bondage (and quoting from Psalm 49), "neither they, nor their Children to all Generations, shall ever be able to do, or to possess and enjoy any Thing, no, not even Life itself, but in a Manner as the Beasts that perish." A year later, a similar group protested that they were unjustly "held in the bowels of a free and Christian country" and "deprived of every thing that hath a tendency to make life even tolerable." The abolition movement would not become widespread until after American independence, but African Americans would not allow the campaign for liberty to stop at the color line.

The Conflict Escalates

Though Americans continued to stress their loyalty, pamphlets, speeches, and mob violence did break into armed rebellion. Boston radicals destroyed a valuable cargo of the British East India Company, and Parliament retaliated by revoking many powers of self-government in Massachusetts. When other assemblies protested, their governors dismissed them, and many Americans predicted that colonial self-rule was disappearing. They responded by creating alternate governments, from local committees of safety to the Continental Congress, that protected themselves by gathering arms. Serious fighting broke out when royal troops tried to seize such weapons from Concord, Massachusetts. Without yet declaring independence, Americans faced full-scale war.

THE BOSTON TEA PARTY AND THE COERCIVE ACTS

Protests of the tea tax eventually faltered, and Americans either paid it or smuggled tea from Holland. Tensions exploded again, however, when Parliament tried to help the powerful East India Company. The Tea Act of 1773 gave the company a monopoly on the sale of tea in America and, by cutting out middlemen, allowed it to undersell the smugglers. Lord North hoped that Americans would pay more taxes by drinking the cheaper legal tea. The Treasury, the company, and the customers would all benefit, and no one would complain but the smugglers.

His lordship was mistaken. In Philadelphia, New York, Charles Town, and virtually every other port, the Sons of Liberty reemerged to tar and feather any merchant who accepted taxed tea from the East India Company. Most captains of ships carrying tea turned back from American harbors before risking their safety and their employers' property. In Boston, however, Massachusetts-born Thomas Hutchinson had become the new governor, and the tea was consigned to his relatives. A proud and sensitive man, Hutchinson resolved to honor the king's trust, protect his family, and defeat the radicals who had leveled his house in the Stamp Act riots. When three tea ships slipped inside Boston Harbor in November 1773, he would not let them leave without paying the hated duty.

For three weeks, crowds met almost daily at the Old South Church to hear fiery denunciations of the ministry's horrid scheme. At nightfall on December 16, 1773, a crowd burst out of the church and headed for Griffin's Wharf. Crudely disguised as Indians, they swarmed aboard the ships and dumped tea worth £11,000 into Boston Harbor. To make sure no one acted for personal gain, vigilant guards enforced the traditional rules for crowd actions of this kind: they took nothing but tea, they made sure it was thoroughly destroyed, they prevented anyone from helping himself to a handful, and they even swept up afterward. Overawed by the crowd, neither the ships' crews nor the king's troops lifted a finger to resist.

King George, Lord North, and Parliament all demanded harsh punishment for the Boston Tea Party. Under the Coercive Acts of the spring of 1774, the port of Boston would remain closed until Massachusetts paid for the drowned tea; town meetings were suspended; an appointed council supplanted Massachusetts's elected upper house; any British official charged with a capital crime in the colonies—one committed while suppressing protests, for example—was promised an English trial; and the army could lodge its soldiers in private homes. General Thomas Gage, commander of British forces in America, replaced Thomas Hutchinson as Massachusetts's governor, with full authority to suppress disorder with his troops.

Dubbed the Intolerable Acts by furious colonists, the Coercive Acts did not subdue Massachusetts, but convinced other Americans that all their representative governments were at risk. They were almost equally alarmed by the Quebec Act, an unrelated piece of legislation that established a nonelected government for the former New France and protected its Catholic Church. It also fixed Quebec's southern boundary at the Ohio River, nullifying the claims of Virginia, Massachusetts, and Connecticut. The Quebec Act respected the customs of French Canadians, but frightened American Protestants with the specter of encroaching tyranny and papism, and outranged colonists who thought they had fought the Seven Years' War to obtain the Ohio Valley for themselves. They quickly associated the Quebec Act with the other Intolerable Acts and demanded their immediate repeal.

THE FIRST CONTINENTAL CONGRESS

Like the Stamp Act, the Coercive Acts inspired American leaders to call an intercolonial meeting to plan common action. In September 1774, the Continental Congress assembled in Philadelphia with representatives from all the mainland colonies from New Hampshire to South Carolina. The 55 delegates included such luminaries as John and Samuel Adams, the cousins from Massachusetts, George Washington and Patrick Henry from Virginia, James Wilson and John Dickinson of Pennsylvania, and Roger Sherman of Connecticut. In its final resolutions, Congress declared that the Coercive Acts violated their rights as British subjects and ought not to be obeyed. To enforce this position, the delegates adopted an agreement they called the Continental Association, which renounced all British imports—including slaves—and threatened to block exports as well until the repeal of the Coercive Acts. The Association also called for local, elected committees to inspect all merchants and customhouses to detect and denounce violations of the agreement. Ominously, Congress sent representatives to Europe seeking money and arms. More theoretically, Congress resolved that Parliament had no right to legislate for the colonies at all, but agreed to respect the Navigation Acts voluntarily. They also pledged their continued loyalty to the king, but petitioned him to seek repeal of the Coercive Acts and other restrictions of their liberties. Uncertain of its next steps, the Continental Congress adjourned after six weeks and promised to reassemble the following May.

Enforcing the Continental Association with elected committees unleashed more popular activity than Congress may have anticipated. Local communities chose as many as 7,000 committee members, many of them ranking far lower in the social scale than those who customarily held colonial office. These committees did not hesitate to use public humiliation and intimidation to get results. In Massachusetts, crowds shut down courts rather than submit to restrictions on provincial self-government imposed by the Coercive Acts. The Pennsylvania militia became the leading political force in Philadelphia, and calls for greater political equality increasingly accompanied demands for liberty. Conservative leaders increasingly worried that inciting popular protests had been a mistake. In the words of William Bull, lieutenant governor of South Carolina, "Men of property begin at length to see that . . . the people . . . have discovered their own strength and importance, and are not now so easily governed by their former leaders." As imperial conflict deepened, Whig leaders began to realize that restoring an acceptable form of British authority might be unattainable, so an independent government led by American gentry would be far better than no government at all.

Without entirely realizing it, delegates to the First Continental Congress had begun to act as the shadow of a national government, adopting the equivalent of laws (e.g., the nonimportation agreements), reaching out to foreign governments, negotiating with the king and Parliament, and even authorizing local bodies to carry out its decisions. The structure of royal authority began to crumble. Six governors had tried to prevent the appointment of delegates to the Continental Congress by disbanding their constitutional assemblies, only to see extralegal provincial congresses take their places. With a larger and more representative number of delegates than the old assemblies, the provincial congresses quickly made themselves the de facto governments of their respective provinces, approving the Continental Association and arranging for local enforcement committees. When surviving royal assemblies continued to resist the Intolerable Acts, governors closed them as well and unauthorized provincial congresses took their places. Congresses and local gatherings outdid one another in sending donations of food to beleaguered Boston, agreeing that, as a Philadelphia meeting put it, "our brethren at Boston [are] suffering in the common cause of America." Wherever possible, the congresses also took charge of public supplies of gunpowder and other weapons, and the Massachusetts Provincial Congress called for companies of minutemen to begin training to defend the public liberties at a minute's warning.

LEXINGTON TO VIRGINIA

These measures enraged the governors, especially General Thomas Gage of Massachusetts. Over the winter and early spring of 1775, Gage felt increasingly isolated on Boston's slender peninsula as the reach of royal authority dwindled to the range of his own guns. To regain the upper hand, Gage decided to send troops to nearby Concord to arrest leaders of the Massachusetts Provincial Congress and destroy their munitions. His secret plans leaked, however, and when 800 redcoats crossed the Charles River on the night of April 18, 1775, Paul Revere, a leading Boston silversmith, and his companion William Dawes galloped ahead to rouse the countryside.

Alerted by the messengers, about 70 minutemen from the town of Lexington gathered on their village green before dawn. They only intended to demonstrate their opposition by standing in arms on the roadside, and they started to obey when the approaching commander ordered them to disperse. Suddenly, in the dim light and tense confusion, an unknown person fired, and the British company followed with a couple of well-aimed volleys. The minutemen got off a few shots, but 8 of them fell dead; 10 others and an Englishman were wounded before the Americans broke for cover.

As blood soaked into the Lexington common, the infantry cheered, re-formed their ranks, and resumed the march to Concord. There they fired on more minutemen, but they had lost the element of surprise and failed to find the powder or the politicians they wanted. Returning to Boston empty-handed, they faced even more trouble as minutemen from the surrounding towns launched continual ambushes from roadside trees, fences, and stone walls. British soldiers were virtually invincible on an open battlefield, but this way of fighting seemed savage, cowardly, and indefensible to them. The close of day left 273 British regulars and about 95 Americans dead or wounded.

Gage was now trapped in Boston. From all around New England, 15,000 militiamen quickly gathered on surrounding hills. A small force commanded by Colonel Ethan Allen captured the British outpost at Fort Ticonderoga on Lake Champlain and hauled its captured cannon into place around the city. On June 17, 1775, Gage tried to break this siege by ordering his men to capture a crudely fortified installation on top of Breed's Hill on the opposite side of the Charles River. In the misnamed Battle of Bunker Hill, British troops charged three times against the withering fire of their entrenched opponents, but did not capture the summit until the Americans had exhausted their ammunition. Of the 2,500 British soldiers involved in the battle, almost 50 percent were killed or wounded.

As fighting broke out in New England, southern slaves mounted their fight for independence by deserting their masters and, with hopes of freedom, offering their services to the British. Facing the collapse of royal authority in November 1775, John Murray, the Earl of Dunmore and last royal governor of Virginia, took a fateful step: he issued a proclamation that offered freedom to all slaves and indentured servants who would escape rebellious masters and fight for the Crown. According to Thomas Jefferson, the prospect of a slave revolt "raised our country to a perfect frenzy." Between 800 and 1,000 blacks eventually enrolled in Dunmore's Ethiopian Regiment, with uniforms bearing the motto "Liberty to Slaves." As many as 30 percent of the runaways were women and children, and eight belonged to Peyton Randolph, Speaker of the House of Burgesses and future president of the Continental Congress. The Ethiopian Regiment soon fought Whig forces "with the intrepidity of lions" at the Battle of Great Bridge, but many then succumbed to virulent smallpox that festered in Britain's Chesapeake fleet. Despite this tragic reprieve, fear and outrage over Dunmore's tactic deeply disturbed white southerners and convinced many that reconciliation was both dangerous and hopeless, but British service attracted even more slaves when the war turned decisively southward after 1779.

Decision for Independence

The Second Continental Congress combined policies of war and peace, creating an American army headed by George Washington while still petitioning the king for a constitutional settlement. As war preparations continued on both sides, Thomas Paine's hard-hitting *Common Sense* appeared, mocking the idea of kingship and dismissing the remaining arguments for reconciliation. As Paine's arguments sank in, one assembly after another instructed its delegates to vote for separation. Congress finally adopted Thomas Jefferson's Declaration of Independence on July 4, 1776. The Declaration's fervent language has inspired and challenged Americans ever since.

THE SECOND CONTINENTAL CONGRESS

The Second Continental Congress assembled in Philadelphia in May 1775, three weeks after the Concord fight. Its members faced an entirely different situation than their predecessors had the previous autumn, for the earlier body had merely coordinated resistance to the Intolerable Acts, but the second faced outright war. In its first major decision, Congress embraced the impromptu gathering of militia units around Boston and proclaimed them the Continental Army. Emphasizing intercolonial solidarity, it gave the army's command to George Washington. The 43-year-old Virginian had military experience, but more important was his air of calm authority and his remarkable ability to inspire trust from almost everybody. Convinced that all North Americans must be as unhappy with British rule as they were, the delegates sent a force to "free" Quebec, but French Canadians failed to respond and the foray failed disastrously. Needing money, Congress sent emissaries to Europe to beg assistance and also ordered the printing of $2 million in paper bills, though it lacked the means to back them up with either coinage or taxation. It also sought Indian allies and undertook to regulate the Indian trade. By organizing an army, launching an invasion, sending out diplomats, issuing currency, and conducting Indian affairs, the Second Continental Congress was already acting like a sovereign national government in the summer of 1775, though all but a handful of delegates still insisted they rejected the goal of independence.

In a final bid for imperial unity, Joseph Galloway, a delegate from Pennsylvania who later became a Loyalist, proposed parallel legislatures for Britain and America under a common king. His idea resembled Benjamin Franklin's Albany Plan of Union and the future British Commonwealth, but it strained against conventional beliefs in an undivided sovereign, or ultimate authority in government, and no one showed much interest. In effect, Franklin's radical concept of 1754 had become the conservative compromise of 1775. Instead of seeking a new structure, Congress sent the king the Olive Branch Petition, calling again for the loosely jointed empire of 1763. Noting Americans' actions instead of their words, King George refused to receive the Olive Branch Petition and proclaimed that the colonies had broken into outright rebellion and were no longer under his protection. Lacking an army of sufficient size, his ministers hired mercenaries from the German principality of Hesse and continued their plans to reduce the American colonies by force.

COMMON SENSE

Sentiment for independence began to crystalize in January 1776, with the appearance of an inflammatory pamphlet entitled *Common Sense*. Its author was Thomas Paine, a hard-pressed English radical and former artisan who arrived in Philadelphia in 1774 after numerous personal and professional failures at home. The imperial crisis gave Paine a new identity as a freelance revolutionary, and he went on to distinguish himself in both the American and French Revolutions. Unlike earlier pamphleteers, Paine did not cite philosophers or theorists but drew his arguments from the Bible and the "common sense" of ordinary literate Americans. Upholding popular demands for political equality as well as liberty, Paine implicitly asserted that ordinary people could judge their institutions by the rules of reason as well as European philosophers.

Common Sense ridiculed the "balanced" government of king, Lords, and Commons, and denied that the king's authority came from God. In Paine's view, Old Testament kingship violated the covenant between God and Israel, and the monarchy founded by William the Conqueror in 1066 was no better. "A French bastard landing with an armed Banditti, and establishing himself king of England against the consent of the natives, is in plain terms a very paltry rascally original," he sneered. "It certainly hath no divinity in it." Continuing, Paine attacked hereditary power itself as "an insult and an imposition on posterity. For all men being originally equals," he reasoned, "no *one* by *birth* could have a right to set up his own family in perpetual preference to all others." And how could a return to the system of 1763 atone for the suffering inflicted at Lexington and Concord? Instead, Paine called on his adopted countrymen to reject "the hardened, sullen tempered Pharaoh of England for ever; and disdain the wretch, that with the pretended title of FATHER OF HIS PEOPLE can unfeelingly hear of their slaughter and composedly sleep with their blood upon his soul." He thus called boldly for an American republic, or elected government without a king, and included a proposed constitution. *Common Sense* closed by predicting a world-historical destiny for the new nation. Freedom was disappearing throughout the world, he claimed. "O! receive the fugitive," Paine begged his readers, "and prepare in time an asylum for mankind."

Common Sense sold as many as 120,000 copies in three months. Paine's strong language shocked readers who were more accustomed to respectful political discourse, but to those who snapped it up, *Common Sense* seemed to break the psychological bonds that still tied Americans to the idea of kingship. When he read the pamphlet, and heard simultaneously about Britain's destruction of coastal towns in Maine and Virginia, George Washington was ready to put reservations about style and decorum to the side. "A few more of such flaming arguments as were exhibited [in the burning] of Falmouth and Norfolk, added to the sound doctrine and unanswerable reasoning contained in the pamphlet *Common Sense*, will not leave members [of the Continental Congress] at a loss to decide upon the propriety of separation."

In part, *Common Sense* was so popular because Paine voiced ideas that many Americans believed already, including the linkage between liberty, or freedom from British domination, and equality, or a broader distribution of political power within America. Paine's ridicule of kingship and hereditary power clearly implied a republican government for America, and strengthened the "revolution from below" by insisting that the citizens of a new American nation should be both free and equal.

Public meetings and protests agreed, and increasingly demanded independence to escape from Britain and redistribute power in America. The anti–Stamp Act mobs had protested the authority of men like Thomas Hutchinson as much as the claims of Parliament. Five years later, in 1770, Boston's artisans had denounced the merchants who wanted to abandon nonimportation, and defended their voting rights in town meetings by declaring, "If they had no property, they had liberty, and their posterity might have property." In the spring of 1775, the citizens of Mecklenburg County, North Carolina, not far from the centers of Regulator activity, proclaimed "the former civil Constitution of these colonies for the present wholly suspended," and created their own provisional government, with voting based on militia membership rather than landownership. The next fall, the Philadelphia militia made similar demands, and New York radicals echoed them when the state began to write its own constitution. John Adams, Samuel's more conservative cousin, had to admit in the spring of 1776 that "a more equal liberty than has prevailed in other parts of the earth must be established in America."

THE DECLARATION OF INDEPENDENCE

Still the Second Continental Congress hesitated. Several middle colonies were not ready for independence, and the others would not move without them. The last holdouts were wavering by June 7, 1776, when Richard Henry Lee of Virginia moved a resolution "that these United Colonies are, and of right ought to be, free and independent States." Instead of debating the resolution right away, however, Congress appointed a committee to prepare a declaration of independence: John Adams, Benjamin Franklin, Roger Sherman, Robert Livingston, and Thomas Jefferson.

Thomas Jefferson was a 33-year-old lawyer and planter from piedmont Virginia. His father had been a respected mapmaker and land surveyor who had risen to moderate prominence and to membership in the House of Burgesses, and Jefferson had gained from his father's estate the rare opportunity of education at the College of William and Mary. A gifted though eclectic scholar, Jefferson had embraced the ideas of the Enlightenment and England's Country Party. He especially loved the rational and philosophical study of law, government, and history. Though he inherited most of his father's land and slaves, he practiced law until marriage with Martha Wayles Skelton doubled the size of his estate and enabled him to begin the plantation he called Monticello. In Virginia's House of Burgesses, Jefferson gravitated to the radical Whig faction led by Patrick Henry and Richard Henry Lee, but distinguished himself as a brilliant political writer rather than speechmaker. Jefferson's service at the Second Continental Congress was his first appearance in politics outside Virginia.

At the committee's request, Jefferson composed a stirring draft that skillfully blended Whig theory, Enlightenment philosophy, and popular demands from American crowds and legislatures. It opened by asserting that "all men are created equal," for all possess the same God-given, "unalienable rights." Legitimate government must respect these rights, or the citizens could change it. Jefferson then insisted that King George had indeed broken the contract and cited a long list of specific violations. This section of the Declaration drew on the old radical Whig notion of a conspiracy against liberty by listing "a long train of abuses and usurpations" that supposedly "evinces a design to reduce them under absolute despotism." Jefferson blamed these actions on the king instead of Parliament, not because George III was truly responsible for all of them, but because he was the last link Americans still accepted with Great Britain.

Receiving Jefferson's text, the committee made some revisions and passed it on to Congress, which had approved Lee's resolution on July 2. Congress polished it still further by clarifying and simplifying several important passages. It also deleted some of Jefferson's more fanciful complaints, including his claim that the king had foisted the slave trade on innocent Americans, only to incite the slaves against their masters. Jefferson never fully forgave his colleagues for tampering with his words, but he swallowed his resentment for the sake of solidarity. Well aware of the penalty for treason but nervously putting their lives on the line, the delegates adopted the United States Declaration of Independence on July 4, 1776, and signed it in the weeks ahead.

LIBERTY, EQUALITY, AND SLAVERY

Through almost constant repetition and invocation, the text of the Declaration of Independence has become a classic, some would say sacred, statement of American values. Certainly its affirmation that "all men are created equal" has become a touchstone of American idealism and a demanding standard for national self-scrutiny. Especially in the twentieth century, however, Americans became painfully aware of the discrepancy between the stern but inspiring demand of human equality and the failure of Jefferson and his society to live up to this standard, particularly on the subject of slavery and race.

Paradoxically, there were powerful links between liberty and slavery. As we have seen, seventeenth-century planters had recruited allies against slave revolts by expanding the rights of common white men. Foreign visitors to the colonial South frequently remarked that the powerful experience of personal mastery lent special force to the desire for independence in the slaveholding elite. "They are haughty and jealous of their liberties," one observer wrote as early as 1759, "and can hardly bear the thought of being controlled by any superior power." Despite their passion for autonomy, however, Virginia's planters were almost all in deep debt to the British merchants who sold their tobacco and purchased their supplies. The indebted gentry writhed in self-reproach at this situation, claiming that the "Root of our misfortunes is our Pride, our Luxury and Idleness," but they could not curb the extravagance that proved their rank in a slave society. Thomas Jefferson was no exception to this rule, and he remained deeply in debt his whole life, though never sparing expenses at Monticello. The conflict between the masters' love of autonomy and ostentation and their embarrassed dependence on their creditors undoubtedly fed their psychological discomfort with colonial subordination and contributed to their support for American independence.

In varying degrees, Virginia's gentry were also aware of the incongruity of demanding liberty for themselves while holding others in bondage. Patrick Henry, who cried "give me liberty or give me death," called slavery an "abominable practice . . . as repugnant to humanity, as it is inconsistent with the bible, and destructive to liberty," yet admitted that he could not abandon "the general inconvenience of living without them." Jefferson expressed similar sentiments, and supported measures to end the African slave trade and to encourage masters to free their slaves voluntarily. His efforts grew weaker over time, however, and he could never bring himself to take a forthright public stand for emancipation or racial equality. What then could Thomas Jefferson and his fellow white Americans have meant by the declaration that "all men are created equal"?

Thomas Jefferson knew perfectly well that all people were not alike, but he believed that "all men" had an equal and God-given right to a government that protects their "life, liberty, and the pursuit of Happiness." It probably never occurred to him to expect the same for women, whom he left to the government of their husbands. He did see the conflict between his grand ideals and African slavery, and though he questioned their intellectual abilities, Jefferson never explicitly denied blacks' fundamental right to liberty. He did believe, however, that rights applied to men within political communities, and blacks were outside the American political community in 1776. Instead of going free immediately, blacks should receive their rights under a government of their own, as soon as white safety would allow it. As Jefferson later put it, "We have the wolf by the ear, and we can neither hold him nor safely let him go." His pledges in the Declaration of Independence are thus good examples of statements whose meaning has grown over time, and whose fullest import has rightfully expanded beyond the imaginations of the people who first composed them.

The Military Challenge

The revolutionaries faced a dual challenge. They had to win a war against the most formidable army and navy of the Atlantic world, and build a republican government and society that would retain popular support and justify their daring rebellion. They pursued the two tasks simultaneously, but the military effort had the greatest immediate urgency (see chapter 6 for republican government). The war would not be easy, and both armies faced serious military challenges. Both sides competed for the allegiance of undecided Americans, whose choices would be crucial to the outcome.

THE CONTINENTAL ARMY

George Washington took command of the Continental Army on July 2, 1775. In the years since his youthful scrapes with the French and Indians, he had grown in judgment and estate. His older brothers had died, leaving him substantial property, including the plantation at Mount Vernon and its large force of slaves, and he acquired more by marrying Martha Dandridge Custis, a wealthy widow. As the imperial crisis mounted, Washington had devoted himself to plantation management, served on his Anglican parish vestry, and entered the House of Burgesses. Regarded as strong and wise rather than brilliant, Washington brought to his command maturity, judgment, and steadfastness, in addition to his military experience.

The soldiers around Boston were militiamen who expected to go home when the crisis had passed. Reckless civilians boasted that courageous American militiamen, devoted to liberty and hardened by the wilderness, could easily defeat the king's degraded mercenaries. Washington knew better. In an open battlefield, the iron discipline of professional troops would enable them to stand in crisp blocks firing volley after volley with murderous effectiveness, while the independent-minded militiamen would be all too inclined to break and run.

Washington's first task was to create a permanent force trained to follow orders and execute maneuvers without question or delay. It was not an easy task for an army committed to liberty, and Washington and his officers never had more than partial success. As the war continued, they enticed enlistees with cash bounties and 100-acre land grants, some for three-year terms and others for the duration of the war. Desertion remained a problem and recruiting efforts could never slacken. High costs kept both armies small, however, causing British and American generals to launch major battles with less than 2,000–3,000 men on a side.

States ultimately required quotas of soldiers from each community, and local committees of safety chose individuals for the service. Sensitive to community pressures, they leaned heavily on the poor and powerless, and allowed affluent draftees to hire substitutes. Over time, the American army increasingly resembled its adversary, filled with disadvantaged young men with limited prospects in the civilian world. Fearful of losing his men, however, Washington never subjected them to the full rigors of British discipline, which included lashings for disobedience and unflinching use of the firing squad against mutiny, cowardice, and desertion.

THE BRITISH DILEMMA

The British Army faced serious problems as well. Most Americans were unfriendly and the terrain was unfamiliar. Transatlantic supply lines were long and fragile. The army could not subdue the dispersed population by capturing a capital city; the rebellion would continue until all rebel armies were destroyed, and each colony pacified. British critics questioned the rationale for the war, arguing that the empire existed for commerce, and that Americans would need to trade their raw materials for British manufactures whether they were independent or not. Why waste lives and money to keep an empire that was already too expensive?

Several times before surrender, the king's generals and ministers were ready to accept this logic, but King George refused to give up. His determination led to difficulties, for the old empire had largely depended on consent. Could an army restore consent by force? If it tried to woo the Americans with gentleness, the impact of force disappeared. If it punished them harshly, it alienated Loyalists and neutrals, and consent would never return. Could the empire survive a fight to preserve it?

This dilemma brought indecision and inconsistency to British policy. Generals could never make up their minds about where they wanted to be or what they wanted to do, marching endlessly around the country without ever making much progress. Officers often had contempt for all colonials, underestimating the enemy and neglecting their supporters. The treatment of occupied territory shifted from leniency to scorched earth and back again, leaving neutrals with the growing conviction that nothing would return to normal until the British left. Without a clearer idea of why they were in America and what they wanted to accomplish, it was always hard for the British to devise a winning strategy.

THE LOYALISTS

America's loyal population was a potential British advantage. Known as "Tories" and "traitors" to their enemies, the king's friends were a mixed group. At the highest level of government, royal governors and other officials deeply believed in the order, justice, and glory of the British Empire. While many leading merchants supported independence, others preferred their business connections to Britain. Some of the "better sort" feared that order, rank, and civility could not survive in republican society. Some ethnic groups did not trust the Anglo-Americans and counted on royal protection. Quakers and the German pacifist sects hated war on principle. Particularly in the South, some backcountry settlers distrusted the planter elite, and clung to the king when the gentry turned rebellious. Also in the South, thousands of slaves were potential enemies of revolutionary masters. All along the frontier, Indian tribes had more to fear from expanding colonists than from distant royalists

Many potential supporters had little interest in the principles of monarchy but might respond to tact and persuasion. Neutrals would live with either side. When diehards persisted, states levied heavy penalties on Loyalists, including extra taxation, confiscation of property, and even banishment for those who refused to swear oaths of allegiance to the new governments. In rough fractions, perhaps three-fifths of the American population truly supported independence, one fifth gave active support to the Crown, and the remainder showed varying degrees of neutrality.

The Course of War

For three years, revolutionary fighting centered in the middle Atlantic region, as successive British commanders pursued the Continentals through New Jersey and Pennsylvania. Americans also defeated a British invasion from Canada, an impressive victory with important diplomatic consequences. The war then shifted to the South, where a British offensive destabilized slavery and sparked fierce guerilla warfare but could not destroy its adversary. When Britain's weary army camped by the Chesapeake for resupply by sea, quick maneuvers by French and American forces trapped them at Yorktown, Virginia. Britain then conceded defeat and recognized American independence in 1783.

FIGHTING IN THE NORTH

After the fiasco at Bunker Hill, the ministry replaced General Thomas Gage with his subordinate, General Sir William Howe. Trapped in Boston for the winter of 1775–1776, Howe withdrew by sea to Nova Scotia and then decided to attack New York. Joining with an overland force from Canada, he planned to occupy the Hudson Valley, isolate New England, and choke the rebellion. In July 1776, Howe began landing 32,000 men, including 8,000 Hessians, on Staten Island. Marching from Boston in pursuit, the Continentals could not prevail when Howe attacked them on Long Island in late August. The Americans retreated to Manhattan and then to northern New Jersey, where Howe followed and defeated them whenever he made contact, but they always slipped away before suffering a deathblow. When Washington's army reached safety in Pennsylvania, Howe gave up the chase and returned to New York, leaving a Hessian garrison to hold Trenton, New Jersey. Then Washington turned the tables. Recrossing the Delaware River with a small force of 2,400 men, he surprised and captured the Hessians on December 26, 1776. The victory lifted American spirits and demonstrated that quick movements and clever escapes could preserve the Continental Army and its fragile revolution.

Britain resumed the offensive in the summer of 1777, but stumbled from miscommunication. In England, General John Burgoyne revived the idea of cutting off New England by seizing the Lake Champlain/Hudson River corridor from Canada to New York City. He won command of the march south from Canada while another force would come from Lake Erie to join him at Albany. Success depended on Howe's presence in New York City, but Howe did not hear about these plans and sailed his army to Philadelphia instead.

Washington could not prevent Howe's capture of Philadelphia, but the rest of the summer and fall went more successfully. An American force in New York's Mohawk River Valley repulsed the invasion from Lake Erie. Burgoyne descended from Canada and retook Fort Ticonderoga on Lake Champlain, but collapsed farther south at the Battle of Saratoga, and surrendered his entire army to General Horatio Gates in October 1777. Far away in Paris, the Saratoga victory proved American strength to the French government, leading to French recognition of the United States and a crucial French-American alliance.

To spend the approaching winter, Washington's army found a hilly, unpromising refuge called Valley Forge, Pennsylvania, which was easily defended but lacked convenient supplies of water, food, fodder, and most other necessities. While the British warmed themselves in Philadelphia, Washington's 11,000 men suffered bitterly for lack of food, clothing, and shelter. They were sure that neighboring farmers had plenty to eat and were selling ample supplies for British money, but like his British counterparts, Washington refused to seize supplies for fear of a backlash. There was no solution but to drill and suffer, and the soldiers did both until the spring of 1778, when General Sir Henry Clinton replaced William Howe as senior British commander and moved the army back to New York. Washington attacked his troops on the way, but could not halt their progress.

DIPLOMACY AND THE FRONTIER

The major land battles of the American War for Independence took place along the Atlantic seaboard, but conditions in Europe and the trans-Appalachian frontier both had major implications for its outcome. As early as 1775, the First Continental Congress had used agents to seek money and weapons in France and elsewhere in Europe. To the west, American settlers pressed continuously against the Indian lands, and Britain angered Americans when it responded with the Proclamation Line of 1763. With the outbreak of war, the United States pressed harder for European support, and the British recruited Indians to attack Americans from the rear.

Britain and France were traditional adversaries, and a chance to undermine Britain always appealed to French diplomats. In the Seven Years' War, Britain and Spain had taken France's American empire, so American independence could even the score by salving French pride and injuring British commerce. American merchants had long wanted to defy the Navigation Acts and trade directly with France, moreover, so a wartime partnership could interest both sides. Cooperation would not come easily, however. Louis XVI had no love of republican revolutions (he later lost his head in one) and Protestant Americans had deep-seated fears about French Catholicism.

After declaring independence, the Second Continental Congress named a commission headed by Benjamin Franklin to negotiate with France. Franklin was immediately popular in Paris as a plainspoken emblem of American simplicity, but his commission worked without success for nearly a year to win French recognition of the United States and entry into its war. When Americans proved their staying power at the Battle of Saratoga, King Louis and his advisors put caution aside, recognized American independence, and signed a treaty of alliance and a treaty of amity and commerce in February 1778. A few months later, France declared war on Britain and sent an army and navy to America. Eventually, France's ally Spain also declared war on Britain (without a formal treaty with the United States), giving additional support to the campaign for independence.

If France and the United States had common interests, so did the British and the Native Americans. French defeat in the Seven Years' War had cost the Indians an ally and encouraged American efforts to cross the mountains into the Ohio Valley. The intruders included squatters who built homes and farms without a legal title, and large-scale land speculators who would need legal authorization to resell plots to more cautious settlers. North Carolina hunter Daniel Boone served the Transylvania Company, which sought to buy most of modern Kentucky from the tribes who hunted there. In 1775, Boone defied the Proclamation Line and marked a trail that became known as the Wilderness Road, across the North Carolina mountains, through the Cumberland Gap, and into central Kentucky's lush bluegrass region, where he founded the town of Boonesborough.

Indians tried to take advantage of the colonial dispute to reverse such incursions. Armed by the British, the Cherokees attacked white settlements in what is now eastern Tennessee in 1776. Militia from the Carolinas, Georgia, and Virginia struck back hard, inflicting numerous casualties, and burning over 50 Cherokee towns along with their food, fields, and livestock. Most Cherokees sought peace in 1777 and surrendered their lands in South Carolina and much of Tennessee, but the Chickamauga band of Chief Dragging Canoe kept fighting until 1794.

Similar events unfolded among the Iroquois. In 1775, the Continental Congress had sought the neutrality of the Six Nations by assuring them, "This is a family quarrel between us and Old England. You Indians are not concerned in it." With longstanding ties to Britain, most Iroquois thought otherwise. Thayendanegea, a talented Mohawk chief and Anglican convert whom the English called Joseph Brant, had been educated among whites, visited Britain, and served as a British interpreter. His sister Molly Brant joined him in building ties between the British and the Iroquois. Joseph Brant led Indian fighters in damaging raids on western New York and Pennsylvania in 1779, but had no more lasting success than the Cherokees. In 1779, an American punitive expedition destroyed 40 Iroquois towns while their inhabitants sought shelter with the British at Fort Niagara. Shawnee and Delaware warriors likewise fought with the British in the Ohio country. Kentucky militia under General George Rogers Clark captured British posts in the future Illinois, but white Americans did not control most of the Trans-Appalachian West when fighting finally ended. Indians thus expected the British to protect their land claims in peace negotiations.

That moment was still distant when France declared war in 1778, but French and Spanish participation had major implications for the military struggle. War with France required the British to keep forces at home to prevent a cross-Channel invasion, leading some strategists to worry that British power was spread too thin to prevail. King George would not hear of defeat, however, so strategy changed again. Stalemated in the North, Britain fought in the South instead.

WAR IN THE SOUTH

British planners believed that southern Loyalists only waited for a chance to rally to the king. They also knew that southern slaves were potential allies who terrified their rebellious masters. General Clinton tested the potential of a southern campaign by sending a small force to Georgia in November 1778. They quickly captured Savannah and then the rest of Georgia, reestablishing a loyal legislature and the semblance of colonial rule. A year later, Clinton followed up with an attack on South Carolina. Sailing from New York, his expedition captured Charleston in May 1780 and fanned out across South Carolina. Clinton then returned to New York, leaving General Lord Charles Cornwallis in charge. The new commander scored a crucial victory at the Battle of Camden on August 16, 1780, when he smashed the American army of General Horatio Gates. Gates had been the hero of Saratoga three years earlier, but he and his men collapsed at Camden, running pell-mell from the British charge and apparently opening the South to full-scale occupation.

Cornwallis did find Loyalists in South Carolina. The state had embraced independence reluctantly in 1776, and some leaders still favored a cooperative or coordinate linkage with Britain. Severe class and sectional divisions split the whites and led some to side with Britain simply because their enemies supported the Continental Congress. Even some prominent Whigs concluded that British victory was inevitable, and either pledged allegiance to the Crown or accepted Clinton's invitation to lay down their arms without reprisals.

Cornwallis mustered sympathizers into Loyalist militias, but soon found their loyalty unreliable and their power to reestablish order even weaker. Wherever Loyalist units emerged, Whig militias formed nearby, and the two sides began robbing and butchering one another. British officers tended to treat all Americans as the enemy and plundered the property of Whigs and Loyalists alike, driving their victims to the Whig camp. Cornwallis decided that Clinton had been too lenient, and decreed that all defeated Whigs must not only stop fighting but give him active support, a decision that turned many sidelined Whigs against him. Militia units switched sides, sometimes more than once, and both armies faced gangs of bandits who killed and looted indiscriminately.

Social disruption badly undermined the occupation of South Carolina. Whig guerillas erupted everywhere behind Cornwallis's lines, attacking supply trains and isolated soldiers. British and Tory forces tried to intimidate their enemies with unsparing violence against prisoners, civilians, and private property, and Whigs retaliated in kind. At King's Mountain, for example, in October 1780, a party of "overmountain" men from what later became Tennessee surrounded and defeated a Loyalist force on the border of North and South Carolina but slaughtered many of their prisoners. "Such scenes of desolation, bloodshed and deliberate murder I never was a witness to before . . . !" exclaimed one Continental officer. "For want of civil government the bands of society are totally disunited, and the people, by copying the manners of the British, have become perfectly savage."

THE AFRICAN AMERICANS' WAR

African Americans recognized the War for Independence as an opportunity to find their own freedom, and weighed their options carefully. Like Solomon, the son of Venture Smith of Connecticut, a certain number of northern blacks fought for American independence, including about 150 free men of color at the Battle of Bunker Hill and eventually as many as 500 from Massachusetts alone. George Washington initially accepted blacks in the Continental Army but expelled them when white southerners objected. He slightly relented six weeks later, still closing his ranks to slaves but accepting free men of color. In 1777 and 1778, as many as one-fourth of Rhode Island's enslaved men of military age joined an almost all-black regiment when offered freedom at war's end, and fought successfully all the way to Yorktown.

Far more African Americans served the British. As early as 1774, Abigail Adams reported to her husband, John, that a number of enslaved Bostonians had conspired to fight for Governor Gage in exchange for arms and the promise of freedom. Lord Dunmore began to gather his Ethiopian Regiment a year later, and the scale of black support for the British soared when the war moved south in 1779.

British strategists had long seen slaves and Indians as potential allies who could attack the revolution from within. In January of 1775, the House of Commons had discussed emancipation as a means of "humbling the high aristocratic spirit of Virginia and the southern colonies," but the proposal only seems to have stiffened colonial resistance. When South Carolina's provincial congress heard the news that May, it added "the dread of instigated insurrections at home" to the news from Lexington and Concord as grounds "to drive an oppressed people to the use of arms." North Carolinians quickly echoed them and dispatched patrols "for the more effectually disarming and keeping the negroes in order." Jefferson likewise mentioned the alleged incitement of "merciless Indian Savages" as one of the causes that justified the Declaration of Independence.

Even as they recognized the potential uses of black allies, British leaders did not want to alienate slaveholding neutrals or Loyalists, much less to start a race war. A general assault on southern slavery was therefore unlikely, even if the British had favored it in principle. To encourage desertions, they decided to free the slaves who fled to them from rebel owners but to keep captured slaves as booty. The slaves of Loyalists would remain with their masters. Clear in theory, these distinctions proved difficult to maintain in practice.

Slave escapes subsided after Dunmore's defeat and withdrawal, but immediately began again with the invasion of Georgia in 1778. Throughout the South, both Whigs and Loyalists took thousands of slaves from their enemies, along with livestock, wagons, and food supplies. In the confusion, some black Georgians headed for British-held Florida, where Spain had sheltered runaways in the past. Others built maroon communities in swamps or forests, but more joined the British forces. Women and children joined the exodus, though in smaller numbers than men. So many escaped that commanders could not use them all, but many worked as laborers or servants, and some served in pioneer units building roads, bridges, and fortifications. Of Georgia's 15,000 slaves, as many as 5,000 escaped in the first three months of the invasion, joined by 5,000 more by war's end.

Escapes only multiplied when Cornwallis entered the Carolinas and Virginia. Well-versed in the paths and waterways of the low-country, black guides steered his troops to Charleston, and then up the main rivers into the piedmont. Desperate to avoid capture and to keep their human property, Whig planters scattered before the enemy and brought as many slaves as possible along with them. As in Georgia, those left behind could seek their freedom in Florida, in the woods, or with the invaders. A few fought in British uniforms. Anxious to preserve social order, British commanders put captured slaves to work on confiscated plantations, gave some to Loyalists to cover their losses, and sold some as personal property. Fighting back, Whig commanders assembled militia units by promising captured slaves as soldiers' pay or as enlistment bounties. Tragically, however, disease still raged in British ranks. Fugitive blacks got the worst food, clothing, and shelter available, so pestilence took thousands who had just grasped their liberty. Across the entire South, perhaps as many as 80,000–100,000 enslaved African Americans left their masters in the American Revolution, but only about 20,000 departed with the British in 1782. Of these, perhaps half found freedom in Canada or Africa and half faced re-enslavement in Florida or the West Indies. Faced with lashings, death, or sale if recaptured, a probable majority of southern slaves decided to remain in place, but the war had badly disrupted the institution of bondage.

VICTORY AND THE TREATY OF PARIS

Realizing that guerillas alone could not stop Cornwallis, Washington sent his ablest subordinate, General Nathanael Greene, to reconstitute the Continental Army in the South. Greene reached North Carolina in November 1780 and began to reassemble the army's fragments. By a series of bold maneuvers, he and his deputies drew Cornwallis out of South Carolina and into a wild goose chase across the interior of North Carolina, into Virginia, and back again. He paused for battle at Guilford Courthouse, North Carolina, in March 1781, and inflicted heavy casualties before another retreat. Cornwallis did not pursue him but marched his bloodied and exhausted troops to the North Carolina coast and pondered what to do. His withdrawal from Georgia and the Carolinas had ceded all the British gains of the past 15 months, leaving them with no more than a few southern ports. To complete this achievement, Greene turned away from Cornwallis to mop up remaining resistance in South Carolina.

Cornwallis rested briefly in the coastal town of Wilmington and then headed north. Hoping for a fresh start, he looked for a spot beside the Chesapeake where supplies could reach him by sea. In August 1781, he settled on the village of Yorktown, located on a peninsula formed by the York and James Rivers.

It was a fatal mistake. The French fleet sailed from the West Indies and closed the entrance to Chesapeake Bay. Washington slipped away from Clinton in New York, and sped his army south. With a French force under General Rochambeau, the allies sealed the neck of the York Peninsula in September 1781 and began bombarding the British camp. Hopelessly surrounded, Cornwallis accepted defeat within a month and surrendered his entire army of 7,000 men on October 19, 1781.

Yorktown did not end all fighting, for there were still strong British armies in New York, Charleston, Savannah, and elsewhere in North America, but Parliament had no more stomach for the contest. Lord North resigned and King George replaced him with the Marquess of Rockingham, who had managed repeal of the Stamp Act.

Rockingham agreed to peace, and the Continental Congress sent Benjamin Franklin, John Adams, and John Jay to Paris, where they slowly hammered out a settlement with their British counterparts. On November 30, 1782, over a year after Yorktown, the negotiators signed a preliminary agreement in which Britain recognized American independence and set the new nation's boundaries at the Canadian border, the Mississippi River, and the 31st parallel, north of Florida. Both sides promised to honor their prewar debts to the other, and the United States made an empty promise to request the state legislatures to return the confiscated property of Loyalists. Violating a promise to the northwestern tribes, Britain did not require Americans to recognize Indian claims in the Ohio country. "It was an act of cruelty and injustice that Christians *only* were capable of doing," tribal spokesmen protested, who now faced expansionist Americans with only token support from British Canada and Spanish Florida.

It took another year for France and Spain to work out their own differences with Britain, including the return of Florida to Spain, so the final treaty was not signed until September 3, 1783. When British vessels finally sailed from New York, Charleston, and Savannah, they carried over 30,000 white Loyalists and as many as 20,000 African Americans to new homes in Florida, Canada, Nova Scotia, and Sierra Leone, a British African colony for free blacks.

*

The American War for Independence had finally ended. Jubilant citizens celebrated with toasts, bonfires, parades, and public speeches. The war had cost thousands of lives: 6,824 American fighters fell in battle, diseases took another 10,000, and 8,500 died while prisoners of war. British losses were about the same, but the toll among escaped and captured slaves was far higher. Economic historians estimate that the United States spent as much as $400 million just to pay its troops, while Britain's costs may have reached £250 million. France and Spain also spent vast sums, and the costs of boycotts, property damage, and lost opportunities were proportionately high. To cover its costs, the United States had borrowed heavily from foreign governments and its own citizens; these creditors would now demand repayment from a struggling economy, while consumers borrowed more to regain what they had lost. The state and federal governments had also issued millions of dollars and pounds in paper money, which had largely lost its value, giving the new nation little hard currency with which to rebuild. At war's end, George Washington made a widely praised gesture of self-restraint by relinquishing power and resigning his commission. As he did so, citizens asked themselves anxiously if other Americans would always act so virtuously, especially in economic matters.

No one had planned for independence when colonial protests had begun, for the British had no desire to "enslave" the Americans and Americans felt genuine loyalty to Britain. Americans were deeply fearful of plots against their liberty, however, and after 1763, British steps to consolidate the empire seemed to follow a well-rehearsed script for the approach of despotism. Even if the colonists' fears were overblown, the centralization that British leaders wanted was incompatible with the degree of liberty and self-government that the colonists thought they deserved. The American gentry expected to govern their homelands, but Parliament wanted "to bind them in all cases whatsoever." These sets of expectations were fundamentally irreconcilable.

The American gentry did not win independence by themselves. The "better sort" had sought support from ordinary free Americans, and they had responded, both for the sake of their interests and their liberties. The war ended in 1783, but the revolution did not, for these Americans would demand a place in the republic that replaced British rule.

CHAPTER 6

A Federal Republic, 1783–1789

The evening of St. Patrick's Day 1784 was raucous in Charleston, South Carolina, especially in the tavern of Captain William Thompson, veteran of the recently concluded War of Independence. The local Society of the Sons of St. Patrick had assembled for its annual banquet, and news of the final peace treaty with Great Britain had just arrived. Cannons boomed in the harbor, revelers filled the streets, and American and Irish patriots crowded the tavern to toast the triumph of liberty and equality over British tyranny.

Unfortunately for Captain Thompson, the evening celebration touched off a quarrel with John Rutledge, former governor of South Carolina, current member of its legislature, future United States chief justice, and one of the low country's wealthiest and most powerful gentlemen. Rutledge was invited to the banquet but stayed home, sending a female slave with the excuse that he was ill. Upon returning, the messenger complained that William Thompson had ignored her. When her angry master demanded an explanation the next day, tempers flared, insults flew, and the feisty tavern keeper wound up in Charleston's jail, threatened with banishment for insulting the mighty John Rutledge and, through him, the dignity of the legislature itself.

Uncowed, William Thompson poured out his rage in a local newspaper. Sarcastically he claimed that the incident proved that "a *wretch* of no higher rank in the commonwealth than of Common-Citizen" could be attacked and humiliated by "those *self-exalted* characters, who affect to compose the *grand hierarchy* of the State . . . for having dared to dispute with a *John Rutledge*, or any of the NABOB *tribe*." According to Thompson, men like Rutledge were unfit for public leadership, for "their pride, influence, ambition, connections, wealth and political principles" were "calculated to subvert *Republicanism*."

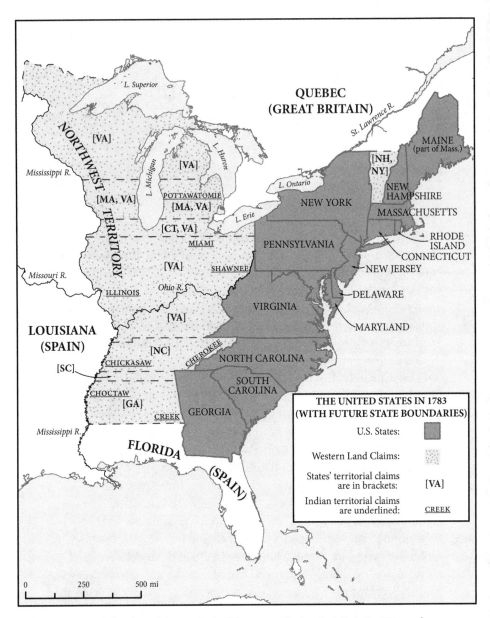

MAP 3. The borders of the new United States stretched to the Mississippi River when it gained independence in 1783. Eastern states eventually ceded their western land claims to the federal government, but Indians continued to inhabit parts of these territories until their expulsion in the 1830s and 1840s. Map by Gabriel Moss.

The St. Patrick's Day incident had erupted in an atmosphere of rising political tension in Charleston. In the years of pre-Revolutionary protest, white merchants and artisans had joined together in the Sons of Liberty. During the recent war, Governor John Rutledge had taken a hard line against Loyalists and British merchants. When peace returned, however, he and his equally powerful brothers Edward and Hugh wished to restore normal commerce. To promote the orderly sale and export of plantation products, they pressured the legislature to halt confiscations and allow British merchants to collect their debts and stay in business. Merchants and planters supported these measures, but the town's white artisans and shopkeepers opposed them bitterly, fearing that a wave of cheap British imports would rob them of the fruits of liberty. The Marine Anti-Britannic Society began protest meetings at William Thompson's City Tavern, infuriating gentlemen like the Rutledges who believed that their social inferiors had no understanding of the issues and no business challenging their wisdom. For them, the Revolution had unleashed an audacious and even dangerous challenge to civil order and gentry power. Determined to nip such insolence in the bud, John Rutledge surely welcomed the opportunity to silence his upstart critic with jail and banishment.

In the short term, Rutledge won out. The Marine Anti-Britannic Society defended Thompson "for his *spirited, manly*, and *patriotic* conduct . . . , when *Aristocratical principles* endeavored to subvert and destroy every *genuine idea* of real *republicanism*," but the planters proved more powerful. William Thompson was not legally banished, but he lost the gentry's business and then his lease. By 1785, he had disappeared from Charleston.

The Rutledge-Thompson quarrel raised crucial questions for republican society and government. How much "natural" inequality was tolerable in an egalitarian republic? How could the rights of ordinary men withstand the power of entrenched privilege? From the perspective of men like John Rutledge, the property rights of British merchants, the treaty obligations of the United States, and the orderly flow of international trade were all at risk from the ignorant and impertinent brawling of men like William Thompson and the Marine Anti-Britannic Society. If turbulent war and giddy rhetoric had distracted such men from a proper sense of subordination to their betters, they had to be taught a lesson both personally and politically. A private quarrel thus became a public controversy. Three years later, in 1787, John Rutledge joined with gentlemen from other states to write the

US Constitution, hoping that a new national government would provide even firmer lessons about the proper place of tavern politicians in a federal republic.

From the perspective of William Thompson, of course, America's future was in even more danger from the arrogance and presumption of those who still called themselves "the better sort." What did republican liberty mean if a patriotic citizen could be jailed for rebuking a public official? How could the people control their republic if the gentry stayed on top? When the new constitution was submitted for ratification by the states, many men like William Thompson would call for its defeat.

And what of the unnamed messenger, now forgotten in the midst of public controversy? William Thompson had asserted his liberty by claiming the right to bully a slave woman. How many other white men would define equality as their common right to abuse everyone else? What would happen to the legacy of independence if privileges based on race and gender replaced those of wealth and social class? By 1783, the War for Independence was over, but in the largest sense, the ongoing struggle over these and similar questions prolonged the American Revolution for at least the rest of the 1780s and possibly longer. The questions were not easy, and the early republic's answers would not endure, but wrestling with these issues absorbed the energies of the next generation and decisively affected the legacy of the American Revolution.

Revolution and American Society

Victorious Americans greeted the coming of peace with loud public rejoicing. Speeches, parades, sermons, and hymns of thanksgiving pealed forth in celebration of independence. "How wonderful, how gracious, how glorious has been the good hand of our God upon us," exulted the Reverend Ezra Stiles, preaching to the Connecticut state legislature, "in carrying us through so tremendous a warfare!" With much less solemnity, the citizens and gentlemen of New Bern, North Carolina, joined together in an uproarious victory celebration, in which everybody drank together and feasted on barbecued pork. "It is impossible to conceive without seeing it a more democratic assemblage," a foreign visitor marveled, "and one which fulfills to a greater extent what the poets and historians of ancient Greece tell us of similar events among those free people." Between the prayers and the toasts, a rough-edged poet captured a widely shared feeling that radiated the joy and optimism felt by thousands of Americans:

> With drums and trumpets sounding
> Liberty and joy abounding . . . ,
> The road's made plain, march on, march on,
> Huzza for peace and Washington.

Despite the joy and optimism brought on by the peace treaty, the road to the future was not quite as plain as the poet suggested. Perhaps the solemn warnings of ministers best captured the note of anxiety beneath the rejoicing. Drawing on the legacy of Puritanism, many preachers compared America to Israel, the favored nation of the Old Testament, only to remind their congregations of the special burdens imposed when republican principles were joined to a national covenant. "We cannot be a happy, unless we are a virtuous people," the Reverend Samuel McClintock warned the legislature of New Hampshire. "As virtue is the basis of republics, their existence depends upon it, and the moment that the people in general lose their virtue, and become venal and corrupt, they cease to be free." The struggle to define national virtue in the face of widespread social and economic diversity, and to devise social and political structures to maintain it, would become the foremost American task in the generation following independence.

GENTLE AND SIMPLE

The Revolution had unleashed far-reaching changes that undermined the existing rules for an orderly and well-organized society. The revolutionaries did not slaughter or expel a hated upper class, as the French, Russian, and Chinese Revolutions would later do, but the "revolution from below" had led to many incidents like the clash between William Thompson and John Rutledge. Americans struggled with new meanings for liberty and equality in state after state.

Writing his autobiography in 1794, at the age of 61, the Reverend Devereux Jarratt of Virginia described the social impact of the Revolution in a few vivid sentences. The son of a carpenter, Jarratt recalled that "we were accustomed to look upon, what were called *gentle folks*, as beings of a superior order. For my part, I was quite shy of *them*, and kept off at a humble distance. A *periwig*, in those days, was a distinguishing badge of *gentle folk*—and when I saw a man riding the road, near our house, with a wig on, it would so alarm my fears, and give me such a disagreeable feeling, that I dare say, I would run off, as if for my life. Such ideas of the difference between *gentle* and *simple*, were, I believe, universal among all of my rank and age."

Officially, at least, the Revolution had changed such customs. According to the Declaration of Independence, all white men were equal citizens, and freeborn carpenters could teach their children that a head of false hair was nothing to be afraid of. The aging Jarratt was not sure this was such a good thing, however. "In our high *republican times*," he lamented, "there is more leveling than ought to be, consistent with good government."

By 1794, when Jarratt wrote, most "gentle folk" who agreed with him were careful to conceal their opinions, particularly if they were men who aspired to public office. Except in a few places like Charleston, ordinary white men would no longer submit to the worst pretensions of self-styled gentlemen. Louis Otto, the French ambassador to the United States, captured the reality of most communities in 1786, when he informed his government that "although there are no nobles in America, there is a class of men denominated 'gentlemen,' who by reason of their wealth, their talents, their education, their families, or the offices they hold, aspire to a preeminence which the people refuse to grant them."

Distinctions of wealth and talent continued to exist in America, but republican leaders increasingly attributed their success to hard work and personal merit instead of birth and good breeding. Officers of the Continental Army outraged public opinion when they tried to create the Society of the Cincinnati as a hereditary association for themselves and their first-born sons. Samuel Adams called it "as rapid a Stride towards an hereditary Military Nobility as was ever made in so short a time," and George Washington was forced to disavow the effort. Instead, republican intellectuals like Thomas Jefferson insisted on the fundamental equality of men, and thoughtful yeomen and artisans like William Manning of Billerica, Massachusetts, denounced the "Difference of Interest Between those that Labour for a Living and those that git a Living without Bodily Labour." Social class distinctions would hardly vanish in post-Revolutionary America, but the shape of those distinctions would change significantly. Economic, political, and cultural leadership would diverge, so the wealthiest and best-educated men in a community would not always be its highest officeholders.

Accommodating the privileges of some with the supposed equality of many would become a major challenge for the new society.

BLACK AND FREE

White men were not the only ones affected by the promise of equality. Out of three million Americans counted by the first federal census in 1790, three-quarters of a million were black, and 60,000 were free. Most were creoles, that is, American-born. By contrast, Latin American and Caribbean slaves were more likely to be African, because they suffered higher death rates and masters regularly replaced them with new captives. Free blacks and creoles were likelier than new arrivals to have learned the language, skills, and customs of the surrounding white population.

The painful contradiction between American liberty and African bondage inspired a post-Revolutionary antislavery movement. Except for Georgia and South Carolina, the states slapped prohibitive taxes on the Atlantic slave trade. Vermont outlawed slavery altogether in its 1777 constitution. Massachusetts followed in 1781, when Quok Walker and Elizabeth Freeman sued for freedom on the grounds that the recently adopted state constitution had declared that "all men are born free and equal." Both won their cases in the lower courts, and Chief Justice William Cushing endorsed their argument two years later. New Hampshire judges agreed, and slavery began to crumble in both states. In 1780, Pennsylvania adopted a law that gave freedom to all slaves born after its passage when they reached the age of 28. Connecticut and Rhode Island took similar measures, followed by New York in 1799 and New Jersey in 1804. These statutes freed no living slaves, but only promised freedom to their unborn children. The end of slavery did not bring racial equality to the northern states, however, for law and custom continued to bar African Americans from voting, holding office, serving on juries, joining the militia, or worshiping equally in churches.

Even in the South, where slavery was deeply embedded in society and culture, freedom became more available. During the war, thousands of slaves had liberated themselves by escaping to British lines or other places where they passed for free. Chesapeake planters softened their stand on slavery when they shifted from tobacco to wheat, a crop that needed less labor. Virginia changed its laws to permit manumission, or the voluntary release of slaves, in 1782, and by 1790, all the southern states but South Carolina had followed suit. In his will, George Washington offered freedom to his own human chattels upon the death of his wife, Martha. When George died, Martha regained the slaves she had owned when she married him, and these she kept in bondage. Other masters emancipated their favorite individuals, some of whom they had fathered, or allowed slaves to purchase their freedom. Fed by northern abolition laws, self-purchases, manumissions, and escapes, America's free black community more than tripled in size, from 60,000 in 1790 to 186,000 in 1810.

Despite countless forms of discrimination, freedom opened new doors to this small but significant African American community. Restrictive laws and white prejudices barred them from schools, jobs, and equal citizenship, but many still forged ahead. Paul Cuffee of Massachusetts excelled as a sea captain, a prosperous community leader, and a pioneer in establishing African American settlement in Africa itself. After enslavement in Virginia, Philadelphia, and the Caribbean, Olaudah Equiano (or Gustavus Vassa, as he was also known) purchased his freedom, became a British antislavery activist, and published his autobiography, *The Interesting Narrative of the Life of Olaudah Equiano, or Gustavus Vassa, the African*. Benjamin Banneker, a Maryland land surveyor, published an almanac based on his own astronomical calculations, and used it to rebuke Thomas Jefferson's suggestions that Africans were inherently inferior to whites. Jefferson did not retract his libels, but he made an exception for Banneker by allowing him to participate in surveying the District of Columbia.

Free blacks poured energy and resources into new institutions for their own communities. In Philadelphia, Methodist convert Richard Allen established the Free African Society, a combined church and mutual aid association. Ordained by Methodist evangelist Francis Asbury, Allen later founded Philadelphia's Bethel African Methodist Episcopal (AME) Church and served as first bishop of the new AME denomination. A comparable movement in New York saw the formation of an AME Zion congregation in 1796, followed by a distinct AME Zion denomination. The first black Baptist church appeared in Savannah in 1779, followed by congregations in Virginia, Philadelphia, Boston, and New York. Initiated by Freemasons in the British Army, Prince Hall of Boston launched a black Masonic movement that became the African Grand Lodge of North America in 1791. A parallel movement led to the creation of private schools for black children and mutual aid societies for black workers, though educators often met stiff opposition in southern settings. By their hard-won success, these community institutions nourished a free black community that was hard-pressed by continued white hostility. In the years ahead, they would also offer space to support more dramatic efforts to liberate those who were still in bondage, from abolition campaigns to outright slave rebellions.

"REMEMBER THE LADIES"

Female supporters of American independence also used the post-Revolutionary generation to claim a new position in American society. During the years leading up to the war, women and men protested obnoxious taxes both publicly and privately, sometimes together and sometimes separately. Women of all ages and conditions increased their spinning and weaving in response to the boycott movement, and elite women raised funds and renounced luxuries that profited British merchants and supposedly sapped revolutionary virtue. Some followed the army in wartime, working as cooks, laundresses, or prostitutes. Rich and poor, those who stayed at home took on new tasks and responsibilities in the absence of men.

Like many revolutions, the American Revolution disturbed traditional thinking about the relations of men and women. One of the most vivid examples occurred in an exchange of letters between John Adams and his brilliant and spirited wife, Abigail. When John was in the Second Continental Congress, campaigning for American independence, Abigail wrote from their home in Braintree, Massachusetts. "In the new Code of Laws which I suppose it will be necessary for you to make," she remarked, "I desire you would remember the Ladies." Echoing the phrases male revolutionaries used about the British Crown, Abigail urged her husband "not [to] put such unlimited power into the hands of the Husbands. Remember all Men would be tyrants if they could." Adopting a playful tone that softened the gravity of the subject, she warned that "if perticular care and attention is not paid to the Laidies we are determined to foment a Rebellion, and will not hold ourselves bound by any Laws in which we have no voice, or Representation."

John and Abigail Adams shared a loving and respectful relationship, but Abigail's remarks cut too close for her husband's comfort. John protected his dignity by expanding on his wife's jesting tone. "As to your extraordinary Code of Laws," he replied, "I cannot but laugh." The revolutionaries had been accused of stirring up all kinds of social inferiors, from children to college students to Indians to Negroes—

and now women! "Depend upon it," he promised, "We know better than to repeal our Masculine systems," because "you know they are little more than Theory." In reality, he said, men's legal power over women was no match for women's emotional power over men; so men's loss of nominal authority "would completely subject us to the Despotism of the Peticoat."

For the most part, discussions of new political relationships between men and women went no further than John and Abigail Adams's edgy private banter. An exception came in New Jersey, whose early constitution conferred the ballot on "all free inhabitants" who met certain property requirements. Though wives could not own property, land-owning widows used this provision to claim the right to vote in the 1780s and continued to cast ballots until male legislators revoked the privilege in 1807.

Women who could not vote could still claim the role of republican motherhood. If the republic depended on civic virtue, women played a crucial public function by inculcating virtue in their sons and husbands. The republican mother should put aside flirtation, fashion, and gossip in favor of the moral and intellectual uplift of her children. She could not change her legal or political rights, but she could claim more public honor and respect than her colonial grandmother. More tangibly, she could claim the right to an education for herself so she could do the job of child-rearing properly. As educational reformer Benjamin Rush put it in 1787, "Our ladies should be qualified to a certain degree, by a peculiar and suitable education, to concur in instructing their sons in the principles of liberty and government."

Inspired by this ideal, post-Revolutionary Americans founded as many as 196 new women's seminaries and academies between 1790 and 1830. Increasingly, these schools offered the same curricula as the best male colleges. Though barred from government, female graduates sought to influence public opinion by joining reading circles, literary societies, and reform organizations, and by writing for publication. In the 1790s, newspaper essayist Judith Sargent Murray insisted that educated women must know how to earn their own livings if necessary, and they must have the psychological strength to make their way in the world without the constant protection of a man. In Murray's view, the ideal woman *should reverence herself.* More active agitation for gender equality would come in future generations, but the Revolutionary experience had left a mark on gender relations that would not disappear.

INDIANS AND FREEDOM

The Revolution dealt a harsh blow to eastern Native Americans. When European empires claimed the continent, tribes between the Appalachians and the Mississippi skillfully played the English, French, and Spanish against one another to defend their own independence, while still trading furs and deerskins for European products. Though France departed in 1763, Great Britain drew its Proclamation Line to protect trans-Appalachian Indians from American encroachment, and most of these tribes took Britain's side in the Revolution. The Americans never fully occupied their territory during the war, and Indians felt betrayed when the British surrendered it at war's end.

The diverse tribes of the Ohio Valley were largely united in their determination to keep their homes. Early inhabitants had been Shawnees, Miamis, Wyandots, and numerous smaller tribes, but retreating bands of Delawares and others had joined them from the East. The region's villages often contained multiple ethnic groups who were already changing their traditions to protect themselves from white domination. As refugees from the East, they had no desire to move again, and many had previously embraced the spiritual revival and pan-Indian vision preached by Neolin and Pontiac following the Seven Years' War. They would respond once again to calls for unified resistance when American ambitions collided with their own territorial claims.

East of the Ohio country, the Revolution fractured the once-powerful Iroquois confederacy of western New York. Chief Thayendanegea, also known as Joseph Brant, led the Iroquois in battles against the Americans, and brought them safely to British Canada when peace arrived. Soon afterward, Brant organized a multitribal alliance to keep Americans south of the Ohio. Britain initially encouraged the Northwest Indian Confederacy by supplying weapons and refusing to evacuate its forts in the Ohio country, until the cycle of skirmishes and revenge killings between Ohio Indians and white intruders from Kentucky finally broke into open warfare. On Brant's advice, the Iroquois did not participate in the ensuing war, but withdrew to small reservations in New York and Ontario.

Joseph Brant's southern counterpart was Alexander McGillivray, the son of a Creek mother and a Scottish trader who had received a British education in Charleston but fully embraced his Creek identity. Alternately courting the rival empires of Spain and the United

States, McGillivray won support from both while strengthening the Creek confederacy against local chiefs who were tempted to sell their lands piecemeal. Avoiding the fate of the Ohio Indians, McGillivray's maneuvers protected his people's independence for another generation, though internal disputes about relations with surrounding empires would ultimately undermine their solidarity. Skillful diplomacy by Brant, McGillivray, Dragging Canoe, and their compatriots forced the United States to abandon its plans to seize the lands of Indians unilaterally. Instead, the federal government acknowledged the tribes as sovereign nations, and promised that future land transfers would occur through treaties that were at least nominally voluntary. Though frequently violated in practice, these concessions would form the legal basis for future claims of Indian sovereignty.

Devising Republican Government

When royal government crumbled, the revolutionaries faced the immediate task of creating alternate institutions for their individual states, and the Continental Congress had already urged them to begin the process six weeks before the formal adoption of the Declaration of Independence. Connecticut and Rhode Island had been virtually self-governing before the war, and they continued under their earlier plans of government for some time afterward, but the former royal and proprietary colonies began to reorganize themselves in the midst of revolution. The process required the revolutionaries to devise new institutions for self-government and to rethink the relations between members of the same community. White men posed the first challenge, for they now expected some form of public equality to replace the older hierarchy of "gentle" and "simple," or the "better," "middling," and "lower" sorts.

More particularly, Americans divided over the practical meaning of "virtue." They knew in the abstract that republican virtue was a dedication to the common good over personal advantage. When there was no agreement on the common good, however, whose advantage should come first? Could a simple majority define the common good in every case? Was it possible for the majority to err? If so, what protections should exist for the minority, especially the minority who called themselves the "better sort" and controlled the most wealth? The practical meaning of "virtue" had crucial but hidden implications for the nature of equality and class privilege in the new America.

STATE CONSTITUTIONS AND GOVERNMENTS

Disgusted with monarchy, politically active Americans agreed that their new states must be republics, with written constitutions to limit their governments' lawful powers. Written in the summer of 1776, Virginia's constitution came first, and its structure became typical. It provided for a bicameral general assembly, elected annually and responsible for choosing state officers, including a largely powerless governor. The Virginia Declaration of Rights promised "that all men are by nature equally free and independent," but only "when they enter into a state of society," a provision intended to exclude the state's nearly 300,000 slaves. Other clauses protected frequent elections, trial by jury, and freedom of the press. Without disturbing the Anglican Church establishment, Article 16 promised "the free exercise of religion" but admonished Virginians "to practice Christian forbearance, love, and charity towards each other." Little changed at the local level, where county courts composed of permanently appointed magistrates continued to rule.

Virginians continued to agonize over the legal place of religion for another decade. Conservative planters thought the established Anglican Church, called the Protestant Episcopal Church after 1784, was essential to public order and morality. Ever since the Great Awakening, they had struggled to suppress dissenting sects and prevent them from diminishing the church's authority and their own. Baptists and other dissenters continued to protest, however, joined by Enlightenment figures like Thomas Jefferson and James Madison, who argued that religion was a strictly private matter that deserved no public funding. Following the war, some Virginians advocated a compromise that would distribute religious taxes according to the taxpayer's instructions, but support for complete disestablishment grew steadily. In 1786, the General Assembly agreed, and adopted Thomas Jefferson's Act for Establishing Religious Freedom. It began by declaring that "Almighty God hath created the mind free," then branded religious taxes as "sinful and tyrannical," and went on to affirm "that our civil rights have no dependence on our religious opinions any more than our opinions in physics or geometry." The act banned religious taxes, any establishment of religion, and any religious test for holding office, and became the model for future guarantees of religious freedom in the states and the federal government.

Reflecting the "revolution from below," many active citizens demanded state constitutions that expanded equality as well as liberty and that spread political power to a broader circle of citizens. In North Carolina, for example, backcountry residents wanted "a simple Democracy or as near it as possible," and warned their representatives to "oppose everything that leans to aristocracy or power in the hands of the rich and chief men exercised to the oppression of the poor." A New Hampshire pamphlet echoed the same sentiments: "The people best know their own wants and necessities and are therefore best able to rule themselves." Voters elsewhere were equally firm, but many in the "better sort" worried about unchecked popular power. In many respects, state and federal politics would reflect this fundamental tension for the next generation.

Pennsylvania did the most to meet the radicals' demands. In the spring of 1776, the Philadelphia militia had pressed successfully for a constitutional convention based on the votes of all male taxpayers who favored independence, not just the propertied elite. The gathered delegates included farmers, artisans, and shopkeepers from Pennsylvania's major white ethnic groups, with only a sprinkling of lawyers and businessmen. Their constitution gave almost all power to a single-chambered legislature that allowed no upper house for the wealthy, and provided for an executive committee instead of a governor armed with a veto. Annual elections and term limits clipped the power of legislators. The constitution guaranteed the vote to all male taxpayers and required that all laws and legislative debates be published and distributed for public consideration. The finished document horrified conservatives, who thought it meant mob rule, chaos, and the end of liberty. One called it "singular in its kind, confused, inconsistent, deficient in sense and grammar, and the ridicule of all America." Conflict over the Pennsylvania constitution continued until 1790, when the state abandoned it in favor of a more conventional framework featuring a bicameral assembly and a single governor.

Massachusetts had the most procedural difficulty in framing its new government, but made the greatest progress in constitutional theory. In most states, provincial congresses had written the new constitutions and implemented them without popular ratification. Massachusetts's voters spotted the error in this procedure, however. If a legislature could write its own constitution, no legislative action could ever be unconstitutional, and a parliamentary-style tyranny would return. Bay State towns called instead for a special convention to write a constitution, with members elected for that purpose alone. This process made a clear distinction between a constitution and a statute, and between sovereignty and normal legislative authority. In America, the people would be sovereign, not the king, the parliament, or the legislature, so only the people could write and approve a constitution. Once this constitution had established a legislature, the lawmakers could pass statutes or ordinary laws, but they could not amend the constitution or violate it. By making the state constitution a direct expression of the people's will, outside of and superior to ordinary law, Massachusetts established what became standard procedure for ensuring that lawmakers themselves were bound by the law. The process also allowed courts to void specific statutes as unconstitutional, regardless of their momentary popularity.

THE ARTICLES OF CONFEDERATION

America's leaders moved more slowly to create a national government, though everyone agreed that the "United Colonies" were a collective unit and not just a gaggle of separate republics. Congressmen realized that the United States would also need a written constitution and began to compose one in 1776, without following the elaborate procedures later devised by Massachusetts. The delegates immediately encountered a set of problems that would take more than a decade to resolve. Congress had originally given each state delegation one vote. Should that practice continue, giving tiny states the power to block action by those states that contained the majority of Americans, or should larger states have power commensurate with their populations? If power should depend on population, should slaves be counted, even though they possessed no political rights?

The question of western land proved equally vexatious. Several states claimed vast tracts of land beyond the mountains, with the official boundaries of Massachusetts, Connecticut, Georgia, and the Carolinas stretching to the Mississippi. Virginia claimed virtually all the land north of North Carolina and west of the mountains. States like Maryland and New Jersey had no such clauses in their colonial charters, and naturally worried that the larger states would eventually overwhelm them. Several smaller states also hoped that their own land speculators would stand a better chance if western lands were controlled by the central government. The larger states not only protected their own speculators against others, but they also wished to use their western lands to compensate their veterans and pay their public debts.

The quarrel over western lands was not only a debate over the equality of the states within the Union, but also a scramble among rival sets of creditors, land barons, and settler-soldiers.

In between more urgent matters, the Continental Congress struggled with these questions for more than a year, and finally produced the Articles of Confederation and Perpetual Union in November 1777. This document basically formalized the existing arrangement: each state could send between three and seven delegates to the Confederation Congress but only received one vote. A simple majority of seven states could make ordinary decisions, more important matters required nine states, and amendments to the Articles required approval from all thirteen state legislatures. The Confederation Congress had the power to conduct war and negotiate peace. It could borrow money and print currency, but it had no power to impose taxes or coerce any state or its citizens. There was no executive or judicial branch; congressmen expected state courts to enforce the laws and congressional committees to administer the government. Recalling the colonies' proposed alternative to the Stamp Act, the Articles allowed Congress to raise money by asking states for voluntary contributions, or requisitions, based on their land values.

Fearing domination by the others, many state legislatures were reluctant to approve the Articles of Confederation. Maryland held out the longest, insisting that its giant neighbor Virginia first surrender its vast western lands to Congress. In 1780, Virginia finally promised to do so, Maryland ratified, and the first United States constitution began to operate.

FINANCES AND FOREIGN AFFAIRS

The new government faced a serious economic crisis. The war had been very expensive, and Americans had borrowed to pay for much of it. Congress and the states owed back pay and pensions to their soldiers, and wartime loans were coming due to Dutch and French financiers. At the same time, the war had inflicted massive property damage, and Americans longed to restore their farms and businesses with foreign goods. British merchants obliged them with generous credit terms, and the result was a major postwar shopping spree, paid for by a dramatic increase in private debt.

Public and private debts to foreign lenders caught the United States in a web of economic and diplomatic entanglements. Americans needed to sell their products abroad to repay these public and private loans, but normal trade with Britain and its remaining colonies had ended with independence. Without treaties to open trade with other countries, Americans could not find alternate markets, and their commerce faced a serious crisis. The British were in no mood to negotiate, moreover, so long as the states refused to restore the property of Loyalists or require the repayment of prewar debts. Citing these grievances, Britain refused to fulfill its own treaty obligations to evacuate its Ohio Valley forts, with their dangerous potential for encouraging Indian warfare.

Staggering under its debts, the United States fell into a major economic depression between 1784 and 1789. Some historians estimate that the effects of war and depression cut the United States' gross domestic product by almost half between 1775 and 1790. Even if that figure is exaggerated, it is clear that the war had made Americans much poorer, and they paid very dearly for their independence and their principles.

The Confederation Congress struggled against its economic problems with little success. As early as 1781, superintendent of finance and Philadelphia financier Robert Morris had proposed an amendment to the Articles of Confederation that would authorize a 5 percent impost, or import tariff. Morris wanted the money to "fund" the national debt, or, in other words, to guarantee its interest payments with specifically dedicated taxes. When wealthy men could see that lending money to the United States brought a secure return, he reasoned, loans would be easy to obtain and certificates of government indebtedness would become so valuable that they would back up a national currency. Tiny Rhode Island vetoed this idea, fearing that federal taxes would ruin its foreign trade. Congress sought another impost in 1783, but New York refused this time, fearing the creation of a powerful central government. In the absence of a national impost or a common set of trade policies, moreover, each state began to impose its own regulations and taxes on trade, to the despair of those who thought uniform economic policies were essential to national unity. Surveying the confusion, Robert Morris resigned in disgust to become a private banker, but his bank failed, his fortune collapsed, and he ended his life in debtor's prison.

LAND POLICIES

The Confederation Congress had greater success with its land policies. Americans expected white settlement to spill over the mountains and fill their western territory with farms and towns. They assumed Native Americans would abandon the Middle Ground or vanish altogether, as so many tribes had already done in the East. Private speculators had been making purchases from Indian leaders since before the French and Indian War, and still continued to do so. Thousands of pioneer Americans had already moved into the area, many simply squatting, or settling on land without any legal title.

Congress faced two major questions over western lands and territories, in addition to the challenge of Indians. First, should the federal government keep tight control of the territories, administering them like colonies of the eastern states, or should it allow their settlers to govern themselves? Second, should the government sell territorial land for high prices to finance the national debt or other major projects, or should it keep prices low to benefit the pioneers? As chairman of a congressional committee on western lands in 1784, Thomas Jefferson wanted cheap land for self-governing settlers. More cautious congressmen worried that the frontier would need supervision to prevent anarchy and that the nation's most valuable asset must not be given away. Actual policies combined these two perspectives, but the tension between them continued to influence federal land policy throughout the nineteenth century.

The Land Ordinance of 1785 enacted Jefferson's recommendation of a rectangular survey for the West, dividing its forests and prairies into townships six miles square, each one containing 36 sections of one square mile, or 640 acres. This surveying system was extended into future land acquisitions, and it remained in force for the remainder of the period of federal land sales, creating the checkerboard landscape that dominates the West to this day. The act reserved the sixteenth section of each township to support schools, following Jefferson's conviction that republics require an educated populace. Disappointing Jefferson, however, Congress tried to fill its empty treasury by auctioning public land to private buyers, with a minimum price of one dollar per acre and a minimum purchase of 640 acres, far more than ordinary squatters could afford. When sales proved disappointing, Congress decided to sell a single tract of 1.5 million acres to a private group named the Ohio Company for one million dollars in devalued paper money. (Land claims by a different company of the same name had sparked the first skirmishes of the Seven Years' War.) The aggressive role of land speculators remained a controversial aspect of federal land policy for decades to come.

In the Northwest Ordinance of 1787, Congress created a government for the Northwest Territory, defined as the land between the Ohio River, the Mississippi River, and the Great Lakes, or the modern states of Ohio, Indiana, Illinois, and Michigan, plus much of Wisconsin and Minnesota. As its population grew, the territory could be subdivided into three to five smaller territories that would become new states fully equal to the old ones, not colonies ruled from a distance. Each would remain under congressional control until its population reached 5,000 adult men, who could then elect a territorial legislature. With a population of 60,000, the territory could summon its own convention to prepare a state constitution and apply for admission to the Union.

Reflecting Jefferson's thinking, the Northwest Ordinance prohibited slavery in the new territories, but did not emancipate the slaves of the settlers who were already there, and the true status of slavery in the Northwest Territory remained controversial for decades. No single ordinance covered all the region below the Ohio River, but slavery remained secure there. Kentucky split off from Virginia and joined the Union in 1792. Surrendered to Congress in 1789, North Carolina's western lands first became the Territory South of the Ohio River and soon the state of Tennessee. Western Georgia comprised most of the future states of Alabama and Mississippi. Congress mostly followed the precedent of the Northwest Ordinance in framing these governments, but implicitly divided the federal domain into free and slave territories at the Ohio. Despite its inefficiency in other areas, the Confederation Congress's land policy and its system for admitting new states endured.

The Northwest Ordinance opened the way for mass migration to the Ohio country. Army observers counted 177 boats with 2,689 passengers floating past the modern town of Marietta, Ohio, over an eight-month period in 1786-1787, later followed by 146 boats with 3,196 passengers and 308 boats with 6,320 passengers in 1788. In order to prosper, these migrants would need to trade with the outside world, and the Mississippi River was their natural highway to the sea. The United States claimed the Mississippi as its western boundary, but Spain controlled its lower portion, including the port of New Orleans. Through British agreements with Spain, colonial Americans had used New Orleans and the Mississippi freely, but lost those rights with independence. Seeking to curb the strength of a new rival, Spain now refused to open the river to Americans.

In 1785, Spain sent Don Diego de Gardoqui to negotiate with John Jay, American secretary for foreign affairs. Gardoqui refused to yield on the Mississippi question, but did offer other concessions. Sensing defeat, Jay asked if Congress would be willing to give up Mississippi commerce for 25 years in exchange for trade with Spain itself. Angry southerners immediately charged that Jay, a New Yorker, would sacrifice their interests in the West to benefit the East, and the proposed Jay-Gardoqui Treaty died in a storm of sectional outrage. The negotiations that should have added economic substance to congressional land policy only marked another failure of American diplomacy and another sign of the government's weakness.

Conflict in the States

As the national government struggled under the Articles of Confederation, the center of American public life shifted to the states. The Revolution had opened up state governments, and given opportunity to men who might never have won power in colonial days. These new leaders did not always sympathize with the problems of Congress, and viewed the common good from the perspective of their own local constituents. Citizens who longed for a more "continental" approach to American problems worried that the state governments were making matters worse.

DEFERENCE AND AMBITION

In some respects, the new state constitutions responded to popular demands that originated in the "revolution from below" that accompanied the War for Independence. They were far more open and permissive than the colonial governments had been, but fell short of later standards of democracy and equality. Most retained some property requirements for voting and holding office, most denied political rights to free blacks, and all subordinated women to men. They allowed dissenters to worship freely but often retained state-funded churches or religious tests for office holding. Property restrictions on political rights soon diminished or disappeared, however, or only applied to certain offices. If only one-half or two-thirds of free white men could vote in colonial days, at least three-quarters could do so after independence.

The new state governments were also less powerful than their colonial counterparts and more dependent on the popular will. Annual elections kept legislators closely attuned to the wishes of their constituents. Assemblies were much larger than before, with more representatives from western districts. Framers had hoped that members of the smaller upper houses would surpass those of the lower houses in age, wealth, and education, but little distinguished them in practice. Governors lacked the broad military and appointment powers of colonial chief executives, and if they had veto power, legislatures could override them. While the new state governments were not as democratic as they later became, they represented the free population more directly than their predecessors.

While opening the doors to wider participation in government, gentlemen revolutionaries still expected that grateful citizens would continue their deference to the "better sort." They agreed with Alexander Hamilton, for example, that urban workers would never turn the commercial elite out of office, for "they know that the merchant is their natural patron and friend." Unfortunately for Hamilton and his friends, Revolutionary politics turned out differently. Real plowmen and artisans won public office only rarely, but middling farmers, petty traders, successful mechanics, and ambitious country lawyers won elections in all the states. Many were like William Thompson, the captain and tavern keeper of Charleston, who served as a military officer and aspired to civilian leadership as well. Others had made sudden fortunes as military suppliers, purchasers of confiscated property, currency speculators, and the like, but they kept the outlooks of their original communities and occupations. They were also less educated, less well traveled, and less likely to have served in the Confederation Congress or the Continental Army (as distinct from their state militias), or to share other experiences that would change their perspectives beyond the common sense of their immediate neighbors. Modern historians have therefore called them localists in contrast to their more cosmopolitan opponents.

The localist representatives were much closer to ordinary white Americans than their predecessors and brought far more popular participation to American government than the original revolutionaries had ever wanted. They typically quoted the egalitarian rhetoric first voiced by the elite, and used it to demand more power than their superiors wanted to surrender. "The people," wailed Fisher Ames, a conservative leader from Massachusetts, "have turned against their teachers the doctrines which were inculcated in order to effect the late revolution."

Conscientious republicans did not object when ordinary men got ahead in life, but they also wanted the newly rich or prominent to acquire the education, taste, and manners of established gentlemen before they claimed the right to lead society. "To rise from the cellar to the senate house, would be an unnatural hoist," complained the Princeton-educated novelist Hugh Henry Brackenridge, after he lost an election to William Findley, a former weaver. "It would be a reversion of the order of things," he protested, but it seemed to be happening anyway. Instead of accepting mere equality, a Connecticut writer complained, ambitious Americans jostled for a little something extra to set them above their neighbors. "Every man wants to be a judge, a justice, a sheriff, a deputy, or something else which will bring him a little money," he fumed, "or what is better, a little authority." The gentry often charged that ambitious office seekers lacked virtue because they put their local or personal needs ahead of the elite's ideas of the common good. Localists replied that the wealthy would easily confuse their private interests with public benefits, and that majorities were more likely to recognize virtue than the privileged few.

ECONOMIC CONTROVERSIES

Localists and cosmopolitans clashed repeatedly over economic policy, beginning with the question of Loyalist property. Most states had punished Tories by confiscating their estates, but in the Treaty of Paris, Congress agreed to recommend an end to such policies. Many states refused, however, citing wartime outrages and the interests of struggling revolutionaries, so Britain retaliated by refusing to complete its own treaty obligations, including the evacuation of forts in the Ohio country. Popular majorities often approved harsh measures against Tories, shocking more conservative gentlemen who saw confiscation as wanton theft. Some fretted that if angry majorities could plunder the Tories, their own wealth might disappear next. More realistically, men like the Rutledge brothers of South Carolina hoped that improved relations with British merchants would restore Atlantic trade, and resented interference by those they saw as vengeful riffraff.

The question of debt and paper money was another source of controversy, and here the questions of virtue and class interest arose most powerfully. Some states responded to the economic crisis with stay laws, or statutes that restricted the rights of creditors to collect their debts. Hoping to make debts easier to pay, states also issued their own paper money, sometimes lending it to farmers on the security of their lands, or using it to pay state debts and accepting it for payment of taxes. Merchants accepted this money when it kept its value and served its purpose, but refused it when excessive currency issues brought runaway inflation. In the process, states discovered how hard it would be to address fiscal and monetary controversies without treating one class better than another.

UPHEAVAL IN NEW ENGLAND

Rhode Island had the worst experience with paper money. When inflation sapped the value of its notes, the legislature tried to restore them with a legal tender law that blocked the collection of a debt when the creditor refused payment in paper money. The law created a ludicrous situation in which debtors chased their creditors with offers of worthless currency. If the hapless creditor managed to escape, the debtor could discharge his obligation by depositing his bills with a state court. Rhode Island's disastrous experiment convinced merchants, lawyers, and other men of property that democracy would always undermine public virtue by tempting the many to rob the few. Their opinion spread widely in the press, giving Rhode Island a notorious reputation for recklessness and dishonesty.

Neighboring Massachusetts took the opposite approach. Heavily influenced by Boston creditors, the legislature decided to pay the public debt by raising taxes instead of printing money. Authorities hauled those who could not pay into court, often sent them to debtor's prison, and sometimes took their farms. Pressure grew so great in 1786 that Connecticut River Valley farmers repeated the actions of the Carolina Regulators from a generation earlier and formed mobs to close courts and prevent the seizure of property. They too called themselves Regulators. Authorities identified Daniel Shays, an insolvent farmer and former captain in the Continental Army, as the ringleader and dubbed the movement Shays's Rebellion, but Shays was only one of several important leaders. After several court closings, the climax came when 1,200 Regulators attempted to seize the federal armory in Springfield in January 1787 but fled before the defenders' artillery. Determined to preserve order and enforce the law, Governor James Bowdoin sent a militia of 3,000 volunteers who defeated and scattered the Regulators after a brief skirmish.

Men like Daniel Shays obviously questioned the virtue of public policies that enriched Boston creditors by ruining hard-working yeomen, but conservative officials were horrified. Suddenly, it seemed, men of the "revolution from below" had turned on their legitimate leaders and raised the prospect of a revolution gone mad. General Henry Knox misinformed George Washington that the protestors were "determined to annihilate all debts public and private and have agrarian laws" that would redistribute private property. Others warned of anarchy, the collapse of the republic, a return to the state of nature, a collapse into savagery. Such charges were absurd if taken literally, but they accurately reflected the fear that popular majorities were indeed unsuited for self-government. From their perspective, the real danger was that Massachusetts and other states could become like Rhode Island, where men like Shays ran the legislature, and laws threatened property more seriously than riots ever could. As Noah Webster put it, illegal disturbances were not as worrisome as "so many legal infractions of sacred right—so many public invasions of private property—so many wanton abuses of legislative powers!"

Reacting to the troubles in Rhode Island and Massachusetts, more and more thoughtful revolutionaries, not all of them conservatives in a narrow sense, began to doubt the unfettered wisdom or virtue of the voters, and to believe that democratic majorities in the states must somehow be restrained. In Philadelphia, humanitarian Benjamin Rush reflected that "in our opposition to monarchy, we forgot that the temple of tyranny has two doors. We bolted one of them by proper restraints; but we left the other open, by neglecting to guard against the effects of our own ignorance and licentiousness." In reality, the Massachusetts protests were not the fault of a weak central government. In their aftermath, however, men who had resisted modest measures to strengthen the Articles of Confederation began to reconsider. Most of them knew that simple repression was no solution to the problem of political conflict, whether in petty matters like the jailing of William Thompson or in grander events like the Massachusetts Regulator movement. They also realized that taxing foreign trade was the best way to pay the national debt, and that required the power to set uniform duties and regulations. After a long and painful struggle, the United States Constitution became their chosen remedy to these problems.

The Movement for a Stronger Union

Cosmopolitan Americans of the 1780s hoped that a stronger central government would right the new nation's finances and allow the commercial economy to recover. Firm national authority and a sound economy would enable the United States to hold its own with rival nations, expel the British from the Northwest, and subdue the Native Americans who vied to control it. Above all, the central government should restrain what the "continentally minded" saw as the follies and abuses of state governments. The task called for difficult wrangling and tedious negotiations, so creating the American Constitution would be the most challenging political exercise of the Revolutionary generation.

JAMES MADISON COMES FORWARD

Virginia's James Madison became the most influential leader of the movement to correct the problems of the Articles of Confederation. Like his friends Washington and Jefferson, Madison grew up in a respectable planter family. Unlike Jefferson, Madison was physically slight and painfully shy, and his intellectual interests did not embrace every field of learning but focused on history, government, and law. Showing early academic promise, Madison graduated from Princeton University (then called the College of New Jersey) in 1772 and returned to his father's estate in search of a career.

The young Virginian soon found his vocation in Revolutionary politics. He fought the Intolerable Acts on local committees, and then rose to the Governor's Council and the Continental Congress, all before turning 30. After the war, he served in Virginia's General Assembly and thought he saw how the self-interest, narrow-mindedness, and parochialism of his fellow lawmakers could repeatedly frustrate good government and the best interests of the whole Union. "How easily are base and selfish measures masked by pretexts of public good and apparent expediency," he later protested. "Individuals join without remorse in acts, against which their consciences would revolt if proposed to them under the like sanction, separately in their closets [i.e., in private]." Moving to the Confederation Congress, Madison witnessed the paralyzing weakness of the Confederation government, but also remembered the specific interests of Virginia and the need to protect local liberties. As he saw it, the problem was to devise a system of government that would strengthen the nation and curb the misbehavior of the states without crushing popular liberty or legitimate rights of the states—a system he would later call "partly national and partly federal." He began by persuading the Virginia legislature to invite representatives of all the states to meet at Annapolis, Maryland, to recommend a common set of commercial regulations.

Only five states attended the Annapolis Convention of September

1786, so the delegates issued a report on the weakness of the existing government and called for a larger convention at Philadelphia in May 1787. Madison then won the endorsement of the Virginia legislature and the Confederation Congress. He coaxed George Washington to lend his presence and his prestige, and Washington ultimately presided over the convention. One by one, all the states except Rhode Island agreed to meet, and 55 of America's most distinguished statesmen slowly converged on Philadelphia, the recent din of Shays's Rebellion still ringing in their ears.

DELEGATES TO THE FEDERAL CONVENTION

Almost all the men who attended the federal convention favored a stronger central government, for state leaders who opposed the idea showed little interest in coming. Patrick Henry said he "smelt a rat," and like-minded localists like Samuel Adams of Massachusetts and Richard Henry Lee of Virginia probably shared his suspicions. The Virginia delegation was one of the most distinguished, and included Washington, Madison, Governor Edmund Randolph, and George Mason, the principal author of Virginia's constitution and its Declaration of Rights. The aging Benjamin Franklin headed the Pennsylvania delegation, but active leadership fell to legal scholars James Wilson and Gouverneur Morris. John Dickinson joined them as a representative of Delaware, while John Rutledge, the autocratic Charlestonian, came from South Carolina. Other active delegates included Alexander Hamilton of New York, William Paterson of New Jersey, Roger Sherman of Connecticut, and Rufus King of Massachusetts. Missing were John Adams, minister to Great Britain, and Thomas Jefferson, minister to France.

Like Madison himself, who had put in long weary hours at the Confederation Congress, most delegates had significant "continental" experience that taught them to see American problems from a national instead of a local perspective. As a group, they firmly supported stronger government but also cherished the interests of their individual states, so agreement between them would not be easy.

THE VIRGINIA PLAN

Madison carefully prepared for the convention with thorough research in classical political theory, the history of ancient republics and confederacies, and the current politics of the states. The delegates were only authorized to suggest revisions to the Articles of Confederation, but Madison resolved to ask for something bigger, and when the convention agreed to deliberate in secret, he pressed for an entirely new frame of government.

The Virginian began by persuading his own delegation. He urged them to abandon the fundamental principle of the Articles, that the central government was simply a league in which each member state had a single vote and whose decisions only operated on the member governments rather than on the general population itself. In his view, the "one state, one vote" rule had given small states the power to frustrate the will of the majority, while the idea of a league of states made it impossible for a majority of the American people to take shape and assert themselves. In place of the Articles, Madison wanted a government derived from the whole American electorate, making laws to bind the people themselves instead of issuing recommendations to the state governments. In effect, his proposal would bring the concept of a single "American people" into legal existence for the first time, as distinct from the separate peoples of thirteen discordant states.

Going further, Madison proposed that the central government consist of three distinct branches—executive, legislative, and judicial—each with its own powers, but each with significant checks upon the powers of the others. His new congress would have wide-ranging authority, including the power to levy taxes, to regulate interstate and foreign commerce, and even to veto state legislation. To limit the power of small states, he wanted to distribute all the seats in the congress on the basis of population. When the Virginia delegation agreed to Madison's broad outline, Governor Edmund Randolph presented it to a startled convention in his opening speech, and the proposal became known as the Virginia Plan.

Discussion quickly revealed that some representatives thought the Virginia Plan went too far, especially in using population to allocate votes in both houses of the new congress. Still fearing that the possession of western lands would enable the larger states to monopolize wealth, population, and political power at the expense of the landless, William Paterson of New Jersey presented an alternative, the New Jersey Plan. His proposal kept the basic framework of the Articles of Confederation, including the unicameral congress based on "one state, one vote," but added executive and judicial branches and the power to legislate for states and individuals. When the New Jersey Plan failed to attract a majority, its supporters acquiesced in Virginia's overall frame-work, though they continued to contest the distribution of congressional seats on the basis of population.

SLAVERY AND REPRESENTATION

The convention divided more deeply over the question of slavery. Human bondage was dying north of Maryland, but African slaves composed a large portion of both population and property in the southern states, so how should these slaves be counted? Northern delegates argued that counting slaves like citizens would only inflate the power of their masters. Southerners replied that slaves were valuable property. As South Carolina's Charles Coatesworth Pinckney put it, "property in slaves should not be exposed to danger under a Government instituted for the protection of property," so masters deserved more seats to defend their property interests. The two sides reversed their arguments on the subject of taxation. Southerners did not want to count their slaves for tax purposes while northerners insisted they must. Though the delegates did not discuss the outright abolition of slavery, some wanted to ban the African slave trade to the United States. Pennsylvanian Gouverneur Morris was especially vehement, calling slavery a "nefarious institution" that contradicted "the most sacred laws of humanity" and blighted the economy wherever it flourished. Southerners would not budge, however, so the delegates allowed the slave trade to continue for another twenty years. Later on, Madison himself admitted, "The real difference of interests lay, not between the large and the small [states], but between the Northern and Southern states. The institution of slavery and its consequences formed the line of discrimination."

The question of representation nearly split the convention irreparably, but Roger Sherman of Connecticut suggested a compromise that eventually proved acceptable. He proposed to give each state two members of the upper house, or Senate, to be chosen by their state legislatures for terms of six years. Members of the lower house, or House of Representatives, would be allocated among the states by population and chosen by the voters for two-year terms. By design, short terms and direct election would keep the representatives closely attuned to popular opinion, while long terms and indirect election would insulate the senators from public pressure. The lower house would have exclusive power to initiate money bills, giving an upper hand to the more populous states in matters of taxation and finance. To determine population for the purposes of taxation and representation, Sherman employed a formula debated by the Confederation Congress, and apportioned each on the basis of all free persons and three-fifths of all "others." His three-fifths compromise thus gave special protection to the interests of slaveholders without using the word "slave" in the Constitution itself.

THREE BALANCED BRANCHES

Most delegates assumed that the new government would not be able to take any actions that were not explicitly authorized in the founding document, so they finished their work by spelling out the specific powers of each government branch. In a post tailor-made for George Washington, a single executive officer called the president would exercise unprecedented powers over war and peace, federal law enforcement, the final approval of legislation, and the overall direction of the government. Like senators, he would not be chosen by the voters directly, but by a special body called the Electoral College in which each state had as many members, or electors, as the combined number of its senators and congressmen. Each elector, or member of the Electoral College, would cast two votes; the majority winner became president, and the runner-up, vice president. Since a state's electoral vote depended on its number of congressional representatives, the three-fifths compromise also boosted the South's power in choosing the president. In the beginning, most state legislatures chose their electors but later passed the choice to their voters.

The Constitution's final draft also stripped state legislatures of their powers to issue paper money, pass legal tender laws, interfere with contracts, or impede the collection of debts. The federal government could suppress rebellions in the states, whether by slaves or by free insurgents like Daniel Shays. As further concessions to slaveholders, the Constitution declared that "No Person held to Service or Labour in one state" could gain freedom by escaping to another, once again avoiding the word "slave."

Congress would have exclusive power over interstate and international commerce, and its laws and treaties and the Constitution itself would be the "supreme Law of the Land." To avoid an excessive concentration of power, a series of checks and balances allowed each branch of the government to limit the powers of the others. The president could veto legislation, for example, but Congress could override him by a two-thirds vote. The president also had the power to negotiate treaties, but they would not go into effect until ratified by two-thirds of the Senate. Though the president was potentially quite powerful, Congress could impeach him and remove him from office for "Treason, Bribery, or other high Crimes and Misdemeanors." A loosely sketched judiciary branch, staffed by judges appointed by the president, confirmed by the Senate, and serving for life, would enforce the Constitution and the laws. Shrewd lawyers realized that the federal courts could thus invalidate state laws by declaring them unconstitutional. Madison never got the congressional veto over state legislation he wanted, but the power of judicial review, as it came to be called, became an almost equally powerful substitute. In effect, the proposed Constitution strictly limited the direct influence of voters on the government and settled almost all major controversies over debts, paper money, and national finances in favor of cosmopolitans over localists. Not surprisingly, its reception was controversial.

The convention adjourned on September 17, 1787, and submitted its work to the Confederation Congress. Thirty-nine delegates signed it, three refused, and the others went home early. The document proposed a new ratification procedure that reflected the ideas of sovereignty developed in the Massachusetts constitutional debate of 1780. Each state would choose a ratifying convention that was independent of its legislature. The Constitution would go into effect when nine of the thirteen states had ratified it, and the Confederation government would disappear. Without passing judgment on the new proposal, the Confederation Congress submitted it to the states, launching a sweeping national debate over ratification.

The Ratification Debate

Friends of the new Constitution quickly assumed the misleading name federalists, which suggested that their support for a federated government of separate states was stronger than it really was. This move left their opponents with the awkward and uninspiring label of antifederalists. Of the two sides, federalists enjoyed intellectual facility, enormous prestige, unity of purpose, and dominance of the press, while antifederalists were frequently isolated and disjointed, even from each other. Three leading federalists—James Madison, Alexander Hamilton, and John Jay—would use their advantages to the fullest in writing a brilliant set of essays that became known as *The Federalist Papers,* which expounded the Constitution's basic tenets and sought to convince doubters that the new government would not endanger liberty but protect it. The federalists triumphed, but the antifederalists won a supremely important concession. In the aftermath of victory, and almost as an afterthought, federalists agreed to mollify their defeated opponents by amending the Constitution to include a bill of rights.

FEDERALISTS AND ANTIFEDERALISTS

The debate between federalists and antifederalists featured two rival visions of the United States' future. Federalists looked forward to a strong and united republic in which the interests of average Americans were balanced and overseen by traditional leaders from the "better sort" of people. They were friendly to the needs of commerce, creditors, and economic development, and while they genuinely believed that the people must rule themselves, they also believed that popular majorities must be firmly guided by a well-trained and respected elite. More frankly elitist than most, Alexander Hamilton of New York had explicitly voiced their leanings in the convention. "All communities divide themselves into the few and the many," he declared. "The first are the rich and well born, the other the mass of the people. . . . Give to the first class a distinct, permanent share in the government . . . [and they] will ever maintain good government." Antifederalists accepted the idea of union, but they still believed that strong state governments were the only reliable protection for popular liberties. As one North Carolina antifederalist put it, "I know the necessity of a federal government, I therefore wish this was one in which our liberties and privileges were secured." Some antifederalists were locally distinguished members of the "better sort" who feared that more distant cosmopolitans would somehow displace them under the new order. Building on the "revolution from below," others were less prominent Americans who had found a way to influence their state governments but worried that the new central government would be too distant for them to master.

For many antifederalists, the struggle over the Constitution also resembled a replay of earlier English rivalries between the Court and the Country Parties. The federalists wanted to create a strong central government, or "court," that favored banking, commerce, and high taxes, while the antifederalists played the role of the "country" opposition, defending liberty and the blessings of a simple agricultural way of life. It is hard to reduce support or opposition to the Constitution to narrow economic interests, for men of greater or lesser property took both sides. In effect, however, William Thompson had known what he was talking about—the federalist leaders stood out for "their pride, influence, ambition, connections, wealth and political principles," while antifederalists were conspicuous for humbler qualities. In that broad sense, the debate over the Constitution was indeed a class struggle between aristocracy and democracy.

Federalist and antifederalist constituencies differed even more than their respective leaders, for federalist districts were much more likely to hug the economically advanced sections of the coast, while antifederalists predominated in the backcountry, except in the most remote frontier regions where inhabitants wanted a stronger government to protect them from the Indians. Within the different districts, however, distinct groups of citizens often saw their interests in similar ways and class lines were less sharply drawn. In coastal cities, merchant groups generally favored the Constitution, hoping that the new government could foster commerce, pay the national debt, and protect private property. Within the same communities, federalist artisans also supported the Constitution because they wanted tariff protection from British imports. In rural areas near navigable water, commercial farmers and planters joined their city neighbors in favor of the Constitution because they anticipated improved foreign trade. In the backcountry, however, prosperous community leaders were still locally minded and often led their neighbors in opposing ratification. Low voter turnout in the election of delegates to the ratification conventions suggests that many of the poorest voters were ill-informed about the issues and did not care strongly about the outcome.

Federalists began the ratification process with a few quick and easy victories in small states that could never hope to go it alone in a weakened union: Delaware (December 7, 1787), New Jersey (December 18, 1787), Georgia (January 2, 1788), and Connecticut (January 9, 1788). In Pennsylvania, a pro-federalist faction had perfected a political machine that hastened through the ratification process before the opposition had time to organize. Virginia and New York presented serious obstacles, however, for the new union could never function effectively without them both, and their conventions generated a long and serious debate about the Constitution's merits.

THE FEDERALIST PAPERS

New York City and the lower Hudson Valley were highly commercialized areas, but upstate counties were much less enthusiastic about a stronger union, and Governor George Clinton was a committed localist whose opposition had killed the second proposal for a congressional impost in 1783. In an effort to swing public opinion, Alexander Hamilton, John Jay, and James Madison joined forces to produce a series of 85 newspaper essays in favor of ratification, using the signature "Publius." Republished in book form, the essays became known as *The Federalist Papers*, and they are still recognized as the most eloquent and authoritative exposition of the US Constitution ever written. The authors discussed the Constitution's implications both large and small, but the most far-reaching arguments came in Madison's discussions of the new government's benefits, particularly in Federalist No. 10. Struggling with eighteenth-century political concepts to explore a new set of problems, Madison used these essays to explain how the US Constitution could restrain the unpropertied majority without creating a tyranny of the few.

Theorists had long assumed that republican government could only function in small homogeneous states. A large republic would either succumb to despotism, because it was more efficient, or be torn apart by faction, because its people were too diverse to agree. In Federalist No. 10, Madison pointed out that small size had not protected Rhode Island from factionalism, and suggested that a large republic might be safer than a small one. He began by defining "faction" in classic fashion, as a political group motivated by its own self-interest or passion instead of the common good. Significantly, a faction for Madison could even compose a majority of the electorate, so long as it was motivated by self-interest instead of virtue. His task was to show how a large, federated republic could prevent domination by a selfish majority.

Madison admitted that people could never abandon self-interest entirely, so the Constitution could never prevent the formation of factions, but only control their effects. In a large continental republic like America, he predicted, people would not divide neatly between the rich and the poor, or the few and the many, for social and economic diversity would ensure that no single interest could ever predominate. Representatives would come from relatively large districts where supporters of petty causes would suffer in comparison to the broad-

minded, well-traveled, well-connected, and cosmopolitan "fit characters" that Madison pinned his hopes on. Sent to join similar gentlemen
at a distant congress, these men would be more qualified to recognize
the general good and carry it out than narrow-minded demagogues.
And if some representatives lacked virtue themselves, Congress would
never approve their selfish projects because their factions would be
too small to command the majority.

Clearly recalling the Rhode Island experiment in paper money and
the eruption of the Massachusetts Regulators, Madison predicted
that the operation of the Constitution would frustrate any nationwide
movement for the "improper or wicked project[s]" so popular in the
states, including "a rage for paper money, for an abolition of debts, [or]
for an equal division of property." "In the extent and proper structure
of the Union," Federalist No. 10 concluded proudly, "we behold a Republican remedy for the diseases most incident to Republican Government."

Antifederalists understood Madison's logic but feared its consequences. Still thinking of a society divided between the many and
the few, they insisted that the Constitution was the product of a selfish minority. Like Madison, they realized that a national elite would
dominate all three branches of the government, but feared they could
never join it. "Unhappily for us," charged a North Carolina antifederalist, the federal officeholders "will have too much weight for us; they
will have friends in the government who will be inclined against us,
and thus we may be oppressed with impunity." Others worried that
traders would benefit more than subsistence farmers. As one federalist
groaned, "The common people have unhappily taken up the idea that
the system is formed for commerce and not for them." Like the British
ministry, which could not imagine how colonies and Parliament could
divide sovereignty between them, antifederalists also found it hard to
understand how two sets of authority could coexist in the same realm.
Either the states or the federal government must be supreme, they
reasoned, and the new Constitution would give all the advantages to
the latter. Drawing on classical republican theory, they reasoned that
the democratic branch of government must "represent" the people to
their "sovereigns," and even the US House of Representatives was too
distant and immobile for such purposes.

Here the federalists neatly turned the tables. Building on the constitutional experience of states like Massachusetts, they argued that
neither the state nor federal governments were sovereign in them-

selves, but both were creatures of the sovereign people. The people could delegate some powers to the states, some to the federal government, and retain others for themselves, making every government and every officer their "representative," state as well as federal. In this sense, the federal government would be just as republican as the states and equally protective of public liberty. By insisting that the US Constitution was as much a product of "we the people" as the smallest unit of local government, federalists deflected the argument that the new government was somehow antirepublican, while they helped legitimize an institution that was actually intended to resist popular influence. As an intellectual achievement, the Constitution was therefore both democratic and conservative at the same time.

A BILL OF RIGHTS

In the end, the outcome probably had more to do with political organizing than intellectual arguments, but the ideas discussed in *The Federalist Papers* and similar works did have a powerful impact on the ways Americans thought about their government. As the campaign proceeded, antifederalist opposition began to center on the absence of a bill of rights like the parliamentary statute that had limited royal power after the Glorious Revolution of 1688–1689 and similar features in the state constitutions. George Mason, who wrote Virginia's Declaration of Rights but left the federal convention disenchanted, led the campaign for a bill of rights. Federalists called this addition unnecessary, insisting that the federal government could never take actions that the Constitution did not authorize, including interference in matters like speech or religion. They worried instead that a list of explicitly protected freedoms would imply that unlisted rights were not protected. To win over doubtful delegates, Madison finally relented and promised to support a bill of rights after ratification, based on state suggestions for amendments. Reassured by this pledge, eleven states ratified the Constitution by the end of July 1788. The next challenge would be to implement the new document, and to test its meaning.

*

Scholars have often asked if the Revolution changed American society as much as it influenced its government. The Revolution did not overthrow the nation's social foundations, but its consequences for ordinary men and women were still profound. The abolition of northern slavery enabled free African Americans to strengthen their own communities and to lay the groundwork for a longer struggle against slavery in the South. Women still lacked political rights, but the rhetoric of liberty and virtue strengthened their demands for more education and expanded roles in their families and in public. For American Indians, the war destroyed old protective arrangements and forced new efforts to unify the tribes and protect Indian lands.

The Revolution made its greatest social changes among white men. The colonial gentry had not intended the rhetoric of liberty to empower their social inferiors, but the momentum of equality moved steadily in that direction. The electorate expanded and, as the clash between William Thompson and John Rutledge demonstrated, ordinary voters grew much less submissive to upper-class dominance. Many white men from the middling and lower classes increased their economic and political standing and won public offices they could never have gained before. In the state legislatures, they responded to economic crisis with measures that benefited their own constituents, but that in the view of cosmopolitan leaders, violated the rights of property and made national problems worse.

The movement to create a stronger central government arose in this turbulent social and political climate. Federalist leaders hoped that a powerful national legislature, controlled by wealthy, educated, and well-connected men like themselves, would rein in the states and balance liberty with their own version of order. Antifederalists hotly replied that the US Constitution would reverse equality and impose a cosmopolitan tyranny. James Madison replied that the United States would be too large and complex for any one group to dominate. Was he right? Could the American republic adopt a strong central government without crushing democratic localism? Put another way, could men like William Thompson live freely under a government designed by men like John Rutledge? On both sides, many Americans believed that the answer depended on how the new administration of George Washington would implement the new constitution.

CHAPTER 7

Federalists and Republicans, 1789–1815

John Adams and Thomas Jefferson were once great friends. They met in 1775, when both pushed reluctant members of the Second Continental Congress to support American independence. They worked together to prepare the Declaration of Independence, but Adams asked Jefferson to write its first draft because of his "happy talent for composition."

Leading the new republic drew Adams and Jefferson even closer. When the Confederation Congress sent them both to Europe as America's first diplomats, Adams called Jefferson "an old Friend . . . in whose Abilities and Steadiness I always found great Cause to confide." It was especially ironic in hindsight that he praised Jefferson's freedom from "Party Passions." And Jefferson felt just as warmly about Adams. "He is profound in his views, and accurate in his judgment," he told James Madison. Admitting to Adams's personal quirks, Jefferson still assured his fellow Virginian that Adams "is so amiable . . . that you will love him."

Foreign service kept Adams and Jefferson from attending the Philadelphia convention of 1787, and both had their criticisms of the Constitution it produced, but they both favored ratification. When George Washington took office as the nation's first president, they served his administration together—Adams as vice president and Jefferson as secretary of state.

By 1800, everything had changed. Adams was president by then and Jefferson was vice president, but Jefferson was seeking the nation's highest office himself to deny his old friend a second term. George Washington was dead and the national unity he symbolized seemed gone as well, shattered by bitter partisan warfare between Adams's Federalists and Jefferson's Democratic-Republicans. (The supporters

FIGURE 5. In 1798, hostility between congressional Federalists and Democratic-Republicans brought violence to the floor of Congress. American cartoon print filing series, Prints and Photographs Division, Library of Congress, LC-DIG-ppmsca-31832.

of ratification and the members of President Adams's political party shared a name but were not always the same people, so it is convenient to call the former "federalists" and the latter "Federalists.") As the party in power, Federalists were jailing their most vocal opponents, while undaunted party presses hurled invective back and forth. Democratic-Republicans described Federalist economic policies as "rapine, fraud, and plunder" carried on by "a system of speculation, fraud, and bankruptcy," while Federalists urged every voter to ask himself a simple question: "Shall I continue in allegiance to GOD — AND A RELIGIOUS PRESIDENT; Or impiously declare for JEFFERSON — AND NO GOD!!!" One newspaper concluded that "there is scarcely a possibility we shall escape a civil war."

Thomas Jefferson defeated Adams. A procedural quirk in the Electoral College left the election unresolved, however, so as the Constitution directs, the House of Representatives made the final decision, going through 36 fruitless ballots before finally deciding for Jefferson. John Adams was so embittered by defeat that he refused to attend his rival's swearing-in. On Inauguration Day, March 4, 1801, he boarded a public stagecoach at four o'clock in the morning and turned his back on the infant city of Washington, DC. Eleven years would pass before Adams and Jefferson could begin to repair their old friendship.

For the rest of his life, Thomas Jefferson referred to his victory as "the Revolution of 1800" and believed that the United States had narrowly escaped a return to monarchy. For all its explosive animosity, the election did see the nation's first free transfer of power from one party to another, and Jefferson stressed reconciliation as his term began. Yet the framers of the Constitution had not anticipated that popular votes or political parties would choose the president. The election's divisiveness was at least as remarkable as its peaceful resolution.

The election of 1800 might not have surprised observers of the state conventions that ratified the Constitution in 1787 and 1788. As they debated the new frame of government, federalists had denounced a spirit of anarchy and radical democracy apparently unleashed by the Revolution. Antifederalists shot back that the proposed Constitution would strangle the liberty of common citizens. Following ratification, probably no one but the deeply respected George Washington could have persuaded winners and losers to come together.

Washington's appeal to national unity did not endure. Rival visions of the future divided his administration and put Jefferson and Adams on opposite sides. Hostility spread from the administration to Congress and from there to the state legislatures and the voters themselves. Disputes over foreign policy made domestic divisions even worse, until Federalists and their newly organized rivals the Democratic-Republicans (often simply called Republicans) were at each other's throats. Despite some overheated predictions, however, civil war did not break out in 1800. While some of Jefferson's supporters had once been antifederalists, they had accepted the Constitution's framework, and determined not to overthrow their opponents but to outvote them.

Electoral rivalry allowed a mostly peaceful expression of deep-seated differences. Organized opposition checked the Federalists' most undemocratic impulses and ensured that the new government would not become the aristocratic tyranny that the antifederalists had feared. Instead of undermining the Constitution, Federalists and Republicans both praised it as a sacred charter, and each claimed to be its true champions. When the United States survived a second war with Great Britain between 1812 and 1815, constitutional government emerged much stronger than anyone could have predicted when George Washington took office.

Launching the Federal Republic

The air was heavy with anxiety on April 30, 1789, when George Washington stood on the balcony of Federal Hall in New York City to take his oath of office. The new president questioned his own abilities for the immense task ahead and reminded his fellow citizens that preserving "the sacred fire of liberty" now depended on "the experiment intrusted to the hands of the American people." Many in his audience undoubtedly shared his worries, but Washington inspired their confidence as he began to flesh out the Constitution's prescriptions.

CREATING PRECEDENTS

The new government began to form in 1788, as soon as nine states had ratified the Constitution. State legislatures chose their new senators and arranged for elections to the House of Representatives. Most also chose their presidential electors, but Pennsylvania and Maryland left this decision to the voters. George Washington was the electors' unanimous choice for president, and John Adams became vice president.

Congress followed the Confederation government by creating three departments for federal business. The Treasury was the largest, befitting the role of finances in the government's creation, and Washington asked his trusted aide Alexander Hamilton to lead it. Thomas Jefferson, minister to France, became secretary of state, and General Henry Knox of Massachusetts continued in his previous post as secretary of war. Washington sought regular advice from these officials, but they were not called the Cabinet until they started meeting as a group. An attorney general and a postmaster general completed the list of major appointments.

To establish respect for his office, Washington partly modeled his conduct on a king's. His journey to the inauguration resembled a royal procession, with endless ceremonies, speeches, toasts, banners, flowers, and anthems, and he later repeated the ritual in regional tours. He required visitors to come to him, did not return their calls, and held regular receptions, or levees, in royal style. An elegant coach with six matched horses and liveried attendants carried him through the streets. Not to be outdone, Congress spent its first month debating how the president should be addressed, with John Adams favoring "His Highness the President of the United States of America, and Defender of their Liberties." Despite his adoption of some royal trappings, Washington was relieved stern simplicity prevailed and Congress settled for "Mr. President."

The addition of a bill of rights to the Constitution remained as unfinished business from the ratification process. From his seat in the House of Representatives, James Madison carefully sifted the modifications that the state conventions had requested. Discarding all that curbed essential powers like taxation, he composed twelve amendments that mostly limited the federal government's power over individuals. Ten won state approval and became known as the Bill of Rights. The best-known features of the Bill of Rights guaranteed freedom of speech, freedom of the press, freedom of religion, the right to bear arms in state militias, trial by jury, and barriers against self-incrimination. In addition, the Tenth Amendment declared that "the powers not delegated to the United States by the constitution, nor prohibited to the states, are reserved to the states respectively, or to the people." This provision became and remained controversial, as Americans disputed how completely it limited the actions of the federal government. The Bill of Rights soothed the suspicions of North Carolina and Rhode Island, and they ratified the Constitution in 1789 and 1790 respectively.

The federal Bill of Rights did not restrict state governments at first. States freely violated the spirit of the First Amendment, silencing critics of slavery in the South, for example, and supporting established churches in New England. Federal courts did not apply the Bill of Rights to the states until the end of the nineteenth century.

The First Congress also established a system of federal courts, since the Constitution had only sketched the outlines of the judicial branch. The Judiciary Act of 1789 established thirteen district courts, two circuit courts above them, and a six-member Supreme Court. State courts were supposed to handle most federal cases, and each state retained its own body of law and legal traditions. The Judiciary Act did allow parties in state courts to appeal their cases to federal courts if they claimed that a federally protected right was at stake. This provision became crucially important, for it allowed the Supreme Court to rule on the constitutionality of state laws, eventually making the judiciary an immensely powerful branch of the federal government.

HAMILTON'S PLANS

The need for money had been an important reason for adopting the Constitution, and it remained a central problem. Congress quickly passed the 5 percent impost on imports that reformers had vainly sought from the Confederation. Together with some higher duties on specific products like distilled spirits and a tax on incoming ships based on their size, or tonnage, the impost finally gave the government some reliable revenue, payable in coined money, or specie.

Treasury Secretary Alexander Hamilton was responsible for the public debt. Unlike most of the founders, Hamilton was an outsider in American society who had been born out of wedlock in the West Indies. Charitable merchants discovered his talents as a clerk when he was in his teens and arranged for his education at King's College in New York, now Columbia University. During the Revolution, Hamilton left college for the army and distinguished himself as a field commander and staff officer for General Washington, and that record allowed him to marry into one of New York's leading business and political families and become a prominent attorney.

Hamilton was one America's strongest supporters of a privileged elite and a centralized state, who praised the British Crown and nobility and frankly doubted the effectiveness of republican government. He always thought the Constitution was too weak, calling it "a frail and worthless fabric" in 1802, but he fought for its ratification by coauthoring *The Federalist Papers* with James Madison and John Jay. To the best of his considerable ability, Alexander Hamilton worked all his life to raise America as a great urban and commercial empire, rivaling the strength and wealth of Europe's foremost kingdoms.

Hamilton used a series of reports to Congress to outline his plans for the nation's finances and economy. In January 1790, his "Report on the Public Credit" revived Robert Morris's earlier call for a funded public debt, guaranteed by the impost and new taxes on coffee, tea, and imported alcohol. He also wanted the federal government to assume, or promise to pay, the remaining war debts of all the states. The national debt already stood at $54 million and state obligations would add another $25 million, but Hamilton argued that they all had paid for independence so the whole nation should repay them.

Complicating these proposals, most state and federal IOUs no longer belonged to those who had first offered credit. Some of the original lenders were common soldiers who were paid with certificates instead of cash. Others were domestic or foreign investors who got bonds in exchange for large loans. Over time, many former soldiers had to sell their certificates for ready money, often for a small fraction of their face value. The purchasers would gain enormous windfalls at public expense if the debts were repaid at par, or face value, so many believed that speculators should get less than original lenders when the debts were repaid. Hamilton rejected this argument, insisting that the government must establish its credit by repaying all creditors at par.

Hamilton's larger vision reached further than his individual proposals. He believed that generous repayment would bring the government indispensable support from the bondholders, who included foreigners and some of the wealthiest and most powerful Americans. A fully funded debt would make federal bonds as valuable as money itself, moreover, so bonds could become collateral for new loans to support business expansion. Commercial farmers would benefit as cities grew and swelled demand for their products. Like the policies that provoked the Massachusetts Regulators, Hamilton's plan would tax ordinary Americans to reward a small number of financiers, but he thought the results would justify this sacrifice. If successful, his policies would use the national debt to leverage a prosperous future based on business, manufacturing, and trade, much as Sir Robert Walpole had done with the British national debt some seven decades earlier. When properly managed, he declared, "A public debt is a public blessing."

MADISON'S RESPONSE

James Madison rejected the ideas that lay behind funding and assumption. In Congress, he fought unsuccessfully against repaying second-hand certificates at par, and opposed assumption because Virginia and several other states had already repaid their own debts, and, more fundamentally, because he could not believe that debt was ever a "blessing." He was willing to compromise, however, and he and Hamilton reached agreement at a dinner arranged by Jefferson. Southerners wanted to locate the national capital on their own turf, especially on the Potomac River, a potential water highway to the West. When Hamilton conceded this point, Madison promised to find more votes for assumption and to minimize his own objections. This bargain moved the government from New York to Philadelphia for ten years, while the federal city of Washington, DC, began to rise from a Maryland swamp. Far removed from the commerce, culture, and pomp of big cities, rural patriots hoped that the new government would also escape the moral pollution of urban life.

Another of Hamilton's reports called for a Bank of the United States, modeled on the Bank of England, with a charter, or legal authorization, lasting 20 years and a capital of $20 million. The government would buy one-fifth of its shares and private investors would purchase the rest, using specie and the new federal bonds created by funding and assumption. The Bank would make loans to merchants in the form of paper notes they could exchange for specie and use to pay taxes, so these could circulate as a national currency. Merchants and businessmen would use their loans to expand operations and create new wealth. The Bank would also serve the government by holding its deposits, making payments, transferring funds, and selling or repaying its bonds. Like the Bank of England, the Bank of the United States would help make an agrarian economy more urban and commercial, and implement the goals of funding and assumption.

Not surprisingly, Madison opposed a national bank as well. He not only questioned its benefits but called it unconstitutional because the Constitution gave Congress no explicit power to charter a corporation. The charter passed anyway, but Washington sought constitutional advice before signing it. Hamilton countered Madison's arguments with an expansive interpretation of the Constitution that limited the force of the Tenth Amendment. He reminded the president that the Constitution permitted unspecified government actions that were "necessary and proper" to carry out its more explicit responsibilities, and claimed that Congress's power to create money, collect taxes, borrow funds, and pay expenses implied the power to create a bank to perform those functions.

Long after settling the Bank issue, Americans continued to debate Madison's and Hamilton's diverging views of the Constitution. Lawyers have called Madison's narrow definition of federal powers strict construction (i.e., interpretation) of the Constitution, and Hamilton's broader approach broad construction. Creating another precedent, Washington accepted Hamilton's reasoning and signed the bill chartering the Bank of the United States in February 1791.

Hamilton completed his economic proposals with reports calling for higher taxes on luxuries, especially distilled spirits, and direct subsidies and higher tariffs to encourage the growth of a manufacturing economy. His "Report on Manufactures" became a classic statement of the importance of industrial development for America's future. To raise more revenue, Congress did tax liquor (not realizing how unpopular that would be) and increased some tariffs, but did not subsidize industry as Hamilton recommended. Madison opposed Hamilton's "Report on Manufactures," but when he was president in 1816, Congress adopted its first protective tariff to encourage American industry.

Important differences in values and outlook inspired the debate between Madison and Hamilton. Unlike the New Yorker, Madison and his friend Jefferson were countrymen at heart, with no love for cities, no admiration of debt, grave suspicions of merchants, bankers, and financiers, and no desire for a society they dominated. Instead of regarding speculation as a normal business activity, they despised clever traders who snapped up securities for a song and redeemed them at par. Unlike Hamilton, they distrusted all things British and wanted more trade with France. They were not "antifederalists," for Jefferson supported the Constitution and Madison had done more to write and ratify it than virtually anyone. Once the Constitution was adopted, however, both men interpreted it more strictly than Hamilton, favoring limited government, dispersed power, and landed interests both large and small. Jefferson especially believed that yeoman farmers were the ideal republican citizens. "Those who labor in the earth are the chosen people of God, if ever he had a chosen people," he declared, "whose breasts he has made his peculiar deposit for substantial and genuine virtue." In short, Jefferson and Madison were the heirs of England's Country Party and believed that Hamilton's measures would destroy American liberty.

Unlike the two Virginians, Hamilton's career was entirely commercial, legal, and military. He had no ties to the landed gentry or to the customs of a particular place. His powerful personal ambitions were exclusively linked to the United States and its commerce, and he had no patience for limited government or the simple joys of farming. He thought America's weakness made ties to Britain inescapable, unless it used British methods to become a mighty empire. Like Walpole and his Court Party, Hamilton thought centralized government, high taxes, high finance, and a national bank would make America wealthy and powerful.

THE FIRST PARTY SYSTEM

Americans of the early republic associated the idea of "party" or "faction" with a small group working for its own interests, contrary to virtue and the common good. In *The Federalist Papers*, Madison and Hamilton had blamed factions for the problems of the 1780s and promised that the Constitution would cure them. To everyone's surprise and hurt, however, Madison and Hamilton introduced factional divisions themselves. When Madison could not defeat Hamilton's plans in Congress, Jefferson fought them in the Cabinet and urged the president to cast his veto. His unsuccessful efforts bred fierce personal hatred, until Hamilton regarded Jefferson as an ambitious demagogue and Jefferson accused Hamilton of plotting to restore monarchy. Seeing no other way to save the country from ruin, both organized their friends to fight their adversaries, and reluctantly created the nation's first, rudimentary, political parties.

Madison and Jefferson took the first steps. Consistent with their grassroots sympathies, their supporters called themselves "Democratic-Republicans," and sometimes just "Democrats" or "Republicans," insinuating that their enemies favored aristocracy or even monarchy. Hamilton's followers moved more slowly, first calling themselves "the friends of government," and later adopting "Federalist" to imply that they alone supported the Constitution. In fact, like Madison himself, many of the new Republicans had been dedicated federalists when the Constitution was adopted, and Hamilton's Federalists did not really want a king. (The modern Democratic Party descends from Jefferson's Republicans, while the modern Republican Party dates from the 1850s.)

To rally sympathizers around the country, Madison invited poet Philip Freneau to move to Philadelphia in 1791 and launch an anti-Hamilton newspaper. Jefferson supported Freneau with a job in the State Department, and the *National Gazette* soon brimmed with partisan attacks, charging, for example, that Hamilton's plans were "calculated to aggrandize the few and the wealthy, by oppressing the great body of the people . . . with unlimited impost and excise laws . . . copied from British statute books." Hamilton struck back in John Fenno's *Gazette of the United States*, accusing Republicans of anarchy, class warfare, and even treason.

Hating personal confrontation, Jefferson resigned from the Cabinet in 1793, followed by Hamilton in 1795, but both led their parties from retirement. Congress soon split into Federalist and Republican camps, and so did the electorate. Republicans took the lead in drumming up mass meetings, adopting slogans and resolutions, sponsoring party newspapers, and organizing party caucuses, or closed meetings, to nominate candidates for office. Admiring tradition and established order, Federalists hated these tactics but copied them halfheartedly to avoid defeat.

Generally speaking, Republicans and Federalists held opposing views on class and race that may appear paradoxical. Like William Thompson in his 1784 quarrel with John Rutledge of Charleston, Jeffersonians favored equality for all white men, but they were less likely to grant equality to nonwhites and usually accepted slavery. By contrast, Federalists took social class ranking for granted. Hamilton had hailed government by the "rich and well born" in the Constitutional Convention, and his fellow New York Federalist John Jay often declared that "the people who own the country ought to govern it." Many northern Federalists disapproved of slavery, without endorsing full racial equality. Though Jay owned several slaves himself and so did Hamilton's in-laws, for example, both were founding members of the New-York Society for Promoting the Manumission of Slaves.

The paradox arose because Republicans usually saw citizenship as an all-or-nothing proposition. For them, "half equality" was meaningless, so an individual either had full civic rights or none at all. Republicans thus condemned anything less than complete political equality for all white men as "aristocracy" but imposed inequality on nonwhite men and all women. Federalists had a more traditional view, however, and saw society as an extended hierarchy based on multiple factors like race, property, and culture, with different rights and duties at each level. The established gentry took first place, and respectable blacks fell below middling whites but above white paupers. Federalist lawmakers could thus oppose slavery and support property requirements for voting by blacks and whites alike, while Republicans usually would not.

The parties' policy differences clearly resonated with their positons on class and race. Jefferson and Hamilton had originally divided over economic measures that pitted northeastern urban and commercial interests against southern and western farmers. These differences inevitably implicated slavery, for agrarian Republicans' policies drew planters and yeomen together, while everyone seemed to assume that slavery and Federalist-style development were incompatible. Both sides were also well aware that the Constitution's three-fifths clause bolstered the electoral power of southern Republicans and penalized northern Federalists. Slavery itself was usually not an explicit issue between Federalists and Republicans, but it hovered behind their other disputes. When issues related to slavery did appear, southern Republicans defended the institution more often than northern Federalists.

Not surprisingly, the parties drew most of their votes from different sections of society. Support for commerce and shipping made Federalists especially popular among merchants and city dwellers and commercializing farmers in the rural Northeast. Federalists also attracted the traditional gentry, including some planters like George Washington and the Rutledges of South Carolina. New England's religious establishment supported Federalists as defenders of tradition, but Baptists and other dissenters favored the religious liberties offered by Republicans. With a few holdouts in the tidewater and low country, most southern planters supported the Republican party of their fellow slaveholders Jefferson and Madison. Since the aftermath of Bacon's Rebellion, they had benefited from the trend toward white equality and racism that Republicans favored, and they also came to realize that small, weak government would be safer for slavery and agriculture. The Republican pledge of equality also attracted white artisans and yeoman farmers, especially in the middle states and the southern backcountry, and wealthy men who rose from humble origins.

Historians have called the rivalry of Federalists and Republicans America's First Party System, but these parties were still rudimentary. They were not as well defined or well organized as their later counterparts, and none of their participants accepted party competition as a normal or beneficial aspect of free government. Jefferson compared Republicans and Federalists to "the parties of honest men and rogues, into which every country is divided," and his Federalist opponents thought likewise. Both looked forward to the day when their party enemies would be vanquished entirely, and polite consensus could return, but party competition became permanent, and gradually reduced more irregular forms of dissent like mob violence.

Trials of Strength

Washington's administration soon faced challenges that sharply tested its authority. In 1789, a revolution broke out in France that ignited war in Europe and led to attacks on American commerce. To the west,

Britain still encouraged Indian attacks from its Ohio forts. The tax on liquor aroused furious and violent opposition. The challenges were so severe that party leaders suspected their opponents of conspiring with the nation's enemies and wondered if the government would survive.

THE FRENCH REVOLUTION AND
AMERICAN DIPLOMACY

Just as the Washington administration began in 1789, French revolutionaries overthrew the absolute monarchy of King Louis XVI and launched a radical transformation of French society and government. Most Americans were pleased at first and hoped that their own republican example would spread across Europe. The French Revolution horrified Europe's conservatives, however, and Britain was soon leading other powers in a war to restore the "Old Regime." When the king sided with his nation's enemies, revolutionaries beheaded him and his wife, Queen Marie-Antoinette, and proclaimed France a republic. Inspired by the Enlightenment's cult of reason and deism, they also attacked the Catholic Church for defending the old order with what they called "superstitions." These events unleashed a storm that swept the Atlantic world for most of the next generation.

Federalists quickly turned against the French Revolution and its violent assaults on established society and religion. Republicans were more sympathetic, for they prided themselves on support for class equality and opposition to conservative traditions. They also remembered French support for American independence and hated to imitate Britain. Jefferson was so enthusiastic that he forgave the revolution's excesses and later claimed that "rather than it should have failed, I would have seen half the earth desolated." To celebrate equality in both republics, supporters formed Democratic-Republican Societies that reminded Federalists of France's revolutionary Jacobin Clubs.

Attacked in Europe, France dispatched Citizen Edmond-Charles Genêt to seek assistance from its old American ally, but the clumsy emissary threatened to drag the United States into war by licensing and equipping privateers, or armed private vessels, to attack British shipping. Unwilling to risk America's existence for France, Washington issued a Proclamation of Neutrality in 1793. Genêt would not accept this decision and kept recruiting supporters, warmly courting the Democratic-Republican Societies, and hinting at Washington's overthrow. The infuriated president demanded Genêt's recall, and the

Genêt Affair convinced Federalists that French revolutionaries could never be trusted. Soon afterward, Genêt's party fell from power in France, and he only escaped the guillotine by staying in America as a private citizen.

WESTERN AND ATLANTIC CHALLENGES

The Washington administration juggled two military conflicts as it contended with Citizen Genêt—both involving Britain. To the west, Britain had surrendered its claims on the Ohio country at the end of the American Revolution and, contrary to its promises, failed to defend Indian interests in the peace treaty. It had not abandoned its forts and trading posts in the area, however, and used them to encourage Indian resistance to American expansion. From the Indians' perspective, the American Revolution had not been a principled fight for liberty but another imperial war much like the Seven Years' War and its predecessors. In both cases, the victors threatened Indian lands and autonomy. After the British defeat at Yorktown, therefore, Miami chief Little Turtle, Shawnee chief Blue Jacket, and Iroquois leader Joseph Brant followed the previous example of Pontiac and organized what whites called the Northwest Confederacy to maintain control of the Ohio country. Though Brant eschewed warfare, Little Turtle and Blue Jacket led 1,000 Indian fighters in 1791 against an equal number of Americans commanded by General Arthur St. Clair. In a breathtaking victory that shocked and angered George Washington, the Indians prevailed overwhelmingly, killing or wounding all but 24 of St. Clair's men. St. Clair's Defeat, or the Battle of the Wabash, was the biggest defeat that American forces ever suffered at the hands of Native Americans.

It took the Washington administration two years to recruit and train another army, the 2,000-man United States Legion, commanded by General Anthony "Mad Anthony" Wayne. Their forces met in 1794 at the Battle of Fallen Timbers, and this time, the Americans prevailed against a body of 1,500 Shawnees, Delawares, Miamis, Wyandots, Ojibwas, Ottawas, Potawatomis, and Mingos, plus a detachment of white Canadians. In 1795, the chiefs of the Northwest Confederacy surrendered most of modern Ohio and parts of Indiana and Illinois at the Treaty of Greenville. White settlement of the ceded territory soon surged ahead, governed by the provisions of the Northwest Ordinance.

The Chickamaugas, a breakaway band of Cherokees, conducted a parallel fight against white expansion in the South. Led by Dragging Canoe, the Chickamaugas had not joined the Cherokee surrender that followed white attacks in 1776 and 1777, but retreated west to new towns along the Tennessee River. When militia commanded by Colonel John Sevier destroyed those settlements in 1782, Dragging Canoe again led the Chickamaugas to safety and then launched a series of raids all along the trans-Appalachian frontier from Tennessee to Indiana. He helped organize the Northwest Confederacy and also allied with the Creeks under Alexander McGillivray. After his death in 1792, Chickamauga raids continued through the 1790s.

Overlapping with the Indian war, Britain and France still attempted to block each other's foreign trade and subjected the United States to assaults from both sides. America's commercial economy had long depended on Atlantic commerce, and American merchants and shipowners did extensive business with both belligerents, but British seizures of American ships were more serious and demanded effective response. Finally, Americans had never repaid their pre-Revolutionary debts to the British, while Britain still discriminated against American products and refused to pay for slaves who had escaped with them in the War for Independence. When a British crackdown in the French Caribbean seized some 250 American ships in 1793, furious Republicans called for war, but President Washington sent Chief Justice John Jay to Britain to settle these outstanding differences.

In 1795, Jay came back with a treaty that averted war but kept America's economy tied to Britain's. In it, Britain agreed to pay for the ships it had seized, to vacate its western forts, and to give the United States limited trading rights with its Caribbean colonies. In return, the United States gave Britain "most favored nation" status, which gave Britain the best available terms in trading with Americans. The United States also agreed to pay its citizens' pre-Revolutionary debts to Britain. The treaty did not acknowledge Americans' right to trade with France or compensate masters for runaway slaves. General Wayne's defeat of Little Turtle and Blue Jacket probably played an important role in the outcome, for Britain might otherwise have kept its northwest forts and continued to support its Indian allies.

Jay had done his best with a weak hand, but his treaty enraged Republicans. In their eyes, any agreement with England implied American humiliation and betrayal of France, while southerners still resented the loss of slave property. Federalists replied that the treaty's commercial advantages outweighed its defects. While the Senate debated in secret, party presses teemed with abuse and mass meetings burned Jay in effigy. A typical blast came from the youthful Andrew Jackson, still a political unknown in Tennessee. Instead of ratifying the treaty, he snarled, Congress should "have the insulting cringing and ignominious Child of aristocratic Secracy removed Erased and obliterated from the archives of the Grand republick of the United States." Such reactions did not block the Senate's ratification or even the House's vote for implementation funds. They did bring Federalist and Republican doctrines to thousands of ordinary citizens and carried party rivalry from the Congress to the streets. The "people out of doors" had not spoken so loudly since the era of the Revolution.

A second treaty pleased Republicans more, especially in the South and West. Settlers there had long complained that Spanish control of the Mississippi blocked their access to the outside world, and muttered threats of secession unless conditions improved. When Britain agreed to leave the Northwest, Spain retreated as well. A 1795 treaty negotiated by Thomas Pinckney of South Carolina accepted a Florida border at the 31st parallel, allowed free navigation of the Mississippi, and granted the right of deposit, or duty-free storage of goods, at New Orleans.

Domestic protest also tried the government's authority. Congress had raised more revenue for funding and assumption with an excise tax on distilled liquor. The tax angered Scots-Irish settlers in the backcountry who turned their surplus corn into fiery whiskey that accompanied every male activity from business deals to haymaking. Easier to transport than corn itself, whiskey was important to local and long-distance trade, and the tax weighed heaviest on small producers. Republican editors and officeholders fanned the flames of western anger, cursing Hamilton's excise and linking it to Walpole-style corruption and extravagance.

WASHINGTON'S FAREWELL

Complaints were loudest in western Pennsylvania, where antifederalism had been strong, shippers clamored for an open Mississippi, and farmers often distilled their corn into whiskey to export it. In what came to be called the Whiskey Rebellion, irate frontier farmers there treated the liquor tax like the Stamp Act, responding to a 1794 enforcement crackdown by closing local courts and burning the home of their chief revenue agent. As violence escalated, Washington blamed the Democratic-Republican Societies for inciting defiance, and concluded that the federal government must assert its authority or surrender to another Regulator movement. In September 1794, he summoned state militia and personally led a 13,000-man army into western Pennsylvania. Resistance was already waning as alarmed Republican officeholders reminded constituents that the excise was a case of taxation *with* representation, so it must be obeyed until repealed. Military occupation demonstrated the government's authority, and Washington pardoned the only two defendants convicted of treason. Still resenting organized opposition, Washington denounced "self-created societies" in his next message to Congress, an obvious thrust at the Democratic-Republican Societies.

George Washington's election as first president had been taken for granted by everyone. He reluctantly accepted a second term, but Citizen Genêt, the Democratic-Republican Societies, protests of Jay's Treaty, and the Whiskey Rebellion had all tested his reliance on deference and consensus. As a Virginia planter, Washington might have sympathized with Madison and Jefferson, but he shared the Federalists' love of order and increasingly distrusted Republicans as demagogic and irresponsible. As the end of his second term approached, Washington resolved to leave office and return to his beloved Mount Vernon. Before leaving, he tried once more to calm the partisan storm he left behind.

Ghostwritten by Hamilton, Washington's Farewell Address was not a speech but a newspaper essay, published in September 1796. In it, the Founding Father begged Americans to abandon "the baneful effects of the spirit of party," warning that its disruptions could drive them to a despot for the sake of peace. Washington also worried that foreign attachments could lead patriots astray, so he advised Americans to trade with all nations but ally with none. "The great rule of conduct for us in regard to foreign nations," he warned, "is in extending our commercial relations, to have with them as little political connection as possible." As he called for unity and neutrality, however, Washington clearly broke his own rules to favor a Federalist consensus at home and British friendship abroad. His advice proved impossible to follow, both in the 1790s and later, but his criticisms of parties and foreign alliances continued to resonate in American civic culture.

John Adams and Party Conflict

In 1796, Federalists supported Vice President John Adams to succeed George Washington while Republicans endorsed Thomas Jefferson. The canvass was quiet, the candidates did not campaign actively, and legislatures chose most of the electors. Reflecting sectional divisions, Federalists won the Northeast while Republicans captured Pennsylvania and most of the slave states. The Constitution had not anticipated party divisions, however, and gave the presidency to the majority winner in the Electoral College and the vice presidency to the runner-up. This awkward arrangement made Adams the president and his bitter rival, Jefferson, the vice president. The government was divided, international conditions deteriorated, and party hostility intensified. Adams wanted to rise above party like Washington, but he lacked his predecessor's stature, pleased almost nobody, and angered zealots on both sides.

THE QUASI-WAR AND REPUBLICAN DISSENT

Foreign affairs remained a flashpoint, for France answered Jay's Treaty by seizing American ships. In 1797, Adams sent three special envoys to repair the damage, but France's corrupt and cynical foreign minister, Charles-Maurice Talleyrand, evaded them. Three private messengers appeared instead, later called "X," "Y," and "Z," and demanded large bribes before negotiating. The XYZ Affair excited a storm of protest when it became public, with congressmen and editors vowing war before dishonor.

Just as Republicans had done over Jay's Treaty, Federalists howled defiance at France and overrode Republicans to enlarge the army and create the Navy Department. French and American vessels fought what came to be called the Quasi-War for months, while Hamilton's High Federalists railed against Adams's prudent reluctance to seek a formal declaration of war. The president and the friends of peace eventually prevailed. Startled by Americans' reactions, Talleyrand offered to negotiate fairly with new envoys, and they won an agreement that stopped the fighting in 1800 with no repayment for captured ships. The compromise avoided war, but the High Federalists never forgave Adams for bargaining with France.

Political conflict worsened in 1798, as party leaders grew increasingly sure that their opponents would surrender America to one foreign power or the other. Especially frightened by foreign radicals who brought French ideas to America, the Federalist Congress passed a series of Alien Acts that restricted access to American citizenship and allowed the expulsion of suspicious immigrants.

In a further assault on free speech, Congress added the Sedition Act, which banned "any false, scandalous, and malicious writing or writings against the government of the United States, or the President of the United States, with intent to defame . . . or to bring them into contempt or disrepute." Federalists clearly intended the Sedition Act to gag Republicans in the election of 1800, when Adams and Jefferson would oppose one another again, because it did not cover the vice president and expired on the eve of Inauguration Day 1801. Under its terms, authorities arrested 25 Republican editors and jailed 10 of them for criticizing the Adams administration.

The Sedition Act plainly violated the First Amendment, but appeals to Federalist courts seemed useless. Jefferson responded instead with a set of protest resolutions for the legislature of Kentucky, and Madison sent others to Virginia. Retreating from Madison's position in *The Federalist Papers*, the Virginia and Kentucky Resolutions described the Union as a compact among sovereign states (not by the whole American people) and spelled out a states' rights interpretation of the Constitution, which argued that the states alone (not the courts) could rule on violations of their compact. Arguing that the Alien and Sedition Acts did violate the Constitution, they claimed a right to nullify them, or to interpose state authority against them, but did not take any concrete actions or spell out what they meant. For decades thereafter, southern politicians swore by the "immortal principles of '98" and used them to demand a federal government of strictly limited powers — first to oppose the Federalists and later to defend slavery.

"THE REVOLUTION OF 1800"

The election of 1800 thus capped a decade of escalating party conflict that seemed to pit every aspect of American public life against its opposite: Federalists against Republicans, Britain against France, North against South, deference against equality, financiers against yeomen, orthodoxy against dissent, broad construction against strict. Each side could point to actions by its opponents that undermined the Constitution: Federalists jailing editors, Republicans encouraging whiskey rebels. The controversies seemed desperately important because their outcomes might determine the permanent character of the young republic, or even its ability to survive. George Washington had died in 1799, universally mourned but seemingly disconnected from the bitter polarization of public life. Under the circumstances, it is not surprising that Adams's and Jefferson's friendship broke down.

Party nominating procedures did not exist yet. High Federalists opposed a second term for Adams, but a party consensus rallied around him. Republicans united behind Jefferson, and their congressmen met in a party caucus, or private meeting, to nominate Aaron Burr of New York for vice president. The campaign focused on electing state legislators who would promise to vote for electors of one party or the other. The campaign seethed with hostile rhetoric and political interest soared, especially in closely divided states.

Just as the canvass closed, Adams and the government moved from the comforts of Philadelphia to the infant city of Washington, DC. Adams and his family occupied the unfinished executive mansion that later generations called the White House, still so raw that Abigail hung her laundry in the vast and drafty East Room. Congress met in the unfinished Capitol Building, down a muddy, rutted lane called Pennsylvania Avenue. Like-minded congressmen lived with each other in boardinghouse "messes" without their families. Foreign ambassadors deplored Washington's primitive conditions, and it would be many years before the capital seemed habitable.

Adams did not stay in Washington long, for Jefferson bested him, 73 electoral votes to 65. Most of Adams's support came from New England, Jefferson took the South, and the middle were states divided. Voting starkly revealed the consequences of the Constitution's three-fifths compromise, which inflated the power of slaveholding states in the House of Representatives and the Electoral College. The compromise gave Jefferson as many as 12 additional electoral votes, and made him the winner over Adams. The "democratic" candidate thus owed his election to slavery, leading Federalists to jeer him bitterly as the "Negro president."

The election also revealed a fundamental defect in the Constitution's rules for choosing the president. Republican electors all wanted Jefferson as president and Burr as vice president, so all gave one of their two ballots to Jefferson and the other to Burr. The result was a tie in the Electoral College, which triggered a constitutional requirement that the House of Representatives choose a president from the highest vote-getters, with each state delegation casting a single vote. Hoping to block the hated Jefferson, Federalist congressmen voted for Burr and deadlocked Congress for 36 fruitless ballots. As tension mounted, Jefferson sent private assurances to Delaware's Federalist congressman that he would not dismantle the party's achievements if elected. Accepting this promise, Delaware and South Carolina abstained on the next ballot, allowing Jefferson to win and settling the election only two weeks before John Adams left office. In the aftermath, Congress approved and the states ratified the Twelfth Amendment to the Constitution, requiring electors to cast separate ballots for president and vice president.

A footnote to the election of 1800 led to Alexander Hamilton's death. Burr sought rehabilitation by running for governor of New York in 1804. During the campaign, Hamilton dropped an insult and Burr replied with a challenge. Morally opposed to dueling but dreading taunts of cowardice, Hamilton fired in the air, but Burr shot straightest and the genius of Federalism fell mortally wounded. Hamilton's death shocked northern public opinion, but southerners respected Burr's defense of his honor and allowed him to return to the vice presidency. The duel left Burr in disgrace, however, and ruined his once-glowing prospects.

Celebrating his victory, Thomas Jefferson ignored the role of the three-fifths clause and cheered "the revolution of 1800" as a triumph for majority rule. He even called it "as real a revolution in the principles of our government as that of 1776 was in its form." In fact, Jefferson defeated Adams in the six states with popular voting for electors, and Republicans swamped Federalists in the accompanying congressional election, but ten states chose electors in their legislatures, so the majority's true preferences remained unknown. The election did mark the first transfer of federal power from one party to another, however, and Republican rhetoric had championed the role of ordinary citizens. Federalists had resisted popular appeals and they never fully recovered. After 1800, Federalists still dominated New England and other commercial centers, but Republicans contested them everywhere. Federalists would benefit when Republicans blundered, but they never controlled the country again or elected another president. If not a fundamental revolution, the election of 1800 was certainly a significant turning point.

The Jeffersonians in Power

Despite the venom of "the revolution of 1800," Thomas Jefferson did not unleash a reign of terror or a social revolution, but allowed the least popular Federalist measures to die quietly. On the whole, however, American political culture grew increasingly responsive to the wishes and values of ordinary white men. Though judges still defended a Federalist vision of public life, Jefferson and his supporters found that minimal government could bring a sense of freedom and opportunity for men like William Thompson without attacking the privileges of the John Rutledges.

"WE ARE ALL REPUBLICANS, WE ARE ALL FEDERALISTS"

The president began with a famous appeal for conciliation. "Though the will of the majority is in all cases to prevail," he declared in his inaugural address, "the minority possess their equal rights, which equal law must protect." Affirming the rivals' shared values, he assured his listeners that "we are all Republicans, we are all Federalists." He did not mean to deny party differences but only that virtually all citizens preferred a federated republic over disunion or monarchy. Dissenters could "stand undisturbed as monuments to the safety with which error of opinion may be tolerated where reason is left free to combat it." Privately, Jefferson still called Federalist leaders "monocrats" and "Anglomen," but he hoped that gentle persuasion would wean away their followers and restore political harmony.

Jefferson avoided radical shifts in government policy. The Sedition Act expired and Congress relaxed the Alien Acts' requirements for naturalization. Republicans sold the government's stock in the Bank of the United States but kept it alive until its charter expired in 1811. Jefferson reassured Federalists that he would shun "entangling alliances" with foreign powers and preserve the Constitution, but would not use the government to remodel society. Unlike Hamilton, Treasury Secretary Albert Gallatin began to pay off the national debt instead of using it for development capital. Congress also cut the Federalists' expensive military establishment and their hated excise taxes. Finally, Jefferson abandoned the government rituals cultivated by Washington and Adams. He walked from his boardinghouse to the inauguration and rode a horse around Washington instead of a coach. Receiving the British minister in slippers and a dressing gown, the president cultivated an air of public simplicity without surrendering the comforts of Monticello.

Jefferson forecast his policy changes with a passage in his inaugural address that painted an idyllic vision of personal liberty and limited government. All the country needed, he said, was "a wise and frugal government, which shall restrain men from injuring one another, shall leave them otherwise free to regulate their own pursuits of industry and improvement, and shall not take from the mouth of labor the bread it has earned. This is the sum of good government, and this is necessary to close the circle of our felicities." Future generations would fiercely debate the adequacy of this formula, and its application to nonwhite men and all women.

A CHANGING POLITICAL COMMUNITY

In 1776, Virginia's Declaration of Rights had proclaimed "that all men are by nature equally free and independent," but restricted the ballot to white men who owned 25 acres of improved land or 100 acres unimproved. Thomas Jefferson had opposed such limitations and thought they disenfranchised at least half of Virginia's adult white men, but most early states used similar restrictions. Defenders argued that landownership demonstrated "permanent attachment to the community" or reasoned that property requirements actually curbed the power of the wealthy by preventing them from wielding the votes of their laborers and tenants.

Following the Revolution, new states filled with citizens whose land purchases were incomplete or legally contested but whose tax payments and militia service, or even their willingness to stay put for a year, seemed to prove as much community attachment as a perfect land title. Vermont, Kentucky, and Tennessee all dropped property requirements for voting when they joined the Union in the 1790s, and so did most states that followed them. Despite conservative opposition, the movement for a broader franchise then spread eastward. Political calculations usually drove reform, as office seekers angled for the votes of the newly enfranchised. By the 1820s, most states allowed white men to vote with little more than a tax-paying or residency requirement, and restrictions on office holding fell also.

Colonial gentlemen had assumed that most voters would defer to men of wealth, education, and social distinction. They were shocked when new voters cast ballots as they pleased. "You are a fool, young man," stormed New York Federalist Judge William Cooper to one sturdy freeman in 1792. "You cannot know how to vote as well as I can direct you, for I am in public office." Republican organizers like Connecticut's Abraham Bishop capitalized on such bluster, denouncing "the great, the wise, rich and mighty men of the world" as "agents of delusion," and he raked in votes with appeals to "the laboring and subordinate people throughout the world" whose "toil goes to support the splendour, luxury and vices of the deluders." Bishop's rhetoric horrified conservatives, but forced them to choose between white male equality and risking those treasured offices.

African Americans also used the language of republicanism to claim equal rights. As the northern states gradually ended slavery, a free black population gathered in cities like Boston, Philadelphia, and New York, and some met property requirements for voting. Mindful of the parties' racial differences, most free blacks voted Federalist whenever they could. Even when they could not vote, urban blacks expressed their political values with marches and banquets to celebrate the Fourth of July, the abolition of the slave trade, and their own presence in the community. In reply, northern racists used bogus dialect to ridicule the "bobalition" of slavery, and continued the discrimination that burdened free blacks like Venture Smith. White women also asserted their civic membership by joining Fourth of July celebrations, either alone or with men, and stressing the importance of republican motherhood, but could not vote outside of New Jersey.

THE POWER OF THE COURTS

Republicans won the legislative and executive branches of the federal government when Jefferson took office, but Adams's Federalist appointees kept the judiciary. His most notable choice was Chief Justice John Marshall. The Virginian kept his seat for 34 years and his decisions continued molding a strong federal government long after Federalists had lost power everywhere else.

Republicans charged that Adams had stayed up until midnight on his last day in office, unfairly naming Federalists to vacant judgeships. Efforts to unseat these "midnight judges" brought a very important case to Marshall's Supreme Court. Federalist William Marbury received a midnight appointment as justice of the peace for the District of Columbia but did not get his commission before Adams's term expired. Jefferson instructed Secretary of State James Madison to withhold the commission so he could appoint a Republican instead, but Marbury demanded a mandamus, or court order requiring its delivery. In accordance with a minor provision of the Judiciary Act of 1789, the case of *Marbury v. Madison* went directly to the Supreme Court. Less farsighted judges than John Marshall might have sided with Marbury to slip a fellow partisan into office. The chief justice saw a bigger opportunity, however, and used the case to assert the power of the judiciary and attack the premise of the recent Virginia and Kentucky Resolutions that the states had final authority to interpret the Constitution.

Marshal delivered the court's unanimous decision in 1803. In simple terms, he agreed that Marbury deserved his commission, but decided he had come to the wrong court. More specifically, Marshall ruled that the Constitution did not give Congress explicit authority to send mandamus disputes to the Supreme Court, so that section of the Judiciary Act was unconstitutional, and Marbury must try his luck in a lower court. This was the first time that the Supreme Court used the power of judicial review to invalidate an act of Congress. The Constitution did not mention this power, but Marshall used strict constructionist logic to claim it, by insisting that the Congress could not exercise a power that the Constitution did not grant. He also insisted that the courts alone could settle the Constitution's meaning, for "it is emphatically the province and duty of the Judicial Department to say what the law is." Marshall's decision made the doctrine of judicial review an explicit and crucial component of US government, and a crucial check on Congress by the judiciary.

Subordinating the people's representatives to unelected judges, *Marbury v. Madison* used Republican means to enshrine Federalist principles. Marshall shrewdly made his point in a minor case that blocked a Federalist appointment, overturned a Federalist statute, and limited the Supreme Court's jurisdiction (over mandamuses), all on the basis of strict construction. The unfortunate Marbury lost his position, but his failed lawsuit affirmed the higher Federalist principle of judicial supremacy. Marshall's subsequent decisions would assert the court's power to void state laws, state judicial rulings, and even state constitutions, erecting the Supreme Court as the final arbiter of American constitutional authority.

HAITI AND LOUISIANA

When Jefferson became president, the United States stopped at the Mississippi River. Beyond was Louisiana, founded by France and awarded to Spain at the end of the Seven Years' War. Its vast boundaries nominally stretched to the Rocky Mountains, but Europeans occupied little more than some riverbank trading posts and the country around New Orleans. Pinckney's Treaty had opened the Mississippi in 1795, but river navigation and access to the Gulf remained key concerns of American foreign policy.

The acquisition of Louisiana became the central incident of Jefferson's first term, and linked foreign affairs and slavery to western expansion. It also clearly illustrated Republican and Federalist differences on crucial matters of public policy, beginning when the French Revolution reached the sugar colony of Saint Domingue, later known as Haiti.

When Haiti's free people of color heard the egalitarian principles of the French Revolution, they demanded inclusion in its promises of liberty and equality. Their revolt soon spread to the slaves, and fleeing whites reported extreme violence as they sought refuge all over the United States and the Caribbean basin. Responding to pressure and its own principles, the revolutionary French government abolished slavery in 1794, and Toussaint Louverture, a supremely talented former slave, emerged as the leader of the black forces who battled for liberty against assorted rivals, including whites, free people of color, and British invaders. Toussaint dominated the island by 1798, and as long as slavery remained illegal, he kept it as a nominal colony of France. Toussaint's caution, however, did not disguise the fact that the ideals of the French and American republics had inspired what slaveholders feared most: a successful black revolution.

Disliking both slavery and France, the Adams administration welcomed the revolution in Saint Domingue. In 1798, Secretary of State Timothy Pickering endorsed independence under Toussaint's leadership, and trade with Haiti soon resumed. The Federalist government even sent military assistance, but the tables turned abruptly when Jefferson took office. Fearing that slave revolt might spread to the mainland, the new president cut off support, downgraded diplomatic contacts, and eventually banned US trade. Throughout the slave states, terrified whites shuddered at tales of "the horrors of St. Domingue," and worried that the slave attendants of planter refugees might carry revolt to local blacks. Whites immediately suspected Haitian and radical French influence in 1800, for example, when a literate slave blacksmith named Gabriel organized an unsuccessful revolt in Richmond, Virginia.

As Toussaint Louverture rose in Saint Domingue and the election of 1800 approached in the United States, General Napoleon Bonaparte seized dictatorial power from a corrupt and ineffective French government. A brilliant strategist, Bonaparte won repeated victories on land, but the British navy controlled the seas, and war continued between France, Britain, and the other European powers. Seeking to rebuild France's empire, Bonaparte sent a 40,000-man army to recapture Saint Domingue, reinstate slavery, and resume sugar production. He also reclaimed Louisiana from Spain to feed the restored colony. French forces captured Toussaint and he died in captivity, but yellow fever destroyed their army and Bonaparte gave up his plans. Without Saint Domingue, moreover, he had no more use for Louisiana. In 1803, Bonaparte surprised the United States with an offer to sell the entire territory for $15 million, approximately $0.13 an acre. Soon afterward, Toussaint's leading subordinate Jean Jacques Dessalines proclaimed the independent republic of Haiti.

Though Federalists had defended the Haitian Revolution, many criticized the Louisiana Purchase. Party members noted that the Constitution did not explicitly authorize the acquisition of new territory and denounced Jefferson for violating his own principles of strict construction. Congressman Manasseh Cutler of Massachusetts called it a "flagrant violation of the principles of the Constitution." New England Federalists also feared the creation of new slave states and dilution of their region's influence. More fundamentally, Federalists worried that western expansion would undermine the refinement and stability they thought a republic needed, and tilt the new nation toward barbarism. "We rush like a comet into infinite space," warned Massachusetts's Fisher Ames. "In our wild career, we may jostle some other world out of its orbit, but we shall in every event, quench the light of our own." Jefferson replied that the Constitution gave unlimited power to make treaties and snapped up Napoleon's proffered bargain. He called Louisiana "an empire for liberty," and thought it would protect the republic by providing enough land for future generations of yeoman farmers to continue their way of life. As Federalists feared, he also surely realized its potential for expanding slavery.

To explore the new territory, Jefferson sent an expedition under his personal secretary, Captain Meriwether Lewis, and Lieutenant William Clark up the Missouri River in 1804. He ordered Lewis and Clark to collect as much scientific information as possible about the animals, plants, geology, and Indians of Louisiana, and to find a route from the Missouri to the Pacific. Aided by Sacagawea, a Shoshone Indian woman who had learned multiple Indian languages while living with the Mandan tribe, Lewis and Clark returned after two and a half years of perilous travel. Passing over the Rocky Mountains, their Corps of Discovery descended the Columbia River and spent the winter of 1805–1806 on the Pacific coast of Oregon, before regaining St. Louis the following fall. The voyage of Lewis and Clark laid a basis for American expansion to the Pacific Ocean that would not be formalized until 1846.

The Trans-Appalachian West

After independence, settlers began flooding the lands between the Appalachians and the Mississippi. Native Americans resisted unsuccessfully, and the government scrambled to accommodate the newcomers. Pioneers struggled for livelihoods and some became unruly without eastern constraints. In the years after 1800, however, a new wave of religious revivals reinforced order in frontier communities, and spread eastward to enlist a new generation of converts throughout the nation.

WHITES AND INDIANS BEYOND THE MOUNTAINS

Euro-Americans had taken almost two centuries to move from the Atlantic to the Appalachians, but raced from there to the Mississippi in less than a generation. As early as the 1770s, hunters and trappers like Daniel Boone had entered eastern Tennessee from North Carolina and Virginia. Independence erased the Proclamation Line of 1763, allowing thousands to follow Boone's trail to the fabled hunting grounds that Native Americans called Caintuck. In the late 1780s, parties of Revolutionary veterans floated down the Ohio to claim lands and establish camps at Marietta and Cincinnati. The territories that Americans later called the Old Northwest and the Old Southwest filled rapidly, for the census counted fewer than 110,000 people west of the mountains in 1790 but nearly 2 million in 1820. The settlers organized new states to govern themselves: Kentucky in 1792, Tennessee in 1796, and Ohio in 1803. Seven more entered the Union between 1812 and 1821, all but Maine from beyond the mountains.

The migrants came from eastern regions where large families, high land prices, and limited soil fertility had endangered prosperity in the late colonial era. New lands thus allowed them to escape a return into European-style poverty. President Jefferson welcomed the chance to multiply yeoman farms, and his views were widely shared. "If the cause of the happiness of this country was examined into," Republican Albert Gallatin of Pennsylvania declared in 1796, "it would be found to arise as much from the great plenty of land in proportion to the inhabitants which their citizens enjoyed, as from the wisdom of their political institutions."

Whites could only expand at Indian expense. In theory, the United States recognized Indians' rights to the land for as long as they wished to remain on it. In practice, federal officials assumed that Indians would have to sell as the white population increased. Like other nations, tribes could be forced to sign an unfavorable treaty after losing a war, but negotiators normally used bribery, threats, and alcohol to obtain a "voluntary" cession. Skillfully plying these methods, they gained title to most of Ohio at the Treaty of Greenville in 1795, and they steadily won more of the Northwest and Southwest in the next quarter century.

But what should happen to the Indians themselves? Few whites would accept a perpetual Indian presence on the land. Some hoped that western Indians would simply disappear like so many had done in the East, but President Jefferson wanted Indians to embrace "civilization" and blend into white society. Forgetting that Indians had farmed for centuries, he repeatedly urged them to stop wandering and plant. He also wanted them to give up traditional gender roles, with men replacing women in the fields and women spinning and keeping house. An all-farm economy would require less land, so Jefferson believed that transformed Indians would happily sell their surplus acreage to whites. He also wanted them to turn their common fields into private property and give up tribal governments for white men's laws.

To encourage such changes, the administration gave seeds, tools, and instructions to the tribes and invited churches to send them teachers and missionaries. Jefferson's "civilization" policy did not work as planned, however, for technological change did not make the Indians more willing to sell. Especially in the Southwest, it gave them more resources for land protection, and strengthened them for later confrontations.

THE PROCESS OF SETTLEMENT

As the government took possession of the West, federal surveyors marked it off in squares as provided by the Northwest Ordinance. The land law of 1796 continued existing sales policies but raised the minimum price to $2.00 per acre. If land failed to sell at auction, purchasers could buy it at the minimum price and take one year to pay. Reacting to steady pressure, Congress liberalized credit terms and gradually lowered the price and the minimum purchase until 1820, when a pioneer could buy as few as 80 acres for $1.25 an acre. The auctions were not always honest, for speculators might pay surveyors for inside information or collude to keep bidding low. Cash-poor squatters had to hope their little clearings would escape the auctioneer's hammer and sell for minimum prices later on. Illegal settlers who lost their claims usually tried to sell their improvements to the new owners and squatted again a little farther westward, but potential for conflict between squatters and speculators was naturally high.

Western migrants brought diverse cultures with them. Beginning in western New York, rural New Englanders dominated the northern Midwest and spread their values and customs as far as Michigan and Iowa. Upper South migrants took southern Ohio, Indiana, and Illinois, and some clamored to bring slavery there. Other southerners carried slavery to Kentucky, Tennessee, and points south. New Englanders brought Congregational churches and village covenants with them; southern yeomen brought log cabins, split-rail fences, and rangy hogs to fatten in the woods. Their two streams joined in the early Midwest, but the Deep South reflected South Atlantic culture, spiced by French and Spanish influences.

THE GREAT REVIVAL

The settlement process included Indian warfare, animal attacks, backbreaking labor, gnawing hunger, and extremes of heat and cold. Pioneers included a disproportionate number of young men whose activities emphasized aggressive masculinity: militia musters, hunting trips, clearing forests, and guiding the plow. Whiskey was indispensable at every gathering and disputes erupted easily, not only over land titles but also over status and physical power. Violence and disorder could dominate frontier life.

Disruption troubled sober-minded male and especially female migrants who longed for the civilizing influences of schools, governments, and churches, since religion seemed to falter in the post-Revolutionary generation. In the South, national independence had broken the weak Anglican establishment without providing any substitute. Leaders like Thomas Jefferson embraced Enlightenment deism, and the revolutionary writer Thomas Paine turned from political tracts to mockery of Christian revelation. New Englanders still used taxes to support their churches, but ministers bemoaned the "coldness" of their congregations.

In 1798, a Scots-Irish Presbyterian minister named James McGready began fervent preaching in the roughhewn Green River district of southern Kentucky. Like a backwoods Jonathan Edwards, McGready offered vivid descriptions of heaven and hell that attracted crowds where sinners shouted, sobbed, and begged forgiveness. By the summer of 1800, his congregations were gathering in outdoor camp meetings to hear teams of preachers around the clock. Participants experienced a spectacular outpouring of religious emotion that ranged from the anguished guilt of penitent sinners to the ecstasy of the saved. The most spectacular occurred at Cane Ridge, Kentucky, where 20,000–25,000 people celebrated a four-day revival in 1801.

The Great Revival, or Second Great Awakening, as it came to be called, spread rapidly over Kentucky, Tennessee, and southern Ohio. Reversing the pioneers' route, it crossed the mountains to the Carolinas and Virginia, and then moved northward to western Pennsylvania. Helped along by rousing hymns and ardent personal pleas, revivals appealed especially to those with lower status in the secular world— women, youths, poor whites, and slaves.

Like their predecessors in the First Great Awakening, the revivalists were evangelicals who valued a sincere conversion experience above complex doctrine. As preachers, they preferred immediate inspiration and emotional fervency over dry book learning and formally prepared prayers or sermons. Though some favored schooling more than others, many successful revivalists lacked traditional theological training, and trimmed the classic Calvinist conversion from a period of months or years to a few days or hours. Salvation became democratized as self-taught preachers took the gospel beyond a predestined few to all who opened their hearts to God and valued personal devotion over dry reason or distant church authorities. Irresistible feelings swept some participants into "exercises," or uncontrollable tears, laughter, paralysis, or fits of violent trembling called "the jerks." These displays could repel conservative Christians, and resulting disputes produced new denominations like the Disciples of Christ and the Cumberland Presbyterians. Many Methodists and Baptists embraced the new measures and eventually displaced Presbyterians as America's largest evangelical denominations. The evangelicals' emphasis on personal experience over abstract doctrine matched the democratic spirit of the era and continued to energize American Protestantism.

The revival's greatest impact came when the shouting died down. Much like the Puritans, evangelical churches kept close watch on their members and punished misbehavior with penance or expulsion. Some converts inevitably relapsed, but ministers reported that most reformed their lives and worked to build the churches, schools, colleges, voluntary associations, and local governments that would bring order to a rapidly growing frontier. Writing in 1810, a typical account from backcountry North Carolina reported that "from 1800, up to the present time, the progress of civilization And literature has been greater, than for perhaps fifty years Antecedent to that time. The great revival of religion about that period seems to have contributed much to the dissemination of morality, sound principles and good order in Society." A later phase of the Second Great Awakening carried revivals to eastern towns and cities in the 1820s and 1830s, with important consequences for culture and politics. The reforming efforts of western and southern evangelicals took decades to fulfill, and their churches did not dominate their societies for many decades, but Cane Ridge had clearly launched a vital movement.

In most ways, the revival movement shared little with the intellectual world of Thomas Jefferson, who venerated reason, balance, and moderation, shrank from emotional displays, and abhorred what he saw as fanaticism. Nevertheless, evangelicals ignored Federalists who charged Jefferson with atheism. Still an embattled minority, they remembered the burdens of an Anglican or Congregational establishment and applauded Jefferson's defense of religious freedom. During his first year in office, Connecticut's Danbury Baptist Association congratulated Jefferson on his election and protested the discrimination they still faced under state law. In reply, the president praised the First Amendment for "building a wall of separation between Church & State," and encouraged the Baptists' fight against church establishment. While Federalists defended orthodoxy, Jefferson's Republicans attracted religious dissenters, from radical skeptics like Thomas Paine to fervent revivalists, and supported the nation's increasingly voluntary approach to the support of religion.

A Second War for Independence?

As in the 1750s and the 1790s, American western expansion in the Jeffersonian era linked Indians' defense of their homelands with European power politics. When Americans cast longing eyes on Canada, Indians and the British again came together to defend the Great Lakes region, the remnants of what had once been known as the Middle Ground. War in Europe stimulated demand for American foodstuffs and products, but exposed American shipping to attacks and interference by the warring parties. Conflict over American ambitions in the Atlantic and on the frontier eventually brought another war with Britain.

The first two Republican presidents, Thomas Jefferson and James Madison (who succeeded Jefferson in 1809) struggled to defend American interests on both fronts. Fearing Britain more than France, they adopted a series of economic measures to force British respect for neutral trading rights. They also struck back hard when northwestern and southwestern Indians united to resist American expansion. When economic measures failed against Great Britain, Jefferson and Madison both worried that national weakness sapped confidence in republicanism. They also faced unrelenting opposition from a Federalist minority who still admired Britain and despised all things Jeffersonian. Led by President Madison, the Republicans eventually decided that the preservation of republican government, control of the West, and true American independence required a second war with Great Britain. Every aspect of the War of 1812 would also reflect the deep-seated hostility between America's political parties.

COMMERCE AND CONFLICT

After selling Louisiana and abandoning his effort to reclaim Haiti, Napoleon Bonaparte dropped the remaining vestiges of the French Republic, and proclaimed himself "Emperor of the French" in 1804. Still seeking to curb his ambition, Britain led a coalition of other European nations against Napoleon, so continued fighting drew men from farmwork and generated huge demands for food and resources. On the oceans, competing navies seized ships and sailors from merchant fleets, while military suppliers increased their orders for foreign goods. As the world's leading neutral, the United States claimed the right of doing business with both sides, opening great opportunities and serious risks.

The Napoleonic Wars advanced the dreams of Alexander Hamilton despite the political dominance of his opponents. Shipbuilding boomed in America's ports, and sales of flour and salted meat soared wherever Americans could find a market. The value of American exports rose from $33 million in 1794 to $97 million in 1801 and to $108 million in 1807. American sailing vessels probed ever farther, carrying cargoes to the Baltic, the Mediterranean, the Middle East, and even as far as China, as well as to the battling superpowers of western Europe. The United States not only remained Great Britain's leading trade partner but its vessels transported French colonial products to Europe and dominated the Atlantic carrying trade.

Mediterranean trade put Americans in contact with seagoing raiders from North Africa, where the rulers of Algiers, Tunis, and Tripoli had long allowed the capture of European ships, crews, and passengers. The so-called Barbary pirates held their captives as slaves and demanded cash payments to buy off further attacks. The United States paid when its navy could not resist, but the pasha of Tripoli declared war when Jefferson stopped payment in 1801. In the First Barbary War, the US Navy and Marines fought Tripoli in a series of land and sea battles later remembered in the "Marines' Hymn." Tripoli agreed to peace in 1805, but Algerian raids persisted until the Second Barbary War of 1815.

International conflict stalemated after 1805, with Britain controlling the seas and Napoleon invincible on land. Striving to end the deadlock, each side broke international law as it tried to restrict American trade with its adversaries. Based on longstanding resentments, America's Republican majority hated Britain's measures more, but Federalists felt the opposite.

A key issue stemmed from Britain's efforts to man its navy. Many British seamen sought relief from poor pay and brutal treatment by deserting to American vessels. Britain denied its subjects the right of renouncing their allegiance, however, and intercepted American ships to arrest or impress alleged deserters. Americans claimed that Britain impressed as many as 6,000 genuine Americans as well, and the US government seemed powerless to protect them.

Another problem arose in 1806, when Napoleon proclaimed the Continental System, which forbade trade with Great Britain and ordered the seizure of neutral vessels that stopped there before sailing to Europe. Britain retaliated with the Orders in Council, which blockaded French-controlled ports and required neutrals to pay a fee before trading with Europe.

Napoleon then ordered the seizure of any ship that obeyed the Orders in Council or even submitted to a British search. These competing decrees put all American trade with Britain or France in violation of one set of rules or the other, and led to the seizure of some 900 American ships between 1806 and 1812. British harassment punished France, but also protected British shippers by preventing neutral competition. Americans suspected that British actions were inspired more by economic calculation than by military necessity.

Tension between the United States and Britain almost boiled over in 1807, when the British *Leopard* attacked the USS *Chesapeake* just outside the harbor of Norfolk, Virginia. The attack killed three American seamen, injured eighteen, and allowed the British to arrest four sailors they accused of desertion. Enraged by this humiliation but hoping to avoid war, Jefferson revived the tactics that defeated the Stamp Act. At his request, Congress passed a series of increasingly drastic Embargo Acts that eventually forbade all American commerce with foreign countries. Naively believing that America's trading partners needed its products more than America needed theirs, Jefferson thought his policy would protect American shipping until other nations respected its rights. Instead, the Embargo Acts distressed the US economy as exports dropped from $107 million in 1807 to $22 million in 1808. The embargo failed to change British behavior but embittered New England, which heavily depended on international trade. Just as Jefferson left office in 1809, Congress replaced the Embargo Acts with the Non-Intercourse Act that only banned trade with Britain, France, and their colonies.

As in the 1790s, international tension in the Jefferson and Madison years reverberated on the frontier and spawned rumors of secession, conspiracy, and foreign intrigue. After leaving the vice presidency in 1805, for example, Aaron Burr traveled up and down the Ohio and Mississippi to recruit participants in a shadowy plot to invade Spanish Texas or seize the lower Mississippi—no one was ever sure. The administration arrested Burr before his plans matured, but could not convict him of treason.

TECUMSEH AND THE RED STICKS

European and Atlantic conflicts intertwined with Native American resistance. After surrendering most of Ohio in the Treaty of Greenville (1795), the remaining northwestern tribes had retreated to new towns in modern Indiana and Illinois and the upper Great Lakes region, where they struggled with disease and demoralization. Beginning in 1805, however, a Shawnee spiritual leader named Tenskwatawa, or "the Prophet," launched a new spiritual movement to revive Indian culture and reclaim Indian independence. Reviving the earlier teachings of Neolin, the Delaware preacher who inspired Pontiac's War, Tenskwatawa urged the tribes to purify themselves by renouncing white culture, including tools, clothing, food, and alcohol, and prepare for an apocalypse that would destroy the whites and restore their former greatness. Also like Pontiac after the Seven Years' War and Little Turtle in the wake of the American War for Independence, the Prophet's brother Tecumseh began to add that Indians should unite, expel the whites by force, and create their own independent state in the Ohio Valley. The two brothers had lost their father in a pre-Revolutionary fight with pioneers, and then lost home after home when invading frontiersmen attacked their villages. Small wonder that Tecumseh had fought against Americans in their War of Independence and once more in the Northwest Confederacy of the early 1790s.

Battered by smallpox and defeat, many Ohio Valley tribes thrilled to the message of Tecumseh and Tenskwatawa, and began to pull together in a new tribal confederacy. When less determined chiefs approved a massive and probably fraudulent surrender of land in 1809, Tecumseh traveled from village to village denouncing all land sales. In 1810, he and 300 warriors confronted William Henry Harrison, governor of the Indiana Territory, at his home and demanded the land's return, insisting that "no tribe has the right to sell [land], even to each other, much less to strangers." "Sell a country!" he reportedly continued. "Why not sell the air, the great sea, as well as the earth? Did not the Great Spirit make them all for the use of his children?" Rebuffed by Harrison, Tecumseh took his campaign southward and urged the Creek Confederacy to join him in war against the whites.

Harrison worried increasingly that Tecumseh and the Prophet could indeed incite a war to reclaim the Middle Ground. His anxiety grew as tensions rose with Britain, prompting rumors of an Indian-British alliance in case of war. Unwilling to wait, Harrison struck first. In 1811, when Tecumseh was away, he marched on Tenskwatawa's home village of Prophetstown, defeated the Indians at the ensuing Battle of Tippecanoe, and found a cache of British muskets. With Tecumseh still alive and active, reports swept the West that British agents had incited and supplied his followers, and pressure mounted for a full-scale war.

Tecumseh had also won followers among the Creeks. Following the American Revolution, the Creek economy had suffered as the deer population thinned and whites moved ever closer to the tribal heartland in modern Alabama. Spotting an opportunity, successive administrations tried to supplant the tribes' traditions with gifts of plows, seeds, spinning wheels, and looms, hoping that Indians who lived like whites (whom they called "civilized") would be more willing to surrender their lands. Closer to the advancing whites, inhabitants of the Creeks' Lower Towns more readily accepted these overtures and increasingly substituted cattle ranching, cotton planting, and African slavery for older patterns of hunting and agriculture. Their leaders were often men of mixed parentage, whose Creek mothers gave them tribal membership while their fathers taught them skills and values from the white world that helped in gaining personal wealth, contrary to traditional notions of community property. They experimented with the gender roles preferred by whites, as men abandoned hunting and war and took over farming, leaving women with more domestic duties. The same men moved to create a strong tribal government that could protect their new possessions and enforce peace with the United States.

Farther west, inhabitants of the Upper Towns resisted these changes and clung to traditional technology, gender roles, and notions of communal property. They especially resented white incursions and tribal laws to restrain their resistance. They accordingly listened carefully when Tecumseh urged them to reject white culture and join him in expelling the encroaching Americans. As tension mounted between the two Creek factions, traditionalists took the name Red Sticks after an ancient emblem for war. With supplies from British traders in Spanish Florida, the Red Sticks edged closer to a civil war with their tribal opponents, with significant repercussions for the growing conflict between America and Britain.

THE ROAD TO WAR

In 1808, a solid Republican majority passed the presidency—and growing international conflict—from Jefferson to his longstanding lieutenant and secretary of state, James Madison. Many Republicans still believed that economic sanctions could protect American commerce from Britain without Hamiltonian measures like high taxes, expensive navies, standing armies, or war. Searching for a winning formula, Congress dropped restrictions on trade with France and England in 1810 but authorized the president to reimpose sanctions against one if the other promised to respect neutral rights. Napoleon offered misleading gestures of compliance but Britain refused to follow.

The elections of 1810 brought a number of younger Republicans to

Congress who would dominate ensuing decades. Men like Henry Clay of Kentucky and John C. Calhoun of South Carolina were too young to remember the Revolution, and even the party battles of the 1790s were distant memories to them. They would not tolerate American inferiority, however, and railed against British arrogance and Indian resurgence. "No man in the nation desires peace more than I," Clay told the Senate. "But I prefer the troubled ocean of war, demanded by the honor and independence of the country . . . to the tranquil, putrescent pool of ignominious peace." Congressman Hugh Nelson agreed, and thought war would "shew that our republican government was competent to assert its rights, to maintain the interests of the people, and to repel all foreign aggression." Quickly labeled War Hawks, the insurgents stirred westerners to frenzy and promised to punish Britain by seizing Canada, but forgot that Republicans' long neglect of the military had left them with few land forces and no navy to speak of. Still hating Hamilton's Bank of the United States, they also created financial obstacles by allowing its charter to expire in 1811.

Federalists fervently opposed war. Since losing in 1801, their party had contracted to a narrow base among the economic and political leaders of New England, and held about a quarter of the seats in Congress. Still convinced of their superior fitness for leadership, they viewed Republican measures with suspicion and contempt. Boston Federalist Josiah Quincy Jr. explained his opposition to the Louisiana Purchase, for example, by commenting that "nothing . . . can seem politically good whose root springs on the other side of the political Equator. . . . A pure stream cannot issue from a corrupt source." Though their own merchants were badly injured by British seizures, Federalists hated trade restrictions far more. Preferring a prosperous junior partnership with Britain to a costly war, they correctly argued that the nation was unprepared to fight and unprotected from attack. Going further, many Federalists saw the war as a Republican political stunt and an act of aggression to conquer Canada. "I regard this war, as a war of party, and not of the country," concluded Senator Rufus King of New York as the war began. "Whether we consider our agriculture, our commerce, our moneyed systems, or our internal safety," warned the party's *Alexandria Gazette*, "nothing but disaster can result from it."

The advocates of peace did not prevail. When impressments continued and the Orders in Council remained, Madison asked for war on June 1, 1812. Congress agreed, with most Republicans voting in favor and most Federalists opposed. Ironically, word arrived weeks later that the British ministry had finally lifted its Orders in Council, but war continued for the sake of national dignity, and its results were nearly disastrous.

THE COURSE OF COMBAT

Fighting began with a luckless, three-pronged invasion of Canada. General William Hull invaded Ontario from Detroit, but hastily retreated before a combined force of British and Indians, led by Tecumseh. Chasing the Americans back to Detroit, the British and Indians briefly besieged its fort before a terrified Hull surrendered without firing a shot. Farther east, New York aristocrat General Stephen van Rensselaer crossed the Niagara River between Lakes Erie and Ontario, but had to return when his militia refused to follow. A third column under General Henry Dearborn headed for Montreal via Lake Champlain, but also faltered when militiamen halted.

The Americans began to recover in 1813, when General William Henry Harrison recaptured Detroit, pursued Tecumseh and the British into Ontario, and defeated them at the Battle of the Thames. There Tecumseh lost his life, but supply problems prevented the victorious Harrison from following up his victory. To remedy such problems, the British and Americans both sought to control the Great Lakes with freshwater navies, leading to an American raid on shipyards in York (modern Toronto), Ontario, which ended in sacking the town. At the end of the summer of 1813, a hard-fought naval battle by Commodore Oliver Hazard Perry secured American command of Lake Erie and anchored American's defense of its northwestern frontier.

After another summer of inconclusive fighting, the war's low point came in August 1814, when a British invading force penetrated Chesapeake Bay, landed in Maryland, and retaliated for the destruction of York by burning Washington, DC. Only prompt action by First Lady Dolley Madison and domestic slaves and employees saved some White House art and furnishings from the flames, including a copy of Gilbert Stuart's famous portrait of George Washington that now appears on the one dollar bill. The Capitol was left in ruins. Soon afterward, an unsuccessful British assault on Baltimore inspired the composition of "The Star-Spangled Banner," later adopted as the national anthem.

America's weak performance in the Great Lakes and Chesapeake theaters risked serious disaster, but its forces did much better in the

Southwest. When the Creek government attacked supporters of Tecumseh, the Red Sticks retaliated with a broad attack against their tribal enemies, culminating in an 1813 attack on Fort Mims, Alabama, that killed as many as 500 whites, allied Creeks, and their slaves. In the aftermath, pro-American Creeks sought US government assistance, and the governor of Tennessee summoned militia general Andrew Jackson, a planter politician with fierce resolve and personal charisma. Quelling threats of mutiny and desertion, Jackson cornered the Red Sticks at the Battle of Horseshoe Bend in early 1814 and inflicted 800 casualties. After wresting a vast land cession from his Creek allies, he continued south to defend the Gulf coast.

With an army of 10,000 men, Admiral Sir Alexander Cochrane and General Sir Edward Pakenham hoped to strike a decisive blow in late 1814 by capturing New Orleans, the economic choke point for the entire western territory. Jackson invaded Spanish Florida and expelled a small British force from Pensacola before racing to New Orleans. The British attacked on the morning of January 8, 1815, but Jackson's polyglot force of frontier militia, skilled artillery, free blacks, and pirates from the surrounding bayous inflicted terrible damage on their bungled charge, with 2,000 British casualties but only 70 American. General Pakenham died in combat and the surviving troops had to retreat. National honor seemed vindicated at last, and Americans celebrated Jackson's triumph far beyond its actual military significance.

Much about Jackson's wartime performance presaged what his friends loved and his enemies hated about his later career as president. He began the war by trumpeting American superiority. *"Who are we?"* he thundered in his 1812 proclamation to the Tennessee militia. *"And for what are we going to fight?"* The answer followed immediately. "We are the free born sons of america, the citizens of the only republick now existing in the world; and the only people on earth who possess rights, liberties, and property which they dare call their own." Federalists surely groaned at such bombast but pugnacious frontiersmen cheered it. When pursuit of the Red Sticks carried that same militia deep into Creek country, supplies ran short, enlistment terms expired, and some troops demanded to go home. Despising weakness, Jackson would have none of it, and when six militiamen were condemned to death for desertion, he approved their sentences unflinchingly. Soon afterward, the Red Sticks too faced the bloody consequences of his wrath. Preparing to defend New Orleans, Jackson had proclaimed martial law, and refused to lift it after victory was secured. When a legislator protested, Jackson arrested him. When a federal judge intervened, the unbending general jailed him too, outraging defenders of the rule of law but pleasing admirers of a strong will and decisive results.

In short, Andrew Jackson could be violent, ruthless, and indifferent to the rules when they stood in his way. He embodied frontier patriotism, championed the equality of white men with each other and their superiority over everyone else, scorned self-doubt, brooked no dissent, thrilled his admirers for defending their rights, and frightened his critics as a moral monster and potential dictator. His complex, polarizing character would leave a deep mark on American public culture, representing what some saw as the best and others the worst of his era.

PROTESTS AND PEACE

Federalist opposition to the war never abated. New England congressmen and legislators opposed new taxes, discouraged enlistments, blocked the use of their state militias, impeded war loans, and, imitating the Virginia and Kentucky Resolutions, threatened to interpose state power against a draft. When these measures failed, some Federalists suggested that New England leave the union or negotiate a separate peace, and the Massachusetts legislature called a regional meeting to discuss those steps in Hartford, Connecticut. Assembling in December 1814, the Hartford Convention took no immediate action but demanded a series of constitutional amendments to limit Republican power, including repeal of the three-fifths clause that benefited southern slaveholders.

Unknown to all participants, the Hartford Convention and the Battle of New Orleans both occurred after British and American diplomats had already signed a peace agreement in the Belgian city of Ghent. The treaty did not mention any of the war's major causes, but Britain and its allies had finally toppled Napoleon, so further bloodshed seemed pointless. Retreating from earlier pledges, the British did not demand an Indian buffer state around the Great Lakes, and left Tecumseh's followers to face the Americans alone. Jubilant Republicans scoffed at the Hartford Convention, for Federalists seemed thoroughly discredited by their antiwar stance, and Republicans' future dominance seemed secure.

Peace brought widespread rejoicing. Contrary to predictions, Americans had failed to conquer Canada or humble Great Britain, but their triumph at New Orleans vindicated their citizen-soldiers. The outcome seemed to embody what headlines called "The Rising Glory of the Republic." A typical editor boasted, "This second war of independence has been illustrated by more splendid achievements than the war of the revolution." Others linked British defeat with Federalist overthrow. "The triumph over the Aristocrats & Monarchists is equally glorious with that over the enemy," wrote one. "It is the triumph of virtue over vice[,] of republican men & republican principles over the advocates and doctrines of Tyranny." At the very least, the war had made his countrymen "more American," Albert Gallatin reflected. "They feel and act more like a nation; and hope that the permanency of the Union is thereby better secured."

*

In 1789, Americans began to implement their Constitution with great concern about the character and stability of their republic. Treasury Secretary Alexander Hamilton led an effort to strengthen the government with economic programs to consolidate and pay its debts, raise its revenues, and administer its finances through a national bank. Virginians James Madison and Thomas Jefferson feared these measures would endanger liberty by creating a corrupt and despotic government that favored urban commerce over agriculture. They began opposing Hamilton inside George Washington's administration and took their opposition across the country when their arguments did not prevail.

The resulting party system pitted Hamilton's Federalists against Jefferson's and Madison's Democratic-Republicans. The parties differed over more than economic policy, for Federalists trusted the established elite and Republicans favored greater power for common white men. Strongest in the South, Republicans defended slavery and benefited from the three-fifths clause over bitter Federalist objections. The French Revolution and its consequences drove party divisions ever deeper, as each side saw its opponents as the tools of foreign enemies in a worldwide struggle.

As Republicans gained the upper hand, they sought a more loosely connected union than the Federalists, with room for popular power, local variations, rural interests, slavery, western expansion, and voluntary participation in unifying institutions like the churches of the Second Great Awakening. The War of 1812 severely tested this model of national unity and nearly broke it, but Republicans survived and so did their vision of for the republic. Limited government did not eliminate social or economic equality, but it did encourage white men like William Thompson and John Rutledge to feel equally free and respected, and allowed party rivals to compete politically without personal rancor. A Republican political monopoly was not sufficient for harmony, however, for Federalist decline required new channels for the debates that a changing society would generate.

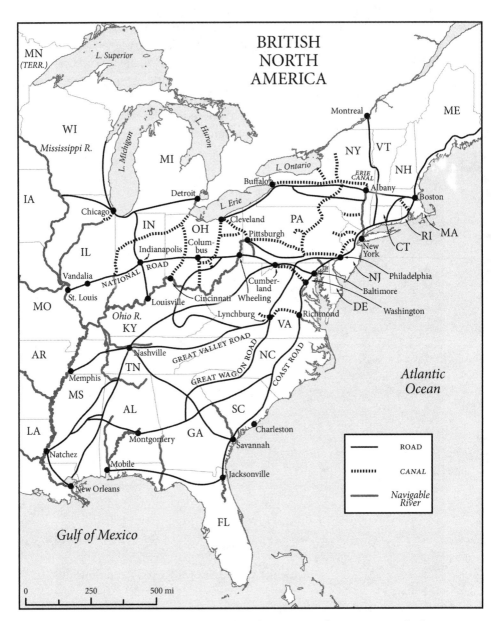

MAP 4. Between 1815 and 1840, a broad expansion of transportation facilities sparked a major burst of economic change known as the Market Revolution. Map by Gabriel Moss.

CHAPTER 8

Market Revolution in the North, 1815–1860

"I never cared much for machinery," Lucy Larcom remembered. "The buzzing and hissing and whizzing of pulleys and rollers and spindles and flyers around me often grew tiresome. . . . In the sweet June weather I would lean far out of the window, and try not to hear the unceasing clash of sound inside." Larcom's feelings were not surprising, for in 1835 she had started factory work at the age of eleven and a half, working fourteen hours a day spinning cotton for the Lawrence Corporation of Lowell, Massachusetts. She later admitted that the mill was "not the right sort of life for a child," but she had little choice. Her widowed mother badly needed Lucy's wages of one dollar per week, as well her other daughters' meager pay, to supplement what she earned by keeping a boarding house for Lowell "mill girls."

Hardship did not embitter Lucy Larcom, and she never lost her love of books and gift for poetry. As she grew older, Larcom published numerous poems and stories in the *Lowell Offering*, the workers' literary magazine. She eventually became a teacher on the distant prairies of Illinois, gained higher education, and supported herself as a writer. For Lucy Larcom, mill work led to independence and fulfillment.

Sarah Bagley's experience was very different. In 1837, Bagley arrived at Lowell from a failing New Hampshire farm, and began work as a spinner to help her family. Over the next seven years, conditions deteriorated as managers cut costs. The work day shortened from fourteen hours to twelve, six days a week, but the mills slashed wages, doubled the number of machines per worker, and crushed the ensuing strike. When the company restored men's wages but not women's, Bagley led the Lowell Female Labor Reform Association in demanding legislation for a ten-hour day.

With Bagley as president, the LFLRA bombarded the Massachusetts legislature with petitions signed by thousands. The "mill girls" could not vote or even speak in public without scandal, but they seized on republican political principles to condemn the mills' "system of tedious and protracted toil" as violating "the great principles of justice, equality and republicanism . . . so essential to the moral, mental and physical well-being of society, and the existence of a free and virtuous people." When lawmakers would not act, Sarah Bagley kept agitating for labor reform, prison reform, the abolition of slavery, and the end of capital punishment until she finally left the mills in 1848.

Lucy Larcom and Sarah Bagley lived at the intersection of converging changes in America's society and economy. Their workplaces were technological marvels that belonged to corporations, an increasingly powerful business structure. They spun slave-grown cotton that came to Lowell on newly constructed canals, steamboats, and railroads. The same carriers took their cloth to consumers, including the slaves who had grown its fiber. New forms of communication, including cheaply printed newspapers and handbills, had lured a woman from Ireland to work in Mrs. Larcom's boardinghouse. Millions of other immigrants made similar journeys. And finally, the mill owners reinvested their profits in a continual process of capitalist development that made America a world industrial power by 1860.

Historians have given the name "Market Revolution" to the interlocking sets of changes that introduced Americans to the "buzzing and hissing and whizzing" of early industrialization. Americans had always bought and sold in far-flung markets, for transatlantic trade had supported the colonies from the start, but geographical barriers had hampered commercial expansion. Historians have also identified the "Transportation Revolution" and the "Communication Revolution," for improvements in these areas greatly expanded the scope and scale of market activities. They also speak of the "Industrial Revolution," for machinery transformed both manufacturing and the nature and meaning of work. All these terms are useful for specific developments, but "Market Revolution" seeks to embrace them all by emphasizing the role of expanding markets in driving change throughout the society and the economy.

These "revolutions" had far-reaching consequences. When cheap, abundant goods arrived from far away and undersold local products, Americans had to put aside what others could do cheaper, concentrate on making and selling what they did best, and buy their other necessities from those distant, unseen rivals. These were the market forces that sent slaves to Mississippi, cotton and "mill girls" to Lowell, machine-made textiles to every neighborhood, and homespun cloth to oblivion. As the new methods spread, buying and selling intensified, and the importance of markets, prices, cash, and credit rose dramatically. The consequences included western expansion, urban and rural transformation, a new class structure, new shapes and meanings for homes and workplaces, and dramatically new roles for women.

The changes of this period are also called the expansion of capitalism, or the economic system based on private ownership of capital (the money and equipment needed to make things) and on free markets for products, labor, land, and capital itself. In a capitalist economy, business owners, or capitalists, employ workers and compete for profits, often by replacing older methods with more efficient newer ones, a process economists call creative destruction. As capitalism continued to grow and spread, American public discourse would often revolve around its complex burdens and rewards.

Because the years 1815 to 1860 immediately preceded the Civil War, historians also call these years the antebellum, or prewar, period. The label can be distorting, for the era was important in itself and not just for what followed. The term is convenient and often appropriate, however, for the sectional conflict became more and more serious in these decades, inflamed in many cases by economic change.

The Market Revolution affected the free and slave states differently. This chapter focuses on the impact of economic change on northern society between the end of the War of 1812 and 1860. Chapter 9 treats social reform and cultural change in the North, and chapter 10 examines the South.

Technology and the New Economy

Household production still dominated the American economy at the end of the eighteenth century. Joined by a servant or two and sometimes a slave, farm families combined limited self-sufficiency with the sale of surplus crops. Most townspeople lived on the same scale, in homes that were also workshops, where the master ruled his family and a handful of journeymen and apprentices. The household economy could be stifling or supportive to its members, but it rested on face-to-face relationships and an intimate scale of life.

A number of factors eroded the household economy, especially after 1815. A growing population strained existing resources. Ambitious leaders applied lessons from the War of 1812 to domestic economic problems. New technology stimulated competition over long distances, breaking barriers between communities that had fostered both isolation and independence. Americans responded by dramatically increasing the pace of economic change.

THE HOUSEHOLD ECONOMY

Household independence was the most important product of the small farm in the early nineteenth century. The male head enjoyed the most liberty, but an adequate farm also freed his wife and children from the poverty and servility of tenant farming or wage labor. Seeking a competency, or enough land and tools to keep them decently fed, clothed, and sheltered, families also wanted to leave their children enough property—land for the boys, cash or household goods for the girls—to allow them to establish their own independent households when they married. Though women lacked independence almost everywhere, most Americans shared Thomas Jefferson's view of yeoman farming as a free man's ideal life and the essential social foundation for a republic, because it freed men from "the casualties and caprice of customers" and allowed them to avoid the "subservience and venality" that ruined good citizens. With care, most rural families could reach this limited goal, but only a few surpassed it.

In many parts of the countryside, many families still grew most of their food, made many things themselves, and limited their outside purchases. Farm women could make work clothing, for example, first raising cotton, wool, or flax, then spinning and weaving it, and finally sewing it into garments. Those who could not afford a loom or spinning wheel bartered for homespun with neighbors and bought imported fabrics for special occasions. Women also produced butter and cheese for sale in nearby towns, and their men did the same with corn whiskey, lumber, or wood ashes to make soap and glass. Americans called these products home manufactures, meaning things that were made by hand, not grown from the earth.

When they needed extra help or something they could not make, farm families pooled labor or swapped tasks with neighbors, keeping intricate accounts with each other and often allowing months to pass between repaying the loan of an ox, for example, with a load of firewood. Similar barter arrangements with rural craftsmen and storekeepers limited outside trade, so New Englanders sold no more than

25 percent of what they grew outside the region. Some gained enough wealth to stand above their neighbors, but in contrast to plantation districts, northern rural inequality mostly varied with men's ages, as farmers accumulated property over time and then passed it to their children.

In this environment, costly innovations promised great risks and few rewards. Borrowing money for more land or better equipment might swell the harvest, but a shortage of harvesters could ruin it and rural isolation would limit sales. The credit crisis that sparked the Massachusetts Regulators (or Shays's Rebellion) was still a fresh memory, moreover, and warned farmers against economic risks that endangered their land and liberty. Avoiding dangerous innovations, safety-first farmers clung to tradition, though outsiders bewailed their "backwardness."

Urban households resembled their country cousins. Even the largest import-export firms were family businesses held together by networks of brothers, uncles, and nephews. Smaller businessmen often lived with their clerks above their shops or offices. Americans still imported luxuries from Europe and China, but towns and cities also supported skilled artisans who produced everything from fine furniture and silver tea sets to candles, wagons, barrels, clothing, and shoes. Artisans treasured the hard-won skills that turned raw materials into finished products. Like other small businessmen, the typical master lived over his shop, with live-in apprentices who began to learn his trade as early as age 12 or 14. Gaining freedom at age 21, the male apprentice became a journeyman who worked for wages until he could start his own shop and gain the urban equivalent of the farmer's precious independence. Workingwomen sometimes entered this world through trades such as dressmaking or millinery (hat-making), though self-supporting women more commonly toiled in low-paying positions as seamstresses, washerwomen, or domestics. Like safety-first farming, the master mechanic's workshop fostered a sense of masculine independence that reinforced the promise of republican liberty.

In Philadelphia, New York, and other major cities, craft associations assisted masters and journeymen in sickness and hard times, and gave them political leverage as they marched together in grand parades, to demand adoption of the federal Constitution, for example, or to celebrate victory in the War of 1812. Artisans championed republican equality and stressed the combined importance of workers and their tools with their motto "By hammer and hand, all arts do stand." They played key political roles in organizations like the Sons of Liberty and the Democratic-Republican Societies, and they continued their civic activities as the nineteenth century opened.

Below the ranks of skilled craftsmen, were the carters, draymen, and laborers who kept urban commerce moving by land, as throngs of sailors did by sea. Poor black and white women could join the workforce as domestic servants. Possibly disenfranchised by laws that limited voting to property holders, the poorest white workers enjoyed the privileges of race without full republican equality. They suffered galling poverty in the best of times, and serious want when business slackened, competing with penniless widows and disabled veterans for meager public assistance. Northern cities still held a scattering of slaves but gradual emancipation had freed the rising generation. Criminals, beggars, and prostitutes filled the lowest ranks of urban society.

Despite its resistance to change, the household economy faced rising pressures, beginning with population growth. The United States held about 8.4 million people in 1815, and their numbers doubled almost every 25 years. The Louisiana Purchase had more than doubled the country's land area, but 85 out of every 100 Americans still lived east of the Appalachians, and the ratio of people to land was growing tight for the existing technology. In every generation, northeastern farms grew smaller as fathers divided their lands among heirs, and the urban economy could not easily absorb many rural migrants. Struggling to make ends meet and worried for their children's future, farm families sought new strategies for preserving independence, gaining a competency, and providing for the next generation. New transportation technology would offer them a possible solution.

THE TRANSPORTATION REVOLUTION

Spurred by population growth and the pressures on households, entrepreneurs in every field tried sell their products cheaper, faster, and farther away. They especially tried to expand the size and scope of their markets with big transportation and communication projects that Americans called internal improvements. The earliest were turnpikes, or privately financed toll roads, that tied cities to the countryside with well-drained gravel surfaces that could bear heavy traffic in bad weather. In 1794, the Lancaster Turnpike linked Philadelphia to its hinterland, and a thin network of similar roads quickly spread out across eastern Pennsylvania, southern New York, and southern New England.

Traveling by water was even easier than traveling by turnpikes, so British experiments in canal building drew widespread attention. In 1816, a Senate committee complained that "a coal mine may exist in the United States not more than ten miles from valuable ores of iron and other materials, and both of them be useless until a canal is established between them, as the price of land carriage is too great to be borne by either." Early canals were very short, but in 1817, New York undertook an artificial waterway running 364 miles from Lake Erie to the Hudson River at Albany. Under the leadership of Governor DeWitt Clinton, the Erie Canal became the engineering marvel of the age, using a complex series of locks to regulate its flow of water and an extensive series of bridges and aqueducts to traverse valleys and streams. Even before its completion in 1825, tolls on the finished portion of the Erie Canal were paying for construction of the rest, as upstate farmers raised more wheat and millers floated cheap flour to New York City. The completed canal linked the Great Lakes basin with Atlantic markets and brought commercial farming to the Ohio country, where the English, French, and Indians had fought only two generations before. Success spawned dozens of imitators, and a wave of canal construction spread across Pennsylvania and the Ohio Valley.

More innovations came from steam. By heating water in sealed boilers, eighteenth-century inventors had used steam to drive the pistons of pumps and factory equipment. In 1807, after numerous failures, Robert Fulton successfully sent his steam-powered *Clermont* up the Hudson from New York to Albany. Within five years, a steamboat had paddled from Pittsburgh to New Orleans, and by 1830, steamboats dominated America's navigable rivers. Steam defied wind and currents and turned rivers into highways, stimulating production of corn, wheat, pork, and cotton, and making it possible for farmers to purchase goods from distant manufacturers. Steamships began crossing the Atlantic in 1838, and a voyage that once took months now took fifteen days, though service remained costly and unreliable for decades. Steam engines also created an enormous market for the energy of wood and coal, with immediate impact on mining and timbering.

When canals and steamboats funneled western trade to New York City, Boston, and Philadelphia, Baltimore sought overland alternatives to avoid eclipse. The earliest "rail roads" used horses to pull cars along a railed track, but in 1825, English inventor George Stephenson replaced the horses with a rolling steam engine. The Baltimore and Ohio Railroad brought his invention to America in 1830, and a South Carolina line that diverted trade from Savannah to Charleston soon followed. Railroads crossed terrain that waterways could not and outdistanced canals by 1840. Over 30,000 miles of track had opened by 1860, creating a seemingly endless market for iron. An expanding network covered the Northeast and Midwest, and long feeder routes connected the richest plantation districts to southern ports. The fastest passenger railroads did not go much faster than 30 miles per hour in 1860, and freight moved only a third as fast, but the speed of both had dramatically improved while the cost had plummeted.

THE COMMUNICATION REVOLUTION

Improved communications proved just as important as better transportation, and dramatically expanded American newspapers. In 1790, 92 newspapers—almost all of them four-page weeklies—had reported on the Washington administration. Forty years later, 650 journals were hotly debating the conduct of President Andrew Jackson, 65 of them dailies. By the eve of the Civil War, the number of American newspapers exceeded 3,700.

Early newspapers had limited circulation, for a single issue cost between six and eight cents and copies were sold only at the printer's office. A yearly subscription cost almost a week's wages for a common laborer, so many readers followed the news at their local tavern or lending library. Most papers were proudly partisan, reprinted long, dense speeches by political favorites instead of news stories, and freely mixed editorial comments with factual reporting. Editors spread information over long distances by exchanging free copies and reprinting the stories they received.

Densely peopled streets and sidewalks formed new settings for reading and discussing information that encouraged more popular kinds of news than dry accounts of business or politics. Beginning with Benjamin Day's *New York Sun* in 1833, innovative editors linked these new reading tastes with new methods of printing, papermaking, and distributing printed material to produce sensationalist journals that transformed urban communication. Newsboys hawked the *Sun* for only a penny, and its imitators soon flooded cities from Boston to Baltimore. The penny press drew more revenue from street sales and advertising than subscriptions and political patronage, and often ignored politics for dramatic stories of crime, scandal, and freakish accidents. By 1835, Day's *Sun* sold 8,000 copies a day, twice the entire daily circulation of New York newspapers before he began. Mass sales financed a steam-powered cylindrical press that could print 20,000 copies a day. Presses were spinning even faster by mid-century, using molds, or stereotypes, to preserve and quickly reproduce a page of type. In 1841, editor Horace Greeley introduced his *New York Tribune*, which combined the price and format of the penny press with careful reporting and increased separation of news from editorials. Together with the spread of rural weeklies, the cheap new urban papers nearly quadrupled newspaper circulation in the 1840s. Keeping pace, other new machines increased the production of inexpensive paper and unleashed a flood of affordable books, magazines, pamphlets, leaflets, and images.

Communication changed again after 1841, when New England inventor Samuel F. B. Morse perfected a magnetic telegraph that sent instantaneous messages over vast distances. Congress paid for the first telegraph line, running from Washington to Baltimore, but declined to purchase the invention itself, so telegraphy remained a private enterprise. Businessmen quickly saw its value for transmitting commodity prices and business news, but uses of the telegraph soon expanded. When war broke out with Mexico in 1846, New York newspaper readers got battlefield reports as fast as the generals, thanks to the telegraph. The new medium quickly seemed indispensable.

Public Support and Private Initiative

The Market Revolution needed more than new technology. Private fortunes were often too small, or investors too cautious, to assume all the costs and risks of major projects like canals or railroads. Promoters also felt the need for new laws and judicial principles to safeguard their investments and to regulate relations between different businesses. Above all, buyers and sellers needed sources of credit and a dependable currency to do business with each other. Americans combined public and private initiatives to carry out these tasks.

THE ROLE OF GOVERNMENT

One of the most important government contributions came from the US Constitution itself. Devised in part for the needs of commerce, the Constitution laid the groundwork for a national market economy by abolishing commercial barriers between the states, protecting property rights throughout the Union, forbidding anticommercial state policies like stay laws and inflationary paper money, and granting Congress power over postal service, patents, and bankruptcies. Alexander Hamilton went further by harnessing the national debt for development capital and establishing a nearly uniform national currency through the Bank of the United States. Led by Chief Justice Marshall, the Supreme Court endorsed Hamilton's broad construction of the Constitution and affirmed the economic powers of the federal government.

Federalists were not the only supporters of economic development. Jefferson's famous dictate "Let our workshops remain in Europe" acknowledged the need for long-distance trade, and some Jeffersonians thought that a people's government should promote it with direct investments. Congress allotted money from public land sales to road construction in 1802. It drew on these funds in 1811 to begin constructing the National Road, which started at Cumberland, Maryland, and led through the Appalachians to the Ohio River at what is now Wheeling, West Virginia. As intended, the National Road became an important highway for western expansion, and further extensions took it to Vandalia, Illinois, by the middle of the nineteenth century.

The War of 1812 fed demands for federal support of economic change. In 1811, Republican congressmen still thought the Bank of the United States was unconstitutional and would not renew its charter. Without a national bank, the wartime government had trouble borrowing money or transferring it from one region to another. When state banks then faltered and stopped exchanging their paper money for coin, experts warned that specie payments might not resume without guidance from a well-managed national bank. Lacking a national transportation system, moreover, the army was unable to move troops and supplies to the battlefronts, so the Canadian invasions had failed and General Andrew Jackson's forces had nearly collapsed from starvation.

Manufacturing posed other challenges. Even before the war, early cotton mills and steamboats pointed to an industrial future. Jefferson's embargo and the war itself had also stimulated manufacturing by forcing Americans to produce what they once imported. When peace came, the new producers did not want their infant industries to succumb to British competition, so owners and workers begged Congress for protection. Just as important, political and military leaders foresaw that future wars would require foundries to cast cannons, mills to weave sailcloth, and roads to move troops. Regardless of constitutional barriers or agrarian ideals, fostering American industry might be a military necessity. In 1816, a Republican Congress accepted this logic and adopted the United States' first protective tariff, or import tax designed to make foreign goods too expensive to compete with domestic alternatives.

States often created corporations to own and operate internal improvements. With some resemblance to the joint-stock companies that financed colonial explorations, corporations enabled individuals to pool their resources, but the corporation had additional privileges as an artificial legal person. It could own property, conduct business, sue and be sued, and outlive its individual owners, but it could only be established by a special law, or charter, passed by a state legislature. Unlike business partners, investors did not risk their entire fortunes in a corporation, but only the money they spent on stock. Called limited liability, this privilege made it much safer for strangers to invest in new enterprises. Many of the earliest corporations were mixed enterprises, jointly owned and paid for by governments and private investors. Initially, legislatures only granted charters for significant public services like building roads, supplying water, or even creating banks, but corporations eventually dominated manufacturing as well.

Internal improvements could bring great economic benefits, but they were also quite expensive. The Erie Canal cost about $7 million in 1825; competing projects were at least as costly and not nearly so profitable. Even the largest private fortunes could not furnish such sums, especially considering the serious risks involved, so promoters depended on government help. New York paid the entire cost of the Erie Canal with state bonds, while the state of Pennsylvania spent some $65 million on public works before 1860. In 1841, Indiana nearly went bankrupt after sinking $9 million in unprofitable transportation companies. Illinois collapsed the next year. Throughout the era, Americans spent some $200 million in canals, about two-thirds of it from state governments. The federal government also bought stock in companies like the Chesapeake & Delaware Canal on the East Coast and lavished land grants on others, including the Midwest's Wabash & Erie and Illinois & Michigan Canals. Despite the power of individualist rhetoric, economic development in America depended heavily on the government.

The federal government played another indispensable role by developing an effective post office. The colonial postal service had been a moneymaking operation for the colonial government that mostly carried the transatlantic correspondence of seaboard merchants. The Post Office Act of 1792 abandoned the goal of raising revenue and refigured the mail as a crucial means of information for business and self-government. The new law established very low rates for newspapers and allowed printers to exchange newspapers with each other for free. Congress soon insisted on scattering post offices widely to facilitate communication with constituents, and increased their number from 75 in 1790 to over 3,000 in 1816 and nearly ten times that many in 1860. Free exchanges enabled local papers to reprint news from the farthest parts of the Union, while cheap postage and widespread post offices allowed ordinary subscribers to receive the news directly from faraway places. As a result, newspapers took up most of the mail, followed by commercial circulars and correspondence. Since congressmen could send mail free, they sent a steady stream of printed speeches, reports, and newsletters to their home districts. The new system thus created a broad forum for public conversation and debate and permitted national campaigns for public office, social reform, religious conversion, and other causes. It also created a dense network of business communications that aided enterprise throughout the country, as interior trade overtook Atlantic commerce at the center of economic activity.

Most customers continued to pick up their mail at the local post office, but some offices offered home delivery for an extra fee, and private services did the same in some cities. Midcentury rate cuts finally made personal letters affordable for ordinary Americans, allowing them to keep in touch with migrating friends and family members and raising the volume of personal letters from 300,000 in 1790 to 3 million in 1856. Along the way, the Post Office used its power over mail routes to subsidize stagecoach companies and create a national network for overland transportation. Far larger than any private business, the Post Office operated with a vast bureaucracy, and succeeded remarkably well.

MONEY AND BANKING

Banks had a special place in the developing economy. To remedy wartime financial problems, Congress swallowed its constitutional doubts and chartered a second Bank of the United States as a mixed corporation in 1816, providing one-fifth of its $35 million in capital. As the nation's largest bank, the Bank of the United States made private loans and held the government's money interest-free. It could not meet all credit needs, however, so states also chartered banks, ranging from large and conservatively managed institutions in New York, Boston, and Philadelphia, to small and highly unreliable wildcat banks in frontier villages. The number of American banks rose steeply, from none at the end of the Revolution, to 208 in 1815, and to 1,562 in 1860.

Once chartered, a bank was supposed to sell stock for specie, and then start making loans in the form of paper notes bearing promises to pay a given amount of gold or silver on demand. These notes passed from hand to hand throughout the country to provide a currency for the rapidly growing economy. The value of banknotes depended on the issuing bank's ability to keep its promise and exchange them for specie, and those of the national bank were the most dependable. The federal mint issued some gold and silver coins but no paper currency, so legally privileged corporations issued most of the country's cash

Under the assumption that customers would never try to redeem all their notes at once, even the best banks loaned more paper than the specie in their vaults, handsomely multiplying the interest they collected. Some banks held no specie at all, either from fraud or because they had sold their stock on credit. Low specie reserves endangered banks when business instability made coins more trustworthy than paper. Unfortunately, instability is intrinsic to capitalism, because producers in good times eventually make more things than consumers can buy, leading to oversupplies of goods, a sudden collapse of prices, and a preference for specie and other enduring assets.

When this happened, banks could not satisfy everyone who suddenly wanted metal instead of paper, so they suspended specie payments and refused to honor the promises on their notes. Business confidence then collapsed, notes lost much of their value, prices plummeted, individuals and businesses could no longer pay their debts, bankruptcies multiplied, workers lost their jobs, and loans became nearly unobtainable. After a long spell of "hard times," confidence slowly returned and business conditions improved again. Nineteenth-century Americans called these episodes panics, and they were equivalent to modern recessions or depressions. Occasional recessions were (and are) inevitable, but the Market Revolution broadened their impact. A widespread suspension of specie payments had gripped the country during the War of 1812, and severe panics hit the country in

1819, 1837, 1839, and 1857. While the new economy promised greater prosperity, it also exposed Americans to more insecurity than before.

JUDICIAL SUPPORT

Chief Justice Marshall's claims of broad federal power supported the creation of a stable, nationwide marketplace. *Fletcher v. Peck* was an important early case that arose when the Georgia legislature tried to annul a public land sale resulting from massive bribery. Speaking for a unanimous court, Marshall decided in 1810 that the fraudulent sale remained valid because it was a contract, and the Constitution barred states from "impairing the Obligation of Contracts." This was the first time the Supreme Court ruled a state law unconstitutional. A supporting decision came in 1819, when the court blocked a New Hampshire takeover of Dartmouth College because its charter was also an inviolable contract. Both rulings gave invaluable support to the sanctity of business agreements, while the Dartmouth College case protected private corporations from government interference.

An especially crucial decision involved the Second Bank of the United States. In 1818, Maryland tried to privilege its state banks by imposing a stiff tax on the rival Baltimore branch of the national bank. Bank officer James McCulloch insisted that the state had no right to tax a federal institution, and refused to pay. Maryland replied that the Bank of the United States should not even exist because the Constitution gave Congress no explicit authority to create a bank. In *McCulloch v. Maryland* (1819), Marshall ruled for a unanimous court that the national bank was indeed constitutional. Though the Constitution did not mention banking, he reasoned that the Framers could not have listed every subject that might need legislation, so the Constitution permitted actions that were "necessary and proper" to exercise the powers it did list. Since a national bank seemed "necessary and proper" for national finance, Marshall continued, the national bank was constitutional and protected from the states. In 1824, the court reaffirmed this decision in *Osborne v. Bank of the United States*. Infuriating strict constructionists, Marshall affirmed the sweeping claims for implied federal power that Alexander Hamilton had used to defend the First Bank of the United States, and laid the groundwork for the wide authority of the modern federal government.

The Supreme Court also asserted broad federal powers over interstate commerce, not only based on the wording of the Constitution but also on marketplace values favoring competition and innovation. A pivotal case involved a steamboat monopoly that New York granted to Robert Fulton and his backers. Fulton's company sold Thomas Gibbons an exclusive license to operate a steam ferry to New Jersey, so when Aaron Ogden opened a competing line, Gibbons sued to stop him. In *Gibbons v. Ogden* (1824), Marshall reasoned that a principal purpose of the Constitution was "to benefit and improve" "the state of trade and commerce," so it should not be interpreted to stifle progress. He therefore ruled that Fulton (and hence Gibbons, his licensee) had no legal monopoly at all because Congress—not New York—had exclusive authority over interstate commerce. A similar case arose in 1837, after Marshall's death. The Charles River Bridge Company operated a toll bridge between Boston and Cambridge, Massachusetts, and tried to block a competing bridge by claiming that its earlier charter gave it a monopoly. Chief Justice Roger B. Taney rejected this claim and ruled for the new bridge, arguing that the Constitution should not block "those improvements which are now adding to the wealth and prosperity, and the convenience and comfort, of every other part of the civilized world." In both cases, private interests wanted to preserve old legal monopolies regardless of the consequences, but the court used the public interest to rule otherwise. Instead of perpetuating obsolete rights, the outcomes of *Gibbons* and the Charles River Bridge case favored the process of creative destruction.

Markets and Production

The new economy transformed how Americans worked and made things. Farmers changed their methods and grew different crops for new markets. Local artisans lost work to distant businesses and left self-employment for wage labor. Like Lucy Larcom and Sarah Bagley, a few found work in early factories. New ways of working not only changed how things were made but transformed personal relationships and traditional ideas about dependence and independence.

AGRICULTURAL IMPROVEMENTS

Writing in 1794, Assistant Secretary of the Treasury Tenche Coxe deplored the farming methods he observed in the middle states, reporting "innumerable instances of impoverished lands . . . ; a frequent inattention to the making or preserving of manure; as frequent inattention to the condition of the seed grain . . . ; the bad condition of *barns*, stables, and fences . . . ; [and] the neglect of household manufactures in many families." Coxe fumed that *"farming* . . . is too generally speaking, the least understood, or the least economically and attentively pursued, of any of the occupations which engage the citizens of the United States."

As canals and turnpikes stretched out from coastal cities, rural families with too many children on too few acres began to pay more attention to voices like Coxe's. When traditional methods became too unprofitable to protect their independence, farmers began manuring their fields and clearing wood lots to boost productivity. Europe's Napoleonic Wars encouraged their efforts, as armies drafted peasants, crop yields sagged, and prices soared for grain, meat, butter, leather, and other farm products. American farmers with the necessary skills and capital could suddenly prosper more readily by selling their crops in foreign markets. Others could move west for more and better land, or leave their farms for urban employment.

After peace returned in 1815, Europe's farms recovered and its need for imports slackened, so commercializing farmers sought customers in America's towns and cities. Instead of growing many things, they specialized in a few cash crops that gave them what economists call a comparative advantage over competitors. In the fertile Midwest, farmers turned wheat into flour to ship east on the Erie Canal or south on the Mississippi. Their corn fattened pigs for salted pork and gave Cincinnati the nickname "Porkopolis." Unable to match the West in these staples, eastern farmers raised perishables like milk, cheese, butter, fruits, and vegetables for nearby city dwellers. They also turned their least productive fields into pastures to supply cities with beef and woolen mills with fleece.

As inexpensive products became more available from urban workshops, farm women changed their own work. Along the Erie Canal, families gave up homespun for factory cloth. Farm women in the mid-Atlantic states sold butter and eggs in growing cities and turned these traditional female activities into major sources of family income. More and more rural families thus left the world of near-subsistence farming for the cash-dependent world of buying and selling.

Commercializing farmers were constantly alert for improved methods and formed state agricultural societies to publicize every possibility. They imported superior breeds of livestock and penned the animals to control their breeding and collect their dung. They also adopted labor-saving technology. In 1837, Illinois blacksmith John Deere developed a steel-tipped plow that easily broke the thick turf of midwestern prairies, and built an industrial empire based on farm tools. Other inventors came forward with new devices for planting seeds precisely, for mechanical cultivators to replace the handheld hoe, and a cradle scythe for harvesting wheat more easily.

An especially dramatic invention appeared in 1831, when young Cyrus McCormick built on his father's ideas to perfect a horse-drawn device for harvesting wheat. His first machines cut as many as 10 to 12 acres a day, but worked best on the broad, flat fields of the Midwest. Moving to Chicago from Virginia, McCormick sold 1,000 machines a year by 1851. Speed allowed farmers to gather more wheat before it spoiled, leading them to plant more and increase production. One of McCormick's rivals created the first combine, or machine that reaped and threshed in a single process, but his invention was not perfected until after the Civil War.

Many farmers welcomed the shift to a cash economy. In 1852, the president of the New York Agricultural Society rejoiced that old-fashioned practices like barter and sharing chores were disappearing, and boasted that the up-to-date farmer "now sells for money, and it is his interest to buy for money, every article that he cannot produce cheaper than he can buy. . . . His farm does not merely afford him a subsistence; it produces capital, and therefore demands the expenditure for its improvement." By implication, farmers with capital would edge out those without it. Mindful of such trade-offs, others expressed their doubts. The same year, one New Englander told a patent office investigator that "as a general rule . . . it is better that the farmer should produce what he needs for home consumption. . . . He may obtain more money from tobacco, hops or broom corn, than from breadstuffs, but taking all things into consideration will he be better off?" This cautious Yankee knew that if a farmer experimented with some highly specialized crop, a sudden panic might slash the value of his harvest and take his farm when he could not pay his debts. The same circumstances could take a farmhand's job or evict a tenant. In good times, farmers' incomes rose under the new system, but their need for capital and their vulnerability to economic downturns had grown.

FROM ARTISANS TO OPERATIVES

Manufacturing changed even more than agriculture. In colonial times, Americans had imported fine manufactures from England, but local artisans made everyday items, and these blacksmiths, tailors, carpenters, and others were vital members of the household economy. Their livelihoods had depended on slow, expensive transportation, however, for lower shipping charges exposed them to distant competition. The creative destruction brought by more efficient transport and machinery put many craftsmen out of business, blocked journeymen's rise to shop ownership, turned masters back into wage earners, and eventually ended the artisans' world. The change not only damaged their personal status but raised enduring questions of public concern, for republican ideology viewed the class of self-employed artisans—urban yeomen, in a sense—as essential to good government and a good society.

The decline of the artisanal economy began with simple articles like shoes. Traditionally, cordwainers made each pair of shoes by hand for a specific customer. Beginning in the late eighteenth century, enterprising merchants in Lynn, Massachusetts, and other nearby towns began to consolidate shoemaking by paying local families to make dozens of pairs at a time, especially in winter months when farm chores were fewer. To improve speed and cut costs, they applied a principle called division of labor to split shoemaking into a series of very simple tasks, like stitching the upper pieces together or binding them to the sole. Then they paid a few highly skilled artisans to cut out large quantities of standardized shoe parts and "put out" these materials to the homes of less skilled workers, who performed a single step of assembly over and over before passing the unfinished shoes to another worker.

Endless repetition increased workers' speed but eroded their skills when no one made a whole shoe anymore. The outworkers, many of whom were women and children, also commanded lower wages than skilled shoemakers, but shoe production rose, prices fell, and merchants increased their shipments over roads and canals. As early as the 1820s, western pioneers and southern slaves donned cheap New England work boots, while formerly independent shoemakers had become poorly paid hands under constant pressure to work faster. When Elias Howe invented the sewing machine in 1845, Lynn manufacturers used it to replace hand stitching without altering their methods fundamentally.

The division of labor could cheapen and simplify many tasks. Much like the merchants of Lynn, New York City businessmen employed highly skilled men to cut up cloth and put it out for women to assemble into ready-made shirts and trousers. For pennies a day, a seamstress might sew collar after collar in her own home, or a number of clothing workers could toil furiously together in a tiny sweatshop. Sweated workers could also make hats, buttons, artificial flowers, simple furniture, and hundreds of other articles that could be assembled in a series of simple tasks.

TEXTILE FACTORIES

The textile industry was the first to move from "putting out" to true factories. The process began in England, where the invention of the spinning jenny enabled a single worker to make thread on six or seven spindles at once, and subsequent improvements increased this number rapidly. Inventors then developed a power loom that tapped the energy from a water wheel or steam engine to weave much faster than a handworker. These machines did not require great strength or skill to operate, so manufacturers employed unskilled women and children at lower pay than men. They created the first true factories by bringing workers and equipment into one building with a single power source and soon flooded world markets with inexpensive cottons and woolens.

Britain banned the export of textile machinery to safeguard its monopoly, but an ambitious mechanic named Samuel Slater slipped away with the knowledge in his head. In 1790, Slater built America's first water-powered spinning mill at Pawtucket, Rhode Island. Similar mills soon spread across southern New England, using the labor of surrounding farm families. Middlemen put out the finished yarn for local women to weave in their homes.

When Jefferson's embargo blocked Atlantic trade, New England merchants and shipowners moved their capital from commerce to manufacturing. Like Samuel Slater, Francis Cabot Lowell memorized English loom designs and gathered a group of partners called the Boston Associates to launch the Boston Manufacturing Company in 1813. Using waterpower to drive its machines, the company concentrated carding, spinning, and weaving in a single structure in Waltham, Massachusetts. Factories on the "Waltham plan" were very expensive to build, but they produced cloth more efficiently than the putting-out system. In following years, the Boston Associates put Waltham-style factories at the falls of the Merrimack River and built the surrounding town of Lowell to house their workers. Copying their success, textile factories spread rapidly to other waterpower sites throughout New England.

Workers like Lucy Larcom and Sarah Bagley were unique features of New England factories. Managers stopped hiring local families and replaced them with young unmarried women from remote rural districts. These "mill girls" worked long hours amid choking dust, stifling heat, deafening noise, and tight supervision, marking time by the factory clock and whistle instead of the rhythms of nature. English factories and factory towns already had bad reputations for squalid living and working conditions, so American owners sought to head off such criticisms by requiring "mill girls" to attend church and live in strictly regulated boardinghouses like Mrs. Larcom's.

While their time and labor were no longer their own, factory wages gave many women the first cash they ever earned. "Sarah don't I feel independent of everyone!" a New Hampshire farm girl rejoiced in a letter to her friend back home, after her second payday. "The thought that I am living on no one is a happy one indeed to me." Most of the women hoped to work briefly to help a struggling family, educate a brother, or save money for marriage. In the meantime, despite harsh conditions, they somehow managed to conduct sewing circles, reading groups, and missionary societies, and also published a literary magazine, the *Lowell Offering*. Despite the fame of New England "mill girls," their lives were still exceptional in antebellum America. Outside the textile industry, most of the early industrial workforce was male, and more women probably toiled as outworkers in rural homes and urban tenements than as factory workers.

The seemingly wholesome Lowell experience reassured Americans who feared the grim conditions of English factories, and convinced many that manufacturing and commercial agriculture reinforced each other. A Maine editor credited "*a cotton factory*" for "the greater beauty of the farms, and the higher state of cultivation" in a nearby town, because it "furnished the ready home market for the wool, the hides, the fuel, timber, beef, pork, hay, butter, cheese, apples, cider, potatoes, and a great many other vegetables, besides eggs, lamb, veal, and many other things" produced on local farms. For many northerners, the editor's observations proved the benefits of American freedom and the superiority of their own society.

EARLY MASS PRODUCTION

As factories spread across New England, a series of smaller-scale developments prepared the way for greater changes later. In government-owned armories at Springfield, Massachusetts, and Harpers Ferry, Virginia (now West Virginia), a few visionary officers and inventors tried to simplify battlefield repairs by making guns out of interchangeable parts. They faced serious technical hurdles, but began to succeed in the 1820s with elaborate systems for precisely measuring, holding, cutting, and molding metal. Their improvements continued in the following decades, with limited civilian applications before the Civil War.

Other inventors tried using machines to make articles that were more complex than cloth. Unlike military officers, civilian businessmen wanted lower costs more than simplified repairs, so they worked on labor-saving devices instead of interchangeability. After patenting the revolving pistol in 1835, Colonel Samuel Colt used new machine tools to produce thousands of weapons for soldiers and civilians and made the single- and double-shot flintlock pistol obsolete. In the same period, Connecticut manufacturers devised machines to cut large numbers of cheap brass and wooden clock parts, until a simple windup clock cost no more than $1.50 by 1850, and peddlers could sell hundreds of thousands each year. Reversing the customary flow of trade, New England clockmakers even sold their products in Great Britain. Samuel Colt established an arms factory in London and astonished a committee of Parliament by declaring that "there is nothing that cannot be produced by machinery." Interchangeable parts and early machine production paved the way for more extensive mass production later in the century.

The new technology had dramatic effects. Home manufactures probably peaked in 1815, especially on major trade routes, but machine production of cotton cloth rose from 4 million yards in 1817 to 323 million in 1840, while prices fell by three-quarters. The impact of internal improvements and textile manufacturing ricocheted throughout the economy, as demand from railroads and machine production stimulated iron making and coal mining. The value of American manufactures increased by 59 percent in each census year between 1810 and 1840, exploded by 153 percent in the 1840s, and then returned to a growth rate of 60 percent in the final decade before the Civil War. Most Americans still lived on farms, and despite the rise of early factories, most workshops remained small, with fewer than 20 hands each in 1860. Even so, the once primitive American manufacturing economy had reached second or third place in the world when the Civil War began in 1861.

LABOR PROTESTS

Machine production had costs as well as benefits, for artisans lost independence and income as goods became cheaper. Colonial Americans had classed "hirelings" with paupers, servants, and slaves as weak dependents undeserving of full equality. As the proportion of wage earners rose from 12 percent of the workforce in 1800 to 40 percent in 1860, some observers worried that "wage slaves" could never be prosperous or independent citizens. Labor reformer Orestes Brownson went further and condemned wages as "a cunning device of the devil" that gave employers "all the advantages of the slave system, without the expense, trouble, and odium of being slave-holders." He longed instead to make every man "an independent laborer on his own capital, — on his own farm or in his own shop." Unable to avoid wage labor, other workingmen organized to defend what Sarah Bagley's Lowell Female Labor Reform Association called "the great principles of justice, equality and republicanism."

Early labor organizations grew out of eighteenth-century societies that enlisted both masters and journeymen, like New York's General Society of Mechanics and Tradesmen, but as competitive pressures increased, masters pushed for lower wages and longer hours while journeymen defended the opposite. In the first and second decades of the nineteenth century, these pressures led some journeymen to form separate organizations, agreeing with an 1817 declaration by the New York Typographical Society that "the interests of the journeymen are *separate*, and some respects *opposite* to the employers." These early labor unions struggled to uphold craft traditions that celebrated artisans as crucial members of republican society and fought against measures that seemed to undermine them, including wage cuts, the twelve-hour day, and the use of poorly trained workers to underbid skilled mechanics.

The first municipal labor federation, the Philadelphia Mechanics' Union of Trade Associations, took shape in 1827. New York followed soon afterward, and both organizations conducted strikes and political experiments with Workingmen's Parties (see chapter 11). The Lowell workers also "turned out" in 1834 and 1836 to protest wage cuts and rent increases in company-owned boardinghouses, and the same decade saw a wave of strikes by male workers in other trades. Even so, the right to strike was not well established, for in 1806, a Philadelphia court had convicted striking shoemakers of criminal conspiracy. The

Massachusetts Supreme Court affirmed the right to strike in 1847, but employers still used courts to counter union activity. The Panic of 1837 undermined both unions and Workingmen's Parties, but labor militancy became an enduring option for workers in asserting their own vision of republicanism for industrial society.

On the Move

The Market Revolution put Americans in motion as never before. The forces that sent many rural Americans to industrial jobs were also at work in Europe, and launched a new wave of Atlantic migration, often from regions and ethnic or religious groups with little previous presence in America. Many of the newcomers joined native-born Americans in the nation's growing cities, where they took the hardest and lowliest jobs. Americans also sought new lives across the Appalachian Mountains and created new communities on the frontier territories of the Old Northwest and Old Southwest.

IMMIGRATION

Even more than New Englanders, Europeans again strained their available resources in the early nineteenth century, for improvements in farming and sanitation had diminished epidemics and famines and doubled the population between 1750 and 1850. Beginning with Britain, western Europe had also seen improved roads, canals, railroads, and the introduction of factories, and just as in America, these innovations had undermined traditions, transformed agriculture, and revolutionized manufacturing. In the countryside, landlords owned most of the cultivated land, and sought to increase their profits by evicting tenants, consolidating plots, adopting new crops and machinery, and converting fields to pasture. Even more than in America, uprooted country people flocked to cities for new jobs and a fresh start, but often found low pay, grim working conditions, squalid housing, and dire poverty.

Hoping for something better, some five million Europeans moved to the United States between 1815 and 1860, more than the entire US population in 1790. Forsaking their loved ones and native villages for a new country where labor was scarce and wages were higher, three million arrived between 1845 and 1854 alone, proportionately the greatest wave of immigration in the nation's history. A few of these newcomers settled in southern cities, but most headed northward, where they would not compete with slaves and the diverse economy created more jobs. As its population swelled by one-third, America's rapidly growing economy somehow absorbed the newcomers, though not without social, cultural, and political strain.

By far the largest number came from Ireland. Most early Irish immigrants had been Scots-Irish Protestants, but those of the nineteenth century were largely impoverished Catholics fleeing eviction and famine. Even more than elsewhere, most of the land in Ireland belonged to absentee landlords who leased and subleased tracts as small as a single acre to farmworkers who used them to grow potatoes, a prolific and nutritious crop that the Columbian exchange had brought from South America. Seeking more profitable arrangements, ambitious landlords began consolidating these holdings in the 1820s, sending thousands of their former tenants to the cities of England and America.

Departures swelled to a flood after 1845, when a deadly fungus cut the potato harvest by as much as 80 percent. Potato crops suffered everywhere, but especially in Ireland, where the poor ate little else. From a population of seven million, as many as a million people died of hunger and disease as the blight lingered for another seven years. Another million fled to America.

The migrants traveled in the dark holds of American sailing vessels that carried timber and cotton in one direction and people in the other, in voyages that lasted from one to three months. Many were young people who hoped to bring their families later. Few could buy land in America, so they dug canals, built railroads, washed clothes, and served in middle- and upper-class homes. Concentrated in northeastern cities, the Irish-born constituted at least a quarter of the populations of Boston, New York, Philadelphia, and Baltimore by 1850, where poverty sent them to densely packed slums with inadequate water and sanitation. More-established Americans were often horrified and accused the Irish of increasing crime and the costs of public relief. Building on existing prejudices, Protestants often blamed these problems on the Catholic religion of the Irish or even their supposed racial inferiority.

A second wave of newcomers came from the Catholic areas of southern Germany, where more debt-ridden peasants were losing their land to foreclosure and consolidation. Other German migrants ran the gamut from paupers to artisans to prosperous farmers. Some were liberal activists and intellectuals who fled repression after democratic uprisings failed in 1848. A few were Jewish shopkeepers who continued in retailing, often starting as peddlers.

On arrival, most German immigrants headed for midwestern states like Ohio, Illinois, and Missouri. With more resources than the Irish, some got land and returned to agriculture. Others headed for ethnic neighborhoods in new cities like Cincinnati, Chicago, and St. Louis. There, immigrants of every nationality built institutions for themselves, from stores and bars that welcomed their languages and stocked their favorite products, to schools, mutual aid societies, newspapers, theaters, sports clubs, churches, and synagogues.

Less visible than the Irish or Germans, newcomers from Britain were the third-largest immigrant group in antebellum America, and they quickly blended with the existing population. Smaller numbers of antebellum migrants came from Scandinavia, Holland, and Canada.

URBANIZATION

Commerce and industry swelled the cities. The census of 1790 counted only 24 "urban" places of 2,500 people or more, but the 1860 tally put almost 400 towns on that list. Among them was Lowell, Massachusetts, whose locale contained no more than 200 inhabitants when the first factory arrived but 37,000 in 1860. The same census counted 8 American cities of 100,000 or more. In the same period, the number of urban dwellers in the northeastern states rose from one out of ten to one out of three, and the combined population of New York City and Brooklyn broke one million for the first time. Most immigrants had rural roots but settled in cities; at least one-third of urban residents were foreign-born in 1860.

American cities had begun as small Atlantic ports, but those with inland access, like New York, Philadelphia, and Baltimore, gained people along with trade. Boston flourished by supplying raw materials to the textile and shoe industries of surrounding towns. Cities also moved west, as interior ports like Cincinnati, St. Louis, and Chicago arose to handle the products of midwestern farms. Connections blossomed between growing cities until domestic commerce rivaled the importance of transatlantic trade.

Cities also changed their shape and structure. Urban businesses had formerly clustered along the waterfronts, where merchants kept their warehouses, docks, and countinghouses. Rich and poor lived side by side, with wealthy families in imposing homes on major streets and the poor in alleys behind them. Artisans' workshops and households appeared throughout the city. Lacking public transportation, most people walked from place to place, and tried to put their homes and shops as close to the city center as possible, pushing the disadvantaged to the city's margins.

These patterns began to change in the early nineteenth century. By separating home from work, new production methods broke up the artisan household, sending employers to comfortable residential neighborhoods and wage earners to crowded tenements. The distance between homes and jobs undermined the "walking city" and led to horse-drawn streetcars and omnibuses for urban transportation. Downtown centers for business and shopping drew away from industrial and residential neighborhoods, and a few wealthy residents began to commute from homes on the urban periphery that put city convenience in a semirural setting. From the bucolic society of independent yeomen envisioned by Thomas Jefferson, large parts of the United States were becoming the opposite by the outbreak of the Civil War—urban, industrial, wage earning, and dependent for every necessity on the ups and downs of the economic marketplace.

MOVING WEST

Restless rural families could also move west. When the War of 1812 quelled Indian warfare east of the Mississippi, millions of white Americans streamed across the mountains for new opportunities. In 1790, the white population of the Ohio country had numbered in the hundreds, but it rose to seven million by 1860, mostly from migrants and their children. Pioneers had created seventeen new states beyond the mountains by the outbreak of the Civil War.

The federal government supported the pioneers by pressing the remaining Indians to sell their lands, surveying the public domain, and selling it in ever-smaller parcels on increasingly generous terms. Speculation flourished, for land values seemed bound to rise as population grew. In the Michigan Territory alone, pioneers and investors increased their purchases of public land from half a million acres in 1834 to 4.2 million acres two years later. Speculation was especially brisk at proposed town sites. "I have seen detailed plans, with straight streets and fine public squares scrupulously reserved, of cities which do not actually consist of a single street, of towns which hardly contain three houses," marveled French traveler Michel Chevalier in 1836. "[S]everal of them have really become flourishing villages, although the dreams of their founders have not proved true."

Many of these speculative villages vanished, but not all of them. The city of Chicago began with a visionary sketch in 1830 and grew to 4,000 inhabitants in 10 years. Strategic location and a crucial canal gave it control of transportation between the Great Lakes and the Mississippi basin, and key rail lines extended its reach still farther. As the transportation hub of inland America, Chicago became a center for manufacturing, meatpacking, and retail distribution. Its population broke 100,000 by 1860, placing the onetime speculative dream among the top ten cities in the nation.

Speculation in future plantation districts was also fierce, as investors imagined vast future profits from growing cotton. "This country was just settling up," satirist Joseph Baldwin recalled as he later described what he called "the flush times of Alabama and Mississippi" in the 1830s. "Marvelous accounts had gone forth of the fertility of [the region's] lands," bringing unmatched returns to slave labor. "The State banks were issuing their bills by the sheet, like a patent steam-printing press [producing] *its* issues; and no other showing was asked of an applicant for the loan than an authentication of his great distress for money.... Under this stimulating process, prices rose like smoke." Speculation was just as feverish north of the Ohio, until bubbles burst in both the Panics of 1819 and 1837. Prices and credit suddenly collapsed, land sales almost halted, and thousands went bankrupt when no one could sell or pay for the overpriced tracts they had bought with borrowed money.

If they had the funds, more cautious settlers bought a few hundred acres of fertile wilderness to clear for farmland. The less fortunate squatted without paying, rented in hopes of buying later, or bought on credit and struggled to pay. Those who failed tried to sell their improvements to a newcomer and move west to start over. In the beginning, many families lived in crude log shelters and scratched a bare subsistence from tiny corn patches. Like Indians, they might earn cash by selling skins and furs. As settlements thickened and markets opened, they kept raising their own food but sold some for cash, just as safety-first farmers had done in the East. Before long, however, the combination of fertile soils and improved transportation allowed the Midwest to develop as a premier location of family-based commercial farming.

Cheap western lands gave many hard-pressed easterners a welcome alternative to city life or rural poverty, allowed them to renew the ideal of yeoman independence, and incidentally eased competition for urban jobs. For those who moved and those who stayed behind, the combination of growing cities and western expansion calmed older worries that Americans would sink into European-style poverty when too many were crowded on a fixed quantity of land.

Society in the Free States

The new economy reached into almost every corner of American society. Commercial agriculture linked farmers to the business cycle, pushed families west, and broke up old customs of swapping, bartering, and semisubsistence. Manufacturing raised new fortunes, created new occupations, and destroyed old crafts. Immigration diversified religion and culture while increased mobility rocked the stability of communities, traditions, and established elites. In the two generations between the elections of Thomas Jefferson and Abraham Lincoln, eighteenth-century notions of rank and deference gave way to a more impersonal culture of public equality among white men of the free states.

But economic change also shaped a new class structure based on new sources of wealth for some and wage labor for others. Between the extremes, the "middling sort of people" from colonial days gave way to an urban middle class with new tastes, aspirations, and work habits. In middle-class families, changes in women's lives were especially important in reshaping personal values, religious standards, community customs, and eventually the agendas of politics.

EQUALITY AND INEQUALITY

Eighteenth-century Americans had lived in a society of ranks, with a multitude of steps between the lowliest slave, the struggling laborer, the independent yeoman or artisan, and the gentleman with economic, cultural, and political power. In a vertically ranked society, everyone seemed to know who stood above and below, but ties between roughly equal people seemed less important. For example, masters, journeymen, and apprentices in the same trade might feel more in common with each other—despite their inequality—than with economic peers in other lines of work.

Contemporaries frequently boasted that the American Revolution had opened a golden age of democratic equality that eliminated the class distinctions of aristocratic Europe. Foreign visitors frequently agreed. Ignoring the gulf between whites and blacks, and men and women, for example, French nobleman Alexis de Tocqueville opened his classic 1835 account, *Democracy in America*, by pointing to "the general equality of condition among the people." The famous traveler did not mean that all Americans lived alike, but that class distinctions among whites were more open and flexible than in Europe because white men claimed political equality as their birthright.

Certainly hopes of social and economic improvement lay behind the mass migration of poor Europeans to America, and reality anchored these hopes. Visitors seemed uniformly impressed that white Americans were better dressed, fed, and housed than their European counterparts. But while immigrants earned more in America than in the old country, ascent from wage earning to small business ownership was difficult and gaining true affluence was rare. One careful study of Poughkeepsie, New York, in the 1850s found that less than one skilled worker in four moved from earning wages to self-employment. In Poughkeepsie and Philadelphia, only 5–10 percent of manual laborers made this leap, but nonmanual clerks had strikingly better chances, with 25–38 percent of them becoming professionals or business owners in the 1850s.

Stark economic differences therefore mingled with boasts of equality. Americans invented the word "millionaire" in the 1840s. There were 10 such New Yorkers in 1845 but 115 in 1860. John Jacob Astor, the city's richest man, had prospered in the western fur trade, but the bulk of his $25 million fortune came from urban land speculation. In contemporary Boston, the Lowell mill complex made Francis Cabot Lowell and his fellow manufacturers almost as wealthy. By 1860, 1 percent of Bostonians owned 65 percent of the city's taxable property and the top tenth owned 95 percent, but half the city's people had none.

Wealth was more evenly distributed in the rest of the rural North, but the top 1 percent of Americans still owned 29 percent of the country's wealth in 1860. Economic historian Lee Soltow determined that almost two-fifths of America's free men owned less than $100 worth of land or personal property that year, leaving them and their families with little more than their clothing and some meager household goods. Other historians have found that midcentury artisans earned about $300 a year but needed more than $500 for a minimal standard of living. The slim earnings of their wives and children made up the difference. The rise of capitalism thus brought great wealth to a few Americans, modest prosperity to more, and poverty to many in the new working class. In a telling sign that the old system of deference had eroded, free workers stopped referring to their employers as "master" and called them "boss" instead—a Dutch word that meant the same thing but felt less demeaning.

THE BURDEN OF RACE

With hard work and good fortune, some Americans could overcome poverty, but racial inequality was more enduring. The absolute number of free African Americans grew rapidly after the Revolution, leveled off after 1820, and reached 500,000 in 1860. Half the nation's free blacks lived in the North, especially in cities, but the surge in white immigration reduced their proportions in the overall urban population. Northern blacks suffered continued discrimination in employment, housing, education, and political rights, and even faced kidnapping and re-enslavement.

Every sizable northern city held free people of color who succeeded in professions that included business, teaching, law, and the ministry. Others plied their skills as barbers, caterers, and tailors, and in other trades. For the most part, however, free blacks faced inflexible discrimination. White artisans would not train or employ them because other whites refused to work beside them. European immigrants quickly picked up local racial customs and insisted on the privileges of whiteness. Early labor unions would not accept black members or insisted on racially separate organizations. As a result, northern blacks had scant opportunities outside difficult and poorly paid work as laborers or domestic servants.

Blacks faced legal discrimination as well. Laws barred their settlement in some midwestern states. Outside New England, most blacks had no right to vote, to sit on juries, or to serve in the militia. Their children were usually confined to segregated schools, or denied education entirely. Segregation prevailed in hotels, restaurants, stagecoaches, streetcars, railroads, and steamboats. Housing discrimination often confined blacks to the poorest and most dangerous neighborhoods: New Guinea in Boston, Little Africa in Cincinnati, and New York's Five Points. Black neighborhoods were often the targets of white mobs that assaulted the helpless, demolished property, and put residents to flight. After an 1834 riot in Philadelphia, investigators blamed blacks for taking white jobs and behaving too boisterously in public.

Free people of color sustained their communities by continuing to build their schools, churches, and fraternal lodges. A black Order of Odd Fellows organized in 1843, followed by the First Colored Grand Lodge of Masons in 1845. Most large cities featured black self-help associations for men and women, like Baltimore's Friendship Benevolent Society for Social Relief and its Daughters of Jerusalem. African Americans also founded colleges, including the schools that became Lincoln University in Pennsylvania and Wilberforce University in Ohio, and a few enrolled at Oberlin and other white colleges. Launching a tradition that would lead to the civil rights organizations of the twentieth century, the first National Negro Convention assembled in Philadelphia in 1830 to criticize plans for deporting blacks to Africa and pondered moving to Canada instead. Similar conventions met with rising frequency and intensity as the Civil War approached.

Black communities supported antislavery speakers, newspapers, and petition campaigns, and helped runaway slaves by hiding them, finding work for them, and protecting them from professional slave catchers. In 1827, Samuel Cornish and John Brown Russworm founded *Freedom's Journal* in New York, the nation's first black-owned newspaper. Frederick Douglass, William Wells Brown, J. W. C. Pennington, and numerous other runaways founded a rich literary tradition with autobiographies detailing their own experiences as slaves. Douglass, Brown, Pennington, and a host of others also won renown as antislavery speakers and essayists, and in 1847 Douglass started his own newspaper, the *North Star*. When slavery finally fell, northern black communities were poised to send teachers, ministers, and other leaders to assist their newly liberated brothers and sisters.

A NEW MIDDLE CLASS

The division of labor affected nonmanual workers almost as much as artisans. Even in big cities, eighteenth-century retailers had usually carried everything from ribbons to iron ingots, while importers and exporters dealt in every kind of commodity from sugar to hides. By the mid-nineteenth century, urban retailers were more likely to specialize in something like clothing or furniture, or experiment with large, well-organized establishments that foretold the coming of department stores. Wholesale merchants concentrated on particular commodities and spun off specialized occupations: brokers, jobbers, auctioneers, and agents. Business also became more systematic, with improved methods of inventory, bookkeeping, record keeping, and internal organization. Banks and insurance companies underwent comparable transformations, while railroad and steamship lines pioneered in managing great enterprises over long distances. Every new step in specialization required its own skills and bred new occupations for a growing middle class. Within the factories, clerks and managers moved to offices that were closer to customers and far from mechanical din. And as nonmanual work became cleaner, quieter, and detached from production, clerks gained prestige while operatives lost it.

While some Americans had always fallen among the "middling sort" in income and social prestige, the new occupations were among the first to provide comfortable incomes from salaries instead of self-employment. Every growing town also needed lawyers, physicians, ministers, teachers, and storekeepers. These men and their families could lead genteel lives without manual labor, and were numerous enough to shape national standards of consumption, behavior, gender roles, morality, and religion. In the process, they virtually created the middle class as a pervasive American social ideal.

THE HOME AS WOMAN'S SPHERE

The separation of home and work changed households as much as neighborhoods. Middle-class men now left their urban dwellings for work every morning, and their employees had separate lodgings. As households emptied, families embraced the idea of privacy and separated their living quarters from semipublic spaces like the entrance hall. The front room that once held a shop or office became a well-furnished parlor, with comfortable furnishings like carpets, curtains, upholstered furniture, and, the ultimate symbol of respectability, a piano. In very large cities, like New York and Philadelphia, thousands of middle-class homes even boasted running water and flush toilets.

Economic development brought multiple changes to the lives of American women. Poorer women took jobs and earned wages denied to their grandmothers, and like Lucy Larcom, some wrung benefits from their new circumstances. Lacking Larcom's good fortune, others suffered silently while some protested like Sarah Bagley. Women in the urban middle class did not earn wages or work outside their homes, but their lives also changed dramatically in the new economy.

When men's work moved to separate locations, mothers and their children took daytime possession of the middle-class home, joined perhaps by a servant or two. Purchasing consumer goods in stores, these women could give up household manufactures like spinning and weaving to focus on cooking, needlework, and childcare, with time left for visiting friends. Housekeeping standards probably rose as spotless floors and clothing became attainable symbols of affluence. Middle-class women also faced more pressure to produce elaborate meals, fancy needlework, and doting childcare than their overworked grandmothers had time for. Contemporary magazines told them how to train their roughhewn husbands to respect their newly beautified interiors, keeping boots off the furniture and tobacco juice off the carpet. Some women found time for reading, correspondence, and diary keeping, a luxury that has given historians unparalleled access to their thoughts, feelings, and daily routines.

Some early republican women built on the ideal of republican motherhood to claim a more active role in public life. They could read and write political literature, petition their legislatures, join female reading circles, speak and perform in some public ceremonies, and in New Jersey even vote. Increased interest in female education brought hundreds of new schools for young women, many offering the same academic curricula as those for men. As Revolutionary ardor dimmed in the Jeffersonian era, however, women's participation in public affairs contracted again. Lawmakers increasingly defined suffrage as the natural right of all white men, regardless of property, establishing politics as an exclusively masculine arena and pushing nonvoting women to the side. As evangelical religion spread into middle-class northern families, moreover, ministers insisted that women should concentrate on turning their homes into centers of Christian love and virtue where husbands and children could find salvation. Beyond that, women might find a public role in church work and charity, but not in the hurly-burly of masculine politics.

Excluded from public life, middle-class antebellum women forged the idea of home and family as "woman's sphere," where feminine emotions and moral authority held sway. In the words of a popular lady's magazine, "To render *home* happy, is woman's peculiar province; home is *her* world." According to the author, domestic authority brought a form of gender equality, for a woman was "neither greater nor less than man, but different, as her natural vocation is different, and . . . each is superior to each other in their respective departments of thought and action." Thanks to unique feminine qualities, declared another, the whole "Universe might be Enlightened, Improved, and Harmonized by WOMAN!"

In the pages of women's magazines and advice books, plentifully produced by cheap new methods of printing, the world beyond the home was brutal, sordid, and masculine, but "woman's sphere" was pious, pure, loving, and redemptive. Though men were endowed with reason and strength, the authors explained, "true women" were more attuned to emotions, morality, and religion. Wives read that submission to their husbands was their greatest source of strength, for it melted men's anger and dissolved their resistance to feminine influence. Eighteenth-century patriarchs had claimed moral as well as physical superiority, with absolute power over their families, but their antebellum grandsons were more likely to leave child-rearing to their wives and admit that women might uplift men instead of the other way around.

The resulting "cult of domesticity," or "true womanhood," became an important cultural ideal, though it did not spread evenly or to everyone. As the eloquent black abolitionist Sojourner Truth reportedly snapped, no one gave special courtesy to her, "and ar'n't I a woman?" In practice, the cult of domesticity applied to middle- and upper-class "ladies," but not to blacks, servants, mill workers, or the widows who stitched in tenements.

Ironically, the cult of domesticity kept ladies in the home, but control of "woman's sphere" gave some of them an alternate source of authority. In the daytime absence of men, many middle-class women and girls formed powerful friendships with each other that often seemed more emotionally fulfilling than their marriages. Mothers restrained their feelings for their children less, and spoke and wrote much more openly about their intense love for each one, their heartbreak over each loss. They carefully studied the Bible and other religious literature, organized prayer groups and missionary societies, and learned techniques of leadership and communication with other women. They taught religion to their children and dragged their husbands to church, hoping to save those whom the soulless market had degraded. The birthrate fell as middle-class families stopped needing their children's labor, and this may have reflected the heightened autonomy of wives. Ironically, the cloying values of sentimentality and gentility made space for middle-class women to grow and flourish, and build their strength for greater challenges to male power.

∗

The Market Revolution began in the late eighteenth and early nineteenth centuries, with changes in technology that expanded long-distance commerce. Cheaper transportation opened local economies to competition with faraway producers, forcing regions and families to seek their comparative advantages, specializing in cash crops to pay for things made elsewhere. Parallel changes in communication caused information to travel even faster than people or goods, increasing the possibility—and the need—for long-distance decision making. Other developments made it possible to produce things for sale in large quantities, which inspired continuous efforts to make more goods, cheaper and faster. As a result, Americans increasingly based their daily actions on the signals conveyed by impersonal markets. Even more than before, the crops a farmer grew, the products his wife made, the skills and jobs available to their children, and the family's decisions to move or stay put depended on costs and prices shaped by distant events.

Manufacturing changed even more conspicuously, first in traditional crafts like shoemaking and tailoring, and then with machines that made everything from cloth to revolvers. In many fields, new technology made workers' skills less relevant and forced them to work harder, faster, and longer for lower wages. Striking back, journeymen tried to protect their status and income by organizing the earliest labor unions.

These changes transformed northern society. The new economy brought prosperity, but also exposed more Americans to the uncertainty of the business cycle, with attendant bankruptcies and unemployment. The transition from self-employment to wage labor would force artisans to rethink their treasured dreams of independence. Millions of European immigrants arrived in northern cities to take new jobs in a growing economy. Pioneers surged west, and cities grew dramatically, changing their shape as homes and workplaces pulled apart. A new class structure brought great wealth to some and left others as lifelong wage earners. Between these extremes, an urban middle class emerged to shape new national expectations in religion, culture, and women's roles.

The Market Revolution would have important implications for public affairs. Older republican theory maintained that true liberty required a level of equality that prevented the rich from exploiting the poor and a degree of simplicity that reduced the temptations of luxury and selfishness. What then would higher standards of living and rising levels of wealth and poverty mean for the republic? Rapid fluctuations between prosperity and hard times would frighten and enrage many Americans, as did the influx of immigrant culture and religion. Both concerns sparked crucial political reactions. The demand for western expansion likewise drove public debate and sometimes led to war. Perhaps most important, middle-class faith in freedom and perfectibility would inspire hopes for local and national reform, and feed opposition to freedom's greatest enemy — human slavery.

CHAPTER 9

Northern Culture and Reform, 1815–1860

When Congress tightened the Fugitive Slave Act in 1850, one furious abolitionist dared her sister-in-law to act. "Hattie, if I could use a pen as you can," wrote Isabella Jones Beecher, "I would write something that will make this whole nation feel what an accursed thing slavery is." Harriet Beecher Stowe embraced the challenge. According to family recollections, she stood with the crumpled the letter in her hand and vowed, "I will write something. I will write something if I live."

In 1851, Harriet Beecher Stowe was the shy wife of a professor and the mother of six. She had only written magazine sketches before, but she set to work on a blistering novel while her sister Catharine ran her household. Installments of *Uncle's Tom's Cabin* soon began appearing in the *National Era*, a widely circulated weekly. Long and heart-wrenching, her book told contrasting stories of the saintly Uncle Tom, sold down the Mississippi and eventually murdered by the brutal Simon Legree, and the plucky George and Eliza Harris, who saved their family by escaping to Canada. A surprise blockbuster, Stowe's novel sold millions of copies worldwide and left a massive impact on public opinion.

Uncle Tom's Cabin told its readers that bondage violated the fundamental values of domesticity and evangelical religion, destroying slave families and corrupting white ones, teaching masters to sin and slaves to despair. Despite furious southern protests, Stowe's novel played a major role in turning a northern majority against slavery. No one suspected beforehand that this retiring mother could write the world's greatest piece of antislavery literature, but when she met Abraham Lincoln in 1862, the president reportedly greeted her as "the little woman who wrote the book that started this great war!"

Harriet Beecher Stowe came from a remarkable family. Her father

CAMP-MEETING

FIGURE 6. During the Second Great Awakening, some participants in religious revivals experienced powerfully emotional conversions to evangelical Christianity, though others looked on with amusement. Popular Graphic Arts, Prints and Photographs Division, Library of Congress, LC-DIG-ds-030915.

was the Reverend Lyman Beecher, the era's most famous clergyman. Though humbly born, Beecher entered Yale, found conversion, and began to preach in 1799, moving from his obscure Long Island pulpit to one of Boston's leading Congregational parishes in 1826. He plunged into controversy everywhere, denouncing Jeffersonians, Roman Catholics, drunkenness, dueling, and religious indifference with power and fury. Initially skeptical of the Second Great Awakening, Beecher switched to support when he witnessed the effectiveness of revivals, and he became a leading advocate of voluntary organizations to fight sin. He ended his career as president of Lane Seminary in Cincinnati, determined to save the West with a new generation of ministers and missionaries. At every stage, Beecher churned out widely read books, pamphlets, and sermons in the classic Puritan mold, demanding penitence, conversion, and reform for an erring nation.

Lyman Beecher made a deep impression on his thirteen children. Most of his sons became distinguished ministers too, and Henry Ward Beecher succeeded him as the nation's best-known clergyman. His eldest daughter, Catharine, became a leading advocate of women's education, founding a series of outstanding girls' academies. She also wrote widely selling schoolbooks and *A Treatise on Domestic Economy*, which became the leading household manual of its day. Catharine shared her sister Harriet's antislavery principles, but she revered female domesticity and deplored political agitation by women, especially in the controversial cause of abolitionism. She thus could not agree when her sister Isabella became a leading advocate of women's suffrage. Drawing on a rich family tradition, the Beechers embodied the diversity and dedication of antebellum movements for religion and reform.

They were not alone. Throughout the country, and especially in the middle class, antebellum Americans hatched endless plans for reform and improvement. There were movements to distribute the Bible, to build asylums, penitentiaries, and schools, to ban strong drink, to bring world peace, to purify diets, and to commune with the dead. Religious revivals surged from the frontier to city streets, launching new sects and doctrines. Idealists renounced materialism and pledged to live together in loving communities, holding all goods in common. Prophets foretold the Second Coming and dabbled in sexual experiments from free love to total abstinence. Women were among the most outspoken, proclaiming their rights to speak and act in public, even to vote.

The reform ethos was strongest in the North, but the South was not immune. Moved by revivals, white southerners banded together to build schools, aid the poor, stop drinking, and save souls, but they could not equal others' efforts. One reason was that reform grew from the domestic values and new roles for women that the Market Revolution brought to the urban middle class, a limited development in the South. Equally important, as Stowe demonstrated, the reformers' values collided with slavery. North Carolina's conservative senator Nathaniel Macon felt the affinity as early as 1818. "We have abolition-colonizing bible and peace societies," he warned a friend. "Their intentions may not be known; but the character and spirit of one may without injustice be considered that of all." The senator was right. Before long, the reform movements did culminate in the epic attack on African American slavery.

Uncle Tom's Cabin was also part of a revolution in American literature, one of thousands of inexpensive newspapers, magazines, books,
pamphlets, handbills, and sheets of music that flooded stores and post
offices. Critics praised this outpouring as a declaration of literary independence that showed how America no longer depended on Europe
for ideas. More subtly, the new literature also taught that determined
individuals could remake themselves for the better. Repeated through
thousands of sources, this message suffused a new American culture.

The Fate of the Republic

Many Americans greeted the end of the War of 1812 with a burst of
patriotic optimism that seemed to wipe away military embarrassments
like the failed invasions of Canada and the burning of Washington,
DC. Enthusiastic speechmakers and editors converted the war's dubious beginnings, spotty results, and bitter political divisions into an un-
broken triumph over Europe's strongest forces, and in the heady aftermath, many predicted a glorious future for America and the principles
of republicanism.

While praising the republic's potential, some Americans were also
very concerned about its fragility. The fiftieth anniversary of independence would arrive in 1826, and the Founding Fathers were passing
away. Would the rising generation be equal to the achievements of
their heroic parents? Would republican virtue survive the temptations
of prosperity, complacency, and sin? Fears that the republic might fall
even faster than it rose drew attention to America's imperfections and
stimulated religious revivals and a wide-ranging movement for reform.

THE POSTWAR MOOD

President James Monroe captured an important facet of the national
mood in his 1816 inaugural address in which he ignored obvious evils
to boast "how near our government has approached perfection." Other
public figures agreed and pointed to the war's results as signs of divine
favor. "Was not the Lord of Hosts with our republican armies?" cried
a Vermont orator. "Did it not 'please the Almighty' to give victory?"
On July 4, 1815, the first Independence Day since the coming of peace,
similar sentiments echoed in village assemblies from Maine to Georgia.

National pride reached beyond military and political achievements
to embrace the economic and technological improvements brought by

the Market Revolution. In 1824, Massachusetts orator Edward Everett spoke for many when he reminded Harvard's Phi Beta Kappa chapter of "the intensest activity" in American cities, the agricultural innovations in the countryside, and the spreading network of roads and canals that linked the two. "Abroad," he boasted, "our vessels are beating the pathways of the ocean white; on the inland frontier, the nation is journeying on, like a healthy giant, with a pace more like romance than reality." In short, beamed Everett, "the country is growing with a *rapidity* without example in the world," while "arts, letters, agriculture, all the great national interests, all the sources of national wealth are growing in a ratio still more rapid."

Beneath all the fanfare, not everyone was confident and some were even worried. In the spirit of Puritan jeremiads, cautious observers warned once again that a successful republic depended on virtue, and loss of it meant ruin. Boston's 1815 Independence Day orator remembered that "military corruption or political depravity, the mad ambition and profligacy of rulers, or the degeneracy and debasement of the people, can . . . eradicate the principles of liberty, blast the hopes of refinement, and bring back another age of darkness and barbarism." Lyman Beecher was more direct. "The bible is denounced," he cried. "The sabbath is profaned; the public worship of God is neglected; intemperance hath destroyed its thousands, and is preparing the destruction of thousands more; while luxury, with its diversified evils, with a rapidity unparalleled, is spreading in every direction, and through every class." Wealth and progress were especially perilous, for without moral and religious restraints, the golden calf of riches could bring wickedness and retribution. "All which is done to stimulate agriculture, commerce, and the arts," Beecher thundered, "is . . . but providing fuel for the fire which is destined to consume us. The greater our prosperity, the shorter its duration, and the more tremendous our downfall, unless the moral power of the Gospel shall be exerted to arrest those causes which have destroyed other nations." In the minds of moral and political sentries like Beecher, America teetered on a brink. A glorious future beckoned, but one false step and the world's only major republic could perish.

TROUBLING SYMPTOMS

Throughout the country, social and economic changes associated with the Market Revolution were inflaming the evils that critics deplored. As the children of marginal yeoman families trekked away from long-settled areas, they also left the restraining influences of traditional homes, churches, and local governments. Was it surprising that the president of Yale accused Maine frontiersmen of "prodigality, thoughtlessness of future wants, profaneness, irreligion, immoderate drinking, and other ruinous habits?" Roughhewn revivalist Lorenzo Dow agreed, calling northern Vermonters "the offscouring of the earth . . . [who] ran hither for debt . . . to avoid prosecution for crimes, and . . . to accumulate money." Another critic called frontier Kentucky "Rogues Harbor," where "murderers, horse thieves, highway robbers, and counterfeiters fled . . . until they combined and actually formed a majority," forcing "the honest and civil part of the citizens" into vigilante justice.

Disorder was especially troublesome in the nation's rapidly growing cities. From 1790 to 1860, the proportion of Americans living in urban areas quadrupled, from 5 to 20 percent. New York grew even faster, doubling its population between 1814 and 1834 while quadrupling its crime rate. Whether they came from rural America or distant lands like Ireland and Germany, the newcomers escaped their employers' oversight as traditional households of masters and apprentices fell apart, and struggled for livelihoods in the sweatshops and "putting out" industries fostered by the Market Revolution. Working-class women who freely roamed the streets and mocked traditional restraints on feminine behavior especially worried urban authorities. With even less supervision, migrant bachelors fanned across the country to labor on large-scale construction projects like the Erie Canal or the growing network of railroads. Roman Catholic immigrants were especially alarming to traditional American Protestants, and many observers likewise worried that the newcomers' tolerant attitudes toward alcohol fostered poverty and crime.

The urban problems that disturbed antebellum reformers were often quite real. Modern historians have verified that Americans of the 1820s and 1830s drank an average of seven gallons of pure alcohol per year—more than twice as high as modern levels and enough for two shots of 80-proof whiskey a day for every American over fifteen. Resulting problems with alcoholism, violence, and domestic abuse could be devastating for the individuals involved and dangerous for their communities.

In addition, the new economy did not provide a decent livelihood for everyone. When new production methods sidelined artisans, poverty could send whole families into ill-paid urban industries that left them hungry and cold. Conditions grew worse in times of financial distress; New York charity workers counted 8,000 paupers during the Panic of 1819 and 13,000 a year later, and estimated that 50,000 were unemployed in New York, Philadelphia, and Baltimore in the same period. Even in good times, the incomes of day laborers and pieceworkers fluctuated wildly with the weather and similar seasonal conditions. Traditional systems of poor relief and charity predictably crumpled under the strain.

Almost inevitably, poverty and urban crowding led to poor sanitation and disease. Urban doctors reported that thousands of poor families lived in single rooms or cellars only 10 feet square, with virtually no light, ventilation, or clean water. "In these places, the filth is allowed to accumulate to an extent almost incredible," reported Dr. John Griscom in his 1845 account *The Sanitary Condition of the Laboring Population of New York.* "The walls and windows . . . become broken, the doors and floors become injured, the chimneys fill with soot, the whole premises populated thickly with vermin, the stairways . . . the receptacle for all things noxious, and whatever of self-respect the family might have had . . . crushed under the pressure of the degrading circumstances." With no knowledge of germs, physicians like Dr. Griscom still knew that these conditions were "productive of the most offensive and malignant diseases," including yellow, typhoid, and scarlet fevers, as well as smallpox, cholera, measles, tuberculosis, and rheumatism. Even worse, according to urban missionaries, crowding exposed children to nakedness and sex, so as one put it, their minds and morals "become greatly debased, and [their] fall before the assaults of vice become[s] almost certain." In the missionaries' view, poverty injured morals as much as health, and both doctors and ministers cried out for urgent remedies.

REVIVALS IN THE NORTH

The Second Great Awakening began in the rural South, but it heavily influenced Americans' responses to antebellum social problems as it spread to the growing towns and cities of the North. As northern ministers watched disorder mount in their own section, they began to see the appeal of revivals as potential answers to what they perceived as a flood of national sinfulness.

National confidence bolstered their efforts. In the optimistic atmosphere of the early republic, Americans increasingly expected to shape their own futures, including their moral lives and spiritual prospects. Even among Calvinistic Congregationalists and Presbyterians, ministers relaxed or even discarded the doctrine of predestination, and taught instead that God would open heaven to all who sought it sincerely. Theologians like Rhode Island's Samuel Hopkins and Yale's Timothy Dwight went further and taught that the best way to demonstrate one's love of God was to show "disinterested benevolence" to others and seek to convert them as well. Fortified by this blessing of individual efforts for personal and social improvement, evangelical religion became a powerful force to reorder a seemingly chaotic society. Beginning in the 1820s, the first and greatest example of its power appeared when the northern phase of the Second Great Awakening blossomed along the path of New York's Erie Canal.

The "Big Ditch" had unleashed rapid social change in a rural backwater populated mostly by migrants from western New England. Canal towns like Buffalo and Rochester grew quickly, moral standards relaxed, and transient canal workers collided with pious country folk. Rapidly expanding commerce rewarded avarice and double-dealing and ignored drinking, cursing, and Sabbath-breaking, while the New Englanders' high moral expectations collided especially harshly with the frontier's imperfect reality. Soon after the canal's completion in 1826, sober residents welcomed the revival ministry of the Reverend Charles Grandison Finney, a tall, handsome preacher with a riveting gaze and commanding personal presence. Befitting the new nation's confidence in personal freedom, Finney ignored the riddles of predestination and put the responsibility for salvation squarely on the individual, titling his most famous sermon "Sinners Bound to Change Their Own Hearts." After successful appearances throughout the canal district, Finney led a climactic six-month campaign in Rochester in 1830–1831 that brought thousands to repent their sins and embrace new lives committed to God and personal reform.

Most of Finney's converts were not the transient laborers whom many residents associated with disorder, but leading townspeople who seemed to blame themselves for a lack of moral leadership. Prosperous women came first, followed by their husbands and other male relatives. Ambitious clerks and workingmen came next, perhaps influenced by the example of their employers. Inspired by the revival, converts rushed to join churches and reform their personal behavior. The women dedicated themselves to creating Christian homes and bringing their families to Christ, while their wayward menfolk swore off idle diversions like liquor and cards and pledged to purify their working lives by dedicating their business pursuits to God. If they could not persuade all their rowdy employees to imitate them, they would enforce evangelical morality with strict regulation of taverns and working-class amusements.

The formula worked. In the next generation, the fires of revival and reform swept western New York so often it became known as the "Burned-Over District," and Finney carried revivalism to his own enormous church on Manhattan's Broadway. Finney became so good at leading revivals that he wrote an instruction manual for others, *Lectures on Revivals of Religion*, and baldly admitted that revivals were not spontaneous acts of God but human contrivances to be used for God's purposes.

Initially, orthodox clergy like Lyman Beecher complained of Finney's exuberant methods and slipshod theology, but they could not resist his success. Beecher became the foremost advocate of moderate revivalism in New England, and convinced most rural and small-town Congregationalists that ardent preaching and sincere efforts at personal and social reform could update and reestablish Puritan values in a changing world. He carried the same message to Ohio when he accepted the presidency of Cincinnati's Lane Seminary in 1832. Influenced by Finney, Beecher, and their imitators, the northern middle class embraced evangelical Protestantism and tried to bring their version of moral seriousness to a turbulent American society.

Revivals and Reform

The success of evangelical religion strengthened the drive to reshape America. For an influential minority of citizens, evangelical Protestantism became an inspiration for social improvement, and even social perfection, supporting new efforts in education, charity, and care for the disabled. Most important, the evangelical reform movement inspired a struggle against slavery and inspired female activists to challenge the restrictions of domesticity.

NEW DENOMINATIONS AND COMMUNITIES

Religious upheaval was not limited to the genteel families of mill owners. The democratic ethos of the revival touched thousands of

Americans whose spiritual longings were unsatisfied by a growing economy and whose worldly fortunes suffered in the midst of apparent prosperity. Convinced that property and sexuality were instruments of the devil, for example, thousands separated from their spouses and possessions and joined communities of Shakers, who held all property in common and replaced conjugal marriage with vigorous community dancing. In the heart of the Burned-Over District, William Miller identified October 22, 1844, as the day on which the world would end. His prediction fell through but the Seventh-day Adventist church formed amid the fallout. In Boston and other New England cities, wealthy and sedate Congregationalists rejected the emotionalism of the revival, even as softened by Lyman Beecher. With a subdued and intellectual form of worship, these churches abandoned theological mysteries like the Trinity in favor of Unitarianism, while Universalist preachers taught rural and working-class Christians that God would save everybody.

The most far-reaching denominational development of the Awakening era came from the prophecies of Joseph Smith Jr., a visionary youth whose impoverished family moved from Vermont to Palmyra, New York, in 1826. Located in the heart of what would become the Burned-Over District, Palmyra teemed with religious excitement as Presbyterians, Baptists, and Methodists all sponsored revivals and competed for converts. The Smiths struggled hard with meager prospects, and when they finally lost their farm, Joseph announced that an angel had shown him a pair of buried golden plates covered with strange writing, as well as a pair of sacred stones that allowed him to translate them. Over the next two years, Smith produced his translation of *The Book of Mormon*, which described an ancient Christian civilization in the Americas and foretold the Second Coming of Christ. Smith proclaimed *The Book of Mormon* a work of divine revelation equal to the Old and New Testaments, and began to draw believers to a new denomination, the Church of Jesus Christ of Latter-day Saints.

Smith led his followers west in a series of moves, first to Kirtland, Ohio, then Independence, Missouri, and later to Nauvoo, Illinois. Over time, he promulgated the doctrine of "plural marriage," which encouraged male Mormons to take multiple wives. At every stop, the Mormons increased their numbers but also encountered bitter persecution from traditional Protestants who viewed their scripture as blasphemous and their marital customs as immoral. Finally, in 1844, a violent mob murdered Smith and his brother, and Brigham Young assumed leadership of the church. Young decided to leave Nauvoo and led 12,500 refugees to safety in the Far West, reaching the site of Salt Lake City in 1847. Here the Mormons built a new Zion in the wilderness that flourished and eventually became the nucleus of the state of Utah.

Shakers and Mormons were not alone in building utopian settlements. Dozens of planned reform communities flowered in the antebellum decades, especially in New England. Each was slightly different, but most renounced the individualist ethic of marketplace society and held all their property in common. In New Harmony, Indiana, a secular group under British reformer Robert Owen offered a utopian socialist community as an alternative to the factory system. In West Roxbury, Massachusetts, an adventurous group of intellectuals led by George Ripley founded Brook Farm in 1841 to practice Transcendentalism, a vague but influential philosophy that revered the spiritual power of "transcendental" forces in nature. At Oneida, New York, a particularly colorful group of idealists gathered around John Humphrey Noyes, who preached that the monogamous family hindered human improvement as much as private property, and practiced a kind of communal marriage among themselves.

All told, at least 100 planned, utopian communities took shape in the United States between the Revolution and the Civil War, with the greatest number founded in the 1840s. Those with a religious basis or a charismatic leader like Noyes tended to last longer, but most broke up after several years. The communitarian movement was an unusual but emblematic example of the era's faith in the power of love and reason to remake society around the principle of human perfectibility.

THE BENEVOLENT EMPIRE

Americans with no desire to renounce marriage or private property still tried to harness evangelical values for social improvement. Even before the War of 1812, conservative ministers had pushed back against irreligion and immorality by fighting to preserve state funding for churches in Massachusetts and Connecticut, the last states to require it. When disestablishment finally came to Connecticut in 1818 and to Massachusetts in 1833, however, ministers had already shifted their attention to voluntary efforts, recognizing that coercive methods would never work in a republic based on liberty.

Outvoted by Jeffersonian democracy and discredited by their

opposition to the War of 1812, New England's fading Federalist elite found new roles by joining with pious merchants and idealistic college graduates to form voluntary associations for evangelical reform. The first was the American Board of Commissioners for Foreign Missions (1812), dedicated to supporting missionaries to the American Indians and to non-Christian countries like China, India, and Burma, as well as Africa. Almost simultaneously, the New York Tract Society and New England Tract Society formed to distribute religious leaflets to the poor, followed by the American Tract Society in 1824. The American Education Society (1816) supported young candidates for the ministry, and the American Bible Society (1816) aimed to place a Bible in every home. The American Sunday School Union took shape a year later to provide both religious and secular instruction to children whose parents needed their labor every other day of the week. The American Peace Society (1828) sought to end war. In 1826, the American Home Missionary Society pledged to send ministers to the unchurched West. The same year, the American Temperance Society began urging Americans to cut back on hard liquor, and it eventually renounced all forms of alcohol. Founded in 1828, the General Union for Promoting the Christian Sabbath fought a hard but unsuccessful campaign to stop business and travel on Sunday, including the operations of the Post Office. Taken together, these organizations wielded serious financial clout; from 1789 to 1828, the nation spent $2.8 million on the thirteen leading benevolent societies, compared to $3.6 million on internal improvements.

Widely known as the "Benevolent Empire" or "Evangelical United Front," these societies consciously imitated parallel organizations that had emerged in Britain a decade or two earlier in response to similar problems. With overlapping membership and common goals, the societies maintained that social disorder sprang from the neglect of evangelical Protestant Christianity. To reform the unruly and help the suffering, these societies resolved to bring them to God and instill the virtues of self-control: temperance, frugality, hard work, church attendance, and education. Especially in the cities, the societies' agents, missionaries, and "friendly visitors" pursued this mission by entering the homes of the urban poor to pass out tracts and Bibles. There they faced the most urgent material needs of the poor, often for the first time. As one dismayed disciple reported, "Almost every-day brings me in contact with cases so appalling and distressing that it requires a nerve of steel to prevent the mind and body from sinking under perpetual excitement." As evangelicals increasingly confronted the number and variety of suffering Americans, some put aside their missionary work for new benevolent societies that addressed these troubles directly.

The practice of tackling common problems through voluntary associations spread beyond the Benevolent Empire to become a characteristic trait of early nineteenth-century America, and caught the attention of French observer Alexis de Tocqueville when he toured the United States in the early 1830s. In his famed analysis *Democracy in America* (1835–1840), Tocqueville marveled that "Americans of all ages, all conditions, and all dispositions constantly form associations. . . . The Americans make associations to give entertainments, to found seminaries, to build inns, to construct churches, to diffuse books, to send missionaries to the antipodes [i.e., the other side of the world]; in this manner they found hospitals, prisons, and schools. . . . Wherever at the head of some new undertaking you see the government in France, or a man of rank in England, in the United States you will be sure to find an association." Tocqueville suggested that voluntary associations were essential to American democracy, because they gave the strength of numbers to otherwise weak individuals and trained them to seek the common good. Besides, he reasoned, the government would become tyrannical if it tried to enforce all the goals that associations pursued voluntarily.

At the very least, voluntary associations won the hearts of critics like Lyman Beecher and reconciled them to religious disestablishment. Once a fervent opponent, Beecher finally decided that the end of state-funded churches was "*the best thing that ever happened to the State of Connecticut*" because "it threw [the churches] wholly on their own resources and on God." Religious coercion, he realized, was as ineffective in America's new democratic culture as other discarded symbols of elite status and moral authority. "By voluntary efforts, societies, missions, and revivals," he concluded, ministers "exert a deeper influence than ever they could by queues [i.e., an old-fashioned hair style], and shoe-buckles, and cocked hats, and gold-headed canes."

EVANGELICAL REFORM

Influenced by urgent revivalism, some reformers came to see the moderate and church-focused efforts of the Benevolent Empire as half-hearted and inadequate. Just as evangelicals required converts to renounce their sins completely and immediately, reformers of the 1820s and 1830s increasingly demanded a more radical "perfectionist" or "immediatist" approach to reform that would bring the immediate perfection of American society. Many believed that if America improved itself enough, Christ would return to earth in the United States and begin his "millennium," or thousand-year reign of perfect peace and justice preceding his Last Judgment. Finney boldly claimed that "if the Church will do all her duty, the millennium may come in this country in three years." Inspired by such fervor and optimism, evangelical converts who might have become ministers became professional reformers instead and demanded new institutions to reclaim damaged souls.

Working in this vein, reformer Samuel Gridley Howe tried to create alternative families or communities for the handicapped, especially in schools for the deaf. Dorothea Dix applied the same theory to the treatment of the mentally ill, and fought to bring the victims of madness out of chains, prisons, and attics to more comforting asylums. Temperance lecturers fought the evils of alcohol by demanding total abstinence instead of moderate drinking. Horace Mann, commissioner of education in Massachusetts, became a national leader in the cause of public schools and worked to make the state system of free public education a fundamental institution of democracy. More eccentric figures promised national redemption if Americans would only change their styles of clothing, take cold baths, and eat their vegetables. Practitioners of Spiritualism even claimed to communicate with the dead, using séances and mysterious rapping sounds from table tops.

Broadly speaking, the reformers carried the ideals of the northern middle class to their logical conclusion, preaching that republican citizens must use their liberty for personal and social improvement instead of selfish indulgence or violent strife. In a time of rapid mobility and expansion, established authorities could not enforce these standards alone, so Americans must practice self-control to become self-governing in a literal sense. The ideal institution for instilling a self-governing conscience was the Christian family, inspired by a pious mother and led by a sober and hard-working father. Children brought up in such an environment would presumably carry their evangelical conscience wherever a turbulent economy or an expanding frontier might take them, but if it failed, an artificial family like the school, the asylum, the temperance society, or even the penitentiary might rescue them.

Reformers adapted evangelical methods, using powerful language and images to break open the sinner's stubborn heart and produce re-pentance. Once penitent, erring souls were urged to renounce their failing (such as alcohol), take action (for example, shun tipplers and their haunts, join a temperance society for support and sober friend-ship), and continue to improve themselves with hard work, self-reliance, self-discipline, frugality, punctuality, and respectability. In the case of temperance, reformers achieved a remarkable success, having persuaded Americans to reduce their consumption of alcohol from 7.1 gallons per person in 1830 to 1.8 gallons per person by 1845. When persuasion failed, some reformers imposed their goals by law, as when Maine banned the sale of alcohol in 1851. Twelve other states adopted the "Maine Law" before the Civil War, but few kept it for long. Without much government enforcement, the reform movement struggled to make evangelical values a national creed, sometimes bat-tling uphill against divergent values among the working class, immi-grants, frontier settlers, and slaveholders.

As they fought, reformers freed public discourse from the exclu-sive control of white male leaders in church and state. While minis-ters and office seekers still pressed their claims, professional advocates and passionately committed volunteers argued for innumerable causes without political or denominational sponsorship. Women and Afri-can Americans joined national debates, even over their adversaries' fiercest objections. New means of communication like cheap news-papers produced by steam-powered printing presses broadened the reach and lowered the cost of public debate, while an efficient Post Office and faster, cheaper transportation spread it to every corner of the country. Impressed by the strength of reform agitation, politicians tried to divert its energies or silence its disruptions, but they never entirely succeeded. Beginning in the antebellum era, voluntary asso-ciations of dedicated citizens became permanent fixtures in American public life.

OPPOSING AND DEFENDING REFORM

The reformers drew skepticism and even condemnation from various opponents. They often tried to bypass fathers and community leaders to make emotional appeals to vulnerable dependents like women and children, and defenders of traditional family and community hierar-chies naturally resented these efforts. The reform movement could appear intolerant and overbearing to outsiders, particularly in campaigns to enforce observance of the Christian Sabbath or to ban strong drink. Americans who celebrated the absolute freedom of every white man hated restraints like temperance laws (or even temperance lectures) and other curbs on liberty or personal choice.

Immigrants and Catholics had their own reasons for distrusting reformers. The Puritan tradition had long opposed Catholicism, and Federalists were suspicious of foreign subversion. Irish and German newcomers were the first major contingent of Catholic immigrants to the United States, and they often voted for Jeffersonians and their successors. Native-born Americans often blamed Catholic immigrants for social problems such as poverty, crime, illiteracy, and alcohol abuse. Zealous Protestants commonly believed that Catholic dogma could silence the individual's conscience, and accused the church of subverting reform objectives. Some Protestant reformers concluded that social ills, immigration, and Catholicism were multiple aspects of the same underlying problem. They filled classrooms and penitentiaries with Protestant tracts and Bible translations while more-secular leaders carried nativist views into politics and argued that Catholics and immigrants should not hold public office.

Targeted Americans naturally resented these campaigns. Catholics and immigrants never welcomed evangelical interference, and few disapproved of moderate drinking. Reformers' efforts to turn the public schools into evangelical bastions incensed Catholic leaders, so they created parochial schools as alternatives. Workers hated campaigns by evangelical employers against public amusements like saloons, theaters, and dance halls, believing that their bosses were less interested in saving souls than time and money. Baffled by this resistance, Protestant advocates assumed that tippling workers were drenched in sin while Catholics favored ignorance and superstition, so they simply redoubled their efforts. Fueled by these controversies, antebellum reform efforts often carried a distinct edge of class animosity and religious and ethnic intolerance.

But though they valued self-restraint, reformers never saw themselves as tyrannical busybodies, capitalist police, or enemies of freedom. In their minds, they were trying to perfect the world by inspiring individuals to escape from deadly traps like immorality, poverty, ignorance, addiction, and infirmity, and bringing them to salvation, or freedom from the bondage of sin. If self-indulgence or traditional hierarchies supported these obstacles to true liberty, they must give way to the promise of the millennium. Reformers were sometimes deluded and self-righteous but they were usually sincere, and they often struggled as hard against evils within themselves or their families as they did in the world at large. Even as they fought to make the middle-class values of the urban and small-town North the creed of the entire nation, the antebellum reformers established a continuing national tradition of collective efforts to solve community problems.

The Assault on Slavery

As reformers made progress against ills like intemperance, they increasingly saw the moral blindness and cruelty of slavery as the greatest and most intractable obstacles to American improvement. Like other advocates, the opponents of slavery began by calling for moderate, gradual improvements, but shifted to calls for immediate abolition as perfectionist ideals grew increasingly compelling. The abolitionist movement met angry opposition in the North and violent resistance in the South, but activists persisted and their movement slowly grew.

EARLY EFFORTS

For most of human history, slavery existed without controversy as one of many kinds of subordination in a world where few people were truly free. As eighteenth-century Britons increasingly boasted of their liberty, however, a few religious leaders began to question the ownership of human beings. Foremost among them were members of the Religious Society of Friends, who believed that God had given everyone an "inner light" to see his truth. Quaker founder George Fox had therefore insisted to his followers that "Christ . . . shed his blood for [Africans] as well as for you; and hath enlightened them as well as he hath enlightened you." An early Pennsylvania meeting asked, "Have these Negroes not as much right to fight for their freedom as you have to keep them slaves?" The same meeting denounced all forms of slave-keeping. Individual Quakers like Anthony Benezet and John Woolman wrote and traveled widely in the early eighteenth century, urging their fellow Friends to liberate their slaves. The Philadelphia Yearly Meeting heeded their message in 1758 and excluded all buyers and sellers of slaves from its leadership. Ordinary Quakers began to abandon the institution altogether, and Philadelphia Quakers formed the world's first antislavery society in 1775. Similar groups spread across the North and even into the Upper South in subsequent decades.

Opposition to slavery spread as the principles of the Enlightenment and the American Revolution underscored the hypocrisy of calling for liberty while holding others in bondage. With few slaves already, northern states gradually gave up the practice after independence, and Congress banned the Atlantic slave trade in 1808. Further progress then began to falter. Where slaves were numerous, slave owners clung to their valuable property and many whites feared a large free black population. Certain that the two races could never live peacefully together, they insisted that slavery could not end until the former slaves left America.

In 1816, a group of leading gentlemen organized the American Colonization Society, a component of the Benevolent Empire that proposed to settle free blacks in Liberia, a settlement the society founded in Africa for this purpose. The colonization movement attracted a mixed group of supporters, including political leaders like Thomas Jefferson, James Madison, Henry Clay, and Bushrod Washington (the first president's nephew), moderate reformers who hoped to encourage emancipation, evangelicals who hoped the migrants would convert the Africans to Christianity, and slaveholders who wanted to rid the country of free blacks.

Colonization even interested some black leaders like Paul Cuffee, the sea captain from New Bedford, Massachusetts, who transported 38 people of color between 1810 and 1820 to Sierra Leone, a British colony like Liberia. African Methodist Episcopal bishop Richard Allen and businessman James Forten supported the movement, but other African Americans insisted that their own claims to American equality were as good as anyone's, and condemned colonization as a plot to strengthen slavery by expelling free blacks. Experience proved, moreover, that the hope of ending slavery by colonization was utterly impractical, for the Colonization Society could never send more than a couple of hundred emigrants to Africa per year, while the slave population grew by 50,000 annually. Right down to the administration of Abraham Lincoln, however, moderate white politicians continued to endorse colonization as the answer to the slavery problem, even while more committed activists looked for another solution.

BLACK ABOLITIONISTS

African Americans hardly kept silent while white Americans debated their fate. New England slaves petitioned their state governments for liberty in the American Revolution, claiming "a natural and inalienable right to that freedom which the Great parent of the Universe hath bestowed equally on all mankind." Slavery collapsed in Massachusetts after Elizabeth Freeman and Quok Walker sued for their freedom and won, citing provisions of the Revolutionary state constitution. African Americans watched carefully when slaves in the sugar colony of Saint Domingue invoked the egalitarian principles of the French Revolution to launch their own revolt in 1791, as did the enslaved blacksmith Gabriel in his unsuccessful 1800 revolt in Richmond, Virginia.

Partly from fear of the Saint Domingue example, antislavery idealism began to falter after the first wave of post-Revolutionary emancipations. Southern states banned voluntary manumissions and gradual abolition laws did not extend below Pennsylvania, but African Americans did not relax their struggles. In 1822, free carpenter Denmark Vesey reportedly organized an extensive conspiracy in Charleston, South Carolina, which was only averted when a participant leaked the secret. Seven years later, in 1829, David Walker, a free black man of Boston, dramatically publicized the radical critique of slavery with his blistering pamphlet *Walker's Appeal to the Coloured Citizens of the World*. He argued that slavery must be abolished everywhere, that whites had no right to send blacks "back" to Africa, and that slaves should reclaim their freedom by force if necessary. The *Appeal* was especially frightening when free black seamen slipped it into southern ports, where slaves and free blacks gathered secretly to read and discuss it. Southern authorities quickly put a price on Walker's head and banned the circulation of such "incendiary" literature.

Walker died soon afterward, but other black abolitionists continued the struggle. Many participated actively in northern abolition societies, both racially mixed and all-black. Maryland runaway Frederick Douglass became one of the country's most renowned antislavery orators after gaining his freedom in the 1840s. Physician and editor Martin Delany and Presbyterian minister Henry Highland Garnet both promoted national conventions of black leaders and revived the idea of black migration to Africa when they decided that whites would never tolerate black equality in America. Black women formed auxiliaries to male abolition societies, and beginning with the free black women of Salem, Massachusetts, they built all-female societies to fight discrimination along with slavery itself. "Conductor" Harriet Tubman took direct action for freedom by entering the South 13 times after her own escape to rescue some 70 slaves through the clandestine network known as the Underground Railroad. Once the Civil War began, black men and women streamed south to aid newly freed slaves with relief work, education, and health care.

IMMEDIATISM

Influenced by black abolitionists and frustrated by the ineffectual methods of the American Colonization Society, a small but deeply committed number of white antislavery radicals rejected the goal of ending slavery gradually. They demanded immediate abolition instead, without compensating masters for lost property (few thought of compensating the slaves), and no deportation of the freed people.

The best-known radical abolitionist was William Lloyd Garrison, a white Massachusetts reformer who had worked for temperance and colonization before free blacks in Baltimore converted him to immediatism. On January 1, 1831, Garrison published the first issue of his newspaper, the *Liberator*, denouncing slavery as a monstrous evil and demanding its immediate abolition. He also condemned racial prejudice and discrimination and insisted on complete racial equality. Garrison renounced the use of force and insisted that his only weapon would be "moral suasion," but he swore that "I will not equivocate—I will not excuse—I will not retreat a single inch—AND I WILL BE HEARD." Founding the American Anti-Slavery Society in 1833, Garrison and his followers welcomed black and female members and shocked moderates by demanding equality for women as well as African Americans. Garrison's harsh rhetoric and uncompromising style angered most white Americans, but won support from free blacks, who composed three-quarters of the *Liberator*'s early subscribers, and leading black abolitionists such as Frederick Douglass.

Borrowing revivalist methods, the American Anti-Slavery Society raised money from sympathizers like Lewis and Arthur Tappan, who were brothers and pious and reform-minded New York business partners, and employed traveling lecturers who toured the North to denounce slavery, organize local chapters, and circulate petitions. One of the most active lecturers was Theodore Dwight Weld, who had led antislavery discussions among his fellow students at Lane Seminary until President Lyman Beecher expelled the participants for stirring controversy. Weld and the other lecturers endured rotten eggs and stoning as they crisscrossed the free states in the mid-1830s, explaining the evils of slavery and establishing local chapters of the society.

Abolitionists aroused furious opposition. When Nat Turner's bloody slave revolt broke out in Virginia only months after the first appearance of the *Liberator,* southerners blamed Garrison for the carnage and the state of Georgia offered a $5,000 reward for his arrest. Even in the North, many established leaders and ordinary citizens hated abolitionists as extreme versions of other unpopular reformers, who flouted white male authority to preach radical equality to women, children, and blacks. Some northern politicians courted southern votes with furious attacks on abolitionism, and many voters in New York and other centers of the cotton trade shared their sentiments. Mobs dragged Garrison through Boston in a noose and, in 1837, killed abolitionist editor Elijah P. Lovejoy for defending his press in Alton, Illinois. Black neighborhoods in northern cities were frequently the targets of racist attacks.

Abolitionism kept spreading despite persecution and eventually outgrew the leadership of any single individual. The movement split when Garrison continued to insist on gender equality and "nonresistance," renouncing of all forms of coercion, including self-defense, laws, government, and voting. Quoting the biblical prophet Isaiah, he condemned the US Constitution as a "covenant with death and an agreement with hell" for its proslavery features. Adopting the slogan "No union with slaveholders," Garrison urged sympathizers to "come out" of all churches and other institutions that refused to condemn slavery wholeheartedly and even called on the North to preserve its moral purity by seceding from the Union.

ANTISLAVERY POLITICS

More-pragmatic abolitionists declined to abandon politics and insisted that the true spirit of the Constitution supported liberty, regardless of its proslavery compromises. They confronted slave owners in Congress by electing antislavery representatives from sympathetic northern districts and petitioning Congress to end slavery in the nation's capital. These petitions so enraged southern congressmen that they imposed a "gag rule" to silence them in 1836, a clear violation of freedom of speech and the right of petition. Frederick Douglass gave personal testimony on the horrors of plantation life and raised funds for the aid of fellow fugitives, finally splitting with Garrison over the issue of nonresistance. Antislavery politicians first took their case to the voters with the Liberty Party, a small splinter group formed in 1840, which broadened into the Free Soil Party in 1848. With the founding of the Republican Party in 1854, antislavery politicians created the organization that elected President Abraham Lincoln in 1860, directly leading to disunion and the Civil War.

Abolitionism never commanded a northern white majority before the Civil War, but dislike of slavery kept spreading in the 1840s and 1850s. With telling effect, orators asked how a system that seemed to require the gagging and murder of white citizens could ever be compatible with American liberty. Influenced by such questions, even white northerners who could not support immediate emancipation grew increasingly resentful of slavery's growth and expansion.

Women and Reform

As the Market Revolution stimulated the growth of an urban middle class, the "cult of domesticity" glorified women's roles as mothers and homemakers. Under the doctrine of "separate spheres," men supposedly ruled the rough world of politics and the marketplace, while "true women" turned their homes into gentle and redemptive spaces to nurture children and men. Even in the middle class, however, women were never disconnected from a wider world. They were very active in the Second Great Awakening, composed most of its first converts, and actively worked for their churches. Building on these experiences, female activists threw themselves into the whole spectrum of evangelical reform associations. There they joined a "public sphere" larger than their private lives but mostly distinct from the business and political arenas that still belonged to men. Eventually, their experience in this public sphere would inspire some women to demand full equality of the sexes, including the right to vote and hold office.

FROM DOMESTICITY TO THE PUBLIC SPHERE

Even the most conservative men conceded the importance of women to the Second Great Awakening. Women almost always outnumbered men on church rolls, both before and after seasons of revival, and preachers counted on women for help in redeeming their men. "Who can so successfully wield the instrument of influence than women?" asked the Utica (New York) Tract Society in 1823, cautiously adding that "a sensible woman *who keeps her proper place* . . . may exert *in her own sphere*, almost any degree of influence that she pleases" (italics added). Women often led in inviting evangelists to their communities, and Charles Grandison Finney reciprocated by encouraging women to pray in each other's homes and to raise money for ministers and their efforts. As they gained confidence, the same women aided the Benevolent Empire by dispensing Sunday school lessons and missionary literature and forming maternal associations to learn better methods of rearing and converting their own children. Before long, the church women of New York's Burned-Over District were editing their own publications, such as the Presbyterian *Mother's Magazine* and the Baptist *Mother's Monthly Journal*, and pushing against the barriers that forbade their speaking in mixed congregations of men and women.

It was a natural step from prompting conversion to supporting more public causes that also preferred a transformed heart over headstrong passions, and internal self-discipline over undependable external authorities, such as urban or frontier justice. All-male societies to promote temperance or Sabbath observance welcomed female auxiliaries; societies for antipoverty relief, prison reform, and colonization did the same. Many men were more doubtful, however, when Finney's wife Lydia organized the New York Female Moral Reform Society in 1834 to denounce the sexual double standard, to rescue "fallen women," and to embarrass their customers. Though male figures like ministers, editors, and politicians denounced "respectable" women who openly raised the subject of sex, the moral reformers pressed on, even publicizing the names of prominent men they spotted entering brothels. "Who among us can tell that our sisters and daughters are safe while the seducer is unhesitatingly received into our society and treated with that attention which virtue can claim?" they demanded, moving far beyond the "proper place" prescribed for them by an earlier generation of husbands and ministers.

ANTISLAVERY WOMEN

Women likewise played a crucial role in the antislavery movement, especially in its Garrisonian wing. Women also formed local antislavery groups, from the large Philadelphia Female Anti-Slavery Society down to village circles all over New England, New York, and northern Ohio. As in other reform efforts, they initially organized lectures and craft fairs to sell their cooking and needlework to raise money that male abolitionists would spend. By the mid-1830s, however, organized female abolitionists were flooding Congress with the antislavery petitions that so enraged the slaveholders' representatives, collecting as many as two million signatures in one two-year period, and many more than that before final emancipation. They also supplied most of the signatures on those petitions. And female abolitionists wrote moving and persuasive antislavery polemics like *An Appeal in Favor of That Class of Americans Called Africans* by popular author Lydia Maria Child and, of course, *Uncle Tom's Cabin* by Harriet Beecher Stowe.

Sarah and Angelina Grimké were two especially distinguished female abolitionists and women's rights advocates from Charleston, South Carolina. Born to a privileged, slaveholding family, Sarah developed an early hatred of slavery, and when she reached adulthood, she became a Quaker and moved to Philadelphia to escape slavery's influence. Her younger sister Angelina joined her there and both became active in Quaker circles. As an eloquent former slaveholder, Sarah drew instant attention when she aired her views in the *Liberator,* and Garrison recruited the two as agents of the American Anti-Slavery Society. Their powerful pamphlets, including Angelina's *An Appeal to the Christian Women of the South* (1836) and Sarah's *An Epistle to the Clergy of the Southern States* (1836), won many readers, and the sisters became prominent public lecturers across New York and New England. In 1839, Angelina married prominent abolitionist Theodore Weld, and the three collaborated in editing *American Slavery as It Is,* a compilation from southern sources that documented slavery's brutality.

Abolitionism had a special appeal to white women like the Grimkés who identified closely with the sufferings of enslaved mothers. Like *Uncle Tom's Cabin,* their writings repeatedly stressed that slaveholders beat women as mercilessly as men, that dealers parted families and sold babies from their mothers' arms, and that enslaved women could never practice the virtues of "true womanhood," or provide their families with ideal homes. Worst of all, abolitionist women did not hesitate to proclaim the sexual sinfulness of slavery: that slave women could be raped at any time without recourse, that they frequently bore their masters' children, that light-skinned "fancy girls" were raised and sold specifically for sexual exploitation, and that white women must live with their husbands' predations without protest.

Perhaps for this reason, many white female abolitionists made special efforts to work closely with black women, joining biracial reform societies more commonly than men and denouncing northern prejudice along with southern slavery. "They *are our sisters,*" wrote Angelina

Grimké. "To us, as women, they have a right to look for sympathy with their sorrows, and effort and prayer for their rescue." Women also admired the uncompromising "nonresistance" and antipolitical principles of Garrison's American Anti-Slavery Society, which some male activists condemned as impractical. Garrison reciprocated by standing firm on the equality of the sexes as well as the races, both in and out of the abolition movement.

The Grimkés' willingness to speak before mixed groups of men and women horrified gender traditionalists. "We appreciate the unostentatious prayers and efforts of woman," Massachusetts ministers protested, "but when she assumes the place and tone of a man as a public reformer . . . her character becomes unnatural." The clergymen particularly opposed any mention of sex. "We especially deplore the intimate acquaintance and promiscuous conversation of females with regard to things 'which ought not to be named,'" they wrote, inevitably soiling that "modesty and delicacy which is the charm of domestic life" and opening the door to "degeneracy and ruin." If flaunting themselves before white men were not bad enough, moreover, the Grimkés' audiences included black men, leading to the ugliest insinuations of interracial promiscuity. Despite their friendship, Catharine Beecher thus condemned the sisters when they left "women's sphere" to speak in public. Like their male counterparts, the Grimkés and other female abolitionists were showered with abuse, insults, and violence, especially when Pennsylvania Hall, the newly constructed headquarters of the Philadelphia Female Anti-Slavery Society, was burned in 1838.

Sarah Grimké responded to attacks on her sister's speechmaking with a blistering series of letters, published in 1838 as *Letters on the Equality of the Sexes*, in which she defended and spelled out the links between equality for blacks and for women. Going further, Angelina soon addressed the Massachusetts legislature on the subject of women's rights, making her the first woman to appear before an American legislative body. Female activists still met insult and rebuff, however, even from other abolitionists. When Garrison appointed Abby Kelley to the business committee of the American Anti-Slavery Society in 1839, financial backers Lewis and Arthur Tappan quit in protest, bringing almost a third of its members to a rival organization, the American and Foreign Anti-Slavery Society. In London the following year, the World's Anti-Slavery Convention refused to seat the American female delegates, including Lucretia Mott and Elizabeth Cady Stanton. It was a slight that neither woman forgot.

WOMEN'S RIGHTS

The debate over gender equality in the antislavery movement meshed with other trends in antebellum culture to support a pathbreaking movement for women's rights. Following the Revolution, women had become more active in civic life, but the doctrine of republican mother-hood still denied them the right to vote or hold office. But republican mothers needed good education, so schools for women spread, and some of their graduates gained the intellectual self-confidence to act on their own behalf. When working-class women protested the wages and conditions in New England textile mills, moreover, they built awareness of their unequal treatment both as workers and as women and learned invaluable lessons in leadership and organizing. Rising alcohol consumption directly led to more domestic violence and family neglect, which drew countless women to the temperance movement.

Economic uncertainty also stimulated the women's rights move-ment. The common law doctrine of coverture merged a wife's legal identity with her husband's. As long as she remained married, she could not own property, sign contracts, make a will, or file a lawsuit in her own name. Her children and her earnings belonged entirely to her husband, and creditors could seize any property she brought to the marriage to pay his debts. Divorce was nearly impossible, even in cases of abandonment. And though the economic gyrations of the Market Revolution brought a flood of middle- and upper-class bankruptcies, it was also very difficult for wealthy fathers to protect their daughters from their husbands' misfortunes. Pushed by fathers and influenced by the calamitous Panic of 1839, Mississippi chipped away at the re-strictions of coverture that year with the first married women's prop-erty act. Women's rights advocates took up the campaign and won a broader law in New York in 1848.

Economic matters were also a central concern of the eccentric Scot-tish heiress Frances (or "Fanny") Wright, one of the most remarkable early advocates of women's rights. Unlike most American reformers, Wright drew her inspiration from Enlightenment and French revolu-tionary principles of reason and religious skepticism instead of evan-gelical Protestantism. She was also a passionate advocate for working men and women and their demands for public education and better pay and working conditions. Most shockingly, she had no use for do-mesticity, respectability, or Christianity. She denounced the restrictions of conventional marriage and instead loudly called for sexual freedom, birth control, and more easily available divorce.

Wright made her second trip to America in 1824, when she traveled with the marquis de Lafayette during his farewell tour of the United States. After visiting Robert Owen, founder of the utopian commune at New Harmony, Indiana, Wright decided to establish her own experimental community in Nashoba, Tennessee, where she hoped that slaves could gain freedom and education before moving to Haiti. When the colony failed, Wright further scandalized conservatives by living openly with Owen's son, Robert Dale Owen, and launching a fiery lecturing career before mixed male and female audiences. Appearing onstage in a long flowing robe, Wright drew 1,500 to her first New York address and poured scorn on the failures of American republicanism, the oppression of women, the exploitation of artisans and workers, and unequal access to education. Wright made a sensational impression with her speeches and her newspaper, the *Free Enquirer*, but her religious and sexual nonconformity won her few friends outside a small circle of radical New York workingmen. The campaign for American women's rights grew more directly from the reform mainstream, especially abolitionism.

SENECA FALLS

Soon after their rebuff at the World's Anti-Slavery Convention in 1840, the famed Quaker abolitionist Lucretia Mott began discussing with Elizabeth Cady Stanton, wife of male abolitionist Henry Stanton, the idea of a women's rights convention. When Mott revisited Stanton in 1848, they joined with three of Stanton's Quaker friends and sent out a call for the world's first women's rights convention to assemble in Stanton's hometown of Seneca Falls, New York, not far from the Erie Canal in the heart of the Burned-Over district.

The Seneca Falls convention attracted about 300 white and black attendees, most of them abolitionists and about one-third of them male, including Frederick Douglass from nearby Rochester. After two days of speeches and debate, 100 participants signed a Declaration of Sentiments modeled directly on the republic's founding document. Beginning with the stirring affirmation that "all men and women are created equal," the declaration proclaimed that "the history of mankind is a history of repeated injuries and usurpations on the part of man toward woman, having in direct object the establishment of an absolute tyranny over her." It protested that wives were "civilly dead" in the eyes of the law, while women could not attend college, enter the higher professions, earn equal wages, or leave their "proper sphere." Most explosively, it demanded for women the right to vote.

The Seneca Falls convention drew widespread ridicule, but unlike Fanny Wright's shocking appearances, this movement did not fade away. Two years later, 1,000 participants attended the first national women's rights convention in Worcester, Massachusetts, and others met every year but one before 1860. In each case, the call for women's suffrage grew more insistent. The demand would not be met until 1920, with the passage of the Nineteenth Amendment to the US Constitution, but the Seneca Falls convention had launched a movement for gender equality that continues to the present.

A Cultural Renaissance

The antebellum United States experienced a burst of cultural creativity that many republicans had hoped for and that paralleled the nation's vigorous economic and geographical expansion. "I must study Politicks and War that my sons may have liberty to study Painting and Poetry[,] Mathematicks and Philosophy," John Adams had mused to his wife, Abigail, in 1780. "My sons ought to study Mathematicks and Philosophy, Geography, natural History, Naval Architecture, navigation, Commerce and Agriculture, in order to give their Children a right to study Painting, Poetry, Musick, Architecture, Statuary, Tapestry and Porcelaine." Adams's hopes were not easily realized. "In the four quarters of the globe," sneered a British critic in 1820, "who reads an American book?" But even as he asked his question, a cultural movement now known as the American Renaissance was beginning that celebrated equality and self-reliance in many new forms of writing, music, art, and entertainment.

Originally applied to a small group of white male writers of the 1850s, "American Renaissance" more usefully describes a diverse cultural flowering in antebellum America that displayed some common themes and many racial, class, and gendered variations. Different kinds of entertainment appealed to country dwellers and urban workers, for example, and the men and women of the urban middle class likewise had their own preferences. The black community created an extraordinary musical legacy and produced a rich literature on resistance to slavery. Especially in Boston and New York, self-conscious writers, artists, and intellectuals tried to produce uniquely American work that would stand comparison with the polished arts of Europe. Within this broad variety, and consistent with their confident boasts to foreign visitors, northern Americans consistently championed the free individual, the opportunities available in a free society, and the value of what they called "free labor." A few prominent examples can illustrate the depth and variety of their creative efforts.

RURAL AND URBAN FRONTIERS

The music, stories, and amusements of rural Americans revolved around their work and their civic rituals. Work parties like cornhuskings and barn raisings were not only crucial to the farm economy, but also welcome occasions for folk arts like music, storytelling, and dancing, often accompanied by homemade whiskey or brandy. The same was true for public events like militia musters, elections, and Fourth of July observances. Though dismaying to temperance reformers, public drinking naturally led to tall tales, boasting, and brawling, in which a celebration of republican virtue led to glorification of men's personal power. Renowned fighters kept their thumbnails sharp to gouge the eyes of their enemies, while western "ring-tailed roarers" bragged of being "half-horse, half-alligator, with a little touch of snapping turtle." Adopting this swashbuckling style in his 1834 autobiography, Congressman David Crockett struck a pose for countless "Wild West" characters of the future. Exaggerated boasts of white male strength and valor became comic raw materials for Mark Twain and other writers known as the "southwestern humorists."

Urban workers' entertainment celebrated white male strength and equality in other ways. Nineteenth-century Americans were passionately fond of the theater, for example. Perhaps surprisingly to modern Americans, the plays of William Shakespeare were highly popular at every level of income and education, but audiences expressed their class and patriotic loyalties through support for rival actors. In 1849, working-class fans of American actor Edwin Forrest tried to block a performance of *Macbeth* by English favorite William Charles Macready at New York's opulent Astor Place Theater. A crowd of 10,000 armed with stones and incited by placards demanding "SHALL AMERICANS OR ENGLISH RULE THIS CITY?" became so unruly that 300 militiamen opened fire. In the Astor Place Riot, 25 New Yorkers died, bloody testimony to workers' hatred of presumed English (and American) aristocracy.

A craze for blackface minstrel shows reflected other values of northern white workers. In 1828, a little-known white actor named Thomas D. Rice disguised himself as a caricatured black man singing, "Weel about and turn about and do jis so, Eb'ry time I turn about I jump Jim Crow." By the mid-1830s, minstrel shows, which featured white men with blackened faces playing stereotyped black characters, had become one of the most popular forms of northern urban entertainment, especially for white male workers. Classic American melodies such as "Swanee River," "Jimmy Crack Corn," "Oh! Susannah," and "Dixie" all had their origins on the minstrel stage.

The typical minstrel show featured clownish plantation characters such as Bones and Tambo, whose songs and jokes made fun of Mr. Interlocutor, a pompous straight man. Zip Coon was a dandified free black character whose oafish attempts to imitate upper-class whites made him (and them) look ridiculous. The antics of imitation black buffoons obviously flattered white racism, but a blackface disguise also made it easier to mock respectable targets like the wealthy or temperance reformers, and to express envy for blacks' imagined carefree playfulness and sexual promiscuity. Depicting a proslavery version of plantation life, minstrel shows celebrated the ideology of President Andrew Jackson's Democratic Party and played a conspicuous part in its campaign events. Like western bragging and theater riots, the minstrel show appealed to American workers who cherished liberty and equality but worried about preserving them in a topsy-turvy world.

Americans also loved mass-market literature that new means of printing and distribution made widely available. Dozens of popular male and female authors turned out hundreds of sentimental novels and stories, mostly intended for women. Filled with lost lovers, swooning maidens, and expiring babes, these tales were easy to mock, but carried important messages. Implicitly struggling with the contradiction between women's moral responsibility and their physical and political powerlessness, the writers of sentimental fiction assured readers that they had the moral force to transform a wicked world without violating the restrictions of "true womanhood."

For young men, journalist E. Z. C. Judson used the pen name Ned Buntline to churn out dozens of thrillers about Indian fighting, New York gangs, slum life, and nautical adventures. Characteristically, perhaps, Buntline was one of the main organizers of the Astor Place Riot. In a similar vein, George Lippard fed men's fantasies with fictionalized historical romances and lurid depictions of city life and social injustice that enjoyed great commercial success. Like the sentimental stories that attracted female readers, sensationalist fiction and journalism offered men a heroic and idealized world with richly imaginative alternatives to any frustrations they may have felt in humdrum daily life.

The glorification of free individuals extended beyond mass entertainment. With political independence confirmed and hopes rising for every kind of improvement, ambitious American writers and painters hoped to match the cultural achievements of Europe. Less concerned than reformers with republican community, these artists were more likely to probe the meaning of freedom and equality for individuals. Many embraced the transatlantic cultural trend called romanticism.

As early as the mid-eighteenth century, many intellectuals had begun to worry that the Enlightenment's cool rationalism had obscured spiritual and emotional truths. Stimulated by German philosophers like Immanuel Kant, romantics asserted that feelings and intuitions could lead to deeper and more powerful knowledge than reason alone. Under these influences, European artists increasingly tried to evoke powerful emotional responses in their work, ranging from the stormy musical compositions of Ludwig van Beethoven to the dreamy and mystical images of English poets like William Wordsworth, Percy Bysshe Shelley, and Lord Byron. Romantics were also less interested in the universal political principles of the American and French Revolutions than in the unique qualities of heroic individuals and nations.

Self-consciously creative Americans embraced the romantic impulse in the generation following 1815. Revivalists and reformers shared the romantic belief that emotional knowledge was deeper and more powerful than mere intellectual reasoning, and relied on feelings to reach their audiences. Romantic nationalists imagined that every people possessed a unique character or spirit apparent in their culture, and cherished their own national identity above all others. New respect for the moral authority of women stemmed from the view that women's emotions brought them closer to spiritual truth than the calculations of men. American painters used awe-inspiring landscapes to suggest that the grandeur of nature could teach deeper lessons than academic instruction. When politicians extolled "the rising glory of the Republic," they shared the message that patriotic feelings said more about national destiny than dry disquisitions like *The Federalist Papers*.

Two of America's first professional authors, the New Yorkers Washington Irving and James Fenimore Cooper, fed romantic nationalism by celebrating the distinctive qualities of America's people and landscape. Irving became popular for his folklore-inspired tales of the Hudson Valley, including "Rip Van Winkle" and "The Legend of Sleepy Hollow." Cooper created an immortal frontier hero, Natty Bumpo, and followed his adventures through five novels, including *The Deerslayer* and *The Last of the Mohicans*. A noble hunter who drew his strength of character from his roots in nature, Bumpo prefigured Daniel Boone and Davy Crockett as a prototype for countless western heroes, from fictional frontiersmen to film stars such as John Wayne and Clint Eastwood.

Romanticism also appeared in the work of a small corps of professional American painters. Beginning in the 1820s, Thomas Cole broke free from the portraits and historical subjects of eighteenth-century artists with sweeping landscapes that evoked the nation's seemingly endless possibilities. Asher Durand and Frederic Edwin Church, Cole's followers in the so-called Hudson River School, continued to paint inspiring landscapes like the Catskill Mountains and Niagara Falls, hoping that vast scenes of natural beauty could elevate humanity to the spiritual greatness that romantics called the "sublime." Conscious of the moral perils hidden in America's vast environment, Cole also used landscape series like *The Course of Empire* and *The Voyage of Life* to warn viewers against the dangers of national or personal complacency. Less grandiose, the likeable people in George Caleb Bingham's paintings of specific locales seemed to demonstrate the benefits of political democracy and the proper balance between wilderness and civilization.

TRANSCENDENTALISM

Romantic inspiration brought an influential group of New England intellectuals to a new philosophical movement they called Transcendentalism. Early in the nineteenth century, a few New England ministers had reacted against evangelical emotionalism by exploring what they saw as a more reasonable and benevolent approach to Christianity. Becoming known as Unitarians, they continued traditional worship but stressed God's love, compassion, and rationality over belief in miracles or the divinity of Christ. By the mid-1830s, a few daring intellectuals around Boston had pushed beyond Unitarianism and gathered to discuss Hindu scriptures, Chinese philosophy, and German free thought in a circle they called the Transcendental Club.

The most prominent Transcendentalist was Ralph Waldo Emerson, a former Unitarian minister who forged a new career as an essayist and popular lecturer. Others included George Ripley, founder of the utopian community at Brook Farm; Margaret Fuller, editor of the groups' journal, the *Dial*; and Henry David Thoreau, a seeming ne'er-do-well who composed enduring classics in American environmental and political thought. The Transcendentalists' teachings remained rather hazy, but they all believed that close contact with nature, a reliance on unfettered genius, and openness to insights from all sources could reveal truths that transcended the materialism and religious dogmatism they found elsewhere in America.

Americans knew Emerson best for his manifestos of individualism. If all men and every generation were truly equal, he demanded, "why should not we also enjoy an original relation to the universe?" His 1837 address "The American Scholar" proclaimed that "we have listened too long to the courtly verses of Europe," and insisted that American intellectuals should be engaged and innovative creators, not the guardians of dead facts. In his 1841 essay "Self-Reliance," Emerson told readers to find truth within themselves, not in tradition or society. "To believe your own thought, to believe what is true for you in your private heart is true for all men,—that is genius," he insisted. "Whoso would be a man, must be a nonconformist." Emerson shocked Americans by dismissing politics and conventional Christianity, but they loved his confidence in their own inner capacities. In later generations, many Americans would share the Transcendentalists' conviction that personal enlightenment could supersede churchly doctrines, and followed this faith into diverse forms of self-help and alternative spirituality.

Between 1840 and 1844, Transcendentalist critic and editor Margaret Fuller wrote her most important book, *Woman in the Nineteenth Century*. In it, she called for equal spiritual growth for men and women, inside and outside the bonds of marriage. Fuller next became a regular columnist for Horace Greeley's prominent newspaper, the *New York Tribune*, where she vigorously called for female equality, including equal education, suffrage, and employment. She likewise championed the rights of slaves, Indians, prisoners, and the poor, and won praise as a major pioneer in feminist thought.

Henry David Thoreau practiced his friend Emerson's individualist convictions by his simple manner of living, his travels in the American wilderness, and his moving descriptions of natural beauty. Observing the frantic search for wealth among ordinary Americans, Thoreau concluded that "the mass of men lead lives of quiet desperation," and took to the woods to find an alternative. After living for two years in a small cabin beside Walden Pond, near Concord, Massachusetts, he hymned the results in his classic account *Walden*, published in 1854.

Thoreau also questioned relationships between individuals and the state that other Americans took for granted. In his 1849 essay "Resistance to Civil Government," later republished as "Civil Disobedience," Thoreau discounted majority rule because majorities were so often wrong. "Must the citizen ever for a moment, or in the least degree, resign his conscience to the legislator?" he asked. "Why has every man a conscience, then?" Thoreau's conscience told him that the United States and Massachusetts were both deeply wrong in tolerating the sin of slavery and conducting an unjust war on Mexico. Unwilling to go along, he drew a night in jail when he refused to pay his taxes in protest. "I think that we should be men first, and subjects afterward," he explained. "It is not desirable to cultivate a respect for the law, so much as for the right."

The principle of civil disobedience had little impact in Thoreau's lifetime, but it became central to political protest in the twentieth century. Citing Thoreau, advocates for an independent India, civil rights for African Americans, and democracy in South Africa all protested oppression by peacefully violating unjust laws to expose the injustice of the governments that imposed them. Thoreau's visit to the Concord jail had long repercussions.

DARKER VOICES

Not all participants in the American Renaissance shared Emerson's sunny optimism. Novelist Nathaniel Hawthorne doubted that America could easily shrug off the weight of its past, and brooded on the problem of recalcitrant evil in human life. In numerous short stories and in novels like *The Scarlet Letter* and *The House of Seven Gables*, his characters struggled to escape the repressive influence of Puritanism and its legacy of hypocrisy, guilt, and self-recrimination. The poems and short stories of Edgar Allan Poe intensified the dark tone of Hawthorne's fiction in their treatment of lost love, murder, remorse, and death. Poe's and Hawthorne's contemporary Herman Melville first won fame with idyllic stories of an American sailor in the South Seas, but revealed a much darker side in *Moby Dick*, the story of a vengeful sea captain consumed by his search for a white whale. Published in 1851, this complex novel explored the dark side of individualism, and suggested that obsessive pursuit of a personal vision might destroy men instead of freeing them. This pessimistic theme attracted few readers in the 1850s, and Melville's later work did not receive praise or careful study until the twentieth century.

Poet Emily Dickinson also dwelt on life's tragedies as she looked inward on the female experience. Perhaps disappointed in love, certainly preoccupied with mortality and immortality, Dickinson secluded herself in the 1850s in her family home in Amherst, Massachusetts, where she poured her wry and sometimes anguished feelings into brief, eloquent poems hidden in her notebooks. Mostly unpublished before her death in 1886, Dickinson's deeply private voice remained mostly unheard until the twentieth century.

DEMOCRACY'S ADVOCATES

New England was not the only literary locale in antebellum America, and neither Transcendentalism nor dark reflections engaged all authors. A group of native and adopted New York writers called themselves "Young America" and clustered around Democratic Party editor John L. O'Sullivan and his literary and political journal the *United States Magazine and Democratic Review*, published from 1837 to 1859. Modeled after contemporary nationalist movements in Europe, Young America shared Emerson's desire for a distinctive American literature, but loudly asserted its devotion to American superiority, democratic equality, majority rule, and geographical expansion. Some members questioned slavery; others took little interest in it. Novelists Nathaniel Hawthorne and Herman Melville, critic Evert A. Duykinck, and poets John Greenleaf Whittier, William Cullen Bryant, and Walt Whitman all played active roles in the *Democratic Review*, Young America, or both. Even when the Democratic Party seemed to lose much of its energy and optimism in the 1850s, the Young America group continued to demand a revitalized commitment to their own views of progress and democratic principles.

New York journalist Walt Whitman was probably the most original member of the Young America circle. In *Leaves of Grass*, published in 1855, Whitman used free verse to celebrate democratic equality and open and sensitive consciousness as keys to a higher human freedom. Bravely admitting the role of physical sensations and even sexuality in opening people to spiritual insights, Whitman referenced his own homosexual desires in language that contemporaries often overlooked but later generations found unmistakable.

Excluded from Young America, a courageous cadre of black writers demanded to join its celebrated democracy, most obviously through autobiographical narratives of their escapes from slavery. Maryland runaway Frederick Douglass published his enduring classic *Narrative of the Life of Frederick Douglass* in 1845 before he became a leader of the abolitionist movement. In it, he showed how he struggled physically and mentally to claim the freedom and independence that America offered its white men. When he did emerge as a major abolitionist speaker, Douglass used his eloquence to excoriate the moral blindness of a nation that boasted of democracy while enslaving one-sixth of its people. In his scathing oration "What to the Slave Is the Fourth of July?," originally delivered as an Independence Day address, Douglass answered the question of its title with what he called "scorching irony." To the slave, he cried to his listeners, "your celebration is a sham; your boasted liberty, an unholy license; your national greatness, swelling vanity; your sounds of rejoicing are empty and heartless; your denunciations of tyrants, brass fronted impudence; your shouts of liberty and equality, hollow mockery." Despite his scorn, Douglass did not denounce the principles of the Declaration of Independence. Instead, he invoked liberty, equality, and natural rights to expose white America's hypocrisy and to demand their extension to everyone.

Harriet Jacobs's *Incidents in the Life of a Slave Girl* portrayed the very different struggle of an enslaved woman, first to protect herself from sexual abuse, and then to preserve her children from sale. Now widely regarded as an outstanding account of the female slave experience, Jacobs's work was largely forgotten after publication in 1861 and was misinterpreted until the end of the twentieth century. Harriet Beecher Stowe drew on the voluminous literature of slave narratives as written by escapees like Douglass and Jacobs to weave emotions and social protest together in *Uncle Tom's Cabin*. Justly renowned for its host of vivid and engaging characters as well as its powerful sentimentality, Stowe's best seller crystallized northern antislavery feeling and brought home the sufferings of slavery's victims to white readers as no other work had yet done.

THE FREE LABOR IDEAL

Writers and artists of the antebellum North drew many of their themes from the liberty, equality, and self-reliance that many white men valued in their daily lives. Even as late as 1860, most Americans still drew their livings from the soil and an estimated 57 percent of free farmers owned their own land. Most industries relied on small workshops with no more than 10 or 12 employees. Public spokesmen thus sang the praises of the independent property-owning citizen. Pennsylvania's Thaddeus Stevens expressed the dominant idea precisely: "The middling classes who own the soil, and work it with their own hands are the main support of every free government." As in politics, it was the struggle of the free average man to define and improve himself that provided the dominant drama of antebellum religion and reform.

In reality, individual improvement eluded many Americans, even in the North's environment of free labor. The ideal of the self-made man specifically excluded women, and the cult of true womanhood kept most middle-class women in their homes. Powerful racial prejudice likewise dismissed blacks, Indians, and Hispanic Americans as hopelessly incapable of true liberty. Factory workers faced industrial subordination, but many observers did not protest so long as most of those affected were young women like Lucy Larcom and Sarah Bagley, not men they regarded as worthy of true independence.

Observers did worry about the future of freedom in a society dominated by wage labor. While antebellum workshops were still small by later standards, the Market Revolution undermined opportunities for independent artisans and kept growing numbers of adult men in the uncomfortable position of lifelong "hirelings," sometimes called "wage slaves." For the least fortunate urban workers, poverty and exploitation were already daily realities, and the "dark satanic mills" of Victorian England were grim reminders of what might be in store for growing numbers of Americans. These developments fostered labor unions and strikes, and brought gibes from the slave states that the liberty and equality of free society were delusions.

Partly responding to these challenges and partly replying to the South, northern politicians and other popular spokesmen began to celebrate the ideal of "free labor." "Free labor" could mean working for wages or self-employment, but orators saw no conflict between them, for they saw the first leading easily to the second. "A young man goes out to service—to labor, if you please to call it so," explained Senator

Zachariah Chandler of Michigan, working "for compensation until he acquires money enough to buy a farm . . . and soon he becomes himself the employer of labor." Abraham Lincoln had lived through the process and echoed the claim. "The man who labored for another last year," he declared in 1856, "this year labors for himself, and next year he will hire others to labor for him." In this view, the unlimited abundance of the American environment guaranteed that every hard-working freeman had the "right to rise," particularly in the boundless West. Cheap and fertile western land seemed to ensure that no one would be trapped in a servile condition, and the middling economic status that underpinned republican government would always be available to the deserving.

Northern spokesmen also stressed that there was no serious class conflict in free society, for everybody was a worker, employers and employees alike. "Why who are the laboring people of the North?" inquired Daniel Webster in 1850. "They are the whole North. They are the people who till their own farms with their own hands; freeholders, educated men, independent men." No bloated aristocrats or degraded slaves existed to block opportunity for others, he implied, and so long as statesmen protected the ideal of free labor, the republic would be safe. Ironically, just as realistic hopes for self-employment were slipping out of reach for millions of Americans, free labor spokesmen like Webster blurred the differences between wage labor and business ownership by lauding paid employment as the gateway to the middle class. As sectional conflict intensified, northern leaders swore to protect the ideal of free labor, to preserve its promise as America expanded, and to protect it from slavery, its sinister opposite.

*

Since the days of the Puritans, visionary Americans had seen their "godly experiment" as an opportunity for the moral and spiritual elevation of humanity. "Wee shall be as a Citty upon a Hill," John Winthrop had prophesied. "The eyes of all people are upon us." Such aspirations gained a secular republican gloss with the coming of the Enlightenment and the success of the American Revolution, but did not lose their spiritual resonance. When Revolutionary fervor led to religious skepticism and political warfare, however, alarmed Americans struggled to restore what they saw as the nation's sacred mission. Their task grew more urgent as the Market Revolution unsettled communities from the cities to the frontier, unleashing problems like greed, violence, crime, drunkenness, unemployment, and poverty, and disrupting institutions like families, churches, schools, and public charity. From a cultural base in the New England heartland, idealistic reformers fanned across the North, drawing inspiration from religious revivals to build voluntary societies to cure the nation's ills. Their movement often relied on the efforts of middle-class women and inspired some to challenge the restrictive bonds of domesticity. Among ordinary families and sophisticated intellectuals, the reformers stimulated a middle-class American culture based on evangelical religion, individual striving, personal virtue, and self-control.

The reform movements had considerable success. Drinking declined, literacy increased, and churches multiplied. Early feminists met ridicule but their ideas took root and slowly gained strength. In the greatest change of all, northern opinion turned against slavery. If immediate abolition still frightened most whites, more and more believed that slavery undermined their own liberties as well as those of blacks, and that a republic based on free labor could not coexist forever with bondage. Hoping for slavery's ultimate demise, northerners increasingly believed that the system should at least stop expanding. That conviction put them into growing conflict with white southerners, a conflict based on rival visions of the ideal American republic.

HORRID MASSACRE IN VIRGINIA.

The Scenes which the above Plate is designed to represent, are—Fig. 1, a Mother intreating for the lives of her children.—2. Mr. Travis, cruelly murdered by his own Slaves.—3. Mr. Barrow, who bravely defended himself until his wife escaped.—4. A comp. of mounted Dragoons in pursuit of the Blacks.

FIGURE 7. In August 1831, a group of slaves led by Nat Turner killed over 50 whites in Southampton County, Virginia, and whites retaliated by killing over 200 blacks. Miscellaneous Items in High Demand, Rare Book and Special Collections Division, Library of Congress, LC-USZ62-38902.

CHAPTER 10

The World of the South, 1815–1860

Young Frederick Bailey was 16 years old when he went to live with Edward Covey, a small farmer on the Eastern Shore of Maryland. Renowned in the neighborhood as a "Negro-breaker," Covey rented spirited young slaves like Bailey for unusually low prices by promising to break their resistance to enslavement.

"If at any one time of my life more than another, I was made to drink the bitterest dregs of slavery, that time was during the first six months of my stay with Mr. Covey," Bailey later remembered. He received his first whipping within a week of his arrival and about once a week thereafter. Work was incessant and there was never enough time to eat or rest. Under this treatment, Bailey felt completely crushed. "I was broken in body, soul, and spirit," he later admitted. "The dark night of slavery closed in upon me," and he became "a man transformed into a brute!"

But Frederick Bailey's destruction was not complete, for sparks of his independence and ambition still flickered. In the middle of August 1834, he collapsed from heat and exhaustion and could not resume work despite serious beating. Briefly escaping, Bailey sought help from his owner and a friendly older slave before summoning the strength to return to Covey. "You have seen how a man was made a slave," Bailey later told friendly audiences; "you shall see how a slave was made a man." This time, when Covey attempted to punish him, Bailey refused to submit. "From whence the spirit came I don't know—I resolved to fight; and . . . I seized Covey hard by the throat," he later remembered. For two hours, the older man and the powerful teenager rolled and struggled across the barn floor. Finally the "Negro-breaker" was broken himself. Covey gave up the struggle and never whipped Bailey again. For the victorious young man, moreover, the battle with Edward

Covey became "the turning point in my career as a slave." The fight "revived within me a sense of my own manhood. . . . It was a glorious resurrection, from the tomb of slavery, to the heaven of freedom." Bailey soon resolved to escape from slavery completely. Four years later, he disguised himself as a sailor and used forged free papers to slip from Maryland to Massachusetts.

Frederick Bailey's adventures did not end there. Taking the name of a popular fictional hero, he became "Frederick Douglass," a thrilling antislavery orator and abolitionist celebrity. His first autobiography, *Narrative of the Life of Frederick Douglass, an American Slave, Written by Himself*, became a contemporary best seller and a classic account of a slave's struggle for freedom, identity, and manhood. As the most famous and respected black man in the United States, Douglass became a persistent influence on Abraham Lincoln, pushing the Civil War president to embrace the cause of emancipation. Over the rest of his career, Douglass was the preeminent public advocate for black civil rights, a bold supporter of women's suffrage, the US minister to Haiti, and the author of two more autobiographies. As he put it in the final words of his *Narrative*, Douglass spent the rest of his life "in pleading the cause of my brethren."

The battle between Edward Covey and Frederick (Bailey) Douglass exemplified the social experience of the antebellum South in several ways. Slavery rested on violence, actual or potential, and on collaboration between common white men like Edward Covey and Bailey's more affluent owner, Thomas Auld. Frederick Douglass's furious battle demonstrated that the love of freedom did not die, no matter how subdued a slave might appear. In their hearts, slave owners knew that superficial acquiescence was not the same as true submission, and they charged their slaves with perpetual deception. "So deceitful is the Negro that as far as my own experience extends I could never in a single instance decipher his character," a Georgia master admitted after emancipation. "We planters could never get at the truth."

Slavery's fierce antagonisms and pervasive influence gave a distinct character to the economy, society, and government of the antebellum South. Slave owners wielded pervasive power over the economy, politics, and culture of the region, even though most southerners were neither slaves nor masters, but whites who lived on small farms like those of the rural North and Midwest. Even in the midst of slavery, these southerners insisted on white liberty and equality, and the planter elite could not ignore them. Masters' efforts to control their slaves and to dominate nonslaveholders without appearing tyrannical suffused the public and private life of the region. The antebellum North and South were similar in many ways, but the institution of slavery made them just different enough to generate serious sectional discord. Managing these tensions became a fundamental task of national leaders in the antebellum years. Eventually the task overwhelmed them, and slave labor and free labor societies went to war.

Southern Contours

In 1815, when Andrew Jackson triumphed at the Battle of New Orleans, the identity and physical dimensions of the American South were still emerging. France and Spain had claimed Louisiana for over a century, but it never flourished like the Atlantic colonies, and only a dozen years had passed since President Jefferson acquired it for the United States. The state of Louisiana had entered the Union just as the War of 1812 began, and it was still the only state south of Tennessee and west of the Appalachians when peace came. A handful of Spaniards held Florida, but Native Americans possessed much of the future Deep South. The South's most populous and densely populated region was still the Chesapeake, where white settlement had begun 200 years before.

By 1860, the territory that Jackson seized from the Spanish and the Indians and defended from the British had changed considerably. Most of the Native Americans had been expelled and their lands had turned into cotton plantations. The 15 slave states held 12 million Americans, nearly 40 percent of the total population, and slavery stretched from tiny Delaware to the frontier states of Texas and Missouri. Most important, the South in 1860 had emerged as a distinct American section with its own internal divisions, drawn together by a common commitment to slavery and a long political struggle to defend it. These differences played an important role in political controversy and the construction of southern identity, beginning in the era of Jackson's victory and continuing through the secession crisis and the Civil War itself.

THE UPPER SOUTH

At least three major geographical divisions crisscrossed the southern landscape, powerfully contributing to regional diversity. The first divided the tidewater, low country, and river bottom land from the piedmont and similar upland districts. Plantation slavery thrived on the fertile soil of the lowlands, but the higher ground held more yeomen and small slaveholders. Beyond the piedmont, the mountainous portions of the South were even more isolated and usually unsuited for plantations. A second major division followed the Appalachian Mountains and separated the long-settled Southeast from the Southwest, sometimes called the Old Southwest, where Americans followed French and Spanish colonizers. The most important division separated the Upper South and its more diversified economy from the Lower South, or Deep South, dominated by cotton, rice, and sugar plantations. Though state lines never coincided exactly with agricultural regions, the Upper South roughly extended from the Ohio River and the Mason-Dixon line (between Maryland and Pennsylvania) through North Carolina, Tennessee, and Missouri, while the Deep South stretched southward from there to the Gulf of Mexico.

Over the course of the eighteenth century, soil exhaustion and changing markets had led many planters in Delaware, Maryland, and Virginia to switch from tobacco to wheat and other crops that required fewer workers, and hopes rose that slavery might disappear from the Upper South as it had farther north. Some masters freed their slaves or allowed them to purchase their liberty, until free blacks outnumbered slaves in Delaware and the District of Columbia, and nearly did so in Maryland. Local societies to promote voluntary manumission dotted the region through the 1820s and support grew for the American Colonization Society.

These conditions changed after the Lower South opened for settlement after 1815. Thousands of Upper South whites bid up the price of slaves when they migrated to the Southwest seeking fresh soils and new opportunities. A massive domestic slave trade sprang up, and the sale of surplus workers became an important source of income to cash-strapped masters. Support for emancipation likewise faltered, as slave sales restored the profitability of worn-out Chesapeake plantations.

Some whites who remained in the Upper South experimented with manufacturing or agricultural reforms, but the region largely retained its traditional economy. Plantations grew tobacco, cotton, corn, wheat, and hemp, and pine forests still yielded naval stores. Small farmers in the up-country leaned toward self-sufficiency, but also hauled a small surplus to fall-line markets. Divisions between up-country and lowlands roiled the politics of the Upper South, as low country planters resisted yeoman demands for greater representation and state expenditures on internal improvements. As sectional tensions increased, family ties, slavery, and the importance of slave sales all tied the Upper South to the Deep South, while proximity and economic similarities drew it to the North. Together with its own internal divisions, these competing allegiances undermined sectional extremism and kept the Upper South's future uncertain.

THE COTTON KINGDOM

In 1858, Senator James Henry Hammond of South Carolina popularized a memorable expression on the floor of the US Senate. While the North was reeling from the Panic of 1857, he boasted, the South remained unscathed and untouchable. "No, sir," Hammond sneered, "you dare not make war on cotton. No power on earth dares make war upon it. Cotton is King."

Hammond was certainly right about the size and importance of the cotton crop. By the time he spoke, cotton cloth had become the world's most important industrial product, and the United States was the leading supplier of raw cotton, producing about 70 percent of the annual harvest. Cotton was by far the most valuable US product, constituting at least half the value of total exports every year, with an annual value of at least $100 million by end of the 1850s. Wealth from the cotton crop not only built the mansions of the cotton planters; it filled the bank accounts of shippers, export merchants, bankers, and textile manufacturers, paid the salaries of their thousands of employees, and fostered the growth of the cities they lived in, both North and South. Economist Douglass C. North has concluded that cotton production was the largest single contributor to US economic growth in the antebellum era and laid the basis for America's future economic power.

African American slaves plowed, planted, hoed, picked, and "ginned" most of this valuable crop. While the Market Revolution propelled northern states toward industrialization and the commercial family farm, the same set of economic pressures brought an expansion of slavery in the southern states. Under the influence of expanding cotton production, the South remained what it had been in the eighteenth century: not merely a society with slaves in it but a thoroughgoing slave society in which the principle of human property dominated the economy, preoccupied the government, and underpinned the values and ideals of the white majority. The antebellum North and South had much in common, but the fundamental institutions of one section depended on freedom while their parallels in the other relied on slavery. That difference ultimately overwhelmed the similarities of North and South.

The most significant economic event of the post-Revolutionary South had been the spread of a new variety of cotton to supply the booming textile industry of New England and Europe. Long-staple cotton grew long delicate fibers with smooth seeds that a pair of rollers could easily separate, but it would not grow outside the semitropical environment of the South Carolina and Georgia Sea Islands. Hardier upland, or short-staple, cotton flourished in the southern interior, but its short fibers clung stubbornly to its seeds, requiring a day's labor to prepare a single pound of lint for carding and spinning. Visiting a Georgia plantation in 1792, Connecticut tutor Eli Whitney overcame this difficulty by combining rollers with wire combs and a toothed cylinder that forcefully pulled out the seeds. Whitney's engine, or "gin," made a single worker 50 times as productive as before and inspired a host of imitators. The cultivation of upland cotton spread rapidly, and the Cotton Kingdom began to rise.

The cotton gin made short-staple cotton a profitable crop from southern Virginia to eastern Texas. Cotton plantations spread from coastal districts to the up-country of South Carolina and Georgia, on to central Tennessee, and then south to the Gulf coast territory that Andrew Jackson had seized from the Creeks in the War of 1812. Jackson further expanded the Cotton Kingdom with two invasions of Florida, which pressured Spain to sell the province in 1819, and by seizing the remaining Indian territory when he became president in 1829.

The new crop sparked a wave of emigration and land speculation, as thousands of whites abandoned worn-out acreage in Virginia and the Carolinas for the deep rich soils of the newly opened Southwest. "The *Alabama Fever* rages here with great violence and has *carried off* vast numbers of our Citizens," a sardonic North Carolinian observed in 1817. "Some of our oldest and most wealthy men are offering their possessions for sale and [are] desirous of removing to this new country."

Farmers could raise cotton with family labor but larger operations were more efficient, so slavery spread in cotton's wake. Congress ended the African slave trade in 1808, but domestic traffic replaced it. Historian Michael Tadman has estimated that the transport of slaves from one region to another rose from 40,000 or 50,000 in the 1790s to 150,000 in the 1820s, and then as high as 250,000 in the 1830s and 1850s. Some migrating slaves moved with families and friends when

Upper South masters transplanted whole communities to the Deep South. As many as 60 or 70 percent, however, were torn individually from their loved ones and delivered to professional slave dealers. The domestic slave trade profited buyers and sellers but tormented its victims, few of whom could ever see their families again.

The Cotton Kingdom never displaced the other staples of the Deep South. Sea Island planters kept growing long-staple cotton for luxury fabrics, and rice plantations persisted nearby. In southern Louisiana, successful planters mastered the culture of sugarcane to amass huge fortunes and slave holdings. Sugar, rice, and Sea Island cotton laid the basis for some of the South's largest fortunes, vast palatial mansions, and largest concentrations of slaves, but their special environmental requirements limited their growth and overall influence.

THE SLAVE ECONOMY

Economic historians have left little doubt that slavery was a profitable institution that was not in danger of internal collapse, especially after the spread of cotton cultivation. Slave prices hit their all-time high on the eve of the Civil War, a good indication of slave owners' confidence in their economic prospects. With high cotton prices, planting was not only profitable but the safest and most prestigious activity a southern investor could pursue. Throughout the South, ambitious nonslaveholders like Edward Covey did not look for alternatives to slavery but hoped to gain land and slaves of their own. Men who made fortunes in business, medicine, or law likewise gained dignity and social standing with the purchase of slave plantations.

Slavery produced short-term profits and painful long-term consequences. Considering the free population alone, the South's per capita income actually exceeded the North's, particularly in the Southwest where very wealthy planters skewed the averages. The average figures plunge, however, when slaves—the most deprived portion of the population—are counted in the comparison. Per capita incomes in the industrializing Northeast were more than twice those of the Southeast, moreover, and most observers who compared the "North" and the "South" were actually comparing these regions. Like many others, New York's senator William H. Seward reported "exhausted soil, old and decaying towns, wretchedly-neglected roads, and, in every respect, an absence of enterprise and improvement" on his 1856 trip to Virginia. A few critical southerners agreed. Summarizing conventional wisdom, North Carolinian Daniel R. Goodloe wrote that "slavery affects the prosperity of the country by its tendency to degrade labor in the estimation of the poor and to engender pride in the rich; and as a consequence, to produce idleness and inattention to business in all."

The South's economy was not all backward. Sizable cities dotted its periphery and funneled regional crops to distant markets. The largest was Baltimore, built on shipbuilding, manufacturing, and trade and holding over 200,000 inhabitants in 1860. The portions of Kentucky and Virginia (now West Virginia) that bordered the Ohio River interacted extensively with their northern neighbors, and cities like Louisville and St. Louis flourished with free labor. A few slave-operated cotton mills appeared at Upper South waterpower sites, and Richmond's Tredegar Iron Works produced weapons, rails, and locomotives with 900 free and enslaved workers. As early as the 1830s, the region's leaders called for more such developments and their numbers grew over time, but observers still complained that the Upper South's economy badly lagged behind the North's.

The slave economy also contributed to northern growth. Cotton was the key raw material for cotton cloth, the most important product of early industrialization in the United States and Europe. The size of the US cotton crop rose from just over 3,000 bales (400–500 pounds each) in 1790 to 3.8 million bales in 1860, and the United States produced two-thirds of the world's supply.

Cotton had been the most valuable American export since 1840, and British factories bought most of it. Southern planters profited from these sales, but so did the northern banks that financed the purchase and sale of the crop and often the purchase and sale of the enslaved workforce. Other beneficiaries included the northern owners of the railroads, steamboats, and merchant vessels that carried the cotton crop to market and across the sea, the northern insurance companies that underwrote it, the northern manufacturers who spun it into cloth, the northern farmers and manufacturers who sold food and supplies to the plantation system, and the millions of free northerners who worked for them, not to mention the millions of other Americans who did not handle cotton themselves but drew their livelihoods from those who did. The slaves who grew this cotton were valued at $3 billion in 1860, about 20 percent of all the wealth in the United States. The profits that northern businesses and individuals reaped from slave labor financed a substantial portion of the growth and income of the antebellum United States.

In technical terms, the South "grew," because its wealth and income continued to increase, but did not "develop" as fast as the rest of the country, because its economic complexity and sophistication (and thus its capacity for future growth) did not improve at the same pace. In other words, while the South became wealthier, it lagged in such things as the growth of cities, construction of railroads, accumulation of banking capital, number of pupils in school, and levels of literacy. Development could lag in any farming region, but the rural regions in the Northeast and Midwest (or Old Northwest) prospered more than the slave states as the frontier receded. Did slavery impoverish the South by hampering economic development?

Historians continue to debate this question. The South's geography was not inherently agricultural, for some southern factories prospered using slaves, and industry grew even more when slavery ended. Even so, some planters actively discouraged industrialization because they feared that urban-dwelling factory slaves would become too independent, while free white factory workers might cast their votes for antislavery agitators. Louisiana sugar planter Samuel Walker expressed these attitudes in his diary in 1856. "Slavery is from its very nature eminently patriarchal and altogether agricultural," he concluded. "It does not thrive with master or slave when transplanted to cities, where is assembled large crowds of indigent and many unprincipled whites, especially where there are many foreigners to earn or steal subsistence."

The slave South paid a social and political price for its choices. Limited industrialization slowed population growth, for immigrants shunned an economy where wage-paying jobs were scarce and tainted by resemblance to bondage. The states south of Pennsylvania contained 51.3 percent of Americans in 1790 (2 million out of 3.9 million) but only 38.9 percent in 1860 (12.2 million out of 31.4 million). As a result, southern representation in the House of Representatives steadily dwindled, from 46 percent of the seats in 1790 to 35 percent in 1860, despite protection by the Constitution's three-fifths clause.

Facing these realities, some southern leaders longed to combine slavery with progress, but their exhortations had limited effect. The slave states subsidized transportation technology to carry exports to market, but not to build cities or internal trade. Wary of expense and dubious of social uplift, southern states lagged far behind the North in establishing common schools and educating white children. Needing to keep their captive workers busy, planters saw little need for labor-saving machinery beyond the cotton gin and imported their farm tools from the North. Tellingly, Cyrus McCormick's business did not thrive until he moved it from Virginia to Chicago, where it evolved into the International Harvester Company. Though factories using slaves enjoyed high rates of return, investors still hesitated to build them. For many, the plantation system was a way of life, not just a way to make a living. No smoky factory could produce the social and psychological satisfactions of a gentleman who surveyed his broad acres and fluffy white fields from the spacious veranda of a plantation "big house."

By reinforcing the system of slavery, the paradoxical effect of the Market Revolution in the South was to hinder its economic development until after emancipation. Slavery generated substantial incomes in the southern states, but failed to stimulate the technological complexity and sophistication that could feed more growth in the second half of the nineteenth century.

The Peculiar Institution

White southerners called slavery their "Peculiar Institution," not because they thought it strange but because it was uniquely theirs. Though slavery once existed throughout the Americas, the northern states and the former Spanish colonies abolished it after gaining independence. The slaves of Haiti threw off their chains in the world's only successful slave revolution, Britain abolished slavery in its colonies in 1834, and France followed in 1848. African slavery survived in Cuba, Puerto Rico, Brazil, and a handful of smaller European colonies, but by 1830 if not earlier, the US South had become the most important slave society in a world based increasingly on free labor.

WORKING LIKE A SLAVE

The enslaved were about a third of the antebellum southern population. Most lived on plantations, defined as farms with 20 slaves or more, but no more than 10 percent lived on plantations with more than 100. Though conditions varied from region to region, the typical slave in 1860 probably lived on a farm with the owner's family, perhaps an overseer, and about 30 or 40 other African Americans.

First and foremost, slavery was a labor system, and slaves did virtually every kind of manual labor available, from skilled woodworking, iron making, and dressmaking, to cooking, cleaning, and childcare. As Frederick Douglass said of his year with Edward Covey, "We were worked fully up to the point of endurance. . . . It was never too hot or too cold; it could never rain, blow, hail, or snow too hard for us to work in the field. . . . The longest days were too short for him, and the shortest nights were too long for him." Wealthy slave owners could afford to take a long view and attempt to keep their chattels healthy, but an ambitious renter like Edward Covey had little use for such pains. Men like Covey typically longed to make enough money to buy their own slaves, giving them even more reason to drive themselves and their rented workers without mercy.

Large planters could allow a few men and women to become specialized artisans or house servants, or to supervise other slaves, but most male and female plantation workers were field hands. Sea Island masters assigned work according to the "task system," designating each hand's daily work and allowing those who finished early to use the extra time as they wished. In practice, most tasked slaves had to use their "free" time to support themselves by hunting, fishing, tending small gardens or livestock, or performing odd jobs for pay. Some Sea Island slaves used their earnings to acquire property that custom — not the law — recognized as their own. In most parts of the South, however, masters strictly regimented slave labor from dawn to dark, and sometimes longer.

On the typical cotton plantation, the master or overseer roused slaves by a bell or horn and marched them to the fields by daybreak. With a short break for breakfast and another for the midday meal, labor continued at a steady pace until sundown, weather permitting, with rest breaks timed to meet the needs of the work animals, not the people. Cotton planters improved productivity by substituting the "gang system" for tasks. Dividing their workforce into small groups, or "gangs," typically led by a single slave "driver," planters used competition and intense supervision to reach maximum output. Exacting masters knew exactly how much plowing or picking to expect from each worker, sometimes rewarding those who overperformed, but certainly punishing those who fell short. By steadily raising their daily work requirements and routinely whipping slaves who did not meet them, Deep South planters forced a phenomenal 361 percent increase in the amount of cotton picked per slave per day between 1811 and 1860. Though improved plant varieties may have contributed to the increase, enslaved men and women clearly had to pick faster and faster, picking with both hands, for example, just to avoid the lash. "No matter how fatigued and weary he may be — no matter how much he longs for sleep and rest—a slave never approaches the gin-house with his basket of cotton but with fear," recalled Solomon Northup, once enslaved in Louisiana. "If it falls short in weight . . . he knows he must suffer."

Most field hands got Sundays off and a holiday between Christmas and New Year's Day, but house servants were always on duty. Free farmers worked hard too, but the unrelenting compulsion of the gang system was the key to slavery's profitability. Its regimentation made slaves significantly more productive than free workers and gave masters a marked economic advantage over yeomen and small slaveholders. In other words, "to work like a slave" in the Old South was very hard labor indeed.

The steadily rising price of slaves reminded most masters to keep their chattels healthy and productive, and even Edward Covey gave his workers enough to eat. Written instructions to overseers usually prescribed a peck of ground corn, three or four pounds of salt pork, and a serving of molasses every week for "full hands," or able-bodied men, and proportionately less for "half hands," or less productive women and children. These rations supplied enough calories for working adults, but like the diets of other laboring Americans, the rations lacked the proper amounts of key vitamins and nutrients. Even under the gang system, most slaves could supplement this diet with gardens or extra work in off-hours, and masters might pay them for surplus vegetables, game, and poultry. Slaves' clothes and houses were likewise crude, and Frederick Douglass remembered suffering from the cold, but sensible masters issued enough clothing for winter protection. Some plantations produced their own shoes and garments, but it was increasingly more efficient to purchase such items from northern manufacturers who made "negro goods" for the southern market. Most plantation slave families lived in the "quarters," a cluster of small, dirt-floored log cabins not far from the master's "big house," but single slaves on small farms probably found living space in odd corners of the master's own dwelling.

Slave labor was relatively inflexible, for slaves had to be supported and supervised whether working or not. Owners of unneeded slaves could rent them to others, usually for one-year terms that began on New Year's Day. Edward Covey hired Frederick Douglass on this basis. Some skilled or urban slaves "hired their own time" by paying their masters a fixed weekly sum for the privilege of living and working independently. Venture Smith worked this way in colonial Connecticut, and Frederick Douglass hired his time in Baltimore after leaving

Edward Covey. Though convenient for individual masters, governments discouraged or forbade this practice as injurious to discipline. As one slaveholder explained to northern traveler Frederick Law Olmsted, hired slaves "got a habit of roaming about and *taking care of themselves*." The result, said a governor of Louisiana, was that slaves gained "liberties and privileges totally inconsistent with their proper condition and good government."

SLAVE FAMILIES

The laws of the slave states did not recognize slave marriages, but most masters encouraged slaves to form marriage-like unions and to live in families. African Americans certainly welcomed this opportunity, and masters thought it discouraged escape. Most slave mothers had their first children about the age of 21, so couples presumably formed shortly before that. Christian slaves could be married by a minister, but most masters conducted a simple ceremony themselves that climaxed when the couple jumped over a broomstick together. Slaves might be required to find spouses on their own plantations, but masters normally permitted "abroad" marriages between men and women on neighboring farms, and they allowed husbands to spend Saturday nights and Sundays with their wives and children. Even when slaves were married in church, ministers generally omitted the binding phrase "till death do you part," for about 15 percent of all slave couples were parted by sale.

Sexual abuse was a particularly distressing aspect of slavery. Its precise extent is impossible to recover, but ex-slaves mentioned it repeatedly in their published recollections, white women often complained about it in divorce petitions, and the census of 1860 described 13 percent of all African Americans as "mulattoes." The open sale of beautiful, well-dressed "fancy girls," often of racially mixed ancestry, was a matter of common notoriety in cities like Charleston and New Orleans. Slave owners who impregnated their female slaves added more slaves to their holdings, and white and black women were mostly powerless to stop them. South Carolina's Mary Boykin Chesnut confined her rage to her diary, but significantly blamed black women more than white men. "Under slavery, we live surrounded by prostitutes," she seethed. "God forgive us, but ours is a monstrous system, a wrong and an iniquity . . . ! Any lady is ready to tell you who is the father of all the mulatto children in everybody's household but her own. Those, she seems to think, drop from the clouds."

Some masters showered privileges on their concubines and freed and educated their children. Others practiced brutal rapes or more subtle forms of coercion, for by law, forcing a slave was not a crime. Certainly the notion of "consensual" sex between a white man and a slave woman was highly complicated by the woman's almost complete inability to refuse. Sexual abuse degraded black women, humiliated black men, embittered white women, and coarsened white men, yet it was an obvious and widespread aspect of the slave experience.

Masters valued slave births and instructed overseers to protect the health of pregnant women, but hard labor pressed heavily on recent and expectant mothers. Slave babies suffered low birth weights and higher than average mortality, and their mothers experienced serious health problems as well, but the total slave population still grew steadily. Mothers nursed their infants in the fields, and an elderly slave cared for older children until they were ready for light tasks such as weeding at about age seven or eight. The work got heavier every year until young people were deemed ready for full field labor in their mid-teens. Slave children did not go to school, and most states made it a crime to teach a slave to read or write.

SLAVE DISCIPLINE

Masters understood that slavery depended on force. "It is like 'casting pearls before swine' to try to *persuade* a negro to work," declared one Arkansas planter. "He must be *made* to work, and should always be given to understand that if he fails to perform his duty he will be punished for it." Even so, writers on slave discipline recommended a system of rewards as well. "I contend that the surest and best method of managing negroes is to love them," wrote one Georgia planter with no apparent irony, and he also observed that kindness could be as useful in training slaves as it is in horses. Whatever they thought of the comparison, diligent slaves could receive extra food, clothing, money, alcohol, or time off. A successful harvest season could bring a party or a feast but poor performance might cancel it. Like employers firing free workers, masters could sell their resisting slaves, and the threat of sale away from family and friends could be a powerful form of discipline, but unlike free workers who could not eat without a job, slaves who were sold remained an expense until the new master could make them work.

Corporal punishment therefore underpinned persuasion, and the whip cracked on virtually every plantation. "The whip was evidently in constant use," reported a *New York Times* correspondent when he visited one Deep South plantation. A Virginian explained why: "A great deal of whipping is not necessary; *some* is." Accepting this reality, the laws of the slave states generally forbade the deliberate murder of a slave but otherwise gave masters a free hand. "It is a pity that agreeable to the nature of things Slavery and Tyranny must go together," sighed a Carolina planter. "There is no such thing as having an obedient and useful Slave, without the exercise of undue and tyrannical authority." Most masters thought that 15 or 20 lashes with a heavy rawhide strap were enough to "correct" an offender, but punishments of 100 lashes were not uncommon and massive sentences of 500 lashes or more were not unheard of. Other penalties could include the use of jails, stocks, chains, and other heavy and painful devices. Slave narratives and travelers' reports repeatedly confirmed cases of extreme brutality. "Often I have witnessed negroes dragged, without regard to age or sex, to the public whipping post," wrote a northern visitor to North Carolina, "and flogged with the cowskin until the ground beneath is dyed with the blood of the sufferer."

Some masters were pathologically cruel. Others struggled with their tempers. The Reverend Charles Pettigrew, for example, admitted that "to manage negroes without the exercise of too much passion, is next to an impossibility." Others indulged in petty tyrannies, like the mistress who always spat in the cooking pots to keep her kitchen slaves from sampling the leftovers. While thousands tried to operate within their own rules of decency, the law made no distinction between them and their sadistic neighbors, for as North Carolina chief justice Thomas Ruffin put it, "The power of the master must be absolute to render the submission of the slave perfect."

SLAVE RESISTANCE

Captured Africans resisted their enslavement from their first moments of captivity, and African Americans did likewise. By the first decades of the nineteenth century, however, most American blacks had been born in slavery and the opportunities for complete escape were rare. Instead, rebellious slaves did what they could to make their lives easier inside the system of bondage, to disrupt their work routines, and to challenge the relentless psychological pressures of enslavement.

State laws defined slaves as "chattels personal," or moveable property like animals, tools, and furniture. Paradoxically, the law also recognized slaves as human because it forbade their murder and punished their crimes. The most profound insults of slavery involved treating humans as things, so anything a slave did to claim humanity could qualify as resistance. Slaves used their own families and communities to remind each other of their common dignity, to cherish children, to honor the elderly, to share the love of husbands and wives. When these family ties were broken by sale, slaves leaned on adopted relationships of "uncle," "auntie," "brother," or "sister."

Slaves retained a rich cultural heritage of African-inspired music and folklore, and they used their art to convey their deepest hopes and frustrations. Influenced by the Second Great Awakening, thousands of slaves converted to Christianity and used this aspect of white culture to condemn the moral pretensions of whites themselves. Most slave Christians joined Baptist or Methodist churches dominated by whites, but many also seized every opportunity for secret prayer meetings in the woods or the quarters, where they could express their own longings for spiritual and temporal liberation.

Besides art, religion, and kinship, the most obvious form of slave resistance was a collective refusal to work harder than necessary. Owners and overseers constantly complained that slaves broke tools, damaged crops, injured work animals, and failed to pay attention. Some blamed black stupidity, but shrewder owners guessed the truth. The slave, one admitted, can "pretend to more ignorance than he possesses . . . [which] serves as an apology for awkwardness and neglect of duty." Slaves could also be adept at feigning illnesses or stealing food and other valuables. Despite the prevalence of such "day-to-day" resistance, however, masters still wrung more labor from slaves than northern farmers got from hired hands.

Escape was the most common form of overt resistance. Runaways' autobiographies celebrated permanent flight to Canada or the North, but such exploits were rarely feasible. Maps and traveling information were scarce, and local governments employed vigilant white patrols, or "paterollers," to ride the roads at night and demand written passes from all blacks found absent from their masters' property. Like the young Frederick Douglass, aggrieved slaves more commonly took to the woods temporarily, to avoid a sale, to escape an unbearable punishment, or to visit a distant family. Runaways could even negotiate the terms of their return by sending messages through other slaves. Such bargaining undermined all the principles of slavery, but harassed masters frequently compromised for the sake of results.

Violence was the most drastic form of slave resistance. Frederick Douglass pointed to his fistfight with Edward Covey as the psychological turning point that inspired him to seize control of his life. Masters and overseers sometimes died in such outbursts, and some also fell to arson, poison, or midnight suffocation. Punishment for murder was swift and severe, but it could not quiet owners' fears of what the most docile slaves might contemplate in secret.

In the Caribbean and South America, the enslaved population was dense enough to support repeated revolts. Of those, the Haitian Revolution was the best known and most successful. North American slaves seldom took such risks, probably because well-armed whites outnumbered them by at least two to one or more in most districts. Four planned or actual uprisings offer proof, however, that the possibility of slave revolt never disappeared. In 1811, as many as 200 slaves led by the Haitian-born driver Charles Deslondes rose on the so-called German Coast of Louisiana, on the Mississippi's east bank. For two days, the rebels marched toward New Orleans, burning plantations on their way, until they were stopped by a white militia. Vengeful whites took almost 100 black lives in the aftermath; Deslondes himself was burned alive. A decade earlier, in 1800, a Richmond blacksmith named Gabriel enlisted many followers in a plot to seize the city and its arsenal, kill the leading whites, and bring in allies from the countryside. In 1822, white Charlestonians shuddered at reports that a free black seaman named Denmark Vesey formed a similar plan in Charleston with the help of "Gullah Jack," an Angolan shaman whose familiarity with traditional African religion won support among the country slaves of the Sea Islands. In both cases, rumors of a planned revolt brought torture and execution to dozens of suspects. In 1831, Nat Turner, a slave preacher of Southampton County, Virginia, became convinced that God would free his people if they only struck the first blow. Turner and his companions attacked a series of surrounding farms and quickly took about 60 whites' lives before an aroused militia crushed them. Like the others, Turner's revolt was followed by mass executions of suspected participants, some by the forms of law and others by simple lynching. Slave revolts were not common in the antebellum South, but the possibility of violence terrified whites and left them susceptible to panicky rumors and vengeful excesses.

The South's Free Society

Slave society left a profound mark on southern whites as well as blacks. The slaveholders themselves were a minority of the population, but slave ownership gave them powerful economic, political, and social privileges. A few slaveholding spokesmen defended the resulting inequality among whites, but racial privileges gave all white men a form of equal superiority that usually masked class differences. Sexual abuse of black women and obsessions over racial purity put a unique burden on white women as the only possible mothers of legitimate white children. White women of the upper classes occupied an elaborate pedestal, rigidly barred from public life but extravagantly praised for the "feminine" virtues. Racism burdened the lives of the South's tiny free black population and kept most of them poor and fearful of re-enslavement.

THE MASTERS

Slaveholders were a declining minority in the South, falling from a third of the white population in 1790 to a quarter in 1860. The average slaveholding increased in the same period, so slaves were concentrating in fewer hands as their prices increased. Historians have used the ownership of 20 slaves or more to distinguish between small slaveholders and planters. The distinction is somewhat arbitrary, but it roughly separates farmers who mostly supervised their slaves from those who worked beside them in the fields. Defined in this way, planter families constituted only 12 percent of all slave-owning households. Planters with more than 50 slaves often hired overseers for daily management and devoted their time to business, leisure, or public service. Less than 1 percent of white households owned over 100 slaves in 1860, creating a planter "aristocracy" of about 2,300 families. At the other end of the scale, nearly half of all slaveholders owned no more than five slaves.

Planters were the richest and most prestigious men in the South. The region's elite also included the merchants who shipped its staple crops from ports like Charleston and New Orleans. In county seats and market towns, the lawyers, doctors, merchants, and ministers who served the planters also belonged to the upper class. Southern planters and professionals held a disproportionate share of political power, monopolizing governorships and congressional seats and dominating the state assemblies. In the climactic year of 1860, for example, the proportion of slaveholders in soon-to-be Confederate state legislatures ranged from 86 and 82 percent in North and South Carolina, respectively, to 42 percent in Arkansas, while the proportion of planters varied between 55 percent in South Carolina and 13 percent in Arkansas. And the "nonslaveholders" counted in these figures included planters' sons who expected to inherit the family estate. Planters were a small proportion of the total population, but they set the tone of public life and exercised great cultural influence as well as political and economic power.

Elite families could enjoy palatial homes and luxurious living standards, especially where the plantation system was old and well-established. Brick Georgian mansions graced the landscape of ancient Virginia counties, while newer regions sported plantation homes in the popular Greek revival style with wide verandas and tall white columns. Ostentation triumphed along the lower Mississippi, where Louisiana sugar planter John Andrews built his 75-room mansion Belle Grove in the late 1850s to overshadow neighboring Nottoway with its 64 rooms. Such displays were exceptional, however. Most of the Lower South was only a generation away from the frontier in 1860, and pretensions to ancestral polish had little basis in reality, no matter how wealthy a family might be. Some of the most ambitious southwestern planters were so intent on building up their fortunes that they ignored physical comforts and installed their families in houses made of logs or unpainted wooden boards.

Small planters in many parts of the South did not live much differently from ordinary farmers, as journalist Frederick Law Olmsted discovered in a trip through the Red River country of Louisiana in the late 1850s. "The house was a small square log cabin, with a broad open shed or piazza in front, and a chimney, made of sticks and mud, leaning against one end," the traveler reported of a typical dwelling. "A smaller detached cabin, twenty feet in the rear, was used for a kitchen. . . . About the house was a large yard, in which were two or three China trees, and two fine Cherokee roses; half a dozen hounds; several negro babies, turkeys and chickens, and a pet sow, teaching a fine litter of pigs how to root and wallow. . . . The house had but one door and no window, nor was there a pane of glass on the plantation." The owner's family lived in a single room, 16 feet by 20, but they owned at least 20 slaves. The reporter probably found an extreme example, but among ordinary slaveholders simple quarters were far more common than pillared mansions.

THE MISTRESSES

Slaveholders took special pride in the place of privileged women in their society. No political gathering or Fourth of July celebration was complete without an eloquent toast to "the fair," and plantation men boasted that the southern lady was so well-honored that feminist complaints would never be heard in Dixie. "A Southern matron is ever idolized and almost worshipped by her dependents and beloved by her children, to whom no word ever sounds half so sweet as *mother* and for whom no place possesses half the charms of her *home*," promised one proslavery author. Fond regards came at a high price, however. To fulfill the ideal of the "lady," planter women were expected to combine beauty, fashion, wealth, refinement, etiquette, charity, and submission with loving motherhood and efficient household management, all with effortless grace. Writing in the *Southern Literary Messenger*, a female teacher warned her pupils to practice unfailing "self-control, gentleness and benevolence of disposition, purity and rectitude of conduct, [and] courtesy and politeness of manner," especially within the family. More bluntly, George Fitzhugh declared that "woman, like children, has but one right and that is the right to protection," balanced by "the obligation to obey . . . her husband, lord, and master." No wonder that another leading Confederate insisted that "each Planter is in fact a Patriarch—his position compels him to be a ruler in his own household."

In the spirit of republican motherhood, female academies spread across the South in the post-Revolutionary generation so future mothers would be prepared to train their sons for leadership. The best of these schools joined sound academic education with instruction in polite accomplishments like music, needlework, and French, as *DeBow's Review* explained, "to improve their [students'] minds and manners without robbing them of . . . delicacy and refinement." In late adolescence, parents might halt formal schooling at any time for a round of balls and social engagements designed to introduce young ladies to society and lead them to the most important decision of their lives—the choice of husband. Antebellum families allowed a free choice in these matters, but did their best to ensure that young people found partners with similar backgrounds, education, and wealth. To avoid the extensive division of estates, some families encouraged children to marry their first or second cousins. To safeguard the land and slaves that fathers often gave their daughters upon marriage (either from the son-in-law's bad habits or bad luck), Mississippi passed the first law protecting a married woman's property from her husbands' debts in 1839, and some other southern states did likewise.

Once married, plantation mistresses certainly enjoyed more opportunities than other women for leisure activities such as visiting, reading, or gardening, but most also faced the difficult responsibility of running a plantation household. Slaves performed the hardest parts of cooking, preserving food, cleaning, sewing, weaving, health care, and childcare, but like masters and overseers, mistresses faced steady resistance from unwilling workers. Protected from housework since childhood, many new brides struggled to control slaves and operate large households efficiently. The letters and diaries of planter women clearly show that they often felt lonely and overwhelmed, and longed for the company of friends and relatives, but the far distances that prevailed in rural society made visits as rare as they were welcome.

Unlike urban businessmen, planters did not leave home for the working day. Ruling their homes as well as their fields, they routinely called their dependents "our family, black and white." Southern women learned the ideas of "true womanhood" from the same books and magazines as their northern counterparts, but they did not have the same opportunity to rule their homes as a "separate sphere" or to claim the moral authority that encouraged reform activities among some northern women. When they could, however, many southern women from all classes embraced the Second Great Awakening and threw themselves into church work. The Presbyterian and Methodist denominations remained popular with the elite, but Methodists and Baptists attracted members from all classes, including slaves, middling white women, and plantation mistresses. Urban women could undertake benevolent activities through Sunday schools, Bible and tract societies, orphanages, poor relief, and religious missions, and they also pressed for public schools in cities such as Charleston, Mobile, and Natchez. Even so, the early women's rights movement found no public echo in the antebellum South.

Despite the prerogatives of patriarchy, some planter women enjoyed the loving marriages praised in ladies' magazines. "Thank God for the unity of spirit which exists between Patrick and myself," wrote one. "With him I am really better, more sensible, more entertaining than I am to any other mortal besides." Unluckier wives raged helplessly against their husbands' infidelities and vented their feelings on enslaved victims. "Patsey wept oftener, and suffered more, than any of her companions," wrote former slave Solomon Northup of his master's sexual victim. "Nothing delighted the mistress more than to see her suffer. . . . To be rid of Patsey . . . by sale or death or any other manner . . . seemed to be [her] ruling thought and passion." Humiliated wives had little legal recourse, however, since divorce was nearly impossible, and South Carolina banned it entirely.

NONSLAVEHOLDERS AND POOR WHITES

Though slaveholders controlled a disproportionate share of the South's wealth, the majority of southern households owned no slaves but enough land and equipment to live in simple comfort. Yeomen and artisans might resent the planters' airs but did not quarrel with the fundamental institutions of their society. Even the "poor whites," who owned little or no property, and whose standards of food, clothing, and shelter were often little better than those of slaves, usually accepted the privileges of race without questioning slavery. The effects of bondage could protect nonslaveholders, for underdeveloped transportation and marketing networks shielded yeomen from competition and cushioned artisans from some of the pressures that sent many northerners into wage-paying jobs with lower status, skills, and income. For the same reason, wives and daughters on small farms continued to support the family's independence with home manufactures long after most northern women had laid aside their looms and spinning wheels. Even in cotton-growing areas, nonslaveholding farmers grew significantly smaller crops of cotton and larger crops of corn than pure business logic would dictate, indicating that safety-first farming still ruled the economic strategies of yeomen.

To the extent that slaveholders were concentrated in the lowland parts of the South and nonslaveholders in the up-country, social and political rivalry spawned intrastate sectional rivalries, with up-country and low country legislators battling over banks, internal improvements, taxes, and legislative apportionment. Expressing equal measures of racial and class resentment, a North Carolina mountaineer bluntly explained to Frederick Law Olmsted that slavery gave planters too much power. "People out here hates the Eastern people," he confided. "They vote on the slave basis, and there's some of them nigger counties where there ain't more'n four or five hundred white folks, that has just as much power in the Legislature any of our mountain counties where there'll be some thousand voters."

Given the obvious class tensions of southern white society, historians have often wondered about the support for slavery among white nonslaveholders. For the most part, yeomen supported the system even if they resented the inequality it created. Many nonslaveholders hoped to own slaves themselves someday. Sharing the racism that made slavery possible, most southern whites feared an onslaught of black violence if slavery ended. Finally, white nonslaveholders probably sensed that slavery protected their own independence. Looking north, they could see a free labor society where more and more men like themselves were becoming dependent wage earners, and they did not like what they saw.

FREE PEOPLE OF COLOR

Not all free southerners were white. Most numerous in the Upper South, "free people of color" usually descended from mixed-race couples of the early colonial-era, the children of masters and slaves, slaves who purchased their freedom, and a lucky few liberated by Revolutionary idealists. Some combined black, white, and Indian heritage. To preserve a strict barrier between the races, most state legislatures set the proportion of black ancestry that barred free people of color from the privileges of whiteness at one-sixteenth or less and made no legal distinction between blacks and mulattoes. Beginning in the 1830s, the federal government forced most Indian tribes west beyond the Mississippi, but a few scattered communities of Native Americans remained in isolated corners of the South, mostly without tribal lands or governments, and state laws often classified them as free people of color as well.

Free blacks were anomalous in a society where all African Americans were presumed to be slaves and only whites were presumed to be free. Most legislatures eventually regretted the relaxed manumission laws of the late eighteenth century and took steps to reduce or tightly control the free black population. In 1806, Virginia gave all newly emancipated blacks 12 months to leave the state or return to slavery. Other states passed similar laws and limited manumission powers to the courts or the legislature itself. These measures limited the growth of the free black population, but the 1860 census still counted over a quarter million free people of color in the slave states and the District of Columbia, approximately 2 percent of the total population.

Lawmakers adopted a complex web of restrictions to control free blacks and prevent them from leading slaves in a challenge to the racial order. State laws barred them from voting, bearing arms, serving on juries or in the militia, testifying against white people, and preaching or holding meetings without white supervision. County courts routinely apprenticed free black children without their parents' consent. State laws discouraged free blacks from fraternizing with slaves and imposed harsher penalties on blacks than on whites for the same offenses or banned certain acts for blacks but not for whites. Most slave states made it illegal for a free person of color to speak or act disrespectfully to a white person, for example.

Most free blacks lived in the southern countryside, but a disproportionate number gravitated to towns and cities. The most successful became skilled artisans and shopkeepers, like North Carolina cabinetmaker Thomas Day or Natchez barber William Johnson. Some white fathers, especially in French-speaking Louisiana, lavished property and education on their mixed-race children, but racial discrimination kept most in casual day labor, domestic service, and other menial occupations. A handful of free blacks owned slaves themselves. In most of these cases, a free person had purchased his or her spouse or children and held them as slaves because manumission was impossible. Other free blacks bought slaves for straightforward economic purposes. Despite their disadvantages, free blacks tried to take full advantage of their few liberties to create community institutions such as churches or benevolent societies

Slavery and Culture

White Americans of the North and South shared many common convictions. Slaveholding southerners like Thomas Jefferson and James Madison had composed many of the nation's founding documents and articulated Revolutionary ideals for all Americans. With significant variations, the evangelical religion that stoked the North's First Great Awakening spread into the South, where it evolved, gained energy, and moved north again in the Second Great Awakening. Despite these core similarities, northern and southern societies embraced diverging ideals in the antebellum period. In some cases, as in convictions about race, the difference was mainly a matter of emphasis and intensity. In others, as in their ideas on social reform and human liberty, southern intellectuals differed profoundly from their northern counterparts. Both kinds of differences converged as southern leaders constructed a defense of slave society to rebut abolitionist criticism. Especially after the 1820s, southern writers and thinkers worked to prove that a society based on slavery was in every way superior to a society based on free labor.

RACE

Eighteenth-century intellectuals agreed that blacks and whites were all descended from Adam and Eve, and attributed racial differences to environmental factors like tropical weather. Despite this reasoning, most whites took racial inequality for granted and did not try to explain it. Stung by abolitionist attacks, however, southerners of the 1820s and 1830s developed elaborate justifications for slavery, arguing that blacks were inherently different from and inferior to whites, that slavery was blacks' God-given destiny, and that they were better off in slavery than freedom. Despite banning slavery itself, many northern whites adopted similar views and used them to defend discrimination.

As he did in so many other areas, Thomas Jefferson led the way to new ideas about race. "I advance it as a suspicion only," he observed in his *Notes on the State of Virginia*, written and published in the 1780s, "that the blacks, whether originally a distinct race, or made distinct by time and circumstance, are inferior to the whites in the endowments of body and mind." Jefferson always disapproved of slavery, and in his last public letter, written in 1826, he still insisted that "the mass of mankind has not been born with saddles on their backs, nor a favored few booted and spurred, ready to ride them legitimately, by the grace of God." Even so, he did not believe that the two races could live equally and peacefully in the same country, and refused to publicize his antislavery views until more whites shared them and a way appeared for blacks to leave America.

Later southerners were less reticent and defended slavery on plainly racist grounds. In 1835, Governor George McDuffie shared an increasingly popular consensus with South Carolina's legislature. "The African negro is destined by Providence to ... servile dependence," he proclaimed. "It is marked on the face, stamped on the skin, and evinced by the intellectual inferiority and natural improvidence of his race." Blacks were brutal and savage when left alone or incited by others, he went on, but under slavery, they "are cheerful, contented and happy much beyond the general condition of the human race." South Carolina's Senator John C. Calhoun firmly agreed, and told his colleagues in 1837 that "never before has the black race of central Africa ... attained a condition so civilized and so improved" as under slavery.

A few scholars formed elaborate theories of race based on physical differences, developing a now-discredited school of thought known as "scientific racism." University of Pennsylvania professor Samuel G. Morton measured hundreds of human skulls, and declared in his 1839 book *Crania Americana* that whites, Indians, and blacks could be ranked by their brain sizes, with whites having the largest brains and greatest intelligence and blacks having the smallest and the least. The races were so different, he concluded, that God must have created them as separate species. Alabama physician Josiah Nott and Egyptologist George Gliddon admired Morton's work and elaborated on his theory of "polygenesis," or separate creation, in their 1854 work *Types of Mankind*. Some southern intellectuals embraced scientific racism as a justification of slavery, but ministers rejected it as unscriptural and taught instead that God had cursed Noah's son Ham, supposedly the ancestor of all Africans, and condemned his descendants to racial inferiority and perpetual servitude. Scientific racism gained wider currency in the later nineteenth century, however, and was widely used to justify racial discrimination and white domination of other races.

Racial prejudice was also widespread in the North. Most Revolutionary-era constitutions reserved political privileges for white men, not simply freemen. When blacks did win their freedom, they were rigorously barred from public facilities like steamboats and stagecoaches. Racial segregation in housing, work, schools, and public accommodations was common in the North, and some midwestern states joined Missouri in passing laws to prevent free black people from entering the state at all. Many northerners sincerely rejected slavery, but others could tolerate it when it stayed far away and blacks did not compete with whites.

RELIGION

Colonial southerners had neglected their established churches, but the First Great Awakening introduced them to evangelical fervor. By 1790, about a fourth of white southerners and 3 percent of blacks had joined churches, especially evangelical congregations of Baptists, Methodists, and Presbyterians. A few gentry families clung to the forms of the Church of England and founded the Protestant Episcopal Church as the American branch of Anglicanism. This core group of believers prepared the way for an enthusiastic plunge into the Second Great Awakening.

Late eighteenth- and early nineteenth-century southern evangelicals often condemned slavery. They called it a "horrid evil" and "contrary to the laws of God, man, and nature," though they gave blacks separate seats and inferior roles within their churches. In 1784, Methodists made plans to excommunicate all members who had not freed their slaves within the next two years. Presbyterians asked for slavery's "final abolition" in 1787, and Baptists in 1789 called slavery "a violent deprivation of the rights of nature and inconsistent with republican government."

These professions gradually faded. Methodists could not enforce their proposed exclusion and other denominations did not try. Slaveholders decided that Christian slaves made better workers, and welcomed their conversion if ministers dropped their criticisms. Slaveholding women listened carefully to the gospel message and labored like northern women to convert their worldly sons and husbands. When they succeeded, evangelical planters made doubly sure that ministers left slavery alone.

While northern evangelists stressed individual freedom and tried to implant an inner moral compass so their converts could guide themselves, southern ministers increasingly stressed the benefits of social rank, order, and control. All were equal before God, admitted the *Southern Presbyterian Review*, but not in this world. "If a man is justly and providentially a ruler," it continued, "he has the rights of a father; and if a slave, only the rights of a slave." Quoting Saint Paul, southern ministers also reminded potential dissidents that God commanded servants to obey their masters just as he ordered wives to submit to their husbands and children to their parents. Like all human institutions, slavery was not perfect, but if men rejected all God-given institutions for mere imperfection, civilization itself would collapse. Masters and slaves could both be sinners, but if both accepted their Christian duties, slavery could be a blessing as much as marriage or parenthood. Beginning as critics of slavery and inequality, the southern evangelical churches eventually embraced them.

Divergence between northern and southern churches was painfully apparent by the 1840s. Pointing to general biblical principles like "love thy neighbor as thyself," northern churches increasingly denounced slavery as sinful and unchristian, but southerners rejected such abstractions. "If 'do unto others as you would they should do unto you' is to abolish slavery," argued Virginia Baptist minister Thornton Stringfellow in 1841, "it will, for the same reason, level all inequalities in human condition." Relying on "strict construction" in biblical as well as constitutional interpretation, he and other southern ministers claimed to follow the literal word of God while northerners worshiped fallible human reason and the vain pursuit of heaven on earth.

Rupture finally came in 1845, when the Methodist and Baptist denominations both split over northern efforts to brand slaveholding as an unacceptable sin for ministers. Presbyterians had already split into

Old School and New School segments in 1837 over other theological issues. Most southern Presbyterians had sided with the Old School because of its more conservative position on all issues relating to human reform, including abolition of slavery.

Differences over secular reforms paralleled disputes over theology. Throughout the antebellum period, southern churches strictly punished members for sins like drunkenness, profanity, Sabbath-breaking, and sexual immorality, but hesitated to endorse projects of wider social improvement. Some southerners eventually accepted the temperance crusade, but no antebellum southern state passed a "Maine Law" to ban alcohol entirely. Southern legislatures were slower than northern ones to build common schools, mental hospitals, asylums for the deaf and blind, and reformed penitentiaries, though all these measures met some success in the 1850s. Reforms that seemed to challenge the principles of social hierarchy, especially abolitionism, women's rights, and utopian communities, were either illegal or highly unpopular in the southern states.

EQUALITY AND INEQUALITY

White southerners faced an awkward contradiction between republican ideals of equality and the unequal realities of slave society. A few simply rejected white equality. Others claimed that slavery gave white men more equality than free society did. All agreed that slave society was vastly superior to its northern rival.

Some states retained property requirements on the rights to vote and hold office for some years after independence, but in both sections, most states abandoned them in the early nineteenth century and only used race and sex to separate political equals from inferiors. Georgia dropped its property requirement for the suffrage in 1789, followed by Maryland in 1801, and South Carolina in 1810. The newer states of the trans-Appalachian South dispensed with such restrictions from the beginning.

On the whole, antebellum voters in both sections participated much more actively in elections than modern citizens, and ballot restrictions had less impact on participation rates than overall interest in a given election. Only 26.5 percent of adult white males cast ballots in the muddled presidential canvass of 1824, and southern rates ranged from 11.5 percent in Virginia to 53.7 percent in Maryland. In the hotly contested campaign of 1840, hosts of professional and volunteer organizers drummed up every possible vote, and the national participation rate hit 78 percent of adult white men. Southern rates were similar, ranging from 39.4 percent in Louisiana to 89.6 percent in Tennessee. Stiff property requirements always limited participation in Virginia, but participation still hit 54.6 percent in 1840.

Legislative representation had close links to voting rights. The earliest state constitutions gave extra legislative seats to plantation counties, just as the three-fifths compromise gave the South more representatives in Congress. In Virginia, for example, each county elected two representatives to the House of Delegates, so the 620 whites of the Tidewater's Warwick County had as much clout as the 17,000 whites of Shenandoah County in the west. When representation was so unequal, nonslaveholding communities had minimal legislative power no matter who voted.

Planters opposed legislative reapportionment far more than white male suffrage. The noisiest and most dramatic campaign took place in the Virginia constitutional convention of 1829-1830. The existing state constitution denied the ballot to as many as half of the Old Dominion's white men and gave most legislative seats to the Tidewater. Backcountry representatives fought hard in the convention, battling Tidewater conservatives for political equality.

Eastern delegate Benjamin Watkins Leigh boldly avowed that slavery required white inequality, for with equal voting rights, westerners would impose ruinous taxes on eastern slaveholders to pay for extravagant internal improvements. Going further, Leigh compared eastern slaves to those he scornfully called "the peasantry of the west." "In every civilized country under the sun," he declared, "some there must be who labour for their daily bread." Whether they were slaves, peasants, or Virginia mountaineers, civilization would not survive if these underlings gained equality. Unfazed by this radical rejection of its Jeffersonian heritage, the Virginia convention tinkered modestly with suffrage and representation requirements but the most glaring inequalities remained until 1850.

In 1831, a year and a half after the convention adjourned, Nat Turner's slave revolt reawakened Virginians to slavery's dangers and reopened their debate over liberty, equality, and the future of slavery. Thomas Jefferson Randolph, grandson and namesake of the sage of Monticello, proposed to make all slaves born after July 4, 1840, state property and to hire them out to defray the costs of resettling them outside the United States. Packed with spectators, the House of Delegates seriously debated the proposal for two weeks in January 1832. Mindful that the recent convention had preserved white inequality for the sake of slavery, western representatives assailed the system's backwardness and injustice, but conservatives fended them off. Finally the House decided that Randolph's plan would be "inexpedient." Professor Thomas R. Dew of the College of William and Mary followed the vote with a pamphlet demonstrating the utter impracticality of any proposal to colonize Virginia's slaves abroad. This outcome ended all public discussion of a peaceful and voluntary end to slavery in the nation's largest slave state.

Whatever they thought in private, most defenders of slavery maintained publicly that slavery made whites more equal, not less. Judge Abel Upshur argued that slavery granted the poor white man something more precious than the right to vote. "However poor, or ignorant, or miserable he may be," the judge offered, "he has yet the consoling consciousness that there is still a lower condition to which he can never be reduced." Going further, politicians often claimed that whites' equal superiority over blacks obliterated class distinctions in white society. "Let us keep the white race as they are here now and ever ought to be," cried an Alabama congressman, "free, equal, and independent, socially and politically, recogniz[ing] no subordinate but those whom God made to be such—the children of Ham [i.e., Africans]."

Despite such boasts, white men were not really equal in the Old South. Economic inequality was greater in the South than the North because slavery enabled masters to gain a disproportionate share of wealth, land, and political power. Great planters deployed refinements in education, dress, manners, religion, artistic taste, and genealogy (both real and imaginary) to distinguish themselves from the multitude. Class lines were less stable in the Southwest than the Southeast, for huge cotton crops could outweigh traditional symbols of taste and family. Even there, however, the backslapping politician who invited everyone in the district to an annual barbecue never admitted the poorest voters to his parlor. These devices enabled wealthy southerners to maintain an uneasy balance between the potentially conflicting principles of white democracy and social inequality.

LIBERTY, HONOR, AND VIOLENCE

The presence of slaves constantly reminded white men of what the loss of liberty entailed, and encouraged them to cherish their own public and private liberty. Slave society also linked liberty to the power of command, for true freemen gave orders while chattels followed them. Freemen also demanded equal respect from each other, and those who settled for less joined the powerless and unfree. Southern politicians frequently won elections by campaigning against real or imagined threats to public liberty. As discussed in detail in chapter 11, President Andrew Jackson denounced the Bank of the United States for attacking liberty, and Jackson had scores of state and local imitators.

The linkage of liberty to personal authority, plus the violence of slavery itself, invited southerners to glorify male power, masculine pastimes, and "manly" virtues. Noticeably more than other Americans, southern men delighted in hunting, fishing, gambling, horseracing, and cockfighting. The temperance movement came late to the South and had less impact there. Southern evangelicals struggled to win male converts, who resented the humility and contrition that sincere conversion required. Southerners flocked to the nation's military academies, stressed military education in their own colleges and boarding schools, and dominated the army's and navy's officer corps.

Above all, southern society tolerated a high level of personal violence. If insulted or challenged, white men were expected to fight for their "honor," or their public reputations for courage, strength, honesty, and the willingness to protect their dependents, especially women. "Their code of honour is so exceedingly strict that it requires the greatest circumspection to escape its violation," reported a Scottish visitor to Virginia. "An offence which elsewhere would be regarded as of homeopathic [minor] proportions, is very apt to assume in Richmond the gravity of colossal dimensions." Honor was intimately tied to social rank, for slaves could have no honor, and freemen who submitted to insults were humiliated and demeaned. Common whites defended their reputations with rough-and-tumble bouts of eye-gouging or nose-biting. A gentleman offended by a social inferior revenged himself with a cane or a horsewhip, but settled differences with other gentlemen by the meticulous ritual of the dueling ground. Laws forbade the practice, but dueling became a virtual rite of passage for young men who knew that facing an enemy's bullet demonstrated manhood and bravery, while submitting to an insult could bring humiliation and ostracism. The culture of honor encouraged the belief that flexibility and compromise were demeaning, an attitude that southerners carried with them into politics.

THE POLITICAL DEFENSE OF SLAVERY

In the era of the Revolution and the early republic, white southerners rarely mounted a thorough defense of slavery and often called it a necessary evil. Virginians like Jefferson admitted that slavery was un-just but blamed New Englanders or the British for introducing it and claimed that blacks had become too numerous and dangerous to lib-erate. Perhaps if slaves were allowed to spread out, or "diffuse," across a broad expanse of western territory, Virginians sometimes suggested, whites would eventually outnumber them so completely that emanci-pation would become safe. Until then, abolition without compensat-ing the masters and deporting the freed people was out of the ques-tion, and any public discussion of it might incite a revolt.

South Carolinians and Georgians had never been as ambivalent about slavery as the Virginians, and vigorously defended it in the Con-stitutional Convention and the Congress. After the Missouri crisis of 1819–1820 (see chapter 11) and especially after the rise of radical abo-litionism, most southern spokesmen discarded the tone of apology and launched a passionate defense of their Peculiar Institution. Some southern intellectuals eventually favored slavery so strongly that they abandoned the basic principles of republican equality, even for white men.

A pivotal moment came in 1837, when South Carolina's eminent senator John C. Calhoun called on his colleagues to ignore all anti-slavery petitions. "I do not belong to that school," he proclaimed, in language taken directly from the pugnacious culture of dueling, "which holds that aggression is to be met with concession. . . . Those who act on [that] principle are prepared to become slaves." Reject-ing the slightest compromise, he repeated Benjamin Watkins Leigh's view that "there never has existed a wealthy and civilized society in which one portion of the community did not . . . live upon the labor of the other." In Calhoun's view, American slavery was simply a vari-ant on this universal principle, so allegedly free laborers in Europe and the North were slaves in fact if not in name. Slavery was a kinder form of exploitation than freedom, he believed, because masters cared for slaves in sickness and old age, while "free" laborers faced starva-tion when they could not work. Unlike free workers, moreover, slaves could never go on strike or agitate for rights they did not deserve. As a result, Calhoun famously concluded, slavery was no necessary evil but "a good—a positive good."

Southern spokesmen continued to repeat and expand on Calhoun's "positive good" theory in ensuing decades. Senator James Henry Ham-mond, also of South Carolina, sharpened the argument with a particu-larly grating expression when he declared that "Cotton is King." "In all social systems there must be a class to do the menial duties, to perform the drudgery of life. That is, a class requiring but a low order of intellect and but little skill," he explained in 1858. "It constitutes the very mud-sill of society and political government; and you might as well attempt to build a house in the air . . . except on this mud-sill." Black slaves played the role of "mud-sill," or structural foundation, in the South, but white wage earners did the same in the North. The southern system was superior, he claimed, because blacks were fitted by nature for servitude, and their enslavement allowed poor whites to enjoy the liberty and equality they deserved.

Virginia planter George Fitzhugh took the proslavery argument to its furthest extreme. In several pamphlets and two major books, *Sociology for the South, or the Failure of Free Society* (1854) and *Cannibals All! Or, Slaves without Masters* (1857), Fitzhugh moved beyond race to defend slavery "in the abstract," boldly declaring that enslavement would benefit all inferior people, white as well as black. Deploring the suffering of free but poverty-stricken wage laborers and denouncing the competitive economy that left them starving, Fitzhugh condemned free society as merely giving "license to the strong to oppress the weak." In his view, the strong should *own* the weak, for masters would care for human property of any race, love them as a father loves his family, protect them in sickness and old age, and require no more labor than was good for them. He therefore challenged the advocates of slavery to stop defending bondage for one race only and to forthrightly call for enslaving all workers, including whites. As he put it, radically reversing Jeffersonian equality, "'Some [people] were born with saddles on their backs, and others booted and spurred to ride them'—and the riding does them good."

Fitzhugh remained a marginal figure, for the enslavement of white people was just what successful politicians promised to prevent, but his ideas showed how far some defenders of slavery were willing to go in rejecting the republican principles of the American Revolution. In effect, Fitzhugh's argument overturned the cliché that black slavery created white liberty and suggested the opposite: black slavery *threatened* white liberty, for it showed why *all* inferiors should be enslaved, white as well as black.

By 1860, Fitzhugh, Hammond, Calhoun, Leigh, and their countless imitators had constructed a proslavery version of republicanism at odds with the North's free labor version. Both made the liberty of the individual white man indispensable for the common good, but the southern version based liberty on racial superiority and the power of command, not on the dignifying and empowering role of work. Pro-slavery republicanism infuriated northern voters, for just when figures like Abraham Lincoln were glorifying free labor as the stepping-stone to real equality and personal improvement, southerners like Hammond mocked white workingmen as no better than slaves. Hearing his gibes, thousands of northerners became increasingly convinced that slave owners not only oppressed blacks but despised their own aspirations as well.

A handful of white southerners criticized slavery in defiance of public opinion. Kentucky slaveholder James G. Birney freed his slaves, joined the American Anti-Slavery Society, and published an anti-slavery newspaper in Cincinnati. After breaking with William Lloyd Garrison over women's rights, he served as presidential candidate for the Liberty Party in 1840. Birney made an ethical case against slavery, but southern critics more commonly avoided moralizing and blamed bondage for depressing the South's economy and stifling opportunities for poor whites.

North Carolinian Hinton Rowan Helper made this case most powerfully in his 1857 book *The Impending Crisis of the South: How to Meet It*. Coming from a yeoman piedmont family, Helper used elaborate statistical comparisons to prove that slavery grossly damaged the southern economy, but he directed his fiercest rhetoric against the political power of slaveholders. "Too long have we yielded a submissive obedience to the tyrannical domination of an inflated oligarchy," he railed, "too long have we tolerated their arrogance and self-conceit; too long have we submitted to their unjust and savage exactions. Let us now wrest from them the sceptre of power, establish liberty and equal rights throughout the land, and henceforth and forever guard our legislative halls from the pollutions and usurpations of proslavery demagogues." Northerners who feared the expansion of slavery welcomed his words, but southerners responded with death threats, book burnings, and imprisonment of those who distributed his work. Especially after anti-slavery slavery politicians endorsed *The Impending Crisis*, Helper could no longer live in the South, and critics cited his treatment to prove that slave society could not tolerate freedom of speech. Adding references to Hammond and Fitzhugh and contemporary events, they made the broader case that slavery did more than mistreat blacks, for it inevitably undermined white rights too. This idea became the most powerful antislavery argument in the politics of the 1850s.

*

The antebellum South was geographically and economically diverse, but its most important crop was short-staple cotton, heavily demanded by the booming textile industries of Europe and the North. Cotton culture expanded dramatically after 1815, created a market for the underused slaves of the Upper South, and ended hopes that slavery might die quietly. Instead, slavery grew stronger, inhibited the growth of southern cities and industry, and heightened differences with the North.

Slavery imposed bitter toil and heartbreak, which African Americans continually resisted. It also encouraged a distinctive culture among whites, where status was associated with slave ownership and the power of command, where reform and women's rights were limited, and where the demands of honor made compromise seem disgraceful. As criticism of slavery grew, white southerners mounted a defense that emphasized racism, literal readings of scripture, disdain for free labor, and occasional support for white inequality. While the slave and free states still had much in common, their diverging commitments to slavery and free labor inspired sharply opposing views on the meaning of republican liberty and the best ways to preserve it.

FIGURE 8. Supporters of President Andrew Jackson praised his "Bank War" as the embodiment of democracy, but opponents denounced him as authoritarian and destructive. American Cartoon Print Filing Series, Prints and Photographs Division, Library of Congress, LC-USZ62-809.

CHAPTER 11

The Transformation of Politics, 1815–1836

In the summer of 1834, a bitter and noisy election contest split the sleepy little river port of Fayetteville, North Carolina. The town's businessmen longed for a railroad to bring them more customers, and their state representative had fought hard for a legislative subsidy. Success seemed guaranteed if the town remained united, so a sudden challenge to the incumbent legislator dumbfounded them. Two months before the balloting, a local newspaper announced that "the town election is to rest on Political grounds," and "a Jackson man" would defy the little town's establishment.

General Andrew Jackson had been president for six stormy years when Fayetteville's "Political" conflict broke out. Firmly rejecting the policies of his predecessor, John Quincy Adams, Jackson had systematically cut federal aid for the Market Revolution, including support for internal improvements and the Bank of the United States, and his policies had stirred raucous approval and furious opposition. There was no official connection between Jackson's policies and the Fayetteville town election, but participants saw them as interdependent, with national issues reappearing at the village level. Village politicians thus set to work and organized rival campaigns linking Jackson's opposition to the Bank with opposition to Fayetteville's railroad subsidy. This was no transient squabble, moreover, for debate over economic change would dominate public discourse for decades. In Fayetteville and across the country, disputes between Democratic-Republicans (increasingly called "Democrats"), who supported President Jackson, and their opponents in "the Bank or Whig party" would dominate public life for the next two decades.

Fayetteville's contest raged all summer and the local papers rang with charges and countercharges. Some saw an older conflict re-

appearing, like the Jacksonian who declared that "those who are opposed to the United States bank are as they have always been, republicans; those in its favor are as they have always been, *federalists*," while
Whigs denounced the president's policies as "violation[s] of Law . . .
[with] a direct tendency to subvert the Constitution." Reaching out
to voters who might ignore printed appeals, both parties held excited
nightly meetings in every neighborhood, climaxed by a rollicking
Whig ball on election eve.

"Never had the old borough witnessed such excitement as on the
day of the election," one participant recalled almost 60 years later.
"Party distinctions were *strongly drawn*," reported another, "and but
few, if any men who voted at the election, left any doubt as to how
they voted." Democrats wore pink ribbons and the Whigs sported blue
ones. Marching bands led voters to party headquarters, where "liquor,
from pure French [brandy] to mean whiskey, flowed freely." A railing
separated rival camps at the polling place, but fights still exploded in
the rising din, and a bloody duel almost resulted when a leading Whig
answered a Jacksonian orator with a call for "three groans." When a
general brawl erupted, one eager participant tried to join the fray by
leaping from a balcony but landed on the ballot box instead, smashing the fragile symbol of republicanism as badly as Fayetteville's lost
tranquility.

The Whigs claimed a narrow victory when order returned, but the
shattered ballot box remained an apt symbol for the fractured community. Fayetteville's future elections would not be quite so tumultuous, but Whigs and Democrats continued to dominate both local
and national politics. The two sides kept using the same devices to stir
up enthusiasm, moreover, from the speeches, newspapers, party ribbons, brass bands, and incessant rallies, to the liquor, the groans, and
even the fights. In Fayetteville, the party rivalry was so intense that the
two parties cancelled each other's influence, and the little town never
got its railroad subsidy.

Historians call the political rivalry that disrupted antebellum Fayetteville and the rest of the United States the Second American Party
System to distinguish it from the contest between Thomas Jefferson's
Democratic-Republicans and Alexander Hamilton's Federalists. It fit-
tingly appeared in Fayetteville in a dispute over public support for
a bank and a railroad, both vital engines of the Market Revolution.
Throughout the United States, similar developments pushed against
older principles of republicanism and generated conflicts that needed

a public response. Most Whigs believed that the government should provide material support for economic development. Democrats worried that federal aid would enrich a privileged few at public expense and attack the liberty and equality that republicanism required. Today we recognize that "Jacksonian democracy" excluded American women, blacks, and Indians, but most contemporary leaders focused on the liberty of white men. The excluded would inherit their rhetoric and fight similar battles in later years.

The Framers had detested parties, or "factions," but the Electoral College made them almost inescapable. The need to win a majority pressured politicians to form two broad coalitions, each potentially large enough to succeed, and the need to unify these coalitions pushed supporters to sacrifice personal convictions for partisan success. The imperative of party unity distressed Americans who thought republican virtue depended on personal independence, especially Federalists and many Whigs, but most accepted it in the Second Party System. Thoughtful politicians knew that party divisions were inevitable but hoped to avoid a split over slavery, since that dispute could wreck the Union. They looked instead for political divisions that would focus popular energies without destroying the republic. They found what they wanted as citizens responded to the economic challenges of the Market Revolution and the moral imperatives of the Second Great Awakening with the intellectual and political tools of Revolutionary republicanism. When those controversies subsided, the slavery question erupted again and split the nation more deeply than anyone ever intended.

An Era of Good Feelings?

The roots of the Second Party System lay in the aftermath of the War of 1812. Disgraced by its opposition to the war, the Federalist Party ran its last presidential candidate in 1816. Thereafter, virtually all politicians called themselves Republicans, and the United States entered a period of one-party politics known as the Era of Good Feelings, despite its very serious personal and policy disputes. Unthreatened by Federalism, Republicans began to test Jeffersonian orthodoxy in ways that brought sharp controversies and opened the way for a strong counterreaction.

NEW LEADERS, NEW CHALLENGES

As they celebrated the coming of peace in 1815, farsighted American leaders worried about problems the war had exposed, and pushed for government aid to economic development (see chapter 8). Congress faced these demands with new leadership. Antiwar sentiment and threatened secession made the Federalist Party seem hopelessly unpatriotic. Innovative Federalists like Daniel Webster held on in New England, but the party collapsed in other regions. Rufus King of New York won 34 electoral votes as the Federalist candidate for president in 1816, but his Republican opponent, James Monroe of Virginia, swamped him with 183, and the Federalists never proposed another candidate.

As Federalism faded, Congress and the Cabinet filled up with younger Republicans, many from the South and West. Men such as Henry Clay of Kentucky, John C. Calhoun of South Carolina, and John Quincy Adams of Massachusetts had been too young to serve in the Revolution, or even to participate in the ratification of the Constitution. Many of them had been War Hawks in 1812 and ardently longed for economic and territorial expansion. Unlike some of their Federalist predecessors, these younger Jeffersonians embraced universal white male suffrage, though some still counted on local elites to deliver their votes and believed that wise leaders could overrule public opinion. Some were highly educated, like Adams and Calhoun; others were mostly self-taught, like Henry Clay. Whatever their origins, the most prominent postwar Republicans felt a need for economic development and did not cling to older party dogmas like small government and strict construction.

When the Fourteenth Congress assembled in the fall of 1815, President Madison proposed three departures from Republican orthodoxy. Though he had strongly opposed the First Bank of the United States, he now asked Congress for a new national bank to repair the government's finances. To protect the struggling industries fostered by war, he asked for a mild protective tariff to make foreign imports more expensive than American manufactures. Finally, he asked Congress for a constitutional means to build a national system of internal improvements. Wartime problems had proved the need for such Federalist-style measures, and the death of Federalism itself had removed them from partisan contention.

Congress responded favorably. In 1816, it chartered a new and larger Bank of the United States for a term of 20 years. The government would supply one-fifth of its $35 million in capital, select 5 of the 25 directors, and grant it a monopoly of its banking business. In return for these privileges, the Bank would pay the government a bonus of $1.5 million and issue paper notes for a uniform national currency. The protective tariff won approval a few weeks later but internal improvements proved harder to achieve. The Constitution gave Congress power to "*establish* post Roads" (italics added) but did not mention *building* them, so strict constructionists would not act without a constitutional amendment to authorize federal spending on transportation. The friends of internal improvements resisted that step, fearing that the amendment process was too risky and too cumbersome. Instead, Representative John C. Calhoun proposed to devote nontax funds—the dividends and bonus from the Bank—to an internal improvements fund, but his reasoning did not satisfy President Monroe (who succeeded James Madison in 1817), so he vetoed the Bonus Bill as unconstitutional.

Monroe's veto did not satisfy traditional Jeffersonians, who called themselves Old Republicans and clung to earlier party doctrines. "Who could have supposed when Mr. Jefferson went out of office," mourned North Carolina senator Nathaniel Macon in 1818, "that his principles . . . would so soon have become unfashionable?" Led by Representative John Randolph of Roanoke, a brilliant though eccentric Virginian, the Old Republicans railed that power might corrupt anybody and frankly worried that broad construction would lead to meddling with slavery. As Macon put it, "If Congress can make banks, roads and canals under the constitution; they can free any slave in the United States." In the heady days after 1816, few heeded the Old Republicans, so a new generation eagerly looked forward to the energetic use of government.

To crown its handiwork, the Fourteenth Congress gave itself a raise. "To attract and secure ability and integrity to the public service," Calhoun explained, congressmen deserved a salary of $1,500 a year instead of an allowance of $6.00 per day, even though laborers earned only $0.50 for 12–14 hours of toil and $2.00 would buy an acre of public land. The pay raise was a symbol of lingering elitism among the post-1815 crop of Republican leaders. Much to their astonishment, the action infuriated ordinary Americans who thought that ability and integrity should not be so costly among a virtuous people. Reeling from grievous crop failures inflicted by the brutally cold summer of 1816 ("eighteen-hundred-and-froze-to-death"), angry voters expelled two-thirds of their extravagant representatives in the fall elections. It was a display of democratic rebellion that national political leaders were completely unused to, but would witness again in the future.

FLORIDA AND THE FIRST SEMINOLE WAR

Elected in 1816, President James Monroe was a Virginia neighbor of Jefferson and Madison. He was the last president to wear the powdered wig and knee breeches of an eighteenth-century gentleman and nearly the last Revolutionary in high office. To conciliate Federalists who still resented the recent war, Monroe toured New England shortly after his inauguration and attracted widespread popular applause. A Boston paper rejoiced that Federalists and Republicans who had not spoken for years were coming together to welcome the president, and proclaimed an "Era of Good Feelings." This label for Monroe's administration survived, but events proved that tensions still boiled beneath the surface.

Indian warfare and geographical expansion provided an early example. After defeating the Red Sticks in 1814, General Andrew Jackson had forced the Creek Indians to surrender vast territories along Georgia's border with Spanish Florida and north into Alabama and Mississippi. He had also won sizable cessions from the Choctaws, Chickasaws, and Cherokees, until the southwestern tribes had lost as many as 50 million acres by 1820. Several bands of displaced Creeks then sought refuge with their Seminole relatives in Spanish Florida and continued attacks on American settlers. Even more ominously from the American perspective, a former British outpost near the Gulf coast had become the "Negro Fort," sheltering hundreds of runaway slaves. Spain seemed powerless to stop either group.

An American expedition destroyed the Negro Fort in the fall of 1816, killing most of the occupants and reenslaving the rest, but clashes with the Seminoles continued to escalate. The First Seminole War formally began in early 1818, when Monroe ordered Jackson to enter Florida and subdue the Indians without disturbing the Spanish. The headstrong general not only laid waste to the Seminoles' towns, but went on to exceed his orders by seizing most of the Florida panhandle, occupying its Spanish settlements, and executing two British subjects whom he accused of arming and inciting the Indians. These actions naturally outraged the Spanish and British governments and provoked a storm of criticism in Congress and the Cabinet. Jackson narrowly escaped an official rebuke by claiming secret authorization from the president, but he thrilled expansionists and proved that Spain had lost its hold on Florida. President Monroe and Secretary of State John Quincy Adams may have disapproved of Jackson's methods, but they welcomed the result and used it to pressure Spain for its thinly settled colony. In 1819, Secretary of State John Quincy Adams and Spanish minister Luis de Onís signed the Adams-Onís Treaty, granting Florida to the United States and settling the border between the Louisiana Purchase and New Spain. In return, the United States agreed to cover up to $5 million of Spain's debts to American citizens. Still defiant, the Seminoles fled deeper into Florida's wilderness to fight twice more in the Second Seminole War of 1835–1842 and the Third Seminole War of 1855–1858.

PANIC AND ITS REMEDIES

The United States acquired Florida in a period of postwar economic boom. Europe's demand for American foodstuffs, cotton, and wool briefly stayed high, sustaining prosperity for New England farmers and southern planters alike. Settlers were especially hungry for the new cotton lands that Jackson had wrested from the Indians. The government encouraged speculation by extending credit to land buyers, and banks offered generous loans to expansive merchants. Prosperity seemed endless and Americans who embraced the market economy reveled in their good fortune.

The bubble inevitably collapsed as a European recession and recovery by its farms cut demand for American products. The tipping point came in late 1818, when the Bank of the United States sought specie from its debtor banks to make the final payment for Louisiana. To comply, the state banks denied new loans and pressed their borrowers for repayment, but the combination of weaker demand and tighter credit drove down prices for cotton, lands, and slaves, and sent thousands of planters and speculators into bankruptcy. Customers rushed to trade banknotes for coins, but the banks suspended specie payments again. The Panic of 1819 had frozen the commercial economy.

The panic hit unevenly. It hardly touched yeomen who grew their own food and owed no money. Wage earners suffered unemployment until wages and prices reached a new equilibrium. Land buyers who had gambled on continuously rising prices faced destruction, and distress was probably greatest on the cotton frontier. Suffering from early years of poor management, the Bank of the United States struggled to maintain its own solvency and pushed its debtors relentlessly. Throughout the South and West, defaulting borrowers watched helplessly as farms and property vanished under the auctioneer's hammer. "The Bank was saved but the people were ruined," one commentator noted bitterly, and the Bank won many enemies.

The panic renewed debate over government support for economic development. Old Republicans repeated their criticisms of banking, commerce, speculations, and industry. Congressman Philip P. Barbour of Virginia praised old-fashioned citizens—property owners, not wage earners—"who do not receive their daily bread from the hand of another, but from their own voluntary labor upon their own soil; who have some stake in the Government, who feel and take an interest in public affairs, and are ready and willing to defend themselves as men and citizens in their rights of property, and civil and political liberty." He and other Old Republicans wanted to fight the panic by reviving strict construction, withholding aid from manufactures and commerce, and returning to a simple and virtuous landholding economy. Only slaves, he suggested, should work for others or follow orders.

More-optimistic Republicans disagreed and called for more economic change instead of less. As the depression began lifting in 1824, President Monroe endorsed this approach by favoring a higher tariff. Henry Clay of Kentucky, Speaker of the House of Representatives, became the measure's greatest advocate and proposed an even broader plan for national development. Clay called his program for government guidance of economic change the "American System" in contrast to what he called the "British System" of "laissez-faire," a French expression meaning no government control of the economy. The American System became the leading theme of Clay's long career in American public life.

Replying to Barbour, Clay rejected crude self-sufficiency and proclaimed instead that "the greatest want of civilized society is a market for the ... produce of the labor of its members." To create this market, the American System would raise tariffs to stimulate industry, support the Bank of the United States as a source of credit and currency, and sell public lands at high prices to pay for a national transportation network. With flourishing manufactures, credit, and transportation, farmers could sell more crops to cities, and city businesses could sell farmers more goods, so the whole country would benefit, even southern planters. Clay countered Barbour's critique of hired workers by insisting that "idleness and vice" posed "the greatest danger to public liberty," not wage earners. Congress accepted these arguments in 1824 and raised the tariff to an average of 37 percent on most imports, but the debate over economic development was far from over.

Conflict Returns

Party conflict ebbed in the so-called Era of Good Feelings, but policy disputes continued. The Bank, the tariff, internal improvements, and the congressional salary increase proved more unpopular than ambitious young Republicans had imagined, and angry voters punished them in 1816. The panic brought widespread distress just as a bitter dispute over slavery revealed sectional animosity. The presidential election of 1824 seemed to show that greed for office and neglect of founding principles had replaced republican virtue with corruption. At the end of the 1820s, most voters would heed these apparent omens and embrace a leader who claimed that unfettered popular democracy—like the vote against Congress's pay raise—could restore the republic's purity.

MISSOURI COMPROMISE AND MONROE DOCTRINE

Western settlement had passed the Mississippi after 1815, leading the territory of Missouri to seek statehood in 1819. When the House considered approval, Representative James Tallmadge Jr. of New York startled his colleagues with amendments to prohibit the further importation of slaves into Missouri and to free the unborn children of those who lived there already.

Talmadge's proposals drew ready support from northern congressmen, for their states had ended slavery with similar laws. While they did not want racial equality or claim any power over slavery in existing states, they believed that southerners had implicitly promised to follow their example. So far, the three-fifths clause had helped southerners elect every president but one, so northerners also longed to reduce that advantage. A few northern congressmen went further and attacked slavery on moral grounds. Senator Rufus King of New York, the last Federalist candidate for president, claimed that slavery defied the laws of God so no human law could justify it. Arthur Livermore of

New Hampshire called slavery "a sin which sits heavy on the souls of every one of us."

Southerners furiously rejected these sentiments. No matter how they felt about slavery—and some still claimed to deplore it—they denied that the national government had any power to end it in Missouri or anywhere else. The Constitution made new states equal to the old, they argued, so Missouri had the same right to slavery as Georgia, and northerners only raised the issue to gain power. Besides, they claimed, slavery would be easier and safer to end if slaves were widely and thinly dispersed, so extending it westward would hasten its disappearance. Meanwhile, agitating the question could inspire a slave revolt. Other southerners defended bondage in more positive terms. Slavery was a benevolent institution that benefited both races, they insisted. It was economically necessary, not only in the existing slave states, but also in the West. The Bible authorized it, and the Declaration of Independence did not apply to blacks. The antislavery argument, cried Senator John W. Walker of Alabama, "unhinges the Union at a dash."

Though most whites probably worried more about the Panic of 1819 than slavery in Missouri, the issue overwhelmed Congress in 1819 and 1820. The House adopted the Tallmadge amendments but the Senate refused, and all other business ground to a halt. Congressmen shocked one another with explosions of passion and freely discussed the possibility of disunion. "If you persist," Georgia Congressman Thomas W. Cobb grimly warned the restrictionists, "the Union will be dissolved. You have kindled a fire which all the waters of the ocean cannot put out, which seas of blood can only extinguish." James Tallmadge retorted, "If civil war must come, I can only say, let it come!"

Hoping to settle the crisis, Henry Clay supported the Missouri Compromise in 1820: Missouri would be admitted to the Union with slavery, but slavery would be barred from the Louisiana Purchase north of 36°30′, Missouri's southern boundary. Detached from Massachusetts, Maine would also gain statehood, and thus the equal number of slave and free states in the Senate would be maintained. Thinking they had won a victory by protecting slavery in Missouri, 39 southern congressmen agreed to give up slavery in the rest of the Louisiana Purchase, but went down to defeat in the next election. Of the northern congressmen, 18 broke sectional ranks as well and voted to permit slavery in Missouri. Instead of thanking them for this support, Virginia representative John Randolph of Roanoke mocked the mavericks as cowardly "doughfaces," and the name stuck for decades to describe "northern men with southern principles." On both sides, congressmen who made concessions to the other side faced bitter criticism at home in a telling sign of slavery's divisiveness.

The Missouri crisis was the first major sectional controversy since the secret slavery debates in the Constitutional Convention, and it shocked Americans who thought that real political controversy pitted Republicans against Federalists, not Republicans against each other. "This momentous question, like a fire bell in the night, awakened and filled me with terror," the aging Jefferson admitted. "I considered it at once as the knell of the Union." Once a moral principle divided the Union into rival sections, he feared, rancor would increase until his life's work collapsed. Less philosophical politicians tried to put the issue behind them. Southerners decided that the compromise protected them. Northerners continued to disapprove, but most concluded that fighting slavery would not be worth the cost. Both feared its powerful divisiveness.

President James Monroe offered little public leadership in the Missouri crisis, but left his name instead on a foreign policy that cast a long shadow on future American diplomacy. Independence movements had appeared in most of Spain's American colonies during the Napoleonic Wars, but Spain tried to reclaim its territories when French power collapsed in 1815. Britain and the United States opposed Spain's move because independence would open Latin America to their trade. Britain thus asked the United States for a joint declaration against Spain's return, but Monroe and Secretary of State John Quincy Adams refused to become lesser participants in a British initiative. Instead, the president used his annual message of 1823 to proclaim what became known as the Monroe Doctrine. While the United States would not interfere in European affairs, including its republican revolutions, it would oppose all efforts to establish new colonies or reestablish old ones in the Americas. On the surface, Monroe's declaration supported the independence of fellow republics, but it subtly implied that the United States should dominate Latin America itself. It thus became the rationale for future American interventions.

THE ELECTION OF 1824

Personal rivalries also ruffled the Era of Good Feelings. No one opposed Monroe's reelection in 1820, but a crowd of Washington insiders jostled to succeed him in 1824. Secretary of the Treasury William H.

Crawford of Georgia was the first choice of many southerners and Old Republicans, as well as Republican Party bosses like Senator Martin Van Buren of New York. The New England favorite was John Quincy Adams, secretary of state and son of former president John Adams. Congressman Henry Clay of Kentucky sought to represent the West. Secretary of War John C. Calhoun of South Carolina also aspired to the White House but ultimately accepted the vice presidency instead. In previous elections, Democratic-Republicans had used a caucus, or meeting, of all Republican congressmen to unite behind a single candidate, but this device had come to seem dictatorial by 1824. A small caucus eventually gave its nod to Crawford when other candidates' supporters refused to attend, but the prize did him little good in the end.

When the Tennessee legislature added the name of General Andrew Jackson to the list in 1822, no one but Jackson himself expected his candidacy to go very far. Standing apart from the other candidates, Jackson had grown up on the Carolina frontier without the social, educational, or economic advantages of the "better sort." He served as a boy in the American Revolution, lost his family in the war, and worked his way into the legal profession on his own. Moving to Nashville, Tennessee, the hot-tempered Jackson married well and gained a fortune from legal practice, planting, and land speculation, while fighting duels and trading slaves on his way to the top. He tried his hand at civilian politics but much preferred the office of major general of the Tennessee militia, which brought him victory at New Orleans and the status of national hero. Along the way, his soldiers nicknamed him "Old Hickory" since his wartime endurance matched the toughest timber in the forest. Quietly accepting adulation, Jackson began to think of himself as the one man who could clean up the antirepublican corruption embodied in the scramble to succeed Monroe. Previous presidents had always risen through polished family backgrounds and distinguished civilian service, however, so experienced politicians did not take the frontier general seriously.

Campaigning was dignified and discreet in 1824 because republican customs forbade expressions of ambition or self-promotion. The candidates corresponded instead with influential friends who pressured other leaders, wrote for newspapers, gave speeches, and held rallies. Some states still chose their electors in their legislatures, and Jackson might well have triumphed if every state had held a popular vote, but in the end Jackson astounded his rivals by outstripping them where popular elections did take place. He also won the plurality of electoral votes, mostly from the South and West, but not a majority, so the House of Representatives had to choose a victor from the top three finishers. Jackson, Adams, and Crawford thus faced the House, with Speaker Henry Clay seeming to hold the balance of power.

Clay and his supporters mostly voted for Adams, the second-place finisher, and made him president. Their choice reflected honest policy differences and perhaps the preferences of their states, but Jacksonians cried foul when Adams then made Clay his secretary of state, the usual stepping-stone to the presidency. Though rewarding allegiance with prized appointments became routine to later generations, republican sentiments condemned such behavior in 1825. Newspapers screamed "Bargain and sale!" and Henry Clay spent the rest of his life denying that he and Adams had struck a "corrupt bargain."

"THE SPIRIT OF IMPROVEMENT"

President Adams quickly made things worse for himself. Like Monroe, he wanted to rise above factions, and rejoiced upon taking office that "the baneful weed of party strife was uprooted," but he found that his refusal to play favorites left him friendless. Devoted to duty above popularity, the president used his first annual message (now known as the State of the Union address) to sketch an ambitious vision of national progress steered by a powerful federal government. He called for a national bankruptcy law, a uniform national militia, an expansion of the navy, more internal improvements, a national university, a federally funded program of scientific discovery, adoption of the metric system, and even an astronomical observatory. "The spirit of improvement is abroad upon the earth," the president proclaimed, and "liberty is power." Echoing covenant theology, he maintained that the United States could not preserve its liberty without using it constructively. If the voters resisted his grand visions, Adams told Congress to ignore them. "Were we to slumber in indolence or fold up our arms and proclaim to the world that we are palsied by the will of our constituents," he asked, "would it not be to cast away the bounties of Providence and doom ourselves to perpetual inferiority?" In effect, Adams asked Congress to embrace broad construction of the Constitution and use its own wisdom to uplift a misguided populace. For politicians who were learning to steer by public opinion, the president's views were starkly suicidal.

Congressmen and the newspapers pounded Adams for his allegedly unconstitutional and undemocratic proposals, and the president achieved little in his single term. When he asked Congress to approve sending representatives to a gathering of Latin American diplomats in Panama, southerners denounced any meeting with racially mixed delegations. Adams's efforts to negotiate a more favorable commercial treaty with Great Britain were likewise fruitless. Between his father's presidency and his own, the terms of American political culture had decisively shifted, for the government could no longer function without the trappings, at least, of popular democracy.

Jackson Takes Charge

Jacksonians began to shape a new vision of politics and government from the moment John Quincy Adams took office. Convinced that Adams and Clay had stolen the previous election, Jackson demanded vindication in 1828. His advisors responded with a new kind of election campaign, bypassing traditional elites and directly promising voters that Jackson represented "the will of the people" over the "corrupt bargain" made by Adams and Clay. Their efforts won Jackson a landslide in 1828, and the new president began remaking the office of president to reflect the new importance of party organization and popular appeal.

REVIVING THE DEMOCRATIC PARTY

Together with a circle of Tennessee friends, Senator Martin Van Buren of New York organized the general's 1828 campaign. A tavern keeper's son from the upstate village of Kinderhook, Van Buren embodied the republic's open opportunities and rose in politics by diligent service to New York's Democratic-Republican Party. There he learned the need for unity and discipline, since factionalism and personal quarrels would divide the party and allow the hated Federalists to triumph. His "Bucktail" faction (renamed the "Albany Regency" when he left for Washington) controlled New York with county, district, and state conventions to make party decisions and by using jobs and contracts to reward its friends and punish its enemies. Van Buren believed at heart that his Democratic-Republicans led the "many" in their eternal struggle against the "few," but he valued party loyalty above all else in most practical matters. The openness of post-Revolutionary society allowed him to create the role of American professional politician.

In 1824, party discipline led Van Buren to support the caucus candidate William H. Crawford, but 1828 was another matter. When John

Quincy Adams abandoned Republican partisanship, Van Buren quickly switched to Jackson and vowed to unite Republicans against Adams and Clay. He began by writing Thomas Ritchie, Virginia's most prominent editor, to insist that "we must always have party divisions and the old ones are best." Why? "If the old [parties] are suppressed," he candidly explained, "prejudices between free and slave holding states will inevitably take their place." To quiet what Jefferson had called "a fire bell in the night," Van Buren proposed the *"substantial reorganization of the old Republican Party,"* based as in Jefferson's day on an alliance "between the planters of the South and the plain Republicans of the north." Appealing to Virginia's Old Republicans by implying a revival of strict constructionism, Van Buren vowed to brand his opponents as Federalists, a role that fit John Quincy Adams perfectly.

Ritchie, Calhoun, and Crawford accepted Van Buren's logic and so did most of their followers. Pro-Jackson editorials blossomed everywhere, and a Nashville corresponding committee mailed reams of letters urging support and spreading campaign news while avoiding policy commitments. The Jacksonians stressed that Adams, Clay, and their friends had abandoned republican virtue to think only of themselves. Ordinary voters could recognize the common good and act on it far better than these "aristocrats," so the only way to cleanse the republic was to honor "the will of the people" and make Jackson president. In the words of the *U.S. Telegraph*, Jackson's chief Washington newspaper, Old Hickory's cause was "the great cause of the many against the few, of equal rights against privileged orders, of democracy against aristocracy."

Adams's supporters denounced Jackson as a gambler, a duelist, and a bloodthirsty tyrant who executed deserters without mercy. They even called Jackson and his wife, Rachel, adulterers and bigamists who married before her divorce became final. Democrats struck back with absurd charges that Adams was a degenerate aristocrat who put a billiard table in the White House for immoral gambling, and had pimped for the czar of Russia while growing up abroad. They likewise turned his European diplomatic experience against him, claiming "it was there that he learned the superiority of a monarchical over a democratic government . . . and [that] the people were not calculated to govern themselves."

These wild charges sprang from the sudden need to stretch over the heads of established leaders to reach the voters directly. The politics of mass appeals had overturned the courteous discourse of gentlemen and would not be abandoned, whatever the costs in logic or civility. When Rachel Jackson died soon after her husband's victory, the general blamed Henry Clay for the sexual smears that seemed to have broken her heart, and branded him "the basest, meanest scoundrel that ever disgraced the image of his god."

In the end, Jackson triumphed easily, with 56 percent of the popular vote and 176 out of 261 electoral votes. Once again, his support came from the South and West, joined by New York and Pennsylvania. Adams limped in with New England and the tariff-conscious states of Kentucky and Louisiana. Without committing himself to specific actions, the Old Hero had captured republican nostalgia. When he arrived in Washington, still in mourning for his wife, Massachusetts Senator Daniel Webster made an accurate prediction: "I think he will bring a breeze with him."

THE SPOILS SYSTEM

Andrew Jackson's inauguration became a legendary symbol of the people's rise to power. After a solemn ritual at the Capitol, crowds thronged to the White House reception. "*The Majesty of the People* had disappeared," shuddered one society matron, replaced by "a rabble, a mob, of boys, negros, women, children, scrambling, fighting, romping." Aides hustled the nearly smothered president back to his hotel, but destruction continued until waiters set tubs of punch on the lawn and the crowd followed. Official Washington looked on in horror and warned of worse to come.

Unfazed by this embarrassment, the new president immediately turned on his critics in Washington's tiny bureaucracy. Convinced that corrupt careerists had conspired against his election, he proclaimed that no one had a permanent right to office, and dispatched aides to uncover embezzlement, fraud, or incompetence. He quickly replaced suspected culprits with loyal Democrats, leading Adams men to charge that he practiced New York–style machine politics by substituting cronies and hacks for experienced civil servants. Jackson defended "rotation in office" as essential in a people's government, but a New York senator coined a more memorable phrase. "To the victor belong the spoils of the enemy," crowed William L. Marcy, and ever since, the "spoils system" has meant the use of government jobs to reward political operatives. Jackson did not invent the spoils system and he did not abuse it as badly as many of his successors, but he fought corruption with a practice that eventually increased it.

INDIAN REMOVAL

Jackson also moved quickly to change Indian policy. The federal government had long desired Indian lands, but also declared that peaceful Indians could keep their homelands as long as they wished and provided them with tools like plows and looms to permit survival without departure. Sharing his constituents' contempt for native culture and denying that so-called savages had any rights to land wanted by white people, Jackson had vowed to end this contradictory program. Soon after taking office, he moved to expel all Native Americans from east of the Mississippi to an "Indian territory" now in Oklahoma.

The new policy applied to all the eastern tribes but especially affected the "Five Civilized Tribes" of the Southeast: the Cherokees, Creeks, Choctaws, Chickasaws, and Seminoles. These nations had always been more populous and unified than those of the Northeast, and they still controlled some 50 million acres when Jackson took office. Their customs were also changing rapidly by the 1820s. Urged by missionaries and the federal government, Indian women were leaving agriculture to work indoors, while men abandoned hunting and replaced them in the fields. Along with white gender roles, many Indian families adopted white religion, clothing, and houses, and some leaders operated cotton plantations with black slaves and brick mansions. Such changes did not reduce their determination to keep their traditional territories and to hold them in common, however, but only strengthened their resistance to white demands.

Cultural adaptation had spread most among the 15,000 Cherokees, who lived on 10 million acres in northwest Georgia and nearby areas of North Carolina, Alabama, and Tennessee. Though whites frequently declared that the Indians were simply wandering hunters, one leader insisted in 1826 that "there is not to my knowledge a solitary Cherokee to be found that depends upon the chase for subsistence." By 1825, a Cherokee silversmith and blacksmith named Sequoyah had devised a system for writing the tribal language, and the *Cherokee Phoenix*, a newspaper printed in English and Cherokee, circulated widely. Led by Principal Chief John Ross, a prosperous and well-educated "mixed blood," Cherokees adopted a written constitution, with an elected government and a professional police force to keep order and repel intruders. A new tribal law imposed the death penalty on anyone who tried to sell tribal land.

White Georgians did not welcome these changes, for in 1802 they had surrendered their far western land claims on the condition that the federal government would soon give them title to all the remaining Indian land in the state. After years of fruitless waiting, Georgia decided to force the issue when prospectors found gold in Cherokee territory. Knowing Jackson would sympathize, Georgia passed laws to abolish the tribal government in 1830, to subject all Indians to its own laws, and to grant all tribal lands to white Georgians by a lottery. State law barred Indian testimony against whites, so a wave of white intruders assaulted Cherokees and freely seized their property. Jackson announced that he could not help because Georgia had unlimited power over its inhabitants; to keep their sovereignty and lands, the eastern tribes must make new homes in federal territory, beyond the Mississippi.

In 1830, Democrats introduced a bill in Congress authorizing the president to negotiate removal treaties, pay individuals for improvements such as houses and fields, assign new tribal territories, and transport the Indians westward. Inspired by missionaries to the Indians, northeastern congressmen resisted without success. Early in 1830, the Indian Removal Act passed the Senate easily but squeaked through the House, 102 votes to 97.

Cherokees fought back in court, with two important results. Chief Justice John Marshall dismissed the case of *Cherokee Nation v. Georgia* (1831) by deciding that a tribe could not sue a state, but he did recognize tribes' limited rights of self-government as "domestic dependent nations." When Georgia required licenses for all missionaries, two refused and appealed their convictions. In *Worcester v. Georgia* (1832), Marshall ruled for the missionaries, declaring that federal laws and treaties superseded the states in Indian affairs, so Georgia's effort to rule the Cherokees had been unconstitutional.

Georgia denied the court's jurisdiction, however, and observers agreed that the state would never obey the court's decision. To avoid a constitutional crisis which might destroy the principle of judicial review, intermediaries negotiated a settlement whereby Georgia's governor pardoned the missionaries and they left the state, leaving no case for the court to settle or for Georgia to defy. In later years, the story spread that Jackson had flouted the Supreme Court by remarking, "John Marshall has made his decision, now let him enforce it." Jackson did side with Georgia in these cases, but legally speaking, there was nothing for him to enforce.

Faced with these defeats, a few prominent Cherokees decided that continued resistance was useless. Falsely claiming to speak for the tribe, they agreed to removal in the 1835 Treaty of New Echota. Despite this fraud, the federal government enforced the treaty by rounding up the Cherokees in 1837 and sending them across the Mississippi on the "Trail of Tears." Nearly one-fourth of them died along the way. Upon their arrival in Indian Territory, unknown assailants carried out the penalty for selling tribal land by killing the leaders of the "treaty party." Jackson's successors continued his policy until most Indians had left the East and only scattered communities who submitted to state authority remained.

INTERNAL IMPROVEMENTS AND NULLIFICATION

Jackson had soft-pedaled economic questions while campaigning, but he privately believed that government support for economic change would tempt lawmakers and businessmen to trade favors corruptly. He acted on this view in 1830 by vetoing a bill to buy stock in Kentucky's Maysville Turnpike Company. In his eyes, the project was local rather than national, the Treasury was empty, and repaying the national debt was more important. Above all, he cited the same concern as Presidents Madison and Monroe: the Constitution did not mention federal aid to internal improvements, so it must be unconstitutional. Friends of internal improvement swore political revenge, but even Kentuckians accepted the Maysville veto and Jackson gained popularity as a friend of strict construction.

The protective tariff posed a more serious problem. Northern manufacturers wanted protection from European imports, and northern farmers did not object because prospering factories boosted their crop sales. Most planters hated the tariff, however, because they grew far more cotton than northerners could buy. Protection only raised their costs while cutting their revenues, they thought, since Europe bought less cotton when Americans shopped at home. When Congress raised rates in 1828, southerners condemned the measure as a "Tariff of Abominations," and they were not satisfied by modest reductions in the Tariff of 1832.

South Carolinians were especially angry. Planter grandees blamed the tariff for their weak recovery from the Panic of 1819, but worried even more over slavery. With a population that was mostly enslaved, more than 90 percent in some coastal parishes, the state's gentry were hypersensitive to economic burdens. Slavery could not last if the tariff consumed its profits, they reasoned, and how could whites survive if blacks ran free to seek vengeance? In South Carolina, the tariff was more than an economic or constitutional issue; it seemed to be a question of survival.

Andrew Jackson made no commitments on the tariff. Like the South Carolinians, he was a cotton planter who believed in states' rights, strict construction, and slavery, but thought both sides exaggerated the tariff's effects. He also still remembered supply problems in the War of 1812. Jackson also hated the national debt, wanted tariff revenue to pay it, and needed support from both sections. He had thus backed a "judicious" tariff in the campaign and left voters to decide what that meant.

As South Carolina's leading politician, Vice President John C. Calhoun held a difficult position. Personal disputes had soured his friendship with Jackson and ended his policy influence. He badly wanted to be president himself, but had no chance without solid backing from his own state. When reckless planters began threatening secession unless the tariff was ended, Calhoun sought an alternative that would save the Union and his own career. Turning away from the broad national vision that had marked his postwar years, he embraced strict construction, states' rights, and the Old Republican argument that a stronger federal government might interfere with slavery, and used these principles to attack the tariff. In the summer of 1828, Calhoun spelled out his new position in an anonymous "Exposition," which, along with a more concise "Protest," soon defined South Carolina's position in the gathering crisis.

The "Exposition and Protest" refined several ideas from earlier anti-tariff thinkers. Calhoun had to admit that the Constitution gave Congress clear authority to impose tariffs and other taxes, but insisted that the power only existed to raise revenue, not advance some economic interests over others. If protectionism did not break the *letter* of the Constitution, the "Exposition" claimed, it violated the Framers' *intentions*, which made it unconstitutional.

Knowing that Chief Justice Marshall would never accept this inference, Calhoun declared that the states did not need the courts to interpret the Constitution. Recalling the Virginia and Kentucky Resolutions of 1798 and 1799, the "Exposition" called the Constitution a "compact" that states could interpret for themselves. If a state considered some federal law unconstitutional, it could "nullify" it with a special convention and block enforcement within its boundaries. A national constitutional convention must then rule on the dispute, but the injured state could secede if it could not accept the outcome. Calhoun hoped that the threat of nullification would mollify his state's hotheads long enough to negotiate a settlement. Instead, Carolinians embraced his theory wholeheartedly and called a state convention that nullified the tariffs of 1828 and 1832.

Even fellow southerners questioned Calhoun's constitutional reasoning, and most Americans thought Massachusetts Senator Daniel Webster effectively demolished it in a debate with his South Carolina counterpart Robert Y. Hayne. Webster insisted that the Constitution was not a compact of the states but an agreement among "we the people," who had given the courts the power to interpret it. Above all, he denied that membership in the Union and respect for its laws truly abridged the freedom of a state or its people. Coining a classic patriotic slogan, Webster cried for "Liberty *and* Union, now and forever, one and inseparable!"

Andrew Jackson did not like protectionism but hated defiance of his authority even more. He also despised Calhoun, and when Congress considered the Force Bill to implement the tariff, he loudly threatened to march into South Carolina at the head of an army and hang its leaders if necessary. A bloody civil conflict suddenly seemed imminent, until Senator Henry Clay found a solution in early 1833. Though he strongly favored protectionism, Clay proposed to lower his treasured tariff gradually until protection ended in 1842. This compromise gave manufacturers time to adjust but promised to end the system that nullifiers hated. As part of the agreement, Congress asserted federal supremacy by passing the Force Bill. Calhoun agreed to the plan, and Clay won credit as the "Great Compromiser" who had once more saved the Union, just as he had in the Missouri controversy. While Jackson's support of the Force Bill frightened many southern conservatives, South Carolinians realized they were not yet ready for the most extreme assertions of states' rights, at least so long as controversy focused on economic matters instead of slavery itself. Determined to have the last word, however, South Carolina nullified the Force Bill, a closing gesture that everyone else ignored.

War on the Bank

The most dramatic controversy of the Jackson administration was the president's effort to destroy the Bank of the United States. The Bank War was so divisive that it precipitated formation of the Whig Party and disturbed national politics from Washington down to little towns like Fayetteville, North Carolina. The struggle marked the era's clearest confrontation between republican traditions and the economic forces of the Market Revolution.

THE MONSTER

The charter of the Second Bank of the United States would expire in 1836, the last year of Andrew Jackson's second term. Under its latest president, Philadelphia patrician Nicholas Biddle, the Bank still profited its private stockholders, but it also sought to stabilize the currency and economy like a modern central bank by lending to state banks when credit was tight. When business conditions improved, the Bank discouraged excessive lending and note issue by promptly demanding specie when it received state banknotes from its customers. A stable currency was increasingly important as more and more Americans depended on paper money, so many saw the Bank as crucial to the nation's affairs. Old Hickory and other traditional Republicans thought otherwise, and saw the "Monster Bank," or "Hydra of Corruption," as a gigantic private entity with far too much power over public business. Eventually many Jacksonians spoke of the Bank as part of a far larger financial network they dubbed the "Money Power" that conspired to enrich insiders and subvert the republic by manipulating credit and currency. In their eyes, all banks juggled prices and the money supply by issuing or withholding loans, tempting individuals to overextend themselves, and then ruining them with panics. They fostered a "moneyed aristocracy" built on paper instead of land. Above all, they bred inequality because they depended on privileges such as corporate charters and limited liability, and their need for legislative protection led inevitably to corruption. Rather than the "rag money" of the "Money Power," Jackson wanted a more reliable currency of gold and silver. "The bank . . . is trying to kill me," he swore to Van Buren, "*but I will kill it!*"

Congress sent Jackson a bill to recharter the Bank of the United States in early July 1832, and he replied with a thunderous veto message excoriating special privileges. Using strict constructionist logic, the message condemned the Bank as unconstitutional, despite Supreme Court approval in *McCulloch v. Maryland* (1819) and *Osborn v. Bank of the United States* (1824). Most significantly, Jackson branded the Bank as undemocratic. "The rich and powerful too often bend the acts of government to their selfish purposes," he noted. Though some inequality was natural and inevitable, "when the laws undertake to make the rich richer and the potent more powerful, the humble members of society—the farmers, mechanics and laborers—who have neither the time nor the means of securing like favors to themselves, have a right to complain of the injustice of their Government."

The looming presidential election of 1832 would pit Jackson against Henry Clay, whose supporters now called themselves the National Republicans. The veto was a brilliant cornerstone for Jackson's campaign. It spoke directly to millions of voters who feared that economic changes had subjected them to "monsters"—invisible and unnatural forces that lifted the corrupt few above the virtuous many. These voters cheered the veto message at noisy rallies, parades, and barbecues, and rejoiced at defeating a presumed aristocracy. Deaf to the cheering, National Republicans badly misgauged the veto's impact. Biddle compared it to a wild manifesto from the French Revolution and even circulated it as campaign literature, convinced that the president's words would destroy him. Instead, Jackson defeated Clay handily and girded himself for a final battle against the Bank.

The Bank of the United States remained in business under its old charter. Fearing that Biddle would use its funds to buy another charter from a friendlier Congress, Jackson struck first by ordering withdrawal of the government's deposits, depriving the Bank of its biggest customer and seriously trimming its power. Demanding strict obedience, the president fired two secretaries of the Treasury until his third agreed to place the government's funds in five "pet" banks, all managed by reliable Democrats.

Deposit removal proved immensely controversial. Many congressmen saw it as a blatant violation of the Bank's charter, a dangerous usurpation of power, and even a step toward dictatorship. "We are in the midst of a revolution," Clay warned the Senate, "hitherto bloodless, but rapidly tending toward a total change of the pure republican character of the government, and to the concentration of power in the hands of one man."

Matters worsened when Biddle denied new loans and demanded repayment of old ones. The loss of federal funds required some adjustment, but Biddle contracted more than necessary in a deliberate effort to extort a new charter. Deprived of credit in the winter of 1833–1834, businesses reduced their purchases and laid off workers, generating reams of angry petitions from crippled trades and industries. Jackson was unmoved. "Go to Nicholas Biddle!" he roared to protestors. "We have no money here, gentlemen." Biddle would not relent either. "Nothing but the evidence of suffering abroad will produce any effect in Congress," he noted grimly. "All the other Banks and all the merchants may break, but the Bank of the United States shall not break."

DEPOSIT REMOVAL AND THE PARTY SYSTEM

Deposit removal galvanized Jackson's opponents. Recalling the Revolution, a coalition of National Republicans, nullifiers, and pro-Bank Democrats began to call the president "King Andrew the First" and themselves "Whigs," after the British and colonial faction that resisted the Crown. At Clay's urging, the Senate censured Jackson in the spring of 1834, and the Whigs contested local elections from New York City to villages like Fayetteville, North Carolina. Jackson's financial tampering had inspired a permanent opposition party with far greater appeal than National Republicans had ever enjoyed.

Biddle's disdain for elected government enraged Democrats even more. "I for one say perish credit, perish commerce," one congressman roared. "Give us a broken, a deranged, and a worthless currency rather than the ignoble and corrupting tyranny of an irresponsible corporation." Calling himself "the direct representative of the American people," Jackson claimed that presidential authority was more democratic and thus more legitimate than the power of Congress, which was too often captured by local or special interests. Both parties defended themselves with republican traditions, but Democrats cited the superior virtue of the people while Whigs demanded respect for the law and limits on executive power.

The early Whig Party was a motley assortment of Jackson's critics, but most Whigs eventually rallied to Henry Clay's American System and the broad constructionist theories that justified it. They demanded a strong currency and a stable banking system, preferably under a revived Bank of the United States, and federal support for internal improvements, paid for by the sale of public lands. Led by Henry Clay and Daniel Webster, the Whigs insisted that the economic interests of North and South, city and countryside, were all complementary and reconcilable by compromise, and spoke for citizens who embraced the Market Revolution and wanted the government to promote it.

By contrast, Democrats worried that corporations, banks, and industry could subvert republican equality. While they did not resist all economic progress, especially at the state level, they usually opposed federal subsidies and listened to voters like the Massachusetts worker who feared that "manufacturing breeds lords and Aristocrats, Poor men and slaves." Paradoxically, Jackson strengthened the presidency, but used its powers to reduce government direction of economic activity. His party likewise celebrated strict construction and proclaimed that "the best government is that which governs least." That slogan would later defend business interests from government regulation, but antebellum Democrats used it to inhibit state-sponsored development and preserve the republic. The connection between the Democratic Party and "big government" did not appear until the twentieth century.

Generally speaking, Democrats were also more proslavery than Whigs. Small government and strict construction had clear implications for the Peculiar Institution, and Van Buren had explicitly hoped that his North-South alliance would silence its critics. As with the Jeffersonians, Jacksonian claims of white equality implied inequality for nonwhites, because rights for other races might dilute those of white men. A minority of northern Democrats did oppose slavery, usually on economic or political grounds. Their convictions mattered more as the sectional crisis worsened, but they mostly hid their feelings in Jackson's heyday. When Democrats boasted of supporting "the people," they universally meant white men.

Most antislavery voters found a better home in the Whig Party. Some northern Whigs were committed abolitionists; most of the rest disliked slavery without supporting immediate abolition or racial equality. As a party, southern Whigs swore fidelity to slavery as much as Democrats, but slavery's rare southern critics usually came from Whig ranks. Henry Clay, their perennial favorite, was a prosperous planter and large slaveholder, for example, but he began his career by calling for gradual emancipation in Kentucky and led the American Colonization Society for most of his life. By the same token, some Whigs could imagine permitting blacks some rights without conceding full equality, such as voting rights with a property requirement. Going further, northern Whigs clearly sympathized with evangelical reforms, including antislavery.

Democrats were likewise stronger supporters of western expansion. Jefferson had welcomed the opportunity to purchase Louisiana and Jackson seized Indian land avidly, while Democratic racism favored Indian Removal and the growth of slave territory. In the 1840s, Democrats wanted to fight for Texas, California, and Oregon, and a Democratic journalist coined the phrase "manifest destiny" to justify continental empire. By contrast, Whigs often resisted expansion. In part, strategists realized that the question of slavery in the new territories would split the party and damage their electoral prospects. More fundamentally, they tended to fear the wilderness as a source of disorder and barbarism, and preferred to improve the existing America instead of stretching it too far.

Praising "the people" above the elites, Democrats learned the tricks of popular mobilization more quickly than the Whigs. Activists used eye-catching emblems like hickory poles and hickory leaves to symbolize Old Hickory's party, and excited their supporters with barbecues, music, and mesmerizing oratory. Committed volunteers and party professionals organized county, district, and state conventions to choose nominees and drum up support, and senior officials used patronage and government contracts to enforce the conventions' decisions. Party members claimed that conventions were more democratic than private bargaining, but they also learned new forms of elitism by manipulating outcomes to suit themselves. Many Whigs despised partisanship for undermining republican independence, and adopted campaign stunts and party discipline very reluctantly. As the Whigs of Fayetteville demonstrated, however, they swallowed their doubts when nothing else would win elections.

As both parties intensified their electioneering efforts, interest in national politics soared among ordinary voters. Only about one out every four white men had cast a ballot in the presidential election of 1824, but the number more than doubled in the partisan excitement of 1828. By the presidential election of 1840, voter participation had risen to a remarkable 78 percent of the eligible voters, and with a few exceptions, it remained in that range until the twentieth century.

Economic interests affected political choices without entirely controlling them. The richest Americans were mostly Whigs, but the party won its most votes where the Market Revolution had improved opportunities for all citizens. Whigs endorsed evangelical virtues such as temperance, thrift, hard work, and piety, and often embraced the moral reforms inspired by the Second Great Awakening. By contrast, Democrats preferred personal liberty and often resented the reformers' efforts to close saloons or send them to church. Free blacks voted Whig when they could, and Democrats enrolled vast numbers of Irish and German immigrants. Democrats were also popular among farmers, artisans, and urban workingmen who feared that economic change could end their opportunities and independence. In the Upper South, Democrats usually controlled the tidewater regions, where conservative planters feared the reach of government power, but the Whigs were strong in the upland regions where internal improvements were popular and plantations were scarce. Conditions were often the reverse in the Lower South, where extremely wealthy planters in the Black Belt admired Whig ideas on banking and the economy while yeomen in the hill country embraced the egalitarian slogans of the Democrats.

The specific complexion of the Second Party System varied from state to state and constantly threatened to break down, but it held together for a pivotal generation and fulfilled Van Buren's desire to bind "the planters of the South and the plain Republicans of the north." As long as the Whigs and Democrats of one section thought they had more in common with distant fellow party members than with all southerners or northerners, they were not likely to put sectional interests before the concerns of their parties. The Second Party System thus promoted national unity by debating the issues raised by the Market Revolution instead of the far more divisive issue of slavery. The parties likewise cemented public opinion and mass voting as the only paths to national political power, even when they manipulated public opinion and practiced a new elitism once in office.

THE AFTERMATH

Biddle's recession did not last long, for the number of pet banks increased and expanded lending to counter contraction by the Bank of the United States. Whigs continued to protest, but the pet banks kept the government deposits and the federal charter of the Bank duly expired in 1836. Biddle's bank remained in business with a new charter from Pennsylvania, but its economic power had seriously diminished.

The economy expanded rapidly in the Bank War's aftermath. Crop prices rebounded, land speculation resumed, and paper money poured from unreliable wildcat banks. Whigs assumed that irresponsible pet banks loaned the government's money too freely, while Democrats blamed Whig bankers for the profligate "Flush Times." In fact, banks lent more because changes in the flow of international trade allowed American banks to import more Mexican silver, which then supported more lending, but few Americans understood these details. They interpreted the "Flush Times" by their own experience and scrambled to benefit as best they could.

In 1836, prosperity and Jackson's frugality allowed the United States to pay off its federal debt for the only time in its history. The nullification settlement made tariff levels politically untouchable, so with no debt to repay, a surplus built up in the Treasury. Congress distributed this surplus to the states, and most invested their share in banks and internal improvements, sometimes devoting the profits to public education. The same bill expanded the number of pet banks to almost 90, dramatically increasing the difficulty of supervising their custody of the public funds. The resulting burst of new loans and construction projects further stimulated the business boom, much to the president's disquiet. To cool speculation and promote a metallic currency, Jackson issued an executive order, the Specie Circular, in 1836 that required gold or silver for the purchase of public lands. The circular angered speculators and Whigs cursed the president for another interference with the nation's currency, but paper money remained popular and the "Flush Times" roared on.

As the aging and ailing Jackson approached the end of his second term, he copied the example of George Washington and issued an earnest farewell address. In it, the president warned against sectional strife and government overreach, but focused on the lessons of the Bank War. He denounced all banks for encouraging excessive borrowing with a get-rich-quick spirit that corroded popular virtue. Sudden demands for repayment would inevitably follow, he warned, leading to panic, foreclosures, and worthless paper for wage earners. If allowed, banks would attempt to control the government as the Bank of the United States had done, and once more threaten the republic. The solution, Jackson believed, was to unite "the planter, the farmer, the mechanic, and the laborer," or those he called "the great body of the people . . . the bone and sinew of the country," against "the moneyed interest" and "the multitude of corporations with exclusive privileges." It was one of the most explicit appeals to class conflict ever heard in mainstream American politics. Without saying so in public, Jackson bequeathed this endless struggle to the Democratic Party, led by his loyal lieutenant and handpicked successor, Martin Van Buren.

Outside the Party Fold

Many Americans of the 1830s did not think of the Whigs or Democrats as natural or inevitable. Dissidents challenged and resisted the mainstream parties, offered alternatives, and tried to supplant them. Three of the most powerful challenges came from the remarkable anti-Masonic movement of the late 1820s and early 1830s, the Workingmen's movement of the same period, and the steadily mounting slavery conflict. These movements responded to the same pressures that produced the major parties, but none gained the same success in the short term. Their records illustrate the many influences on Jacksonian politics and the power of the mainstream parties to silence or absorb their critics.

THE "BLESSED SPIRIT" OF ANTI-MASONRY

The Masonic order developed as a benevolent fraternity in eighteenth-century Europe, serving as something like a rationalist church for Enlightenment deists that offered secret rituals and an optimistic faith in human improvement to its all-male membership. Masonic lodges spread into late colonial America, enrolling distinguished patriots like George Washington and Benjamin Franklin, and sending impressively costumed dignitaries to ceremonies like the laying of cornerstones.

The order grew rapidly after independence, possibly numbering 100,000 in the 1820s. Lawyers, judges, and officeholders flocked to Masonry, and it also attracted many mobile men who enjoyed the food, drink, and camaraderie they could always find in lodges. Members hoped that fellow Masons would help them in business, and non-members sometimes worried that the secret order gave its members unfair advantages in the market's topsy-turvy scuffle for success.

These suspicions boiled over when William Morgan, a disgruntled former Mason and unemployed stoneworker from Batavia, New York, suddenly went missing in September 1826. Morgan was jailed when he threatened to reveal Masonry's secrets, and then whisked away by carriage and never seen again. Many suspected that vengeful Masons had murdered the hapless artisan and conspired to conceal their crime. All over western New York, Masons seemed implicated as sheriffs refused to investigate, grand juries refused to indict, and judges let suspects off with guilty pleas to minor offenses. Equally dominated by Masons and Martin Van Buren's Democrats, the state legislature ignored all complaints.

Masonic stonewalling fed anti-Masonic activism. Over the summer of 1827, local meetings denounced the alleged conspiracy and Masonic officeholders. Continued frustration led to a statewide convention in 1828 that warned of a secret conspiracy to obstruct justice, suppress liberty, and even overthrow the republic. The Anti-Masons then turned to politics themselves, nominating their own presidential candidate in

1828 and threatening Democrats and National Republicans through-out the Northeast. Their gubernatorial candidates took 45 percent of Pennsylvania's vote in 1829 and 45 percent of New York's in 1830, and carried Vermont between 1831 and 1834. Gathering in the United States' first national political party convention, Anti-Masons nomi-nated another presidential candidate in 1832, campaigned throughout the Northeast, and actually carried Vermont.

Anti-Masonry had clearly transcended protests over Morgan's dis-appearance to reflect the features of other contemporary movements. It originated in the Burned-Over District just as the Second Great Awakening caught fire, and spread like the revivals in regions of dis-location and anxiety. Activists denounced the secret machinations of the supposed Masonic aristocracy just as Democrats condemned the Bank of the United States and blamed its conspiratorial elite for dan-gerous and uncontrolled economic forces. Unlike Jacksonians, how-ever, the Anti-Masons also feared the Masons' nonsectarian quasi-church, their distaste for evangelical religion, and their fondness for a friendly drink. Whatever they had in common, Anti-Masons would not mix with Democrats, not simply because Jackson was a Mason and New York Democrats ignored their concerns, but because their evangelical moralism conflicted with the Jacksonians' freewheeling machismo.

The Anti-Masons succeeded too well, for all but 48 of New York's 507 lodges disbanded in the next decade, and state membership dropped from 20,000 to 3,000. Active Masons had to leave churches, pulpits, jury rolls, and elected offices. When the order collapsed, what was the need for a party? Pragmatic politicians like New York's Thur-low Weed and Pennsylvania's Thaddeus Stevens soon recruited most Anti-Masons for the nascent Whigs. By 1838, the "blessed spirit" was virtually defunct, but its electoral base and crusading energy had be-come vital components of northern Whiggery.

THE RISE OF THE WORKINGMEN

The Market Revolution bore especially hard on urban artisans. Even outside the early factories, putting-out methods cheapened their skills and undermined their hopes for economic independence. Many struggled with unemployment and survived on the labor of their wives and children. The poorest workers endured real suffering, and the more fortunate knew that misery was as close as the next serious illness or economic downturn. Even in good times, workingmen complained that contempt for manual labor had undermined republican equality. In the words of a Massachusetts writer, "The laboring classes in our country, in consequence of the inroads and usurpations of the wealthy and powerful, have for years been sinking in the scale of public estimation."

In the larger cities, masters and journeymen had long joined together to celebrate artisans' role in a republican state and society. After the Panic of 1819, some went further and formed all-journeyman societies to resist any pay cuts or extensions of the working day. In 1827, the Philadelphia Mechanics Union of Trade Associations brought several of these early labor unions together to protest an announced lengthening of the workday from ten hours to eleven, with no increase in wages. They further resolved "to raise the mechanical and productive classes to the condition of true independence and equality" and establish "a just balance of power, both mental, moral, political, and scientific, between all the various classes and individuals which constitute society." The following year, they organized the Workingmen's Party, the first explicitly labor-oriented political party in the world.

The "Workies" spread to other northeastern cities and elected officials from New York to Northampton, Massachusetts, before slowly declining. Some local groups split between radicals and moderates, and others decided that confronting employers directly would help more than winning elections. The early Workingmen had spurned both major parties, but Democrats quickly lured them with their own class-conscious rhetoric. Inside the New York Democratic Party, for example, the most far-reaching opposition to banks and corporations came from the "Loco-Focos," a faction of former Workingmen known for their use of newly invented "loco-foco" matches to illuminate a meeting when their opponents turned off the gaslights. With this exception, the Workingmen's movement of the 1830s died when a new recession struck in 1837, deflecting workers' energies from political action to the struggle for simple survival.

WRESTLING WITH SLAVERY

The Anti-Masons and the Workingmen each attempted to escape the two-party straitjacket, but the Whigs and the Democrats absorbed them both. Mainstream parties had more trouble with the strongest attackers and defenders of slavery. Party leaders longed to silence the slavery dispute, but dissidents wanted just as much to rouse it.

The American Anti-Slavery Society spread rapidly after Jackson's reelection, growing from 225 local affiliates in 1835 to 1,346 in 1838, and 1,650 in 1840, with a total membership of 130,000–170,000. Copying evangelical techniques, it first attempted to convince individual slaveholders by "moral suasion," but white southerners proclaimed that death awaited any abolitionist who preached in a slave state, and posted large rewards for the capture of leaders like Garrison and the Tappan brothers. Changing tactics in the summer of 1835, the society mailed bundles of abolitionist literature to leading slaveholders throughout the South, with gory illustrations seemingly designed to inflame illiterate bondsmen. When these materials reached Charleston, city officials led a mob to the post office and burned the offending pamphlets in the street, immediately challenging the Jackson administration.

Jacksonian officials had no sympathy for abolitionism, but the law required them to protect and deliver the mail. Should there be an exception for antislavery literature? Without success, slavery's defenders demanded that the free states ban "incendiary" speech and writing just as the slave states did. Congress refused to bar antislavery literature from the mails, but Jackson and his postmaster general got the same result by forbidding delivery of any materials thought dangerous in a given community. Proving the white South's considerable power to silence criticism, abolitionists lacked free use of the mails until the Civil War.

Denied entry to slaveholders' homes, abolitionists turned to Congress. Virtually everyone agreed that Congress lacked power over slavery in the states, but the Constitution gave it the power of "exclusive Legislation" for the District of Columbia. Slavery had remained legal in the district since its formation from parts of Maryland and Virginia. Since then, traders had made Washington a major center for the sale of slaves from the Chesapeake to the Deep South, horrifying visitors with jails and auction houses in sight of the Capitol itself. Simply attacking this traffic would give the abolitionists a major opportunity to publicize their case, and success would hand them a major victory. In the winter of 1835–1836, they flooded Congress with at least 176 petitions with almost 34,000 signatures, including those of some 15,000 women, all respectfully calling for the abolition of slavery and the slave trade in the nation's capital.

In the past, Congress had buried such petitions in committee. By 1835, however, the spread of abolitionism, the mixed success of nullification, and, above all, the desire to force other southerners to choose section over party drove proslavery zealots to demand stronger action. In 1835, freshman South Carolina representative James Henry Hammond won instant notoriety when he moved for a routine antislavery petition to "be not received." He claimed that abolition in the capital would be unconstitutional, so no one had the right to ask for it. Instead of legitimizing abolitionists, Hammond's so-called gag rule would require Congress to ignore all their petitions. John C. Calhoun echoed Hammond's demands in the Senate, and Congress fell into a major debate over the right of petition and the legitimacy of antislavery speech.

In the course of this debate, the South Carolinians sharpened the defense of their Peculiar Institution. Rejecting Jefferson's lament that slavery was a necessary evil, Calhoun praised it as a "positive good." Hammond hailed slavery for producing "the highest toned, the purest, best organization of society that has existed on the face of the earth." Both insisted that enslavement had brought Christianity and civilization to savages, uplifted blacks as far as they could go, and turned white men into racial equals, regardless of their economic status.

According to its defenders, however, this perfect society was so fragile that it could not withstand public controversy. Contented slaves would turn violent if they heard that Congress debated their status, and honorable southern congressmen could not endure the insults of deranged fanatics. Northern congressmen who could listen to antislavery petitions must hate the South, Carolinians charged, and moderate southerners were traitors to their section. These accusations had their intended effect and locked Congress in a monumental battle over the gag rule.

On the other side of the argument, former president John Quincy Adams heroically defended the right of petition. The sixth president was now a mere congressman from Massachusetts, and though he professed to disagree with the petitioners, he insisted on their right to be heard. The stalemate finally ended when South Carolina's Henry Pinckney broke ranks and suggested a slightly milder gag rule that dismissed all petitions about slavery as "inexpedient," not unconstitutional. This change made no practical difference, but northern Democrats liked it better and it gave a potential opening to abolitionists if circumstances changed. Calhounites therefore hated it and denounced Pinckney's "treachery," but most southern Democrats believed that party unity with northern Democrats provided slavery's best defense and their own best chances for higher office. Pinckney's gag rule swept the House because the approaching presidential election of 1836 pushed northern and southern Democrats to find common ground.

Congressman John Quincy Adams continued to struggle against the gag rule almost single-handedly, but it would be nine years before this monument to the power of partisan compromise over pro- and antislavery principles would finally collapse. John C. Calhoun likewise kept fighting to tear southern politicians out of both parties and unite them in a proslavery bloc to defend sectional interests, but outside South Carolina itself, he did not succeed in his lifetime. As their builders had hoped, the allure of the national parties usually prevailed over sectional loyalty.

*

Americans had greeted the end of the War of 1812 with jubilant celebration and proud assertions of national greatness. Congress felt especially assertive and approved a number of measures that Republicans had once spurned as unconstitutional, especially a national bank and a protective tariff, while nearly adopting a national policy on internal improvements. All three policies became hotly controversial, however, when the Panic of 1819 revealed the most destructive side of the Market Revolution. At the same time, the Missouri crisis revealed the explosive power of the slavery question, especially its tendency to stir violent disputes that might consume the republic in its infancy. In the presidential election of 1824, Andrew Jackson led his rivals, but the eventual victory of John Quincy Adams brought charges of corruption and linked government support for economic development to undemocratic political practices. Lauding "the will of the people" over his enemies' "corrupt bargain," Jackson swept to victory in 1828.

Jackson and his supporters turned their electoral coalition into a permanent political party by reaching out to ordinary voters with parades, rallies, and entertaining speeches, and by disciplining activists through patronage, nominating conventions, and newspaper coverage. In reaction to Jackson's Bank War, opposing Whigs created their own party to resist the Democrats, and a Second American Party System emerged to debate the issues aroused by the Market Revolution. The two parties likewise widened access to politics beyond the ranks of eighteenth-century-style elites, and guaranteed that no one could inherit political leadership by default, but must earn it through the noisy, messy rituals of mass democracy. Critics assailed this system for its own elitism and for limiting the range of political debate, but party leaders hoped it could widen a controlled democracy while dampening the slavery dispute.

The Jacksonian political system was still unfinished when Old Hickory left office. Both major parties had unstable features, and firmer structures would only emerge under Jackson's successor, Martin Van Buren. But Jackson had laid the basis for the two-party arrangement of American public life that governed the republic until the eve of Civil War and remained as a general pattern ever afterward. The issues that had brought angry villagers to blows in places like Fayetteville, North Carolina, a decade earlier reached across the nation and become manageable, even routine. Party songs and banners did not reverse the Market Revolution, but gave many Americans a reassuring sense of control in this wrenching period of transition. Future generations would find that these creations of the contemporaries of Andrew Jackson had become indispensable aspects of their public life.

The Second Party System did collapse eventually. Over the next two decades, Americans would find that the slavery issue would not disappear as easily as the question of a national bank, and the policy of geographical expansion would drive that controversy beyond the power of Whigs and Democrats to control. They began that discovery in the 1840s, when they carried their quarrels across the Mississippi to the unknown territory of the Great West.

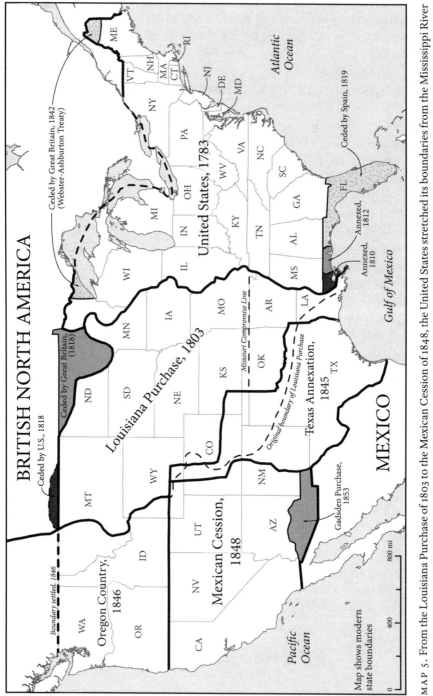

MAP 5. From the Louisiana Purchase of 1803 to the Mexican Cession of 1848, the United States stretched its boundaries from the Mississippi River to the Pacific Ocean, opening new lands for white settlement and plantation slavery, and sparking major disputes over slavery in the new territories. Map by Gabriel Moss.

CHAPTER 12

Wars for the West, 1836–1850

Once a novelty, the political party nominating convention had become a routine feature of American public life by the 1840s. Baltimore's central location made it a favorite spot for these regular gatherings, and May of 1844 brought three separate national conventions to the city, along with the state convention of the Maryland Democratic Party. The Whigs came first and nominated for president their beloved "Prince Hal," Senator Henry Clay of Kentucky, now 67 years old and seeking the office for the third time. A second gathering endorsed the wan ambitions of "His Accidency," John Tyler of Virginia, who had risen from the vice presidency to the presidency upon the death of William Henry Harrison but spoiled his chances for an elected term by quarreling with all comers.

The most significant assembly convened in Odd Fellows Hall on May 27 to choose a presidential candidate for the Democratic Party. The leading contender was former president Martin Van Buren. The New Yorker was a faithful Jacksonian, a key founder of the Second Party System, and a master of the compromises and patronage agreements that held it together. General William Henry Harrison had ruined Van Buren's hopes for reelection in 1840, but "Little Van" returned in 1844, ready for a second campaign based on the old Jacksonian slogans that denounced special privileges and the banking system.

But Martin Van Buren was also vulnerable, and a handful of rivals ardently hoped he would stumble. Many Americans remembered Van Buren's earlier presidential term for the Panic of 1837 and the hard times that followed it. As the depression slowly lifted, party professionals did not look forward to defending the former president's economic record and few longed to refight old battles that now seemed settled. More voters were attracted instead by western expansion, especially the opportunity to annex the breakaway Mexican province of Texas. Mostly populated by Americans and their slaves, Texas had declared independence in 1836 and sought to join the United States, but Mexico had never accepted its loss and American leaders had stalled to avoid war. Looking for a winning issue in 1844, President Tyler had opened the subject again. Always seeking more slave territory, moreover, Secretary of State John C. Calhoun had inflamed matters by calling annexation essential to the security of slavery. By the time the Democratic convention assembled, the question of slavery and Texas dominated the election and riveted the delegates' attention.

Sensing the divisive potential of the Texas question, Van Buren and Clay tried to soft-pedal the issue by warning of war and calling for delay, but southern Democrats longed for Texas and refused to back down. As soon as the Democratic convention assembled, southerners seized control and imposed a rule requiring a two-thirds majority for the presidential nomination, enough to give them a veto over the outcome. The result was fatal to Van Buren, for the New Yorker fell short in the first round of voting in the sweltering hall. His share kept dwindling over seven tense and weary ballots, as one rival after another first surged and then faltered in pursuit of the necessary two-thirds. By nightfall, Van Buren had clearly lost, but who would take his place?

When the convention recessed on the evening of May 28, candidates from Michigan, Pennsylvania, and Kentucky had exhausted their strength, and the friends of an obscure Tennessean named James K. Polk came forward. All day they had whispered around the hall that the former congressman and Bank War leader would make an excellent vice president. Just as they had hoped, others now suggested that this potential running mate might be the only candidate that all Democrats could support for the top spot. After all, Polk was an ardent expansionist, slaveholder, and Jacksonian who had not offended the Van Burenites. He had keen intelligence but little imagination, steady work habits, excellent political instincts, and support from Old Hickory himself. The following morning, Polk's name won a few votes on the eighth ballot and swept the convention on the ninth, and delegates wore themselves out with cheering and giddy relief that their daunting job was done. Polk would triumph in November by calling for "the reannexation of Texas and the reoccupation of Oregon," slipping past Henry Clay by a mere 39,000 votes out of nearly 2.6 million cast.

The story of "Young Hickory's" nomination and election taught several lessons for the future. Polk was the nation's first dark horse, or unexpected, presidential nominee, but the private deals in smoke-filled rooms that brought him forward would only grow stronger in later years. Party nominating conventions and even the Second Party System itself were still new, but the race between Polk and Clay reinforced these institutions and brought out voters in increasingly familiar patterns, as party loyalty grew stronger. Popular republicanism would no longer give automatic preference to distinguished statesmen like Washington or even familiar figures like Van Buren or Clay, for a fickle national mood could overturn anyone. Above all, western expansion now excited Americans far more than economic questions, even at the cost of war.

Democrats, Whigs, and the West

The issues of 1844 had worried few Americans when Andrew Jackson left office in 1837. The fierce rhetoric of the Bank War still dominated politics, and no one knew how long the Whig and Democratic Parties would endure. Answers began to emerge, however, after Vice President Van Buren stepped forward to succeed the man he called his "Old Chief." The financial boom of Jackson's final years suddenly gave way to a severe panic, or depression, and hard times solidified the structures and ideologies of the rival parties. Reluctant Whigs learned the tricks of electioneering pageantry, and used them to defeat the Democrats as prosperity remained elusive. Recovery did not take the nation back into financial controversy, however, but fed the appeal of territorial growth.

MARTIN VAN BUREN AND THE PANIC OF 1837

Andrew Jackson had long preferred Martin Van Buren as his successor, and nine years before James K. Polk's successful maneuvers, the Democratic Party had ratified his choice at another Baltimore convention in May 1835. The Whigs faced a harder decision that year. No single party member stood out above all others as a suitable candidate for president, and many Whigs disapproved of party conventions and caucuses to force a partisan choice upon reluctant freemen. Instead, Whigs in each major section supported a locally popular candidate. If they had any national strategy, it was to use local candidates to deny Van Buren an electoral majority and once more force a final choice upon the House of Representatives.

General William Henry Harrison of Indiana became the favorite of western Whigs. Like Jackson, Harrison was a popular frontier general who had made his reputation fighting Indians in the War of 1812. Unlike Jackson, Harrison's public career had faltered after the war, and he was working as the clerk of an Indiana county court at the time of his nomination. Undeterred, Whigs made the most of the military exploits of "Old Tippecanoe." Harrison did not spell out his views on national policy, but broadly hinted that he favored the main outlines of Henry Clay's American System, including a return to a national bank, a protective tariff, and generous expenditures for internal improvements. In the South, Whigs supported Judge Hugh Lawson White of Tennessee, a former Jacksonian who claimed that the wily Van Buren had led the Old Hero astray. White appealed to southerners who doubted the New Yorker's commitment to slavery and bridled at the new structures of party discipline, but his strongest backers were orthodox Whigs who shared their party's views on banking and internal improvements. Daniel Webster led his party in Massachusetts, but the three candidates' efforts were to no avail. Van Buren took a clear majority of electoral votes, 170 out of 294, and proudly stepped forward as Old Hickory's successor.

Van Buren's triumph was short-lived. Soon after his inauguration, overheated cotton prices began to chill and merchant houses in New Orleans, New York, and Liverpool started failing. Prices were soon in free fall and the nation's financial system collapsed into the Panic of 1837. Banks suspended specie payments once again, thousands of urban workers lost their jobs, farmers and planters could not make payments on their overvalued acreage, bankruptcies multiplied, and the parties fell to blaming one another for the catastrophe. Whigs assailed Jacksonian currency experiments as unmitigated disasters, from the Bank veto to deposit removal to the Specie Circular. Democrats replied that traders, bankers, and speculators had no one to blame but themselves, that greed for instant riches had fed the inflationary spiral, and that the highfliers had reaped what they had sown. In fact, like the "Flush Times" that preceded it, the Panic of 1837 stemmed from international factors that were not comprehended by most American politicians and largely beyond their control in any case. The main political effect of the panic was to reinforce existing opinions about financial policy and strengthen the party lines that had already formed in the Jackson administration.

The economic effects of the panic were painful and lingering, however. A weak recovery in 1838 led to an even deeper collapse in 1839. Pennsylvania's Bank of the United States became a conspicuous casualty, closing its doors at last in 1841. Times remained hard until well into the 1840s, as farmers lost their lands, merchants and shop owners faced bankruptcy, banks slashed their lending, and many states could not repay the funds they had borrowed for massive projects of internal improvement. Within these states, Whigs blamed Democrats for destroying the public credit, but Democrats denounced the whole scheme of reckless economic development they identified with Whiggery, refusing to charter new corporations and sometimes seeking to abolish the banking industry altogether.

At the federal level, President Van Buren rejected Whig demands that he act to revive the economy. Insisting that he lacked the constitutional power to intervene, Van Buren declared that the depression should run its course, forcing dishonest and reckless operators out of business and purging the nation of corruption. Honest Americans who sought no easy riches but labored hard to feed their families from the products of their own farms or workshops, he suggested, would not be touched by fluctuations in market prices and were thus immune from the depression's worst effects.

Van Buren did worry, however, that federal funds now lay trapped in private banks that paid unredeemable paper notes instead of specie. His solution called for the creation of the Independent Treasury in order to enact a "divorce" between the government and the banks. Summoning Congress into special session in the fall of 1837, he asked for authorization to keep the government's money completely out of banks and to lodge it in regional government offices called subtreasuries instead. Whigs resisted furiously, realizing that the banks used the government's deposits to make profitable loans in the credit-starved economy. If the government withdrew its money from the banking system, these loans would disappear, credit would become even scarcer, and recovery would be that much more difficult. Dismissing Whig arguments as a smoke screen from greedy bankers who only wanted to feast on the people's money, Democrats sided with the president but could not deliver enough votes. Van Buren spent most of his single term struggling patiently for the Independent Treasury. When he finally won it in 1840, the prize was politically useless, for hard times had scarcely abated and Whigs looked forward to the next election with undisguised jubilation.

"TIPPECANOE AND TYLER TOO"

Confident of success, Whigs assembled their own convention in December 1839. Party stalwart Henry Clay longed for the nomination, but unsentimental power brokers realized that his enemies were too numerous and chose William Henry Harrison instead. To balance the ticket, they named John Tyler of Virginia as his running mate. Tyler was a conservative planter with Old Republican leanings who had gravitated to the Whigs for fear of Jackson's bellicose stand on nullification, but Whigs gave his opinions little thought as they organized for victory. Embellishing the methods that Democrats had long used to enliven their own campaigns, Whigs gathered in enormous rallies for "Tippecanoe and Tyler Too" and derided "Little Van" as a "used up man." Popularizing a deathless expression, they proclaimed that the country would be "O.K.," or "Oll Korrect," when the "Little Magician" was finally sent "off to Kinderhook," his New York home. A Democratic newspaperman handed the Whigs an indispensable symbol when he dismissed their aging candidate as a doddering old fool who would rather sit by the fire in a log cabin and sip hard cider than run the country. In fact, Martin Van Buren had risen from obscurity, while Harrison was a Virginia planter's son whose father signed the Declaration of Independence. Gleeful Whigs ignored these facts and trumpeted their man as "the log cabin candidate" who shared the dwelling of the poor and contented himself with simple cider while Van Buren rioted in White House luxury. Whigs drenched themselves with the exhilarating beverage, pushed ten-foot leather balls across the country to "keep the ball rolling" for Harrison, and put up log cabins everywhere to symbolize their campaign, even in the heart of Manhattan. Without success, frustrated Democrats denounced these stunts as deceptive nonsense. Aroused by fierce party competition and irresistible entertainment, an astonishing 78 percent of eligible voters came to the polls and handed William Henry Harrison the victory. "They have at last learned from defeat the art of victory," the *Democratic Review* admitted. "We have taught them how to conquer us!"

Harrison won a landslide in the Electoral College, 234 votes to 60, and 53.1 percent of the popular vote. Previous elections had been lopsided contests within most states, but the parties in 1840 were strongly competitive almost everywhere. Nearly every citizen could see that his own vote mattered, and party operatives struggled to bring every last voter to the polls. The Second Party System had reached its maturity, and party competition had brought its restricted electorate to an astonishing level of political participation.

Whig euphoria did not last long. Seeking perhaps to dispel Democratic charges that he was too old and frail to be president, Harrison stood in a raw March wind without an overcoat to deliver the longest inaugural address in American history. In the following weeks, he trudged through Washington's slushy streets until he fell ill. Four weeks after he took the oath of office, President William Henry Harrison was dead of pneumonia, and Vice President John Tyler took his place.

Tyler immediately had trouble, for he had virtually no personal support in the country and was neither an orthodox Whig nor Democrat at a time when party support had become essential for political success. Whigs in the Capitol followed Senator Henry Clay, but President Tyler had no sympathy for Clay's unchanged plans for an activist federal government. Under Clay's leadership, Congress repealed Van Buren's Independent Treasury and twice rechartered a national bank. Tyler consented to the Treasury bill but vetoed the bank charters, forcing the government to leave its funds in unreliable state banks. Tyler also clashed with Congress over taxes, for the combined effects of the depression and the tariff reductions of 1833 had thrust the government into a revenue crisis. Tyler reluctantly agreed that the tariff had to go up again, but he drew the line against Clay's proposal to allow the distribution of the proceeds of public lands for the purposes of internal improvement.

Infuriated by Tyler's rejection of the doctrines that voters had apparently endorsed in 1840, congressional Whigs denounced the president, and all of Harrison's cabinet appointees resigned except Secretary of State Daniel Webster. When Webster completed work on the Webster-Ashburton Treaty, settling the US border with Canada, he too quit and left President John Tyler with no more than a "corporal's guard" of states' rights southerners to keep him company.

The Jacksonian political system seemed deeply entrenched by the presidential election of 1844. National party conventions chose both major candidates, party organizations dominated the campaign process from the presidential contest down to local battles among legislators and aldermen, party newspapers spelled out the respective platforms, and the contest was close in virtually every state. Having originated in a bitter controversy over the tension between republican traditions and new demands for economic programs, the parties had shown they could adapt to additional concerns and offer voters a meaningful choice on other issues such as Texas annexation. The power of the Second Party System proved ephemeral, however. Over the next two decades, Americans would find that the slavery issue was not so easily quieted as the question of a national bank, and the policy of geographical expansion would drive that controversy beyond the power of the Second Party System to control. The process began when Polk pursued the consequences of Texas annexation.

THE EMERGENCE OF MANIFEST DESTINY

In July of 1845, New York Democratic editor John L. O'Sullivan coined a memorable phrase in an article proclaiming the United States' "manifest destiny to overspread the continent allotted by Providence for the free development of our yearly multiplying millions." Other writers and speakers latched on to "manifest destiny," for the words seemed to encapsulate a popular conviction that American territorial expansion was natural, inevitable, and glorious, and would eventually embrace the entire North American continent. O'Sullivan himself had long promoted this idea in his journal, the *United States Magazine and Democratic Review*. There he insisted that America was unique among all nations, its universal democratic principles would exempt it from prior human ills, and its future would be the salvation of all mankind. "The far-reaching, the boundless future will be the era of American greatness," O'Sullivan had predicted in 1839.

> In its magnificent domain of space and time, the nation of many nations is destined to manifest to mankind the excellence of divine principles; to establish on earth the noblest temple ever dedicated to the worship of the Most High—the Sacred and the True. Its floor shall be a hemisphere—its roof the firmament of the star-studded heavens, and its congregation an Union of many Republics, comprising hundreds of happy millions, calling, owning no man master, but governed by God's natural and moral law of equality, the law of brotherhood—of "peace and good will amongst men."

O'Sullivan's enthusiasm was grandiose even in the 1840s, but similar sentiments spread widely. White Americans had long imagined themselves as a people set apart from others and distinguished with a special mission. While Puritans had conceived this mission in religious terms, Jacksonian Americans like O'Sullivan found sacred meaning in a republican crusade. To the distant nations of Europe, America might lead by the force of its example. Within the Western Hemisphere, however, O'Sullivan and many of his fellow Democrats foresaw a policy of expansion that would bring distant territories under the rule of American democracy and open them to a spreading population of white Americans. Like O'Sullivan, many expressed this hope with spread-eagle optimism, but others warned that America must expand or shrivel, and that the security of its people and its institutions depended on the subjection of supposedly inferior neighbors, particularly Mexicans and Native Americans.

During the 1840s, O'Sullivan's version of American nationalism seized the public imagination, and "Manifest Destiny" became a powerful political slogan that legitimized a quest for continental empire. As Americans extended their institutions to the Pacific, however, a virulent question took over the public debate. Whose institutions would move west—the North's or the South's? Would O'Sullivan's "law of brotherhood" make room for slavery? Or was the republic's growth inseparable from the spread of human property? Whether slave or free, didn't the destiny of the United States depend on the fate of its Great West? Eventually Americans could not evade these questions, but they began the debate over territorial expansion in the conventional way, within the structure of the two-party system, and consequently, by attempting to downplay the sectional implications of continental growth.

The Great West

What was the land that Americans coveted in the 1840s? Who lived there already? Beyond the Mississippi floodplain, the North American continent sloped upward beneath a vast sea of grass and scrubland to the crest of the Rocky Mountains. The true deserts of the Great Basin came next, followed by more ranges that lined the Pacific coast. This vast sweep of territory became the object and the prize of Manifest Destiny. Its harsh landscape initially intimidated eastern travelers, who labeled it the "Great American Desert." In fact, the Great Plains had been as much a highway as an obstacle to those who knew how to cross it, and had long offered pathways for Indians, Spaniards, traders, trappers, and wildlife. After centuries of dispute between Native Americans and multiple European empires, claims to the vast region from the 49th parallel to the 31st at the Rio Grande, and then down the river to the Gulf of Mexico, would fall to the United States in the decades before the Civil War and make the former seaboard colonies a transcontinental republic. For well over a century, the struggle to occupy and subdue this territory bred myths and folklore about western expansion and American identity. More immediately, the American drive to possess the West would displace its earlier inhabitants.

GEOGRAPHY AND EARLY PEOPLES

The West's many regions varied widely from each other and supported diverse human cultures. On the Pacific coast, food sources were so abundant that native peoples practiced little agriculture and lived almost entirely by hunting and gathering. Acorns were the favorite food of the California Indians. Rivers in the rainy forests of the Pacific Northwest attracted annual swarms of salmon, which members of the Chinook, Kwakiutl, Haida, and Tlingit tribes harvested and dried to last all year. Living from Puget Sound to southwest Alaska, these tribes established elaborate hierarchies of social class, built wooden plank houses, and produced highly distinctive art to cover their dwellings, clothes, boats, ritual objects, and the monumental carvings that whites called totem poles. In the southwestern desert, where the upper Rio Grande flows south before turning eastward to the Gulf, ancestors of the Pueblo Indians had been among the first to adopt the culture of maize, or corn, from Central America. Benefiting from ingenious systems to catch every available drop of rainwater, maize supported elaborate towns made of stone and adobe brick, safely perched on mesa tops or cliff faces, or tucked away deep in protected canyons. Not far away, the Navaho people also farmed and tended sheep they acquired from the Spanish, while their relatives the Apaches alternately fought and traded with Spaniards, Mexicans, and Anglo-Americans alike.

The most widely known of western Indians were the horseback riders who hunted the bison, or buffalo, across the Great Plains. The Plains people used dozens of plant and animal species but depended most conspicuously on the vast buffalo herds that dominated the environment. Pursuing the animals on horseback, they ate fresh or dried buffalo meat and used the hides for clothing and for their distinctive portable dwelling, the teepee. Their mounts had originally come by purchase, escape, or capture from early Spanish settlers and from

Pueblo Indians, who seized large Spanish herds at the time of their 1680 revolt and traded them eastward to the southern Plains. There the Comanches brought horse culture to perfection, pushed the Apaches westward toward New Mexico by the mid-eighteenth century, and then used their superb horsemanship to create a raiding and trading network that dominated most of inland Texas and it surrounding territory. From the Rocky Mountains, Cheyennes and Arapahos also acquired horses from New Mexico and used them to move southward and join the hunting, raiding, and trading culture of the Plains. By contrast, the Lakotas (also called the Sioux) and smaller eastern groups did not acquire enough horses to leave the Great Lakes region and venture extensively across the Plains until the late eighteenth and early nineteenth centuries. The Mandans and similar tribes remained along the Missouri River in permanent villages composed of domed earthen structures, and combined mounted buffalo hunts with tilling corn and other crops.

Horses allowed the Plains tribes to become formidable fighters who presented serious obstacles to white American expansion. At the same time, raiding for horses and competing for pasturage encouraged destructive wars among the tribes. Horses also competed seriously with buffalo for grass and water and enabled a huge market for buffalo hides, badly diminishing the wild herds long before the coming of the transcontinental railroad and professional white hunters. Even so, it would not be until after the Civil War, with the near extinction of the buffalo and a long series of disastrous wars and broken treaties, that the Plains Indians submitted to the far more numerous white Americans.

FIRST COLONIES

Previous European colonizers joined the Native Americans in the human variety of the West. Explorers entered from New Spain as early as 1540, when Francisco Vásquez de Coronado met the Pueblo Indians while Hernando de Soto was crisscrossing the Southeast. When these conquistadores found no precious metals, however, Spain lost interest and only kept a band of frontier outposts from Florida to California to convert the Indians and guard its more valuable colonies to the south. Except for New Mexico, moreover, Spain's western buffers appeared late, when French, British, and Russian trading posts seemed to threaten its hold on the area, and remained small. These colonizing powers all depended on Indian trade or Indian labor, but the coercive methods of the Spanish and the Russians proved far too inflexible and unproductive for permanent success. The British and Anglo-Americans gained far more with voluntary trading, to which they added military conquest and the population pressure of agricultural settlements. This combination of methods finally brought most of the area to the United States.

Spain's first settlements in what became the US southwest began in 1598, when Don Juan de Oñate founded the colony of New Mexico in the upper valley of the Rio Grande. After crushing the Pueblo Revolt of 1680, Spain relaxed its harsh mission program to coexist with the Pueblos and cooperate with them in order to resist the Apaches. With 25,000 Hispanic residents in 1800, New Mexico became Spain's largest outpost in the thinly populated north.

Other Spanish settlements resembled New Mexico on a smaller scale. In the early eighteenth century, Hispanic settlers followed Jesuit missionaries into southern Arizona, but their numbers did not exceed a thousand. About the same time, the Spanish built a handful of forts and missions in Texas to counter the influence of French traders from Louisiana. Texas developed a ranching economy, but the province did not flourish, and there were still less than 2,000 Spanish-speaking *tejanos* in 1763, when the French surrendered Louisiana to Spain at the end of the Seven Years' War, or French and Indian War.

The last Spanish settlement emerged in California. Mostly ignoring Baja (Lower) California, Mexican officials began to eye Alta (Upper) California when they heard that Russians might enter it from Alaska. There the Spanish met as many as 300,000 Indians, a regional population thought to be more numerous than any other north of Mexico. The native Californians lived in hundreds of small bands, supporting themselves on rich harvests of acorns, other seeds, and a variety of game animals. Rarely warring among themselves, they proved no match for the heavily armed Spanish invaders. Converting them to Christianity became a major goal of Spanish colonization.

Led by a military commander and the Franciscan missionary Fray Junipero Serra, a combined expedition of soldiers and friars reached San Diego in 1769 and built the first mission and fort, or *presidio*. Their settlement grew slowly, but the Franciscans eventually constructed 21 coastal settlements between San Diego and the north shore of San Francisco Bay. Cattle ranches later took shape on huge private land grants, but Alta California still grew slowly, with a Hispanic population that did not reach 1,000 until 1790.

The California mission system mixed idealistic goals with brutal methods. Embracing lives of extreme poverty and self-denial, determined friars urged Indians to move into mission settlements with churches and farms. Indian residents, or "neophytes," received food, clothing, shelter, and intense indoctrination in the Spaniards' faith and culture. In return, they were bound to a lifetime of labor, with chains and beatings for those who tried to escape. They also had to speak, dress, and behave like Spaniards, including observance of Spanish gender roles and marital practices. Unmarried women faced special burdens, including nightly imprisonment to safeguard their chastity, and soldiers enforced the rules at every mission. Joining the missions could bring early death from diseases, but when Spanish horses, cattle, and hogs degraded their natural food supply, increasing numbers of Indians had to take the chance. By the time Mexican independence put an end to the mission era in 1821, the number of neophytes had reached 21,000, while the number of other Indians in the mission districts alone had fallen from 72,000 to 18,000. The total number of California Indians fell by half during Spanish and Mexican rule, from around 300,000 to around 150,000.

Spain's fears of a Russian threat to California proved groundless, for its Alaskan outpost lacked all resources for an invasion. The northernmost colony in Pacific America had grown up as a distant extension of Russia's long conquest of Siberia. Pursuing sables and other fur-bearing animals across the vast cold forests of northern Asia, Russian merchants reached the Pacific in the early seventeenth century, during the early decades of English settlement in Virginia. Instead of the voluntary barter offered by the French and British, the Russians seized native hostages and demanded furs for their release. As the numbers of sables and Siberians inevitably dwindled, eighteenth-century Russians ventured into the north Pacific for fresh sources. Sailing for the czar, Danish Captain Vitus Bering and a Russian subordinate made separate landings on the Alaskan mainland in 1741, but Bering could not reach home before winter. Some of his crewmen survived their frigid layover in the Aleutian Islands, but not Bering. Their reward was an impressive cargo of sea otter pelts that sold in China for a bountiful profit.

Pursuing Bering's discoveries, the Russians took skins from the Aleutian Islands with their customary forceful methods for four decades without attempting a permanent settlement. In 1784, however, shortly after the United States won independence from Britain, 130 Russian settlers established an enduring outpost on Kodiak Island, just off the Alaskan mainland. Their presence grew slowly until 1812, when they finally reached northern California, established a trading post at Fort Ross, and remained there 30 years. Over the same period, Russian Orthodox missionaries mitigated the worst abuses of the fur trade and gained some local converts whose descendants maintain the faith today. Russian America remained Europe's smallest and weakest colony on the Pacific.

THE ARRIVAL OF ANGLO-AMERICANS

Sustained American attention to the land beyond the Mississippi began in 1803, when President Jefferson purchased the vast province of Louisiana from France, and dispatched the Corps of Discovery led by Captain Lewis and Lieutenant Clark to cross it and trace a path to the Pacific coast. Their expedition returned in 1806 without discovering an easy waterway across the continent, but did bring back exciting tales of vast mountains, huge plains and rivers, radically diverse climates, strange peoples, teeming wildlife, and beckoning opportunities.

Trappers were the first to follow in Lewis and Clark's path. In 1808, New York businessman John Jacob Astor founded the American Fur Company with the intention of gaining control of the entire US fur trade. To compete with the British Hudson's Bay Company, he began with a seaborne expedition around the southern tip of South America to establish Fort Astoria at the mouth of the Columbia River in 1811 and followed with an overland expedition to find a practical land route. On their way back to St. Louis in 1812, a party from this expedition discovered South Pass in the future state of Wyoming, which was the lowest and most accessible opening through the Rocky Mountains and the key to a wagon trail to the Pacific.

Hoping to sell their quarry to Astor, trappers soon fanned across the upper reaches of Missouri in search of smaller streams where the beavers built their dams and lodges. The most knowledgeable became known as mountain men, renowned for their hunting skills and deep understanding of the peaks and forests. Often marrying Indian women, the mountain men hunted all winter and then converged by the thousand at a company-sponsored rendezvous in midsummer to sell their peltry, buy supplies, and raucously celebrate the end of a successful season. With mountain men as his advance guard, John Jacob Astor monopolized the American fur trade by 1830 but sold his stake in 1834 when the fashion for beaver hats began declining. Investing his gains in New York real estate, Astor became the wealthiest man in America, with a fortune of $20 million when he died in 1848.

By the 1820s, a well-marked trail stretched from Independence, Missouri, up the Missouri River, and across the plains to Oregon by way of South Pass. In 1836, Dr. Marcus Whitman and his wife, Narcissa, followed this path to become missionaries to the Indians in modern Washington State. In the same year, the first wagon train took the Oregon Trail as far as Idaho, and Whitman himself led the first large wave of 1,000 emigrants from there to Oregon's Willamette Valley in 1843. The settlers created a prosperous agricultural society with a growing population, but with no clear demarcation between British and American sovereignty, diplomatic pressure on both nations' leaders to find a solution increased. Farther to the south, Mormon pioneers followed part of the Oregon Trail in 1846 and 1847 to the valley of the Great Salt Lake in modern Utah. There the church regrouped, established the society it had been seeking, and continued adding residents through foreign and domestic missionary efforts.

Before the coming of the transcontinental railroad in 1869, as many as 400,000 emigrants had followed the Oregon Trail to the Pacific. Adding to the traffic, the California Trail branched from the main route in 1843, followed by the Mormon Trail to Utah in 1847 and the Bozeman Trail in 1863. The passage of these pioneers brought the development of western states, including California, Oregon, and Washington, but naturally increased conflict with intervening Indian tribes and opened the way for destruction of the buffalo herds.

As Americans approached Oregon, the crumbling of the Spanish Empire also drew them to the Southwest, especially to the Mexican province of Texas, where 20,000 Comanche Indians had built up a vast commercial empire the Spanish called Comanchería. Ever since the eighteenth century, the Comanches had used mounted hit-and-run raids to dominate their neighbors and amass huge herds of horses, which they traded, along with buffalo skins and captives, all around their domains. As the unquestioned masters of central Texas, they had effectively halted most Spanish settlement north of the Rio Grande.

After independence in 1821, the Mexican government began recruiting settlers to contest Comanche dominance. Moses Austin of St. Louis quickly won permission for a settlement of 300 families, and his son Stephen F. Austin led them to Texas when his father died soon afterward. Other *empresarios* won generous land grants and followed them. Most of the new settlers were slaveholding southerners, for the fertile plains of eastern Texas were ideal for cultivating cotton. Though independent Mexico had abolished slavery, it exempted Texas to gain more settlers, and the tactic worked. By 1835, some 30,000 Anglo-Americans and their 5,000 slaves dramatically outnumbered the territory's 3,500 Hispanic *tejanos*. Like the Austins, some of the newcomers were reasonably conscientious immigrants who learned Spanish, promised to become at least nominal Catholics, and intended to support their new homeland. Others were footloose squatters with no strong loyalty anywhere and a sketchy commitment to law and order. Whatever their loyalties, most of the newcomers hugged the Gulf coast and refused to tangle with Comanchería.

INDEPENDENT TEXAS

By the end of the 1820s, Mexican authorities realized that American immigrants might take over Texas and reversed their earlier hospitality. New laws forbade the importation of more slaves and directed new immigrants away from the volatile borderland. When General Antonio López de Santa Anna seized power in 1835, he centralized all government decision making and revoked the autonomy of the Mexican states, including Coahuila y Tejas, which embraced modern Texas. Few *tejanos* welcomed these moves after experiencing long neglect by the central government in the face of repeated Comanche attacks. When Santa Anna went further and announced that he would enforce the laws against slavery, Hispanic and Anglo-American Texans exploded in resentment and proclaimed their independence in March 1836. Santa Anna immediately sought to crush this rebellion with an invasion that led to the capture and execution of insurgent forces at the town of Goliad and at the Alamo, a former Spanish mission in San Antonio. Soon after the fall of the Alamo, however, General Sam Houston ambushed Santa Anna's army at the Battle of San Jacinto and captured the Mexican commander, forcing him to sign a treaty of independence that implied a Texas-Mexico border at the Rio Grande. Santa Anna repudiated this coerced agreement as soon as he got free, but victorious Texans quickly asked the US Congress for annexation.

Texas's new president, Sam Houston, was an old friend and protégé of US president Andrew Jackson. Old Hickory longed to gratify his friend and add the Lone Star Republic to the United States, but he knew that annexation would arouse charges of a plot to extend slavery and provoke Mexico to war. Not wanting to damage Van Buren's prospects in the upcoming election of 1836, Jackson limited himself to recognizing Texas's independence. For the next ten years, Mexico refused to accept the loss of its northern province and promised its eventual reconquest, but never carried out these threats. Instead, the Comanches avoided the Anglo-Americans and continued to weaken northern Mexico with unrelenting raids. Texas survived as an independent republic and the question of annexation lay dormant.

War with Mexico

Most white Americans had long gloried in western expansion. They celebrated when independence stretched the nation's boundaries from the Appalachians to the Mississippi. They rejoiced again when Thomas Jefferson added the Louisiana Purchase to the "empire for liberty." Democrats were most enthusiastic, and most critics were Federalists or Whigs, but support for expansion spread widely among the voters. More than mere wealth or power, each new acquisition seemed to promise the spread of republican principles, a new field for national identity, unity, and pride. The prospect of Texas annexation was no exception.

TEXAS ANNEXATION

The issue of Texas annexation revived when Virginian Abel P. Upshur replaced US Secretary of State Daniel Webster in 1843. The new secretary was an ultra-conservative supporter of slavery and states' rights who shared the president's hunger for Texas. Tyler's alienation from each of the major parties made both Whigs and Democrats unwilling to hand him a victory, however, and Upshur made no progress until rumors of British plots began to circulate. Britain had abolished slavery in its own colonies in 1834 and favored the end of slavery everywhere. If Texas masters were willing to give up their relatively few slaves, diplomats whispered, England might advance the funds to compensate them and persuade Mexico to recognize their independence. As a British quasi-protectorate, Texas would then be flooded with British immigrants and capital, fully making up for any losses occasioned by the sacrifice of slavery.

Having just fought a revolution to defend their slaves from Mexico, it is doubtful that white Texans would so easily surrender them to Britain, but Houston and his diplomats used the rumors to great effect in Washington. Officials began to wonder aloud what would happen to the American Southwest if Texas were "abolitionized." Runaways from the Black Belt would gain a haven, they predicted. Slaveholders could never take the plantation system beyond Louisiana. White yeomen would flock to the new free labor paradise, leaving planters and slaves behind them in an ever-blacker, ever more dangerous South. British adventurers would mingle with the Indians and runaway blacks as they had in Spanish Florida, inciting forays into the slave states and possibly creating a beachhead for a serious British invasion. These thoughts greatly alarmed Secretary Upshur as he reached out to other proslavery leaders to rally support for a treaty of annexation. The proslavery meaning of annexation grew even stronger in early 1844, when Upshur suddenly died and President Tyler appointed John C. Calhoun to take his place. Calhoun blasted the British with proslavery arguments and condemned their alleged abolitionist plots, effectively polarizing the issue for northern and southern Americans.

Having alienated both parties, John Tyler had almost no chance of election to the presidency in his own right in 1844. The presumed candidates of the two major parties were Democrat Martin Van Buren and Whig Henry Clay. Sensing the divisive potential of the Texas question, they each moved to neutralize it by agreeing to postpone annexation in order to prevent a war with Mexico. Unfortunately for these plans, however, Calhoun had done his work so well that it was nearly impossible to placate anti-Texas northerners without offending pro-Texas southerners, especially among Democrats. Andrew Jackson himself repudiated Van Buren's anti-Texas waffle, and southerners abandoned him at the Democratic convention. The New Yorker could not gain the nomination without southern support, so after eight fruitless ballots, the convention turned to former governor James K. Polk of Tennessee, an annexation stalwart whom Van Buren had considered as a possible running mate.

The election of 1844 thus emerged as an excited referendum on territorial expansion. The little-known Polk called for the "reannexation of Texas and the reoccupation of Oregon," on the dubious theory that Texas had actually been part of the Louisiana Purchase of 1803 but exchanged for Florida in 1819. The theory was useful because it enabled Polk to ease away from Calhoun's position and cast the Texas question as matter of trans-sectional nationalism rather than a morally tainted land grab for slavery. As for Oregon, that country extended from northern California to the southern boundary of Russian Alaska at latitude 54°40' north. The United States and Britain had earlier agreed to leave it open to traders of both nations, but Polk claimed that the Lewis and Clark expedition had given the United States a "clear and unquestionable" title to the whole region. The area would obviously be free territory if it ever joined the American Union, so northern Democrats salved their discomfort over Texas with the belligerent chant "fifty-four forty or fight!"

Henry Clay resisted the frenzy for expansion. The Whig candidate looked for unity by promising northerners not to wage war for what some were beginning to call the "Slave Power," and assuring southerners that Texas would be theirs eventually, but his tactic only seemed evasive. A small number of antislavery Whigs cast votes for James G. Birney of the Liberty Party, probably costing Clay the electoral votes of New York and Michigan, and thus the election itself. Polk swept most of the South and West, and took New York and Pennsylvania, for 170 electoral votes to Clay's 105. The popular vote divided more closely, with Polk gaining 49.6 percent, Clay 48.1 percent, and Birney taking the rest. The mandate for "Polk and Texas" was narrow but clear, and the president-elect prepared to make the most of it.

In fact, John Tyler beat him to the punch. The lame-duck president had submitted an annexation treaty, but Senate Whigs denied him the votes he needed to ratify it. Taking another tack, Tyler declared that a simple congressional majority could "add states" with a joint resolution, though treaties with foreign nations (like Texas) required ratification by two-thirds of the Senate. Congress accordingly authorized Tyler to acquire Texas by treaty or joint resolution, whichever he preferred. Unsurprisingly, Tyler chose the resolution method and offered statehood to Texas in his last days as president. Polk soon endorsed the plan, and Texas accepted it on July 4, 1845. Manifest Destiny and the Slave Power had won a major victory, but its costs would be far greater than anyone imagined in 1845.

POLK TAKES CHARGE

Besides the conflict over Texas, President Polk had four major objectives for his administration. He wanted to settle the Oregon boundary dispute with Britain and to reduce the tariff to a level that gave the government just enough revenue to operate but no more. As an orthodox Jacksonian, he also wanted to reestablish the Independent

Treasury that Martin Van Buren had obtained but a Whig Congress had later abolished. Most ambitiously, Polk desired one more acquisition from Mexico: the fabled land of California. Like Texas a decade or two earlier, California was a thinly populated Mexican province, but Polk knew it was a potentially fertile country with a good harbor at San Francisco to protect America's Pacific trade and other interests. A strong believer in Manifest Destiny, Polk had no doubt that US citizens would soon flood the area as they had already done in Texas and were beginning to do in Oregon, and he was confident that the Mexican government would have to give way somehow. In his single term in office, President Polk accomplished all four of these major objectives and more besides, which gave this secretive, almost furtive Tennessean more success in gaining his own objectives than most presidents in US history.

Polk focused on foreign affairs, leaving his tariff and Treasury goals to congressional lieutenants who eventually achieved them. He took up Oregon first, for the Democrats had campaigned on the demand for "all Oregon," and the pugnacious chant "fifty-four forty or fight" was getting cheers at barrooms and militia musters all over the country. Even so, Polk did not want to fight Great Britain, the world's most powerful nation, for a marginally valuable territory. He was willing to divide Oregon by stretching the existing boundary on the 49th parallel to the Pacific, but British trappers and settlers occupied the land between there and the Columbia River and did not want to give it up. Ultimately unwilling to fight for such a distant and seemingly insignificant spot, Britain eventually backed down and agreed to extend the existing boundary to Puget Sound while retaining Vancouver Island.

FIGHTING MEXICO

The boundary with Mexico might also have been compromised but Polk and his Mexican counterparts would not back down. The traditional southern boundary of Mexican Texas had been the Rio Nueces, but the Republic of Texas wanted a more southern boundary on the Rio Grande del Norte. The difference seemed trivial where the two streams met the Gulf of Mexico, only 100 miles apart, but the Rio Grande was far longer than the Nueces and looped almost 2,000 miles to the north and west. A boundary there would give the United States far more land than the Texans had actually settled, but Polk was determined to have it. Compared to the United States, Mexico was poor and weak but also proud and very sensitive. Its unstable government could not recapture Texas, but any leader who surrendered it would be overthrown, so it might be preferable to fight a losing war against the United States than admit defeat in advance.

To appear flexible, Polk sent John Slidell as minister to Mexico with an offer that was actually an ultimatum: $25 million and assumption of Mexico's debts to Americans in exchange for a Rio Grande border, plus the provinces of New Mexico and Alta California (i.e., the modern US state of California). He also ordered General Zachary Taylor and 4,000 American troops to seize the disputed territory and occupy the north bank of the Rio Grande. With national honor at stake, Mexican officials would not back down and refused to meet with Slidell. He accordingly withdrew, and the Mexican army marched northward to expel what it regarded as a hostile invasion.

In the spring of 1846, Taylor built a small fort on the north bank of the Rio Grande and trained his guns on the village of Matamoros on the opposite shore. Responding to this unmistakable dare, a Mexican force crossed the river and surprised an American patrol on April 25, 1846, killing or wounding 15 Americans and capturing most of the rest. Taylor counterattacked and pushed the Mexicans back across the river. Slidell's failure had already persuaded Polk to ask Congress for a declaration of war, but the news of actual fighting strengthened his hand. When Taylor's dispatches reached Washington in early May, the president informed Congress that war already existed because "Mexico . . . has invaded our territory and shed American blood on American soil."

Democrats in Congress shared the president's enthusiasm and quickly proposed a bill to authorize 50,000 volunteer soldiers and $10 million to pay for them. Whigs were willing to support American troops, but they had always been less eager for geographical expansion than their opponents, and they felt that Polk had picked a fight by seizing Mexican territory. They bitterly protested when Democrats fastened a preamble to the appropriation bill declaring that "by the act of the Republic of Mexico, a state of war exists between that government and the United States." With a firm majority, unrelenting Democrats forced Whigs to vote for the preamble or go on record as opposing the rescue of embattled American troops. In the end, most Whigs surrendered to political logic. The war bill passed the House by 174 votes to 14 on May 11 and the Senate by 40 to 2 on the following day, though furious Whigs still fumed that Polk's orders to Taylor had provoked an "illegal, unrighteous, and damnable war."

The Mexican War proved widely popular with Democrats and southerners, but far less so among northern Whigs. The army received far more volunteers than it could take, and eventually enlisted 112,000 troops. Two-thirds came from the South, but others condemned the war as proslavery aggression. Abraham Lincoln, then a freshman Whig congressman from Illinois, tried to shame the administration with his Spot Resolution, which demanded the exact spot of the initial skirmish, hoping to show it was not American soil as Polk had claimed. Going further, Henry David Thoreau served a night in jail instead of drilling with his town militia, and defended the protest in what has become a classic essay, "Civil Disobedience." Other Whigs joined in the fighting to win their share of glory while still deploring its origins.

Unperturbed, Polk launched a strategy to occupy as much of Mexico as possible, and ordered attacks at the mouth of the Rio Grande (where the war had started), in New Mexico, and in California. General Taylor won quick success at the first target. Demoralized by years of Indian attacks, the local population put up little resistance when Taylor crossed the Rio Grande, the Mexican Army retreated, and Americans captured the city of Monterey in September 1846, after a five-day siege marked by furious hand-to-hand fighting.

The other two incursions were even more successful. Long accustomed to more trade and closer contact with Comanchería and St. Louis than Mexico City, the residents of Santa Fe welcomed their invaders with oaths of allegiance to the United States. In California, a group of mostly American insurgents took advantage of worsening US-Mexican relations to overthrow the province's weak administration in 1846, raise a flag featuring a California grizzly, and proclaim their own "Bear Flag Republic." An American exploring party led by Captain John C. Frémont soon reinforced them and crushed Mexican resistance, while US naval forces replaced the Bear Flag with the Stars and Stripes. The United States had secured the Pacific coast by the end of 1846.

Mexico would not capitulate despite these losses, and the hardest fighting still lay ahead. Temporarily out of power, General Santa Anna hinted that he would arrange a Mexican surrender if Americans would help him regain the presidency. Polk cooperated, but once in office, the crafty general changed course and led an army northward against Taylor. In February 1847, Taylor's smaller forces triumphed at the Battle of Buena Vista, but when Santa Anna vowed to fight on, Polk concluded that the war could not end without the capture of Mexico City.

To achieve this goal, the American commander General Winfield Scott landed at Veracruz on Mexico's Caribbean coast in March 1847, and inflicted heavy civilian casualties when he bombarded and captured the city. Fighting their way over the mountains, his troops faced heat, humidity, insects, disease, a dearth of supplies, and fierce resistance, but finally reached the capital's outskirts in August 1847. A series of desperate battles followed, climaxed by the siege and capture of the fortress of Chapultepec. Americans entered Mexico City and its "halls of the Montezumas" on September 14, 1847. Among them was Nicholas Trist, a secret peace commissioner dispatched by Polk. His instructions called for a settlement much like the one John Slidell had demanded: New Mexico, California, and a Rio Grande border, in exchange for $20 million.

Goaded by victory, some excited supporters of Manifest Destiny demanded that the United States press forward until it could annex "all Mexico." "It is an outrage, for the Mexicans to own such a country," ran a common sentiment, repeated in the letter of an Alabama volunteer. "They are too lazy to till the soil, they make no improvements in the implements or mode of culture and make but few improvements whatever in the useful or mechanic arts or in civilization." Casually adapting older notions of white superiority over Native Americans, another concluded, "The same fate will await them that happen to the Indian tribes of our own frontier. They will naturally vanish before civilization." The *Illinois State Register* was even harsher. Mexicans "are reptiles in the path of progressive democracy," it proclaimed. "They must either crawl or be crushed." Opponents replied that inferior Mexicans could not be American citizens or ruled against their will. Henry Clay led most Whigs to decline all annexations.

The war sputtered on as arguments continued, despite the capture of Mexico City. Guerillas harassed the American occupiers and General Santa Anna made a final, unsuccessful attempt to cut Scott's supply lines to the coast. Provoked by continued resistance, Polk decided that his instructions had been too generous and recalled Trist before he reached an agreement. Remarkably, Trist refused to obey and kept negotiating, convinced that the president did not understand how excessive demands would only lead to more bloodshed. Just as remarkably, Trist's defiance paid off. In February 1848, he and Mexican negotiators signed the Treaty of Guadalupe Hidalgo, giving California, New Mexico, and the Rio Grande border to the United States in exchange for $15 million and US payment of Mexico's debts to Americans. The United States also promised to respect Mexican land grants and property rights, to extend US citizenship to Mexican residents of the area, and to protect the new border from Indian raids, but later resisted the implementation of those pledges. Despite his larger ambitions and his anger at Trist, Polk decided to accept the deal as the best he could get, knowing that congressional Whigs might block a resumption of fighting. The Senate ratified the treaty a month later, officially ending the US-Mexican War.

The Poisoned Fruits of Manifest Destiny

The Mexican War brought 619,000 square miles of new territory to the United States, including virtually all of the modern states of California, Arizona, Nevada, and Utah, with large parts of Texas, Colorado, and New Mexico. It cost the lives of 13,000 Americans, 2,000 from wounds and the rest from disease. By securing Oregon as well, President Polk increased American territory by almost one-third and stretched US boundaries to the approximate contours of the contiguous 48 states of the twentieth century. Americans were not yet sure what they could do with so much unfamiliar wilderness, but they were delighted to have the prize and eager to imagine its future. They quickly, discovered, however, that some of their plans for the region were radically incompatible. The Comanches and other Plains Indians would violently resist the American takeover. More pressing in the short run, would the new lands have a place for slavery, the cherished institution of white southerners? Or should the nation declare its preference for freedom by excluding slavery from the West?

The new lands touched off a massive national debate over the expansion of slavery, even before they were firmly in hand. Ever deepening over the 1850s, the dispute would finally end in civil war. Many practically minded leaders deplored this debate, insisting that climate and terrain made plantation slavery impossible in the West, no matter what the government did, but their pleas could never quell the controversy. Western geography was so poorly understood that no one really knew what would grow there. It was also possible that western states where slavery was legal might support the South without containing many actual slaves. Most fundamentally, the struggle over slavery in the territories expressed Americans' deepest desires for the future of the republic. In this desperate clash of dreams and fears, geographical details had limited significance.

THE WILMOT PROVISO CONTROVERSY

In the years since the rise of abolitionism, antislavery sentiment had spread unevenly across the North. Few white northerners wanted immediate emancipation or racial equality, yet many admitted that slavery was unjust to blacks and gave masters too much power over other whites. Others simply tired of slaveholders' seemingly endless and arrogant demands for deference and protection. Without embracing abolitionism, they increasingly favored a policy called "free soil," which would limit slavery to the existing slave states and reserve the West for freedom. If slavery stopped growing, they reasoned, it might disappear eventually. Even if it did not, free soil and free labor would protect the West from the blighting effects of slavery.

In keeping with their reform traditions, northern Whigs were most receptive to antislavery ideas, but free-soil principles were also spreading among northern Democrats who resented southern domination of their party. Party activists remembered that southerners had barred Martin Van Buren from the presidential ticket in 1844 because he would not risk a war for Texas, a future slave state. They wondered why Polk had given up half of "their" Oregon territory, only to fight for all of Texas and then some. They also complained that Polk favored the South on tariffs, internal improvements, and patronage. The most sensitive began to suspect the existence of a conspiratorial "Slave Power," even more sinister than Nicolas Biddle's "Money Power," that could twist the government in a proslavery, pro-southern direction at every turn. In December 1845, some of these free-soil Democrats joined northern Whigs to repeal the hated gag rule against antislavery petitions, but the president ignored their underlying complaints.

As Congress approached adjournment in August 1846, the president requested a last-minute appropriation of $2 million in response to rumors that Mexico would make peace and surrender vast territories for the right price. The House was about to agree when Representative David Wilmot, a disgruntled Democrat from Pennsylvania, proposed an explosive condition. Polk could have the money, Wilmot offered, under the following condition: "*Provided*, That, as an express and fundamental condition to the acquisition of territory from the Republic of Mexico by the United States . . . neither slavery nor involuntary servitude shall ever exist in any part of said territory, except for crime, whereof the party shall first be duly convicted."

The so-called Wilmot Proviso enjoyed historical precedent, for it simply applied to the Mexican Cession the antislavery policy that Thomas Jefferson had proposed for the Old Northwest in 1784 and Congress had adopted in the Northwest Ordinance of 1787. Wilmot was no abolitionist, however, and held no sympathy for African Americans. He simply wanted to protect white settlers from black competition. As he boasted later, "I plead the cause of the rights of white freemen. I would preserve for free white labor a fair country, a rich inheritance, where the sons of toil, of my own race and own color, can live without the disgrace which association with negro slavery brings upon free labor." Regardless of its motive, the Wilmot Proviso landed in Congress like a bombshell and outraged southern representatives. It clearly implied that a slave-based society was inferior to freedom. Though southern volunteers had won the Mexican War, under the proviso their cherished way of life would be banned forever in the lands they conquered. Southerners stridently denounced Wilmot's disruptive ploy, but free soil was so popular that northern congressmen dared not vote against it. The Wilmot Proviso quickly passed the House of Representatives on a strictly sectional vote, but died in the Senate as the session expired.

Congress reassembled in December 1847. Once again, Polk requested money to end the war, and once again, his opponents countered with the Wilmot Proviso. No one had changed his mind, and the ensuing debate revealed four basic approaches to the controversy. First, northern free-soilers embraced the proviso and insisted that Congress could and should exclude slavery from all federal territories, including those surrendered by Mexico. Some boasted openly that a free West would undermine slavery in the South. "We will establish a cordon of free states that shall surround you," an Ohio congressman taunted his southern rivals, "and then we will light up the fires of liberty on every side until they melt your present chains and render all your people free."

Second, southerners denounced such predictions, but feared they might be true. If slavery were bottled up, masters could not export a growing black population. Slave prices would collapse and many whites would flee, forcing the others to abolish slavery or face a race war. Southern Democrats were especially convinced that slavery must expand or die. Always less keen for expansion and less sure of the need for it, southern Whigs still resented the proviso's moral stigma. Planting their feet, angry southerners insisted that Congress had no right to ban slaves from *any* federal territory.

Senator John C. Calhoun made their case in a series of Senate resolutions. The federal territories were the common property of all the states, he declared, and all US citizens had equal rights within them. That included the equal right to bring in their property, including slaves. Any law blocking slavery from the federal territories was therefore unconstitutional, including the Wilmot Proviso or even the Missouri Compromise.

Third, President Polk and Secretary of State James Buchanan of Pennsylvania wanted an alternative to the sectional extremes represented by Wilmot and Calhoun, and offered to extend the Missouri Compromise line to the Pacific, banning slavery north of 36°30′ and permitting it to the south. Despite their constitutional scruples against banning slavery from any territory, southerners accepted this solution but free-soilers did not. They would not tolerate any expansion of slavery, especially since the West was already free territory under Mexican law.

Senator Lewis Cass of Michigan proposed a fourth solution called "popular sovereignty." He suggested that Congress respect both northern and southern sensibilities by refusing to adopt any blanket policy on slavery in the territories. Instead, the settlers in each territory should decide the question for themselves. Like the extension of the 36°30′ line, however, popular sovereignty clashed with the constitutional argument against allowing anyone—whether Congress or the voters—to ban slavery from territory that belonged to all the states alike. Cass also failed to specify just when a territory could exercise the free-soil option. Was it during the earliest phase of territorial self-government? If so, the two sides might launch a race or even a battle to see who could settle the territory fastest. Or was it afterward, when a territory prepared to enter the Union as a state? Slavery would then remain legal to the moment of statehood, allowing slaveholders an initial foothold that later settlers might never dislodge. As attractive as it seemed on the surface, the doctrine of popular sovereignty was fraught with opportunities for bitter conflict.

THE ELECTION OF 1848

Congress finally granted Polk the money he needed to conclude the Mexican War without including the Wilmot Proviso. Free-soilers promised to keep raising the issue of slavery in the Mexican Cession, however, as attention turned to the presidential election of 1848.

James K. Polk was not a candidate because his health was failing, and he had always promised not to seek a second term. Ill and exhausted, Polk would die only months after leaving the White House.

In his place, Lewis Cass captured the Democratic nomination by equivocating about the meaning of popular sovereignty to gratify voters in both sections. The Whigs also sidestepped controversy by adopting no platform and nominating General Zachary Taylor for president. Taylor was popular in the North as a war hero with no political record, while southerners liked the pair of cotton plantations and over 100 slaves he owned in Louisiana and Mississippi.

In the North, three dissenting factions joined in the small but significant Free Soil Party. They included some New York Democrats known as "Barnburners" who still resented Van Buren's defeat in 1844, a group of "Conscience Whigs" from Massachusetts who resented the proslavery leanings of those they called "Cotton Whigs," and abolitionists from the old Liberty Party of 1844. Nominating Martin Van Buren (even though the former president had always hated party dissidents and shrugged off slavery), the Free Soil Party championed the Wilmot Proviso and foreshadowed the political alignment that would dominate the North by the end of the following decade.

Zachary Taylor triumphed in this three-way contest. With the Democrats split, northerners could support him as a Whig and a war hero, while southerners saw him as one of their own. The Free Soil Party lost everywhere, but out-polled the Democrats in New York, Massachusetts, and Vermont, a forceful reminder that proslavery stances could alienate the North and fracture its party alignments.

DEADLOCK FOLLOWS PEACE

After the election, a deeply divided Congress reassembled to confront additional complexities. The war was fully over by this time, the peace treaty ratified, and the territories had officially changed hands. Following up on their Bear Flag Revolt, Californians were demanding immediate statehood without going through the stage of territorial government. They certainly needed settled government of some kind, for they had just found gold in the riverbeds east of Sacramento. The fabled California gold rush of 1849 brought thousands of new settlers of all nationalities to California and, with them, a need for public order as they scrambled over each other searching feverishly for riches. Their arrival brought even worse calamities to the California Indians, whose population had fallen from 300,000 at the time of Spanish contact to 150,000 by the middle of the nineteenth century. In the first 30 years of American occupation, disease, starvation, enslavement, white massacres, and ruthless land seizures took the lives of all but 30,000 survivors, or only about 10 percent of the original native population.

Southerners brightened at the possibility of using slave labor in California gold mines, but most "forty-niners" recoiled at the idea of black competition and demanded admission as a free state. Southerners hated this prospect, for the admission of California without a balancing slave state would give the North a permanent advantage in the US Senate. With a majority in both houses of Congress, southerners feared, free-state forces could fasten the Wilmot Proviso on all the remaining territories and prevail in every subsequent sectional controversy. Someday, they might even pass a constitutional amendment to abolish slavery

Congress might have used the Missouri Compromise line of 36°30' to divide California into two states, one slave and one free. In principle, leading southerners now rejected the Missouri Compromise and denied the right of Congress to ban slavery from any part of the federal territory, but they might have accepted this compromise for the sake of peace. Instead, northern congressmen were unbending and refused to admit slavery to any part of the Mexican Cession.

A confusing tangle of other issues also needed attention. As before, Texas wanted its state boundary to follow the Rio Grande all the way to the Rocky Mountains, giving it half of New Mexico and extending slavery to Santa Fe. Texas bondholders wanted assurance of repayment since its old government had disappeared. With the gag rule ended, abolitionists revived the petition question and demanded abolition of slavery and the slave trade in the District of Columbia. Congress was so divided that the House took three weeks and 59 ballots to elect a Speaker. Militant southerners angrily threatened to leave the Union before accepting free soil in the Mexican Cession.

The issue of fugitive slaves roused the most divisive emotions. Slaves had always hated their enslavement and attempted to escape it. Their efforts were good examples of the way slaves themselves acted to intensify the slavery dispute and keep forcing whites to grapple with an issue they might have preferred to avoid. The US Constitution had recognized masters' rights to recapture runaways and return them to slavery, but some southerners had used this provision as a pretext for kidnapping free blacks and enslaving them. Upsetting many northerners, some had also employed professional slave catchers to go north and reclaim their human property. As support for slavery declined, northern states struck back with personal liberty laws to outlaw kidnapping and protect fugitives with jury trials, including the right to give testimony and use attorneys. Southern leaders bitterly protested that these laws violated their constitutional rights, and in 1842, the US Supreme Court agreed with them in the case of *Prigg v. Pennsylvania*. In response, many northern states passed new personal liberty laws that forbade their courts or officials from participating in the capture or return of fugitives, forcing masters to rely on federal authorities instead.

Going beyond state laws, black and white abolitionists formed the Underground Railroad, a network of sympathizers to smuggle fugitives to Canada and safety. By risking her own life and freedom by entering the South to rescue the enslaved, Harriet Tubman became the most famous of these courageous activists. Historians are unsure of the scope and effectiveness of the Underground Railroad, for propagandists on both sides had incentives to exaggerate. Supporters boasted of 50,000 escapes, for example, but the slaveholders themselves, who bitterly protested assistance to runaways, only reported about a thousand fugitives each year to US census takers. For angry and frightened owners, however, any assistance to fugitives was outrageous, and tales of the Underground Railroad assumed a symbolic importance far exceeding the number of successful escapes. Southerners bitterly protested both personal liberty laws and the Underground Railroad, steadily claiming that northerners were violating their constitutional obligations, and calling for federal remedies.

CONTENDING RESPONSES

Ducking the issue of fugitives, President Taylor offered his own solution to the territorial dispute. The South had counted Taylor as an ally, but unlike other southern politicians, Taylor the professional soldier was not afraid of the Wilmot Proviso and did not believe that the security of slavery in the South depended on expansion. Nor did he have much respect for the ground rules of the Second Party System, blundering on patronage matters and ignoring the need for party unity in his plan for the West.

In his first annual message to Congress, delivered in December 1849, Taylor proposed to neutralize the controversy over the Wilmot Proviso by organizing no territorial governments in the Mexican Cession.

California could be admitted right away with its free-state constitution and New Mexico could soon follow. If these governments banned slavery as sovereign states, he reasoned, the South could not complain that the federal government had insulted its institutions. In the rest of the cession, Mexican laws against slavery would remain in force until those areas attained statehood or the courts ruled otherwise.

Northern Whigs liked Taylor's plan because it protected free soil without the offensive language of the Wilmot Proviso. Still determined to carry slavery to at least part of the West, southerners of both parties opposed the president and angrily demanded an extension of the Missouri Compromise line of 36°30′, with freedom required to its north and slavery allowed to the south. Northern Democrats were happy that Taylor would admit more free states, but they hoped to satisfy the South by requiring territorial governments with popular sovereignty. None of these factions controlled a congressional majority, and tempers mounted as the combination of crosscutting disputes wrecked all efforts to forge one.

Early in 1850, Senator Henry Clay returned to his role as the "Great Compromiser" and proposed a modification of Taylor's plan that would give territorial governments to the unorganized parts of the cession but leave their Mexican laws against slavery in place. Like the president, Clay left some room for slavery in the West, but he tried to balance the demands of each section with a complex settlement for all related disputes, including the boundary of Texas, the slave trade in the District of Columbia, Texas bonds, and fugitive slaves. Clay also tried to link his proposals in an omnibus bill, so all sides would have to support the entire package and give up something to their enemies in order to gain their own objectives. Unfortunately for Clay, few representatives could make such concessions in 1850, and Congress fought bitterly over the whole range of issues until midsummer.

A trio of major speeches by veteran senators John C. Calhoun and Daniel Webster, joined by Senate freshman William H. Seward of New York, illustrated the problems facing compromise. Ill and dying, the 68-year-old Calhoun sat in the Senate on March 4, 1850, as a friend read his condemnation of the omnibus bill. Compromise could not save the Union or end the sectional dispute, the unyielding old nullifier insisted, until the North stopped questioning slavery, allowed it to spread west regardless of popular sovereignty, and gave the South a veto in national affairs. "California will become the test question," he insisted, since the Golden State would end the balance between freedom and slavery in the Senate. "If you admit her," he warned the

North, "your real objects are power and aggrandizement," and secession would soon be inevitable. The speech was Calhoun's last public act; tuberculosis claimed him a few weeks later.

Three days after Calhoun's threat, Daniel Webster rose in reply and summoned all his rhetorical powers to stoke the Senate's patriotism. "Mr. President," he began, "I wish to speak to-day, not as a Massachusetts man, nor as a Northern man, but as an American. . . . 'Hear me for my cause.'" He denied any hostile northern feelings and begged senators to put aside pointless quarreling, since laws allowed slavery in Texas already while climate and geography would always bar it from California and New Mexico. No one should threaten to secede over such settled questions, for "peaceable secession is an utter impossibility."

But Webster's evenhandedness collided with political reality when he tried to make peace by recognizing grievances on both sides. Though he criticized the South for defending and expanding slavery, Webster shocked his own constituents by denouncing their reluctance to surrender fugitives. He even condemned his section's abolition societies. "I do not think them useful," he blasted. "I think their operations for the last twenty years have produced nothing good or valuable." Unfortunately for Webster, the concessions in his "Seventh of March Address" did not impress the South and appalled his leading constituents. The poet John Greenleaf Whittier called him a "fallen angel," and Ralph Waldo Emerson compared him to a prostitute. With reelection now impossible, Daniel Webster soon left the Senate for a brief stint as secretary of state and, like Calhoun, died within the year.

Known as the "Great Triumvirate" for their eloquence, intelligence, and statesmanship between the War of 1812 and 1850, Clay, Calhoun, and Webster were leaders from a past age in American public life. What they all had in common was their belief that the Constitution protected slavery and their willingness (or in Calhoun's case, his demand) for bondage to survive and spread in order to bring political peace to white America.

On March 11, 1850, Senator William F. Seward stepped forth to represent the next generation, to reject the toleration of slavery, and to demonstrate that fierce assaults now won more support than calls for compromise. Seward denounced the idea that the Constitution protected slavery but then proclaimed, "There is a higher law than the constitution"—the law of God and fundamental morality. "There is no Christian nation, thus free to choose as we are, which would establish slavery," he cried. For him, slavery contradicts "the security of

natural rights, the diffusion of knowledge, and the freedom of industry . . . , subverts the principle of democracy, and converts the state
into an aristocracy or a despotism." The Founding Fathers condemned
it and would never have imposed it on the West. Seward demanded
that his colleagues do the same and admit the free state of California "without conditions, without qualifications, and without compromise." Seward's evocation of a "higher law" thrilled slavery's foes but
horrified southerners who thought their safety depended on northern
veneration for the Constitution itself.

THE COMPROMISE OF 1850

Eloquent as they were, Calhoun, Webster, and Seward changed few
minds; only an accident broke the impasse. President Taylor suddenly
fell ill, died in July, and was succeeded by Vice President Millard Fillmore. Unlike Taylor, Fillmore was a seasoned party hand who knew
how to compromise and how to win friends through patronage. Calhoun was dead, Webster had resigned, and Clay left Washington with
shattered health. Led by Stephen A. Douglas, Democrat of Illinois, a
new group of senators stepped forward to find a solution.

Realizing that the omnibus could never pass because too many
senators found one or more of its features intolerable, Douglas and his
allies broke the bill apart and found a different coalition to approve
each component. As expected, Congress admitted California as a free
state and gave New Mexico a territorial government with the option
to adopt slavery. Other parts of the Mexican Cession would eventually
get the same privilege of popular sovereignty, including the Mormon
colony around the Great Salt Lake. These measures were blows to the
South, for no one thought these territories would choose slavery. As a
result, the Far West would remain free soil, even without the Wilmot
Proviso. The admission of California without slavery gave the Senate
to the North, moreover, and its power would increase with each new
state from the region. The South's major compensation was a much
stronger Fugitive Slave Act. Congress also banned public slave auctions in the nation's capital, funded the Texas bonds, drew the western boundary of Texas in favor of New Mexico, and paid Texas for its
other land claims. The entire package of trade-offs became known as
the Compromise of 1850.

Most Americans hailed the compromise with relief and celebration.
No congressional majority had supported the whole package, and
northern congressmen who supported its pro-southern features met

derision as cowardly "doughfaces" controlled by the "Slave Power." Even so, crowds wept, cheered, and toasted the results as a final settlement that would end the bitter disputes about slavery. In South Carolina, Georgia, and Mississippi, southern rights advocates denounced the admission of California and the loss of the Mexican Cession, and summoned state representatives to Nashville to consider resistance and even secession. Much to their disgust, however, moderates captured the Nashville Convention and blocked all radical action. On the other side, abolitionists excoriated the Fugitive Slave Act and grimly vowed to resist it, but received little attention. Whig president Fillmore and Democratic senator Douglas both called the compromise a "final settlement" and fondly predicted that the slavery debate would fade away.

*

A painful panic had checked both the financial exuberance of the 1830s and the ideological struggles of the Jackson administration. By the time conditions improved, certain things seemed settled. No one would or could roll back the Market Revolution, but for the present, the federal government would do little to subsidize it. There would be no national bank, and the Independent Treasury would hold the government's money. State banks would continue to supply the nation's paper currency, while states and private investors would fund most transportation development. At the same time, the political parties formed around these issues would endure and shape the republic's affairs for the foreseeable future.

The competition between Whigs and Democrats constantly threw up new issues and controversies for public decision. The most immediate was western expansion. Should the United States annex Texas? What about Oregon? If these regions joined the Union, could a continental republic survive? Would republican institutions thrive in the Great West, which easterners mistakenly thought of as wasteland? In the 1840s, Americans took a chance in favor of Texas, Oregon, war with Mexico, and continental dimensions. The republic survived the controversies over war and expansion, but an underlying question almost broke it. Would the new territories be slave or free? Americans tried to compromise this question in the Mexican War's direct aftermath. The following decade showed how the "compromise" was illusory and unstable, and only paved the way for an even greater crisis.

CHAPTER 13

The House Dividing, 1850–1861

Charles Sumner could stand it no longer. In the spring of 1856, reports had reached Washington that "border ruffians" from Missouri had launched full-scale attacks on antislavery settlers in the Kansas Territory. Proslavery Senator David Atchison of Missouri had openly vowed to send enough gunmen "to kill every God-damned abolitionist in the Territory" and ensure a proslavery victory in the upcoming elections. As faraway violence mounted, the senior senator from Massachusetts delivered one of the most scathing speeches ever heard in the Senate, condemning what he called "the Crime against Kansas" in language that no one could forget.

At the age of 45, Charles Sumner stood six feet four inches tall, with a sturdy frame and good looks to match. He sprang from ancient Puritan stock and inherited a Puritan's confidence in his own righteousness. He rivaled his predecessor Daniel Webster in legal knowledge and rhetorical power, but unlike Webster, he was bitterly hostile to slavery and made his reputation in the Senate for his passionate attacks on the Fugitive Slave Act of 1850. When Sumner stood for recognition on the afternoon of May 19, 1856, spectators expected a blistering address, but the outcome far exceeded their expectations.

Dropping the Senate's customary decorum, Sumner ripped into southerners' claims of cultural superiority. In his view, the resort to violence had revealed them as sexual monsters who committed "the rape of a virgin territory, compelling it to the hateful embrace of slavery . . . force being openly employed in compelling Kansas to the pollution." Proslavery raiders were not polished aristocrats but "hirelings picked from the drunken spew and vomit of an uneasy civilization." And southern inferiority was no accident, he scoffed, for the "shameful imbecility of slavery" could never equal "the manifold and endless intellectual activity" that prevailed in Massachusetts.

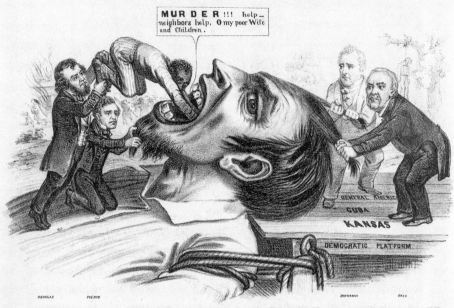

FIGURE 9. In 1856, antislavery voters thought President James Buchanan (*second from right*) and other leading Democrats were courting the South by forcing slavery into Kansas and elsewhere. Cartoon Prints, American Rare Book and Special Collections Division, Library of Congress, LC-USZ62-92043.

Sumner did not stop there. Undoubtedly remembering that southerners had already called him a "serpent," a "filthy reptile," and a "leper," he laced his critique with personal attacks and sexual innuendo. His chief target was Senator Andrew Pickens Butler of South Carolina, a popular and affable 60-year-old who had strongly defended the attackers from Missouri. "The senator from South Carolina has read many books of chivalry, and believes himself a chivalrous knight," Sumner began. "Of course he has a mistress to whom he has made his vows, and who, though ugly to others, is always lovely to him; though polluted in the sight of the world, is chaste in his sight. I mean the harlot Slavery." Going further, Sumner even mocked his opponent for "the loose expectoration of his speech," alluding to a facial condition that caused Butler to lose saliva when he spoke.

Sumner's oration created an instant sensation. Democratic adversaries immediately denounced Sumner's abusive language, but Representative Preston S. Brooks of South Carolina went further. For him,

Sumner had defiled the honor of South Carolina and his family. Butler was both out of town and too frail to act for himself, so the duty of revenge fell on Brooks, his distant cousin. As the Carolinian said later, "I should have forfeited my own self-respect, and perhaps the good opinion of my countrymen, if I had failed to resent such an injury."

A duel was out of the question, for Sumner would only have Brooks prosecuted. Besides, only gentlemen could fight duels, and by South Carolina standards, Sumner did not qualify. In his case, the code of honor demanded a flogging. Brooks was younger than Sumner but shorter, weaker, and handicapped by an injury from the Mexican War. Nevertheless, he selected a gold-headed walking stick made of "guttapercha," a kind of hardened rubber, and stalked his target.

Two days after the speech, Brooks found Sumner in the Senate chamber signing papers after adjournment. Quickly advancing, Brooks accused Sumner of insulting his state and his relative and began raining blows on the senator's head and shoulders. Knees pinned beneath his desk, the victim could not rise until, with an immense heave, he ripped the bolted furniture from the floor. It was too late. By his own account, Brooks struck Sumner at least 30 times until he shattered his cane. When onlookers finally pulled him away, the senator from Massachusetts lay sprawled across the floor, bloody and unconscious.

How could this have happened? The representatives of Massachusetts and South Carolina had once fought together for independence and the Constitution. Now, less than seven decades later, they were spilling blood in the Capitol itself while the citizens of the rival sections applauded. "Are we to be chastised as they chastise their slaves?" asked a prominent New York newspaper. The *Richmond Enquirer* replied affirmatively, pronouncing Brooks's deed "good in conception, better in execution, and best of all in consequence. The vulgar Abolitionists . . . must be lashed into submission." Farther south, tumultuous meetings showered Brooks with replacement canes, inscribed with slogans like "Use knock-down arguments." Though North and South still professed support for their common republican ideals, rival interpretations had brought them to the brink of war.

Old Parties Decline

By the time of Brooks's attack on Sumner, sectional antipathies had almost killed the Second Party System. Racial prejudice still flourished in the North, but moral distaste for enslavement had intensified. Even more, white northerners dreaded the possibility that slavery's penetration of the western territories would bar them from fresh opportunities by denying free society its room to grow. Finally, northerners resented the South's seemingly endless and arrogant demands for special treatment, and worried that a Slave Power conspiracy had gained control of the government. In this climate, northern politicians who cooperated with the South (as the Second Party System demanded) risked political destruction.

For their part, white southerners could not forget the abusive speeches of abolitionists and free-soilers and the painful sensation that the civilized world had raised its hands against them. To win elections in this hypersensitive climate, southern politicians vied with one another to see who could deliver the fiercest defense of slavery, thereby sending a steadily mounting number of sectional extremists, or "fire-eaters," to Washington. As sectional tension continued to build, northern Democratic "doughfaces" seemed to be the only candidates with a prayer of nationwide support, despite the "final settlement" promised by the Compromise of 1850.

THE FUGITIVE SLAVE ACT

Public response to the new Fugitive Slave Act illustrated how the Compromise of 1850 fed hostility instead of peace. Infuriated by northern assistance to runaways, slaveholders had demanded a stronger Fugitive Slave Act in return for the admission of California and insisted on its strict enforcement. Overturning many personal liberty laws, the new legislation required state officials and local bystanders to help recapture fugitives and imposed criminal penalties for refusing. In an open invitation to kidnapping, owners could capture and enslave an alleged fugitive with a simple oath to a commissioner, without a jury trial or proof of ownership. Under the act's crassest feature, the commissioner who returned an alleged runaway to his or her captors received a ten-dollar fee, while deciding for liberty only brought five dollars.

As soon as the new law passed, vigilant masters and professional slave catchers swooped down on free black communities in search of their legal chattels. In several well-publicized cases, they shocked public opinion by dragging peaceful and law-abiding blacks from their families and returning them to plantations they had not seen for years. In 1851, white and black vigilantes successfully fought a highly publicized battle with Boston police to seize a jailed fugitive named Shadrach and whisked him off to Canada. A similar effort spirited William and Ellen Craft to England but failed to prevent the re-enslavement of Anthony Burns in 1854, despite mass attacks on the Boston courthouse by angry crowds of black and white abolitionists. Southerners who viewed the Fugitive Slave Act as their only tangible gain from the compromise observed these struggles with fury. If northern mobs could "nullify" a federal law, where could the South find protection? Compared to the total slave population, the number of escaped slaves was never large, but those who did escape had a political importance far disproportionate to their numbers. By continually testing the strength of their chains, the runaways exposed the illusion of black docility and put human faces on the slavery controversy. Their courageous efforts thus kept public attention on the slaves' plight, tempting southern leaders into foolish extremism and undermining northern efforts to ignore the problem.

The most eloquent opponent of the Fugitive Slave Act was Harriet Beecher Stowe, daughter of the famed evangelist Lyman Beecher and wife of an antislavery minister. In 1851, after years of work among free blacks and runaways in Cincinnati, Stowe reacted to the new law with an explosive novel. First published in installments by an abolitionist newspaper, *Uncle Tom's Cabin* appeared as a book in 1852 and became a runaway best seller in the North and in Europe, but laws banning antislavery publications kept most southerners from ever seeing it. By 1860, over 3 million copies circulated in America and 3.5 million in Europe, though an unfavorable contract and permissive copyright laws denied its author any profits.

Stowe's gripping tale intertwined the pathetic story of saintly Uncle Tom, sold from his happy Kentucky home to the Louisiana plantation of the monstrous Simon Legree, with the intrepid saga of Eliza Harris, who ran across the ice-choked Ohio River to prevent the sale of her lovely child. Occasionally mawkish and sentimental, the novel nonetheless conveyed the horrors of slavery and the humanity of slaves by a dazzling array of colorful and convincing characters. Stowe did not vilify white southerners as innately immoral, but made Legree, her greatest villain, a transplanted northerner. Fundamentally, she argued that the system of slavery blinded otherwise decent people and drove even the best masters into actions with unspeakable consequences. Southern critics denounced *Uncle Tom's Cabin* as dangerous rubbish, but millions of northerners embraced the book itself and the traveling stage versions that soon crisscrossed their section.

THE ELECTION OF 1852

Despite the furor over runaways, most veteran politicians turned to the presidential election of 1852 as if the established patterns of the Second Party System would easily resume. Unable to choose among prominent leaders Lewis Cass, Stephen A. Douglas, and James Buchanan, Democrats united behind the little-known Franklin Pierce of New Hampshire. Whigs were less fortunate in their search for party unity. Their convention tried to please the South by endorsing the Compromise of 1850, including the Fugitive Slave Act. For the sake of balance, however, it abandoned the pro-compromise incumbent Millard Fillmore in favor of General Winfield Scott, the conqueror of Mexico whose antislavery leanings appealed to northern Whigs.

This outcome pleased nobody, for northern Whigs despised the platform and southerners hated the nominee, leading voters in both sections to abandon the ticket in droves. As a result, Franklin Pierce won handily in 1852, capturing all but four states. Whigs also suffered serious losses in Congress, especially in the Deep South, where local Whigs were blamed for the antislavery speeches of their northern colleagues. As southern voters moved heavily toward the Democrats after 1852, the South's influence over the Democrats grew dramatically.

Beneath the façade of normal party competition, political professionals began to realize uncomfortably that the old grounds of party rivalry had eroded. The depression of the 1840s had lifted, and the two parties could no longer win votes by blaming it on each other. The Bank of the United States had been dead for over a decade, and even diehard Whigs had no reason to revive it. Gold from California fed an economic boom that fueled the growth of banks and railroads. Heedless of old party principles, Democrats joined with Whigs in nearly every state to bring corporate charters and railroad construction to their constituents. Awash with new revenues, state governments suspended party animosities and agreed on new systems of public schools and reform institutions like penitentiaries, orphanages, and mental hospitals. As party hostility declined, moreover, many states were able to agree on constitutional reforms that replaced appointive officers with elected ones, expanded voting rights, and streamlined the granting of corporate charters. Despite their obvious benefits, each of these new policies weakened the existing parties, either by removing the grounds for their disputes or reducing the patronage power of their bosses. Making matters worse, a wave of financial scandals fed doubts about all established politicians.

As consensus grew among officeholders and cynicism spread among voters, close observers noticed that declining party differences made the parties themselves less interesting. "The real grounds of difference upon important political questions no longer correspond with party lines," complained Rutherford B. Hayes, an Ohio Whig who would gain the presidency in 1877. "The people's progress, progress of every sort, no longer depends on government." A writer in the prestigious *North American Review* agreed. "These party names of Whig and Democrat now mean nothing and point to nothing," he complained in 1853. "The contest between them, in respect to principles and measures, has virtually ceased, and the opposition is only kept alive as a means of political intrigue and an avenue for the attainment of public office." As such thinking spread, ambitious politicians began looking for new problems or threats that would mobilize voters more effectively.

THE KANSAS-NEBRASKA ACT

Senator Stephen A. Douglas, Democrat of Illinois, stood foremost among this rising political generation. Standing only five feet four inches tall, the "Little Giant" had outsized ambitions for the presidency and knew he needed southern and northern Democrats in order to realize them. As in the days of James K. Polk, support for western expansion might do the trick by appealing to Democrats of both sections and fueling differences with anti-expansionist Whigs. Douglas also wanted a railroad from Chicago to California, but no company would touch this daring project without a local government to protect its investment. Trying to combine the interests of the railroad, his party, and himself, Douglas thus proposed a territorial government for the land between the Missouri River and the Rocky Mountains. If Congress agreed, he would also propose a federal subsidy of the railroad and grants of free land to settlers along the way. With his Jacksonian upbringing, Stephen A. Douglas might have known that federal aid to a railroad should bring trouble to a Democrat, but in the atmosphere of party consensus that reigned in the 1850s, he forgot this lesson from the past.

When Congress reassembled in December 1853, Douglas introduced a measure to organize the Nebraska Territory in the remaining portion of the Louisiana Purchase lying north of 36°30'. To please the South, he included a provision for popular sovereignty over slavery, which removed the guarantee of free soil provided by the Missouri Compromise. The change was harmless, Douglas reasoned, for hostile voters and unfriendly climate would always keep slavery off the plains. He also told critics that the Compromise of 1850 had made popular sovereignty the new national policy for slavery in the territories and rendered the Missouri Compromise obsolete. Allowing the people to choose for themselves was the only sound doctrine for Democrats, he insisted, and the only way to respect both sections equally. "The great principle of self government is at stake," he assured a friendly Georgian, "and surely the people of this country are never going to decide that the principle upon which our whole republican system rests is vicious and wrong."

Southerners of both parties had long resented the antislavery features of the Missouri Compromise and joined together in favor of Douglas's bill. President Pierce supported it too, hoping that the principle of popular sovereignty would unify the Democrats and ease the passage of his other favorite measures. The bill's final version created two territories, Kansas and Nebraska, and declared the Missouri Compromise "inoperative and void." It passed in May 1854, with most southerners and half the northern Democrats voting in favor.

Defying its sponsors' calculations, the Kansas-Nebraska Act enraged large portions of the northern electorate and split the Democratic Party. Opponents charged that spineless northerners had once again submitted to a shadowy force they called the Slave Power and revoked a solemn national covenant to protect free soil. Six members of the Free Soil Party rallied opposition with a scorching manifesto, "The Appeal of the Independent Democrats in Congress to the People of the United States." Drafted by Ohio congressman Salmon P. Chase, the appeal condemned the Kansas-Nebraska Act as "a gross violation of a sacred pledge" and "a criminal betrayal of precious rights." It was "part and parcel of an atrocious plot," Chase charged, to exclude yeomen farmers from the frontier's land of shining opportunity and reduce it to a "dreary region of despotism, inhabited by masters and slaves." Pledging undying resistance to "the domination of slavery," signers of the appeal reminded readers that "the cause of human freedom is the cause of God." Voters showed their approval when 66 northern Democratic congressmen lost their seats in the 1854 elections.

Taking up the cry, mass rallies denounced the Kansas-Nebraska Act throughout the North, more convinced than ever that a Slave Power conspiracy would bar northern freemen from the West. If the Slave Power could overwhelm the territories, moreover, could it somehow capture the states as well, and fasten its hideous system throughout the country? Suddenly such thoughts no longer seemed paranoid. Once again, the liberty of white Americans seemed in danger, and thousands of angry northerners rallied to save it. At the height of the furious protest, Stephen A. Douglas admitted ruefully that he could travel from Washington to Chicago by the light of his burning effigies.

New Parties Arise

The Kansas-Nebraska Act split both parties on sectional lines, and disillusioned voters sought political alternatives. Many southern Whigs left their party for the Democrats, and southern rights supporters grew more vocal. In the Northeast, a sudden influx of immigrants troubled many Protestant voters and drew many Whigs into a movement against foreigners and Catholics. Slavery in the nearby territories bothered more midwesterners than the largely urban problem of immigration, and there the free-soil Whigs and Democrats forged antislavery alliances that soon coalesced as the Republican Party. The combined effects of these political movements would eventually put an end to the Second Party System.

IMMIGRANTS AND KNOW-NOTHINGS

From 1845 to 1851, a devastating blight destroyed Europe's potato crop, with especially harsh effects in rural Ireland, where peasants had little else to eat. As many as 1 million Irish starved to death in the resulting Great Famine, and about the same number found refuge in America. Impoverished by disaster, most of these exiles lacked the resources to farm and took whatever jobs they could find, often as laborers or domestic servants. Each wave of migrants drew friends and relatives to join them, until chain migration had brought nearly 3 million more Irish to America by the end of the nineteenth century. As many as 1.5 million German immigrants also came between 1840 and 1860. Not quite so poor as the Irish, Germans gravitated to midwestern towns and cities and looked for work in their growing industries. In the decade that followed 1845, the United States absorbed almost 3 million immigrants, or 14.5 percent of its population.

The newcomers entered a society with little recent experience of massive immigration. Many of the Germans and almost all the Irish were Roman Catholic, while most native-born Americans were Protestants with tenacious prejudices against "popery." In recent decades, the Second Great Awakening had convinced many of them that evangelical conversion was not only necessary for salvation but also essential for industry, frugality, sobriety, and worldly success. In addition, many working-class Protestants resented competition for jobs and housing, especially when a sudden recession struck in 1854 and idled thousands of Irish laborers in remote communities that were ill prepared to absorb them. As immigration mounted after 1850, complaints intensified that the foreign-born were filling up America's prisons and almshouses and that Europe must be dumping its least desirable inhabitants on US shores. Nativists also worried that foreigners and Catholics drank too much and that their clergy would demand tax support for parochial schools and control the votes of their parishioners.

Leading political parties reacted differently to immigration. Upholding economic and moral improvement, Whigs felt strong ties to evangelical Protestantism and lauded middle-class virtues that immigrants supposedly lacked such as industry, frugality, and temperance. Whig employers needed immigrant workers but often wanted to control them on and off the job, and Whig reformers worried that poverty, superstition, and alcohol blinded the immigrants to the need for self-improvement. With important exceptions like Abraham Lincoln and William Seward, many Whigs lumped together Catholics, foreigners, and unruly workers as equally undesirable. By contrast, Democrats had deep roots among religious minorities and deistic Jeffersonians, defended liberty and equality, and resisted the mixture of faith and politics. Though often steeped in racial prejudice, Democrats tolerated cultural differences among whites and made republican principles their only test of a good American. Most Irish voters had been staunch Democrats since the 1790s, and those in the latest wave were no different.

When party politicians seemed more concerned by slavery than immigration, fearful citizens turned instead to the Order of the Star-Spangled Banner, a New York secret society founded in 1849 and pledged to exclude all foreigners from public office and require 21 years for naturalized citizenship. Members answered prying questions with the bland denial "I know nothing," which led others to call them "Know-Nothings." Spreading rapidly across the North after 1853, the Know-Nothings often stunned established leaders by routing conventional candidates with massive blocs of votes delivered without warning to political unknowns. For a brief period in the mid-1850s, between

800,000 and 1.5 million American men poured into Know-Nothing lodges. They abandoned secrecy in 1855 and campaigned openly as the American Party, or Know-Nothing Party.

Know-Nothings enjoyed a brief but spectacular success. Attracting antislavery voters and disillusioned Whigs, they chose the governor of Massachusetts in 1854 and the majority of its legislature the following year, along with most of the elected officials in New England. In the same period, they closely trailed Democrats in the mid-Atlantic states and offered a home to ex-Whigs in the Upper South. Millard Fillmore, their candidate in the 1856 presidential election, won 21.2 percent of the popular vote, even though many supporters were diverted to John C. Frémont of the equally upstart Republican Party. By 1857, however, the American Party was virtually dead, replaced by the rapidly growing Republicans.

THE REPUBLICAN CHALLENGE

Coalitions of Democrats, Whigs, and Free Soilers had rallied all over the North to protest the Kansas-Nebraska Act, often using names like the People's Party or the Union Party. In July 1854, one state-level gathering in Michigan adopted a platform that called slavery a "relic of barbarism," cheered defiance of the Fugitive Slave Act, and demanded the end of slavery's expansion. Stressing slavery's threat to whites, the delegates proudly claimed the nation's Revolutionary heritage. "In view of the necessity of battling for the first principles of republican government, and against the schemes of aristocracy the most revolting and oppressive with which the earth was ever cursed," they concluded, "we will co-operate and be known as Republicans until the contest be terminated."

The new name caught on, and the Republican Party spread rapidly across the North in 1854 and 1855, absorbing other anti-Nebraska groups and often supplanting the Whigs where the Know-Nothings lacked support. From the beginning, Republicans concentrated on the North and made no effort to attract southern votes or appease southern interests. Their bedrock demand was an end to the expansion of slavery into the territories. Some Republicans also denounced the injustice of slavery for blacks, but all agreed that it gave unfair advantages to slaveholders and allowed them to deny opportunity to other whites. Cut off from the bounty of the West, party orators went on, ordinary white Americans would fall into urban poverty and class oppression, ending the promise of the republic and its free labor ideals. Republicans agreed that the federal government had no constitutional power to abolish slavery in the states, but they joyfully predicted its collapse if expansion only stopped.

Slavery and free labor had created antagonistic social structures and rival economic aspirations in each section. Many on both sides agreed that southern slavery encouraged agriculture over industry, while the northern economy fostered workshops, cities, and wage labor in addition to numerous family farms. Fearing that the freewheeling northern economy would slowly squeeze family farmers into industrial work, the South's defenders praised slavery as the protector of white men's liberties and denounced "free labor" as a euphemism for permanent "wage slavery" for white men, women, and children alike. From the opposite perspective, Free Soilers insisted that slavery oppressed ordinary white families, first because the ownership of slaves gave masters an insurmountable economic advantage, and second because the association of slavery with hard work tainted the dignity of labor. As a New York Republican described the South's common whites, "They are depressed, poor, impoverished, degraded in caste, because labor is degraded."

The elections of 1854 brought 108 anti-Nebraska candidates to Congress, many of them avowed Republicans and all of them potential recruits. Key newspapers embraced the movement, including the formerly Whig *New York Tribune* and the *New York Evening Post*, once a tower of strength for the Democrats. Regional leaders like the Whigs William H. Seward of New York, Benjamin Wade of Ohio, and Abraham Lincoln of Illinois voiced their support, joined by prominent Free Soilers and antislavery Democrats like Charles Sumner of Massachusetts, Salmon P. Chase of Ohio, and John P. Hale of New Hampshire. No party had a majority when Congress assembled in 1855, but after many ballots, the House chose Republican Nathaniel Banks of New York as its Speaker.

For most of 1854 and 1855, Republicans and Know-Nothings vied to replace the Whigs as the principal opponents of northern Democrats. Several factors finally tipped the balance to the Republicans. Many native-born Americans rejected the Know-Nothings' bigotry. Foreign-born Protestants could dislike Catholics but still reject nativism and Know-Nothings, a liability when every vote counted. Once in office, moreover, Know-Nothings could rarely satisfy their followers' demands for radical measures against "subversive" influences and seemed as ineffective as the party hacks they replaced.

Fundamentally, the slavery issue proved more powerful than nativist debates. When the American Party endorsed the Kansas-Nebraska Act in 1856, northerners bolted from its convention, dubbed themselves the "North Americans," and chose their own presidential candidate. Rushing to pick up the pieces, Republicans wooed unhappy Know-Nothings with coalition tickets, temperance legislation, and nativist platform planks, recognizing them as like-minded foes of the Democrats whose party loyalties were still fluid. After losing the 1856 elections, the American Party declined rapidly as most of its northern supporters joined the Republicans.

THE FIRE-EATERS RESPOND

The rise of the Republicans seriously frightened white southerners. Few believed that Republicans only intended to prevent the growth of slavery and would not interfere where it already existed. Even if Republicans kept their promises, however, southerners agreed that an end of slavery's expansion would indeed doom it everywhere. With the federal government in antislavery hands, moreover, who could predict the consequences? Would Republicans enforce the Fugitive Slave Act or preserve slavery in the nation's capital? Would they abolish the interstate slave trade or open the mails to abolitionists? Would previously docile slaves, unnaturally stirred by white abolitionists, rise in revolt? Even if they did not, who could dare to take the chance? As Republicans grew steadily after 1854, the task of a southern politician grew increasingly simple: promise the voters a credible plan to keep them from power.

Anxious southern voters did not form a new party but sympathized increasingly with southern rights extremists and avowed secessionists. In the Deep South, many Whigs left their party for the Democrats and gave their former rivals a near monopoly of power. In 1848, for example, Deep South voters had given Whig slaveholder Zachary Taylor almost half their presidential votes, but the Whig share dropped to 35 percent in 1852, when Winfield Scott refused to endorse the Compromise of 1850. Southern Whigs almost disappeared after 1854, when northern Whigs outraged the South by rejecting the Kansas-Nebraska Act and its repeal of the Missouri Compromise. In the Upper South, geographical divisions allowed some Whigs to survive by using the American Party label to represent upland yeomen against lowland planters, but this tactic did not work in the Deep South, where slavery was more widespread and Democrats had always been stronger. When southern Know-Nothingism could not stem the Democratic tide, the region's moderates stopped looking for a party label and simply called themselves "the Opposition." Their own strategy for thwarting the Republicans was to downplay their appeal, seek cooperation with northern conservatives, and assure the voters that quick defeat at the next election would follow any temporary Republican success.

The Democratic Party had long been popular in the South, and it grew even stronger after 1854. Southern Democrats only picked up two congressional seats that year, but the loss of 66 northern Democrats gave them much more influence in national party councils and seemed to lift a lid on sectional extremism. Prior to the Mexican War, for example, few southern office seekers openly endorsed secession, or withdrawal from the Union, but fire-eaters took a leading role in debating the future of slavery in the territories and made the idea ever more respectable.

Joined by some others in the Deep South, for example, South Carolina threatened to secede in response to the Compromise of 1850. Regional leaders defused the movement by endorsing the "Georgia Platform," a far more radical program than southerners once supported, and pledged secession if Congress took any more steps against slavery in the territories. As the Republican Party grew stronger in the North, moreover, secessionist threats from southern Democrats grew louder. Former Alabama congressman William Lowndes Yancey, for example, joined Robert Barnwell Rhett, editor of the *Charleston Mercury*, in calling explicitly for secession in 1850 and organizing Southern Rights Associations to spread their views. The movement faltered but the two leading fire-eaters spent the remainder of the 1850s agitating for a separate southern nation. By the end of the decade, Yancey was calling openly for a federal slave code and reopening the African slave trade, and accused less radical leaders of being traitors to the South, while Rhett demanded immediate secession if the Republicans elected the president in 1860.

"BLEEDING KANSAS"

Events in the new western territories favored Republican growth. Immediately after the passage of the Kansas-Nebraska Act, opponents of the new law announced a drive to populate Kansas with antislavery settlers who would vote to preserve free soil. "We will engage in competition for the virgin soil of Kansas," promised New York senator

William H. Seward, "and God give the victory to the side which is stronger in numbers as it is in right." The New England Emigrant Aid Society quickly organized to lead the effort, but proslavery forces were just as determined to stop them. "If we win we carry slavery to the Pacific Ocean," Missouri senator David Atchison predicted. "If we fail we lose Missouri Arkansas Texas and all the territories."

Most early Kansans were nonslaveholders from the border states. Their greatest desire was cheap land and a fresh start, and they probably lacked strong feelings about slavery. Distrusting their ambivalence, Senator Atchison's hard-drinking, pistol-packing "border ruffians" left nothing to chance and decided to jam the polling places. At the first territorial election, officials counted twice as many votes as the number of bona fide voters and installed an overwhelmingly proslavery legislature. Once in office, these fraudulently elected lawmakers expelled the antislavery minority and adopted a draconian slave code that made antislavery speech a felony and imposed the death penalty for aiding a fugitive slave. Mindful of his southern supporters, President Pierce ignored these widespread abuses and replaced the governor who complained about them. Despairing of official justice, the antislavery settlers then called their own convention and formed another government. By January 1856, Kansas had two competing legislatures, each claiming to be the sole legitimate government of the territory.

These events inspired Massachusetts Republican Charles Sumner to deliver his scorching condemnation of "the Crime against Kansas" in the Senate and led to his caning by Preston Brooks. Almost simultaneously, news arrived in Washington that proslavery forces had attacked the antislavery town of Lawrence, Kansas, on May 21, 1856, destroying two newspaper offices, a hotel, and the homes and stores of prominent citizens. President Pierce ignored both affairs, but the twin incidents convinced thousands of horrified northerners that proslavery forces would never respect the rights of their opponents, and only Republicans would stand up to their outrages.

Out on the plains of Kansas, a zealous abolitionist named John Brown responded to the "sack of Lawrence" with an act of violent revenge. Joined by four of his sons and one son-in-law, Brown conducted a midnight raid on May 24–25, 1856, kidnapped five proslavery inhabitants from their homes along Pottawatomie Creek, and hacked them to death with broadswords. In the polarized environment of "Bleeding Kansas," proslavery authorities could not arrest the perpetrators and antislavery authorities would not. Grimly satisfied, Brown began to tell his associates that slavery would never end without bloodshed.

REPUBLICANS REACH FOR THE PRESIDENCY

The first Republican national convention met in New York in the month following these events. In a prearranged maneuver, the Republicans nominated John C. Frémont for president while Nathaniel Banks, the nominee of the northern, or "North American," faction of the Know-Nothings, dropped out of the race in his favor. The youthful explorer who had brought California to the Union in the Mexican War, Frémont was a dashing hero who had spoken out against slavery in the territories, and he had Democratic connections through his wife, the daughter of Missouri Jacksonian Thomas Hart Benton. Party managers deftly constructed a platform with lip service to nativism and the moral critique of slavery, but reserved its strongest language for the injuries that expanding slavery inflicted on whites. Among the Democrats, President Pierce and Stephen A. Douglas bore heavy responsibility for the Kansas fiasco and each effectively blocked the other from the party's nomination. The choice went instead to James Buchanan, a colorless Pennsylvania doughface with a long record of party service dating back to Andrew Jackson's day.

The election of 1856 marked the national death of the Second Party System, though fragments persisted in some states. In the North, the contest essentially pitted Buchanan the Democrat against Frémont the Republican. Northern Whigs vanished and mostly turned Republican, along with former Democrats, Free Soilers, and North Americans who saw no other alternative to southern domination. Below the Mason-Dixon line, most Whigs professed to become Know-Nothings and renamed themselves the American Party, running Millard Fillmore against Democrat James Buchanan. The South contained few immigrants, but nativists tried to play on southern Protestants' anti-Catholicism in hopes that a common fear of Rome could keep the North and South together and away from the Democrats. For the most part, Fillmore's southern supporters were former Whigs who used the Know-Nothing perch to warn against Republicans and fire-eaters.

Old alignments between Whigs and Democrats persisted in this guise, but the Whigs/Americans were not widely competitive beyond the Upper South. Democrats argued convincingly that Fillmore could never win, so every state he carried would simply subtract from

Buchanan's total and contribute to victory for the hated "Black Republicans." If that happened, they predicted that the South would have no choice but secession, so a vote for Buchanan was both a vote for southern rights and a vote for the Union. Unable to refute this logic, the Americans carried Maryland but failed to win much more than 40 percent of the vote in any other southern state. Instead, Democrats carried all the other slave states by loudly boasting of their party's proslavery record in Kansas and warning that Frémont's victory would bring abolition, secession, and civil war.

Republicans triumphed easily in New England and the upper Midwest, but faced serious difficulties elsewhere in the North. To soothe popular prejudice, they stressed slavery's harm to whites rather than blacks, but Democrats warned that a vote for Frémont was a vote for secession and Negro equality, for "Black Republicans" were racial fanatics whose inexplicable fondness for Negroes would break up the Union. These arguments enabled Buchanan to add Pennsylvania, New Jersey, Illinois, Indiana, and California to his solid southern base and to win the election with 174 electoral votes over 114 for Frémont and 8 for Fillmore.

Beginning in 1856, the Third Party System pitted Democrats against Republicans. It would not take its final shape until after the Civil War, when most white southerners became Democrats and black men used their new rights to vote Republican. The Republicans had nevertheless ejected the Know-Nothings as the Democrats' only credible opponents in the North. They did so in part with concessions to nativism, but mostly because slavery, their defining issue, was a much more urgent question than immigration. Powerful and important debates over economic development once stifled the slavery debate, but when opponents reached a rough consensus on these questions, they no longer distinguished between the parties or distracted Americans from the insistent question of slavery.

The emergence of the Republican Party as a northern sectional bloc in 1856 terrified white southerners. With no southern wing to placate, victorious "Black Republicans" might abolish southerners' most valuable property, incite insurrection, and promote race war. Even without these fears, southern moderates found it increasingly hazardous to minimize the danger of "Black Republicans" for fear that fire-eaters would attack them for weakness.

The election of 1856 also left the Democrats as the only major political organization with strong ties to both sections. Republicans worried that southerners would use those ties to extract endless concessions from northern Democrats who would do anything for high office. At the opposite extreme, genuine secessionist fire-eaters had the same concern in reverse, worrying that northern offers of sectional coopera- tion would blind opportunists to the need for southern independence. The fears of both groups of rivals would shape events in the next four years, as the national ties of the Democratic Party eroded.

Buchanan's Frustrations

These events were already unfolding as James Buchanan took office in 1857 and confronted dilemmas that had baffled his predecessors. Could he settle the slavery dispute, satisfy all sides, and keep his party together? His personality and background ill-prepared him for this challenge, for Buchanan was a cautious man with little imagina- tion who had long depended on party loyalty and evasive language to climb the political ladder. Fond of the fine points of law, he could never understand why anyone would quarrel with the fairness or jus- tice of something that was technically legal. He longed to take slavery out of politics, but clung to dogmas like popular sovereignty that had brought on "Bleeding Kansas" and made matters worse. As he took the oath of office, however, Buchannan could hope that the Supreme Court would resolve his dilemmas by deciding the case of *Dred Scott v. Sandford*.

THE CASE OF DRED SCOTT

Dred Scott was the slave of an army surgeon who had taken him to the free state of Illinois and also to the future state of Minnesota, then a part of the Wisconsin Territory that the Missouri Compromise had declared free soil. After some years, the surgeon brought Dred and his wife, Harriet, to St. Louis in the slave state of Missouri, where the couple sued for their liberty, claiming that residence in a free state and a free territory had made them free. They filed separate suits, but the courts focused on Dred's case since one decision would cover both.

Dred Scott lost in the courts of Missouri, but when he passed by in- heritance to a man from New York, he gained a second trial in federal court because his suit now involved parties from two different states. There Scott lost again, but he appealed to the US Supreme Court in 1854. Distinguished attorneys represented both parties at two hear- ings in 1856.

The case raised a tangle of legal issues that took the court a long time to decide. First, was Dred Scott a US citizen? If not, the decision to allow him a retrial had been wrong, because citizens alone could sue in federal court. Second, was Dred Scott a slave or a free man? He was certainly free by the laws of Illinois, but did he become a slave again when he moved to Missouri? Or did residence in the Wisconsin Territory make him free? Perhaps it did, but only if Congress had the constitutional right to adopt the Missouri Compromise, which had banned slavery from the part of the Wisconsin Territory where Scott had lived.

Judging the constitutionality of the Missouri Compromise thrust the court into Democratic Party politics by forcing it to choose between two conflicting meanings of popular sovereignty. Southerners claimed that the Constitution protected bondage until a territory became a state, allowing it time to get established. By contrast, northerners assumed that Congress or a territorial legislature could protect free soil at once by excluding slavery in the early days of settlement. Which interpretation was correct? Northern and southern Democrats could both claim that popular sovereignty guarded their interests so long as this question stayed unanswered. Whatever the court decided, however, Democrats could no longer keep their party together by interpreting popular sovereignty differently in the North and South, so the last major political organization that spanned both sections might collapse. On the other hand, if North and South both accepted the court's decision, the debate over slavery in the territories might end.

The chief justice was 79-year-old Roger B. Taney, a Jackson appointee from Maryland. The four northern and five southern justices all wrote separate opinions, but Taney spoke for the majority on most issues. He first ruled that African Americans could never be US citizens, for in his words, when the Constitution was ratified, blacks were "regarded as beings of an inferior order . . . so far inferior that they had no rights which the white man was bound to respect." Not being a citizen, Dred Scott could not sue in federal court. He might be free in Illinois, but he lived in Missouri and remained a slave by its law. Living in Wisconsin had not freed him either, Taney continued, because Congress had no right to ban slavery from the territories. The Missouri Compromise was unconstitutional because slaves were property, and according to the Fifth Amendment, Congress could not deprive persons of their property without due process of law.

Republican commentators denounced the reasoning in *Dred Scott* and modern scholars agree. Taney's denial of black citizenship was particularly faulty, since blacks had rights and even citizenship in many states, and the Constitution requires that "the citizens of each state shall be entitled to all privileges and immunities of citizens in the several states." The *New York Tribune* gave the decision "just as much moral weight as would be the judgment of a majority of those congregated in any Washington bar-room." Other northern papers blasted Taney's "gross historical falsehoods," "wicked and false judgment," "atrocious doctrine," and "deliberate iniquity." Opponents fired back that "Southern opinion upon the subject of Southern slavery ... is now the supreme law of the land." Most observers forgot about the Scotts, but St. Louis friends soon quietly purchased their freedom.

The proslavery decision in *Dred Scott* seriously threatened popular sovereignty, and frightened Democrats who relied on the policy to win votes in both sections. If slavery were legal in all the territories, they reasoned, slaveholding settlers would gain early control and free-soil opponents would stand no chance. This prospect pleased southerners, but unless Democrats could offer northern voters some practical way to avoid it, they would turn en masse to the Republicans. By contrast, Republicans worried about freedom in the states. If the Fifth Amendment protected slavery in the territories, did it do the same throughout the North? Republican orator Abraham Lincoln thought it might. "A house divided against itself cannot stand," he warned, and "this government cannot endure, permanently half *slave* and half *free*." Lincoln denied the government's power to interfere with slavery where it already existed, but to keep it from overrunning the nation, Americans must vote Republican, reverse *Dred Scott*, and stop the spread of slavery to put it "in the course of ultimate extinction." Between the views of Lincoln and the southern supporters of *Dred Scott*, Democrats like Douglas had less and less room to maneuver.

BACK TO KANSAS

The *Dred Scott* decision did not affect Kansas, where proslavery forces were already in charge. In the waning days of the Pierce administration, its territorial legislature had called for a constitutional convention under the same proslavery officials who had stolen the last election. Knowing that news of more fraud would drive more northern voters to the Republicans, Buchanan appointed a new governor, Robert J. Walker of Mississippi, and told him to ensure a fair election. Disbelieving Walker's assurances, free-soilers refused to participate, so proslavery voters—only one out of five in the electorate—chose an equally proslavery convention.

Gathering in the town of Lecompton, Kansas, the convention prepared a state constitution that described slave property as "inviolable" and forbade any constitutional amendments for seven years. Determined to adopt this document, the convention refused to submit its whole text to the voters but only allowed them to choose between two clauses on slavery. One permitted slavery without restrictions, and the other retained the 200 slaves already in Kansas plus their descendants and (free-soilers charged) any other slaves who slipped in later. Critics scoffed that either clause would put slavery in Kansas indefinitely.

Republicans and many northern Democrats denounced this outcome as a farce. Genuine popular sovereignty required a free and fair choice between slavery and freedom, which the Lecompton constitution denied. Southerners demanded its approval, however, and James Buchanan knew where his political support came from. Early in 1858, he submitted the Lecompton constitution to Congress and forced Democrats to choose between their northern and southern supporters. Stephen A. Douglas professed not to care if Kansas became a slave state so long as it did so fairly, but he slammed the Lecompton constitution as a "flagrant violation of popular rights." Southerners spoke just as fiercely in favor of Lecompton. The proposed constitution was perfectly legal, they claimed, and disapproving its contents was no grounds for rejection. "If Kansas is *driven out of the Union for being a Slave State*," thundered Senator James Henry Hammond of South Carolina, "can any Slave State remain in it with honor?" Furious congressmen armed themselves, and at one point, 50 joined a brawl on the floor of the House. After months of argument, the House of Representatives finally rejected the Lecompton constitution, 120 to 112. When they got the chance, Kansas voters did the same and joined the Union as a free state in the early months of the Civil War.

THE FAILURE OF DISTRACTIONS

Like Martin Van Buren before him, James Buchanan could not unify his party or the nation without a program to combine "the planters of the South and the plain Republicans of the north." Also like Van Buren and the Jacksonians, he did not need consensus so much as a public disagreement about something more urgent than slavery, for it was rival visions of the public good that mobilized voters most effectively.

During the Second Party System, the debate over economic development had distracted Americans from slavery by offering a clear choice between rival visions of the public good. With economic questions apparently settled, however, few rivalries seemed more compelling than the contest between freedom and slavery. Buchanan's dilemma as president and party leader was to find a safe subject for political disagreement when the slavery issue entered into every other public discussion.

Buchanan's best hope for redirecting politics came with a financial collapse in 1857. The US economy had enjoyed booming prosperity for most of the 1850s, fed by bountiful shipments of California gold and the outbreak the Crimean War, which cut Europe's production and fed its demand for American products. American banks doubled in number and tripled in size, while factories and railroads grew proportionately. Industrial expansion was concentrated in the North, but banks and railroads spread into the South as well and planters reveled in high prices for cotton, land, and slaves. By 1857, however, the prices of stocks and commodities had risen too far. The sudden bankruptcy of a single large trading company sparked a wave of concern and sent depositors racing to withdraw their funds from banks. Faced with panic, banks froze credit and suspended specie payments, sending the economy into recession.

The most immediate effect of the Panic of 1857 was a wave of repentance that swept through northern cities, prompting sober businessmen to wonder aloud why they had abandoned themselves to the spirit of greed. Bells tolled and thousands turned out for midday prayer meetings at downtown churches. For the first time since the Second Great Awakening, a major religious revival brought waves of urban clerks and businessmen to conversion. Participants were possibly influenced by the nation's political troubles as well as the panic, though party leaders who tried to turn the recession to political advantage found that every argument they raised turned relentlessly back to slavery.

Jacksonian Democrats had drawn their greatest energies from attacks on banking and financial speculation, but these targets could not rally the party in 1857. The seductive prosperity of the previous decade had won Democratic votes for bank bills and railroad charters in every legislature, and campaigners could not attack the institutions their own party had founded. Recent Congresses had also cut tariffs, so Republicans blamed the recession on Democratic policies of free trade. Northern workingmen should save their jobs, they argued, by voting for Republicans and the old Whig doctrine of protectionism.

Republican demands for higher tariffs squarely collided with southern Democrats' longtime resistance. Instead of treating the issue as a simple conflict between industrial and agrarian interests, however, Republicans could now argue that submission to the Slave Power had blinded northern Democrats to the needs of their constituents. Republicans and Democrats also collided over the use of western land grants to stimulate railroad construction, finance education, and provide new farms for would-be pioneers. Such measures to revive prosperity brought almost unanimous support from northern congressmen, but died because southerners thought that cheap western land would reduce federal revenue and create pressure for high tariffs. When a bill to grant federal lands in support of public colleges finally reached Buchanan's desk, the president bowed to southern pressure and vetoed it. Instead of convincing voters that a greedy Money Power was attempting to exploit Americans by monopolizing their lands, as Andrew Jackson might have done, President Buchanan could only splutter helplessly when Republicans charged that a selfish Slave Power had denied relief to suffering whites.

Democrats had also won past victories calling for territorial expansion, and nationalist Democrats had long hoped to continue this tradition by annexing Cuba and other parts of Latin America. Before becoming president, Buchanan had served the Pierce administration as minister to Britain, and contributed to designs against Cuba by joining in 1854 with other US and European diplomats in the Belgian port of Ostend to draft a proposal for buying Cuba or seizing it from Spain. When it became public, Republicans denounced the "Ostend Manifesto" and continued to work against annexation efforts, well knowing that the greatest of all sugar colonies could only join the Union as a slave state. Undaunted, proslavery adventurers known as "filibusters" launched ambitious but unsuccessful attacks on Cuba, Nicaragua, and Yucatan, confident that a private conquest would bring quick annexation of more slave territory. Like Whigs before them, Republicans deplored such efforts as unprovoked aggression against weaker people, inspired by the lust for more plantations. Like debating the economy, politicians of the 1850s found that the issue of territorial expansion only brought more recriminations over slavery. After secession, the dream of a southern empire in the Caribbean would continue to tantalize the Confederacy.

Disunion Approaches

As the Third Party System tensely took shape, Republicans and Democrats vied for power in the North while Democrats ruled most of the South. Aside from the exceptional decade that followed the Civil War, this overall pattern survived until the 1960s. The new political structures did not bring sectional peace, however, since Republicans and southern Democrats had much to gain and nothing to lose by attacking each other. Democrats were the last major party with significant support in both regions, but each sectional faction wanted policies on slavery that the other found intolerable. Northern and southern figures vilified each other, and their arguments turned to violence when a band of abolitionists tried to start a slave revolt by attacking a federal arsenal. When Republican Abraham Lincoln won the presidential election of 1860, seven southern states felt compelled to leave the Union.

RIVAL SECTIONAL VISIONS

Americans of the late 1850s wrote and spoke increasingly as if the slavery question had remade them into separate societies, each grossly inferior to the other. These were the years when Virginian George Fitzhugh suggested that white and black workers should both be enslaved, and South Carolina senator James Henry Hammond lumped free workers with slaves as the "mud-sill of society." An Alabama newspaper took the idea further. "Free society!" its editor snorted. "We sicken at the name. What is it but a conglomeration of greasy mechanics, filthy operatives, small-fisted farmers, and moon-struck theorists? All the northern, and especially the New England states, are devoid of society fitted for well-bred gentlemen." For him, the yeoman farmers championed by Thomas Jefferson were "small farmers who do their own drudgery, and yet are hardly fit for association with a southern gentleman's body servant." The *Richmond Examiner* agreed. "We have got to hating every thing with the prefix free," it growled in 1856, "from free negroes, down and up: through the whole catalogue. Free farms, free labor, free society, free will, free thinking, free children, and free schools, all belong to the same brood of damnable *isms*."

Republicans were especially delighted when their fundamental critique of slave society appeared in the writings of a white southerner. Hinton Rowan Helper was the son of a yeoman farmer in Piedmont North Carolina who published *The Impending Crisis of the South: How to Meet It* in 1857. Helper used statistics from the 1850 census to show that the North outstripped the South in every measure of wealth and culture, and blamed slavery for the yeomanry's plight. "In the South," he wrote, "no kind of labor is either free or respectable. Every white man who is under the necessity of earning his bread by the sweat of his brow, or by manual labor . . . is treated as if he was a loathsome beast, and shunned with the utmost disdain."

Vehemently racist in his view of blacks, Helper still proclaimed that immediate abolition of slavery was the only way to avoid a violent racial cataclysm. When Republicans reprinted his volume as campaign literature in 1859, southern leaders denounced Helper furiously and threatened him with death if he ever returned to his homeland. Tempers ran so high in Congress that southerners blocked the election to the speakership of any Republican who had endorsed *The Impending Crisis*, and the House went unorganized for two months in 1859 as the parties deadlocked and representatives brought weapons to the floor of Congress once again.

THE LINCOLN-DOUGLAS DEBATES

One of the most dramatic illustrations of the centrality of the slavery question appeared in 1858, when Stephen A. Douglas sought reelection to his US Senate seat from Illinois. State legislatures chose US senators before 1913, so Douglas did not face the electorate directly. As a test of party strength, however, Illinois Democrats gave Douglas a formal nomination and Republicans selected Abraham Lincoln to oppose him. Each candidate campaigned for legislators of his own party, urging voters to vote for legislative candidates who shared their preferences for US senator.

The tall, lanky challenger was a living testimonial to the promise of free labor. Born to poverty in Kentucky, Lincoln had moved with his family to Indiana and then to Illinois. With the barest rudiments of education, he supported himself by common labor and fiercely drove himself upward, splitting rails first, then keeping store, and finally reading law. Attracted to Whig respect for self-improvement, Lincoln served several terms in the Illinois legislature and one term in Congress, where he attacked the illegality and injustice of the Mexican War. After leaving Congress, Lincoln returned to his law practice until the 1854 passage of the Kansas-Nebraska Act moved him to speak and organize for the Republican Party in Illinois. He was winning recognition as an orator when Republicans chose him to oppose the Little

Giant, but there were still few obvious signs of his potential for national greatness.

To reach the voters, Lincoln and Douglas agreed to a series of seven outdoor, face-to-face debates across rural Illinois. Oratorical contests like these were popular campaign devices, for isolated citizens hungered for entertaining spectacles, and thousands of listeners were willing to gather for lively exchanges that continued for hours in the summer sun. Political rallies could also feature musical interludes, crude humor, and free food and drink, but the center of the Lincoln-Douglas debates was the future of slavery and its effects on the liberty of white Illinoisans. Each candidate struggled to make the most convincing case possible for his party's position and succeeded in spelling out stark alternatives for the nation's racial future.

One of Lincoln's most famous thrusts occurred at the town of Freeport, when he asked Douglas how western settlers could keep a territory free soil without violating the *Dred Scott* decision. Repeating a popular Democratic position, Douglas replied that territories could keep out slaveholders by refusing to pass any laws to protect human property, such as banning aid to runaways or creating nightly patrols. Becoming known as the Freeport Doctrine, this position hurt Douglas among southerners, who concluded that his alleged tolerance for slavery was insincere. More fundamentally, the debates turned on the issue of slavery and race, and whether the oppression of black Americans was detrimental to whites, as Lincoln argued, or essential to their well-being, as Douglas claimed.

Douglas challenged Lincoln's notion that the United States could not continue "half slave and half free," for the country had flourished that way since its founding. The idea proved that Lincoln was an abolitionist, Douglas charged, and the success of his doctrines would either split the nation or free the South's slaves to roam through Illinois, voting and claiming equality with its whites. "I would not blot out the great inalienable rights of white men for all the negroes that ever existed," Douglas boasted. "Those of you who believe that the negro is your equal . . . of course will vote for Mr. Lincoln."

Douglas's race-baiting put Lincoln in a bind. The Republican candidate did abhor slavery, he was determined to check the political power of slaveholders, and he thought that racist demagoguery was a smoke screen to preserve the privileges of the Slave Power. Nevertheless, Lincoln did not yet believe in racial equality, and he knew the Illinois electorate did not either. Backed into a corner, Lincoln acknowledged his conviction that "there is a physical difference between the races which I believe will forever forbid the two races living together on terms of social and political equality." Contrary to Douglas and Chief Justice Taney, however, Lincoln insisted that black Americans did have precious rights. "In the right to eat the bread, without leave of anybody else, which his own hand earns, *he is my equal, and the equal of Judge Douglas, and the equal of every living man.*" Those who thought otherwise were enemies of liberty and defenders of aristocracy, Lincoln proclaimed, and therefore faithless to American principles of republican government. Agreeing that Lincoln spoke for their own aspirations against southern pronouncements that white and black workers were all "the very mud-sill of society," audiences supported him with banners proclaiming themselves "SMALL-FISTED FARMERS, MUD-SILLS OF SOCIETY, GREASY MECHANICS FOR A. LINCOLN."

The Lincoln-Douglas debates spellbound Illinois audiences. Widely reprinted in popular newspapers, they also attracted national attention. Without embracing racial equality or the most radical convictions of the abolitionists, Lincoln forced his listeners to consider that the endless oppression of African Americans was not only a betrayal of their dearest principles but an active injury to white society and republican government. In reply, Douglas insisted that a good society for white Americans could not exist without keeping blacks in slavery.

In the end, the debates did not change the political complexion of Illinois. Republican legislative candidates received more votes, but Democrats still kept the legislature and returned Douglas to the Senate. The national consequences were significant, however, for Douglas's support for the Freeport Doctrine showed southerners the limits of his tolerance for slavery and badly damaged his presidential prospects. Lincoln gained national stature for the first time, moreover, and won the attention of Republican kingmakers who were already thinking hard about the presidential election of 1860.

JOHN BROWN'S RAID

Unknown to the readers of Helper's *Impending Crisis*, an effort to provoke revolutionary violence was indeed at hand. John Brown had spent the years after Pottawatomie raising funds for the free-state forces in Kansas, but then decided on more. By 1858, a handful of black and white abolitionists had joined him in a secret plan to seize the federal arsenal at Harper's Ferry, Virginia (now West Virginia). Once possessed of arms and ammunition, Brown and his followers would rally slaves from the surrounding countryside in revolt. They would rid the land of slavery or die trying.

Brown found distinguished supporters, including prominent abolitionist Thomas Wentworth Higginson, Unitarian minister and Transcendentalist Theodore Parker, and advocate for the blind and deaf Dr. Samuel Gridley Howe. With their cooperation, Brown diverted money from the cause of Kansas to the purchase of guns and simple iron pikes to arm the slaves he expected to follow him. He tried to enlist Frederick Douglass, America's leading black abolitionist, but Douglass would have nothing to do with the scheme. "You will never get out alive," he warned, but Brown had moved beyond such reservations, and his plan went forward.

On the night of October 16, 1859, John Brown and 18 black and white comrades slipped across the Potomac River from Maryland and seized the federal weapons factory at Harper's Ferry. No local slaves would dare join, but white militias soon converged on the village, killing 8 of Brown's party and forcing the others to retreat to the armory's tiny brick firehouse. That evening, Colonel Robert E. Lee and Lieutenant J. E. B. Stuart arrived with a company of US Marines and captured the last survivors. John Brown's raid was over in a day and a half.

The Commonwealth of Virginia quickly tried Brown for treason and condemned him to death. White southerners initially reacted to the attack with a touch of panic, but relaxed a bit when they realized that Brown's plot had never come close to success. They recoiled in horror, however, when northerners treated him as a martyr instead of a madman. At his trial, the condemned man contrasted the simplest teachings of Christianity to "the blood of millions in this slave country" and moved northern readers to veneration. Bells, prayers, memorials, and funeral bunting marked the hour of his death, while Ralph Waldo Emerson affirmed that Brown would "make the gallows as glorious as the cross." Leading Republicans like Abraham Lincoln and William H. Seward condemned the resort to violence, but the South forgot their disavowals when investigators traced Brown's funds to prominent New Englanders. Just as "Bleeding Kansas" and the caning of Charles Sumner convinced many northerners that slavery destroyed republican values like tolerance for dissent and respect for majority rule, so the response to John Brown convinced many white southerners that their lives were not safe with Republicans in power.

THE ELECTION OF 1860

The approaching presidential election found the United States as divided in politics as it was in spirit. Republicans had successfully established themselves as the majority party in the free states. Democrats ruled the South, but as in 1856, they could not win nationally without some northern support. President Buchanan had declined to seek a second term, leaving Stephen A. Douglas as the Democratic candidate with the greatest appeal across the sectional divide. Secessionists hated Douglas as a faithless former friend, however, who betrayed them with his Freeport Doctrine and condemnation of the Lecompton constitution, and prominent proslavery Democrats like Mississippi senator Jefferson Davis grew closer to their views. Finally convinced that the Union was doomed, Davis and his friends grimly foresaw that Republican victory could inspire southern voters to demand secession, while the election of Douglas could lead to more vacillation. Davis of Mississippi accordingly introduced a series of Senate resolutions calling for a federal slave code in the territories that would frustrate the inaction of the Freeport Doctrine. He knew that Douglas and his followers could never support his proposal, but southern voters needed a test to separate their true friends from mere pretenders.

The Democratic national convention met in April 1860 at Charleston, South Carolina, a hotbed of secessionist sentiment. The convention's rules gave the North a majority of delegates, though most Democratic votes now came from the South. Led by Alabama fire-eater William Lowndes Yancey, southern delegates echoed Davis's demand for a federal slave code in the territories, but most northern delegates refused, knowing that consent would doom them back home. When Douglas supporters forced adoption of their own platform, 50 Deep South delegates walked out. The remainder struggled through 57 fruitless ballots to find a nominee, but neither Douglas nor anyone else could gather the necessary two-thirds majority. Jubilant secessionists jeered when the convention finally collapsed and agreed to try again in Baltimore six weeks later.

Even deeper divisions split the Baltimore convention. When the northern majority still refused to accept proslavery demands, most southern delegates gave up and assembled separately, where they nominated the incumbent vice president, John C. Breckinridge of Kentucky, on a platform endorsing a federal slave code. Northern Democrats could then give their own nomination to Stephen A. Douglas, but returned home furious and depressed, certain that the split in their ranks would forge a Republican victory.

The Republicans gathered in Chicago. Their frontrunner was Senator William H. Seward of New York, the distinguished ex-Whig whose endorsement of a "higher law" than the Constitution had given him a radical reputation in the lower North. Having lost these key areas in 1856, Republicans were determined not to make the same mistake. When Seward failed to win the first ballot, other candidates scrambled forward. Passing over several regional favorites, the delegates finally settled on Abraham Lincoln of Illinois. "Honest Abe" was not well-known, but he did have a genuine reputation for honesty and ability, his record was clear, his humble origins personified the promises of free labor, and he came from a crucial swing state. He was not a nativist, moreover, and immigrant votes would help him carry northern cities. The nomination was a remarkable victory for a man who had not held public office for eleven years and whom many Americans had not yet heard of. In their party platform, Republicans condemned John Brown's raid "as among the gravest of crimes," but denounced the *Dred Scott* decision as "political heresy" and denied anyone the right "to give legal existence to slavery in any territory of the United States." They also endorsed a spate of other northern preferences, including a protective tariff, a transcontinental railroad, and federal support for internal improvements. Reflecting their desire to populate the West with free, independent farmers, they also endorsed the Homestead Act to give small portions of public land to settlers.

A fourth contestant emerged from a gathering of old-line Whigs, mostly from the Upper South, who called themselves the Constitutional Union Party. Loath to join their ancient enemies in either wing of the Democrats and equally estranged from the supposed radicalism of "Black Republicans," this Whig remnant endorsed no platform but "THE CONSTITUTION OF THE COUNTRY, THE UNION OF THE STATES, AND THE ENFORCEMENT OF THE LAWS," and chose John Bell of Tennessee as its presidential nominee. In effect, Bell's candidacy gave the United States two presidential elections: Lincoln against Douglas in the North and Bell against Breckinridge in the South.

The ensuing campaign generated unusual excitement. Republicans recruited new voters into "Wide-Awake" clubs and equipped them with inexpensive uniforms for marching in vast torchlight parades. Both Democratic organizations did likewise and Constitutional Unionist demonstrators clanged bells in honor of their candidate. Republican campaigners dared not venture into the South, and Breckinridge Democrats were scarce in most parts of the North. Consistent with tradition, Lincoln did not campaign personally, but Douglas toured the country and called himself the only truly national candidate. Playing their strongest card against the Republicans, Douglas Democrats repeatedly accused Lincoln of favoring racial equality, often in the crudest terms. Some Republicans fought the Democrats with racist slogans of their own, but others held fast to a moral critique of slavery. Perfectly aware of white Republicans' shortcomings, Frederick Douglass still endorsed Lincoln and reminded black Americans that Lincoln's election "must and will be hailed as an antislavery triumph."

Southern voters were especially convinced of the Republicans' abolitionist leanings. Though the party platform disavowed any federal power over slavery in the states, southern voters heard repeatedly that Lincoln's victory would spell disaster. Republicans would repeal the Fugitive Slave Act, orators predicted, then abolish slavery in Washington, DC, ban the interstate slave trade, and appoint abolitionist postmasters to organize a southern Republican Party by stirring up the slaves and poor whites. Homes would be torched, infants slaughtered, wives and daughters raped. Rumors swept the region that plots were already afoot, that barns were afire and wells poisoned. Most whites drew a simple conclusion. As Georgia's Benjamin H. Hill put it, "This government and Black Republicanism cannot live together." Lincoln's victory would force the South to save itself by leaving the Union. For their part, Republican voters ignored such talk. They thought the southern charges were absurd and they had heard the threats before. Instead, Douglas and the Republicans tried to warn the South that northerners of both parties viewed secession as profoundly illegal, even treasonous, and would not allow it to succeed. Their efforts fell on deaf ears.

In the canvass itself, Lincoln won 54 percent of the free states' popular votes and all but three of their electoral ballots, for a total of 180 out of 303 electors. He took only 40 percent of the total popular vote, but Lincoln's majority in the Electoral College would have given him victory even if all his opponents had united against him. Breckinridge, his closest competitor, swept most of the South but gained only 70 electors, while Bell and Douglas fought over scraps among the border states. The strength of the Slave Power seemed crushed.

SECESSION WINTER, 1860–1861

As soon as the election results became clear, South Carolina summoned a secession convention. Long a hotbed of disunion, the Palmetto State had hoped for independence as early as 1850, but its movement had faltered when other states refused to join. Refusing the risks of delay this time, the South Carolina convention immediately passed a unanimous ordinance of secession on December 20, 1860, amid widespread public rejoicing. Years later, planter's wife and daughter Mary Boykin Chesnut remembered the moment vividly. "South Carolina had been so rampant for years," she reflected. "She was the torment of herself and everybody else. . . . Come what would, I wanted them to fight and stop talking."

Other Deep South states hastened to follow South Carolina's lead. Mississippi seceded on January 9, joined by Florida, Alabama, Georgia, Louisiana, and then Texas on February 1. Convention elections in these states often pitted immediate secessionists against "cooperationists" who preferred a coordinated action by the whole South to separate action by individual states. Some of the cooperationists probably hoped that delay would cool tempers until the crisis passed; others shared the convictions of the immediate secessionists and simply thought a joint movement would have greater impact. Overall, lines between secessionists and cooperationists followed existing political lines, with Breckinridge Democrats supporting immediate action and Constitutional Unionists and Douglas Democrats favoring delay.

Secessionist rhetoric revealed a variety of motives and ambitions. Demands for the right to carry slaves into the territories had long fed the southern rights movement, but withdrawal from the Union would put that goal out of reach, so the secessionists of 1860–1861 reached for deeper motives. Many repeated campaign warnings that slave uprisings and racial equality would follow the Republican victory. Others stressed that submission would degrade southern honor. By choosing Lincoln, the northern majority had declared that southern institutions were inferior to their own, and no self-respecting southerner could accept such a verdict.

With no sense of paradox, secessionists appealed to traditional republican values of liberty and equality and linked their cause to the principles of the American Revolution. "We are either *slaves in the union or freemen out of it*," one Georgian exclaimed. "Defending and protecting the rights . . . which our fathers bequeathed to us," Jefferson Davis likewise argued, southerners will "renew such sacrifices as our fathers made." For secessionists, white liberty depended on black slavery, even for white men who did not own slaves. "Our Abolition enemies . . . are pledged to prostrate the white freemen of the South down to equality with negroes," they charged. In a society without an enslaved mud-sill, moreover, poor white men would be driven to social depths where equality and self-mastery were impossible. "Freedom," one secessionist declared simply, "is not possible without slavery." If such abstractions seemed confusing, other orators made the issue plainer. After Lincoln's election, they warned, "in TEN years or less our CHILDREN will be the *slaves* of negroes," and "abolition preachers will be at hand to consummate the marriage of your daughters to black husbands." In later years, Confederate sympathizers sometimes explained secession as a defense of "states' rights." Participants would surely have agreed, only adding that it was the state's right to preserve slavery that Lincoln's election had endangered.

Initially, at least, Upper South voters resisted the secession movement. The states of Virginia, North Carolina, Tennessee, and Arkansas contained deep divisions between upland and low country districts and lower concentrations of slaves and slaveholders than those of the Deep South. Opposition to planter power and slaveholders' privileges—if not slavery itself—roiled their politics and dampened secessionist fever. Internal diversity drove sharp party rivalries there, preserved distinctions between Whig and Democrat through the late 1850s, and dampened the kind of feverish unanimity that gripped the Deep South. Accustomed to trading places with an opposition, Upper South politicians reasoned that the next election would send Republicans packing if the South would keep its head. The region also had economic ties to the North that secession would rupture. Trapped in the geographic middle, Upper South leaders well knew the passions on both sides and accurately predicted that secession would lead to a long and bloody war that could destroy slavery instead of saving it. Farther northward, the slave states of Missouri, Kentucky, Maryland, and Delaware were even more reluctant to disturb the Union.

Upper South states refused to participate, therefore, when the seven seceding states met in Montgomery, Alabama, in February 1861 to form the Confederate States of America, installing Jefferson Davis of Mississippi as its provisional president. Despite his militant posture in recent years, Davis had not been a genuine fire-eater but a "national Democrat" who had hoped to defend southern rights within the Union through control of the Democratic Party. Until shortly before his election as president of the Confederacy, Senator Davis had been in Washington, DC, exploring possible compromises with prominent Republicans. When fire-eater William Lowndes Yancey stood on the steps of the Alabama capitol and welcomed Davis by proclaiming, "The man and the hour are met," he surrendered control of "his" movement to a man who had consistently resisted it.

Even after the Confederacy's foundation, Upper South loyalists scrambled for a compromise that would keep their own states in the Union and persuade the secessionists to return. Senator John J. Crittenden of Kentucky led a congressional committee that devised a series of "unrepealable" constitutional amendments to guarantee the future of slavery and protect its indefinite expansion, either in the West's new territories or in Latin America. Abraham Lincoln would not accept such arrangements, for the Crittenden Compromise would require the Republicans to renounce their platform of nonexpansion. "We have just carried an election on principles fairly stated to the people," he reminded Republican leaders. "Now we are told in advance, the government shall be broken up, unless we surrender to those we have beaten." The Crittenden Compromise repudiated majority rule, Lincoln insisted, and thus America's republican principles. "If we surrender, it is the end of us," he warned, and efforts at compromise collapsed. Making no promises, the president-elect slipped secretly into Washington to avoid several threats against his life and prepared to take the oath of office on March 4, 1861.

*

Americans struggled without success to heal the sectional rifts exposed by western expansion. The Compromise of 1850 was an elaborate set of trade-offs that supporters praised as a "final settlement" of the slavery issue, but parts of it were deeply offensive to one section or another and few citizens could accept all of it. In 1854, Congress quit searching for an acceptable package of rewards and concessions to offer each section. In the Kansas-Nebraska Act, it tried instead to hand the problem to the western settlers themselves, a solution known as popular sovereignty. When that approach brought open warfare to Kansas, the Republican Party arose on the belief that slavery threatened free government itself. Republicans vowed to end the expansion of slavery with no compromises whatsoever, and when Republican

Abraham Lincoln won the presidency in 1860, seven states seceded from the Union.

The president-elect faced a deeply ruptured Union, for both sides had come to question their rivals' commitment to republican values. In fact, slavery burdened American culture, government, and society with intolerable contradictions, and forced the two sections to defend competing aspects of the same Revolutionary heritage. Secessionists defended self-determination for communities of white men, claimed they all benefited from slavery whether they owned human property or not, and demanded protection for their way of life. Republicans countered that slavery bestowed advantages denied to nonslaveholders and allowed masters to create an unrepublican aristocracy. If these privileges ended, all white men would gain equal opportunity to enjoy the republic's full benefits. Very shortly, war would test these rival visions.

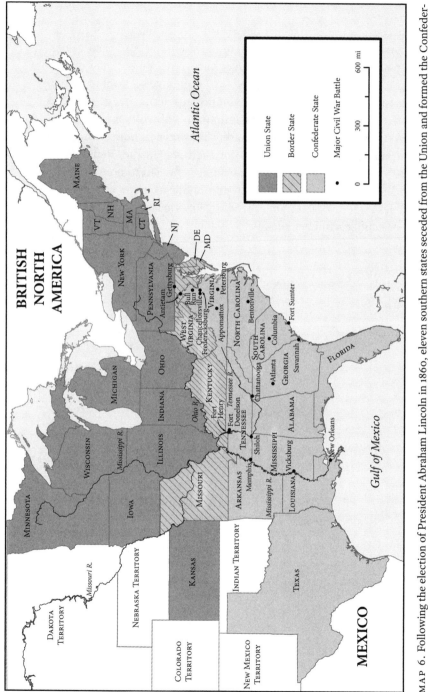

MAP 6. Following the election of President Abraham Lincoln in 1860, eleven southern states seceded from the Union and formed the Confederate States of America. Four slaveholding states remained in the Union, and West Virginia broke away from Virginia to become a new Union state. Map by Gabriel Moss.

CHAPTER 14

"A New Birth of Freedom,"
1861–1865

On January 12, 1862, nine months after the beginning of the Civil War, John Boston of Owensville, Maryland, scratched out a halting but joyful letter to his wife, Elizabeth. "This Day I can Adress you thank god as a free man," he exulted. The journey to freedom had not been easy. "I had a little truble in giting away," Boston admitted. "But as the lord led the Children of Isrel to the land of Canon So he led me to a land Whare fredom Will rain in spite of earth and hell."

John Boston's Promised Land was the 14th New York militia regiment, filled with Brooklyn abolitionists and camped near Upton Hill in northern Virginia. Many Union soldiers had no interest in freeing slaves, but John Boston and fugitives like him could discover those who did. "I am With a very nice man and have All that hart Can Wish," Boston told Elizabeth. "But My Dear I Cant express my grate desire that I Have to See you I trust the time Will Come When We shal meet again"

When the war began, Union officials had not anticipated or welcomed the initiative of men like John Boston. Everyone knew that slavery had led to war, but not all slave states had seceded, not all slaveholders were disloyal, and not all northerners wanted abolition. In fact, John Boston's owner claimed to be a unionist from the loyal slave state of Maryland. Seizing or intercepting Boston's letter, he showed it to state officials who used it to support their protests that elements in the army were violating government policy and attacking private property.

Abraham Lincoln hated slavery but declared the anti-emancipation policy himself. In his first annual message to Congress, delivered only weeks before John Boston's escape, the president called "the integrity of the Union . . . the primary object of the contest." Probably dreading the race war freely predicted by the opponents of abolition, he insisted that the conflict must not "degenerate into a violent and remorseless revolutionary struggle." Before long, however, the war's revolutionary implications seemed inescapable, due in large part to the actions of people like John Boston and his army friends.

The fugitives ran to the army because they knew instinctively that a war for the Union could not spare slavery. Regardless of official policy, moreover, Union commanders had no interest in returning these able-bodied workers to their masters, whether loyal or not, and soon the runaways were building fortifications, preparing food, driving wagons, and tending animals for the Union Army. Their work did not stop with civilian tasks. "They are acquainted with all the roads, paths fords and other natural features of the country and they make excellent guides," admitted a spokesman for General Abner Doubleday, later known (erroneously) as the inventor of baseball. "They will not therefore be exclude[d]." And finally, after much debate, some 200,000 African American men entered the US Army and Navy, where they fought directly for the freedom of themselves and their families.

Men and women like John and Elizabeth Boston redefined the Civil War. If blacks fought for the Union, how could the Union desert them? As this insight sank in, Abraham Lincoln gained legal and political justification for turning a war for the Union into a war against slavery. A year before the Emancipation Proclamation, John Boston was certain that freedom was his. Like many others in the army, he painfully remembered the wife and children he left behind, but he urged Elizabeth to be patient. "Dear you must make your Self content," he counseled. "I am free from al the Slavers Lash"

Momentous as it was, emancipation was not the only revolutionary outcome of the Civil War. Both sides needed huge armies, professionally trained and disciplined for unquestioning obedience. They needed the latest in modern weapons, produced by advanced machinery, distributed through efficient bureaucracies, and transported by smoothly coordinated systems of railroads. The armies and their weapons would cost the winners colossal sums that required a vast new system of federal loans and taxes, administered by more federal bureaucrats, and a giant system of national banks, concentrated on Wall Street. The result would be a radically new federal currency, an ever-stronger industrial economy, and an economic transformation that made the Market Revolution of Andrew Jackson's day look trifling. The mechanical, disciplined style of the Union Army would mesh with the regimented demands of a new age of industry and capital, making efficiency, sub-ordination, and centralization into cultural ideals. No aspect of American public life would ever be the same.

Launched to preserve American traditions, the Civil War pro-foundly transformed them. The end of slavery stemmed from the ac-tions of ordinary Americans like John and Elizabeth Boston as much as decisions by Abraham Lincoln and Jefferson Davis. The war they joined took as many as 750,000 lives and convinced the survivors that many of their oldest traditions had become incompatible with republi-can government. As President Lincoln would put it on the battlefield at Gettysburg, the war required "a new birth of freedom" to guaran-tee that "government of the people, by the people, and for the people, shall not perish from the earth."

"And the War Came ..."

The Union and Confederate governments both hoped to avoid war when Abraham Lincoln took office, but neither would surrender its core demands. Southern leaders swore that disunion was permanent and demanded that the remaining states accept their independence. Northerners insisted just as firmly that secession was illegal and that the South's departure would spell the end of majority rule and republi-can government. These differences exploded into open warfare when the North refused to surrender federal military bases on southern soil. The attack on Fort Sumter released years of mounting tension, as both sides rushed to prepare for what they believed would be a quick and easy victory.

LINCOLN'S INAUGURATION

As southern states responded to the election of Abraham Lincoln by seceding one by one, the federal government lay virtually paralyzed. Though elected in November, the Republican candidate would not take his oath of office until March 4, 1861. After a lifetime of compli-ance with southern demands, President James Buchanan drew the line at secession itself and declared that no state could legally leave the Union on its own, but he took no action to end the stalemate or coerce the seceding states.

In the absence of presidential leadership, congressional figures struggled with a now-familiar reflex to seek a compromise. In January, Senator John J. Crittenden of Kentucky suggested a series of unrepealable constitutional amendments to divide the United States along the Missouri Compromise line and guarantee slavery in all current or future territories to its south, but secessionists and Republicans were equally uninterested. In Virginia, senior statesmen from both sections gathered in the Peace Convention to discuss similar measures, but they too foundered on a fundamental fact: the seceding states had no interest in returning, while Republicans opposed slavery in all the territories and would not retreat from the principle that had won them the election.

Democrats and some Republicans implored Lincoln to make a public statement to quiet southern fears and stop or reverse the Union's dissolution, but the president-elect firmly refused. Biding his time in Springfield, Illinois, Lincoln repeated Republican pledges and made no further commitments. When Inauguration Day approached, he slowly traveled to Washington, with frequent stops to address the anxious crowds who gathered around his train. Before arriving, however, he donned a disguise and slipped secretly into the capital to avoid a serious assassination plot. The decision was prudent but created an impression of cowardice that sarcastic observers did not hesitate to mock.

Just as Jefferson Davis and other southern leaders had used the moment of secession to spell out their reasons for seeking independence, Lincoln used his inaugural address to make a clear, firm case for the Union. He repeated that the federal government had no powers over slavery in the states and affirmed his support for the Fugitive Slave Act. Southerners, he promised, should not fear for their lives or property under a Republican administration. He did insist, however, that the Union must not break. Like Andrew Jackson before him, Lincoln called the federal union a perpetual government, not a mere compact to be broken at will. The Declaration of Independence and the Articles of Confederation had created the Union, he said; the Constitution had only made it "more perfect," which to him meant more permanent. "Clearly the central idea of secession is the essence of anarchy," Lincoln reasoned, for if the minority would not submit to the majority, elections were pointless, democracy was meaningless, and the nation could splinter indefinitely. Without binding majority rule, in other words, "anarchy or despotism . . . is all that is left," and the American experiment in republicanism would end. In effect, Abraham Lincoln had committed himself to a literal version of Daniel Webster's famous slogan: "Liberty *and* Union, now and forever, one and inseparable!"

A bit naively, Lincoln believed that the majority of white southerners remained loyal and would soon return. Until then, he would continue to collect federal revenues and "hold, occupy, and possess the property and places belonging to the Government." He would not be the first to use force. In closing, Lincoln invoked the solemn memory of the American Revolution and urged southerners to return to the national family. "We are not enemies, but friends," he pleaded. "The mystic chords of memory, stretching from every battlefield and patriot grave to every living heart and hearthstone all over this broad land, will yet swell the chorus of the Union, when again touched, as surely they must be, by the better angels of our nature."

Even while ducking the emancipation issue, Lincoln would use his first annual message to repeat the Republicans' defense of free labor. While slavery's advocates contended that civilization required a class of degraded laborers, Lincoln denied any need for permanent social hierarchy. "Labor is prior to and independent of capital," he insisted. Though wage earners served their employers, hard work and diligence could make them property holders and employers themselves. "The prudent, penniless beginner in the world," he explained, "labors for wages awhile, saves a surplus with which to buy tools or land for himself, then labors on his own account another while, and at length hires another new beginner to help him." In other words, capital could not oppress labor because every employer was a former worker and every worker a potential employer. So long as labor was not degraded by enslavement, the "right to rise" lifted free society over every alternative based on privilege.

Lincoln thus defended the Union on the basis of democracy, or majority rule, and on the moral superiority of freedom over slavery, not only for the slaves, but for all workers and citizens. While directed against slaveholders, his arguments persisted in American culture as a rebuke of foreign inequalities and a reply to Americans who protested "wage slavery." The North's faith in its own moral, political, and economic preeminence became a lasting pillar of postwar civic life and a key theme in America's response to foreign and domestic challenges.

No matter how soothing in tone, the inaugural address carried deadly menace to Confederates. Lincoln's refusal to abandon the symbols of federal authority in the South—especially military installations—struck southern leaders as a slap in the face. As they saw it, the Confederacy must now seize these places or create expectations of eventual surrender. Studying the president's subtle promise to answer force with force, the *Richmond Dispatch* concluded grimly that "the Inaugural Address . . . inaugurates civil war. . . . The sword is drawn and the scabbard thrown away. . . . Ere long Virginia may be engaged in a life and death struggle for independence, honor, and for all that makes existence worth living."

FORT SUMTER AND THE RUSH TO WAR

State troops had occupied most federal military positions in the South soon after secession. The most important exception was Charleston's Fort Sumter, whose commander, Major Robert Anderson, had sheltered his forces by moving to the island stronghold. South Carolinians denounced his action as a clear sign that he would fight to stay in Charleston. President Buchanan sent supplies and reinforcements soon after the move, but South Carolina artillery drove the steamer away. Unable to assist, Anderson held his fire, and an anxious truce settled over the city.

Lincoln hoped that the seceding states would eventually return voluntarily, but Anderson quickly reported that he only had provisions for six more weeks. The news made a lengthy standoff impossible and presented Lincoln with three stark choices: First, he could order Anderson to surrender and accept the reality of disunion. Alternatively, he could fight for Sumter and take the blame for starting a war. But he took a third option and informed the governor of South Carolina that he would send a ship with food and water only. Others would follow with arms and reinforcements, but they would not approach if the first ship completed its mission. If shooting must come, Lincoln would force the Confederacy to begin.

Meeting in Montgomery, President Davis and his cabinet accepted the challenge. If Lincoln would not surrender, they reasoned, it was better to show resolve and take the fort. When the relief ship neared, Confederate bombardment began on the morning of April 12, 1861. Bad weather kept the armed escort at bay and Union gunners could not return fire effectively. Anderson finally surrendered when a day and a half's pounding had reduced Fort Sumter to rubble, though his men escaped all casualties. Upon hearing the news, President Lincoln proclaimed an insurrection and called for 75,000 volunteers to suppress it.

The fall of Fort Sumter and the president's call for troops electrified both sections. Years of tension gave way at last to action, and millions threw themselves into war with relief. Like Lincoln himself, the great body of northern voters believed that secession would destroy America's republican experiment. They were also heartily sick of what they saw as southern arrogance and welcomed the chance to strike back. Governors and legislatures scrambled to provide the troops that Lincoln had requested. Volunteer militia units intensified their preparations and new units sprang up daily. Spontaneous meetings cheered the flag and resolved to make every sacrifice. Journalists rejoiced as they felt that the era of degrading submission to southern insolence had ended at last. "Since the landing of the Pilgrims," a Boston editor exulted, "nothing has occurred on the American Continent equal in grandeur and sublimity to the uprising of the people during the last seven days." "At last we have a government!" cried others.

Democrats matched Republicans in patriotic fervor. Northern Democrats had long relied on southern votes and steadily pleaded for compromise, but like their hero Andrew Jackson, they always assumed that the South could settle its grievances within the Union. When Sumter fell, northern Democrats immediately denounced the rebellion and endorsed the war to crush it. Stephen A. Douglas pledged support in person, and then told a Chicago rally, "There can be no neutrals in the war, *only patriots — or traitors.*" From prominent politicians to common soldiers, northerners called the war essential for defending republican principles. Many shared the feelings of one unusually eloquent New Jersey private, who wrote to his family, "We will be held responsible before God if we don't do our part in helping to transmit this boon of civil & religious liberty down to succeeding generations."

Confederates welcomed war with equal zeal. Like Abraham Lincoln, Jefferson Davis had stressed in his inaugural address that the South was defending American rights of self-government. Confederates included slavery in those rights and firmly believed that white liberty required black bondage. Even the nonslaveholding majority could not imagine sharing freedom with nearly four million African Americans. As the guns in Charleston Harbor fell silent, therefore, white southerners also rushed forward to defend their vision of the republican experiment. Bands played, orators declaimed, crowds cheered, regiments formed, and beautiful girls presented silken banners as southerners rushed to what they too trusted would be a short and easy war.

The Second Party System still survived in the nonseceding slave states. Unionist candidates had done well there in the recent elections, and the Constitutional Union Party had won in Virginia, Kentucky, and Tennessee. After Lincoln's victory, the Upper South's "conditional unionists" predicted that Republicans would be powerless and lose the next elections, so their states should "watch and wait" until he actually attacked slavery or attempted to coerce the Confederacy. Despite this moderate advice, secession sentiment had spread through the Upper South in the early months of 1861 as the crisis fed pressure for action.

Lincoln's proclamation swept indecision away. Crowds poured into the streets of Richmond, Raleigh, and Nashville, waving the Confederate flag and madly cheering southern victory. Governors spurned the call for troops and called for secession instead. With a state convention already assembled, Virginia set the pace with a secession ordinance on April 17. Official action by North Carolina, Tennessee, and Arkansas took longer, but all acted as though they had seceded already. "The division must be made on the line of slavery," declared former unionists from North Carolina. "The South must go with the South. . . . Blood is thicker than Water."

The four remaining slave states of Delaware, Maryland, Kentucky, and Missouri teetered on the brink of secession but ultimately held back. Leaving nothing to chance, Lincoln declared martial law in Maryland to protect the national capital. Slavery was limited or declining in all the border states and Republican views gained a hearing, though volunteers joined the armies of both sides. Union sentiment was so strong in western Virginia that most Appalachian counties left the Old Dominion to form the loyal state of West Virginia. Unionism also flourished among mountain whites in North Carolina, Tennessee, and Arkansas, bringing bitter internal warfare to those regions.

Fighting Begins

The Union surpassed the Confederacy in most measures of military strength, but the South benefited from its defensive position, shorter supply lines, and abundant military talent. Geographic factors like the shape of the landscape, the South's agricultural economy, and the location of the two sides' capitals heavily affected the war's conduct and inspired the Union's early decision to seize the Mississippi and impose a naval blockade. Intangible factors like the quality of leadership also mattered enormously, as Lincoln discovered in a long struggle with his first general-in-chief, Major General George B. McClellan.

RESOURCES FOR COMBAT

The 23 northern states seemed to have overwhelming advantages as the war began, starting with 71 percent of the total US population of 31 million. Slaves made up 40 percent of the Confederate population;

they could not bear arms but their labor freed whites for uniformed service. The Union also held 86 percent of the nation's factories and 71 percent of its railroad mileage. Besides these advantages, the North also surpassed the South in food production and the number of essential work animals, and the Confederacy would eventually have much more trouble with scant food supplies than shortages of weaponry.

The South had its own advantages. Operating defensively, the Confederacy did not need to conquer the North but only to survive until it gave up. The South possessed interior supply lines that quickly carried provisions and reinforcements from one region to another. Existing technology favored defenders, moreover, for newly accurate rifles gave entrenched troops the power to stop attackers before a charge could reach them. And southern soldiers had the psychological advantage of fighting on their own soil, for their own way of life.

Southerners also benefited from plentiful military experience. Trained leadership came from southerners in the regular US forces and the graduates of state military academies. Many rural southerners were expert horsemen and marksmen already. Southern states had also kept their militias ready to counter slave revolts. Finally, military historians have traditionally credited Confederate generals Robert E. Lee, Thomas J. ("Stonewall") Jackson, and J. E. B. Stuart with remarkable military talent, while Union forces searched long and hard before discovering comparable ability in men like Ulysses S. Grant and William T. Sherman.

Lincoln's initial call for 75,000 volunteers proved woefully inadequate. Using his authority as commander in chief, Lincoln expanded the regular army and navy in early May and called for 42,000 three-year volunteers. Congress eventually gave him permission to enlist as many as 700,000 men. Confederates bragged that one southerner could whip ten Yankees easily, but leaders knew that victory would take more than empty boasting. The Confederacy had already summoned an army of 100,000 before the attack on Fort Sumter, and added 400,000 more a month later.

Both armies began with volunteers but turned to conscription when recruitment lagged. The Confederacy adopted America's first general conscription law in the spring of 1862, drafting all able-bodied white men between the ages of 18 and 35. The ages of eligibility later stretched to 17 and 50. The law exempted key occupations and allowed draftees to hire substitutes. It also offered an exemption for every holding of 20 slaves or more. Supporters argued that slaves needed white male supervision, but nonslaveholders bitterly objected that the "twenty Negro law" made the struggle for independence "a rich man's war and a poor man's fight."

The more populous North filled its armies more easily than the South. Union soldiers typically served three years, for example, but Confederates fought for the war's duration. Unlike the South, the North did not require service from all men of military age but did force state militiamen into the regular army if their states failed to meet their quota of volunteers. Draftees could also hire substitutes. In the end, the two sides drafted relatively few soldiers, for most men volunteered when faced with the stigma of conscription. Over the course of the war, a little more than half of eligible northerners served in uniform while three-fourths to four-fifths of eligible southerners did so. Though northern armies were numerically larger, the North's need to occupy captured territory and guard its supply lines kept the two sides' fighting forces almost equal.

The Union and Confederate presidents were a study in contrasts. Like Abraham Lincoln, Jefferson Davis had been born in Kentucky under modest circumstances, but his family moved south and rose into the planter class of Mississippi. A West Point graduate and combat hero of the Mexican War, Davis had represented his adopted state in the US Senate and served as secretary of war in the cabinet of Franklin Pierce. Trained as a soldier, he yearned for military command but accepted the presidency as his duty. Davis was intelligent, hardworking, and supremely conscientious, but his health was poor, he was blind in one eye, and headaches and facial pain frequently immobilized him. He was also proud, stubborn, tactless, hypersensitive to criticism, and inclined to blame others for difficulties. Davis drew increasing criticism as Confederate fortunes waned, but the unbending president had few gifts for deflecting it.

Like Davis, Lincoln was renowned for integrity and principle but owed much to his sense of humor, affability, and tactical flexibility. Surmounting serious childhood hardship, Lincoln had combined hard work, deep ambition, and folksy good humor to win distinction in Illinois politics. He worked patiently with unsuccessful generals, scheming politicians, and unending applicants for public office, straining to win over his numerous critics rather than alienate them further. He had a supreme gift for expressing complex truths in simple, inspiring language. As a political leader, Lincoln was incomparably superior to Davis.

The two presidents also faced radically different political circumstances. In the North, party competition continued between Democrats and Republicans, and Lincoln relied on his fellow Republicans for support in Congress, in the press, and across the country. The so-called War Democrats supported the struggle for the Union while the Peace Democrats were more reluctant, but both offered concrete alternatives to unpopular policies. By contrast, Confederate leaders followed the example of John C. Calhoun, renounced political parties as corrupt and unprincipled, and tried to govern by consensus alone. As in the misnamed Era of Good Feelings, however, the absence of clear policy choices from a disciplined opposition fed personal factions and complaints of favoritism. Fiercely independent, Davis's rivals clung to states' rights and plagued him with unceasing criticism.

GEOGRAPHY, STRATEGY, AND DIPLOMACY

Fundamental political and geographic factors shaped all aspects of the war. The Confederacy made a critical decision, for example, when placing its capital in Richmond, Virginia, scarcely a hundred miles from Washington. The oldest English colony in America and home to a venerated dynasty of presidents and heroes, Virginia held important symbolic status, but the move to Richmond made the Confederate government seem temptingly vulnerable to direct assault. With northern editors crying "On to Richmond!," most major battles of the war's eastern theater pitted the North's Army of the Potomac against the South's Army of Northern Virginia inside the narrow corridor that fell between the two cities, the Blue Ridge Mountains, and Chesapeake Bay. Beyond the Blue Ridge, Virginia's fertile Shenandoah Valley pointed diagonally toward the northeast, forming a refuge and breadbasket for Confederate forces and, even more, a sheltered invasion route pointed straight at the federal capital. In this theater, renowned Confederate generals like Robert E. Lee, "Stonewall" Jackson, J. E. B. Stuart, and James Longstreet played daring and dramatic games of cat-and-mouse with blundering Union adversaries until President Lincoln finally discovered in Ulysses S. Grant a military genius who could equal and finally best them. In the war's vast western theater, several Union armies sought first to capture the Mississippi River, and then struggled to control the southern interior, starting with control of Kentucky and Missouri, pushing into Tennessee, then eastward through Georgia, and finally to the Carolinas. Other Union and Confederate armies struggled to dominate the area beyond the Mississippi, with engagements as far west as New Mexico.

When the war began, General Winfield Scott, hero of the Mexican

War and general-in-chief of the US Army, proposed to take advantage of the South's agrarian economy by blockading its ports and seizing the Mississippi River. Unable to transport its plantation products or import essential weapons and industrial goods, he reasoned, the South would eventually collapse. The Union adopted both of Scott's measures, but his "Anaconda Plan" would not work quickly and left the Confederate Army and government untouched. Editors and politicians mocked Scott's plan and clamored for quicker action, though professional soldiers protested that the army was not ready to fight. A veteran politician himself, Abraham Lincoln understood the importance of public opinion. "You are green, it is true," he admitted to his commanders, "but they are green also; you are all green alike," and he urged them to attack.

Trade and diplomacy also figured in Confederate plans for early victory. Southern orators swore that Britain's factory economy depended on a steady supply of southern cotton, so Britain would certainly intervene on their behalf. "You dare not make war on cotton," South Carolina senator James Henry Hammond had sneered in 1858. "No power on earth dares make war upon it." Unfortunately for the South, however, British manufacturers held large stockpiles of raw fiber and imported more from India and Egypt. As the Union blockade tightened, the decline of the cotton trade injured southerners far more than Europeans.

Confederate leaders still worked hard for diplomatic recognition, confident that foreign intervention would end the war quickly. Britain's upper classes seemed to admire the South's aristocratic tone and disliked the North's bumptious democracy. As long as Lincoln refused to attack slavery, moreover, some British leaders saw no reason to prefer the Union. Confederate chances for international recognition probably peaked in the fall of 1861, when a Union naval commander seized Confederate diplomats John Mason and James Slidell from the British steamer *Trent*. British public anger might have led to intervention, but Lincoln released the two and apologized. After the Emancipation Proclamation made the end of slavery an official Union goal, chances for British aid crumbled, and the South faced its war for independence single-handed.

BULL RUN

As the Confederate government moved from Montgomery to Richmond, General P. G. T. Beauregard prepared to defend the capital with 20,000 men placed north of the city around a key railroad crossing named Manassas Junction. One line ran to Washington, while the other reached a second Confederate army of 12,000 men in the Shenandoah Valley commanded by General Joseph E. Johnston. General Irwin McDowell faced them with 35,000 men around Washington, while a much smaller Union force under General Robert Patterson eyed Johnston from the northern end of the valley.

At Lincoln's urging, McDowell ordered his soldiers southward on July 16, 1861. His invasion went badly from the start. Newspapers published his troop movements. Veterans traveled two and a half times faster than raw recruits. Sight-seeing ladies and congressmen followed the army with picnic baskets and binoculars to savor their anticipated triumph. Perhaps most important, General Patterson did not confine Johnston to the valley, allowing him to reinforce Beauregard by rail.

The Confederates dug in along a series of hilltops above a small stream called Bull Run, which McDowell's men crossed on the morning of July 21. Fighting raged back and forth all day across the summit. At one point, a South Carolina officer rallied his wavering troops by pointing to those of Virginia's General Thomas J. Jackson, standing firm "like a stone wall." The South Carolinian soon fell, but "Stonewall" Jackson survived as a Confederate icon and inspiration for two more years.

By late afternoon, Johnston's reinforcements began to arrive by train and McDowell had to withdraw. Most units made orderly retreats, but some panicked and collided with astonished congressmen as they blindly ran for their lives. By sundown, the Union's proud army had nearly disintegrated as frightened and dispirited soldiers stumbled back to Washington through a downpour. The First Battle of Bull Run (called First Manassas by the South) had dealt the North a costly and sobering defeat.

An ebullient Jefferson Davis urged his army to counterattack, but the task was too much for Beauregard's famished, exhausted, and disorganized soldiers. Each side had sent about 18,000 men into battle. The Confederacy suffered 2,000 casualties (that is, men captured, killed, or wounded) and the Union more than twice that, with about 600 killed on each side. These were small numbers by later standards but shocking to a nation more accustomed to nearly painless victories over weaker enemies. First Bull Run bloodied both armies but left them angry and full of fight. The path to victory would be long, tragic, and brutally violent.

MCCLELLAN IN CHARGE

The Bull Run fiasco bolstered those who claimed that the Union Army needed much more training. Lincoln gave that job and the position of general-in-chief to George B. McClellan, a brilliant West Point graduate and Mexican War veteran who had left the army to build railroads. With dashing good looks and vanity to match, the 34-year-old McClellan was a talented administrator who zealously drilled the Army of the Potomac. "Little Mac's" men loved his careful attention to their welfare, and he reciprocated so warmly that he hated to send them into battle. Like McClellan, southern generals also paused after Bull Run to regroup and train. Confident of his own military abilities, Davis chose no general-in-chief at first but designated one senior commander for each theater of the war. He clashed endlessly over personal and strategic issues with General Joseph Johnston, his chosen leader in Virginia, but left him in place for nearly a year.

While eastern armies drilled through the winter of 1861–1862, an obscure Union general struck in the west. The son of an Ohio tanner, Ulysses S. Grant had a mediocre record at West Point, an undistinguished peacetime career, a reputation for heavy drinking, and none of the dazzling social or family credentials of some of his Confederate counterparts. Named a brigadier with a congressman's help, however, Grant silenced doubts by using a fleet of gunboats to seize a pair of key forts on the Tennessee and Cumberland Rivers. The capture of Forts Henry and Donelson in February 1862 were the Union's first significant victories, and Grant exploited them by following Tennessee's major rivers to its southern border with Mississippi.

P. G. T. Beauregard parried Grant's thrust at the Battle of Shiloh on April 6–7, 1862, at a cost of 20,000 killed or wounded on each side, but failed to expel him from the southern heartland. Surveying the carnage afterward, Grant gave up hope for a short, painless war, and recalled "an open field so covered with the dead that it would have been possible to walk across the clearing, stepping on dead bodies, without a foot touching the ground." Over the following year, he slowly gained control of the Mississippi River. *"I can't spare this man,"* responded Lincoln to Grant's critics. *"He fights."*

Prodded, perhaps, by Grant's success, McClellan renewed the drive on Richmond in the spring of 1862. Leading an amphibious expedition down the Chesapeake, he landed near the Confederate capital on the peninsula between the York and James Rivers, but soon bogged down in the swamps around the Chickahominy River. Exploiting McClellan's excess caution, Confederate commanders once more used railroads to bring reinforcements from the valley and repelled the invasion in a weeklong series of clashes known as the Battles of the Seven Days. McClellan lingered on the peninsula a while longer but finally sailed his defeated army back to Washington.

Much of the credit for McClellan's humiliation belonged to General Robert E. Lee. A former unionist from a famous planter family, Lee too had distinguished himself at West Point and in Mexico. Declining Lincoln's invitation to command Union forces, Lee followed his state into the Confederacy after Fort Sumter. His gray beard and calm bearing cloaked a fierce appetite for attack, sometimes regardless of the consequences. With his trusted subordinates Stonewall Jackson and James Longstreet, Robert E. Lee would frustrate the Union for most of the next three years.

On August 29-30, 1862, Jackson stopped another move toward Richmond at the Second Battle of Bull Run. Lee followed up by striking western Maryland, where he hoped to feed his troops, pull Maryland out of the Union, influence the North's elections, and perhaps win foreign recognition. McClellan confronted him at Antietam Creek near Sharpsburg on September 17 and drove him back across the Potomac in one of the war's fiercest battles. Hours of ferocious charges and countercharges around sites known simply as "the Cornfield," "the Dunker Church," and "Bloody Lane" took 12,000 Union and 10,000 Confederate casualties. The Battle of Antietam (called Sharpsburg by the South) marked the bloodiest single day in American military history, with more killed or wounded than the War of 1812, the Mexican War, and the Spanish-American War combined, and more than four times as many as on D-Day in World War II. Despite this staggering sacrifice, or perhaps because of it, McClellan once more hesitated to pursue his advantage. Finally losing patience with his lagging general, Lincoln relieved him and renewed his long, dispiriting quest for a victor. As he searched, the sheer magnitude of the Civil War gradually engulfed the whole country and forced drastic changes on the Union and Confederacy alike.

The War on Slavery

Fearing the results of abolition, many white northerners resisted moves against slavery, but runaway slaves undermined them by escaping to Union lines, serving the Union Army, and eventually joining it. Commanders first decided they were useful enemy property. Building on that logic, Lincoln eventually concluded that slavery benefited the South too much to be protected and that his wartime authority included powers over property he would never use otherwise. The Emancipation Proclamation transformed the purposes of the war and made the end of slavery a crucial part of saving the Union.

UNION DISSENT

Lincoln faced opposing challenges as the war intensified. One group of critics became known as Radical Republicans and demanded more forceful attacks on the South. Led by Senator Benjamin Wade of Ohio, they formed the Joint Committee on the Conduct of the War in late 1861, and began to ask if McClellan's reluctance to attack stemmed from the Democratic general's secret southern sympathies. Fed by such suspicions, Radical Republicans steadily prodded Lincoln for aggressive military action and sterner measures against slavery.

From the opposite direction, the need to appease the border states discouraged antislavery measures. In Congress, War Democrats supported the Union but not emancipation or conscription. Peace Democrats denounced the war itself. Stigmatized as "Copperheads" by Republicans, northern opponents of the war appeared among immigrant workers in eastern cities and in regions of the lower Midwest that were largely settled by white southerners. When he could, Lincoln tried to soothe his critics by calling the war a conservative battle for the Union. When that failed, he cited his constitutional powers during wartime, suspended the writ of habeas corpus, and imprisoned Copperheads and southern sympathizers without trial when he feared they could help the Confederacy. In the most notorious case, Democratic congressman Clement Vallandigham ran for governor of Ohio from his jail cell after he condemned "a war for the freedom of the blacks and the enslavement of the whites." Dismissing sticklers for civil liberties, Lincoln asked, "Must a government of necessity be too *strong* for the liberties of its own people, or too *weak* to maintain its own existence?"

Political dissent could lead to irregular fighting beyond the paths of marching armies. Violence broke out in Missouri as early as May 1861, as both sides in a divided populace battled to rule the state. When Union troops shot 28 pro-southern rioters in St. Louis, southern sympathizers began to "bushwhack," or ambush, their rural counterparts.

As terrified victims fled to neighboring Kansas, armed Kansans known as "jayhawkers" surged into Missouri to defend their fellow unionists and exact revenge for proslavery attacks in the recent era of "Bleeding Kansas." Control of the strategic juncture of the Ohio and Mississippi Rivers hung in the balance as irregular fighters traded midnight raids, murders, and robberies. Some marauders abandoned all military or political objectives for simple plunder. One such band of pro-Confederate raiders in Missouri gave rise to Jesse James's legendary outlaw gang at war's end. Union forces finally gained the upper hand, but not before southern sympathizers in both Missouri and Kentucky formed alternate governments that claimed to join the Confederacy.

Serious violence also erupted in New York City between July 13 and 17, 1863, as the recently passed conscription act went into effect. With Irish roots and strong Democratic sympathies, the city's white poor seethed when Republicans prepared to draft their youth to fight slavery, especially when wealthy men could buy an exemption for $300. When officials began to draw names, workers struck to halt conscription and punish its advocates. Draft offices, African American homes and businesses, Republican newspaper offices, Protestant churches, and the New York Colored Orphans Asylum all went up in flames. Mobs beat and lynched blacks and attacked abolitionists, Republicans, and those they suspected of buying exemptions. Violence raged for four days until battle-tested regiments rushed from the recent Union victory at Gettysburg to reclaim the nation's largest city. Total casualties amounted to 119 killed and 300 wounded, putting the New York draft riots among the worst incidents of civil unrest in US history.

THE CONTRABANDS MOVE

Despite such opposition, African Americans had always seen the Civil War as an opportunity for freedom. Frederick Douglass voiced their hopes as early as the summer of 1861. "Freedom to the slave should now be proclaimed from the Capitol," he wrote. *"The simple way . . . to put an end to the savage and desolating war now waged by the slaveholders, is to strike down slavery itself, the primal cause of that war."* White abolitionists heartily agreed. Even if the North did not realize it, William Lloyd Garrison insisted, "this is fundamentally a struggle between all the elements of freedom on the one hand, and all the elements of despotism on the other." Reversing his previous denunciation of the Constitution as a "covenant with death and an agreement with hell," Garrison proclaimed, "I am now with the Government, to enable it to constitutionally stop the further ravages of death, and to extinguish the flames of hell forever."

As early as May 1861, General Benjamin Butler of Fortress Monroe, Virginia, found legal grounds to protect fugitives like John Boston. While not technically free, he decided, they were "contraband of war," or useful enemy property he could confiscate. Butler paid the "contrabands" for their labor, and Congress soon endorsed his policy with the First Confiscation Act, permitting the seizure of all property used for rebellion, including slaves. Word spread, and thousands of men, women, and children fled to the Union Army wherever it went. As their numbers climbed, the Union gained valuable helpers while Confederates lost them, and border state masters raged helplessly as the cultural and psychological underpinnings of enslavement disintegrated. Building on that development, some Union commanders pushed beyond the contraband formula. As early as August 1861, General John C. Frémont proclaimed freedom to the slaves of Missouri's rebels, and in May 1862, General David Hunter did the same for slaves in Georgia, Florida, and South Carolina. Lincoln overruled both generals and reserved that decision for himself.

Though blacks had served in every American war, law and custom opposed their use as soldiers. The surge of contrabands coincided with mounting Union casualties, however, and soon led whites to call for black enlistments. "Let the slaves and [free] colored people be called into service," Frederick Douglass had proposed early on, "and formed into a liberating army to march into the South and raise the banner of Emancipation among the slaves." Other advocates were less high-minded and crudely preferred blacks over whites as cannon fodder. Without waiting for explicit federal permission, black regiments formed in individual states such as Kansas, Massachusetts, and occupied Louisiana in the fall of 1862, as pressure mounted for unlimited black enlistment and moves against slavery itself.

PROCLAIMING EMANCIPATION

Lincoln's initial reluctance to emancipate had stemmed from his respect for the Constitution and his fear of alienating the border states. He also thought slavery would disappear peacefully and legally if it could not expand and the Union endured. In the first half of 1862, however, the contrabands' service to the Union Army and white calls for black enlistment convinced him that law and public opinion would support a sweeping blow against slavery on military grounds. Armies had a well-known right to the enemy's fighting resources, so a wartime commander in chief held far more power over slavery than Congress or a peacetime president. In the spring and summer of 1862, Congress signaled its sympathy for emancipation by authorizing payments to loyal masters in the District of Columbia who freed their slaves voluntarily, and by the Second Confiscation Act, which freed the slaves of all those found to be "traitors."

Lincoln discussed his decision with the cabinet in mid-1862 but delayed his announcement until a convincing Union victory gave him a position of strength. In the meantime, he released an enigmatic letter to Horace Greeley, Republican editor of the *New York Tribune*. "If I could save the Union without freeing *any* slave I would do it," he insisted, "and if I could save it by freeing *all* the slaves I would do it; and if I could save it by freeing some and leaving others alone I would also do that. What I do about slavery, and the colored race, I do because it helps to save the Union; and what I forbear, I forbear because I do *not* believe it would help to save the Union." The letter appeared indifferent to black freedom, but Lincoln had already chosen his course and prepared the way by presenting liberty as a path to victory.

Antietam gave Lincoln the backdrop he wanted. Five days after the battle, he issued the Preliminary Emancipation Proclamation that promised freedom to the slaves in all parts of the South that were still rebelling on January 1, 1863. In effect, he offered the Confederacy a bargain: lay down your arms and save slavery, or keep fighting and lose it. At the same time, Lincoln endorsed black enlistment in the armed forces. Shortly afterward, he offered to pay the border states for releasing their slaves and colonizing them in South America. Confederate and border state leaders refused both bargains, so Lincoln signed the Emancipation Proclamation on the following New Year's Day.

Then and later, Lincoln's critics assailed the proclamation as too little, too late, too empty. It made no moral case for freedom and reduced emancipation to mere confiscation. It spared large parts of Louisiana, Tennessee, and eastern Virginia by only applying to unoccupied territory. Lincoln "has proclaimed emancipation only where he has notoriously no power to execute it," scoffed the *New York World*. "The exemption . . . renders the proclamation not merely futile but ridiculous." The editor scored a point but missed deeper truth. The

Emancipation Proclamation transformed the moral dynamics of the war and the Union itself by launching a crusade for freedom. In its aftermath, every Union advance broke more chains and dealt another blow to the war's essential cause. By permitting black enlistment, moreover, it opened the armed forces to almost 200,000 black recruits who proved their worth to doubters and laid a claim to broader rights thereafter. Recognizing the proclamation's shortcomings, Congress adopted the Thirteenth Amendment to the Constitution in 1865, banning slavery everywhere in the United States, and sent it to the states for ratification.

In the proclamation's wake, recruits streamed into all-black regiments led by white officers. One of the most outstanding was the 54th Massachusetts Volunteers, led by white abolitionist and Boston blueblood Colonel Robert Gould Shaw. In July 1863, the 54th Massachusetts led the assault on Charleston's heavily defended Fort Wagner, and held its outer walls for about an hour before Shaw and half his men had died. Their sacrifice proved beyond question that black men could fight courageously and effectively.

African American soldiers still faced hostility in uniform. Black soldiers earned less than whites at first, could not become officers, and often toiled in subordinate roles. Confederates might re-enslave or execute them if captured, and their officers faced trial for inciting insurrection. When the Confederacy refused to treat captured black soldiers as prisoners of war, and sold them into slavery or even executed them as rebellious slaves, the North halted prisoner exchanges and a huge prison population was generated on both sides. The South's inability to feed and shelter its captives brought mass starvation and disease, especially at the notorious stockade in Andersonville, Georgia. After the war, Andersonville commander Captain Henry Wirz was the only ex-Confederate tried and hanged for war crimes by the victorious Union.

The Home Fires Burning

The Civil War had a massive impact on both home fronts. It did not transform the northern economy by itself, but mobilization fed changes that had started already. Freed from the objections of states' rights purists, Republicans enacted key policies from the old Whig Party. From a less developed starting point, the Confederacy forged new industries and a powerful central government while struggling with deprivation and painful social change. War exposed the fissures in slaveholding society and sparked explosive protests.

THE ECONOMY OF VICTORY

Federal revenue totaled $41 million in 1861, but the North eventually spent that much on the war every ten days. It began the fight with a Jacksonian financial system, no national bank, no standardized currency, and almost no income but land sales and customs duties. The government paid its own debts in gold and silver, but citizens relied on paper currency from 1,600 state banks of wildly differing dependability.

Secretary of the Treasury Salmon P. Chase set to work by selling bonds to large and small investors alike. When this was not enough, the government imposed a land tax, higher excise taxes, and America's first income tax. With lasting repercussions, Congress authorized $450 million in unsupported greenbacks, or paper money, and made them legal tender, or acceptable for all debts. Leaving gold and silver was a radical departure from Jacksonian traditions, justified only by wartime emergency.

Chase next proposed a national banking system to establish a uniform currency, market government bonds, and secure public debt. Avoiding the monopoly features of the old Bank of the United States, the National Bank Acts of 1863 and 1864 offered a national charter, with authority to issue federal notes and receive federal deposits, to any bank that invested a third of its assets in government securities and accepted regulation of its capital reserves. Going further, the Bank Act of 1865 ended a major source of economic instability by imposing a 10 percent tax on state banknotes that effectively stopped the use of private paper money. Wall Street objected at first, but eventually embraced the more secure and uniform currency of the national banks.

Republicans adopted many old Whig policies when states' rights Democrats seceded. "Government need not be and should not be an institution of purely negative, repressive usefulness and value," Horace Greeley exulted, "but . . . it should exert a beneficent, paternal, fostering influence upon the Industry and Prosperity of the People." In 1861, the Morrill Tariff Act raised import duties and made tariff protection a banner Republican policy until far into the twentieth century. The following year, Congress revived the idea of using public lands for internal improvements by promising generous loans and land grants to the Central Pacific and Union Pacific Railroads to finance their transcontinental railroad. Stephen A. Douglas had introduced his Kansas-Nebraska Act in part to support this project, but sectional tension unleashed by the law made route selection impossible. Under the new plan, the Union Pacific built westward from Omaha as the Central Pacific built eastward from Sacramento on a course that gave them the right-of-way and every other section of public land along its entire extent. The two lines joined in 1867 and opened the West to a dramatic new era of development. Other railroads quickly demanded equivalent favors, and Congress eventually gave them 94 million acres in the next decade. Later critics condemned these subsidies as massive giveaways to private interests, but Civil War Republicans thought them essential to national progress.

Senator Justin Morrill, Republican of Vermont, not only gave his name to the new tariff law but also sponsored the 1862 Morrill College Land Grant Act, which gave western lands to support state colleges of agriculture and engineering. That same year, the Homestead Act offered 160 acres of free public land to every pioneer who would occupy and till it, though many plots were too dry, remote, or infertile for effective cultivation. By 1900, some 600,000 homesteaders had received the government's bounty.

In the short run, war's death and destruction slowed the growth of the North's economy. Even so, government expenditures stimulated sizable growth in specific industries like railroads, iron, and steel, and laid a foundation for more growth later. Responding to military needs, the largest railroad companies coordinated their operations, standardized their tracks, and replaced iron rails with more durable steel. The results brought dividends to stockholders that exceeded $100 million in the last three years of the war. Military contracts for iron, steel, food, clothing, shoes, and oil enriched manufacturers and launched the careers of future industrial giants like Andrew Carnegie and John D. Rockefeller.

Some northern factories had hundreds of employees, but small workshops with no more than a dozen hands produced most manufactures. Few of these workers belonged to labor unions, despite the strenuous efforts of a handful of organizers, and their dreams of personal advancement proved elusive. Despite prevailing praise for free labor, the *New York Times* likened wage earners to slaves, and observed that "the capitalists or masters are becoming fewer and stronger and richer . . . [and] the laborers or slaves are becoming more numerous or weaker and poorer." Squeezed by wartime inflation and the loom- ing military draft, some skilled workers struck successfully for higher wages. Others, like the 30,000 seamstresses of New York City, could toil as long as 14 hours a day for no more than $1.00 to $3.00 a week. Despite these hardships, plentiful job opportunities kept immigration high throughout the war. Despite the antiwar sentiment of some im- migrants, moreover, many newcomers joined all-Irish or all-German regiments to fight bravely in the Union cause.

Beyond cities and factories, northerners of every rank and condi- tion threw themselves into the war effort. Women everywhere took up the challenge of knitting and sewing for the troops, and struggled to manage farms and businesses in the absence of soldier husbands. Others stepped forward as military nurses, expanding the sphere of domesticity to the tending of the sick and dying. One of these was Clara Barton, a former teacher and government clerk who began to serve the wounded by collecting medical supplies, went on the operate field hospitals, and later founded the American Red Cross. The North's greater population allowed many farmers to remain in their fields to produce bumper crops of corn, wheat, and hogs to feed the army. The growing use of farm machinery like the new McCormick reaper in- creased their productivity.

THE CONFEDERATE HOME FRONT

Despite its fund of military experience, total war stressed the Confed- eracy far more than the Union. The South lacked weapons factories, and its railroads were both shorter and less interconnected than the North's. The Union's sophisticated financial system, already centered on New York's Wall Street, boasted twelve times the capital of south- ern banks. Perhaps most seriously, the South's public culture of states' rights and flamboyant individualism undercut moves toward stricter discipline and uniform effort. The Confederacy made impressive prog- ress in mobilization but its efforts finally fell short, so the war that stimulated the northern economy would leave the South in poverty and ruin.

Confederate state and national governments bought as many as 600,000 weapons in Europe before the Union perfected its blockade. Under the leadership of Brigadier General Josiah Gorgas, the Ord- nance Bureau created numerous government-owned factories and armories to make rifles, gunpowder, cannons, and other weapons.

As a result, Confederate soldiers never lacked sufficient arms, though food, clothing, blankets, shoes, and tents might be scarce or nonexistent. "When I say that they were hungry," a Virginia woman remembered about Lee's passing troops, "I convey no impression of the gaunt starvation that looked from their cavernous eyes. All day long they crowded to the doors of our houses, always with the same drawling complaint: 'I've been a-marchin' and a-fightin' for six weeks stiddy, and I ain't had n-a-r-thin' to eat 'cept green apples an' green cawn, an' I wish you'd please to gimme a bite to eat.' . . . That they could march or fight at all seemed incredible." By contrast, Union supplies were so plentiful that rushing soldiers freely discarded them.

Since many prewar southerners had raised their own food, tillage suffered when farmers entered the army, and poor facilities hindered transportation and distribution of the harvest. Financial failures brought other shortages. Like the Union, the Confederacy borrowed from its citizens, but a low-cash farm economy left them little to lend. The Confederacy did not make its paper money legal tender, but issued so much of it that inflation reached 700 percent by January 1863. Respectful of states' rights, the government hesitated to impose high taxes or collect them with a strict and efficient bureaucracy. When taxes did come, the Confederacy refused its own currency and levied a tax in kind that took one-tenth of all farm products. Confederate forces also had the power to seize, or impress, civilian property— including slaves—whenever needed, offering written promises of postwar compensation in exchange. As defeat loomed ever closer, the inadequacy of these promises grew harder and harder to ignore.

Economic problems fell heaviest on the poor, whose wages lagged while the cost of daily necessities soared, many women lacked cash incomes, and soldiers' pay stagnated. Suffering was greatest in towns without food supplies and in nonslaveholding areas where blacks were not available to replace absent farmers. Beginning in 1863, resentment boiled over in a series of urban food riots, one in Richmond itself. Often led by axe-wielding women, protesters demanded that merchants sell flour, salt, and other necessities at affordable rates instead of waiting for higher prices. Worried that civilian suffering could undermine the war effort, state and local governments struggled to find charity for soldiers' families, but with little success.

White men's military service left Confederate women with heavy responsibilities. Before the war, southern law and custom made the male head of each household the ruler and protector of all the women, children, and slaves within it. Privileged women had gloried in the title of "lady" and traded any potential claim to independence for support, protection, refinement, and exemption from physical labor. The war revoked this bargain and forced white women to operate farms and businesses in addition to caring for children and homes. Slave-owning women had to supervise their human property, and many quailed at a task that always implied violence. "Where there are so many negroes upon places as upon ours," one Alabama mistress wrote, "it is quite necessary that there should be men who can and will controle them, especially at this time." "I shall not farm myself," worried another. "I cannot get along with negro men."

Even so, southern white women threw themselves into service, knitting and sewing for the troops and struggling to revive the nearly vanished arts of spinning and weaving by hand. Cajoling and threatening their slaves or joining their children and old men in the fields, they did their best to feed their households and the army. As the Union blockade tightened, they gave up imports and accepted deprivation with a mixture of resentment, zeal, and resignation. "Everyone is kept in such anxiety of mind by this dreadful war," wrote South Carolinian Mary Legg to a friend, "that it is not strange when we see the body sometimes give way when so much rests upon the mind." As the war ground on and misery intensified, some women despaired and urged their husbands to desert. "I would not have you do anything wrong for the world," one North Carolina woman wrote her husband near the end of the war, "but before God, Edward, unless you come home we must die." Combined with even worse conditions in the army, such letters fueled an escalating Confederate desertion rate, especially in the final months of combat.

Slaves reacted guardedly to the war's outbreak, leading many white diarists to wonder quietly what they might be thinking. As Union armies approached, of course, many seized the chance for escape. Others lingered but their owners complained of growing defiance. "The negroes are worse than free," Alabama's Susanna Clay informed her son. "We cannot exert any authority. I beg ours to do what little is done. . . . Alfred told me this morning that if your father . . . let the overseer attempt to punish [slaves] for disobedience that some one would kill the overseer!" While threats of violence frightened whites, they were fortunate that most slaves who could fight for freedom chose military enlistment over acts of private vengeance. In later years, planter families fondly remembered their faithful retainers, but increased resistance seemed more evident to contemporaries.

CONFEDERATE DISSENT

Shortages, conscription, and the fear of defeat inevitably affected Confederate government and stirred conflicting protests against the "tyranny" and ineffectiveness of the Richmond government. Disaffection and outright disloyalty ran highest in the South's interior uplands, where unionism had always been strong, invaders were absent, and the government pressed heavily for men and provisions. Prewar slaveholders had won yeoman support by honoring their freedom and independence. Once the war began, however, the Confederacy interfered with private life far more than the US government had ever done, by forcing men into its armies, extracting high taxes, issuing worthless currency, dictating economic decisions, seizing civilian property, and failing to fend off invasion. West Virginia was the only disaffected region to leave the Confederacy outright, but dissidents in western North Carolina and eastern Tennessee defied conscription, sheltered deserters, and even joined the Union Army, leading to serious guerilla warfare in many counties where whites were poor and slavery rare.

The governors of disaffected states struggled hard to sustain popular morale by sheltering their constituents from Richmond's heaviest demands. "Now Govr.," Private O. Goddin demanded of North Carolina's Zebulon Vance in February 1863, "do tell me how we poor soldiers who are fighting for the 'rich mans negro' can support our families at $11 per month? How can the poor live? . . . I am fearful we will have a revolution unless something is done as the majority of our soldiers are poor men with families who say they are tired of the rich mans war & poor mans fight." Joined by Governor Joseph Brown of Georgia, Vance became especially famous for defying the central government, hindering conscription, resisting appointees from other states, retaining state troops for home defense, and endlessly feuding with tax collectors and army officers. While resisting Richmond, however, state officials organized draft-exempt men in aggressive Home Guard units to suppress more-dangerous disloyalty.

The Confederacy also fought dissenters by suspending habeas corpus, using the army and Home Guard to enforce the draft and arrest deserters, and resorting to martial law. Like Lincoln, Davis drew charges of dictatorship, but he had no political party to support him and no personal warmth to disarm his critics. His own vice president, Alexander H. Stephens of Georgia, accused Davis of "aiming at absolute power" and denounced the suspension of habeas corpus as a "blow at the very 'vitals of liberty.'" Devotion to states' rights remained so wide-spread that one beleaguered official suggested that a tombstone for the Confederacy might read, "Died of a Theory."

Like their counterparts in the border states, some southern dissi-dents moved beyond disagreement to assist the enemy through espio-nage, sabotage, interference with military recruitment, and theft or destruction of supplies. North Carolina unionists organized a secret society known as the Heroes of America, or Red Strings, to collabo-rate actively with the Union, encourage desertion, and spirit recruits to the Union Army. In time, draft resisters, armed deserters, and pro-Union guerillas made parts of the state too dangerous for Confederate forces to enter. Punishment or retaliation for these activities easily led to violence against civilians by regular army units, poorly trained and undisciplined Home Guards, or other civilians. Sent to combat disloyal activity in North Carolina, for example, one Confederate colonel ex-plained how he gained information from one guerilla's wife: "I slapped her jaws till she put down her baby & and went with [my men]," he re-ported later. "They tied her thumbs behind her back & suspended her with a cord tied to her two thumbs thus fastened behind her to a limb so that her toes could just touch the ground. . . . After . . . a while she said . . . she would tell all she knew." Wherever it occurred, guerilla violence and its suppression brought wartime trauma and suffering to civilians who never experienced a formal battle, leaving deep resent-ment in its wake.

UNION-HELD DIXIE

Month after month as the war continued, Union armies stretched deeper and deeper into the Confederacy. The federal government never lost control of Fortress Monroe at the mouth of the Chesa-peake and immediately protected itself by occupying Alexandria, Vir-ginia, and adjacent territory near Washington, DC. New Orleans fell in 1862, and early naval assaults created small Union toeholds on the coasts of Florida and the Carolinas. Grant's capture of the Tennessee and Cumberland Rivers brought in most of Tennessee, and Union pos-session of the Mississippi brought control of its shoreline communi-ties. Over time, more and more of the South became occupied Union territory.

Prewar fears led white southerners to expect John Brown–style treatment from their captors. One northern Virginian predicted "fanatics and lawless ruffians ready for every outrage and violence," while another feared for "the lives and liberties of our people generally, and the horror of our women." Led by slaveholders, large numbers of whites fled the northern approach and brought with them as many slaves and valuables as possible. Adrift in the Confederate interior, these refugees sought shelter with family and friends when they could and seriously strained local resources throughout the war.

Other whites remained in place, some to guard their property, some with Union sympathies, and others with no resources for flight and no place to go. Contrary to predictions, the first waves of occupiers tried to treat civilians gently, still convinced that the majority were loyal at heart, deluded by a secessionist minority, and ready to re-embrace the Union if treated fairly. "I am laboring industriously to undeceive the people," one optimistic officer wrote from Arkansas. "A few weeks work here will make this region safe for the Union forever."

Conciliatory policies soon gave way to sterner treatment, as the occupiers discovered that support for secession and hatred of the invaders reached far beyond the plantation elite. Whites in the occupied territories refused to take loyalty oaths, spat upon soldiers, and publicly prayed for Confederate victory. If anything, women's hostility seemed more virulent than men's, as "ladies" used their privileges of rank and gender to escape its consequences. In New Orleans, General Benjamin Butler attacked those privileges directly by ordering that any woman who insulted his troops would be "treated as a woman of the town, plying her profession," or in other words, as a prostitute.

No matter how provoking, women's insults were less dangerous than violence by male assailants. Just as opposition guerillas attacked behind the lines of the Confederacy, secessionist irregulars harassed Union occupiers by assaulting patrols, destroying bridges and railroads, looting supplies, and murdering Union sympathizers. In some areas, unionist poor whites did the same to secessionist planters. In Arkansas, where one officer had predicted easy conciliation, another soon reported that "the countryside seems to have degenerated into bushwhackers.... It is hardly safe to go out of our lines a mile." Commanders responded with a "hard policy" of harsh retaliation, seizing or destroying supplies from local farms, burning barns and houses of suspected opponents, and executing captured guerillas. In wide swaths of both Union- and Confederate-occupied territory, irregular forces hunted each other relentlessly, all civilians were suspects, and no one could be trusted.

Civilians suffered from temporary enemy incursions as well as long-term occupations. In the spring of 1864, for example, Ulysses Grant sent troops to occupy Virginia's Shenandoah Valley, a major source of Confederate provisions and a proven invasion route to the North. Fighting raged up and down the valley all summer until General Philip H. Sheridan took command of Union forces in August and forced Confederate defenders high into the nearby Blue Ridge Mountains. Sheridan then turned to his real assignment, which was to make "the Shenandoah Valley [into] a barren waste . . . so that crows flying over it for the balance of this season will have to carry their [food] with them." In an episode still remembered locally as "the Burning," Union troops swarmed across the fertile valley until they had burned over 2,000 barns filled with crops and farm tools, destroyed over 70 flour mills, and killed or seized over 7,000 farm animals, without distinguishing between the property of northern or southern sympathizers. Confederate guerillas fought back fiercely but unsuccessfully, and Sheridan climaxed the campaign with a decisive victory that smashed the army of his Confederate opponent, General Jubal Early.

If white southerners met Union occupiers as bitter enemies, blacks welcomed them as heroes and liberators. Even before the troops' arrival, whites complained that slaves were becoming "insolent" and "insubordinate," refusing to work or deserting their plantations to serve the Union. Before the Emancipation Proclamation, slavery did not legally end when the federal army took over an area, but many commanders refused to enforce the laws of bondage. After the proclamation, the army's advance destroyed legal slavery, but former masters struggled to continue it. In many occupied towns and cities, newly freed African Americans celebrated with speeches, parades, and special church services. According to one observer, Nashville's "procession was composed of both sexes and all ages, on foot and riding in carriages . . . and vehicles of all kinds. Two fine brass bands were with them." The marchers hailed freedom as "the year of jubilee."

As the cheers gradually fell silent, the problem remained of what to do next. In areas of early Union control, commanders organized "freedmen's colonies" where fleeing ex-slaves could find emergency rations, simple housing, schools, medical care, and army recruiters. One of the most famous of these experiments in freedom began in 1862 at Port Royal in South Carolina's Sea Islands, where 10,000 blacks had stayed on their rice and cotton plantations when their masters fled from Union occupation the previous year. Northern reformers and missionaries quickly flocked in to establish schools and churches and aid the newly freed in building new lives. Contrary to predictions by slavery's defenders, the liberated slaves did not become idlers, but divided their time between continued plantation work and cultivating individual plots the army assigned them.

By January 1865, General William Tecumseh Sherman had occupied the same region and seized some 400,000 coastal acres for the use of former slaves, promising 40 acres to each family and help in finding them a work animal. Sherman's Field Order No. 15 applied temporarily in only one place, but it opened the question of what economic aid the government could offer the newly freed. It also led to a widespread misunderstanding that the government had promised all freed families "forty acres and a mule." Fully conscious that their unpaid labor had enriched the South and the nation, freed people eagerly embraced this notion as simple justice.

Most commanders preferred to see blacks return to the plantation as wage workers. In South Carolina, Louisiana, and elsewhere, they invited northern businessmen—most of whom knew nothing of cotton planting—to rent "abandoned" plantations and employ the former slaves to till them. Reliable planters who did not flee could do the same. When blacks protested these arrangements, unsympathetic officers compelled them to submit to low wages and harsh discipline that closely resembled bondage. Though some blacks managed to gain their own land in the aftermath of war, most learned bitterly that this result would be much less common than more plantation labor.

"This Mighty Scourge of War"

Lincoln removed General McClellan in the fall of 1862 but his immediate successors were no more successful. Nevertheless, the Confederacy's failure at the Battle of Gettysburg and its simultaneous loss of Vicksburg, Mississippi, brought a turning point in its military fortunes. When Ulysses S. Grant took command of the Union forces, he inflicted a series of increasingly bloody defeats that eventually led to a siege of Richmond. Facing defeat, Confederate leaders desperately considered arming and freeing slave soldiers, but could not fight off Grant or avoid surrender in the spring of 1865. By that point, Lincoln had rejected his former support for black colonization and openly called for including freed African Americans in the nation's political community. Murder blocked his leadership of that momentous task.

FIGURE 10. Massive casualties in the Civil War shocked Americans on both sides who expected a short, painless conflict. Civil War Collection, Prints and Photographs Division, Library of Congress, LC-DIG-cwpb-01099.

"GRANT IS MY MAN"

Lincoln replaced McClellan, who would not attack, with a series of generals who attacked but could not win. Famed for his magnificent side-whiskers (better known as "sideburns"), General Ambrose Burnside sent his troops across the Rappahannock River near Fredericksburg, Virginia, on December 13, 1862, and up the opposing hilltop. Lee's artillery and infantry easily cut them to pieces from their entrenched positions, leading the Confederate commander to remark grimly, "It is good that war is so terrible, or we should grow too fond of it." The Battle of Fredericksburg took 13,000 casualties from a Union army of 114,000, while the Confederacy lost no more than 5,000 out of 72,000.

General Joseph Hooker replaced Burnside and recrossed the Rappahannock in the spring of 1863. "May God have mercy on General Lee," he boasted, "for I will have none." Audaciously, Lee divided his outnumbered men and sent Stonewall Jackson to attack Hooker's rear in the Battle of Chancellorsville (May 2–6, 1863). In twilight at the end of the first day's fighting, Jackson received an accidental wound from his own men that later took his life, but Lee's daring tactic disorganized his opponents and successfully repelled them. Triumphant after these victories, the South would later suffer from a giddy conviction of Lee's invincibility.

Even without Jackson, Lee flaunted his confidence by repeating the tactic that had failed the previous year at Antietam. Passing over the Potomac, his 75,000 rebels romped into Maryland and Pennsylvania, feasted on plentiful provisions, and scooped up all the clothes, shoes, tents, blankets, and work animals they could find. They also captured black civilians whom they took to be runaways and sent them back to slavery. Without cavalry for reconnaissance, units from the two armies unwittingly collided outside the little town of Gettysburg, Pennsylvania. As General George Meade, the new federal commander, hastened north from Washington, the two armies began the greatest battle of the Civil War on July 1, 1863.

After a day of charges and countercharges through the town and its fields, the Union Army retired to the summit of Cemetery Ridge, a U-shaped string of hills on the south side of town. A second day of very fierce fighting did not dislodge the defenders but saw legendary incidents in military history, including a controversial delay by Confederate General James Longstreet that later critics blamed for the South's defeat, and a heroic defense of Little Round Top, a key hill, by Colonel Joshua Lawrence Chamberlain and the 20th Maine Volunteers. On the climactic third day, Lee tried to weaken Meade's hilltop position with a massive but ineffective artillery barrage. When the cannons fell silent about three o'clock that afternoon, the troops of General George Pickett advanced across the low valley separating the two armies and into a deadly curtain of lead. A few attackers reached the summit but nearly half died in Pickett's Charge. The next day, Lee's dispirited warriors turned back to Virginia in a driving rain, having lost their last chance to destroy the main body of the Union Army and menace Washington. A different outcome would certainly have strengthened the war's northern opponents and heightened the impact of the New York draft riots, which broke out a week later. Instead, the so-called high-water mark of the Confederacy had passed and the war had reached its turning point. Between the two armies, 60,000 were missing, killed, or wounded

Jubilant northerners soon learned of another victory. Earlier that spring, the army of General Ulysses S. Grant and the gunboats of Admiral David Dixon Porter had trapped a large rebel force in Vicksburg, the last Confederate stronghold on the Mississippi River. After a bitter siege reduced its inhabitants to eating rats and living in caves, the city fell on July 3 and gave the Union control of the South's river highway. "Grant is my man," Lincoln exulted, "and will be mine for the rest of the war." That October, Lincoln gave Grant command of the Army of the Potomac, and raised him to general-in-chief the following March.

In November of 1863, Lincoln traveled to the recent battlefield at Gettysburg to dedicate a national cemetery for the Union soldiers who had fallen there. Massachusetts Senator Edward Everett was the featured speaker, but the president also had a moment, which he used for a short but overwhelming statement of the war's enduring meaning. He began by invoking the Declaration of Independence, the republic's founding scripture: "Four score and seven years ago, our fathers brought forth on this continent, a new nation, conceived in Liberty, and dedicated to the proposition that all men are created equal." Previous generations of Americans had usually cited the Constitution as embodying their principles, but Lincoln implicitly saw the original Constitution as a bundle of flawed compromises—including its acknowledgements of slavery—that did not match the Declaration's loftier promise of equality. For him, the war's great purpose was to prove that the "proposition" of equality was strong enough to hold the United States together and preserve the possibility of republican government for future generations. As he put it, the war was "testing whether that nation, or any nation so conceived and so dedicated, can long endure." Since the men who had died at the battlefield had already sanctified it, Lincoln humbly denied that he could say anything to magnify their achievement. Instead, he asked his audience to complete "the great task remaining before us," and honor the fallen by defeating disunion, slavery, and inequality, republicanism's worst enemies. Victory would bring "a new birth of freedom," he concluded, and ensure "that government of the people, by the people, and for the people, shall not perish from the earth." In a few cadenced phrases, Lincoln's Gettysburg Address had put the ideals of the Declaration of

Independence at the center of the war's purpose and projected them into the future as crucial expressions of the mission that Americans claimed for themselves.

THE TIDE SLOWLY TURNS

As the Union triumphed at Vicksburg and Gettysburg, it also pierced the Confederate heartland. Federal forces had repelled a great Confederate invasion of Kentucky in 1862 and kept shoving the rebels southward in the year that followed. Pushed into northwest Georgia, the Confederates turned and dealt the Union a smashing defeat at the Battle of Chickamauga on September 19–20, 1863, only to resume their retreat later that year. By July 1864, General William Tecumseh Sherman had trapped the Confederate Army of Tennessee in the city of Atlanta.

Grant reached the outskirts of Richmond that summer. The season's fighting had begun in May, when Lee struck again near Chancellorsville but fumbled in a scrubby tangle known as the Wilderness. Unlike his predecessors, Grant followed up by skirting Lee's right flank, attacking at Spotsylvania Courthouse (May 8–12, 1864) and again at the hamlet of Cold Harbor (June 1, 1864). Union losses in these gruesomely bloody battles exceeded 50,000 men, but Grant would not bend. "I intend to fight it out on this line if it takes all summer," he declared, not realizing that final victory would take ten months longer than that. Well aware of the odds against them, northern troops fought furiously but fatalistically, even pinning name tags on the backs of their uniforms the night before the Battle of Cold Harbor because they expected their faces to be blown off the next morning. The Confederates lost "only" half as many men in that summer, but could not afford to spare them.

Constantly marching left to get around Lee's right, Grant kept forcing his opponent southward until Lee dug in on the eastern side of Richmond. There the armies entered a long and miserable siege in which Grant kept pushing to the south and west and defenders stretched thinner and thinner between the capital and nearby Petersburg.

The approach of the 1864 fall elections saw both armies deadlocked at Atlanta and Richmond. Stalemate favored the South by demonstrating the Confederacy's survival and the Union's failure. Both sides were tired of futile bloodshed, and peace candidates railed against the folly of continued war. In the North, eager Democrats nominated General George B. McClellan to challenge Lincoln for the presidency, and hinted that he might end the war by agreeing to Confederate independence. Anxious to broaden their support, Republicans reached out to War Democrats by briefly renaming themselves the National Union Party and nominating Senator Andrew Johnson of Tennessee, a unionist Democrat and the only senator from a seceding state who remained in Congress throughout the war, for vice president. Even so, Lincoln glumly prepared himself for defeat. Suddenly, on September 2, Atlanta's defenses cracked open and Sherman's troops poured into a flaming city. Lincoln and the Republicans swept to victory on this news, and the North's determination revived.

Atlanta's defenders retreated to Tennessee, but Sherman did not follow. Instead he attacked the fabric of slaveholding society by leading his army across Georgia in its famous March to the Sea. Without external supplies, his 62,000 men fed themselves by foraging 25 miles in each direction along the way. Delighted to despoil the slavocracy, Sherman's "bummers" destroyed everything of military value, quite a bit of everything else, and helped themselves to considerable personal property. Trying to keep his men within limits, Sherman still shrugged off all but the worst excesses, reasoning that the war would never end until southern whites paid a personal price for their rebellion. As in other theaters, thousands of slaves rushed to join the Union advance. Whole families rejoiced in the "Day of Jubilee," and men enlisted eagerly in the army of liberation.

After reaching Savannah, Sherman turned northward to inflict an even harsher thrashing on the arch-rebels of South Carolina. He took Columbia on February 17, 1865, and fires jointly fed by Union, Confederate, and African American hands quickly consumed the capital. Without a pause, Sherman moved on to North Carolina, sweeping before him a tiny Confederate force under General Joseph Johnston. By April 1865, he was poised in Raleigh, North Carolina, hoping for news from Virginia.

"TO FINISH THE WORK WE ARE IN"

As federal troops closed in, the Confederacy punctuated its impending defeat with a bitter debate over slavery. Was it possible, some asked, that extreme military necessity might justify arming the slaves, even with the promise of freedom in return? After all, a Mississippi editor had reasoned in 1863, "It is better for us to use the negroes for our defense than that the Yankees should use them against us. . . . Although slavery is one of the principles that we started to fight for," he acknowledged, "if it proves an insurmountable obstacle to the achievement of our liberty and separate nationality, away with it!" Officers of the Confederate Army of Tennessee formally discussed the concept as early as January 1864, and the idea spread as the year progressed.

Confederate proponents of black enlistment and emancipation warned that defeat would bring radical abolition and its untold horrors, while partial emancipation after a Confederate victory would protect white supremacy and leave blacks working for their former masters. The very idea still horrified most Confederates. The *Richmond Whig* called freeing slave soldiers "a repudiation of the opinion held by the whole South that . . . that servitude is a divinely appointed condition for the highest good of the slave." "If slaves will make good soldiers," Georgia senator Howell Cobb agreed, "our whole theory of slavery is wrong." "Victory itself would be robbed of its glory if shared with slaves," wailed a Mississippi congressman. "If such a terrible calamity is to befall us," a Virginia newspaper concluded, "we infinitely prefer that Lincoln shall be the instrument of our disaster and degradation, than that we ourselves should strike the cowardly and suicidal blow."

Staring at defeat, however, senior leaders reluctantly disagreed. In February 1865, two months before his final surrender, General Robert E. Lee endorsed black enlistment and advised, "It would be neither just nor wise . . . to require them to serve as slaves." President Davis endorsed the idea to his cabinet, and a close vote in the Confederate Congress authorized him to obtain black soldiers from the states, without specifying if freedom would be their reward. Two black companies formed in Richmond, but the war ended before they saw combat.

The end came faster than Richmond debaters could imagine. Grant had spent the winter of 1864–1865 inching slowly around Petersburg, trying to block Lee's access to railroads and prevent him from joining Johnston in the Carolinas. Lee's troops had grown thinner and more exhausted, finally leading thousands of once stalwart but now disheartened warriors to make peace privately by a quiet departure for home. By April 2, with desertions mounting and Grant growing stronger, Lee could hold the city no longer and notified Davis he intended to retreat. Still hoping to survive, perhaps in Mexico as a government-in-exile, Davis and his senior officials boarded trains as the army limped westward.

It was not enough. Pursuers trapped the remnants of the Army of Northern Virginia at Appomattox Court House on April 9, 1865. To formalize surrender, the two generals met in the parlor of a local home, Lee in his finest dress uniform, Grant in his fatigues and muddy boots. Refusing Lee's sword, Grant gave generous terms to his adversary. Pending a final settlement, surrendering Confederates could simply stack their weapons and go home. Soldiers could also keep their own horses and mules for spring plowing, and officers retained their side arms. Eight days later, Johnston surrendered to Sherman near the modern city of Durham, North Carolina. Union troops captured Davis and Vice President Stephens soon afterward and resistance sputtered out across the South. On June 19, 1865, the last federal troops reached Texas and liberated the slaves of Galveston, an event still celebrated as Juneteenth. The war for the Union was finally over.

After winning reelection in November, Lincoln had taken the oath of office on March 4, 1865, with a haunting second inaugural address. Passing over northern victories with scarcely a comment, he reminded America that its sufferings had come from slavery and suggested that its sins had incurred divine punishment. Lincoln prayed for the killing to stop. "Yet, if God wills that it continue," he went on, "until all the wealth piled by the bondsman's two hundred and fifty years of unrequited toil shall be sunk, and until every drop of blood drawn with the lash shall be paid by another drawn with the sword, as was said three thousand years ago, so still it must be said 'the judgments of the Lord are true and righteous altogether.'" Though he gave sacred significance to Union victory, Lincoln would not gloat. "With malice toward none," he concluded, "with charity for all, with firmness in the right as God gives us to see the right, let us strive to finish the work we are in, to bind up the nation's wounds, . . . to do all which may achieve . . . a just and lasting peace among ourselves and with all nations."

While he called for charity, Lincoln's invocation of divine support showed his enduring commitment to the war's goals. Shortly before his death, he also showed how his view of those goals had changed as his racial views evolved. Lincoln had once denied blacks' equality and the government's right to free them. From there he moved to supporting emancipation with colonization. In his last public address, Lincoln ignored colonization but acknowledged that black men deserved more than just freedom. Speaking of the right to vote, he said, "I would myself prefer that it were now conferred on the very intelligent, and on those who serve our cause as soldiers."

Hearing Lincoln's support for limited black suffrage, actor and southern sympathizer John Wilkes Booth vowed to stop him and organized a coordinated assault on the Union's senior leadership. Secretary of War Edwin Stanton fought off his assailant, Secretary of State William H. Seward survived a stabbing, and Vice President Johnson's attacker apparently lost his nerve, but Booth's bullet found Lincoln in Ford's Theater on the night of April 14, 1865. By early next morning, Abraham Lincoln lay dead.

*

The Civil War erupted from a conflict over slavery's place in the republic. The Republican Party viewed slavery as blighting opportunity for white men. Seeing the western territories as essential places for overcrowded easterners to flourish, Republicans hoped openly for slavery's collapse and vowed to protect white equality by excluding slavery from the West. Southerners replied that the exclusion of slavery made slaveholders unequal citizens and deprived them of equally needed room for expansion. If Republicans gained the presidency, vowed sectional extremists, the South must leave the Union to avoid the danger and disgrace of inequality.

Slavery itself became a casualty of the war. Runaways like John Boston confronted the North with slavery's contradictions by fleeing to Union lines and working for Union victory. In doing so, they taught the North the importance of African Americans for the victory of one side or the other and the impossibility of returning the contrabands to bondage. Hating slavery but baffled over how to end it, Lincoln embraced emancipation as a military necessity.

Emancipation transformed the Union that the North had fought to preserve. Once a slaveholders' republic, the United States became legally committed to equality, an achievement that later failures could not erase. The nation's new citizens made new demands on its public sphere and forced the government to exercise new powers in its halting efforts to meet them. Reconstruction would not succeed in the short run, but it established the constitutional basis for further struggle in later generations.

CHAPTER 15

Reconstructing the Republic, 1865–1877

Easter Sunday morning, April 13, 1873, was not a day of peace in the tiny hamlet of Colfax, the seat of government in Grant Parish, Louisiana. Two rival governments of Louisiana, one supported by ex-Confederate Democrats and the other by black Republicans and their white allies, had emerged from a racially charged election dispute. In Grant Parish, each set of claimants demanded the surrender of the other, and both sides were preparing to fight.

Grant Parish lies in north-central Louisiana, between the Red River and Bayou Darro. In 1873, its black population lived on waterfront cotton and sugar plantations while most white families lived on smaller upland farms, leaving the parish almost evenly divided between white and black. The Red River country had a rough reputation for African American slaves, but conditions there had radically changed since the antebellum days. Freed by the Civil War, the black men of Grant could vote in 1873 and swore to defend their chosen government by force if necessary. As a New Orleans newspaper put it, "The years of freedom which they have enjoyed have had their effect on them, as well as the military education which many of them received in the United States Army. The time is past, if ever it existed, when a handful of whites could frighten a regiment of colored men."

When Republicans and Democrats both claimed victory in the state elections of 1872, black Republicans expelled white Democrats from the Colfax courthouse, but whites recruited their neighbors to fight back. "When that Tytantic Black Hand was sweeping over the Red River Valley in 1873 we Catahoula Parish boys—then known as the Old Time Ku Klux Klan—were called to the Test of White Supremacy and rescue of the town of Colfax," one participant remembered much later. When sufficient forces arrived—variously estimated at 125–300

FIGURE 11. As northern support for Reconstruction faded in the 1870s, violence by the Ku Klux Klan and similar groups brought former Confederates back to power in the southern states, and reversed many of the gains won by freed people. Miscellaneous Items in High Demand, Prints and Photographs Division, Library of Congress, LC-USZ62-128619.

men—white sheriff Columbus Nash summoned black organizer Levi Allen for a parley.

"I give you two hours to get your negro women and children and all the negroes who do not want to fight out of town," Nash demanded. "We are going to get 'em." Astride his handsome horse and flourishing an impressive sword, Allen remained defiant. "I'll see you when you get 'em," he shot back and galloped to his lines. The contenders traded rifle and cannon fire for two hours without effect until 30 white men slipped around the defenders and attacked from the rear. Caught in a cross fire, the black fighters fell back to the courthouse and kept shooting until the whites set its roof ablaze.

Then the killing began in earnest. According to the recollections of white participants, fleeing blacks "were ridden down in the open fields and shot without mercy," while bayonet thrusts dispatched the wounded. Fighting finally ceased around 4:00 p.m., and white leaders decided to hold the 40 or so black survivors for a later trial. But after most whites had gone home, a band of "young, reckless, and irresponsible men," filled up with liquor, decided not to wait for courtroom justice. With gunshots crackling "like popcorn in a skillet," they killed their prisoners on the spot. No one can be sure how many died in Colfax that day, but New Orleans police later buried over 60 bodies, and families buried others privately. The Colfax Massacre was the bloodiest single incident in the violence-torn years that followed the Civil War, the era of America's Reconstruction.

How was the Colfax Massacre possible? Why was the control of local government worth so much bloodshed? How, only ten years after the Emancipation Proclamation, had African American men won the power to carry arms and cast ballots? All these questions were central to the issues raised by the effort to reconstruct the Union after the Civil War.

The struggle in Grant Parish was part of a much wider conflict between whites and blacks, southerners and northerners, Democrats and Republicans, over how to rebuild American society. Even before the Civil War began, Americans had used the word "reconstruction" to describe the process of bringing the seceding states back into the Union. They continued this legal usage at war's end, but the end of slavery meant that full reconstruction would include social and economic transformation as well as political and constitutional reunification. As the battle in Colfax illustrated, social and political change blended, for participants could not implement their visions for a post-slave society without invoking local, state, and national governments.

In the spring of 1877, conservative white southerners won a major political victory, as blacks lost support from northern white Republicans and the federal government abandoned formal efforts to remake the South. Despite the withdrawal of federal troops and the formal readmission of the seceding states, the society and economy of the South were still profoundly changed from the days of legalized slavery. Social, economic, and even political questions were not fully settled in 1877, and struggles continued until 1900 and beyond as Americans wrestled over the structure and traditions of their transformed republic for generations to come.

Binding Up the Nation's Wounds

Putting the United States back together again was a monumental task. The seceding and border states suffered serious physical damage that needed repair. More profoundly, emancipation had overturned the South's fundamental institution but left the practical meaning of freedom unclear. White northerners, white southerners, and the four million former slaves all differed over what should replace slavery. Black Americans' role in the new national order became a deeply charged political issue with profound consequences for the postwar world.

War and emancipation had also strained the nation's constitutional fabric. If secession was illegal (as the North had always insisted), were the former Confederates guilty of treason? If so, how should they be punished? Or forgiven? Did the seceding states still have "states' rights," or were they more like conquered provinces? Who should determine the meaning of black freedom—white northerners, white southerners, or blacks themselves? And who should settle these questions—Congress or the president? Debates over these issues would lead to more violence and the first impeachment of a president of the United States.

FREEDOM AND DESTRUCTION

War's end brought widespread rejoicing for the victors, mingled with grief and anger over the death of President Abraham Lincoln on April 15, 1865, just five days after the major Confederate surrender at Appomattox Court House in Virginia. As fighting sputtered out, Union generals Ulysses S. Grant and William T. Sherman brought their armies to Washington for a grand victory parade, and most of their soldiers soon left for their homes. A small number of Union troops, many of them black, remained behind to police the defeated South. Stretched very thin and kept under constant political pressure, they would be responsible for protecting the fragile experiment of Reconstruction.

Returning Union veterans knew they were lucky to be alive. Just over 2.2 million men—about half of those eligible—had worn blue uniforms, but at least 360,000 had died in service, and 275,000 had suffered wounds. These casualties were an immense sacrifice by the standards of earlier and later wars. The 4,800 Americans who died in one day at the Battle of Antietam, for example, had exceeded the 4,000 battle deaths in the entire Revolutionary War. As many as 750,000 Americans perished in the Civil War, almost twice the number who died in World War II. Unlike their Confederate counterparts, former Union soldiers would receive generous federal pensions in the years ahead, though southern state governments would do what they could for their aging veterans.

Historians once believed that the Civil War enriched the North, as large military expenditures stimulated the production of iron and steel and fostered the growth of a powerful industrial economy. In fact, these developments had begun before the war, and the destruction of lives and property probably did more to slow economic growth than hasten it. After a sharp recession caused by the cancellation of military contracts, growth resumed by the beginning of 1868 as railroad construction boomed, cities expanded, European immigration continued to expand, and settlers flocked to the Great Plains. In the decades to come, northern workers would feel the sting of poverty and deprivation as their employers struggled to keep costs down and profits up, and protests would reverberate through northern society, but most northern Americans would escape the grinding want that afflicted many black and white southerners.

In politics, northern voters split unevenly between a Republican majority and a Democratic minority. The Republicans had formed in 1854 to oppose the Kansas-Nebraska Act and the spread of slavery to the territories, and their victory in the presidential election of 1860 had sparked southern secession. Strongly appealing to Union veterans and native-born, middle-class whites, Republicans had fervently supported the war for the Union and wanted to protect what their sacrifices had achieved. Especially in Congress, a small but determined group of Radical Republicans pressed for strong antislavery measures in wartime and active aid to the newly freed thereafter. Moderate Republicans preferred to move more gradually but often became more radical when white southerners resisted even limited change.

Like their southern counterparts, northern Democrats praised white men's equality, states' rights, and a weak federal government. Many had southern sympathies and strongly objected to emancipation and racial equality as wartime goals. Their party was popular among foreign-born urban workers and native-born Americans—often midwesterners with southern roots—from isolated or underdeveloped rural districts. The war's political legacy gave a strongly partisan cast to Reconstruction policies. Especially among Republicans, the war's goals had changed over time. At first, most northerners had fought to restore "the Union as it was." As the war continued, many realized that they could not restore the old Union and had to establish a new one without slavery, the cause of the Union's rupture. Even before the war, slavery had shaped rival visions for America, and northerners now expected their own vision to prevail. Without entirely realizing it, they wanted southerners to concede a moral as well as a military victory, to surrender their principles along with their guns and admit they had been wrong. To do so, northerners wanted southerners to renounce slavery completely, reject their secessionist leaders, embrace surviving unionists, and treat their ex-slaves fairly. Few ex-Confederates could willingly pass this test of loyalty.

Defeated Confederates faced a far different future from their Union counterparts, and despair gripped many. "We have nothing on earth to look forward to," mourned Sarah Hine of Savannah, Georgia. "We have no future, no country, we are slaves to the will of others & must do their bidding. . . . May God forgive me for there are times when . . . I feel as if I could not accept his will in the matter." Physical destruction alone surpassed anything felt in most parts of the North. Advancing and retreating armies had burned bridges, factories, and homes. Mile after mile of railroad track had been heated in bonfires and twisted around trees to make "Sherman's neckties," and the condition of most railway bridges and rolling stock was no better. Assault and capture left nothing but forests of blackened chimneys and charred walls across Atlanta, Charleston, Columbia, and Richmond. Rival armies had demolished many of the Confederacy's new arsenals and factories and put an end to the South's ambitious efforts at government-sponsored industrialization.

Outside southern cities, four years of combat had left barns, fences, ditches, fields, and farm equipment to the forces of weeds and decay. The armies had taken thousands of horses and mules, and grain and other livestock had fed the hungry. Family valuables had disappeared, and Confederate bonds and currency were worthless. Their capital gone, southern banks collapsed and left merchants without credit to reopen their businesses. The South's farms suffered less than its cities, but the crucial question of farm labor remained unanswered.

The South's human casualties were more serious than its property damage. While roughly half of northern men remained civilians, almost every southern white male of military age—as many as 1.5 million men between the ages of 17 and 55—had entered Confederate service in some form or another. Of these, at least 250,000 were now dead and 225,000 more had suffered wounds. The number of amputees was so great that the largest single item in the Mississippi state budget for 1866–1867 was an appropriation of $30,000 to purchase artificial legs for the survivors.

Northern observers reported that the South had accepted its defeat, but the end of fighting was not the same as a change of heart. New York journalist Whitelaw Reid toured the South in the summer of 1865 and agreed that the former Confederates had submitted to defeat. But "question them as to everything for which the war was fought," he warned, "the doctrine of secession, the rightfulness of slavery, the wrongs of the South, and they are found as full of the sentiments that made the rebellion as ever." Carl Schurz, another touring northern Republican, found that "the loyalty of the masses and most of the leaders of the southern people consists in submission to necessity. There is, except in individual instances, an entire absence of that national spirit which forms the basis of true loyalty and patriotism." Republicans ambitious to remake the South would soon find that this degree of submission was less than what they had hoped for.

Despite the war's destruction, peacetime brought jubilation to one key group of Americans. The wartime Emancipation Proclamation promised freedom to most African Americans, though the Thirteenth Amendment to the Constitution, abolishing slavery throughout the United States, was not ratified until December 1865. As Union troops advanced and slavery crumbled, planters usually asked their former chattels to remain at work, promising them wages at harvest time. Many agreed, but some struck out immediately. Almost 200,000 African American men had joined the Union Army or Navy. Like the black veterans in Colfax, military service strengthened their determination to defend and assert their liberty in peacetime, and bolstered their claim to full civic and political equality. The newly freed also began to travel, some seeking work or lost family members, others simply tasting liberty and hoping to see the world a bit. As a cook explained to her protesting former owner, "No, Miss, I must go. If I stay here I'll never know I'm free."

PLANNING FOR RECONSTRUCTION

Reconstruction had started informally during wartime, when Union commanders had begun to administer the occupied parts of the Confederacy. President Lincoln sought to formalize this process in December 1863. Though the Constitution defined treason as "making war on the United States," he offered to pardon all but a few Confederate leaders if they would accept the end of slavery and swear future loyalty to the United States. Under this offer, when 10 percent of a state's electorate had taken this oath, they could reestablish a state government and reenter the Union.

Lincoln tried out his Ten Percent Plan in parts of Virginia, Tennessee, Arkansas, and especially Louisiana, which was mostly under Union control by 1864, but the resulting governments still resisted the end of slavery. On July 2, 1864, Congress responded with a new law known as the Wade-Davis Bill after Radical Republican senator Ben Wade of Ohio and Congressman Henry Winter Davis of Maryland. It allowed a state to elect a constitutional convention when half its electorate swore loyalty to the Union, but limited convention membership to those who swore an "iron-clad oath" that they had never supported the Confederacy in any way. If the convention wrote a new state constitution that abolished slavery, repudiated (that is, forever refused to repay) the Confederate debt, and barred high-ranking Confederates from holding office, Congress and the president could recognize the new government and restore it to the Union. Hoping that his much more tolerant Ten Percent Plan would persuade Confederates to lay down their arms, Lincoln refused to sign the Wade-Davis Bill, and plans for political reconstruction remained deadlocked.

In the meantime, Congress created the Bureau of Refugees, Freedmen, and Abandoned Lands in March 1865, better known as the Freedmen's Bureau, and gave it jurisdiction over all matters related to the former slaves. In the immediate aftermath of war, the Freedmen's Bureau established hospitals, schools, and settlement camps for the homeless and distributed some 13 million emergency rations to both whites and blacks. Its agents' most important duties were helping blacks make wage labor contracts with white farmers, but whites often criticized it for treating the freed people too generously. Some bureau agents were abolitionists who sympathized with the former slaves; some sided with former masters and others tried to be impartial, but whites who still expected the prerogatives of ownership resented all their activities.

From Thomas Jefferson to Abraham Lincoln, American leaders had once believed that free blacks could never live peacefully or equally with whites, so African Americans would have to emigrate if slavery ever ended. By war's end, however, most Americans had abandoned this idea. The sheer size of the black population, the enormous costs of colonization, the economic importance of black labor, and the freed people's almost universal unwillingness to move all discouraged mass colonization. Most now realized that African Americans would remain in the United States and press for their own definition of freedom in a racially mixed society. But what should this mean in practice?

Southern whites, northern whites, and African Americans all differed widely in their expectations for black freedom. Many ex-Confederates still believed that slavery had benefited both blacks and whites, so black "freedom" should be very much like bondage. One former agent of the Freedmen's Bureau later remembered, "Many of the planters seemed to be unable to understand that work could be other than a form of slavery, or that it could be accomplished without some prodigious binding and obligating of the hireling to the employer." For these ex-masters, only some form of forced labor would allow the South to regain prosperity and tranquility, and anything like legal equality for freed people seemed inconceivable. As they saw it, the South's traditional leaders should quickly return to power and impose special laws to govern black conduct. If Negroes must be free, they reasoned, their "freedom" must be a kind of tutelage or serfdom under the control of their former masters.

Northern whites differed among themselves about the future of African Americans. Many northern Democrats sympathized with the racial views of white southerners. Former abolitionists often thought that the freedmen should enjoy absolute legal equality with whites, including the right to vote and hold office. Some, like Pennsylvania congressman Thaddeus Stevens, wanted to punish the southern ruling class by confiscating their plantations and distributing the land to their former slaves, but few other Republicans agreed. They assumed instead that free blacks would work for wages like other laborers, doing the same tasks as before, and enjoying equal rights to move about, choose employers, change jobs, acquire property, make contracts, sue and be sued, and testify in court. They distinguished this *legal* equality from what they called *political* equality, which included the right to vote, hold office, and serve on juries, and also from *social* equality, meaning the right to be received equally in private social circles and, above all, to marry white people.

The former slaves had their own notions of freedom. Over and over, they spurned the accusation of laziness. "The necessity of working is perfectly understood by men who have worked all their lives," a black editor remarked tartly. They certainly rejected any system of forced labor, but even working for wages reminded them too much of slavery itself. Instead, they wanted lands of their own. "We have a right to the land where we are located," Virginia freedman Bayley Wyat insisted. "Our wives, our children, our husbands, has been sold over and over again to purchase the lands we now locates upon; for that reason, we have a divine right to the land." Ex-slaves also gathered in state-level meetings over the summer of 1865 to demand legal and political equality. Some simply asked for the legal rights supported by most northern whites, but others wanted the right to vote, which Virginia representatives called "our inalienable right as freemen, and which the Declaration of Independence guarantees to all free citizens of this government." In the end, the structure of black "freedom" did not match the expectations of southern whites, northern whites, or the freed people themselves, but blended all three.

LAND AND LABOR

The first task of most freed people was to support themselves. Even before formal emancipation, the Union Army and the Freedmen's Bureau had helped refugees with emergency shelter, meals, and medical attention. Some help continued into peacetime, but military and civilian authorities tried to end it as soon as possible. Hopes for widespread black land ownership sagged in the fall of 1865, when President Johnson revoked the allocation of 40-acre tracts to formerly enslaved families in South Carolina and Georgia and returned the land to its previous owners. Affected families protested bitterly. "Why do you take away our lands?" they wept. "You take them from us who have always been true to the Government! You give them to our all-time enemies! That is not right." Fearing black self-sufficiency, planters also tried to prevent blacks from renting their own lands. A convention of South Carolina planters demanded that the army force freed people back to work on their old plantations and resolved "that under no circumstances whatsoever will we rent land to any freedmen."

Denied their own farms, most freed people negotiated annual work contracts with a white landowner, often with the help of a Freedmen's Bureau agent. Typical agreements offered food and rations very similar to those provided to slaves, and wages that ranged from about $10 per month for adult men down to a small fraction of that for children. Typical contracts required workers to be "respectful to [the planter] and his family or Superintendent," as a North Carolina agreement put it, while imposing stiff fines for "time lost by idleness or absence without leave," partial payment of wages until harvest, and forfeiture of all back wages if the worker quit. Assisted by these agreements, southern farmers planted spring crops in 1865 and began to restore the South's agricultural economy.

The contract system quickly collapsed. Northern farmhands faced no such restrictions, and southern workers despised them. Laborers and employers quarreled over the work of family members, with many black women refusing field labor to care for their own children. Above all, field hands resented the return to gang labor under the strict gaze of an overseer and complained that many planters still used the whip. According to a plantation journal of 1869, free workers were "anxious to rid themselves of all supervision on the part of the white race, and look upon it as a sort of continual badge, or remembrancer, of their former condition of servitude."

The alternative was a system of tenancy known as sharecropping. Instead of working directly under the planter's supervision, each black family leased a small plot of land for one year, and their landlord supplied seed, tools, fertilizer, a work animal, and a house in return for half the crop. Tenants who managed to supply some or all of these necessities themselves could increase their share to as much as three-fourths of what they grew. Sharecropping contracts required the tenant to plant a staple crop, usually cotton, which the tenants could not eat but commanded a ready sale.

Tenancy allowed families to control their own time and decide who would or would not work in the fields, but carried a burden of its own. Sharecroppers raised little or no food but purchased necessities on credit from the country stores that sprang up at every crossroads, frequently paying exorbitant rates of interest and offering their own shares of the growing crop as collateral. When the time came to settle up, the landlord took his half of the crop as rent and the merchant took all or most of the rest in payment for his loan. As landowners opened stores and storekeepers bought farmland, moreover, the landlord and merchant might become the same person. Left with little or nothing at the end of the year, the tenant had to sign up for another round, beginning each January with no more savings than the last. Sharecropping left most African Americans impoverished and dependent on white landlords and storekeepers, and trapped large portions of the rural South in a seemingly hopeless cycle of poverty. Tenancy combined some aspects of black, northern white, and southern white conceptions of freedom by allowing some family autonomy (as blacks wanted), creating a nominally free labor market (as northerners wanted), and leaving ultimate power with the old planter class (as white southerners wanted). In the declining farm economy of the late nineteenth century, moreover, millions of white yeoman families lost their lands and entered sharecropping as well.

FAMILY, SCHOOL, AND CHURCH

Another crucial goal for African Americans was to reestablish and protect their families. State laws had not recognized slave marriages, sales had divided husbands and wives from each other and parents from children, and the first thought of many freed people had been to find lost loved ones. Couples also flocked to ministers or government officials for legally binding weddings and struggled with former masters for custody of their children.

Within black families, free husbands could claim patriarchal authority that once belonged to masters. As blacks chose surnames, most wives adopted the names of their husbands, just as whites did. Some wives refused to work outside the home, preferring to care for their own children and avoid sexual exploitation in the workplace, while others challenged the power of their husbands and asked federal officials to settle their disputes. Unlike white women, no one had taught black women that politics lay beyond their "sphere," so they freely joined public meetings. The law favored men, however, and black men eventually claimed the same gender privileges as white men.

Regardless of age or family status, all northern observers agreed that the freed men, women, and children of the South were desperately eager for education. Most slave states had made it a crime to teach slaves to read, so learning was a prized symbol of liberty as well as an invaluable survival skill. "Too much cannot be said of the desire to learn among this people," reported an Alabama agent of the Freedmen's Bureau. "Everywhere to open a school is to have it filled." With bureau support, abolitionists, philanthropists, and previously freed blacks responded with organizations like the New England Freedmen's Aid Society and the American Missionary Association to supply money, teachers, and books for freed people's education.

Without state funds, communities combined charity and self-help to pay for schools. Classes could number as many as a hundred pupils of all ages in a barn or similar makeshift structure. Teachers faced furious white hostility and violence, as southern communities refused to accept them, churches denied them membership, and night riders attacked their homes and schoolhouses. The pursuit of education persisted, however, as black communities struggled to create and perpetuate institutions to serve the race. Over time, communities, churches, and philanthropic groups not only prepared for black inclusion in state public school systems but also for historically black colleges and universities, including Hampton University, Howard University, Tuskegee University, Fisk University, and many others.

African Americans also transformed their religious life by withdrawing from predominantly white congregations, creating their own churches, and worshiping freely. The Baptist denomination remained the most popular, but northern-based and all-black variants of Methodism also grew rapidly, including the African Methodist Episcopal (AME) Church and the related AME Zion Church. The AME Church exploded dramatically, from 20,000 members in 1856 to 400,000 in 1880, and other denominations grew proportionately. Though often struggling to erect the simplest buildings and to pay thinly stretched ministers, churches became central institutions of the black community, enforcing a strict code of morality among their members and anchoring other community activities, from education, charity, and women's leadership to political organizing.

Early in Reconstruction, African American leaders expressed hope that time, patience, and good behavior would lessen white antagonism and promote racial harmony. "We have not come together in battle array to assume a boastful attitude and to talk loudly of high-sounding principles," explained a South Carolina gathering in 1865. "We come together . . . in a spirit of meekness and patriotic good-will toward all the people in the State." The chairman of a North Carolina convention agreed. "We and the white people have to live here together," he pointed out. "The best way is to harmonize our feelings as much as possible and to treat all men respectfully. Respectability will always gain respect."

Unfortunately, many whites did not reciprocate. Steeped in the customs of slavery, former masters attempted to cheat ex-slaves of their wages, to seize custody of their children, to molest black women, to harass black schools and churches, and to assault or murder blacks who defied them. Under these circumstances, African Americans concluded that they needed full political rights to protect the reality of emancipation. Northern journalist Whitelaw Reid captured this basic democratic insight from a North Carolina black man even while black leaders in the state were still counseling moderation. "I tell you sah," he told the reporter, "we ain't noways safe, 'long as dem people makes the laws we's got to be governed by. We's got to hab a voice in the 'pintin' of the law-makers." The need to protect freedom in African Americans' private lives thus led directly toward public affairs and into the intricate political history of Reconstruction.

Andrew Johnson's Approach

Enraged by northern victory and the prospect of black suffrage, the popular stage actor and southern sympathizer John Wilkes Booth took his revenge on April 14, 1865, with a shot that killed Abraham Lincoln and gave the presidency to Vice President Andrew Johnson of Tennessee. Like Lincoln, the new president assumed that reconstructing the Union was a military and executive task that belonged to him. He did not call a special session of Congress to deal with the sudden challenges of peace but attempted to govern the occupied states by presidential decree. The period when Johnson controlled reunion policy is known as Presidential Reconstruction.

THE TENNESSEE UNIONIST

Much like Abraham Lincoln, Andrew Johnson had grown up in severe poverty, serving as a tailor's apprentice in North Carolina before escaping to freedom in the hills of eastern Tennessee. He did not learn to read until he reached adulthood, yet he rose through minor political offices until he reached the House of Representatives, the governorship, and finally the US Senate. A lifelong Democrat, Johnson proudly represented the nonslaveholding yeomen of the upland South and denounced the region's elite as antirepublican aristocrats. The only southern senator who did not resign his seat when his state seceded, Johnson remained fiercely loyal to the Union and joined Lincoln on the National Union Party ticket in 1864 in a show of trans-sectional and bipartisan solidarity. When Lincoln's tragic death suddenly lifted him to the presidency, however, Andrew Johnson revealed that he sadly lacked the tact, flexibility, and wisdom that so distinguished his predecessor.

Once in office, Andrew Johnson was torn by conflicting feelings.

Acutely sensitive to his own humble origins, he burned with resentment of planter aristocrats and longed to call them to account. "Treason must be made odious, and traitors must be punished and impoverished," he swore repeatedly, highly gratifying Radical Republicans who longed to remake the South. But Johnson himself was not even a Republican, much a less a radical one, and he had no sympathy for Radical Republican notions of racial equality. At heart, Andrew Johnson remained devoted to the principles of President Andrew Jackson, his fellow Tennessean who had made states' rights, limited government, and white man's democracy cornerstones of the early Democratic Party. Since his best chances for election as president in his own right lay with the Democrats rather than Republicans, he soon realized that his own Reconstruction policy should emphasize forgiveness rather than punishment of the secessionists, a speedy restoration of the southern state governments, and reliance on states' rights to decide the fate of the freed people.

JOHNSON'S POLICIES

Six weeks after taking office, Johnson launched a surprisingly lenient Reconstruction policy. He did not mention treason trials or confiscations. Instead, he pardoned all Confederates who renounced secession and accepted emancipation, except for major Confederate leaders and the owners of $20,000 in taxable property. A second proclamation named a provisional governor for North Carolina and required him to call a special convention to write a new state constitution. Unpardoned Confederates could neither serve in this convention nor vote for its delegates, but the state's other suffrage laws remained in effect, so black men (and all women) could not vote. The other seceded states received similar instructions. Once a state had renounced secession, accepted emancipation, repudiated the Confederate debt, and written these changes into a new constitution, Johnson decided, it could elect its own governor, legislature, and members of Congress. When the House and Senate admitted the new representatives, legal Reconstruction would be over.

Southern voters signaled their sentiments through the delegates they chose to these constitutional conventions. They mostly avoided ardent ex-Confederates and strict ex-unionists. They turned instead to so-called Conservatives—often members of the old Whig Party—who resisted secession initially, supported the Confederacy eventually, and felt entitled to lead their states without submitting to social change. White voters may have thought that choosing Conservative leaders meant rejecting Confederate diehards, but northerners who viewed the "iron-clad oath" as the true test of loyalty could only see that former rebels were returning to power.

In their conventions, these ambivalent ex-Confederates quickly revealed that they had not grasped the limits of their autonomy. As former unionists, they felt sadly vindicated rather than discredited by the war's outcome and saw no reason why they or their states should suffer further. Instead of thanking the president for his lenity, Conservatives bargained over terms and revived the old slogans of "honor" and "states' rights." Some demanded payment for their lost slaves or declined to ratify the Thirteenth Amendment. Many protested the repudiation of state bonds. Others refused to brand disunion as illegal (as Johnson demanded) and would only repeal the ordinances of secession. Allowing blacks to testify against whites was highly unpopular, and no state would permit them to vote.

With constitutions complete, the new legislatures assembled and turned northern irritation into anger. Assuming that blacks would never work or obey the laws voluntarily, the states adopted special laws, known as Black Codes, to regulate their conduct. Mississippi required all blacks to have a year-long contract on January 1 that bound them to a specific employer, punished them for changing jobs, and penalized employers who tried to lure away contracted workers with better job offers. Every southern state soon had "vagrancy" statutes that punished unemployment with a term of forced labor for a private employer. Other provisions restored slave regulations that banned black preachers, prohibited black social or political gatherings, and barred blacks from hunting, fishing, carrying weapons, and leaving a plantation without permission. Apprenticeship laws allowed courts to bind black children to white masters without their parents' permission. The Conservative legislatures made clear they intended to return blacks to near servitude, candidly calling them inferiors who could not be ruled another way.

The former masters' actions were as harsh as their laws. Every day brought new reports of unfair labor contracts and efforts to replicate slavery. The worst disputes ended in whippings, robbery, rape, or even death. "We are murdered with impunity in the streets," ran a typical plea from Newberry, South Carolina, "and the murderers are walking at large and no notice taken of them. We have no law. We pray to the Government for protection."

Northern anger boiled over when President Johnson began pardoning high-ranking Confederates by the hundreds and southern voters chose them for high offices. Despite his earlier threats to punish and impoverish traitors, the president now seemed willing to return the South's elite to power, if only its members would humble themselves to seek his personal forgiveness. For most Confederate leaders, that was a small price to pay. The new governors of Mississippi, South Carolina, and North Carolina had been a Confederate general, a Confederate senator, and the Confederate state treasurer, respectively. Georgia even sent former Confederate vice president Alexander H. Stephens to the US Senate. "There seems in many of the elections," the president admitted, "something like defiance, which is all out of place at this time." Congress was more emphatic. Using their constitutional power to judge the fitness of their own members, the Senate and House both refused to admit the new representatives in December 1865, barring the South's return to the Union and blocking the president's Reconstruction policy.

REPUBLICANS REACT

Congress reacted to abuses of former slaves by extending the life of the Freedmen's Bureau past its original one-year term and leaving federal troops in the South to enforce its decrees. A second measure, the Civil Rights Bill, countered the Black Codes by granting US citizenship to all native-born Americans of every race (except Native Americans living under tribal governments), with the right "to full and equal benefit of all laws and proceedings for the security of person and property, as is enjoyed by white citizens." This central feature overturned the *Dred Scott* case of 1857, which restricted citizenship to whites. Contrary to modern principles, the Civil Rights Bill of 1866 did not secure political activities like the right to vote, hold office, or serve on juries, but guaranteed the citizen's right to move from place to place, earn a living, make contracts, conduct lawsuits, and testify in court. Moderates assumed that President Johnson would support these steps as part of a minimal program to safeguard the results of the Civil War.

Much to the moderates' dismay, however, Andrew Johnson vetoed both the Freedmen's Bureau Bill and the Civil Rights Bill in February and March of 1866. He called the Freedmen's Bureau unnecessary because, he said, the freed people should learn to take care of themselves. If they needed official protection, they should seek it from their state governments. He criticized Congress for providing more benefits to blacks than it ever offered "our own people" and for legislating for the South while it lacked representatives in Congress. He likewise denounced the Civil Rights Bill for expanding federal power at the expense of states' rights. Defending the principle of racial discrimination, Johnson warned that federal guarantees of nonpolitical civil rights could lead irresistibly to political equality. Even laws against racial intermarriage—a special fear of Johnson's—could be vulnerable. "In fact," he argued, "the distinction of race and color is by the bill made to operate in favor of the colored and against the white race."

Shocked by Johnson's blindness to southern realities and his strident defense of states' rights and racial inequality, congressional Republicans enacted the Civil Rights and Freedmen's Bureau Bills over his veto. Soon afterward, further public violence confirmed their suspicions of the South's new governments. In early May, a routine Memphis traffic accident sparked a battle between black soldiers and city policemen, followed by three days of bloodshed, the deaths of 46 blacks and 2 whites, the rape of at least 5 black women, and the arson of hundreds of black homes and churches. At the end of July, street fighting broke out in New Orleans when members of the state constitutional convention gathered to consider granting suffrage to black men and stripping it from Confederate leaders. White policemen poured rifle fire into the hall as terrified delegates waved white flags of surrender. In the words of General Philip Sheridan, this "absolute massacre" took the lives of 34 blacks and 3 white Republicans. Together with the Memphis riot, it also belied President Johnson's claim that southern conditions had returned to normal and existing governments would protect the rights of blacks and their supporters.

Congress Takes Charge

Andrew Johnson's angry refusal to monitor southern governments or preserve public order convinced moderate Republicans that Presidential Reconstruction had failed and that further inaction would allow ex-Confederates to regain power and nullify the northern victory. Over the spring of 1866, they accepted Radical Republican arguments that Johnson could not be trusted and reluctantly decided to take control of Reconstruction themselves, remove the president's Conservative state governments, and start over with full protection for the war's ostensible winners. The ensuing period is sometimes called Congressional Reconstruction, or Radical Reconstruction, though moderate Republicans made the key decisions throughout.

THE FOURTEENTH AMENDMENT

Congress spelled out its own terms for Reconstruction in a new constitutional amendment that a presidential veto or shifting party politics could not reverse. The Fourteenth Amendment went directly to the states for ratification, since proposed amendments do not require a presidential signature. Ratified in 1868, its provisions immediately became central to Reconstruction policy and have remained crucial to US law and politics ever since.

The amendment's first section wrote the basic features of the Civil Rights Act of 1866 into the Constitution by making all US-born persons "citizens of the United States and of the State wherein they reside." In a brief set of ringing phrases that judges still struggle to interpret, it also barred states from limiting "the privileges and immunities" of US citizens, forbade them from taking any person's "life, liberty, or property without due process of law," and guaranteed "equal protection of the laws" to all persons. These phrases banned blatantly discriminatory laws like the Black Codes, but what else? Future courts would agonize over what "due process of law" required in trials and other legal proceedings. Later courts would decide that the Fourteenth Amendment not only protected "natural persons" but also "artificial persons" like corporations. What would due process mean for them? What were the "privileges and immunities" of US citizens? Were they legally the same as "rights?" And what exactly was "equal protection of the laws"? It certainly meant that states could not make explicitly different laws for each race. But did it outlaw other forms of racial discrimination, like "separate but equal" schools? Or rules for corporations that did not apply to individuals? Or discrimination based on sex or disability? In 1866, Congress did not debate these questions, but all of them would eventually become the subjects of intense political and constitutional disputes in future decades.

The amendment's second section tried to correct an anomaly arising from emancipation. The original Constitution had allotted electoral votes and congressional seats according to a state's free population plus three-fifths of its slaves. The end of slavery thus required the government to count *all* blacks for electoral purposes and reward the South's rebellion by increasing its numbers in the House of Representatives. The second section responded by declaring that states which denied some adult male citizens the right to vote would face a proportionate reduction in their congressional delegations. This provision did not require black suffrage but rewarded states that allowed it. The third section declared that officials who had once sworn to support the US Constitution but then served the Confederacy could no longer vote or hold state or federal office without congressional permission. This feature stripped political power from most of the South's old elite and its current Conservative leadership.

Republicans hoped that the Fourteenth Amendment would establish a fair but reasonably painless process for legal Reconstruction. Southern states could regain their political rights if they ratified the amendment, purged their governments of ex-Confederates, and gave black men the ballot or accepted fewer seats in the House. Instead, the South's Conservative leaders rejected the bargain completely, for they had no intention of leaving office, allowing black suffrage, or accepting fewer congressmen. Strongly encouraged by the president, all the seceding states but Tennessee refused to ratify the Fourteenth Amendment in the summer and fall of 1866. In reply, northern voters returned a two-thirds Republican majority to both houses of Congress in the fall elections of 1866 and set the stage for a more radical reunion.

THE RECONSTRUCTION ACTS

On March 2, 1867, the new Congress responded to the South's rejection of the Fourteenth Amendment by passing the first of four statutes, collectively known as the Reconstructions Acts, that imposed a far stricter Reconstruction policy. President Johnson immediately vetoed this bill and its successors, and just as quickly, Congress overrode him. As Radical Republicans wished, the new law divided the ten nonratifying states into five military districts, each under a general who could overrule the existing state governments, and ordered them to call new conventions to rewrite their constitutions once again. To ensure loyal outcomes, it granted all adult black men the right to vote for and serve as convention delegates, but barred the ex-Confederates proscribed by the Fourteenth Amendment. It required the new constitutions to do the same and promised that the new state governments could reclaim their seats in Congress if they ratified the Fourteenth Amendment. The second, third, and fourth statutes (passed in March 1867, July 1867, and March 1868) basically tightened and fine-tuned the first. Contemporaries agreed that black male suffrage was a radical step, but the new policy did not apply to the North and did not promise lengthy federal supervision or military support.

Even so, the Reconstruction Acts had revolutionary possibilities.

They overthrew the South's planter-politicians and gave control of the region to freed slaves and common whites. If they remained united, these citizens could use their new power to transform southern society. Without economic strength, political experience, or military muscle, however, their hold on power might be brief. It was a breathtaking challenge for the inhabitants of what had been America's most undemocratic region.

THE IMPEACHMENT AND
TRIAL OF ANDREW JOHNSON

Andrew Johnson detested the goal of racial equality as embodied in the Reconstruction Acts, but he could not defy them because Congress had vested enforcement in the War Department. To regain control of Reconstruction policy, Johnson would have to fire Secretary of War Edwin M. Stanton, a reliable Republican holdover from Lincoln's cabinet. To prevent him from doing so, Congress passed the Tenure in Office Act, banning the dismissal of officials whom the Senate had confirmed. Regarding the law as unconstitutional (he was probably right), Johnson fired Stanton anyway. Immediately afterward, on February 24, 1868, the House of Representatives voted to impeach Andrew Johnson of "high crimes and misdemeanors" and remove him from office.

Impeachment occurred because Congress and the president were utterly deadlocked. Radical Republicans had demanded Johnson's removal for months, but moderates had resisted, fearing a backlash from voters. When House moderates realized that Johnson would undo all their handiwork by removing Stanton and other key officials, they resolved to remove him first and adopted eleven articles of impeachment based around his defiance of the Tenure in Office Act. These articles constituted a kind of formal accusation, or indictment. As directed by the Constitution, the trial would take place before the Senate, with the chief justice presiding and a two-thirds vote required for conviction.

At the trial, Johnson's attorneys argued that the president had committed no crime; he only sought to create an ordinary test case against a law he believed to be unconstitutional. The argument seemed plausible, and pragmatic politicians also worried about Johnson's replacement. Without a vice president, the designated successor was Benjamin Wade of Ohio, president pro tempore of the Senate and an active Radical Republican who might seem extreme to some voters and hurt Republicans in the next election. Desperately bargaining for acquittal, moreover, Johnson promised to drop his obstructionism and abide by Congress's policies. With these reassurances, seven Republicans joined all the Senate's Democrats in voting for acquittal in May 1868, and Andrew Johnson escaped conviction by exactly one vote. Before his term ended, Johnson sought but failed to win the Democratic nomination for president in 1868. He spent most of the rest of his life in political obscurity, except for a brief stint in the US Senate shortly before his death in 1875.

Reconstruction and Resistance

Congressional Reconstruction allowed Republican coalitions of blacks, native whites, and northern newcomers to take control of all the southern states but Virginia. They used the opportunity to broaden southern democracy, expand public services, and spread black voting and office holding across the former slave states. Like other state and local governments of the era, however, some Reconstruction regimes were vulnerable to corruption, especially in connection with railroad construction.

Radical reforms sparked violent resistance. Terrorist groups like the Ku Klux Klan used assault and murder to intimidate Republican voters and officials and to recapture southern communities. Fearing these groups might undo everything they had accomplished, Republicans tried to protect black voting with the Fifteenth Amendment to the Constitution, but they could not safeguard the Reconstruction governments indefinitely.

THE REPUBLICAN EXPERIMENT IN THE STATES

War hero Ulysses S. Grant won election as the Republican candidate for president in 1868, and Congressional Reconstruction moved forward with his full support. In every affected state, military authorities conducted a new registration of voters and then held elections for new state constitutional conventions. In response to their new opportunity, southern blacks and their white supporters organized the Republican Party in the southern states and vied with Democrats (as Conservatives were coming to call themselves) for control of state governments. Branches of the Union League, a wartime patriotic organization, also spread widely through the South and worked closely with Republicans to mobilize and educate black voters.

The South's new Republicans came from three groups. Most were former slaves who saw Republicans as the party of liberation and Democrats as tools of their former masters. Next came native white opponents of the planter class. Often condemned as renegades, or "scalawags," southern white Republicans typically came from the yeoman, or poor, white classes, from the nonslaveholding upland districts, or from business interests anxious to transform the southern economy. A few, like Governor James L. Alcorn of Mississippi, had been Whig members of the antebellum elite who accepted the war's outcome and wanted the South to start afresh. Finally there were northern newcomers, both black and white, who had moved south during or following the war, often with the Union Army, the Freedmen's Bureau, or private relief agencies, or as businessmen looking for investment opportunities. Quickly dubbed "carpetbaggers" by those who saw them as fortune-hunting riffraff who carried all their possessions in cheap suitcases made of carpeting, northern Republicans in the South were a diverse group who rarely deserved their unsavory reputations. Many were sincere if inexperienced idealists, others were practical men of affairs, and a few turned out to be scoundrels. The names "scalawag" and "carpetbagger" both have unfairly negative connotations, but historians continue to use them for the lack of simple alternatives. Of the three groups of Republicans, the native whites were the least committed and might be pushed or persuaded to rejoin their fellow whites in a white majority government.

Republicans dominated the new state conventions. Most were native whites led by a small number of carpetbaggers. Blacks formed a majority of delegates in South Carolina and Louisiana, but only a small minority in most states. Democrats and Conservatives represented the South's pro-Confederate whites, even though the Reconstruction Acts barred most Confederate leaders from this round of constitution making.

The new constitutions differed markedly from their antebellum counterparts. Up-country voters gained more-equal representation in state assemblies. Voters rather than legislatures chose most state officials. Appointed local governments became elective. The wealthy faced higher taxes. Public schools, poor relief, mental hospitals, and orphanages became required where they once had not existed. Prison sentences replaced slavish punishments like whipping, branding, and cropping of ears. Most states expanded the property rights of women and liberalized divorce laws. Seeking to win white support, moreover, most Republican governments quickly relaxed prohibitions on political participation by ex-Confederates.

Most new charters won voter approval in 1868. The affected states then elected Republican governors and state legislatures, ratified the Fourteenth Amendment, and chose mostly Republican congressmen. Details varied by state, but Congress was usually satisfied with these results and seated the new senators and representatives. By 1870, all the seceding states had reentered the Union, though federal troops still occupied parts of them.

At one time, many historians were extremely critical of the Republican governments in Reconstruction, accusing them of incompetence, waste, corruption, and "Negro domination." Much of this criticism was based on racial and partisan prejudice, often drawn directly from the rhetoric of whites who eventually overthrew the Reconstruction governments. In fact, blacks did not capture any legislative majority, except briefly in South Carolina's lower house. Two black men, Blanche K. Bruce and Hiram Revels, both of Mississippi, won election as US senators, and other African Americans joined them in the US House of Representatives. Perhaps most significant to ordinary freed people, blacks also served as state legislators, city council members, county commissioners, justices of the peace, sheriffs, and policemen, putting sympathetic faces on local public authority in the South for the very first time. The critical importance of having officials committed to black freedom at the grass roots had much to do with the willingness of blacks and whites to fight so fiercely for control of local government in incidents like the Colfax Massacre.

Corruption did plague many Reconstruction governments, but the same was true in northern states and in those controlled by Democrats. Republican officeholders suffered from inexperience and a lack of economic power at all levels, but their records in office generally stand a fair comparison with those of their Democratic rivals.

Republicans tried to use state governments to reconstruct the South's society as well as its laws. Legislatures eliminated the vestiges of the Black Codes and other forms of state-sponsored discrimination. They strengthened the rights of tenants and employees against the power of landlords and employers. Several fought to integrate public accommodations like railroads, streetcars, hotels, restaurants, and theaters, without mixing the races in the public schools. Most increased expenditures for education, health care, penitentiaries, and poor relief, and raised taxes accordingly.

Above all, the Reconstruction governments supported economic development through railroad construction. The slave South had lagged in building roads, canals, and railways, and both parties resolved to catch up. Lacking private capital, governments endorsed the bonds of private companies, agreeing to take over their roads and service their debts if they failed. Unfortunately, some states endorsed too many bonds and chartered impractical projects. Rival promoters competed feverishly for public subsidies and many offered bribes for favorable treatment. Hard-pressed for funds, legislators of both races and parties gave in to temptation. Even more damaging, some corporations laid few tracks but diverted borrowed money to their managers and directors. These scams collapsed when economic depression struck in 1873, leaving taxpayers with huge debts and few resources for repayment. Even if both parties were guilty, voters blamed the party in power and listened when Democrats faulted black lawmakers and all state development projects.

WHITE VIOLENCE AND THE KU KLUX KLAN

Corruption, high taxes, and railroad frauds were choice issues for the opposition, but not enough to expel the Republicans. Soon after the adoption of black suffrage in 1868, secret terrorist organizations began to attack the new regimes, using such names as the White Brotherhood, the Knights of the White Camellia, and the Constitutional Union Guard. The Ku Klux Klan was the deadliest and most widespread.

Founded in 1866 as a social club for Confederate veterans in Pulaski, Tennessee, the Ku Klux Klan took its name from *kuklos*, the Greek word for "circle," and spread rapidly when its members realized how their hooded costumes could disguise acts of persecution and terror. Acting independently, loosely organized Klan cells launched midnight raids to beat and intimidate Republican officeholders and the leaders of Union League branches, black schools, and black churches. When considered necessary, murder took the place of whipping or tarring and feathering. Often functioning as the military arm of the local Democratic Party, the Klan sought to reestablish "white supremacy" by driving black and white Republicans underground. Deeply aggrieved by emancipation and black suffrage, Klansmen sometimes suggested that blacks were the tools of unscrupulous whites. "Our warfare was only against the Carpet bagger, Scalawag, [and] Provost Marshals," remembered one white participant in the Colfax Massacre, who had been a member of both the Knights of the White Camellia and the Ku Klux Klan. "[They] were leading the poor negroes in their efforts to overrule the White Citizen for Power and Equality."

The Klan became most active in politically and racially divided neighborhoods like Colfax, Louisiana, where shrewdly applied violence could tip the political scale. Ohio-born judge Albion W. Tourgée counted 12 murders, 9 rapes, 14 cases of arson, and over 700 assaults in one such North Carolina district. Protected by the local sheriff, Klansmen stabbed and strangled a white Republican state senator inside one county courthouse there and hanged a Union League president outside another. Several southern counties each experienced more than 100 political murders in the nine years between 1867 and 1876.

Like the black leaders of Colfax, Republicans fought back across the South. New laws forbade traveling in disguise or conspiring to intimidate others, but enforcement was not easy, especially where the Klan controlled the local government. Anxious to attract white support, governors hesitated to use black soldiers to get control of predominantly white areas. In North Carolina, Republican governor William W. Holden proclaimed martial law and recruited a militia of mountain whites to enforce it. The governor of Tennessee did the same, while Texas and Arkansas restored order with integrated militias. Holden's tactic had limited success, however, for North Carolina Democrats used ensuing white outrage to win legislative elections, impeach him, and remove him from office in 1870.

THE FIFTEENTH AMENDMENT

Beleaguered southern Republicans looked to the federal government. In response, President Grant endorsed a constitutional amendment to guarantee black men the right to vote throughout the nation. Congress had long feared a northern backlash to this measure, but more was at stake than Reconstruction alone, for Democrats had recovered strength everywhere, so the national Republican majority now depended on black votes. Congress accordingly approved the Fifteenth Amendment in 1869 and it won state ratification a year later. This amendment barred all states—including those in the North—from limiting the right to vote by reason of race or slavery, but it did not protect the right to hold office, nor did it prevent disenfranchisement for nominally nonracial reasons like illiteracy or the nonpayment of taxes. These omissions would cripple its later effectiveness, but the Fifteenth Amendment was ultimately crucial to the civil rights movement of the 1960s and afterward.

The Fourteenth and Fifteenth Amendments angered Elizabeth Cady Stanton, Susan B. Anthony, and others in the small but determined band of reformers who wanted votes for women and blacks as part of a broad program for racial and gender equality. They were especially outraged that the Fourteenth Amendment inserted the word "male" into the Constitution for the first time. When the Fifteenth Amendment also failed to provide women's suffrage, some reformers acquiesced, including black abolitionist Frederick Douglass, editor Horace Greeley, and suffragist Lucy Stone, who argued that insisting on votes for women might imperil votes for black men. Stanton, Anthony, and their supporters vehemently disagreed and called for defeat of the Fifteenth Amendment. By failing to include women, they argued, it put an "an aristocracy of sex" in the Constitution, based on the idea that all men were superior to all women. In 1869, the two wings of the women's suffrage movement formed rival organizations, the National Woman Suffrage Association, led by Stanton and Anthony, and the American Woman Suffrage Association, led by Lucy Stone and abolitionist Julia Ward Howe, and did not reunite until 1890. Their cause slowly gathered momentum, however, and in 1869, Wyoming became the first American state or territory to give voting rights to women, closely followed by Utah in 1870.

Though Stanton continued to support suffrage for women and men of all races, she began to argue that "pure" women were better qualified to vote than "degraded" men, especially those from "inferior" races. "American women of wealth, education, virtue and refinement," she warned, "if you do not wish the lower orders of Chinese, Africans, Germans and Irish, with their low ideas of womanhood to make laws for you and your daughters . . . demand that women too shall be represented in government." The dispute over women's suffrage revealed deep divisions between the movements for racial equality and women's rights that frequently erupted in subsequent decades.

Leading Republicans hoped the Fifteenth Amendment would complete the work of Reconstruction by allowing southern blacks to defend themselves with ballots and dispense with northern help. They also sought support from moderate white southerners who would give black suffrage a chance. They found few takers, but widely publicized cases of corruption and factionalism in southern state governments made many wonder if southern state governments were really worth saving. In many cases, moreover, Republican coalitions remained too weak and white violence remained too strong for the Fifteenth Amendment to fulfill its purpose without federal enforcement. Here President Grant faced a political tightrope, for nineteenth-century Americans were still very uncomfortable with federal intervention in local affairs. If he failed to protect black ballots with federal troops, white Democrats would overthrow Republicans and undo Reconstruction. If he used federal troops too aggressively, opponents would freely call him a military despot who would keep his party in office by force. Grant tried to respond judiciously, sending troops in flagrant cases like Louisiana, but holding back when force seemed unnecessary or useless. The nearly inevitable result was that federal policy looked vacillating, or indecisive, further undermining northern support for Reconstruction policy. "It is the general feeling," reflected an Ohio Republican as the Fifteenth Amendment went into effect, "that we have done enough, gone far enough in governmental reconstruction, and that it is best for all that the southern communities should be left to manage themselves."

Still unwilling to give up, Congress backed up the Fifteenth Amendment with the Enforcement Acts to allow federal oversight of state elections in cases of suspected violence, fraud, or intimidation. The 1871 Ku Klux Klan Act made it a federal crime to interfere with a citizen's political rights, including voting, office holding, jury service, and equal protection, and Attorney General Amos T. Ackerman used it to arrest hundreds of suspected Klansmen in Tennessee, Mississippi, and the Carolinas. By 1872, the Ku Klux Klan itself had mostly collapsed, but groups known as "White Leagues," "Red Shirts," and "rifle clubs" continued its violent practices. The Colfax violence claimed the greatest number of victims, but between 1873 and 1875, other incidents took dozens of black lives in Red River Parish, Louisiana; Vicksburg, Mississippi; Clinton, Mississippi; and Hamburg, South Carolina. President Grant condemned these incidents unsparingly, denouncing "the butchery of citizens" at Colfax "which in bloodthirstiness and barbarity is hardly surpassed by any acts of savage warfare." In practice, however, there was less and less that he could do.

These episodes inevitably left their mark. Taxes and corruption had already alienated many moderate white southerners who once tolerated Republican rule. Year after year, the combination of disillusionment and intimidation increased Democratic votes and decreased those of the Republicans. Beginning with North Carolina in 1870, Republicans lost control across the region as white conservatives vowed to "redeem" the southern states with permanent Democratic majorities. By 1876, these self-styled Redeemers had recaptured all the former Confederacy but South Carolina and Louisiana, and nothing protected those states from Democratic takeover but federal troops around their statehouses. And during the second Grant administration, other problems made it increasingly unlikely that federal protection would endure.

Constructing the West

As the high drama of Reconstruction unfolded in the South, a complex set of seemingly separate developments was transforming the western territories. In the 1840s, the acquisitions of Texas, Oregon, and the Mexican Cession extended the United States' boundaries to the Pacific Ocean. Debates over these territories eventually led to the Civil War itself, but events in the West had not stood still while the war raged and Congress and the president wrestled over peacetime policies. The Johnson administration even enlarged the "West" still more when Secretary of State William Seward negotiated the purchase of Alaska from Russia in 1867, though decades passed before Alaska experienced the kinds of changes that were already transforming the trans-Mississippi region. The experiences of the South and West appeared to be very different, but underlying questions of racial justice, economic development, and national unification bedeviled them both.

WAR IN THE WEST

Most members of the so-called Five Civilized Tribes of the Indian Territory, or modern Oklahoma (Choctaws, Chickasaws, Cherokees, Creeks, and Seminoles), had sided with the Confederacy in the Civil War, both because they blamed the federal government for their earlier expulsion from the Southeast and because most of their leaders held African American slaves. Early in the war, all five tribes transferred their allegiance to the Confederacy, which pledged to assume the Union's treaty obligations to them. Though the Creeks and Cherokees also had pro-Union factions, all five tribes contributed troops to the Confederacy, most of them led by the Cherokee brigadier general Stand Watie. Smaller groups in the Indian Territory took similar steps, as did several bands of Comanches and Kiowas farther west. At war's end, the Union resumed its treaty relations with the tribes of the Indian Territory but punished Confederate allies with land seizures. It required slaveholding tribes to relinquish slavery and accept their former slaves as tribal members.

Elsewhere in the West, the Civil War had sharpened the contest between whites and Indians, beginning with events in 1862. Early that year, a southern expeditionary force attempted to secure the Southwest's mineral resources for the Confederacy, only to meet defeat at Glorieta Pass, New Mexico, the war's westernmost battle. In the fall, the Lakota, or Sioux, people of southwest Minnesota attacked neighboring white settlements over stolen land and annuity payments, and in the aftermath, President Lincoln approved the hanging of 38 tribal leaders, the largest mass execution in US history. Also that year, Congress passed the Homestead Act and chartered the Union Pacific and Central Pacific Railroads, both crucial components of western transformation.

The Civil War had originated in struggles over the western territories, and the Union and Confederate governments remained eager to secure their lands and mineral riches. The Union proved more successful in recruiting white westerners' support, however, and organized military forces throughout the area to defend its claims. As the Confederate campaign for the West faltered, these Union soldiers often shifted their attention to fighting Indians. In 1864, for example, a party of local militiamen attacked an encampment of unarmed and sleeping Cheyenne and Arapahoe at Sand Creek, Colorado, killing and mutilating more than 150, mostly women and children. The Sand Creek Massacre brought retaliatory attacks throughout the region that became excuses for wider warfare.

During Reconstruction, President Grant tried to end this violence with an Indian "Peace Policy" that revived earlier plans for changing the cultures of Native Americans. Soon after taking office, he appointed Ely Parker, a Seneca Indian and wartime associate, to be commissioner of the Bureau of Indian Affairs and asked a committee of ten leading Protestants to oversee Indian relations. Their assignment was to persuade the Plains hunters to settle on large reservations, convert to Christianity, and support themselves by farming. Corruption plagued the implementation of this policy, however, and most reservation lands were unfit for cultivation, so warfare soon resumed, most spectacularly in 1876, when the Lakota fighters of Sitting Bull and others completely destroyed the command of Lieutenant Colonel George Armstrong Custer at the Battle of the Little Bighorn.

Eliminating Indian food supplies by wiping out the buffalo herds was an active military tactic. Having moved from Civil War duties to the West, General William T. Sherman called for a "Grand Buffalo hunt" in 1868 to eliminate the animals from the paths of the Union Pacific and Kansas Pacific Railroads. "Until the Buffalo and consequent[ly] Indians are out [from between] the Roads we will have collisions and trouble," he advised a subordinate. Colonel Richard Dodge was blunter. "Kill all the buffalo you can," he told his troops. "Every buffalo dead is an Indian gone." Soldiers did their best to comply and facilitated parties of eastern and European "sportsmen" who wanted to join the fun. The herds were vulnerable because Indians had already overhunted them to supply the commercial market for skins, and military and civilian hunters nearly finished the job. By 1900, the American bison, or buffalo, was almost extinct.

NEW SETTLERS

A vigorous process of railroad construction aided the settlement process. Railroads could not expect to make profits while building through empty lands, so Congress provided support for transcontinental railroads in 1862 by offering to lend them between $16,000 and $48,000 per mile, depending on topography. It also gave them the right-of-way, or the path of the track itself, and as many as 20 "sections," or square miles, of public land in a checkerboard pattern along the right-of-way. Thirty years later, the two railroads repaid these loans, but through a highly favorable method of calculating interest payments, they amounted to a bountiful cash subsidy from the taxpayers. The assistance succeeded when the tracks of the Union Pacific and Central Pacific Railroads met at Promontory Point, Utah, in 1869. The Northern Pacific, the Southern Pacific, and the Santa Fe lines quickly followed, and by 1871 the five had received loans of nearly $65 million and grants of 130 million acres, or 9.5 percent of the public domain, to finance their ventures. Individual states added as many as 50 million acres of their own, and total US railroad mileage increased from 9,000 to 87,000 miles between 1850 and 1885. Extensive corruption eased the way for this legislative bounty, but the railroads used it successfully. Their workers performed heroic feats of construction through towering mountains and blistering deserts at daily rates that could range from eight feet through solid rock to five miles across open prairie.

Population quickly followed the tracks under the encouragement of the Homestead Act, which granted 160 acres to every settler who remained for five years. State agencies encouraged immigration with guides in multiple European languages. Promoters promised recklessly that "rain followed the plow," so the arid prairies would soon blossom like the East. Believers flocked in, driving up state populations by hundreds of percentage points. Huddled on treeless plains in houses made of sod, the newcomers planted wheat and hoped for the best. When their crops came in, flour milling forged the cities of Minneapolis and Chicago.

From the early days of Spanish settlement, cattle ranching had long been a mainstay of the western economy. Texas ranchers had developed a hardy breed of longhorn cow that thrived in the ecological niche left by the vanishing buffalo and was capable of surviving harsh conditions and the tick-borne Texas fever. States near the Mississippi banned Texas cattle to protect their own animals from tick infestations, so the longhorns could not supply eastern markets until cattlemen discovered that a hard northern winter would kill the ticks and fatten the cows a bit. Thus began the legendary western cattle drives, featuring crews of white and black Texas cowboys who drove vast herds over the famed Chisholm Trail and similar routes to winter on the central plains before they took the railroad east from cow towns such as Abilene, Wichita, and Dodge City in Kansas. The cow towns kept moving westward along the tracks to keep ahead of farmers' anti-tick measures until breeds improved and tough, stringy longhorns fell from favor. The cattle business grew even more after 1882, when the refrigerated railroad car made it to possible to slaughter cows in Chicago or Kansas City and then sell them cheaply in eastern cities. Centered on the stockyards of the South Side of Chicago, the Swift and Armour companies created a meatpacking monopoly founded on western cattle.

The people who flocked to the West joined one of the most varied ethnic medleys in America. White southerners and midwesterners had sparked the Texas Revolution, and more kept coming in the postwar years. The California gold rush had attracted prospectors from all over the world, including Mexico, Chile, Australia, China, eastern America, and all parts of Europe. Elsewhere in the West, newcomers railed against the Indians, but some Native Americans remained behind when their tribes accepted reservations. Hispanic inhabitants, many with ancient roots in the region, also remained when Mexico withdrew. Mostly Irish work crews built the railroads as they headed west. Chinese workers, mostly men who planned to save their earnings and go back home, toiled on the lines that headed east from the Pacific. About a third of western cowboys were black. Other African Americans served as "buffalo soldiers" in the Plains Indian wars, and formerly enslaved "Exodusters" found land in Kansas when conditions in the Reconstruction South became too threatening.

RACE AND GOVERNMENT

Like the biracial South, this polyglot West posed a "race problem" for white Americans. The late nineteenth century was the heyday of "scientific racism," and learned scholars were quite sure that measurements of the skull and other body parts proved how white Americans were superior to all others, especially nonwhites or "mixed breeds" like Mexicans. Just to be sure, officials and army officers collected thousands of Indian skulls for racist scholars to evaluate. Just as in the South, white authorities agonized over how the West could be truly unified with the rest of the country when its people were so diverse. Official policy rejected the outright extermination of Indians, but as they did at Sand Creek, local authorities could act otherwise with impunity. The United States had promised to protect private landholdings in the Mexican Cession, but legal chicanery transferred thousands of acres to Anglo owners in the aftermath of annexation. Blacks faced racial segregation and exclusion, and the Chinese endured endless persecution. Laws barred them from public schools, public jobs, and testifying in court, while anti-Chinese riots periodically threatened their lives. Fearing their impact on wages, labor unions denied the Chinese membership and boycotted their employers. In 1882, the federal government responded with the Chinese Exclusion Act, the first law to ban the immigration of an entire ethnic group.

The cultural and political riddles posed by western settlement did not stop with race. Free-soil advocates had wanted the West to serve as an outlet and safety valve to protect freedom and opportunity for free citizens, always understood as independent white men and their families. The conviction that the Union existed to protect opportunities for such citizens had underpinned the North's commitment to Civil

War victory. In reality, however, opening the West to free white men required massive and expensive government investments for Indian warfare, railroad subsidies, and free homesteads, to only name a few. Later generations of westerners would demand further investments in water, energy, and highways, as well as support for powerful mining and timber companies. In the midst of all this government intervention and massive private enterprise, what would happen to the free individuals it supposedly benefited?

From this perspective, the South was clearly not the only region to struggle over the proper relationship between government and individuals or between race and citizenship in the Reconstruction era, for these issues disturbed Americans across the continent. Indeed, issues involving economic development, political corruption, and the proper use of government power tied the West and South together and raised pervasive challenges for a reconstructed nation.

Redeemers Triumphant

By the middle of the 1870s, voters who once demanded southern transformation were tiring of the task's demands. Reconstructing the South had dragged on for over a decade yet the challenge remained immense. Northern whites had never accepted the Radical Republican call for a lengthy undertaking, including prolonged use of federal troops, expensive education programs, and the redistribution of land. When southern Republicans proved too poor and inexperienced to resist their enemies successfully, many blamed racial inferiority and concluded that white supremacy was inevitable. Over the course of President Grant's administration, a number of developments reinforced northern reluctance to continue the Reconstruction process, including government corruption, political factionalism, adverse court decisions, and economic depression.

"GRANTISM"

Ulysses S. Grant came into office determined to protect and carry out the victory his troops had gained on the battlefield. As president, Grant conscientiously sought to protect black rights but was increasingly unsuccessful. He also found that civilian leadership demanded skills different from military prowess, and here the successful general stumbled badly. His most notorious shortcoming was an inability to prevent corruption. Following the Civil War, citizens in every section longed for the joys of peace and prosperity, and industrial growth began to spread from the Northeast. Factories expanded and governments vied to construct more railroads. Just like their southern counterparts, lobbyists promised instant wealth to legislatures in return for special privileges. In the carnival atmosphere that some critics dubbed "the Great Barbecue" and satirists Mark Twain and Charles Dudley Fields called the "Gilded Age," political morality collapsed along with common sense, as lawmakers from all sections and parties helped themselves to bribes, favors, and public funds.

The most conspicuous scandal of the Grant era concerned the Crédit Mobilier, a railroad construction firm owned by the officers of the Union Pacific Railroad. Using large government subsidies, they paid the company to build the road, but inflated its costs, spent minimal amounts on actual construction, and paid themselves the difference. Handsome gifts of stock silenced complaining congressmen until the scandal broke in 1872–1873.

President Grant played no role in this swindle, but his personal friends and advisors were deeply implicated in others. Two leading financiers, Jay Gould and Jim Fiske, conspired with Grant's brother-in-law to corner, or monopolize, the New York gold market and drive up gold's price. They briefly succeeded until the brother-in-law leaked information warning them to sell out and escape ruin just before government sales drove prices back down again. In another incident, William W. Belknap, Grant's secretary of war, resigned to escape impeachment when Congress discovered a kickback system in the licensing of Indian trading posts. The so-called Whiskey Ring conspired to evade the collection of federal excise taxes and avoid discovery by bribing Grant's friend and personal secretary. Grant never engaged in graft himself, but he certainly made poor appointments and the public called the corruption problems "Grantism."

WAVERING REPUBLICANS

Corruption was only one of several factors that threatened Grant's re-election in 1872. Southern and border state Republicans split deeply over their future. Should they still champion black equality, or should they imitate northern Republicans by serving railroads and businessmen? In most states, factionalism pitted blacks and carpetbaggers against scalawags, or native whites. Differences in principle played their part, but an unmistakable hunger for government salaries also influenced the rivalry, for party leaders had little hope of nonpolitical employment, especially if they were black. Patronage battles split every state Republican organization and weakened their resistance to Democrats. A Republican faction backed Democrats in the Louisiana election of 1872, for example, followed by the disputes that created two rival state governments there in the months before the Colfax Massacre.

Republican factionalism reached the presidential level in 1872. A group called the Liberal Republicans believed their party was badly corrupted by business interests and the spoils system of awarding government jobs to pay for political services. Distrusting professional politicians, Liberal Republicans thought the "best men" from well-educated and affluent families of the East and Midwest would put principles ahead of sordid personal interests. They also thought the "best men" should include planter aristocrats but not African Americans, whom they distrusted as susceptible to manipulation. They wanted to fill government jobs through civil service exams instead of the spoils system, but they opposed efforts to overturn race relations or enforce the Reconstruction amendments.

Splitting their party, Liberal Republicans nominated Horace Greeley for president in 1872. Greeley was an ex-Whig and founding editor of the nation's most respected Republican newspaper, the *New York Tribune*. Desperate to topple Grant, most Democrats endorsed Greeley instead of their own candidate, but he was painfully incompetent on the stump and Grant sailed to an easy victory. Even so, the breakaway movement showed that many Republicans were tiring of Reconstruction, questioned government efforts to reform society, and trusted elites over ordinary citizens. Once raised, moreover, the issues of civil service reform and the spoils system did not disappear but agitated state and national politics for the rest of the Gilded Age.

Important Supreme Court decisions also hampered Reconstruction and revealed a shifting national mood. In the *Slaughter-House Cases* of 1873, a group of New Orleans butchers complained that the city's publicly owned slaughterhouse hurt their businesses and violated the Fourteenth Amendment by abridging the "privileges and immunities" of US citizens. They even accused the public facility of violating the Thirteenth Amendment by reducing them to "involuntary servitude." The court disagreed and denied that the Thirteenth Amendment applied to anything but genuine bondage. Going further, it insisted that the Fourteenth Amendment only protected the "privileges and immunities" that stemmed from *national* citizenship, like the right to run for federal office or the right to travel abroad, and not those of *state* citizenship, like the right to run a butcher shop. By the same token, the court's reasoning meant that the Fourteenth Amendment would not protect other local rights like the right to equal treatment on trains and streetcars or in public facilities like schools or restaurants. This decision virtually destroyed the power of the Fourteenth Amendment to defend significant black rights under actual conditions in the Reconstruction South.

Events in Colfax played a crucial role in *U.S. v. Cruikshank* (1876). After the 1873 massacre, federal troops and New Orleans police occupied Grant Parish. Most white perpetrators fled, but the authorities made a few arrests and a lower court convicted William Cruikshank and two others of violating the Enforcement Act of 1870. When Cruikshank appealed his conviction, the Supreme Court freed him and ruled that the Enforcement Act was unconstitutional because the Fourteenth and Fifteenth Amendments prohibited *states* but not *individuals* (like Cruikshank) from violating the rights of blacks. The decision not only freed all white participants in the Colfax Massacre; it also closed the federal courts to other victims of racist violence.

Reconstruction suffered another blow in 1873 when a powerful panic, or economic crisis, hit the nation's financial markets, triggering a deep and long-lasting depression. The Panic of 1873 brought wage cuts, collapsing crop prices, widespread unemployment, and numerous business failures. Voters punished Republicans by shifting to the Democrats, by supporting one of several third parties, like the Labor Reform Party and the Greenback Party, or simply by staying home on Election Day.

Endangered Republicans moved in opposite directions. To honor the death of Radical Republican war-horse Charles Sumner, they tried to shore up black support with an 1875 Civil Rights Act that banned racial segregation in boats, trains, theaters, hotels, and eating places (but not public schools). The Supreme Court struck it down in 1883 on the grounds that its legal protections made African Americans "the special favorite of the laws." To mollify Liberal Republican dissidents, however, mainstream Republicans promised to lighten enforcement of existing Reconstruction laws. When President Grant sought renewal of the expired Ku Klux Klan Act, Congress refused.

THE COMPROMISE OF 1877

The Reconstruction experiment in racial equality hung by a thread as the 1876 presidential election approached. Democratic victory would certainly end the federal search for racial equality, but Republicans might abandon the unpopular project as well. The Republican presidential candidate was Rutherford B. Hayes, a respectable Union war veteran with a clean record as governor of Ohio. The Democrats chose New York's governor Samuel J. Tilden, who had prosecuted and jailed his fellow Democrat "Boss" William M. Tweed of New York City's notoriously corrupt "Tweed Ring." Democrats campaigned against "Grantism," while Republicans mostly "waved the bloody shirt" by blaming Democrats for the Civil War's carnage. They also pandered to ethnic and religious passions by stirring up Protestant fears of Roman Catholic immigrants, who often lived in urban poverty, allegedly tolerated corruption, and usually voted Democratic.

Alarmist tactics were not enough. Tilden won a majority of 300,000 in the popular vote, but only 184 of the 185 votes he needed to carry the Electoral College. Hayes had clearly taken 165 electoral votes, but 20 votes remained in dispute, chiefly from the states of Florida, South Carolina, and Louisiana. In these areas, fraud and corruption by both parties and violent intimidation by White Leagues and Red Shirts had hopelessly confused the results, leading rival electoral canvassing boards from each party to claim the victory. Most independent observers thought that Tilden deserved at least some of the disputed ballots, but if Hayes kept all 20, Republicans would keep the White House by a single electoral vote.

Congress appointed a special commission to weigh the doubtful votes and settle the election. This supposedly balanced body gained a Republican majority, however, when its sole independent member accepted an irresistible seat in the Senate. By strictly party line votes, the commission then gave all the disputed ballots—and the presidency—to Hayes.

It was not certain that Democrats would accept this dubious result, but the potential for a settlement seemed obvious. Republicans could allow Democrats to "redeem" the South if they could accept Hayes's election, crack down on white extremists, end electoral violence, and allow blacks to live and vote peacefully as tolerated but subordinate members of the South's political community. Republicans could then celebrate their final victory over slavery and secession while the Redeemers enjoyed "home rule," racial dominance, and economic power. Ideally, budding southern industrialists would imitate their northern counterparts by joining the Republican Party and replacing Radical Republican carpetbaggers at its helm.

Negotiations supposedly climaxed at Washington's Wormeley House Hotel in a February 1877 meeting between southern Democrats led by Kentucky editor Henry Watterson and Ohio Republicans led by Hayes spokesman (and future president) James A. Garfield. No complete record of these talks ever surfaced, but Republicans supposedly promised that President Hayes would withdraw the last federal troops from South Carolina and Louisiana. Without military protection, the last carpetbagger regimes would inevitably fall, and Republicans would abandon their efforts to remake the South. In return, white southerners would acquiesce in Hayes's victory and respect blacks' legal rights. Additional details gave the South a member of Hayes's cabinet and federal subsidies for a southern transcontinental railroad, while Garfield got promises of support in his upcoming bid for Speaker of the House.

This was the Compromise of 1877. Some historians have suggested that it settled the disputes of the Civil War era and fixed the terms of sectional reconciliation. In fact, Hayes would have won the presidential election even without the Wormeley House agreement, and the terms of the "compromise" were never enforced. No federal aid appeared for the promised railroad, no southern Democrats voted to make Garfield Speaker, and southern businessmen showed no interest in the Republican Party. Most conspicuously, southern Democrats did not protect black rights. Instead, they ignored racial violence when they did not practice it, tirelessly warned of "Negro rule" and the "horrors of Reconstruction," and won the white majority by preserving "white supremacy."

*

The inauguration of Rutherford B. Hayes in 1877 still marked a decisive turning point in the Civil War's aftermath. The new president did withdraw troops from South Carolina and Louisiana and conceded those states to the Redeemers. As he did so, most northern leaders and citizens were turning away from the unfinished business of Reconstruction to focus on dramatic changes in their own economy and society, including a surge of industrialization, dramatic growth of cities, continued European immigration, and labor unrest. To a lesser degree, southern leaders would also embrace the promise of cities and industrialization, and tried to shape a "New South" that upheld white supremacy but focused more on economic development than antebellum nostalgia.

The end of the Civil War had presented the American republic with staggering challenges. The nation not only faced enormous losses of life and property but also the destruction of one of its core institutions, African American slavery. Rebuilding the republic with a new set of laws and values was essential, but the United States undertook that task with republican traditions developed for a simpler, more homogeneous society and a much weaker state. It also faced the reality that the racial beliefs used to justify slavery were far more resilient than the Peculiar Institution itself.

President Andrew Johnson led the first efforts of Reconstruction, drawing on the lessons of states' rights and minimal government he had learned as a Jacksonian Democrat. Congress ultimately dismissed his efforts as inadequate and instituted a far more radical version of Reconstruction based on the assertive use of federal power to promote social change. The most extensive reforms of Congressional Reconstruction ultimately fell before northern fatigue and a wave of violent resistance, as in the Colfax Massacre. Older traditions of white supremacy and limited government obviously survived, but reform-minded Americans had also reworked and expanded those traditions to establish a new and fuller conception of the common good.

The South and North of 1877 had changed a great deal since 1860. If African Americans and their allies did not ultimately preserve all the changes they sought, they did prove that the American republic could change far more than anyone had previously expected, and they forged new traditions to support future changes. Above all, the Thirteenth, Fourteenth, and Fifteenth Amendments remained in the Constitution as sleeping monuments to the crusading zeal of Reconstruction activists. In another, later century, they would reemerge as indispensable weapons for the Second Reconstruction of American society.

Acknowledgments

This book has taught us both many things, none more fundamental than the need for help along the way. Foremost, we are grateful to each other for friendship, patience, inspiration, and good humor in numerous trials along the way. Timothy Mennel, executive editor at the University of Chicago Press, believed in the project and made it stronger, always giving us his unstinting confidence, encouragement, discipline, and, above all, patience. Rachel Kelly, Kelly Finefrock-Creed, and the entire staff of the press brought indispensable technical guidance and attentive concern for every detail. Geri Thoma of Writers House steered us wisely and warmly at crucial stages. And we could have had no better developmental editor than Ann Hofstra Grogg, who kept the book moving through endless drafts with her invaluable judgment, deep gifts for communication and organization, and unlimited supplies of wit, warmth, and insight.

Friends, colleagues, and sharp-eyed professionals have made *Building the American Republic* much stronger with their comments and criticisms. Anonymous reviewers at the press enriched its content, analysis, and accuracy throughout. The early chapters of volume 1 benefited immeasurably from a deeply generous and learned reading by Professor Kathleen DuVal. The hard work and sharp insights of the research assistant for volume 1, Robert Richard, show on every page, and Gabriel Moss created excellent maps. Professor Geoffrey R. Stone of the University of Chicago Law School read every word of volume 2. He cut a lot of them, improved the rest, and shared his wisdom and knowledge freely. Any remaining flaws, errors, or misjudgments are our fault alone.

Above all, we are both enormously grateful to our families, who supported this project with guidance, reassurance, and love for more years than we like to remember.

Harry L. Watson
University of North Carolina at Chapel Hill

Jane Dailey
University of Chicago

For Further Reading

Chapter 1. First Americans, to 1550

Colin Calloway, *New Worlds for All: Indians, Europeans, and the Remaking of Early North America* (1992)

Robbie Ethridge, *From Chicaza to Chickasaw: The European Invasion and the Transformation of the Mississippian World, 1540–1715* (2010)

Brian Fagan, *Ancient North America: The Archaeology of a Continent* (2005)

Peter C. Hoffer, *The Brave New World: A History of Early America* (2006)

Henry Kamen, *Empire: How Spain Became a World Power, 1492–1763* (2003)

Charles C. Mann, *1491: New Revelations of the Americas before Columbus* (2005)

William D. Phillips Jr. and Carla Rahn Philips, *The Worlds of Christopher Columbus* (1492)

William R. Polk, *The Birth of America: Before Columbus to the Revolution* (2006)

David B. Quinn, *North America from the Earliest Discoveries to the First Settlements: The Norse Voyages to 1612* (1977)

Hugh Thomas, *Rivers of Gold: The Rise of the Spanish Empire, from Columbus to Magellan* (2004)

John Thornton, *Africa and Africans in the Making of the Modern World, 1400–1800* (1998)

Chapter 2. The First English Colonies, 1584–1676

Virginia DeJohn Anderson, *New England's Generation: The Great Migration and the Formation of Society and Culture in the Seventeenth Century* (1991)

Bernard Bailyn, *Voyagers to the West: A Passage in the Peopling of America on the Eve of the Revolution* (1986)

T. H. Breen and Stephen Innes, *"Myne Owne Ground": Race and Freedom on Virginia's Eastern Shore, 1640–1676*, 2nd ed. (2004)

Kathleen M. Brown, *Good Wives, Nasty Wenches, and Anxious Patriarchs: Gender, Race, and Power in Colonial Virginia* (1996)

David Brion Davis, *Inhuman Bondage: The Rise and Fall of Slavery in the New World* (2006)

Andrew Delbanco, *The Puritan Ordeal* (1989)

John Demos, *A Little Commonwealth: Family Life in Plymouth Colony*, 2nd ed. (2000)

David D. Hall, *Worlds of Wonder, Days of Judgment: Popular Religious Belief in Early New England* (1989)

James Horn, *A Land as God Made It: Jamestown and the Birth of America* (2005)

Karen O. Kupperman, *Indians and English: Facing Off in Early America* (2000)

Jill Lepore, *The Name of War: King Philip's War and the Origins of American Identity* (1998)

Kenneth A. Lockridge, *A New England Town: The First Hundred Years: Dedham, Massachusetts, 1636-1736*, 2nd ed. (1985)

Charles C. Mann, *1493: Uncovering the New World Columbus Created* (2011)

Sidney Mintz, *Sweetness and Power: The Place of Sugar in Modern History* (1985)

Edmund S. Morgan, *American Slavery, American Freedom: The Ordeal of Colonial Virginia*, 2nd ed. (1995)

Gary Nash, *Red, White, and Black: The Peoples of Early North America*, 7th ed. (2014)

Daniel K. Richter, *Facing East from Indian Country: A Native History of Early America* (2001)

Alan Taylor, *American Colonies: The Settling of North America* (2001)

Camilla Townsend, *Pocahontas and the Powhatan Dilemma: An American Portrait* (2004)

Stephen Saunders Webb, *1676: The End of American Independence* (1984)

Chapter 3. The Emerging Empire, 1676–1756

James Axtell, *The Indians' New South: Cultural Change in the Colonial Southeast* (1997)

C. R. Boxer, *The Dutch Seaborne Empire, 1600-1800*, 3rd ed. (1991)

Richard S. Dunn, *Sugar and Slaves: The Rise of the Planter Class in the English West Indies, 1624-1713*, 2nd ed. (2000)

William J. Eccles, *The French in North America, 1500-1783* (1998)

J. H. Elliott, *Empires of the Atlantic World: Britain and Spain in America, 1492-1830* (2006)

Alan Gallay, *The Indian Slave Trade: The Rise of the English Empire in the American South, 1670-1717* (2002)

Ramon A. Gutiérrez, *When Jesus Came, the Corn Mothers Went Away: Marriage, Sexuality, and Power in New Mexico, 1500-1846* (1991)

Ned C. Landsman, *Crossroads of Empire: The Middle Colonies in British North America* (2010)

David S. Lovejoy, *The Glorious Revolution in America* (1972)

John A. Moretta, *William Penn and the Quaker Legacy* (2007)

Robert C. Ritchie, *The Duke's Province: A Study of New York Politics and Society, 1664-1691* (1977)

Daniel J. Usner Jr., *Indians, Settlers, and Slaves in a Frontier Exchange Economy: The Lower Mississippi Valley before 1783* (1992)

David J. Weber, *The Spanish Frontier in North America* (1992)

Richard White, *The Middle Ground: Indians, Empires, and Republics in the Great Lakes Region, 1650–1850* (1991)

Peter H. Wood, *Black Majority: Negroes in Colonial South Carolina from 1670 through the Stono Rebellion*, 2nd ed. (1996)

Chapter 4. Colonial Society and Culture, 1676–1756

Ira Berlin, *Many Thousands Gone: The First Two Centuries of Slavery in North America* (1998)

Patricia U. Bonomi, *Under the Cope of Heaven: Religion, Society, and Politics in Colonial America*, 2nd ed. (2003)

Paul Boyer and Stephen Nissenbaum, *Salem Possessed: The Social Origins of Witchcraft* (1974)

Colin G. Calloway, *One Vast Winter Count: The Native American West before Lewis and Clark* (2003)

William Cronon, *Changes in the Land: Indians, Colonists, and the Ecology of New England*, 2nd ed. (2003)

Thomas S. Kidd, *The Great Awakening: The Roots of Evangelical Christianity in Colonial America* (2007)

Allan Kulikoff, *Tobacco and Slaves: The Development of Southern Cultures in the Chesapeake, 1680–1800* (1986)

Phillip D. Morgan, *Slave Counterpoint: Black Culture in the Eighteenth-Century Chesapeake and Lowcountry* (1998)

Gary B. Nash, *The Urban Crucible: Social Change, Political Consciousness, and the Origins of the American Revolution* (1979)

Mary Beth Norton, *In the Devil's Snare: The Salem Witchcraft Crisis of 1692* (2002)

Daniel K. Richter, *Ordeal of the Longhouse: The Peoples of the Iroquois League in the Era of European Colonization* (1992)

James Brewer Stewart, *Venture Smith and the Business of Slavery and Freedom* (2010)

Laurel Thatcher Ulrich, *Good Wives: Image and Reality in the Lives of Women in Northern New England, 1650–1750* (2011)

Chapter 5. The Era of Independence, 1756–1783

Fred Anderson, *Crucible of War: The Seven Years' War and the Fate of Empire in British North America, 1754–1766* (2000)

Bernard Bailyn, *The Ideological Origins of the American Revolution*, enl. ed. (1992)

T. H. Breen, *The Marketplace of Revolution: How Consumer Politics Shaped American Independence* (2004)

Colin G. Calloway, *The American Revolution in Indian Country: Crisis and Diversity in Native American Communities* (1995)

Kathleen DuVal, *Independence Lost: Lives on the Edge of the American Revolution* (2015)

Douglas R. Egerton, *Death or Liberty: African Americans and Revolutionary America* (2009)

John E. Ferling, *Almost a Miracle: The American Victory in the War of Independence* (2007)

Woody Holton, *Forced Founders: Indians, Debtors, Slaves, and the Making of the American Revolution in Virginia* (1999)

Maya Jasanoff, *Liberty's Exiles: American Loyalists in the Revolutionary World* (2011)

Linda Kerber, *Women of the Republic: Intellect and Ideology in Revolutionary America*, 2nd ed. (1997)

Pauline Maier, *American Scripture: Making the Declaration of Independence* (1997)

Pauline Maier, *From Resistance to Revolution: Colonial Radicals and the Development of American Opposition to Great Britain, 1765–1776*, 2nd ed. (1992)

Michael A. McDonnell, *The Politics of War: Race, Class, and Conflict in Revolutionary Virginia* (2007)

Edmund S. Morgan and Helen M. Morgan, *The Stamp Act Crisis: Prologue to Revolution*, 3rd. ed. (1995)

Gary B. Nash, *The Unknown American Revolution: The Unruly Birth of Democracy and the Struggle to Create America* (2005)

Mary Beth Norton, *Liberty's Daughters: The Revolutionary Experience of American Women, 1750–1800*, 2nd ed. (1996)

Andrew Jackson O'Shaughnessy, *The Men Who Lost America: British Leadership, the American Revolution, and Fate of the Empire* (2013)

Charles Royster, *A Revolutionary People at War: The Continental Army and American Character, 1775–1783* (1996)

John Shy, *A People Numerous and Armed: Reflections on the Military Struggle for American Independence*, rev. ed. (1990)

Chapter 6. A Federal Republic, 1783–1789

Lance Banning, *The Sacred Fire of Liberty: James Madison and the Founding of the Federal Republic* (1995)

Saul Cornell, *The Other Founders: Anti-Federalism and the Dissenting Tradition in America, 1788–1828* (1999)

Gregory Evans Dowd, *A Spirited Resistance: The North American Indian Struggle for Unity, 1745–1815* (1992)

Woody Holton, *Unruly Americans and the Origins of the Constitution* (2007)

Pauline Maier, *Ratification: The People Debate the Constitution, 1787–1788* (2010)

Jackson Turner Main, *The Antifederalists: Critics of the Constitution, 1781–1788*, 2nd ed. (2004)

Jackson Turner Main, *Political Parties before the Constitution* (1974)

Forrest McDonald, *Novus Ordo Seclorum: The Intellectual Origins of the Constitution* (1985)

Richard B. Morris, *The Forging of the Union, 1781–1789* (1987)

Jack H. Rakove, *Original Meanings: Politics and Ideas in the Making of the Constitution* (1980)

Leonard L. Richards, *Shays's Rebellion: The American Revolution's Final Battle* (2002)

Gordon S. Wood, *The Creation of the American Republic, 1776-1789*, 2nd ed. (1998)

Gordon S. Wood, *The Radicalism of the American Revolution* (1991)

Chapter 7. Federalists and Republicans, 1789–1815

Catherine Allgor, *Parlor Politics: In Which the Ladies of Washington Help Build a City and a Government* (2000)

Joyce Appleby, *Capitalism and the New Social Order: The Republican Vision of the 1790s* (1984)

Lance Banning, *The Jeffersonian Persuasion: Evolution of a Party Ideology* (1978)

Susan Branson, *These Fiery Frenchified Dames: Women and Political Culture in Early National Philadelphia* (2001)

John L. Brooke, *Columbia Rising: Civil Life on the Upper Hudson from the Revolution to the Age of Jackson* (2010)

Colin G. Calloway, *The Shawnees and the War for America* (2007)

Douglas Egerton, *Gabriel's Rebellion: The Virginia Slave Conspiracies of 1800 and 1802* (1993)

Stanley Elkins and Eric McKitrick, *The Age of Federalism: The Early American Republic, 1788-1800* (1993)

John E. Ferling, *Adams vs. Jefferson: The Tumultuous Election of 1800* (2004)

François Furstenberg, *In the Name of the Father: Washington's Legacy, Slavery, and the Making of a Nation* (2006)

Donald R. Hickey, *The War of 1812: A Forgotten Conflict* (1989)

Linda Kerber, *Federalists in Dissent: Imagery and Ideology in Jeffersonian America* (1970)

Matthew Mason, *Slavery and Politics in the Early American Republic* (2006)

Jeffrey L. Pasley, *"The Tyranny of Printers": Newspaper Politics in the Early American Republic* (2001)

Claudio Saunt, *A New Order of Things: Property, Power, and the Transformation of the Creek Indians, 1733-1816* (1999)

Thomas Slaughter, *The Whiskey Rebellion: Frontier Epilogue to the American Revolution* (1986)

John Sudgen, *Tecumseh's Last Stand* (1985)

Alan Taylor, *The Internal Enemy: Slavery and War in Virginia, 1772-1832* (2013)

Laurel Thatcher Ulrich, *A Midwife's Tale: The Life of Martha Ballard, Based on Her Diary, 1785-1812* (1990)

David Waldstreicher, *In the Midst of Perpetual Fetes: The Making of American Nationalism, 1776-1820* (1997)

Sean Wilentz, *The Rise of American Democracy: Jefferson to Lincoln* (2005)

Gordon S. Wood, *Empire of Liberty: A History of the Early Republic, 1789-1815* (2010)

Chapter 8. Market Revolution in the North, 1815–1860

Howard Bodenhorn, *A History of Banking in Antebellum America: Financial Markets and Economic Development in an Era of Nation-Building* (2000)

Jeanne Boydston, *Home and Work: Housework, Wages, and the Ideology of Labor in the Early Republic* (1990)

Richard D. Brown, *Knowledge Is Power: The Diffusion of Information in Early America, 1700–1865* (1989)

Christopher Clark, *The Roots of Rural Capitalism: Western Massachusetts, 1780–1860* (1990)

Christopher Clark, *Social Change in America: From the Revolution to the Civil War* (2006)

Thomas Dublin, *Women at Work: The Transformation of Work and Community in Lowell, Massachusetts, 1810–1860* (1979)

John Mack Faragher, *Sugar Creek: Life on the Illinois Prairie* (1986)

David A. Hounshell, *From the American System to Mass Production, 1800–1932: The Development of Manufacturing Technology in the United States* (1984)

Joan M. Jensen, *Loosening the Bonds: Mid-Atlantic Farm Women, 1750–1850* (1986)

Richard R. John, *Spread the News: The American Postal Service from Franklin to Morse* (1985)

John Lauritz Larson, *Internal Improvement: National Public Works and the Promise of Popular Government in the Early United States* (2001)

John Lauritz Larson, *Market Revolution in America: Liberty, Ambition, and the Eclipse of the Common Good* (2010)

Bruce Laurie, *Artisans into Workers: Labor in Nineteenth-Century America* (1989)

David R. Meyer, *The Roots of American Industrialization* (2003)

Winifred Barr Rothenberg, *From Market-Places to a Market Economy: The Transformation of Rural Massachusetts, 1750–1850* (1992)

Carol Sheriff, *The Artificial River: The Erie Canal and the Paradox of Progress* (1997)

Christine Stansell, *City of Women: Sex and Class in New York, 1789–1860* (1986)

Sean Wilentz, *Chants Democratic: New York City and the Making of the American Working Class* (1984)

Chapter 9. Northern Culture and Reform, 1815–1860

Robert H. Abzug, *Cosmos Crumbling: American Reform and the Religious Imagination* (1994)

Stuart M. Blumin, *The Emergence of the Middle Class: Social Experience in the American City, 1760–1900* (1984)

Nancy Cott, *The Bonds of Womanhood: Woman's Sphere in New England, 1790–1835*, 2nd ed. (1997)

William J. Gilmore, *Reading Becomes a Necessity of Life: Material and Cultural Life in Rural New England, 1780–1835* (1989)

Lori Ginzberg, *Women and the Work of Benevolence: Morality, Politics, and Class in the Nineteenth-Century United States* (1994)

Philip Gura, *American Transcendentalism: A History* (2008)

Karen Halttunen, *Confidence Men and Painted Women: A Study of Middle-Class Culture in America, 1830–1870* (1982)

Nathan O. Hatch, *The Democratization of American Christianity* (1989)

Daniel Walker Howe, *What Hath God Wrought: The Transformation of America, 1815–1848* (2007)

Paul E. Johnson, *A Shopkeeper's Millennium: Society and Revivals in Rochester, New York, 1815–1837*, 2nd ed. (2004)

Mary Kelley, *Learning to Stand and Speak: Women, Education, and Public Life in America's Republic* (2006)

Bruce Levine, *Half Slave and Half Free: The Roots of the Civil War* (1992)

Eric Lott, *Love and Theft: Blackface Minstrelsy and the American Working Class* (1993)

Steven Mintz, *Moralists and Modernizers: America's Pre–Civil War Reformers* (1995)

David S. Reynolds, *Beneath the American Renaissance: The Subversive Imagination in the Age of Emerson and Melville* (1988)

David R. Roediger, *The Wages of Whiteness: Race and the Making of the American Working Class*, rev. ed. (2007)

Mary P. Ryan, *Cradle of the Middle Class: The Family in Oneida County, New York, 1790–1865* (1981)

James Brewer Stewart, *Holy Warriors: Abolitionists and American Slavery*, rev. ed. (1996)

Jane Tomkins, *Sensational Designs: The Cultural Work of American Fiction, 1790–1860* (1985)

Ronald J. Zboray, *A Fictive People: Antebellum Economic Development and the American Reading Public* (1993)

Chapter 10. The World of the South, 1815–1860

Edward Baptist, *The Half Has Never Been Told: Slavery and the Making of American Capitalism* (2014)

Daina Ramey Berry, *"Swing the Sickle for the Harvest Is Ripe": Gender and Slavery in Antebellum Georgia* (2007)

Victoria E. Bynum, *Unruly Women: The Politics of Social and Sexual Control in the Old South* (1992)

Stephanie M. H. Camp, *Closer to Freedom: Enslaved Women and Everyday Resistance in the Plantation South* (2004)

Steven Deyle, *Carry Me Back: The Domestic Slave Trade in American Life* (2005)

William Dusinberre, *Them Dark Days: Slavery in the American Rice Swamps* (1996)

Robert William Fogel, *Without Consent or Contract: The Rise and Fall of American Slavery* (1989)

Lacy K. Ford, *Origins of Southern Radicalism: The South Carolina Upcountry, 1800–1860* (1988)

Elizabeth Fox-Genovese, *Within the Plantation Household: Black and White Women of the Old South* (1988)

Eugene D. Genovese, *Roll, Jordan, Roll: The World the Slaves Made* (1974)

J. William Harris, *Plain Folk and Gentry in a Slave Society: White Liberty and Black Slavery in Augusta's Hinterlands* (1985)

Christine Heyrman, *Southern Cross: The Beginnings of the Bible Belt* (1997)

Walter Johnson, *Soul by Soul: Life inside the Antebellum Slave Market* (1999)

Peter Kolchin, *American Slavery, 1619–1877*, rev. ed. (2003)

Stephanie McCurry, *Masters of Small Worlds: Yeoman Households, Gender Relations, and the Political Culture of the Antebellum South Carolina Low Country* (1995)

Albert J. Raboteau, *Slave Religion: The "Invisible Church" in the Antebellum South* (1978)

Adam Rothman, *Slave Country: American Expansion and the Origins of the Deep South* (2005)

Elizabeth R. Varon, *We Mean to Be Counted: White Women and Politics in Antebellum Virginia* (1998)

Jonathan Daniel Wells, *The Origins of the Southern Middle Class, 1800–1861* (2004)

Deborah Gray White, *Ar'n't I a Woman? Female Slaves in the Plantation South*, rev. ed. (1999)

Heather Andrea Williams, *Self-Taught: African American Education in Slavery and Freedom* (2005)

Gavin Wright, *The Political Economy of the Cotton South: Households, Markets, and Wealth in the Nineteenth Century* (1978)

Bertram Wyatt-Brown, *Honor and Violence in the Old South* (1986)

Chapter 11. The Transformation of Politics, 1815–1836

William J. Cooper, *The South and the Politics of Slavery, 1828–1856* (1978)

Richard E. Ellis, *The Union at Risk: Jacksonian Democracy, States' Rights, and the Nullification Crisis* (1987)

Don E. Fehrenbacher, *The Slaveholding Republic: An Account of the United States Government's Relations to Slavery* (2001)

Robert Pierce Forbes, *The Missouri Compromise and Its Aftermath: Slavery and the Meaning of America* (2007)

Ronald P. Formisano, *The Transformation of Political Culture: Massachusetts Parties, 1790s–1840s* (1983)

William W. Freehling, *Prelude to Civil War: The Nullification Controversy in South Carolina, 1816–1836* (1965)

William W. Freehling, *The Road to Disunion*, vol. 1, *Secessionists at Bay, 1776–1856* (1990)

Michael F. Holt, *The Rise and Fall of the American Whig Party: Jacksonian Politics and the Onset of the Civil War* (1999)

Daniel Walker Howe, *What Hath God Wrought: The Transformation of America, 1815–1848* (2007)

Jessica M. Lepler, *The Many Panics of 1837: People, Politics, and the Creation of a Transatlantic Financial Crisis* (2013)

John F. Marszalek, *The Petticoat Affair: Manners, Morality, and Sex in Andrew Jackson's White House* (1998)

Lynn Hudson Parsons, *The Birth of Modern Politics: Andrew Jackson, John Quincy Adams, and the Election of 1828* (2009)

Leonard D. Richards, *The Slave Power: The Free North and Southern Domination, 1780–1860* (2000)

Peter Temin, *The Jacksonian Economy* (1969)

Anthony F. C. Wallace, *The Long Bitter Trail: Andrew Jackson and the Indians* (1993)

Harry L. Watson, *Liberty and Power: The Politics of Jacksonian America*, 2nd ed. (2006)

Sean Wilentz, *The Rise of American Democracy: Jefferson to Lincoln*, abr. college ed. (2009)

Major L. Wilson, *Space, Time, and Freedom: The Quest for Nationality and the Irrepressible Conflict, 1815–1861* (1974)

Chapter 12. Wars for the West, 1836–1850

Amy S. Greenberg, *Manifest Manhood and the Antebellum American Empire* (2005)

Amy S. Greenberg, *A Wicked War: Polk, Clay, Lincoln, and the 1846 U.S. Invasion of Mexico* (2012)

Pekka Hämäläinen, *The Comanche Empire* (2008)

Robert W. Johannsen, *To the Halls of the Montezumas: The Mexican War in the American Imagination* (1985)

Susan Lee Johnson, *Roaring Camp: The Social World of the California Gold Rush* (2000)

Benjamin Madley, *An American Genocide: The United States and the California Indian Catastrophe* (2016)

Michael A. Morrison, *Slavery and the American West: The Eclipse of Manifest Destiny and the Coming of the Civil War* (1997)

Malcolm J. Rohrbough, *Days of Gold: The California Gold Rush and the American Nation* (1997)

Joel H. Silbey, *Martin Van Buren and the Emergence of American Popular Politics* (2002)

Joel H. Silbey, *Storm over Texas: The Annexation Controversy and the Road to Civil War* (2005)

Major L. Wilson, *The Presidency of Martin Van Buren* (1984)

Steven E. Woodworth, *Manifest Destinies: America's Westward Expansion and the Road to Civil War* (2010)

Chapter 13. The House Dividing, 1850–1861

Jean H. Baker, *Affairs of Party: The Political Culture of Northern Democrats in the Mid-Nineteenth Century* (1983)

Steven A. Channing, *Crisis of Fear: Secession in South Carolina* (1970)

Daniel W. Crofts, *Reluctant Confederates: Upper South Unionists in the Secession Crisis* (1989)

Marc Egnal, *Clash of Extremes: The Economic Origins of the Civil War* (2009)

Don E. Fehrenbacher, *Slavery, Law, and Politics: The Dred Scott Case in Historical Perspective* (1981)

Eric Foner, *Free Soil, Free Labor, Free Men: The Ideology of the Republican Party before the Civil War*, 2nd ed. (1995)

William W. Freehling, *The Road to Disunion*, vol. 2, *Secessionists Triumphant, 1854–1861* (2007)

William E. Gienapp, *The Origins of the Republican Party, 1852–1856* (1987)

Michael F. Holt, *The Political Crisis of the 1850s* (1978)

Joel H. Silbey, *A Respectable Minority: The Democratic Party in the Civil War Era, 1860–1868* (1977)

Kenneth M. Stampp, *America in 1857: A Nation on the Brink* (1990)

Elizabeth Varon, *Disunion: The Coming of the American Civil War* (2008)

Chapter 14. "A New Birth of Freedom," 1861–1865

Iver Bernstein, *The New York City Draft Riots: Their Significance for American Society and Politics in the Age of the Civil War* (1990)

Drew Gilpin Faust, *Mothers of Invention: Women of the Slaveholding South in the American Civil War* (1996)

Drew Gilpin Faust, *This Republic of Suffering: Death and the American Civil War* (2008)

Michael Fellman, *Inside War: The Guerilla Conflict in Missouri during the Civil War* (1989)

William W. Freehling, *The South vs. The South: How Anti-Confederate Southerners Shaped the Course of the Civil War* (2002)

Gary W. Gallagher, *The Confederate War* (1997)

Gary W. Gallagher, *The Union War* (2011)

Joseph G. Glatthaar, *Forged in Battle: The Civil War Alliance of Black Soldiers and White Officers* (1990)

Allen C. Guelzo, *Lincoln's Emancipation Proclamation: The End of Slavery in America* (2004)

Bruce Levine, *The Fall of the House of Dixie: The Civil War and the Social Revolution That Transformed the South* (2013)

Chandra Manning, *What This Cruel War Was Over: Soldiers, Slavery, and the Civil War* (2007)

James M. McPherson, *Battle Cry of Freedom: The Civil War Era* (1988)

James M. McPherson, *For Cause and Comrades: Why Men Fought the Civil War* (1997)

James Oakes, *Freedom National: The Destruction of Slavery in the United States, 1861–1865* (2013)

Phillip Shaw Paludan, *"A People's Contest": The Union and the Civil War* (1988)

Nina Silber, *Daughters of the Union: Northern Women Fight the Civil War* (2005)

Emory Thomas, *The Confederate Nation, 1861–1865* (1979)

Chapter 15. Reconstructing the Republic, 1865–1877

David W. Blight, *Race and Reconstruction: The Civil War in American Memory* (2001)

Jane Dailey, *Before Jim Crow: The Politics of Race in Postemancipation Virginia* (2000)

Gregory P. Downs, *After Appomattox: Military Occupation and the Ends of War* (2015)

Gregory P. Downs, *Declarations of Dependence: The Long Reconstruction of Popular Politics in the South, 1861–1908* (2011)

W. E. B. Du Bois, *Black Reconstruction in America, 1860–1880* (1935)

Laura F. Edwards, *Gendered Strife and Confusion: The Political Culture of Reconstruction* (1997)

Eric Foner, *The Story of Emancipation and Reconstruction* (2005)

Thavolia Glymph, *Out of the House of Bondage: The Transformation of the Plantation Household* (2008)

Steven Hahn, *A Nation under Our Feet: Black Political Struggles in the Rural South from Slavery to the Great Migration* (2003)

Tera W. Hunter, *To 'Joy My Freedom: Southern Black Women's Lives and Labor after the Civil War* (1997)

Leon Litwack, *Been in the Storm So Long: The Aftermath of Slavery* (1979)

Charles Love, *The Day Freedom Died: The Colfax Massacre, the Supreme Court, and the Betrayal of Reconstruction* (2008)

Michael Perman, *Reunion without Compromise: The South and Reconstruction, 1865–1868* (1973)

George C. Rable, *But There Was No Peace: The Role of Violence in the Politics of Reconstruction* (1984)

Roger L. Ransom and Richard Sutch, *One Kind of Freedom: The Economic Consequences of Emancipation* (1977)

Heather Cox Richardson, *The Death of Reconstruction: Race, Labor, and Politics in the Post–Civil War North, 1865–1901* (2001)

Heather Cox Richardson, *West from Appomattox: The Reconstruction of America after the Civil War* (2006)

Allen W. Trelease, *White Terror: The Ku Klux Klan Conspiracy and Southern Reconstruction* (1971)

Heather Andrea Williams, *Help Me to Find My People: The African American Search for Family Lost in Slavery* (2012)

Index

Page numbers in italics refer to illustrations.

Federalist Papers, 224-25, 227-29, 236, 249; *Marbury v. Madison*, 254-55; on a national bank, 238, 390-91; reaction to Sedition Act, 249; as a slave owner, 242, 374; strict construction of Constitution, 238; on tariffs, 390, 391; War of 1812, 263, 268-72. *See also* Democratic-Republicans

Magellan, Ferdinand, 22

Maine: ban on alcohol in, 325; founding of, 396; migration to, 130; social problems in, 316

maize. *See* corn

malaria, 18, 122

Mali, 15

Manassas, First Battle of, 505

Mandan Indians, 433

Manifest Destiny, 430-31, 442, 445

Mann, Horace, 324

Manning, William, 200

manufacturing: Hamilton's "Report on Manufactures," 239; Market Revolution in, 291-92, 309. *See also* textile industry

manumission, 201-2, 354, 373, 511

Marbury, William, 254-55

Marbury v. Madison, 254-55

March to the Sea, 527

Marcy, William L., 402

Marie-Antoinette, Queen, 243

Marietta, Ohio, 213, 258

Marine Anti-Britannic Society, 197

Market Revolution, 275-310; agricultural improvements, 289-91; Communication Revolution, 276, 282-83, 309; creation of the middle class, 305-8; implications for public affairs, 309-10; judicial support for, 288-89; in manufacturing, 291-92, 309; role of banks in, 286-88, 388; role of government in, 283-86, 387; social problems following, 315-17, 416-17; Transportation Revolution, *274*, 276,

280-82, 309; urbanization, 299-300; Whig support for, 410, 412

Marquette, Jacques, 83

marriage: in colonial times, 135; interracial marriage, 25-26, 84, 116, 138, 267, 548; plural marriage, 320; between slaves, 120, 363. *See also* divorce

Marshall, John, 254-55, 284, 288-89, 404

Martinique, 86

Mary II, 75, 97, 109

Maryland: Act Concerning Religion, 54; Baltimore, 281, 358; during the Civil War, 500; colonial government of, 99; Cumberland, 284; economy of, 358; founding of, 50, 53-54, 72; free blacks in, 354; interracial marriage laws in, 138; martial law in, 500; *McCulloch v. Maryland*, 288; naming of, 86; railroads in, 281-82; ratification of Articles of Confederation, 210; religious freedom in, 54; slavery in, 351; tobacco cultivation in, 37, 54, 116; voter participation in, 378; voting rights in, 378; wheat cultivation in, 354

masculinity in the South, 381

Mason, George, 220, 229

Mason, John, 504

Masonic Order: African American, 202, 305; anti-Masonry, 414-16; growth in, 415

Massachusetts: agriculture in, 64; Battles of Lexington and Concord, 174-75, 178; colonial government of, 61, 99; constitutional theory in, 208-9; debt collection in, 217-18; disestablishment of churches in, 321; in Dominion of New England, 96; Great Migration, 60-61; ignoring of English laws in, 95-96; Know-Nothings in, 467; Lowell, 275, 293, 299; Lynn, 292; migration to, 130; Native Ameri-